SUPPLEMENT I, Part 2
Vachel Lindsay to Elinor Wylie

AMERICAN WRITERS
A Collection of Literary Biographies

LEONARD UNGER
Editor in Chief

SUPPLEMENT I, Part 2
Vachel Lindsay to Elinor Wylie

Charles Scribner's Sons, New York

Library of Congress Cataloging in Publication Data
Main entry under title:

American writers.

The 4-vol. set consists of 97 of the pamphlets originally published
as the University of Minnesota pamphlets on American writers;
some have been rev. and updated.
    Includes bibliographies.
    CONTENTS: v. 1. Henry Adams to T. S. Eliot. etc.
PS129.A55   810'.9 [B]   73-1759
ISBN 0-684-15797-7

91113151719 QD/C 2018161412108

Acknowledgement is gratefully made to those publishers
and individuals who have permitted the use of the following
materials in copyright.

"Vachel Lindsay"
Reprinted with permission of Macmillan Publishing Co.,
Inc. from *A Handy Guide for Beggars* by Vachel Lindsay.
Copyright 1916 by Macmillan Publishing Co., Inc., re-
newed 1944 by Elizabeth C. Lindsay. Reprinted with per-
mission of Macmillan Publishing Co., Inc. from "The
Spider and the Ghost of the Fly," "The Santa-Fe Trail,"
and "Abraham Lincoln Walks at Midnight" in *Collected
Poems* by Vachel Lindsay. Copyright 1914 by Macmillan
Publishing Co., Inc., renewed 1942 by Elizabeth C. Lind-
say. Reprinted with permission of Macmillan Publishing
Co., Inc. from "The Chinese Nightingale," "Our Mother
Pocahontas," "The Raft," and "King Solomon and the
Queen of Sheba" in *Collected Poems* by Vachel Lindsay.
Copyright 1917 by Macmillan Publishing Co., Inc., re-
newed 1945 by Elizabeth C. Lindsay. Reprinted with per-
mission of Macmillan Publishing Co., Inc. from "The
Golden Whales of California" and "Bryan, Bryan, Bryan,
Bryan" in *Collected Poems* by Vachel Lindsay. Copyright
1920 by Macmillan Publishing Co., Inc., renewed 1948 by
Elizabeth C. Lindsay. Reprinted with permission of Macmillan Publishing Co., Inc. from "The Tree of Laughing
Bells," "Springfield Magical," "The Knight in Disguise," and "General William Booth Enters into Heaven"
in *Collected Poems* by Vachel Lindsay. Reprinted with the
permission of Nicholas C. Lindsay on behalf of the Estate
of Vachel Lindsay from *The Art of the Moving Picture*,
copyright 1915, 1922, and from a letter from Vachel Lindsay to Carl Sandburg, 13 January 1917, now in the Sandburg Collection of the University of Illinois Library at
Champaign-Urbana. Reprinted from *Letters of Nicholas
Vachel Lindsay to A. Joseph Armstrong*, edited by A.
Joseph Armstrong, copyright 1940, by permission of
Baylor University Press

"James Russell Lowell"
from Leon Howard, *Victorian Knight-Errant: A Study of the
Early Literary Career of James Russell Lowell*, copyright
1952, by permission of the University of California Press;
from Martin Duberman, *James Russell Lowell*, copyright ©
1966, by permission of Martin Duberman and Houghton
Mifflin Company; reprinted from *Literary Criticism of
James Russell Lowell*, edited by Herbert F. Smith by permission of the University of Nebraska Press. Copyright ©
1969 by the University of Nebraska Press; from Edward
Wagenknecht, *James Russell Lowell: Portrait of a Many-
Sided Man*, by permission of the Oxford University Press

"Bernard Malamud"
Selections from the following titles by Bernard Malamud,
*The Magic Barrel, The Assistant, Pictures of Fidelman, A
New Life, The Fixer, Rembrandt's Hat*, and *The Tenants*.
Copyright © 1950, 1951, 1952, 1953, 1954, 1955, 1956,
1957, 1958, 1961, 1962, 1963, 1966, 1968, 1969, 1971,
1972, 1973 by Bernard Malamud. Reprinted with the per-
mission of Farrar, Straus & Giroux, Inc.; A selection from
The Natural by Bernard Malamud. Copyright © 1952 by
Bernard Malamud. Reprinted with the permission of Far-
rar, Straus & Giroux, Inc. and Russell & Volkening, Inc.
From Haskel Frankel "Interview with Bernard Malamud"
© *Saturday Review*, 1966. All rights reserved.

SUPPLEMENT I, Part 2
Vachel Lindsay to Elinor Wylie

Vachel Lindsay

1879–1931

WRITING home from the railroad station at Tipton, Missouri, on Sunday morning, June 9, 1912, Vachel Lindsay describes the opportune moment he chooses for seizing the attention of his hosts. "After the kindling is split and the meal eaten and they lean back in their chairs, a-weary of their mirth, by one means or another I show them how I am knocking at the door of the world with a dream in my hand." Tramping across the Midwest, begging and exchanging his labor and rhymes for meals and lodging during the summer of 1912, Lindsay did not realize that the door of the world would soon swing open and enable him to carry his dream to thousands across the country instead of to a few farm families and hands sitting around a kitchen table. In 1912, a year that marks the opening of a new era in American poetry, Harriet Monroe began publication of *Poetry: A Magazine of Verse*. Lindsay was propelled to national recognition when she printed "General William Booth Enters into Heaven" as the lead poem in the January 1913 number. Lindsay composed this poem at the end of his summer trek west, described in *Adventures While Preaching the Gospel of Beauty,* during a week of writing and rewriting at his uncle Johnson Lindsay's home in Los Angeles.

Like his bardic forebear Walt Whitman, Lindsay did not publish and become well known until fairly late in his life. Lindsay, too, as Ralph Waldo Emerson said of Whitman, "must have had a long foreground somewhere, for such a start." It began on November 10, 1879, in the very house where it was to end, by his own hand, on December 5, 1931: 603 South Fifth Street, Springfield, Illinois. A substantial white frame house on a corner next to the governor's mansion, it was always home for Lindsay, the center of his universe and the source of the values expressed in his writing.

These values, primarily religious, were instilled in Lindsay by his mother, Esther Catherine Frazee Lindsay. His father, Vachel Thomas Lindsay, was a physician. Vachel was the second of six children, born two years after his sister Olive. Three younger sisters died of scarlet fever within three weeks of each other. Although a naturally spiritual woman, the mother's religious ardor was intensified by the sudden deaths of her daughters. She immersed herself in the activities of the First Christian Church, consoled by the faith that permeated the Lindsay household and shaped the lives of her remaining children.

During his first eighteen years in Springfield, Lindsay gave evidence of being talented, but not necessarily remarkable. He did well enough in his subjects and graduated from Springfield High School in 1897. His interest in literature and writing was well developed by then, and indicated his inability to become sufficiently attracted to medicine to follow in his father's footsteps. Both of his parents strongly encouraged Lindsay to become a physician, but even though young Vachel sometimes accompanied his father on his rounds, he never became enthusiastic about tending man's physical infirmities. He dreamed, instead, of healing man's diseased spirit. What Lindsay appreciated in his father was not a technical or scientific professional skill but, rather, the warm humanity in his care and caring for patients. In high school he was more proficient in science courses than in Latin, but his real interest was not in the subject matter at hand. For example, in biology he lavished effort upon his drawings. They anticipate the emblems of the butterfly and the spider that represent, in Lindsay's imaginative world, beauty and the evil of Mammon.

Throughout his life Lindsay remained skeptical of progress in the name of science; his attitude was much like William Wordsworth's "they murder to dissect." A clever poem entitled "The Spider and the Ghost of the Fly" illustrates his fascination with the deadly spider.

> Once I loved a spider
> When I was born a fly,
> A velvet-footed spider
> With a gown of rainbow-dye.
> She ate my wings and gloated.
> She bound me with a hair
> She drove me to her parlor
> Above her winding stair.
> To educate young spiders
> She took me all apart.
> My ghost came back to haunt her.
> I saw her eat my heart.

Lindsay's attraction to the spider relates him to at least two other American poets. Although he could not have known Edward Taylor's work, the heritage of Puritanism in America is as strong in his work as it was in that of Emily Dickinson.

The playfulness in this poem, with its undercurrent of horror and its frightful final line, also is reminiscent of Dickinson.

His parents sent Lindsay and his sister Olive to Hiram College, a Campbellite institution in Ohio, in the fall of 1897. He was to study medicine. He did in fact attend the prescribed lectures; but neither his heart nor his mind was in them, and his performance was desultory at best. Because he was affable, his professors tolerated him. Finally, however, Lindsay persuaded his parents that his lack of success in his courses and his lack of desire made him unsuited for the responsibilities of a career in medicine. He left Hiram in the spring of 1900, but he remained fond of this small Christian college and always regarded it as a model of collegiate experience and education. Thirty years later Hiram recognized the achievement of its erstwhile student when Lindsay returned to receive an honorary degree.

While at Hiram, Lindsay kept extensive diaries in which he explored the question of his own identity. In these soul-searchings he came more and more to regard art as his natural calling. In following this course, Lindsay was fulfilling the wishes of his mother, whose advocacy of medical studies was not as strong as her husband's. Her own art work and reverence for the European masters provided Lindsay with the role that he wished—consciously or unconsciously—to emulate. To this end, he enrolled at the Art Institute of Chicago in January 1901, and remained there until the summer of 1903. In Chicago, Lindsay drew, kept his diary, and read. The latter two activities were more enriching for the future poet, since his highly individualistic talent for the imaginative and dreamlike in drawing was not appreciated by the staff of the Art Institute, which emphasized realistic depiction and technical proficiency.

Never lacking confidence in his artistic talent, Lindsay next moved to New York City, where he enrolled at the New York School of Art. Although he was to remain in New York, off and on, for the next five years, his art studies lasted for only about one year. The New York School of Art was less conservative than the Art Institute and Lindsay received some encouragement. However, he had been writing poetry; and when he confronted his art teacher Robert Henri with an impassioned recitation of his poem "The Tree of Laughing Bells," Henri immediately advised Lindsay to turn his efforts from drawing to poetry.

During these years in New York, Lindsay had to find some means of support. He was in his mid-twenties and grateful for the indulgence of his parents, but he also wanted to ease their financial burden. To this end he lectured on art at the YMCA and guided tours at the Metropolitan Museum; but his most ingenious effort was inaugurated in March 1905, when he sallied forth to peddle his rhymes on the streets of New York. This venture probably cost him more in printing expenses than he earned; and even though he was scoffed at by many, the experience convinced him that there were many ordinary people who, if given the chance, would respond to poetry and be receptive to the message it carried.

In March 1906, Lindsay sailed with a friend to Florida, from which they intended to walk back to New York; but his friend returned by steamer after only a week and left Lindsay on his own. Although he carried no money, Lindsay did take along some decoratively printed copies of "The Tree of Laughing Bells," which he hoped to exchange for food and lodging along the way.

"The Tree of Laughing Bells" describes how a hero is sent to a distant galaxy by an Indian maiden, to procure two bells from the Tree of Laughing Bells. She fashions the hero Wings of the Morning from flowers; and he flies on his perilous mission to the galaxy in Chaos-land, from which he successfully returns with the bells

that "will quench our memory, / Our hope, / Our borrowed sorrow; / We will have no thirst for yesterday, / No thought for to-morrow." This poem's echoes of Edgar Allan Poe and Samuel Taylor Coleridge are worked into a fable expressing Lindsay's desire to "save" Springfield. The setting is "Beside the Sangamon— Rude stream of Dreamland Town." The Sangamon River, which flows through Springfield, is the present-day reality that Lindsay's hero will transform into Dreamland Town through the magic of beauty. This poem is subtitled "A Poem for Aviators" and is a tribute to all those who would overcome the perils of flight in order to weave beauty "From all things fragile, faint and fair," so that chaos can be transformed into the work of art that brings tranquillity in transcending time. It was this ethereal poem that Lindsay bartered with the backcountry folk of the South. He recounted this experience ten years later in *A Handy Guide for Beggars* (1916).

Lindsay's stature as a writer has always rested upon the dozen or so poems that made him famous; and the nature of this fame has, unfortunately, tended to obscure his other works. He published five volumes of prose: *Adventures While Preaching the Gospel of Beauty* (1914), *The Art of the Moving Picture* (1915), *A Handy Guide for Beggars* (1916), *The Golden Book of Springfield* (1920), and *The Litany of Washington Street* (1929).

A Handy Guide for Beggars describes the tramps Lindsay made in 1906 and 1908. The first half relates his "vagrant adventures in the south" during March and April of 1906, while walking from Florida through Georgia, North Carolina, and Tennessee to Kentucky, where he stopped at an aunt's house. The second half, "A Mendicant Pilgrimage in the East," describes a trip from New York to Hiram, Ohio, in 1908. *A Handy Guide* begins with a two-page preface dedicating the book to the "one hundred new poets in the villages of the land," and setting forth Lindsay's rules of the road:

(1) Keep away from the Cities; (2) Keep away from the railroads; (3) Have nothing to do with money and carry no baggage; (4) Ask for dinner about quarter after eleven; (5) Ask for supper, lodging and breakfast about quarter of five; (6) Travel alone; (7) Be neat, deliberate, chaste and civil; (8) Preach the Gospel of Beauty.

Lindsay's rules, to which he was not always faithful, suggest the Populist point of view that was at the heart of his philosophy: an agrarian distrust of industrialism and finance. Even in their practicality there is a quaintness about the rules, the source of which in Lindsay's character made him an engaging beggar as he appeared at back-country doors.

A Handy Guide does not attempt to present a day-by-day account of Lindsay's travels. He composed it from notebook entries made at the time of the actual experiences, which are distilled into discrete stories of his adventures with little in the way of transitional material. The placing of poems between prose episodes suggests that Lindsay's real intention in this work is to evoke and sing the qualities inherent in the land and its people. "Make me to voice the tall men in the corn," he petitions "In the Immaculate Conception Church," and keep "my springtime cornland thought in flower." He knows that the expressions of human sympathy he is seeking are not indigenous to the modern city, so he takes to the country to find the genuine expression of the human spirit necessary to confirm and bolster his beliefs.

These prose pieces are in the tradition of American sketchbooks popularized by Washington Irving. If Lindsay's artistic talent had been in realistic depiction, he no doubt would have accompanied his written impressions with appropriate pen-and-ink drawings. His prose sketches, like Irving's, dwell more on the romantic and picturesque. They focus upon the unself-conscious expression of human sentiment in places that time has passed by. The celebration of those qualities carries with it the denial of the modern—even in the case of tramps: "The modern tramp is not a tramp, he is a speed-maniac. . . . he is sure to be shallow and artificial, the grotesque, nervous victim of machinery."

The appeal and charm of *A Handy Guide* lie in the very fact that the experiences and observations of a beggar are not those of a gentleman. The reader relishes poet-Lindsay's narration of beggar-Lindsay's encounters with ordinary folk. He is such an indisputably odd amalgam that people most often do not know what to make of him. Humor frequently results from these meetings. In his role as beggar, Lindsay retains certain "higher" values; for example, consider his comment on "a soup of luke-warm water, tallow, half-raw fat pork and wilted greens" he was served in a shanty in Florida: "This dish was innocent of any enhancing condiment." But Lindsay is not overly pious; his humor is often self-effacing, as in the case of an Asheville gentleman who suspected Lindsay "was neither artist nor literary man. I assured him my friends were often of the same opinion." Sometimes Lindsay's observations carry a bite reminiscent of Mark Twain. A moonshiner in the Blue Ridge whom Lindsay calls The Gnome "was like a third-rate Sunday-school teacher in a frock coat in the presence of the infant class." Nor does the humor of situation escape Lindsay's eye in a northern Florida cabin, where at family prayers he "peeped and observed the Patriarch with his chair almost in the fireplace. He ignored the fire. . . . The father prayed twenty minutes, while the chair smoked."

The appeal of the narrative voice in *A Handy Guide* is not—in spite of its title—found in a voice of experience authoritatively explaining how to travel the open road; it is found in the quality of the innocent or naïf making his way as best he can. The Gnome tells our adventurer: "You are just a run-away boy, that's what you are." At one point, about to give up his tramping, Lindsay is in a railway station wanting to telegraph home for train fare, but discovers he has only thirteen cents—not enough for a telegram. Instead, he buys gingersnaps. That kind of frivolity ameliorates a tone that is potentially too pious. His unbeggarly appreciation of household amenities—"But how ingenious is a white iron bed, how subtle are pillows, how overwhelming is sleep!"—has the same effect, as does his homesickness "for that great civilized camp, New York, and the sober-minded pursuit of knowledge there."

Though Lindsay reworked the notebooks of his trips of 1906 and 1908 for publication in 1916, the prose retains the immediacy of the jottings that served to record the experiences. It is plain and matter-of-fact, consisting primarily of short, simple, declarative sentences dependent upon simile for expressive character. At times the prose becomes ungainly, but this quality merely reinforces the somewhat awkward figure the beggar-poet cuts. Repetitive and staccato rhythms in other passages—"He was cadaverous. He had a beak nose. He had a retreating chin."—echo the beat of Lindsay's heavily accented verses.

In the final episode of *A Handy Guide,* the grandmother of an industrious farm family admonishes Lindsay for not looking for work. He retorts, "I wanted to paint rainbows and gild sidewalks and blow bubbles for a living. But no one wanted me to. It is about all I am fit for." At the end of his tramp in the spring of 1906, Lindsay was still uncertain about what he was best fitted for; a trip to Europe that summer with his parents was as suitable a diversion as any. In the fall he returned to New York, where he remained until the spring of 1908, when he made his second walking trip. Eventually reaching home, he took up quarters in his old room and stayed in Springfield until 1912. Those four years were an important period for Lindsay. He came home an apparent twenty-eight-year-old failure; he had tried, without success, to make his mark in the world as an artist and a writer. Four years later he would start another walking trip; but this time, after an additional period of apprenticeship, he would have a substantial amount of verse to his credit and a plan to spread the Gospel of Beauty. He was on the threshold of poetic success.

After a year in the "city of his discontent," Lindsay declared war on the philistines. In the lead paragraph of *War Bulletin* no. 1, July 19, 1909, he explained how he felt he had compromised himself in "taking counsel to please the stupid, the bigoted, the conservative, the impatient, the cheap"; but *"the things that go into the War Bulletin please me only. To the Devil with you, average reader. To Gehenna with your stupidity, your bigotry, your conservatism, your cheapness and your impatience."* Four additional *War Bulletins* appeared in 1909. Except for no. 4, they were pamphlets of a few pages printed on inexpensive paper. Lindsay initially tried to sell them for five cents each; but when that failed, he gave them away on the streets of Springfield. They are the utterances of a writer and idealist frustrated by the lack of attention he is able to command, and lashing out at what he feels are the sources of a corrupt, materialistic society. Lindsay's protest pamphlets are thus thematically linked to the revolt against the village that manifested itself in works by such American writers as Sherwood Anderson, Sinclair Lewis, and Edgar Lee Masters.

There was not much reaction to the first two *War Bulletins;* but the third, directed at religion, hit home—earning Lindsay the scorn of Springfield's sanctimonious burghers. In their eyes his transgression was not blasphemy, but the radicalism of taking religious injunctions literally and seriously. In "The Creed of a Beggar" Lindsay declared, "I believe in God, the creeping fire . . . in Christ the Socialist" and "in that perilous maddening flower, the Holy Ghost." Lindsay's Christianity was not the packaged version delivered once a week, but a vital, life-directing force. "Heaven is no goal for me. The Kingdom of God on earth is vastly more significant." Feeling the spirit move him toward the cleansing of the excrescences of money, he exhorted: "Let us enter the great offices and shut the desk lids and cut the telephone wires. Let us see that the skyscrapers are empty and locked, and the keys thrown into the river. Let us break up the cities."

Lindsay's attack on Springfield, his sacred city, derived, of course, from his love for it. His reverence for this holy city of Lincoln and the aspirations he held for it (described in the apocalyptic *Golden Book of Springfield*) were expressed in terms of a lifelong lover's quarrel with his birthplace. He could not remain angry with his townsmen for long, however; and at Christmas, 1909, he announced a truce in *The Sangamon County Peace Advocate*. This broadside contained nine of his poems, including "Springfield Magical," which begins "In this, the City of my Discontent," and continues:

. . . No Citadel of Brass
By Sinbad found, held half such love and hate;
No picture-palace in a picture-book
Such webs of Friendship, Beauty, Greed and
    Fate!

The last paragraph of *War Bulletin* no. 3 announced the availability of *The Tramp's Excuse* (*War Bulletin* no. 4), "a book of about eighty pages which I will give with both hands to anyone who will write to me and confess that he reads poetry." This first book of Lindsay's poems was an inchoate collection from which he was to cull many of the finer poems for inclusion in *General William Booth*. All in all, *The Tramp's Excuse,* with its dozen or so illustrations by the author and the ethereal quality of the poems populated with fairies and other imaginary characters, resembles many of the books of the previous decade. There was little suggestion of novelty in either subject matter or technique. One of the more exquisitely wrought poems, "I Heard Immanuel Singing," stands last in the volume and was later printed in *The Congo*. Lindsay said he wanted *"to plant the Tramp's Excuse where it will take root and grow."* Though the 300 copies of *The Tramp's Excuse* generally failed to take root, one seed germinated in the mind of a fellow Illinoisan. The critic Floyd Dell wrote in the Chicago *Evening Post* that "Nicholas Vachel Lindsay is something of an artist; after a fashion, a socialist; more certainly, a religious mystic; and for present purposes it must be added that he is indubitably a poet!"

Another product of this period was *The Village Magazine*. Lindsay regarded magazines as especially important vehicles for the presentation of his work. While he desired the large audiences they reached, he valued the idea of a magazine even more for its framework, upon which he could hang and display his various talents as rhymer, designer, editorialist, and artist, and yet achieve the coherence of a single vision:

It seems to me the magazine as a unit is as justified as the novel. The magazine idea has a tremendous grip on me, but not in the commercial sense. That is, one collection of pictures, poems and editorials and end-page ornaments, issued by one man, and dominated by his ideas, and as definitely his, as though it were his novel. Only in this way can I unify all my activities in balanced proportion, and introduce what might be called my genuine *public self* to my little public.

The Village Magazine, first issued in 1910, was an interesting collection of Lindsay's poems, drawings, and articles. Of the two dozen or so poems, several were new but many were taken from *The Tramp's Excuse.* It was characteristic of Lindsay to reuse and reshape his own material in his unflagging effort to find the ideal form to convey his ideas effectively. His *Collected Poems* is a good example of how he reordered his poetry from several different volumes into a new arrangement. This practice is also seen in his conception of *The Village Magazine* as a permanent but evolving form. It was reissued in 1920 and 1925 with additional prose and poetry selections.

After four years at home, Lindsay was ready to take to the road again. It had been a productive period of apprenticeship and accomplishment, but he felt chagrined at the failure of his writing to achieve ready acceptance by the popular magazines and at his continuing financial dependence, at the age of thirty-two, upon his parents. Lindsay's evangelical background and crusading spirit brought him ten dollars and the opportunity to address audiences whenever he spoke in favor of prohibition for the Anti-Saloon League of Illinois. His speeches rang with the conviction of his personal abstinence and the evidence of the squalid life he had witnessed among miners who squandered their wages on alcohol. And Lindsay was not completely without success in having some of his prose and poetry published. Sketches that were later included in *A Handy Guide* appeared in *The Outlook,* and a few poems were published in *The Independent* and *American Magazine.* Before leaving on his westward journey, he had two works printed to serve as his currency.

"The Gospel of Beauty" and *Rhymes to Be Traded for Bread* contain the creed Lindsay was preaching in 1912. A broadside of three paragraphs, "The Gospel of Beauty" capsulizes Lindsay's philosophy. The first point is expressed as a prologue:

I come to you penniless and afoot, to bring a message. I am starting a new religious idea. The idea does not say "no" to any creed that you have heard. * * * After this, let the denomination to which you now belong be called in your heart "the church of beauty" or "the church of the open sky." * * * The church of beauty has two sides: the love of beauty and the love of God.

Lindsay's new religious idea is hardly what it professes to be. It is not religious in the conventional sense; it is nondoctrinaire and nonsectarian. It asks for an internal transformation that is nothing less than a rebirth or reawakening to beauty. This idea is perhaps more properly considered as a cultural attitude, since the love of God is seen as manifesting itself in the temporal world through the creation of beauty. Ultimately, beauty creates a culture of beauty, from the local to the national level, that for Lindsay was the achievement of a utopian heaven on earth.

The second aspect of "The Gospel of Beauty" Lindsay terms "the New Localism." This doctrine asserts that "the things most worthwhile are one's own hearth and neighborhood," and admonishes us to "make our own home and neighborhood the most democratic, the most beautiful and the holiest in the world." This is a platform emphasizing individual self-reform and advocating a country of beauty achieved through the aggregation of its beautiful parts. An aesthetic outlook ought to be nurtured in children, who "should believe in every possible application to art-theory of the thoughts of the Declaration of Independence and Lincoln's Getysburg [*sic*] Address." These artist-children should "wander over the whole nation in search of the secret of democratic beauty," then return to their homes to make them "more beautiful and democratic and holy."

Lindsay was faithful to his trinity of values—beauty, democracy, God—throughout his life and witnessed for his own gospel by returning to his family home in 1929, at the age of forty-nine, after having lived for five years in Spokane, Washington (following ten years of intermittent sojourns in Springfield). Lindsay obviously used himself as the model for the wandering child-artist, an Ishmael cast out by a profit-dominated society, who in his "darkest hours" was "made strong by the vision of a completely beautiful neighborhood and the passion for a completely democratic art." This was Lindsay's vision and since, as he observed in *Adventures,* "there has been as yet no accredited, accepted way for establishing Beauty in the heart of the average American," he could be pardoned for trying his own experiment.

Beauty lays a "healing hand" on the ills of American enterprise; and though it "is not directly pious," it "does more civilizing in its proper hour than many sermons and laws." If Lindsay's program were to be successful, he would, as he said, have to establish "beauty in the heart of the average American" by means of "a completely democratic art." Lindsay had faith not only in the essential goodness of man but also in man's capacity, if given the chance, to respond to beauty in the form of poetry. He attests to his own success in reading his poems to families and other small groups on his early tramps; but we wonder, as he occasionally did, whether his listeners were responding to the beauty of the poems or simply being courteous to a strange but entertaining pilgrim. These doubts plagued Lindsay even more in his polished poetry readings to large audiences. Was their enthusiasm an appreciation of poetic beauty or a response to a performer making a spectacle of himself in a circuslike atmosphere?

On his mendicant journey in 1912, Lindsay supplemented his broadside gospel with the reading of three poems that, a year later, appeared as the last selection in *General William Booth* under the heading "A Gospel of Beauty": "The Proud Farmer," "The Illinois Village," and "On the Building of Springfield." He prefaced these poems with the statement that "taken as a triad, they hold in solution my theory of American civilization." The first achieves greater poetic success than the other two through its more controlled, objective, and concrete idealization of subject matter. This is perhaps because "The Proud Farmer" is written, as its subtitle indicates, "In memory of E. S. Frazee, Rush County, Indiana." Frazee was Lindsay's maternal grandfather, and during his youth Lindsay had frequently visited the farm of this imposing pioneer who adhered to the doctrines of Alexander Campbell and for forty years had "preached and plowed and wrought." Frazee is an example of one who practiced the new localism. He strove to make his own home and neighborhood "the most democratic, the most beautiful and the holiest in the world."

If "The Proud Farmer" outlines the qualities of character necessary to implement the new localism, "The Illinois Village" argues the superiority of "clean prairie lands" to the city "Whose sidewalks are but stones of fear." Hope and "Spirit-power" emanate from the village church, "Rural in form, foursquare and plain," with "The whiteness it reflects from God." "On the Building of Springfield" lays more stress on the importance of creating an environment of beauty to provide "food for the spirit" and to nourish the artists and leaders needed in every generation to "start our blood athrill / With living language, words that set us free." And because "A city is not builded in a day," the opening line of the final stanza proclaims that "We must have many Lincoln-hearted men." Though Lindsay spread his gospel by reading these three poems, they were not included in the printed pamphlet that he carried with him in place of money.

Rhymes to Be Traded for Bread squeezes forty-six poems into double columns on sixteen pages of cheap paper. Lindsay referred to them as "new verses," which suggests that most of them had been written during 1910–1912 or since *The Tramp's Excuse* and *The Village Magazine*. These poems reveal the maturity of expression Lindsay acquired during the preceding four years. More than half of them found their way into *General William Booth* and *The Congo* in the next two years. Perhaps the finest of these rhymes was one directly inspired by a former governor whom Lindsay had observed from his bedroom window.

John Peter Altgeld, governor of Illinois (1892–1896), won the sympathy of the downtrodden among his constituents for his zeal in reforming conditions in which the lower classes lived and worked, and the enmity of the power brokers, who saw to it that he was turned out of office after only one term. He displayed progressive views by advocating penal reform and the compulsory arbitration of labor disputes. Conservative forces never forgave him for pardoning the "anarchists"—following an investigation that demonstrated they had been railroaded into jail—who allegedly sparked the Chicago Haymarket Riot of 1886. Lindsay was obviously attracted by Altgeld's political philosophy; moreover, his deeper, mystical bond with that courageous governor was forged by the fact that Altgeld had resided in the city of Lincoln and had trod the ground hallowed by that hero. "The Eagle That Is Forgotten" is a quiet elegiac poem lamenting that only a few years after Altgeld's death, those "that should have remembered forever, * * * remember no more." Nonetheless, there is consolation in the fact that the flame kindled by Altgeld is being kept alive by those following in his steps, and thus "to live in mankind is far more than to live in a name." Since Lindsay was suffering at this time the obscurity not of the forgotten, but of the undiscovered, he must have shared in the consolation of that sentiment.

Lindsay begins *Rhymes to Be Traded for Bread* with a reference to his previous trips in a poem entitled "Upon Returning to the Country Road." He recollects that "Those were his days of glory, / Of faith in his fellow-men. / Therefore, today the singer / Turns beggar once again." The experiences of this return to the country road to restore his faith in man are recorded in *Adventures While Preaching the Gospel of Beauty* (1914). Lindsay's best prose work, it has an immediacy, freshness, and excitement that are not always felt in *A Handy Guide*. This stems from the fact that Lindsay was writing closer in time to the events themselves, and using the letters that he wrote home as the basis for his text. Thus, the prose has some of the brusqueness of telegraphic dispatches and the spontaneity of vivid impressions recorded on the spot.

Adventures, like *A Handy Guide,* is Lindsay's unique synthesis of prose narrative, description, and gospelizing—interspersed with poems, a series of five proclamations, and, of course, the text of "The Gospel of Beauty" incorporated into the first chapter. Lindsay's letters home, with their dated entries, form, as he observed, "a sort of diary of the trip" that begins in Springfield and traces his steps westward through Illinois, Missouri, Kansas, Colorado, and into New Mexico; then he rides a Pullman to Los Angeles and the composition of "General William Booth." Despite that format, *Adventures* is not a daily log devoting equal attention to every experience; more than half of the text focuses upon Kansas. Indeed, *Adventures* may be regarded as an ode to Kansas. For Lindsay it represents "the Ideal American Community! Kansas, nearer than any other to the kind of a land our fathers took for granted! Kansas, practically free from cities and industrialism, the real last refuge of the constitution, since it maintains the type of agricultural civilization the constitution had in mind!" He ignores the grandeur of

Colorado's Rockies in order to celebrate the virtues of an "Ideal American Community" through his encomium of Kansas, "the most interminable plain that ever expanded and made glorious the heart of Man."

Some might deem Lindsay's praise fulsome, but it must be realized that Lindsay's perception transcends everyday realities and is colored by his vision of what the true America should be. While sitting out a rain shower in a railway station, he writes:

I have crossed the mystic border. I have left earth. I have entered Wonderland. Though I am still east of the geographic centre of the United States, in every spiritual sense I am in the West. This morning I passed the stone mile-post that marks the beginning of Kansas.

Though the last sentence brings the reader abruptly down to earth, the initial short, breathless sentences of the passage seem to echo the ecstasy of the famous "transparent eyeball" passage in Emerson's "Nature." Like Henry David Thoreau's experiment in the woods, Lindsay's journey is a spiritual exploration of the American landscape: overly romantic at times and less vividly concrete than some other depictions of nature in America, but nonetheless a truly evocative portrait of the drama of wheat harvesting as it was done in western Kansas in 1912.

Lindsay's utterly transparent prose registers his impressions with just enough detail to authenticate the emotional ambience of his experiences. As in a journal, narrative structure resides in individual episodes. One of the finest of these is the story of a bronco named Dick. Dick, a high-spirited colt that became obstreperous while being broken, was beaten and hitched to a reaper to curb his rebelliousness. However, he fought the harness all day, went mad under the hot sun, and died in a last effort to break free. Lindsay renames Dick "Richard the Lion-Hearted," for his indomitable spirit in continuing to "dance"

until his death, and for refusing to be broken by the beating administered by two drunken men. Lindsay's witnessing of the cruel death of the colt made an indelible impression on his mind, and was later forged into the touching poem "The Broncho That Would Not Be Broken." Lindsay identified with the heroic spirit exemplified by Dick ("I think I want on my coat of arms a broncho, rampant"), both in continuing to dance his own poetry despite a disinterested public and in proving to himself that he could endure—within reasonable bounds—the physical hardships of wheat harvesting.

In a long description of a typical wheat-harvesting day, Lindsay gives his material the epic proportions it demands—"There is nothing small in the panorama. All the lines of the scene are epic"—and memorializes the lore of an American calling much as Herman Melville had done for whaling. Fortunately, the success of *Adventures* is not dependent upon our empathizing with the arcane yet prosaic subject of wheat harvesting. It succeeds by virtue of the extraordinary character of the perceiver of these events: a foolish mendicant, an American original. Lindsay's innocence has the attraction of a grown-up Huckleberry Finn with just enough self-consciousness to keep the devout beggar from appearing smug. He concedes that an automobile ride can be a convenience: "I still maintain that the auto is a carnal institution, to be shunned by the truly spiritual, but there are times when I, for one, get tired of being spiritual." Such humor conveys the sense of a likable character (far less austere and self-righteous than a Thoreau), whose realistic yearning—"Oh, for a hot bath and a clean shirt!"—we appreciate. When Lindsay is invited into a shack after a long tramp in the rain, he observes: "And so my heart was made suddenly light after a day and a half of hard whistling." One has to respond positively to a person like that.

The five "Proclamations" that conclude *Ad-*

ventures expand the ideas of "The Gospel of Beauty": they tout the healing power of rural life for the afflictions of modern urban civilization; the cultural blossoming of the old New England spirit in the West and South; the new village as a self-sufficient cultural center; the artists who will spring from fertile rural lands; and the perfected democracy of equality, beauty, and holiness wrought by the statesman, artist, and priest. About ten years after these proclamations appeared, Lindsay averred that "the great virtue of these proclamations is that they map out my private life for a lifetime, and in none of them is it hinted that recitation is to be my fate!" When Lindsay wrote that statement, he was recuperating at a small junior college in Gulfport, Mississippi, from the accumulated toil of several years of touring to recite his poetry. But in 1912 he could not envision the disenchantment he later experienced in spreading his message, even though his commitment to his gospel never wavered.

Adventures concludes with some final impressions of the "distinctive institution" of harvest time in Kansas—a sympathetic portrait of the men who participate ("the harvester is indeed harvested") and a description of how their presence temporarily transforms "whole villages that are dead any other season." Lindsay, however, does not carry his narrative as far as his journey actually went. He continued to Colorado, where he stayed for several weeks at a camp with his parents before walking to New Mexico. There he reluctantly gave up his original intention of walking to the West Coast. He rationalized that it was no failure to decline to go on foot across more than a thousand miles of desert; moreover, a passing reference in the last chapter of *Adventures* suggests that he was anxious to embark "upon a certain spiritual enterprise, namely, the writing of certain new poems that have taken possession of me."

It is not clear when the idea of a poem on Gen-

eral William Booth took possession of Lindsay. The leader of the Salvation Army had died in London in August 1912, and Lindsay may have heard the news then, or possibly not until he reached Los Angeles about a month later. Whatever the case, a week after his arrival in California, Lindsay had, in a burst of frantic activity, completed "General William Booth Enters into Heaven." This poem was unlike anything he had written before, and its publication caused a sensation because it was so different from the bulk of poetry then appearing in America.

What was new for Lindsay was the successful presentation of poetic tendencies that had long been simmering within him. "General William Booth" is more obviously democratic than his earlier verse in both its theme and its form. His conception of poetry is avowedly democratic, but his own problematic poetic identity and much of his poetry obscure his fervent faith in a democratic poetry.

Lindsay's long apprenticeship might be attributed to his divided allegiance to the two mainstreams of American poetry: the aesthetic craftsmanship of Poe and the democratic idealism of Whitman. In fact, he seems never to have resolved the problem of his identity as a poet. He often claimed and, indeed, wrote to a friend in 1929, "I have never called myself a poet." In the poem "Twenty Years Ago" (from *Every Soul Is a Circus,* 1929) Lindsay protests that "You call me 'a troubadour,' / But I am an adventurer, in hieroglyphics, buildings, and designs." Of course, these disclaimers late in his life may be regarded as a way of escaping the criticism that increasingly came his way after 1920, but they are also consistent with the problems of self-definition that beleaguered Lindsay during his formative years.

Lindsay's mother provided the source for these models. It was her insistence that led him to study art and her ardor for the "classics" of

European art—especially poet-artists, such as William Blake and the Pre-Raphaelites—that made Lindsay so open to the conception of the artist as craftsman and accounted for the years he persisted in his art training. At the same time, the devotion of Lindsay's mother to religious and social causes instilled in her son a zealous commitment to the egalitarian principles and democratic utopianism that he expressed in the social formulation of "The Gospel of Beauty." Between the extremes of art for art's sake and art as propaganda, he clearly emphasized the latter.

When Lindsay argues in "The Gospel of Beauty" that future generations will be made strong by "a completely democratic art," he means not merely a nonelitist art but also an art that nourishes and fosters "the thoughts of the Declaration of Independence and Lincoln's Getysburg Address." Indeed, he subscribes to the notion that poets should be legislators: "It is far more important that artists and poets should be in power, and displace the present business caste, than their particular views would be right. The unwritten law should be 'only artists should hold high office.'" For Lindsay, then, "the issues of Poetry *are* political *issues*"; and to be effective, they must be made accessible to the common man, for "in a democracy, the arts, like the political parties, are not founded till they have touched the county chairman, the ward leader, the individual voter." Considering all of these factors, it is not surprising that Lindsay's definition of the ideal American poet—the poet he aspired to be—incorporates elements of Poe and Whitman, but is modeled on a Populist politician:

Bryan is really the American poet, till we can take the Chautauqua platform, and sing to as many. I suppose the ideal American poet would have the tang of Mark Twain, the music of Poe, the sweep and mysticism of Whitman, and the platform power of Bryan, and a career in verse similar to his in Politics.

Prior to the publication of "General William Booth," Lindsay had been ruminating on the problems of how to sing to the many. In the accounts of his walking tours, he frequently reveals the satisfaction gained from reading his verse to the generally unlettered people who shared food and shelter with him. His desire to make his poetry accessible to common folk led him to the idea of incorporating folk elements—in both subject matter and technique—into his poetry. Lindsay felt that if he based a poem on an already familiar subject or rhythm, the work was at least one step closer to the common reader. A familiar theme or rhythm also provided him with an established emotional base that he could refashion, in conjunction with his own feelings, into a powerful new synthesis. But at this stage in his career, Lindsay's aspirations were frustrated by the limited publication and circulation of his poetry. Driven by a sense of destiny and the urge to reform society, he yearned to make an impact: "I would go through most any contortion, even a conventional one, to grip the vitals of the ultimate consumer of song." Whitman had not achieved this end; he had only "brought the idea of democracy to our sophisticated literati, but did not persuade the democracy itself to read his democratic poems." Exploiting folk materials such as popular songs and gospel hymns would prove to be one means to that end; and in August 1912, Lindsay was ready to begin.

"General William Booth" is to be sung to the tune of "The Blood of the Lamb," with instrumental accompaniment as indicated by Lindsay. The first line, "Booth led boldly with his big bass drum," plunges the reader into a palpitating rhythmic alliance with the flow of Booth's parade. It is not the meter or employment of traditional poetic feet that sustains involvement in the poem; it is rhythm broadly construed as it emerges from alliteration, assonance, and the flow of feeling within the work. Lindsay's directions for the accompaniment of bass drum, banjo, flute, and tambourine are not meant to be prescriptive, but to suggest the voice qualities appropriate for the intended effect in reading and reciting the poem. (Lindsay's phonograph recordings are instructive in this matter.)

Edgar Lee Masters, Lindsay's biographer and fellow poet from Illinois, noted that "music is at the bottom of his poetry." In one sense, of course, the primary appeal of Lindsay's verse is to the ear—rather than the eye or mind—and to the sentiments of the heart beating out the physiology of being. In another sense, music is the core of Lindsay's verse. It is not an overlay. Lindsay objected vociferously to attempts by composers to set his poetry to music, because it would violate the internal music of the poems. The musical quality was to emerge from the phonetic qualities of speech itself. If an existing tune was suitable for his purpose, he would utilize it as part of a new synthesis; however, his verses were not to be fitted arbitrarily to new tunes after the fact. Lindsay once wrote to George Armstrong, his tour manager and friend, that Percy Grainger (whose musical compositions incorporated American folk tunes)

. . . is about the only musician I ever struck who has the remotest notion of the elaborateness of the musical construction of my pieces, just as they stand. Most of the literati are utterly deaf to music, though great scrappers as to "methods of versification." That is "methods" of embalming the corpse of poetry.

Lindsay specified that the distinctive musical effects of his poetry—for purposes of dancing or public reciting—were to be achieved through exaggerating the inherent phonetic qualities and by emphasizing every onomatopoeic feature of the verse.

The effect of Lindsay's throbbing rhythms is to involve the reader in the process of the poem itself. If, as Robert Penn Warren claims, "the basic fact about poetry is that it demands participation," then Lindsay is successful not only in making the poem accessible but also in compelling participation in it. Once we are marching in step with Booth, the refrain—"Are you washed in the blood of the Lamb?"—interrogates us individually. The emphasis, however, is not upon the self as a simple, separate person; it is upon the collective, en masse. Lindsay, as poet, does not use his own life as a model to celebrate himself or the concept of selfhood. He sings of the self as the essential unit of democracy, but reserves his highest praise for the self working selflessly for the establishment of heaven on earth.

Lindsay's heroes—and he is a hero-worshipper—are those who contribute to achieving mankind's millennial aspirations. "General William Booth" is a social view of salvation. Just as Edward Taylor domesticates the process of personal salvation in the images of "Huswifery," Lindsay socializes the process of salvation in the images of community government. "Jesus came from out the court-house door, . . . And blind eyes opened on a new, sweet world." Booth is the truly democratic and Christian general who leads "unwashed legions" of lepers, drabs, and drug fiends from the slums to be washed in the blood of the Lamb. His faith advanced the millennial cause, and his Master came "for Booth the soldier." Lindsay felt that the utopian vision of a golden Springfield was "worth working toward," for "if we are millennialists, we must be patient millennialists. Yet let us begin to-day as though the Millennium were to-morrow, and start our 'Village Improvement Parade' down Main Street, and turn the corner east toward the rising sun to a land of clear pictures and young hearts." Thus the special power of "General William Booth" resides in its hopeful egalitarian vision—we may all be washed in the blood of the Lamb—fused to a comparably egalitarian vehicle the upbeat tempo of which sweeps the reader involuntarily into participating in the ecstatic process of entering heaven: "O, shout Salvation!"

Today, our taste having been refined by modernist poetry, we may feel somewhat cool toward what one critic has called the "crude pietism" of "General William Booth"; but the power of the poem has remained remarkably intact since the time when it was felt as a fresh, new force in American poetry. The poetry of the previous two or three decades in America was singularly undistinguished. After Whitman there was no major poet who dominated the American scene, only the legacy of the New England Fireside Poets. Edgar Lee Masters' acerbic characterization of this "interregnum" period, though perhaps overstated, suggests how intensely a new group of poets, who were to become very well known, felt about the plight of the verse they had to redeem: "The magazine poetry of America for more than twenty years before 1912 I believe to be the most dreadful piffle, the most emasculated trash, the most obvious wax fruit that the world has ever seen."

Harriet Monroe, who inaugurated *Poetry* magazine in October 1912, dubbed the work of these young writers "the new poetry," the title of an anthology of contemporary verse she and Alice Corbin Henderson published in 1917. Though the designation has little usefulness—it includes such disparate talents as Robert Frost, T. S. Eliot, Ezra Pound, Carl Sandburg, and Joyce Kilmer—it does suggest that this poetry was at least self-consciously new. "General William Booth" exemplifies this newness in its subject matter, a realistic look at the underside of urban life—a new theme for poetry at the time—and in its use of the language of everyday speech instead of a conventionalized poetic diction. What made Lindsay's verse seem like the newest of the new was its vitality. Compared with the typically genteel magazine verse of the day, "General William Booth" astounded readers with its driving, insistent rhythms that were akin to the syncopated beats of the era's popular ragtime and jazz. Lindsay had triumphed in "making it new"—to borrow Pound's dictum—and had gained the audience he so earnestly desired. Little did he imagine how well known he was to become and how this achievement sealed his fate in a manner he was to regret.

Though "General William Booth" revealed a new dimension in Lindsay's poetry, the other poems in the volume by that name represent his work of the preceding five years, including "The Eagle That Is Forgotten" and three poems collectively called "A Gospel of Beauty." More than one-third of the poems were grouped in a section headed "Fantasies and Whims." Among these deftly composed, dreamy works are several "moon-poems" (reprinted with others in a section by that name in *Collected Poems*) that describe how different people and different animals find their own essences reflected in the light of the moon. Related to these is "A Net to Snare the Moonlight," subtitled "What the Man of Faith Said." This delicate sixteen-line poem subtly expresses Lindsay's belief in the necessity of man's imaginative life as well as man's dependence upon the sustenance of the workaday world. Since God has blessed man with nature's bounty, the Man of Faith, sounding like a Populist, desires that "all men / Have land to catch the rain" and "Ripe wheat and poppies red." The poppies signify for Lindsay an Oriental, mystical restfulness. They are allied to the lotus in "The Wedding of the Rose and Lotus" (a poem commemorating the opening of the Panama Canal in 1911—a joining of the East and West), in which "The lotus is Nirvana" whose genius "Shall heal earth's too-much fret." Thus, man needs "dreams when toil is done" as well as "A place of toil by day time."

General William Booth Enters into Heaven

and Other Poems was very favorably reviewed and Lindsay's achievement celebrated. In March 1914, at a banquet in Chicago given by Harriet Monroe for W. B. Yeats, the guest of honor, directing his remarks to Lindsay, praised "General William Booth": "This poem is stripped bare of ornament. It has an earnest simplicity, a strange beauty, and you know Bacon said, 'there is no excellent beauty without strangeness.' " Lindsay rose to acknowledge Yeats's remarks, and then stunned the diners by reciting a poem only recently completed—"The Congo." Before the end of the year, this work became the title for another collection of poems.

The renown of "The Congo" rests upon its panoply of sound, somewhat like Poe's "The Bells." It is a poem read with the pulse rather than the mind. As in "General William Booth," Lindsay orchestrates its sound effects through copious marginal directions. "The Congo" was to become the poem that his audiences most frequently and insistently requested. The length of the poem—it takes more than seven minutes to recite—allowed for a complete display of Lindsay's declamatory and dramatic talents in reading lines ranging from a light to a terrified whisper, and from the sound of the "wind in the chimney" to the "literal imitation of campmeeting racket, and trance." The most extraordinary aspect of the poem, however, was its syncopated rhythms, which Lindsay delivered in a singsong fashion much like musical chant. His recitation of this poem was guaranteed to enthrall audiences, who became swept up in the multipaced cadences, the rising and falling dynamics of crescendo and decrescendo, and, cast over all, the aura of witchcraft and voodoo.

"The Congo," subtitled "A Study of the Negro Race," is divided into three sections: "Their Basic Savagery," "Their Irrepressible High Spirits," and "The Hope of Their Religion." Today this view of blacks is tawdry and racially offensive. Unquestionably, Lindsay's poem exploits a stereotyped view of blacks in his day and capitalizes upon a black mystique, which perhaps was originally associated with the mystery of the impenetrable, dark recesses of the jungle. That aspect is, however, conveyed primarily through the overlay of sound and description, and is not the intent of the poem, which clearly envisions the salvation of the black race through its faith in the Bible. This theme may carry a distasteful sense of cultural and religious superiority, but it is not willfully racist.

Lindsay's end note to "The Congo" states that the poem was suggested by an allusion, in a sermon delivered by his pastor, to the death of a Disciples of Christ missionary who drowned in the Congo River. That reference was apparently the catalyst for Lindsay's reflection upon blacks. Blacks composed one-fifth of Springfield's population while Lindsay was growing up, and his family employed blacks in the household. Lindsay was aware of their disadvantaged condition, and was deeply disturbed by the lynching of two blacks at Springfield in 1908, which he protested in letters to the editor of the newspaper. On another occasion, in reference to World War I, Lindsay remarked that it was easier to be a martyr for France than for blacks; but he would prefer to die in the cause of the latter.

"The Congo," however, seems to be less "A Study of the Negro Race" than another version of Lindsay's "The Village Improvement Parade." The depiction of blacks is a mishmash of American and African characteristics. Each of its three sections opens with an American scene and then jumps to the Congo. One effect of this commingling is to recall the dignity and pride of the American blacks' tribal origins; but another, of opposite import, is to present Congolese villages as similar in their needs to American villages. Repentance brings the death of Mumbo-Jumbo in the jungle, and "Pioneer angels cleared the way / For sacred capitals, for temples clean." As a result " 'Twas a land transfigured, 'twas a new creation," which is, of course, Lindsay's utopian goal for the villages of America. The Congo needs to kill its false god, Mumbo-Jumbo, just as America needs to kill its false god, money. One of the banners from Lindsay's drawings of "The Village Improvement Parade" proclaims "A hasty prosperity may be raw and absurd, a well-considered poverty may be exquisite." Thus, "Redeemed were the forests, the beasts and the men"; and "The Congo" brings us back to the Midwest.

The poetry revival originating in the Midwest at this time was championing new themes—or a return to the common man and everyday life—and introducing new rhythms into American poetry. Sandburg rediscovered Whitman's free verse, and Lindsay showed how the rhythms and sounds emanating from the kaleidoscope of American life could be incorporated into verse. "The Congo" was an important illustration of how new rhythms could infuse verse with new life and redeem poetry from its status as magazine filler. Lindsay's chanting of "The Congo" inoculated it with a primitive vitality drawn from folk origins. Using folk materials as a source of poetic inspiration opened up poetry to a public who could identify with the themes and participate in the rhythms with which they were familiar.

The poem that follows "The Congo," in the volume of the same title, is an even better demonstration of the use of everyday American sound in poetry. "The Santa Fé Trail" is a Whitmanesque recording of the sounds of the open road as America moves westward. Its subtitle, "A Humoresque," indicates that it is to be regarded as a playful musical composition; and its marginal notes direct how its lively spirit is to be achieved. Walking across Kansas on the Santa Fe Trail, the poet records the novelty of the intrusive sound of the automobile in American life. "Hark to the *calm*-horn, *balm*-horn, *psalm*-horn. / Hark to the *faint*-horn, *quaint*

horn, *saint*-horn." On each car is a "snapping pennant" naming its place of origin. The catalog of cities is to be read "like a train-caller in a Union Depot." As the poet watches, "The United States / Goes by."

The noises of the racing autos "Blasting the whispers of the morning dumb" and American life passing westward is contrasted with the sounds of nature. "I find in the stubble of the new-cut weeds / A whisper and a feasting, all one needs: / The whisper of the strawberries, white and red / Here where the new-cut weeds lie dead." Those lines have their origin in an experience that Lindsay relates in *Adventures* (for which this poem is an excellent gloss). The epigraph for this poem, also taken from that book, is a brief passage describing how an old black man, in answer to Lindsay's question, tells him that a bird he has heard singing so sweetly is called the Rachel-Jane. The Rachel-Jane is the spirit of nature; it epitomizes the rural life, and its lines are to be sung. "Far away the Rachel-Jane / Not defeated by the horns / Sings amid a hedge of thorns:— / Love and life, / Eternal youth, / Sweet, sweet, sweet, sweet." Even though the theme of this poem argues that "fair dreams fade / When the raw horns blow," it is the sound effects of the raw horns that attract and fascinate the reader. The varying tempos and tonal levels, in imitation of contemporary life, engaged the attention of Lindsay's auditors for his rejuvenation of an old Jeffersonian message.

"General William Booth," "The Congo," and "The Santa Fé Trail" all demonstrate what Lindsay called the "Higher Vaudeville imagination." In a note entitled "Primitive Singing," in *Poetry* magazine, he explains the term as he had formulated it in response to a question that Yeats had asked him: "What are we going to do to restore the primitive singing of poetry?" Lindsay's solution in the form of the Higher Vaudeville was to carry the method of the American vaudeville stage ("where every line may be two-thirds spoken and one-third sung, the entire rendering, musical and elocutionary, depending largely upon the improvising power and sure instinct of the performer") "back towards the old Greek precedent of the half-chanted lyric." Lindsay had read that "music was the handmaid of verse" in all Greek lyrics, and he wanted to create a form, accordingly, in which the verses would contain an inherent musical component that could be exploited in reading or performing. The reader is to use his imagination and follow his instincts in bringing out the melody that each line suggests. Elsewhere Lindsay wrote that the Higher Vaudeville "exaggerates musical effects"; it is "an exaggeration of the phonetic qualities and the metrical form," and in reciting "the chanter should bring out every hint of assonance and alliteration."

There is an ambivalence, though, in Lindsay's attitude toward vaudeville. He embraced its technique, but with reluctance. He wanted to reach the common man, yet felt that vaudeville in itself might be too common for the art of poetry: thus his specious link with Greek poetry and his attempt to dignify his endeavors with the adjective "Higher." There is a reference to vaudeville in his poem "The Knight in Disguise," a tribute to the writer O. Henry. Lindsay's own desire to be a knight in disguise accounts for his adoption of the vaudeville method, in which the characters "over-act each part. But at the height / Of banter and of canter and delight / The masks fall off for one queer instant there / And show real faces: faces full of care / And desperate longing: love that's hot or cold; / And subtle thoughts, and countenances bold." Similarly, Lindsay yearned to convey his thoughts and feelings to his audience through vaudeville; but as he painfully learned, they relished the overacted show and did not appreciate the apocalyptic seriousness that was behind the mask.

Lindsay was more successful in transmitting his thematic concerns to ordinary readers through mythic images. He had the gift of being able to endow figures and events from the American past with legendary significance. One of the best examples of this is the poem "Abraham Lincoln Walks at Midnight," one of six antiwar poems that make up the final section of *The Congo*. The outbreak of World War I in August 1914 shocked Americans, and Lindsay immediately responded with his poetic statements against the war. Lincoln "cannot sleep upon his hillside now" because "The sins of all the warlords burn his heart." He paces the streets of Springfield near the old courthouse, moving past his homestead and through the market. Lindsay recalls the image of the brooding Lincoln stalking the streets of a divided nation's capital:

A bronzed, lank man! His suit of ancient black,
A famous high top-hat and plain worn shawl
Make him the quaint great figure that men love,
The prairie-lawyer, master of us all.

Lindsay invokes the spirit of Lincoln; domesticates his appearance, locale, and actions; and then transforms him into a god who becomes a source of comfort, pride, and support for future Americans. Like a mythic hero, Lincoln assumes our burdens in sorrow "That all his hours of travail here for men / Seem yet in vain." He answers our call for aid, and in turn we must allow him to "sleep upon his hill again" by restoring peace. Characteristically, Lindsay incorporates into this pattern—in the next-to-last stanza—a vision having its source in the mythic belief in American destiny and in a future peace, international in scope and socialistic in nature. World War I is the crisis that calls forth from the American pantheon the model of Lincoln to remind us that we, too, cannot rest from the national mission to which we are compelled by our cultural identity:

He cannot rest until a spirit-dawn
Shall come;—the shining hope of Europe free:

The league of sober folk, the Workers' Earth,
Bringing long peace to Cornland, Alp and Sea.

Lindsay's next book was a study of film, surprising in its subject matter yet a natural consequence of his desire to reach the people and convert them to the visionary prospects of his version of American ideals and destiny that he enunciated in the "Gospel of Beauty." *The Art of the Moving Picture* (1915) is the final phase of Lindsay's creative surge during the middle years of the decade. A new work was published every year from 1913 to 1917, but after *General William Booth* (1913) and *The Congo* (1914) his poetry did not significantly change or develop. Hence, *The Art of the Moving Picture,* appearing one year after *Adventures,* may be regarded as the capstone to Lindsay's creative ferment. The critic Stanley Kauffmann believes that "out of the mass of Lindsay's poetry and prose, this may be the work most worthy of survival. And in the field of film aesthetics, it is the first important American work, still important." Though Kauffmann's estimate of *The Art of the Moving Picture* in the Lindsay canon seems overly favorable, it does point up the stature of Lindsay's pioneering contribution to American film criticism. In addition, that contribution may be regarded as a fortuitous by-product, or natural consequence, of his social and artistic beliefs.

Lindsay had a prophetic faith in film; indeed, of all his visions, those about film have come to pass in the greatest number. In the 1922 revision of *The Art of the Moving Picture* he even adds an introductory chapter in which, somewhat gloatingly, he acknowledges that his theories of film have been adopted throughout the country. Lindsay was attracted to film because he derived immense personal enjoyment from it, and because he discerned its usefulness as a means of disseminating ideas and information in a democracy.

Lindsay's fondness for film derives from his interest in drawing and the visual arts. He regarded film as more closely allied to painting than to drama, and saw it as a means of capturing and reflecting the rich images of American life. He thought Americans were visually impoverished and believed that film would contribute significantly to their visual awareness and cultivate a demand for an art and architecture of beauty. His enjoyment was, nevertheless, also on the visceral level. "I am the one poet who has a right to claim for his muses Blanche Sweet, Mary Pickford, and Mae Marsh," he wrote about those early screen heroines, each of whom had inspired a poem, and added that the two things to be said for those poems was "first, they were heartfelt. Second, any one could improve on them." Lindsay's unabashed Midwestern character enabled him to be one of the first intellectuals to appreciate film as a serious artistic medium. Other critics also enjoyed film, but would not deign to consider that a popular form of entertainment, so appealing to the crossroads taste, could be art.

Exactly, however, because it appealed to all social classes, for Lindsay film was a powerful force in a democracy. It "goes almost as far as journalism into the social fabric in some ways, further in others"; and since "it is scattered like the newspaper," it "penetrates in our land to the haunts of the wildest or the dullest. The isolated prospector rides twenty miles to see the same film that is displayed on Broadway. There is not a civilized or half-civilized land but may read the Whitmanesque message in time, if once it is put on the films with power." Not only does the film serve democratic ideals; it promotes religion and brotherhood, and even reunites lower-class families by striking at alcoholism, the root of their dissolution. The movie theater "offers a substitute for many of the lines of pleasure in the groggery." Once, it seems, Lindsay adopted a cause, he was able to adapt it to his personal program. Notwithstanding its idiosyncrasies, *The*

Art of the Moving Picture goes beyond them to present an argument for film as art.

The standards for judging film, Lindsay maintained, are those "which are taken for granted in art histories and schools." He consciously dignified film by frequently comparing the frames of particular movies to famous paintings, and analyzing the film from a pictorial point of view. His insistence on the efficacy of this approach compelled respect for the legitimacy of film as art and for film aesthetics as practical criticism. In judging film, Lindsay contended that "it must first be good picture, then good motion." His emphasis upon the pictorial quality of film blinded him to the future dominance of the "talkies." He thought films should remain silent, and disliked even the musical accompaniment provided by local theaters. On the other hand, he was one of the first to recognize the uniqueness and significance of film, proclaiming that "Edison is the new Gutenberg. He has invented the new printing." In an especially valuable chapter, "Thirty Differences Between the Photoplays and the Stage," Lindsay further defines the properties of film in contrast with those of drama. "The successful motion picture expresses itself through mechanical devices that are being evolved every hour. Upon those many new bits of machinery are founded novel methods of combination in another field of logic, not dramatic logic, but tableau logic."

In the same year (1915) that *The Art of the Moving Picture* was published, Lindsay employed "tableau logic" in "The Chinese Nightingale," a poem that appeared in *Poetry* and won that magazine's Levinson prize of $250 for the best contribution of the year. It was to be the title poem of a volume of verses published two years later; and because it was Lindsay's favorite long poem, he placed it first in his *Collected Poems*. After the success of "General William Booth" and "The Congo," Lindsay was apprehensive about being typed exclusively as a "Higher Vaudeville" poet. He considered that to be only one of his veins, and not the richest one. "The Chinese Nightingale" was an endeavor to throw off his dramatic mantle and establish his proficiency in a sustained fantasy. Lindsay's imagination had frequently been haunted by the Orient through his reading and through the direct link of his sister Olive, who had gone to China in 1905 with her husband, a medical missionary. There were Chinese in Lindsay's native Springfield, and he had been through the Chinatowns of both New York and San Francisco. Probably the immediate catalyst was his parents' visit to China in the summer of 1914.

The tableau logic of "The Chinese Nightingale" is suggested by its subtitle, "A Song in Chinese Tapestries." The bird's song of love and hope weaves reality and fantasy together in an exotic picture given unity as the dream of a Chinese laundryman, Chang. The poet asks Chang why he irons while the rest of San Francisco sleeps. Chang reveals his secret: "My breast with vision is satisfied, / And I see green trees and fluttering wings, / And my deathless bird from Shanghai sings." The lighting of incense creates a dream-vision atmosphere in which figurines come to life, and a dog conjures up a noble Chinese lady who had been Chang's lover when he was king in a pre-Confucian age. Chang and his sweetheart live in a stately palace by the sea, their love enhanced by magical powers that can charm a dragon upon whose back they are borne to their "secret ivory house." Meanwhile, stony-faced Chang "ironed away in that bower dim" and the bird gives vent to his soul. Chang reflects upon the course of human existence: "Man is a torch, then ashes soon, / May and June, then December, / Dead December, then again June." There is "Sorrow and love, glory and love"; but the poem's final affirmation is that "Spring came on forever, / Spring came on forever." Chang's succor in dream that sustains his daily toil is a frequent theme in Lindsay's poetry, which in this case, with a nod to Coleridge and Poe, is more fantastic than usual. Though this poem is rich in bizarre imagery, it ultimately seems thin. It is a tableau—not a moving picture—and thus it lacks the movement that gives life to Lindsay's other poems. Further, it lacks the American context against which Lindsay's best poems resonate.

Just as parts of "The Chinese Nightingale" were inspired by Lindsay's courtship of the poet Sara Teasdale, so other lines seem to be veiled references to the outbreak of World War I, "When all the world was drinking blood / From the skulls of men and bulls." There are two sections of poems about the war in *The Chinese Nightingale and Other Poems*. They reveal Lindsay's own soul-searching about his noninvolvement and his pacifist persuasion. Probably the best of these twelve poems is "Our Mother Pocahontas." From her grave in England, Pocahontas returns to America to remind us that our roots are native and honorable, and that we should stay free of entangling foreign alliances. "We here renounce our Saxon blood. . . . We here renounce our Teuton pride." We are "The newest race . . . born of her resilient grace." Wherefore, "She sings of lilacs, maples, wheat, / Her own soil sings beneath her feet, / Of springtime / And Virginia, / Our Mother, Pocahontas."

The remaining noteworthy poems in this volume all, like "Our Mother Pocahontas," derive richness from their American setting. "The Ghost of the Buffaloes" evokes the awesome presence of those beasts that darkened the vast American plains and then almost disappeared. "The lords of the prairie" and their Indian hunters, coming to a boy in a dream, represent the terrible power of primitive American nature as it impresses itself like "A scourge and amazement" upon the national psyche. In "The Raft," Mark Twain is eulogized for describing a republic upon a raft; "All praise to Emerson

and Whitman, yet / The best they have to say, their sons forget. / But who can dodge this genius of the stream, / The Mississippi Valley's laughing dream?"

The creation of another American author is recalled in the poem "A Negro Sermon:—Simon Legree," which is the first part of "The Booker Washington Trilogy: A Memorial to Booker T. Washington." The other two sections are "John Brown" and "King Solomon and the Queen of Sheba." The portrait of Simon Legree emphasizes his alliances with the devil, and his seemingly supernatural power over his slaves as seen from the slaves' point of view. It is to be read "in your own variety of negro dialect." The poem is meant to portray the superstitious nature of the slave, for whom Legree "was surely a witch-man in disguise," but just as convincingly establishes his abasement under the white master. "John Brown" is a tribute to the abolitionist leader whose "shot-gun lies / Across his knees." A sense of black racial pride is underscored when the poem is sung, according to Lindsay's direction, by a leader with choral response. Lindsay described "King Solomon and the Queen of Sheba" as "an Afro-American jubilee song." It is a celebration of a future millennium, a time when the black "shall feel goads no more. / Walk dreadful roads no more, / Free from your loads / For ten thousand years." Of additional interest is the fact that this is an example of what Lindsay called a "poem game."

The fifth and last section of *The Chinese Nightingale* is called "The Poem Games" and begins with Lindsay's five-page explanation of what they are. Essentially, a poem game is the acting out of a poem's statement and spirit. An actor may mime while someone else reads the poem, in which case it resembles pantomime, or the reader may act out the poem as he recites, and make it resemble drama. Dancing to the poem as it is read is a third option. Although the poem game is a hybrid form, Lindsay insists that "the English word is still first in importance, the dancer comes second, the chanter third." The "game" element is further reinforced by involving the audience as a chorus in the recitation of given lines. Lindsay was very successful in coaxing unsuspecting audiences into participating in the performance. He would take a few minutes to teach them their lines; and as he declaimed the principal part, they would respond with a refrain. The poem games began in the summer of 1916 in Chicago and flourished through the interest of Mrs. William Vaughn Moody, the Chicago Little Theater, the University of Chicago, and *Poetry* magazine. They represent one outgrowth of Lindsay's belief in taking poetry to the people. He even read "The Potatoes' Dance" to a kindergarten class while the children danced and acted to the words. These poem games were a successful venture for arousing interest and participation in poetry, and Lindsay continued to write them for the remainder of his career. His last book of verse, *Every Soul Is a Circus,* contains several that may have been inspired by his own children, who were then quite small.

The poem games were an extension of the Higher Vaudeville but did not lead in new directions of poetic development for Lindsay, whose next book of verse, *The Golden Whales of California and Other Rhymes in the American Language* (1920), displays a stagnation of his poetic genius. The few memorable poems, such as "Bryan, Bryan, Bryan, Bryan" and "John L. Sullivan," possess the energy of his earlier achievement and exploit memories of the American past for their effectiveness. The title poem is a curiously bland description of California that views the physical features of the state through a veil of partial fantasy, but far less masterfully than in "The Chinese Nightingale." The chanting of the whales proclaims California's abundance of which they partake, fed each day by the "sun-struck." When St. Francis comes to his city at night, however, he "shades his face in his cowl / And stands in the street like a lost gray owl." Finally, with the audience instructed to join in the refrain of *"gold, gold, gold,"* the voice of the earthquake makes St. Francis aghast: "Oh the flashing cornucopia of haughty California / Is *gold, gold, gold.* / Their brittle speech and their clutching reach / Is *gold, gold, gold."*

The cynicism of this poem is indicative of a prevailing weariness and loss of spirit that had settled over Lindsay, and it is instructive to contrast it with Lindsay's comments on California made five years earlier in *The Art of the Moving Picture. The Golden Whales of California* begins with an introduction entitled "California, Photoplays, and Saint Francis," which consists almost entirely of excerpts taken from his chapter "California and America" in *The Art of the Moving Picture.* This is an extremely prescient and insightful work on the phenomenon that was and is California. Even the title of the chapter recognizes California's distinctness and separateness from America, while simultaneously implying that the state epitomizes and foreshadows what America is to become. An especially telling passage from the earlier chapter that Lindsay does not reprint in the later introduction is the following:

California is a gilded state. It has not the sordidness of gold, as has Wall Street, but it is the embodiment of the natural ore that the ragged prospector finds. The gold of California is the color of the orange, the glitter of dawn in the Yosemite, the hue of the golden gate that opens the sunset way to mystic and terrible Cathay and Hindustan.

What happened in five years to tarnish this golden glow? The change in Lindsay's perception of California is not tied directly to California itself, but is symptomatic of changes in his view of his own work. During these years, as his popularity increased, Lindsay began to feel more and more harassed. He was experiencing the dark side of the classic American success story: once he became popular, he became the captive of his audiences. In the beginning Lindsay found his new status satisfying, but soon his recital tours became monotonous and tedious. He was trapped. He was dependent upon the recitals for income and emotional sustenance. His audiences became a narcotic; and even though he began to dislike them, he could not give them up. Lindsay would send the local organizing committees for his recitals elaborate instructions concerning their preparation for his visit; but he would always be disappointed to find that all they wanted was a "show," which meant a performance of the same old vaudeville pieces that tired him to death.

Lindsay even grew to hate "The Congo." Lacking financial stability, however, and the strength of will to define himself and determine his own destiny, he continued to gratify the wishes of his audiences while begrudging their pleasure. Consequently, he became soured on this system that made money the common denominator of human transactions. He needed it but felt tainted by it. As a result of this growing personal unhappiness, Lindsay sought solace either in the past or in the future. The latter manifested itself in the labor he devoted to what he considered his magnum opus, the visionary *Golden Book of Springfield;* the former, in poems that looked back to a happier time. Indeed, the only poems that really come alive in *The Golden Whales of California* are those that recall a lost innocence and a brighter day.

"In simple sheltered 1889," the poet remembers, "John L. Sullivan, the strong boy of Boston" (as the poem is entitled), "Fought seventy-five red rounds with Jake Kilrain." That was the year "The baseball rules were changed" and "We heard not of Louvain nor of Lorraine, / Or a million heroes for their freedom slain." It is a nostalgic catalog description of the pre-World War I landscape as viewed from the poet's ninth year. In the first part of the "Alexander Campbell" trilogy, Lindsay looks back to the even more distant past in "My Fathers Came From Kentucky." This forceful, moving poem, Lindsay's favorite short piece, celebrates the Southern roots of the fires he felt burning within a Northern exterior: "Why do I faint with love / Till the prairies dip and reel? / My heart is a kicking horse / Shod with Kentucky steel." Lindsay's greatest triumph, though, in transforming personal reminiscence into myth is "Bryan, Bryan, Bryan, Bryan."

This poem about the election of 1896, composed in 1919, provided a means for the release of Lindsay's personal frustrations by identifying them with the defeat of egalitarian cultural aspirations. The poem is conceived as a Manichaean drama between the forces of evil and good, east and west. "There were real lines drawn: / Not the silver and the gold, / But Nebraska's cry went eastward against the dour and old, / The mean and cold." The Midwest and West are described as a mythic, Paul Bunyanesque land where the men are of heroic stature and the animals larger than life, "The fawn, prodactyl and thing-a-ma-jig, / The rakaboor, the hellangone, / The whangdoodle, a batfowl and pig"; and "These creatures were defending things Mark Hanna never dreamed."

In the election of 1896, thirty-six-year-old William Jennings Bryan ran on the Democratic ticket, endorsed by the Populists, against William McKinley, who became the Republican nominee through the influence of the power broker Mark Hanna. "The ultimate fantastics / Of the far western slope" were oppressed by the "dour East" until Bryan came striding out of the West, "The bard and the prophet of them all. / Prairie avenger, mountain lion, / Bryan, Bryan, Bryan, Bryan." When Bryan brought his battle against gold to Springfield, Lindsay, then sixteen, stood with his best girl amid the festivities that seemed to embody the ''Hopes of all mankind.'' Bryan's support grew until Hanna, ''Rallying the roller-tops,'' rescued McKinley by ''Pouring out the long green to a million workers.'' For Lindsay, McKinley's victory was the ''Defeat of my boyhood, defeat of my dream.'' The poem ends by using the *ubi sunt* formula to ask where the participants in that epic struggle have gone. The sustained power of this work derives from Lindsay's masterful dramatization of the issues of a national election into a dialectic of cultural values, and his identifying the whole with the American dream of success—an innocent, pluralistic optimism—defeated by an elitist establishment.

Lindsay's other avenue of escape from the discontent of the present was into the future, through the fabrication of the utopia he created in *The Golden Book of Springfield*. He had so much of himself invested in this work that he was unable to objectify his material in a satisfactory form. Its final shape as a prose narrative with a semblance of plot lacks the vitality of Lindsay's poetry and earlier prose. The narrative describes the visions of a group of prognosticators in 1918 concerning the Springfield of 2018. Springfield has realized the objectives of the ''Gospel of Beauty'' and represents the spirit of a world government binding nations through love and brotherhood. Without the leavening of Lindsay's humor and the color of concrete imagery, however, his prose is vapid. What he had intended to be his masterpiece proved to be more than 300 pages of almost unreadable prose. *The Golden Book of Springfield* was published in November 1920, and Lindsay soon became depressed by the generally negative reception from reviewers. He said that it would ''always be dull and unpopular,'' but expected it to help ''form the minds of my most intimate friends as to my real intentions and direction.'' Though Lindsay's commitment to his beliefs never wavered, he could not ignore the fact that neither *The Golden Book of Springfield* nor *The Golden Whales of California*, published earlier the same year, had sold well or received enthusiastic reviews. Nevertheless, he was still in popular demand as an interpreter of his own work.

During the next several years Lindsay recited extensively throughout the United States and Canada. This was a demanding and tiring enterprise in which he invested a total effort. He charged a flat fee for an appearance in a single location, but he would speak to as many groups in one day as he was invited to address. Frequently this would amount to three or four appearances, each of which would be a demanding dramatic performance. Lindsay was celebrated for his dynamic presentations, which gave such force to his poetry that many listeners felt that his poetry could be fully experienced and appreciated only when it was heard in performance, from his own lips. The rigors of traveling and reciting, however, inevitably took their toll of Lindsay's psychic and physical energy; and he collapsed from the strain in the winter of 1922–1923. In January he was taken into the home of a former Hiram College friend who was president of Gulfport Junior College in Gulfport, Mississippi. Lindsay stayed there as poet in residence and remained throughout the following school year, 1923–1924. During that time he gathered his verses together into a volume of *Collected Poems*.

The *Collected Poems* (1923) contains almost all of the verse that had appeared in the four commercially published volumes. Lindsay reorganized his works and placed them in nine sections: Nightingales; Orations, College War-Cries, and Olympic Games; Litany of the Heroes; Verses of an Especially Inscriptional Character; Moon-Poems; Incense, and Praise, and Whim, and Glory; Runes of the Road; Home Town; and Politics. This 390-page work was introduced by an autobiographical foreword, ''Adventures While Singing These Songs,'' which declared that ''this whole book is a weapon in a strenuous battlefield.'' Two years later Lindsay brought out a revised and illustrated edition of the *Collected Poems*. This edition, which has remained the standard collection of his poems, is still in print. The revised edition swelled the original by more than 100 pages with its added illustrations (all by Lindsay), second preface, and two new sections of poems. Lindsay's new preface, ''Adventures While Preaching Hieroglyphic Sermons,'' is a polemical defense of his work, with a few new poems on Johnny Appleseed; but otherwise the new material of the revised edition adds little of merit to the original version.

Actually, the best of more than half a dozen poems on Johnny Appleseed had appeared in the 1923 edition. ''In Praise of Johnny Appleseed'' recapitulates the career of John Chapman as he led the way for settlers ''Over the Appalachian Barricade''; became the friend of Indians and all forest creatures; and, in his old age, saw the fruition of his labor: ''All America in each apple.'' (This poem was the basis for the title of *Johnny Appleseed and Other Poems,* a selection of verse from *Collected Poems* suitable for children, published in 1928.) Lindsay was particularly enamored of Johnny Appleseed because he identified with his work and his vision: ''I am for Johnny Appleseed's United States.'' Lindsay agreed with Chapman's faith in the future, symbolized by the planting of seeds ''Till he saw our wide nation, each State a flower.'' Chapman's concern with the beauty of the states, as well as their prosperity, made him an artist in ''trees that would march and train / On, in his name to the great Pacific.'' In addition to these reasons, Lindsay revered Chapman because he was the ideal American folk hero. He provided the kind of material that Lindsay's genius utilized to endow cultural heroes with mythic stature.

In *Collected Poems,* Lindsay pays tribute to other men he admired in the ''Litany of the Heroes.'' This long poem combines a number of previously published short verses on such figures as St. Francis, Buddha, Shakespeare, and Titian into a new format that traces man's history from the ancient to the modern world. This poem, written in the subjunctive, celebrates the subjunctive—probably the dominant mood of Lindsay's writing. ''Would that we had the fortunes of Columbus,'' he wishes for us collectively, and for himself, in his role as poet and evangelist: ''Would I might rouse the Lincoln in you all.'' A man of such grandiose aspirations is not, however, immune to the pricks of indicative reality. Lindsay was especially sensitive to the charge that he was a jazz poet, signifying that he was crass, low-class, and trivial. Thus, rearranging his verses on heroes for his *Collected Poems* was not only a personal action against that charge, but also a means of offering his heroes as his intellectual credentials in order to defend himself against those who claimed he lacked culture.

In 1923, the year that his *Collected Poems* appeared, Lindsay published a new volume of verse called *Going-to-the-Sun*. The introduction states that it ''is a sequel and a reply to a book by Stephen Graham, explorer-poet, and Vernon Hill, artist.'' In the summer of 1921 Lindsay tramped for six weeks with Graham, a British friend, through Glacier National Park in Montana and over the border into the Canadian Rockies. It was such a marvelous trip that two books resulted: Graham's *Tramping With a Poet in the Rockies* (1922) and Lindsay's slim volume of poems and illustrations named after Going-to-the-Sun Mountain.

This work and Lindsay's three subsequent volumes of new verse were profusely illustrated in his distinctly linear and pictographic style. Lindsay had been interested in Egyptology for many years and had spent hours poring over grammars of hieroglyphics. His goal was to develop a

United States hieroglyphics, and many of his drawings are efforts toward that end. His renewed interest in drawing at this time may also reflect his disenchantment with public recitals and the waning popularity of his latest books of verse. He returned to the endeavors of his art student days as an alternative means of expressing his visions and conveying them to his audience in a new form. He even included this warning in the introduction: "I serve notice on the critics—the verses are most incidental, merely to explain the pictures." Lindsay's lifelong fondness for the West and his later hostility toward the arbiters of taste in the East resulted in the only noteworthy poem in *Going-to-the-Sun*. "So Much the Worse for Boston" records the satiric observations of a saucy mountain cat on Bostonian pretensions.

Lindsay's memories of his splendid trip in the Rockies drew him back to Spokane, Washington, in June 1924. When the time came for him to return to his teaching duties, he found his new surroundings so agreeable that he decided to stay in Spokane, where he was to remain for the next five years. Within a year Lindsay ended his protracted celibacy at the age of forty-five and married Elizabeth Conners, a high school English and Latin teacher twenty-two years his junior. They had two children. Lindsay had felt homeless and dispirited since the death of his mother in 1922, but his marriage produced the spark his creative powers needed. In 1926 he published two volumes of verse. The first of these, *Going-to-the-Stars*, "attempts," Lindsay says, "to be a souvenir" of Glacier National Park. He and his wife spent the better part of August and September 1925 hiking in the park, and this book amounts to a transcript of their observations. They renamed St. Mary's Lake "Going-to-the-Stars" because its waters reflected the sun and nine mountain peaks by day and all the stars by night. However, the three most memorable poems from this souvenir of Glacier National Park are ones that recall the American past. "Old, Old, Old, Old Andrew Jackson" resembles "Bryan, Bryan, Bryan, Bryan"; and "Virginia" celebrates the heroes of the Old Dominion and catalogs the westward migration of their descendants. The effectiveness of these two poems is achieved through the accumulation of emotive detail about the subjects. In contrast, the fifteen lines of "The Flower-Fed Buffaloes" are an incisive, lyrical remembrance of the days when the buffalo and the Indian ranged the prairies.

Following the publication of *Going-to-the-Stars* by just three months, *The Candle in the Cabin* continues to explore poetically and graphically, in "A Weaving Together of Script and Singing," subjects occasioned by the experiences of Lindsay and his wife in the mountains. Since there is little of poetic merit in these verses, they are most interestingly viewed as subtle reflections of the ecstasy of sexual release. There is a sense in which these poems, grouped in such sections as "The Forest-Ranger's Courtship," purify the act of love for Lindsay and make it mountain-clean.

Lindsay's last two books were published in 1929, the year that he returned to Springfield. *The Litany of Washington Street* came out in March, and the following month he moved his family back to his home town and the house of his birth. While in Spokane, Lindsay had continued to tour and recite; but as his debts grew, so did his unhappiness. He felt that he had not been entirely accepted by the people of Spokane, and signed his weekly column in the local newspaper "Vachel Lindsay, Citizen of Springfield, Illinois—Guest of Spokane." He wished to return to the city where he felt the people really knew him, and where his spirit was most at ease. These feelings are evident in the prosy chapters of *The Litany of Washington Street*. Placed in a larger cultural context, they reveal Lindsay's view of himself as the perpetual guest or alienated artist in a grossly commercial society. The chapter "Washington Street Is Forever Against Main Street" explains that Washington Street is the "song and poetry street of every United States town." It is "the rival of Main Street" and crosses it "at a right angle."

Lindsay attributed the plummeting of his poetic fortunes to Main Street's total concern with what would sell. Likewise, he attacks the "relentless realists" whose aim is to debunk the mythic conceptions that Americans hold of the founding fathers. Lindsay vents his personal frustrations, as an artist in America, in the form of Fourth of July orations on Washington, Jefferson, Lincoln, and Whitman, with verses from the last interspersed between chapters. The result is a work that conveys an unpleasant argumentativeness in stilted and sterile prose. Moreover, the abstractness of such notions as "The Mystical Johnny Appleseed Highway" are far less interesting than the real highways Lindsay described in *Adventures* and *A Handy Guide*.

A poetic summary of *The Litany of Washington Street* appeared six months later in Lindsay's final volume of verse, *Every Soul Is a Circus*. "The Virginians Are Coming Again," the most compelling poem in this volume, opens with the ringing declaration that "Babbitt, your tribe is passing away. / This is the end of your infamous day. / The Virginians are coming again." With the vigor characteristic of his earlier verse, Lindsay presents his vision of a younger generation, following in the spirit of Virginia's preeminent leaders, making war on the moneychangers of contemporary society. Two autobiographical poems, "The Song of My Fiftieth Birthday" and "Twenty Years Ago," are the only other verses of interest in this volume. Both reveal how Lindsay identified his mental depression and financial problems with Spokane, and how he looked to Springfield as "A Sangamon palace of the soul." He felt that he had been insulted by Spokane, and that in Springfield his eccentricities

would be tolerated. At the least, he considered he would be more at home among those who knew him.

Lindsay's sensitivity to his alleged ill-treatment by Spokane was symptomatic of the gradual deterioration of his physical and mental health. This became apparent with his breakdown in 1923, and was diagnosed the following year at the Mayo Clinic as epilepsy, or, as he told his wife, "nocturnal seizures." Consequently, it was not realistic to expect that Springfield would prove to be the balm for Lindsay's agitated soul. His expectations of what Springfield owed him for his service and devotion were unrealistic. He continued to be financially pressed, and could expect little improvement in that area after the stock market crash of 1929. Not only were his last books not selling well and their critical reception negative, but the prospect for sales of existing or future works was dim. Beset by these problems and suffering from poor health and mental instability, he finally lost faith in his own talent and took his life, in December 1931, by drinking Lysol. "Everything begins and ends there for me," he had prophetically written about his Springfield home.

Lindsay had left Springfield on his tramp west in 1912 as an obscure poet, was catapulted to fame the following year by "General William Booth," enjoyed the adulation of critics and the general public for over a decade, suffered neglect for several years, and returned to his home in relative obscurity as a "has-been." Certainly, a factor in both Lindsay's decline in popularity and his mental depression was the adverse criticism his work had received. His last four volumes of verse, published between 1923 and 1929, contained hardly a memorable poem; and the reviewers noted the fact. By that time Lindsay also knew as much—although a justifiable charge frequently brought against him was his incapacity for self-criticism. Most of the late verse simply lacks substance, a stricture from which his earlier verse is not altogether free. Lindsay's poetry is uneven, as a glance at the *Collected Poems* makes abundantly clear; and a goodly share of it is rather thin and uninteresting in both form and content.

This deficiency results in part from the lack of a strongly felt presence of mind in many of Lindsay's poems, a quality consistently observed by those writing critically on his verse. But good poetry is not limited to the poetry of ideas, nor was Lindsay short of ideas. The weakness of his poetry in this respect may lie, rather, in the fact that he had a few key ideas that he regarded as a panacea for all problems. In addition, he lacked the probing intelligence that explores the multifarious complexities of the human predicament, seeking original answers. As a result, much of Lindsay's poetry may strike a reader as slight and trivial when other compensating features, such as concrete imagery, rhythm, and significant content, are absent. This lack of complexity is, on the other hand, Lindsay's strength in his best poems, where it manifests itself as an elemental force of pure conviction innocently and simply stated.

Today, Lindsay's critical fortunes are down. A few anthologies of American poetry even exclude him from their pages, but that is too harsh a judgment. He gave us a few splendid moments in American poetry, and those moments deserve to be remembered and preserved. The conventional critical wisdom maintains that a poet's stature rests upon his best poems. By that standard Lindsay earns a place in the anthologies, but it is a place diminished by the critical act of detaching those poems from the enterprise of his life. In the era of modernism, Lindsay's ideals and the figure they make in his poetry have been out of fashion; but if we can see his individual works as part of a whole that represents a unique and compelling expression of American culture,

then we may begin to appreciate his total achievement.

Like Thoreau, Lindsay wanted to wake up his neighbors. His avowed purpose—"To waken world-weary men"—contributed to the poetry revival of the twentieth century's second decade, a development of historical significance for the course of American poetry. Lindsay helped to open up poetry by infusing it with the language, subjects, and rhythms of everyday life. He was also instrumental in moving this rejuvenated poetry from the back pages of magazines and bringing it before the public. A poetry exhibiting new life and vigor appealed to a larger audience, and Lindsay was one of those primarily responsible for revitalizing the craft of poetry and thus enlarging this audience.

During his lifetime Lindsay's poetry so overshadowed his prose that we have tended ever since to regard him only as a poet. This is unfortunate, for the three earliest of his five prose works are enchanting and valuable pieces of Americana. They fit into the strong tradition of nonfiction prose in American literature, and two of them are fine examples of the perennial genre of "adventures on the road." For a complete understanding of Lindsay, one must read his prose to discern the man in his work. He once wrote, in reference to his poetry: "I want to be mixed up with my work. I cannot bear to have my verses just so much print." Those prose works are the prerequisites that enable us to perceive the poet in his verses and that explicitly elucidate his ideas.

In "One More Song," the wistful epilogue to *The Candle in the Cabin,* Lindsay summarizes the bittersweet mission of his life: "I would set right the old world's wrong; / I would outbuild New York and Rome. / But all / I can bring home / Is one / More / Song." This poem expresses his claim on our imagination. It recalls the Puritan origins of the American desire to "set right the old world's wrong'' and to establish the City of God in this new land. Indeed, Lindsay is a representative American Jeremiah who calls his countrymen to task for forgetting the principles of the founders in the hope of advancing the visionary cause. The American way of establishing a golden Springfield is to evoke the heroic efforts of the past as a goad to the present generation. In another poem Lindsay contends that ''The soul of the U.S.A.—that is my life-quest.'' It is the measure of his achievement that we still respond to his quest and to the accuracy and power of his portrayal of the national soul. He bequeathed his vision to us in the form of his songs, which will remain interesting, for when Lindsay comes knocking at our door with a dream in his hand, it is the dream of American culture.

Selected Bibliography

WORKS OF VACHEL LINDSAY

(In print works are indicated by an asterisk.)

VERSE

General William Booth Enters into Heaven and Other Poems. New York: Mitchell Kennerley, 1913.

The Congo and Other Poems. New York: Mitchell Kennerley, 1914.

The Chinese Nightingale and Other Poems. New York: Macmillan, 1917.

The Golden Whales of California and Other Rhymes in the American Language. New York: Macmillan, 1920.

Collected Poems. New York: Macmillan, 1923; revised and illustrated edition, 1925.*

Going-to-the-Sun. New York: D. Appleton & Co., 1923.

Going-to-the-Stars. New York: D. Appleton & Co., 1926.

The Candle in the Cabin: A Weaving Together of

Script and Singing. New York: D. Appleton & Co., 1926.

Every Soul Is a Circus. New York: Macmillan, 1929.

PROSE

Adventures While Preaching the Gospel of Beauty. New York: Mitchell Kennerley, 1914.

The Art of the Moving Picture. New York: Macmillan, 1915; revised ed., 1922.

A Handy Guide for Beggars, Especially Those of the Poetic Fraternity. New York: Macmillan, 1916.

The Golden Book of Springfield. New York: Macmillan, 1920.

The Litany of Washington Street. New York: Macmillan, 1929.

SELECTED EDITIONS

Lindsay, Vachel. *The Daniel Jazz and Other Poems*. London: G. Bell & Sons, 1920.

Lindsay, Vachel. *Johnny Appleseed and Other Poems*. New York: Macmillan, 1928.*

Spencer, Hazelton, ed. *Selected Poems of Vachel Lindsay*. New York: Macmillan, 1931.

Harris, Mark, ed. *Selected Poems of Vachel Lindsay*. New York: Macmillan, 1963.*

Sayre, Robert F., ed. *Adventures, Rhymes & Designs*. New York: Eakins Press, 1968. * (Includes *Adventures, Rhymes to Be Traded for Bread*, and selections from *The Village Magazine*.)

Lindsay, Vachel. *Springfield Town Is Butterfly Town and Other Poems for Children*, edited by Pierre Dussert. Kent, Ohio: Kent State University Press, 1969. (Previously unpublished poems).

Kauffmann, Stanley, ed. *The Art of the Moving Picture*. By Vachel Lindsay. New York: Liveright, 1970.*

BIBLIOGRAPHY

Byrd, Cecil K. ''Checklist of the Melcher Lindsay Collection,'' *Indiana University Bookman*, 5:64–106 (December 1960).

White, William. ''Vachel Lindsay-iana: A Bibliographical Note,'' *Serif*, 8:9–11 (June 1971).

———. ''Lindsay/Masters/Sandburg: Criticism from 1950–75,'' in *The Vision of This Land*, edited by John E. Hallwas and Dennis J. Reader, Macomb: Western Illinois University, 1976. Pp. 114–28.

CRITICAL AND BIOGRAPHICAL STUDIES

BOOKS

Armstrong, A. Joseph, ed. *Letters of Nicholas Vachel Lindsay to A. Joseph Armstrong*. Waco, Texas: Baylor University Press, 1940.

Flanagan, John T., ed. *Profile of Vachel Lindsay*. Columbus, Ohio: Charles E. Merrill, 1970.

Graham, Stephen. *Tramping with a Poet in the Rockies*. London: Macmillan, 1922.

Harris, Mark. *City of Discontent*. Indianapolis: Bobbs-Merrill, 1952.

Massa, Ann. *Vachel Lindsay: Fieldworker for the American Dream*. Bloomington: Indiana University Press, 1970.

Masters, Edgar Lee. *Vachel Lindsay: A Poet in America*. New York: Scribner's, 1935.

Ruggles, Eleanor. *The West-Going Heart: A Life of Vachel Lindsay*. New York: Norton, 1959.

Trombly, Albert Edmund. *Vachel Lindsay, Adventurer*. Columbia, Mo.: Lucas Brothers, 1929.

Wolfe, Glenn Joseph. *Vachel Lindsay: The Poet as Film Theorist*. New York: Arno Press, 1973.

BOOKS DEVOTING CHAPTERS TO LINDSAY

Duffey, Bernard. *The Chicago Renaissance in American Letters: A Critical History*. East Lansing: Michigan State University Press, 1954.

Hallwas, John E., and Dennis J. Reader, eds. *The Vision of This Land*. Macomb: Western Illinois University, 1976.

Kramer, Dale. *Chicago Renaissance: The Literary Life in the Midwest, 1900–1930*. New York: Appleton-Century, 1966.

Putzel, Max. *The Man in the Mirror: William Marion Reedy and His Magazine*. Cambridge, Mass.: Harvard University Press, 1963.

Untermeyer, Louis. *The New Era in American Poetry*. New York: Henry Holt & Co., 1919.

Whipple, Thomas K. *Spokesmen*. New York: D. Appleton and Co., 1928; reprinted Berkeley: University of California Press, 1963.

Yatron, Michael. *America's Literary Revolt*. New York: Philosophical Library, 1959.

ARTICLES

The best place to begin is with the representative selection of fourteen articles compiled by John T. Flanagan in his *Profile of Vachel Lindsay*. (They are not listed below.) The fifth number of the *Indiana University Bookman* (December 1960) is devoted to Lindsay and contains, besides Cecil K. Byrd's descriptive bibliography, an assessment by Edwin H. Cady, a reminiscence by Frederic G. Melcher, and the texts of Lindsay's letters that are held by the Lilly Library. *The Shane Quarterly* (vol. 5, April–June 1944) also devoted an entire number of ten items to Lindsay.

Aiken, Conrad. "A Letter from Vachel Lindsay," *Bookman*, 74:598–601 (March 1932).

Ames, Van Meter. "Vachel Lindsay—or, *My Heart Is a Kicking Horse*," *Midway*, 8, 4:63–79 (Spring 1968).

Armstrong, A. J. "Vachel Lindsay as I Knew Him," *Mark Twain Quarterly*, 5:6–11 (Fall–Winter 1942–43).

Bradbury, David L. "Vachel Lindsay and His Heroes," *Illinois State University Journal*, 32:22–57 (April 1970).

Chénetier, Marc. "Knights in Disguise: Lindsay and Maiakovski as Poets of the People," *MidAmerica*, 2:47–62 (1975).

Edwards, Davis. "The Real Source of Vachel Lindsay's Poetic Technique," *Quarterly Journal of Speech*, 33:182–95 (April 1947).

Kreymborg, Alfred. "Exit Vachel Lindsay—Enter Ernest Hemingway," *Literary Review*, 1:208–19 (Winter 1957–58).

Lee, C. P. "Adulation and the Artist," *Saturday Review of Literature*, 22:7, 18–19 (August 10, 1940).

Massa, Ann. "The Artistic Conscience of Vachel Lindsay," *Journal of American Studies*, 2:239–52 (1968).

Masters, Edgar Lee. "Vachel Lindsay," *Bookman*, 64:156–60 (October 1926).

———. "Vachel Lindsay and America," *Saturday Review of Literature* 12:3–4, 15 (August 10, 1935).

Orel, Harold. "Lindsay and the Blood of the Lamb," *University of Kansas City Review*, 25:13–17 (August 1958).

Rittenhouse, Jessie B. "Vachel Lindsay," *South Atlantic Quarterly*, 32:266–82 (July 1933).

Sayre, Robert F. "Vachel Lindsay," introduction to Lindsay's *Adventures, Rhymes & Designs*. New York: Eakins Press, 1968. Pp. 7–41.

Tanselle, G. Thomas. "Lindsay's *General William Booth:* A Bibliographical and Textual Note," *Bib-*

liographical Society of America Papers, 55:371–80 (4th Quarter 1961).

———. "Vachel Lindsay Writes to Floyd Dell," *Illinois State Historical Society Journal*, 57:366–79 (Winter 1964).

Trombly, Albert Edmund. "Listeners and Readers: The Unforgetting of Vachel Lindsay," *Southwest Review*, 47:294–302 (August 1962).

Viereck, Peter. "The Crack-up of American Optimism: Vachel Lindsay, the Dante of the Fundamentalists," *Modern Age*, 4:269–84 (Summer 1960).

Whitney, Blair. "Vachel Lindsay: The Midwest as Utopia," *MidAmerica*, 1:46–51 (1974).

—JAY R. BALDERSON

James Russell Lowell

1819–1891

ALTHOUGH today's appraisals would be very different, during the years immediately after James Russell Lowell's death, obituary writers and critics spoke of his life and achievements as being admirable in almost every way. Extravagant eulogies were then customary, but this author's background, his achievements, and his contemporary reputation provided unusually convincing evidence.

If traditions, family, and learning outfitted a man for a successful career, Lowell got off to a perfect start. A Cambridge, Massachusetts, mansion, Elmwood—his birthplace (February 22, 1819) and his deathplace (August 12, 1891)—was built in 1767 on Tory Row by an appointee of George III; was seized by village freemen in 1774; was used as a hospital during the Revolutionary War; and was the home of a signer of the Declaration of Independence. The Washington Elm and crucial battlefields were strolls away. Nearby every year, a horseplayful muster—"a Cornwallis"—burlesqued the Yorktown surrender. Each Independence Day, Lowell's grandmother, dressed in black, "loudly lamented our late unhappy difference with His Most Gracious Majesty." Lowell felt that just living in the big Georgian frame building with its tall pilasters, old-fashioned garden, and wide meadows tethered one to the past. He warned a temporary renter: "It will make a frightful conservative of you before you know it; it was born a Tory and will die so." Harvard College was a mile to the east.

Family history strengthened vital ties. Ever since Percival Lowle had moved from England to Newbury in 1639, Lowells had lived in Massachusetts. A Lowell had served in the Continental Congress and the state's constitutional convention. Another had established relationships with three leading families by marrying a Higginson, a Russell, and—still more impressive—a Cabot. Three generations had been Harvard-trained lawyers and clergymen. An uncle, as a founder of New England's textile industry, gave a factory town the family name; another founded Lowell Institute. Lowell's mother traced her ancestry to Sir Patrick Spens in the medieval ballad; and for her children she often recited traditional Scottish tales and sang old Orkney Islands folksongs.

In Cambridge, where learning almost had the look of being catching, Lowell had as a superb live-in teacher a sister who spoke twelve languages. He began to read before his third birthday. At three and a half he toddled off to a private school, and soon was absorbing Latin; at nine he could read French. By the time he was fifteen, he had acquired enough Latin, Greek, and mathematics to pass Harvard's formidable entrance examinations.

At Harvard, Lowell bragged, he completely avoided anything "in the way of college study" for four years. True, he ranked only in the middle of his class, spent much time forming friendships, fell "hopelessly in love" frequently, and often was scolded for breaking college rules. But he did much independent reading (Herodotus, Cicero, Terence, and a dozen unrequired and unanointed British authors), and in an unguarded moment found Italian "enchanting." Lowell helped edit the college literary magazine and won election as class poet. Although he could not read his class poem at commencement because he had been suspended (for, it was rumored, being disorderly in chapel), the poem proved he had learned to comment rhythmically and wittily on the controversies of the day.

Lowell's reading, his facile scribbling, and his favorite studies helped him to decide that he would "love to be able to sit down and do something literary for the rest of my natural life." Other New Englanders, on emerging from college with similar bents, had firmly been told by elders—as Lowell was—that writing in America simply did not pay. Postponing literary careers, others prepared for and carried on more remunerative work before edging into successful authorship: Henry Wadsworth Longfellow, for instance, became a librarian and a professor, Oliver Wendell Holmes—after a brief foray into law—a physician.

Lowell gave thought to the ministry, decided against it, tried business briefly and scurried away from it, then at his father's urging had a go at law. Desultory application led to a degree, admission to the bar, and a few clients. But eager to fulfill what he called his "blind presentiment of becoming independent in some other way," he chiefly busied himself with a literary career.

This started well. Lowell contributed to newspapers and magazines, and collected his verses in *A Year's Life* (1841) and in *Poems,* published in December 1843. Also in 1843 he served as an editor of *The Pioneer: A Literary and Critical Magazine* during its three-month life span. Gossips, some of them college classmates, spread the rumor that here was a comer, and reviewers added support, with the result, journalist N. P. Willis remarked, that Lowell was "the best launched man of his time." A review of *A Year's Life* said that here was the future writer of a great American poem "that shall silence the sneers of foreigners, and write his name among the stars of heaven." *Poems* did even better: "Now he has done it!" a New York commentator exclaimed, and Edgar Allan Poe announced that the book would put an author with possibly "a loftier genius than any . . . *at the very head* of the poets of America." For the era, the book had a large sale—three editions, each of 500 copies. Although *The Pioneer* (like most magazines then) died young, it garnered praise. At its debut there was "only one prophecy and that, success," and Poe called its demise "a most severe blow to . . . the cause of Pure Taste." Other magazines commissioned articles from Lowell; one bid for his exclusive services; a series that he expanded and slightly revised in *Conversations on Some of the Old Poets* had large sales, and was praised extravagantly by three revered Harvard professors.

Both *Poems* and *Conversations* touched on what would be a major theme of Lowell's for two decades—abolitionism. In his class poem, the young man had sniped at contemporary zealots, including antislavery crusaders. But his father's stand against slavery and his own natural inclinations encouraged him to join the cause. Probably an even greater influence was Maria White, a beautiful, frail, and impassioned young activist whom Lowell met in 1839, and whom he married in 1843. With her eager support, he wrote copiously in behalf of abolition for antislavery magazines, as well as for some conservative ones, and became a regular contributor to the *Pennsylvania Freeman.*

Initially his stand alienated some readers, and of course it never pleased many Southerners. But Northern public opinion moved Lowell's way. In 1842, Longfellow, who usually avoided controversy, published *Poems on Slavery*. Disputes about Texas and the war with Mexico led many Northerners to reassess their positions.

Lowell's first widely popular success was a series of poems in Yankee dialect satirizing the Mexican War as "a national crime committed in behalf of Slavery." *The Biglow Papers*, published in newspapers beginning in 1846 and as a book in 1848, were, as he said, "copied everywhere; I saw them pinned up in workshops; I heard them quoted and the authorship debated." *Poems by James Russell Lowell, Second Series* (1848), and two long poems of the same year—*A Fable for Critics*, which wittily praised and pilloried the era's writers, and a moralizing Round Table tale, *The Vision of Sir Launfal*—added to his reputation.

The death of Maria in 1853 hit Lowell hard and, as he said, broke his life in two. During the 1850's, he lovingly edited a memorial edition of her poems; with less enthusiasm, he published essays in magazines and edited or wrote introductions for several editions of British poets. His activity was sluggish until he was asked to give the prestigious Lowell Institute lectures for 1855, an assignment that pushed him into making a new and beneficial start. Having decided to speak on "The English Poets," and becoming aware that the catch-as-catch-can critical methods he had been using were too simple-minded to hold the attention of sophisticated Bostonians for twelve long hours of talk, Lowell prepared himself by a thorough reading of half a dozen critics. New approaches and perceptions, and a graceful and often witty style, made the lectures a success.

Impressed by the praise the lectures received in the press and faculty gatherings, Harvard asked the thirty-six-year-old critic to succeed Longfellow, who had just resigned, as Smith professor of French and Spanish and professor of belles-lettres. After a year of study abroad, Lowell served from 1857 to 1872. He was not, by most accounts, very good in the classroom: at times he yawned as he entered, and students had to struggle not to yawn back. But from informal evening seminars in his private study, he gained a high reputation.

Named the first editor of the *Atlantic Monthly*, Lowell got it off to a rushing start between 1857 and 1861. Later he served with Charles Eliot Norton as joint editor of the *North American Review* (1863–1872). Both his editorial skill and his lavish contributions were much admired. The respected English author of *Tom Brown's School Days*, Thomas Hughes, discovered *The Biglow Papers* for his countrymen in 1859, and blithely placed Lowell way up there with Aristophanes, Cervantes, Molière, and Swift in his fulsome introduction—and, incidentally, boomed the author in an America that still put British approval above that of domestic critics. When *The Biglow Papers, Second Series* came out in the *Atlantic Monthly* in 1862, 1865, and 1866, a London publisher issued them in pamphlet form and combined some of them with the first series in hardback—before the initial American edition came out in 1867; and although American critics were generally kind, British reviewers were for the most part even kinder.

In addition to his writings, his prestigious professorship, and the clout of his influential editorships, Lowell's personality helped his career. As a young man, despite some preciousness, he had been idolized—along with Maria—by a "Band" of intellectual contemporaries who thought he was a charming genius. By middle age he had shucked off affectations and had acquired a great many close (and, as it happened, influential) friends—social, academic, and literary. Barrel-chested, heavily bearded, and ship-shape physically, he was untouched by any illness—except for gout—until his mid-fifties. "He had," wrote an intimate, "a power of enjoyment both mental and physical. He liked good food, drink and tobacco, and was altogether fond of the earth." He went for good company, too: there is much testimony that his ebullience, his wit, his delight in horseplay and in good talk, were most attractive. Fredrika Bremer, the Swedish feminist, wrote after a visit to Elmwood: "He seems to me occasionally brilliant, witty, gay, especially in the evening, when he has what he calls his 'evening fever,' and his talk is then like an incessant play of fireworks." And despite the fact that he had black periods of deep depression, hundreds of his letters—highly informal, droll, informative, and affectionate—attest to great personal charm.

Some of this quality enlivened a collection of familiar essays, *Fireside Travels* (1864). Various other books—a long philosophical poem *The Cathedral* (1870), books of shorter poems, prose works including *Democracy and Other Addresses* (1887), *Political Essays* (1888)—as well as works of literary criticism—*Among My Books* (in two series, 1870 and 1876), *My Study Windows* (1871), *The English Poets: Lessing, Rousseau* (1888), *Latest Literary Essays and Addresses* (1891)—led to frequent statements that Lowell was one of the nation's most versatile writers and the leading man in American letters. As such a figure, Lowell was roughly the nineteenth-century approximation, in general American esteem, of the twentieth century's Edmund Wilson. Some honors that Lowell won, in fact, Wilson could not possibly have duplicated: he served as ambassador to Spain from 1877 to 1880, then as ambassador to England between 1880 and 1885, retiring from diplomacy after the death of his second wife of twenty-seven years. He received honorary degrees from Oxford, Cambridge, Edinburgh, and Harvard; and he was the president of an organization with which Wilson feuded, the Modern Language Association, from 1887 to 1891.

Throughout many years after Lowell's death in 1891, a large share of the estimates by reputable critics of his place in American literature were most impressive: "He wrote the finest single poem yet produced in the country and was our foremost critic. . . . No American author, unless it be Emerson, has achieved a securer hold upon lasting fame" (1891). "Nowhere in literature is there a more magnificent and majestic impersonation of a country . . ." (1892). "As *The Biglow Papers* is the firmest and the finest political satire yet written in the United States, so is the *Fable for Critics* the clearest and most truthful literary satire" (1896). "Our acknowledged foremost man of letters [and] the greatest satiric poet in the English language since the days of Pope" (1899). "His patriotic poetry is unmatched—even unrivalled" (1909). "We surely need not despair of our democracy so long as it can produce men of letters like Lowell and utilize them in the service of the common weal" (1918). "Our most distinguished critic, [he had] a comprehensive vision of the task of the critic . . . sensitiveness to impressions, historical understanding, and an aesthetic-ethical judgment" (1928).

With such hosannas ringing in one's ears, it is startling to come across remarks that this admired critic himself made about his achievements. As an old man he wrote: "I feel that my life has been mainly wasted—that I have thrown away more than most men ever had." This cannot be written off as merely a product of a passing fit of depression; habitually, over the years, Lowell talked about either his failure ("I myself am never pleased with what I do") or reasons for it. Maybe, he said more than once, he was too enslaved by a habit for which he scolded himself in *A Fable for Critics:*

There is Lowell, who's striving Parnassus to
      climb
With a whole bale of *isms* tied together with
      rhyme,
He might get on alone, spite of brambles and
      boulders,

But he can't with that bundle he has on his shoulders,
The top of the hill he will ne'er come nigh reaching
Till he learns the distinction 'twixt singing and preaching. . . .

Perhaps, he thought another time, he was too fluent—had "too many thoughts and too little thought." On the contrary, maybe he was too analytical: "I know so well how certain things are done that I can't do them." On other occasions he wondered (with some reason) whether he was just too indolent to realize his potential.

Lowell's stern judgments were not unique during his lifetime or the years when most critics were praising him. During the period when the above encomiums appeared, some commentators noticed serious flaws in Lowell's essays, critical works, and poems. As early as 1872, for instance, a writer for *Scribner's Monthly* did a neat hatchet job on the criticism; in 1893 a British critic who had been a close friend confessed that he could not in good conscience call the poems "first-rate"; and in 1905 a knowledgeable historian of American poetry found "something lacking in most of his work . . . which he seems always striving after."

As time passed, respect for Lowell's writings declined until it almost vanished. Concluding estimates by three recent students and biographers clearly show this diminution. Leon Howard decided that Lowell lacked "a coherent personality" such as "is required to give words a vital relationship that makes them endure." Martin Duberman, in his superb biography (1966), honors Lowell's "multiple attainments" as "a fine editor, a successful teacher, an admired diplomat, an honest public commentator." But he does not deny that "his achievement as a writer (in which, after all, he invested his greatest energy and his highest hopes) can command only limited admiration. I have found no reason to revise the long-standing consensus which denied him the first rank." Duberman's purpose, he therefore admits, was not "to restore Lowell's stature as a Renaissance figure or a literary giant" but to "restore him as a man. It is Lowell's qualities as a human being which have most attracted me. . . ." Edward Wagenknecht, who has found college students agreeing with those who downgrade Lowell's writings, in 1971 made a less sweeping concession but ended with a similar estimate:

He attempted less ambitious enterprises than Longfellow, and often brought off what he tackled with less complete success, and he seldom achieved the autochthonism which will always keep Whittier alive as an American poet until the character of America shall have fundamentally changed. But he was a more "stylish" poet than either of these others, and in a way he carries an air of greater distinction. In every age, and in every line of human endeavor, there are human beings who impress us in some way more important than the sum of what they do, and it is clear that Lowell was one of them. . . . he was a many-sided man personally as well as professionally.

Wagenknecht says, in conclusion, that although Lowell did not have literary power that achieves the great conquests of the imagination, he was a sterling character, and "What he saw, what he expressed . . . had been passed through the alembic of his own personality and verified, for him, in his own experience."

A discussion of any author's writings does well, of course, to indicate what they are like—their aim (when it can be learned), their content and manner, their qualities and values. Because the appeal of Lowell's work has changed so much, a discussion of the values of his writing must consider, in addition, two questions: Why did his writing seem so obviously praiseworthy in the past? And why is it no longer attractive to modern readers?

For seventy years, it has been almost compulsive for writers about Lowell to call 1848 his *annus mirabilis*. During that year four of his books worked together to bring him a solid reputation before he was thirty years old—*Poems, Second Series* (actually published in late December 1847); *The Vision of Sir Launfal; Meliboeus-Hipponax* (which happily became better known as *The Biglow Papers*); and *A Fable for Critics*. All of these quite different works were alike in an additional and even more important way: they revealed lifelong interests and procedures of the author. And so, more than most of his early works, they repay a very close look.

As Martin Duberman has said, *Poems,* a garnering of verses written since 1845, develops topics that already had established themselves as Lowell's favorites:

the beauty of Nature and its revelation of God's benevolent purpose; the need to rely on individual conscience above man-made laws and institutions; a deep sympathy for the poor and oppressed; the superiority of the "simple human heart" over the subtleties of intellect; the necessity of striving toward the Ideal; the desirability of subordinating the traditions of the past to the needs of the present.

These were not themes that Lowell alone cherished: they were developed in scores of poems and sketches in magazines and fashionable gift books of the 1840's. Henry Wadsworth Longfellow, by all odds America's—and probably England's—most popular nineteenth-century poet, treated the first of the six concepts in dozens of poems, for instance in "Hymn to the Night" (1839). He developed no fewer than four of the themes—the second, fourth, fifth, and sixth—in the prodigiously popular "A Psalm of Life: What the Heart of the Young Man Said to the Psalmist" (1838). His "The Village Black-smith" (1841) and "The Slave's Dream" (1842) had as their burdens the third. And he gave the fourth a classic expression: "It is the heart, and not the brain,/ That to the highest doth attain. . . ." Longfellow, a Cambridge neighbor and friend, and Lowell occasionally commented on mutual beliefs expressed in their poems.

Moreover, the two shared a liking for a structure that they and other poets of the day often used in organizing brief lyrics: (1) An object, scene, legend, or event was described. (2) An analogy was drawn. (3) A spiritual connotation or a moral based upon the analogy was presented. Thus, after telling how the village smith has lived, Longfellow thanks his "worthy friend/ For the lesson thou hast taught"—and he sets it down. And Lowell, in "On the Death of a Friend's Child," tells about the effect of the death upon himself and his friend, then draws a Wordsworthian moral: "Children are God's apostles, day by day/ Sent forth to preach of love, and hope, and/ peace. . . ."

Because of such resemblances and others in thought and form, given many a short poem by either Lowell or Longfellow without a name attached to it, even perceptive readers familiar with the writings of both often will not, with confidence, be able to assign authorship.

Some midcentury poems of Lowell that stirred readers of the day memorialized personal experiences; for example, "On the Death of a Friend's Child." "The Changeling," and "She Came and Went" followed the death of Lowell's daughter Blanche. "After the Burial" (1850) was written following the death of another infant daughter, Rose. Unquestionably these losses deeply stirred the poet. But the period when they were written was one when many readers found elegies for children heartrending. Since 1841, the death of Little Nell in Dickens' *Old Curiosity Shop* had been moving large audiences to tears on both sides of the Atlantic. Since 1843, Scrooge's dream that Tiny Tim had died had decimated readers of *A Christmas Carol*. American newspapers, magazines, and gift books featured numerous poems about dead or dying children, often adorned with mournful illustrations. (When Mark Twain had Huck Finn visit a representative Kentucky family about 1845, he endowed them with a sentimental daughter, Emmeline, whose chief pastime was writing obituary poems, one of which—on a child's drowning—Huck quotes at length.) The year 1852 would bring the most mourned little girl's death in American literature—that of Little Eva in *Uncle Tom's Cabin*. So the matter of these serious poems by Lowell was very popular indeed among writers and readers.

The poem that during Lowell's lifetime became his most widely known and respected, *A Vision of Sir Launfal*, also dealt with popular matter. Long preludes, one to each of its two parts, featured lush descriptions of natural American scenes such as those that had charmed readers of poetry and fiction for several decades. The parable that these preludes introduced was set in a period that had become increasingly popular over the years since eighteenth-century authors such as James Gray, Horace Walpole, and Thomas Chatterton exploited the Gothic tradition. Keats in 1820 (the year of *Ivanhoe*) and Tennyson in the 1840's had told medieval stories in poems that American readers greatly admired. (Tennyson's "Sir Galahad" seems to have triggered Lowell's use of the Arthurian legend, and *The Princess* probably suggested the general outline of *A Vision*.) Thomas Carlyle overpraised medieval monastic life in *Past and Present* (1843); John Ruskin was preparing to glorify Gothic architecture; and soon *Idylls of the King* would delight readers on both sides of the Atlantic.

As Tennyson did in his *Idylls*, Lowell used portions of the Arthurian story to point a nineteenth-century moral. At the start of Launfal's quest for the Holy Grail, he meets a begging leper, loathes him, and scornfully flips a piece of gold at him. When, long after, the knight returns from his wanderings, he again encounters the beggar. Now, seeing in "the grewsome thing . . . an image of Him who died on the tree," Launfal shares water from a brook and his last crust. The leper, transformed—"shining and tall and fair and straight"—puts into a moralizing speech a belief that long had been one of Lowell's favorites:

> "Lo, it is I, be not afraid!
> In many climes, without avail,
> Thou hast spent thy life for the Holy Grail;
> Behold, it is here,—the cup which thou
> Didst fill at the streamlet for me but now;
> This crust is my body broken for thee,
> This water his blood that died on the tree;
> The Holy Supper is kept, indeed,
> In whatso we share with another's need;
> Not what we give, but what we share,
> For the gift without the giver is bare;
> Who gives himself and his alms feeds three,
> Himself, his hungering neighbor, and me."

In this instructive tale, as Horace Elisha Scudder says, Lowell thus "in the broadest interpretation of democracy, sang of the levelling of all ranks in a common divine humanity. . . ."

Did the Cambridge writer just happen to put together a poem that conformed so well to current patterns? It hardly seems so. His very first written mention of it described it to a correspondent as "a sort of story . . . more likely to be popular than what I write generally." There is even better evidence that when he wrote *The Biglow Papers* in Yankee dialect he deliberately fashioned them to fetch the readers of the day.

Lowell in 1842 wrote a poem about a discovery he made when, on a railway car, he watched some "men rude and rough" who were talking about Bobby Burns and listening to a reading of some of the Scottish poet's verse. Their responses showed that the homespun songs, couched in dialect, got to them as high-toned poetry never could. Charles F. Briggs, a friendly editor, in a blunt critique of a long poem that Lowell wrote in 1843, told him that the thing was just too bookish and arty:

It is too warm, rich, and full of sweet sounds and sights; the incense overpowers me. . . . I am too much of a clod of earth to mingle well in such elements. I feel while reading it as if I were on a bed of down with a canopy of rose-colored silk above me. . . .

To this same editor Lowell sent a prose satire written in the style of a hayseed, signing himself Matthew Trueman. The editor advised the use of more wit and versification: "Put all your abolitionism into rhyme; everybody will read it in that shape, and it will do good."

It would have been hard for anybody who read newspapers in the years 1825–1846 not to notice that American satire and humor couched in colloquial language was all the go. George W. Arnold, writing under the pseudonym Joe Strickland, Thomas Chandler Haliburton (Sam Slick), Seba Smith (Major Jack Downing), David Crockett (Davy Crockett), William T. Thompson (Major Jones), and many others were popular practitioners. Lowell referred to one of them in the *Biglow Papers* and stated the formula that all of them followed in a couplet:

Then you can call me "Timbertoes,"—thet's
    wut the people likes;
Sutthin' combinin' morril truth with phrases sech
    ez strikes. . . .

Lowell on several occasions gave details about the origins of *The Biglow Papers*. He had been sadly aware, he admitted, that although he was eager to channel public opinion, his articles and poems for periodicals, let alone his books, were "almost unread" by mass audiences. He thought the Mexican War was "a national crime committed in behoof of slavery," and he wanted to "put

the feeling" he had "in a way that would tell." He was aware that "uneducated men (self-educated they are called) are all the rage." Therefore, he "put on the cap and bells, and made himself one of the court fools of King Demos . . . less to make his Majesty laugh than to win a passage to his royal ears for certain serious things which he had deeply at heart." He proceeded to write in the role of an imagined, unread rustic—"an upcountry man . . . capable of district school English, but always instinctively falling back into the natural stronghold of his homely dialect when heated to the point of self-forgetfulness."

Hosea Biglow—"homely common-sense vivified and heated by conscience," as his creator described him—fell in with a parade of men of gumption who either had little learning or could shuck off learning when they had a mind to. The highly American procession of such characters, stretching back to Ben Franklin, had been popular among the masses because folk on farms and in factories or offices thought better of practical men and women who learned to solve problems by absorbing experience than they did of theoreticians who collected what they knew in lecture halls and libraries. Hosea could base what he said on what, as a worker in fields and barnyards, he figured out for himself.

His rusticity and hardwon horse sense were standard equipment for the common man type. Lowell added some less shopworn traits to make his portrait of a bumpkin more individual and more lifelike than most other comic Yankees, and therefore quite persuasive. Having worked and nooned with farmhands in his youth, Lowell could throw in details that smelled of cattle and haymows. For instance, he could have Hosea jeer at recruiting sergeants for "afollerin' their bell-weathers," or he could offer as a clinching argument against going to war the simple statement "The hay's to mow."

Again, Lowell had heard much countrified

talk; he was an apt and trained linguist; and he believed "our popular idiom is racy with life and vigor and originality, bucksome (as Milton used the word) to our new occasions." And so he was eager and able to make Hosea's word choices and phrasings authentic.

Also, since he was a son of a Unitarian minister, Lowell had often heard artless parishioners talk much as naive medieval mystery playwrights had written, showing homely familiarity with the Deity and sacred revelations. Showing the same comic chumminess, Hosea writes:

> Ez fer war, I call it murder,—
> There you hev it plain an' flat;
> I don't want to go no furder
> Than my Testment fer that;
> God hez sed so plump an' fairly,
> It's ez long ez it is broad,
> An' you've gut to git up airly
> Ef you want to take in God.

What in other admired humorous writings was incongruity born of irreverence was in the *Papers,* therefore, a characterizing touch born of innocence, piety, or—possibly—of bigotry.

A final peculiarity of Hosea is his skill as a verse writer. This enables him to concoct striking rhythms, unusual rhyme schemes, and ingenious rhymes (for example, *to vote, ollers* and *teetotallers; refuse to be* and *used to be; distracted* and *attackted; come on't, thum on't,* and *sum on't*). In addition to writing pieces in the first person, Hosea writes dramatic monologues in which he impersonates various characters and translates their speeches or letters into lively verses. The best drawn of these figures is Birdofredum Sawin, a Yankee ignoramus who lets himself be conned into enlisting and who is corrupted by his army experiences. Sawin (whose name puns on "bird of freedom soaring") becomes a charming reprobate whose frank letters expose rascality so thoroughgoing that it is comical.

When he was preparing *Papers* for book publication, Lowell became pleased and fascinated with a character who, in original printings, had played a very small role—Hosea's pastor and sponsor, Parson Homer Wilbur. By building up this character and assigning him the job of editing the book, Lowell changed the nature of the collection and turned a minor character into a major one. Wilbur's few commentaries were plumped out until they actually took up three-fifths of the volume. In part this was justified because the chief index of the personality of this self-important, bookish old coot was his talkativeness. Lowell had him spout, with reckless abandon and at length, vapid sermonizings, academic jokes, Latin quotations, and sesquipedalian words. The enlargement of Wilbur's role made it possible, as Lowell claimed, "on occasion to rise above the level of mere patois" in order to treat matters "beyond the horizon" of the uneducated Biglow and Sawin. Also, the parson's pedantry and highfalutin prose "complemented" the picture of Hosea, and set up an incongruous contrast with the farmer's lively verses.

Lowell's first mention, in a letter, of *A Fable for Critics,* his fourth book in 1848, indicated that it would somewhat resemble Parson Wilbur's maunderings: "It is a rambling, disjointed affair, and I may alter the form of it." He went on to say that he had high hopes for it anyhow: "But if I can get it ready I know it will take." He was correct on both counts.

Although *The Biglow Papers* did well in book form, *Fable* was a greater success, especially in areas at a distance from the author's home territory. Within twelve months, it went through four editions; and outside of New England it appears to have sold more copies than all of Lowell's previous volumes of poetry combined.

Typically, Lowell never experimented with the form, and the long poem tends to wander. In the fable, Apollo, at a gathering of gods on Olympus, asks a critic to supply him with a lily.

The critic reviews the personal traits and works of the leading American authors; then, as his survey ends, he comes up with a thistle. Disgusted, Apollo makes a speech recalling the good old days before there were critics, and the gods adjourn. About the narrative, Lowell said: "My plot, like an icicle's, slender and slippery,/ Every moment more slender, and likely to slip awry."

In addition to setting down this simple, loosely built, and remotely relevant story, Lowell occasionally threw in a playful digression, sometimes without warning and sometimes with a mocking apology. Readers lacking humor or unfamiliar with the authors being discussed must have found the work annoying. But readers with a fondness for ebullient wit and pithy summaries, provided they were up-to-date in their reading of the era's native literature, were likely to share the reaction of critic Francis Bowen of the *North American Review*. "The author's extraordinary command of Hudibrastic rhymes," he said, "and the easy flow of versification" made it a plausible guess that *Fable* came from the pen of Biglow's creator. Bowen called the book "a very pleasant and sparkling poem abounding in flashes of brilliant satire, edged with wit enough to delight even its victims." Well, some victims were anything but "delighted." Even a less touchy author than Edgar Allan Poe, for instance, might find less than enchanting the comment:

"There comes Poe, with his raven, like Barnaby Rudge,
Three fifths of him genius and two fifths sheer fudge,
Who talks like a book of iambs and pentameters,
In a way to make people of common sense damn metres,
Who has written some things quite the best of their kind,
But the heart somehow seems all squeezed out by the mind. . . ."

Despite some jabs and puffs that were not entirely impersonal or in fact justifiable, the young critic managed to tick off the fatal flaws of scribblers who quite properly would be forgotten, and to hit off the weaknesses and credit the strengths of those who were to endure. James Fenimore Cooper, he saw, made his stiff heroes "clothes upon sticks" figures and his heroines "all sappy as maples and flat as a prairie." All the same,

"He has drawn you one character, though, that is new,
One wildflower he's picked that is wet with the dew
Of this fresh Western world, and, the thing not to mince,
He has done naught but copy it ill ever since. . . ."

Bryant he called "as quiet, as cool, and as dignified,/ As a smooth, silent iceberg, that never is ignified"; but he also mentioned that Bryant achieved grandeur and was "almost the one of your poets that knows/ How much grace, strength and dignity lie in Repose." He saw Emerson as a rare combination of the mystic and the pragmatist—"a Greek head on right Yankee shoulders." Sometimes Emerson was too esoteric to be understandable; but "some poems have welled/ From those rare depths of soul that have ne'er been excelled."

The impressive quartet of books published in a single year, then, made a name for Lowell as a poet, political commentator, humorist, and critic. Contemporaries quite understandably believed that these highly varied and outstanding works of a twenty-nine-year-old guaranteed greater things to come; and Lowell continued to perform in every one of his different roles.

After 1848 Lowell for more than a decade and a half limited himself to editing or introducing collected poems by other authors and writing magazine pieces, lyrics, and reviews. He did not publish another book of his own writings until 1864. In the interval, vital changes in his circumstances, his occupations, and his interests worked to bring several modifications in what he wrote.

Maria Lowell's death had a traumatic effect, and, as he saw later and as his biographers agree, cut a gash between eras of his life. The assignment in 1855 to deliver the Lowell Institute lectures stirred him out of his lethargy and started a chain reaction: he immersed himself as he never had before in reading criticism and literature; he spoke for the first time before large, intelligent audiences whose reactions he could watch; his handling of these lectures led to a Harvard professorship and serious study abroad and at home; long years of living, teaching, and writing in an exclusive academic atmosphere; new and different associations. Also, without leaving Cambridge, he served as the first editor of the *Atlantic Monthly,* which through his guidance became the country's most respected literary magazine.

Never one of hoi polloi except in theory, for a brief period, and then largely because of Maria's influence, Lowell became increasingly skeptical about common men and more of an elitist Brahmin. Like his colleague Oliver Wendell Holmes, but with less ingratiating self-satire, he overestimated the importance of belonging to an old and esteemed family and the virtues of his corner of the country. His conviction grew that New Englanders were the best Americans and that Cambridge folk were the best New Englanders. His ties with his "dear native town" became closer than ever; he was sure that it held the world's best society and that its inhabitants used the finest English spoken anywhere. In a lyrical poem, he rejoiced because "what colleging was mine I had" in an institution that by the greatest good luck was located in his beloved Cambridge.

Like many professors Lowell was led into temptation by having captive audiences in classrooms and lecture halls. To the annoyance of some students and the delight of others, he often wandered away from the subject of his lectures. If a student mistranslated a line, Lowell would do the job correctly, then drift into chitchat about European scenery, architecture, and baptismal fonts until the hour ended. In his essay on Lowell in *Stelligery and Other Essays,* Barrett Wendell, who went on to become a Harvard professor himself, explained:

Now and again some word or some passage would suggest to him a line of thought—sometimes very earnest, sometimes paradoxically comical—that it never would have suggested to any one else; and he would lean back in his chair, and talk away across country till he felt like stopping; or he would thrust his hands into the pockets of his rather shabby sack-coat, and pace the end of the room with his heavy laced boots, and look at nothing in particular, and discourse of things in general.

As his official biographer, Horace Scudder, put it, "He turned the lecture and recitation hour into a *causerie.*"

Outside the halls of learning, social gatherings encouraged similar talk. As the founding editor of, and frequent contributor to, the *Atlantic Monthly,* Lowell was on friendly terms with many leading authors. His chief associates were contributors, especially those who were neighbors, and fellow faculty members, many of whom belonged to the august Saturday Club—Holmes, Longfellow, Richard Henry Dana, William Hickling Prescott, William Dean Howells, and Henry James—"scholars, poets, wits, all choice," as Lowell said in the ode "Agassiz," on the death of a member:

Such company as wisest moods befits,
Yet with no pedant blindness to the worth
  Of undeliberate mirth,
Natures benignly mixed of air and earth,
Now with the stars and now with equal zest
Tracing the eccentric orbit of a jest.

On the basis of his long study of New England life and literature, Percy Holmes Boynton suggested in *Literature and American Life* that there was a causal relationship between Lowell's associations and his later writings:

More and more he inclined to write for this group [of friends], who liked good talk as a sort of intellectual steeplechase and who enjoyed a recondite allusion for their consciousness that it was caviar to the general. Writing for this audience, which was very much less than a reading public . . . [he let] his essays and longer poems meander along . . . with the casual sequence of after-dinner talk uttered in the challenging presence of Oliver Wendell Holmes and his brother John and Tom Appleton and Tom Aldrich, who have a long evening ahead of them and do not care where the talk drifts, so long as it contains plenty of "good things."

Boynton considered it typical of Lowell that the Civil War and controversies about it affected his writing of the second series of *Biglow Papers*. The role of Parson Wilbur, already inordinately expanded, continued to grow. The wordy pedant (who now, ironically, read more and more like an unconscious parody of his professorial creator) delivered long commentaries in the periodical versions (1862–1866); then, in the book, he—and for a good many pages Lowell himself, with his mask removed—engaged in digressions and redundancies. In comparison with the foreword, preface, prologue, introduction, explanations of individual poems, postscript, and glossary, Hosea's poems were dwarfed. Hosea, who at times shared his creator's verbosity, did not completely exaggerate the process when he summarized "the argyment" of his final paper:

Interducshin, w'ich may be skipt. Begins by talkin' about himself. . . . Nex' comes the git-tin' the goodwill of the orjunce by lettin' 'em gether from wut you kind of ex'dentally let drop thet they air about East, A one. . . . Spring interdooced with a few approput flours. Speach finally begins. . . . Subjick staited; expanded; delayted; extended. . . . Ginnle remarks; continooed; kerried on; pushed furder; kind o' gin out. . . . Gits back to whare he sot out. Can't seem to stay thair. . . . Argoos with an imedginary bean thet ain't aloud to say nothin' in repleye. . . . Concloods. Concloods more. . . . Finely concloods to conclood. Yeels the flore.

One poem included in the *Second Series* is, by general agreement, the finest of all those in *The Biglow Papers*—"The Courtin'." Since six stanzas of this had been dashed off to fill a blank page in the *First Series,* it was not entirely new; but six stanzas were added in 1857 and twelve more in 1866 or 1867, so that most of it was. It vividly evokes a chilly outdoor landscape and then a firelit indoor scene in wintry New England. In amusing detail it tells how bashful bumpkin Ezekiel was maneuvered into popping the question to mischievous and canny Hilda. Graphic, lighthearted, and straightforward, it is among the best of hosts of comic accounts of rustic wooings that appeared during the nineteenth century in all parts of the United States.

"The Courtin'," Lowell testified, was the result "almost of pure accident"; and it well may be that the rather unusual way (for him) it came into being helped it achieve a more unified form than did *Second Series* as a whole and other individual poems in it.

The collective volume is episodic and disjunctive. "Sunthin' in the Pastoral Line," a long and tenuously connected monologue, is more representative of the book than "The Courtin'." Hosea starts this unit by scolding American poets for not doing right by the scenery of their homeland. Next, he drifts into a description of a Massachusetts spring, which is the most praised and most frequently quoted portion of the poem:

Fust come the black birds clatt'rin' in tall trees,
An' settlin' things in windy Congresses,—
Queer politicians, though, for I'll be skinned
Ef all on 'em don't head aginst the wind.
'fore long the trees begin to show belief,—
The maple crimsons to a coral-reef,
Then saffern swarms swing off from all the
    willers
So plump they look like yaller caterpillars,
Then gray hossches'nuts leetle hands unfold
Softer 'n a baby's be at three days old:
Thet's robin-redbreast's almanick; he knows
Thet arter this ther' 's only blossom-snows;
So, choosin' out a handy crotch an' spouse,
He goes to plast'rin' his adobe house.

Then seems to come a hitch,—things lag behind,
Till some fine mornin' Spring makes up her
    mind,
An' ez, when snow-swelled rivers cresh their
    dams
Heaped-up with ice thet dovetails in an' jams,
A leak comes spirtin' thru some pin-hole cleft,
Grows stronger, fercer, tears out right an' left,
Then all the waters bow themselves an' come,
Suddin, in one gret slope o' shedderin' foam,
Jes' so our Spring gits everythin' in tune
An' gives one leap from Aperl into June. . . .

Having concluded this leisurely description in twenty-two additional lines, Hosea tells about his enjoyment of a spring walk. He next describes a particular stroll past the school he attended as a boy—the sight of which leads him to cuss out contemporary education and reminisce about his boyhood. He makes some remarks about his habit of having dreams. At last, getting to the message by an indirect route, he recounts a particular dream he had during which a Cromwellian ancestor compared seventeenth-century Great Britain with the United States of the 1860's and made prophecies about the future of the nation that Lowell endorsed. In covering this varied ground at great length (324 lines) as it does, this poem is typical not only of the book but also of longer poems of Lowell's later period.

Another tendency in the longer poems—one carried over from the earlier period—was to disregard the advice Lowell gave himself in *Fable* to make "the distinction 'twixt singing and preaching." And of course the writing of long poems with hefty messages was a predictable activity for a poet who followed the fashions, for the most admired lengthy poems of the period were highly philosophical ones. To cite a few instances, such greatly varied ones as the following were alike in this particular: Emerson's *Threnody* (1847), Wordsworth's *Prelude* (1850), Tennyson's *In Memoriam* (1850), Whitman's *Leaves of Grass* (1855–1892), Matthew Arnold's *Rugby Chapel* (1857), Edward FitzGerald's *Rubaiyat of Omar Khayyam* (1859–1868), Browning's *The Ring and the Book* (1868–1869), Lanier's *The Symphony* (1875), Longfellow's *Morituri Salutamus* (1875), and Bryant's *The Flood of Years* (1876).

Critics, looking for ways to describe the forms of the best of Lowell's longer poems, see resemblances between them and his prose compositions. "A Familiar Epistle to a Friend" and "Epistle to George William Curtis," as their titles suggest, were predictable productions of a man whose personal letters showed him at his best and charmed the recipients. Other long poems had the look of compositions of a kindred sort—familiar essays: "Agassiz," "Under the Willows," *The Cathedral,* and *Ode Recited at the Harvard Commemoration.*

George Arms, the critic who has looked most carefully and sympathetically at this group of poems, generalizes:

All these poems have in common a similarity of structure and language. Upon the surface they appear as awkward in their ordering as many of

Lowell's poems are in essence. In language they also may first seem to be less than satisfactory, for certainly they do not cultivate the native idiom to the extent that *The Biglow Papers* do. But these later poems draw together with a final sense of wholeness, and they exhibit a learned-colloquial style, easy and efficient, that has little trace of the archaic poetical. . . . Lowell admitted the colloquial when it was of good blood, and though we may think his standard of family too high, in these poems we can enjoy the liberated result. . . . Consciously wayward in structure and language, Lowell reveals a new kind of unity. . . . Not only in the whole but in the parts he now displays finish. Even the metaphor shows control. . . .

Arms's analyses of individual poems plausibly support his generalizations. *The Cathedral,* which he believes deserves to be the best known, he shows to be well ordered to develop its thought and notable for its use of homely images. And although in theme it resembles "Stanzas from the Grande Chartreuse" by Matthew Arnold, and suffers when contrasted with Henry Adams' *Mont-Saint-Michel and Chartres* (1904), it proceeds in its own way and reaches quite a different resolution:

O Power, more near my life than life itself
(Or what seems life to us in sense immured),
Even as the roots, shut in the darksome earth,
Share in the tree-top's joyance, and conceive
Of sunshine and wide air and winged things
By sympathy of nature, so do I
Have evidence of Thee so far above,
Yet in and of me! Rather Thou the root
Invisibly sustaining, hid in light,
Not darkness, or in darkness made by us.
If sometimes I must hear good men debate
Of other witness of Thyself than Thou,
As if there needed any help of ours
To nurse Thy flickering life, that else must
      cease,
Blown out, as 't were a candle, by men's breath,

My soul shall not be taken in their snare,
To change her inward surety for their doubt
Muffled from sight in formal robes of proof:
While she can only feel herself through Thee,
I fear not Thy withdrawal; more I fear,
Seeing, to know Thee not, hoodwinked with
      dreams
Of signs and wonders, while, unnoticed, Thou,
Walking Thy garden still, commun'st with men,
Missed in the commonplace of miracle.

Arms calls *Ode Recited at the Harvard Commemoration* the long poem "most closely akin to the familiar verse essay at its best" but dealing effectively, often in colloquial language, with "a subject surely proper for poetry": "He mediates between absolutes and particulars: in a structure in which beneath the haphazardness is a unity that produces pleasure out of the disparateness of the material." The poem, read to a group of friends and alumni who had gathered on July 21, 1865, to pay tribute to the Harvard men who had served during the Civil War, posed and confronted a question raised about all wars: "What possible justification is there for the sacrifices of the men who serve?" Lowell had an emotional interest in the question since he himself had lost three beloved nephews. And whether or not one accepts Lowell's answer, it expresses a passionate belief worthy of respect.

A remarkable aspect of the *Ode,* which was nearly four hundred lines long as it was read, is that although it was composed literally in one night, its form was consciously adapted to the way it was presented. This was not an accident, as Lowell's account of his discovery of the form shows:

A long series of uniform stanzas (I am always speaking of public recitation) with regularly recurring rhymes produces somnolence among the men and a desperate resort to their fans on the part of the women. . . . Now, my problem was to contrive a measure which should not be tedious by uniformity, but which should vary with varying moods, in which the transitions . . . should be managed without a jar. I at first thought of mixed rhymed and blank verses leaving some verses without a rhyme to match. But my ear was better pleased with the rhyme, coming at a longer interval, as a far-off echo rather than instant reverberation, produced the same effect almost, and yet was grateful by unexpectedly recalling an association and faint reminiscence of consonance.

The detailed discussion and Lowell's practice in other poems as well as this one indicate why Gay Wilson Allen, a leading historian of American prosody, has argued that this poet's handling of rhyme and metrics "introduced into American poetry the freedom that we find in the first two or three decades of nineteenth-century English poetry"—"a more varied placing of accents and the combination of different kinds of feet to produce suggestiveness of tone and cadence."

The sixth stanza of the *Ode*, written and inserted soon after the public reading, is the one most often quoted and remembered. It paid an eloquent tribute to "our Martyr Chief," who had been assassinated on April 14. "Nature," wrote Lowell,

For him her Old-World moulds aside she threw,
  And, choosing sweet clay from the breast
  Of the unexhausted West,
With stuff untainted shaped a hero new,
Wise, steadfast in the strength of God, and true.
  How beautiful to see
Once more a shepherd of mankind indeed,
Who loved his charge, but never loved to lead;
One whose meek flock the people joyed to be,
  Not lured by any cheat of birth,
  But by his clear-grained human worth,
And brave old wisdom of sincerity! . . .
Our children shall behold his fame.
  The kindly-earnest, brave, foreseeing man,
Sagacious, patient, dreading praise, not blame,
New birth of our new soil, the first American.

In the forty-eight-line stanza, as Richard Watson Gilder, editor of the *Century*, noted in 1887, the author "was the first of the leading American writers to see . . . and clearly and fully and enthusiastically proclaim the greatness of Abraham Lincoln." Lowell therefore had an important role in creating one of the most enduring American legends.

The concern of the later lengthy poems with current events, personalities, and pressing controversies; their embodiment of arguments, emotional appeals, and prescriptions for action; and their tailoring for immediate audiences have led several critics to argue that they are more rhetorical and declamatory than they are poetic. "The famous 'Commemoration Ode,' " wrote Odell Shepard, for instance, "is superb versified oratory designed for a solemn public occasion."

Not only Lowell's tendency to preach in his poetry but also his magazine commitments encouraged his involvement with current affairs. Among his skills was a journalistic ability to gauge public attitudes well enough to make periodicals appeal to potential subscribers. After the *Atlantic Monthly* was founded to foster literature and to editorialize for a particular group of readers, Lowell as its first editor wrote and accepted articles on elections, policies, abolitionism, women's rights, juvenile delinquency, and the treatment of the mentally handicapped. Even after resigning from the editorship, Lowell often contributed to the magazine—Hosea Biglow's controversial poems, for instance. As coeditor of the *North American Review*, he backed Lincoln's wartime policies and urged his reelection; and he was generous with comments on postbellum legislation.

For a time after retiring from editorial work in 1872, Lowell was relatively quiet about politics. But the scandals of the second Grant administration—and, it may well have been, advancing age and galloping respectability—led him to become increasingly vocal and conservative. A change in his feelings becomes evident when one contrasts the 1869 essay "On a Certain Condescension in Foreigners" with later statements. The essay, published in the *Atlantic,* reproved Europeans for commenting adversely on the American—especially the Cambridge—lack of urbanity, and played up merits and fine achievements of the author's countrymen. A poem for the nation's centennial, by contrast, ironically suggested that Columbia might celebrate by proudly putting on display quite different attractions:

"Show 'em your Civil Service, and explain
How all men's loss is everybody's gain. . . .
Show your short cut to cure financial ills
By making paper-collars current bills;
Show your State legislatures; show your Rings;
And challenge Europe to produce such things
As high officials sitting half in sight
To share the plunder and to fix things
    right. . . ."

Lowell's service to the Republican party and his rhetorical skills brought him diplomatic appointments by President Rutherford B. Hayes. In the England of a kindred spirit, Prime Minister William Ewart Gladstone, he was an especially appealing ambassador—"the pet," as a friend said, "of countesses, the habitué of palaces, the intimate of dukes." Happy in this congenial atmosphere, he was remarkably effective as a graceful and polished speaker on public occasions.

A major address in 1884, "Democracy," had wide circulation and provided a summary of a final attitude. A revealing fact about it: it was best in discussing the defects of a democratic system, notably its tendency to vulgarity, its way of equating truth with statistical majorities, and its leaning toward collectivism. When Lowell turned to ways and means of dealing with these trends, he did not do as well:

The true way is to discover and to extirpate the germs. As society is now constituted these are in the air it breathes, the water it drinks, in the things that seem, and which it has always believed, to be the most innocent and healthful. The evil elements it neglects corrupt these in their springs and pollute them in their courses. Let us be of good cheer, however, remembering that the misfortunes hardest to bear are those which never come. The world has outlived much, and will outlive a great deal more, and men have contrived to be happy in it. It has shown the strength of its constitution in nothing more than in surviving the quack medicines it has tried. In the scales of the destinies brawn will never weigh so much as brain. Our healing is not in the storm or in the whirlwind, it is not in monarchies, or aristocracies, or democracies, but will be revealed by the still small voice that speaks to the conscience and the heart, prompting us to a wider and wiser humanity.

"Full of good things," Matthew Arnold thought the speech, "but lacking in body and current."

Several of Lowell's essays, like the diplomatic occasional speeches, resemble personal letters to friends and have similar appeals. The volume marking the end of the sixteen-year interval between books, *Fireside Travels* (1864), collected some of them. The epigraph by "Richard Lassels, Gent.," which justifies the title, is felicitous: "Travelling makes a man sit still in his old age with satisfaction and travel over the world again in his chair and bed by discourse and thoughts." Reminiscent essays take the author and his readers to Maine and to various parts of Italy, and one—the best—journeys back in time to "Cambridge Thirty Years Ago." Here, directly addressing a Roman friend, "my dear Storg," the author reflects at leisure and at length (14,000 words) on the town as it was in his youth—its geography and its townspeople: "loafers, topers, proverb-mongers, barber, parson, postmaster, whose tenure was for life," the black brewer, grocers, constables, Scottish gardeners, an artist, lawyers, college professors, administrators, philosophers, and eccentrics. "My dear Storg" also is told about old Cambridge's festivities, such as the Muster and Commencement Day; and the Cornwallis masquerade, recalled with amusement, when "Silas and Ezra and Jonas were not only disguised as Redcoats, Continentals, and Indians, but not infrequently disguised in drink also." A small part of the character sketch of a jolly professor imported to teach foreign languages indicates the genial tone:

Perpetual childhood dwelt in him, the childhood of his native Southern France, and its fixed air was all the time bubbling up and sparkling and winking in his eyes. . . . The world to him . . . was like a medal, on the obverse of which is stamped the image of Joy, and on the reverse that of Care. S. never took the foolish pains to look at that other side, even if he knew its existence; much less would it have occurred to him to turn it into view. . . . Nor was this a mere outside good humor; its source was deeper, in a true Christian kindliness and amenity. Once, when he had been knocked down by a tipsily driven sleigh, and was urged to prosecute the offenders, "No, no," he said, his wounds still fresh, "young blood! young blood! it must have its way! I was young myself." *Was!* few men come into life so young as S. went out. . . . What was there ever like his bow? It was as if you had received a decoration, and could write yourself gentleman from that day forth. His hat rose, regreeting your own, and, having sailed through the stately curve of the old regime, sank gently back over that placid brain, which harbored no thought less white than the powder which covered it.

Reading this essay and similar ones that came later (such as "My Garden Acquaintance" and "A Good Word for Winter"), one easily sees not only why Lowell was able to people Hosea Biglow's hometown with lifelike quirky Yankees but also why, as an editor, he was hospitable to local-color fiction and did much to es-

tablish the school of writers who helped prepare the way for realism.

"Emerson the Lecturer," "Thoreau," and several similar pieces combine the stuff of such personal essays with literary criticism. In the former, Lowell concretely describes his own excited response to a lecture by Emerson that he heard as a young man; and he also characterizes and criticizes Emerson's writings. "Thoreau" begins with an amusing evocation of America's 1840's, when transcendentalism flourished and an army of "wild-eyed enthusiasts . . . stood ready at a moment's notice to reform everything but themselves." Lowell next recalls the rise of Emerson and the earthshaking lecture, "The American Scholar," that he gave at Harvard in 1837 when Lowell was a junior: "What enthusiasm of approval, what grim silence of foreign dissent! It was our Yankee version of a lecture by Abelard. . . ." He then turns to Thoreau as "the most remarkable pistillate plant kindled to fruitage by the Emerson pollen," and proceeds to evaluate this disciple's writings by weighing his best qualities against what Lowell felt were quite damning ones. (An effect, historians agree, was "to defer the beginnings of the Thoreau cult for twenty years.")

Although *A Fable for Critics* contains the best-known of Lowell's discussions of contemporary American authors, it was by no means his last word on the subject. In 1849 he reviewed Longfellow's *Kavanagh* for the *North American Review* and Thoreau's *A Week on the Concord and Merrimack Rivers* for the *Massachusetts Quarterly Review*. Over the years he reviewed current books by an impressive list of American authors—Sylvester Judd, Josiah Holland, Richard Henry Dana, Nathaniel Hawthorne, John Greenleaf Whittier, William Cullen Bryant, Rose Terry, Oliver Wendell Holmes, Francis Parkman, William Dean Howells, James Piatt, and others. Many of his assessments are of interest because they state informed attitudes of the period; some, such as the brief comment on

Hawthorne's career in general and *The Marble Faun* in particular in the April 1860 issue of *Atlantic,* are concise and illuminating.

This review (fortunately space limitations kept him from digressing) illustrates some of Lowell's procedures. It starts with a quick overview of Hawthorne's career, not book by book but in broad terms that help place him in context. The keynote: "With just enough encouragement to confirm his faith in his own powers, those powers had time to ripen and to toughen themselves before the gales of popularity could twist them from the balance of a healthy and normal development." Lowell further defines Hawthorne's unique achievements by making some comparisons. He contrasts his "thorough conception of a world of moral realities [that causes] Art [to] become the interpreter of something profounder than herself" with Poe's "masterly adaptation of the world of sense and appearance to the purposes of Art." In at least this perception, Lowell finds that Hawthorne resembles Shakespeare. On the other hand, "that breadth of nature which made Shakespeare incapable of alienation from common human nature and actual life is wanting to Hawthorne." So Hawthorne shows a certain remoteness—like that, say, of John Donne, "but with such a difference that we should call the one super- and the other subter-sensual." The American, "psychological and metaphysical . . . does not draw characters" as Shakespeare, Fielding, and Thackeray do, by representing idiosyncrasies, but subtly and "with what truth to as much of human nature as is included in a diseased consciousness" because he "traces all the finest nerves of impulse and motive [and] compels every trivial circumstance into an accomplice of his art." So Hawthorne's works are acclimated to the New World by their moral purpose, "and perhaps their sadness [which] mark him as the son of New England and the Puritans."

Next Lowell generalizes about a common practice of his fellow New Englander that is related to such a moral purpose, and he does so in terms that look forward to many of the twentieth-century critiques of Hawthorne: "It is commonly true . . . that the interest centres in one strongly defined protagonist, to whom the other characters are accessory and subordinate,—perhaps we should rather say a ruling Idea, of which all the characters are fragmentary embodiments . . . the actors and incidents seem but vistas through which we see the moral from different points of view. . . ."

The application of these generalizations to *The Marble Faun* is perceptive, graceful, and clear:

Nothing could be more imaginative than the conception of the character of Donatello. . . . His likeness to the lovely statue of Praxiteles, his happy animal temperament, and the dim legend of his pedigree are combined with wonderful art to reconcile us to the notion of a Greek myth embodied in an Italian of the nineteenth century; and when at length a soul is created in this primeval pagan, this child of earth, this creature of mere instinct, awakened through sin to the necessity of atonement, we feel that while we looked to be entertained with the airiest of fictions, we were dealing with the most august truths of psychology, with the most pregnant facts of modern history, and studying a profound parable of the development of the Christian Idea.

Everything suffers a sea-change in the depths of Mr. Hawthorne's mind, gets rimmed with an impalpable fringe of melancholy moss, and there is a tone of sadness in this book as in the rest, but it does not leave us sad. In a series of remarkable and characteristic works, it is perhaps the most remarkable and characteristic.

But for the most part the lengthy literary criticisms that Lowell gathered in his books concerned foreign authors of the past. And despite the fact that he said something about many specific works, ranging all the way from 700 B.C. to 1889, his thirty major essays featured earlier—and British—writers and works between

Dante and Thoreau. In the order of their appearance (in the world and not in the capricious order of the essays) these included Dante, Chaucer, *Don Quixote,* Spenser, Marlowe, Shakespeare, Shakespeare's *Richard III* and *Hamlet,* Beaumont and Fletcher, Webster, Chapman, Massinger and Ford, Milton, Milton's *Areopagitica,* Walton, Dryden, Pope, Rousseau, Fielding, Gray, Lessing, Wordsworth, Coleridge, Keats, Landor's *Letters,* Carlyle, Swinburne's *Tragedies, Life and Letters of James Gates Percival,* "Emerson the Lecturer," and "Thoreau."

Putting these essays side by side with Lowell's early critical writings helps describe them. For the callow young critic, what fouled up both creative works and discussions of them was anything that was not instinctive. The best writers were those who wrote before and after "the French Apollo, with powdered wig and gold snuff-box . . . set foot in England and established the reign of hollowness and taste." The reason? Because "the poets of those days" and of the period after the neoclassicists were deposed "knew nothing of 'established principles,' " or disregarded them: "Freedom is the only law which genius knows." The best critics, just as scornful of rules, were the sensitive readers who instinctively recognized fine literature for what it was. And since comments "gather clouds rather than dispel them," what such critics had to do was avoid many comments and "cull out and give . . . the most striking and beautiful passages." The young Lowell's articles on authors were made up mostly of quotations, interspersed with brief encomiums. The expectation was that sensitive readers with superb taste (like Lowell's) would fall in love with quoted passages at first sight. Less perceptive readers were simply out of luck.

This approach, and witty comments based upon it, as well as puns, topicalities, ingenious rhymes, and tricky metrics insured the success of *A Fable for Critics.* But in 1855, eager to make the Lowell Institute lectures systematic and in-

structive, as his notebooks show, the thirty-six-year-old apprentice put himself through a home study course in criticism. He certainly read Gray, Johnson, Coleridge, and Schelling. Probably, too, he either recalled or reread Emerson, a favorite former teacher, Edward Tyrrel Channing, and Harvard textbook writers Hugh Blair and Dugald Stewart. The lectures showed that after intensive preparation Lowell had learned new ways to read and discuss literature and, as Leon Howard says, he was able to "make his entrance into the brotherhood of critics" as "both a diagnostician and a judge":

His arrangement of ideas did not constitute a formal critical system so much as it represented a series of definitions, a formality of relationships, and a hierarchy of values which could guide his thoughts toward fresh critical opinions even though he might not directly apply them. They referred primarily to the capabilities of a writer, who was required to possess such fundamental qualities as an active "fancy" and a factual "understanding" in order to collect and use the materials from which literature was formed. These materials might be shaped by the structural "poetic faculty" or informed by the "poetic sense," but before they could be turned into the highest form of literature they had to be transformed by an "imagination" which could be either "narrative" or, at its best, "dramatic." No single work of literature could be characterized by a display of all six of these qualities, but a consideration of any piece of writing with reference to them would enable the critic to make a thorough diagnosis of its merits and shortcomings. These terms and the various synonyms which Lowell used for them, in short, formed what the older rhetoricians would have called the "commonplaces" which enabled him to achieve copiousness without chaos as a lecturer in 1855 and also during his later years as a space-filling editor or as a contributor paid at journalistic space rates.

A valuable perception, as Howard says, was that the qualities of an author might be classified and the writings praised and condemned "within the limits of that classification."

These basic distinctions between the differing ways that writers collect, use, and shape materials were supplemented in due course by other distinctions and ways of looking at works. Helped by classical critics, especially Aristotle and Horace, and by such later figures as Ben Jonson and Goethe, Lowell made illuminating statements about "images," "types," and "actualities"—about historical milieus and (with a special bow to Goethe) about "teleology, or the argument from means to end, the argument of adaptation."

When Lowell, as was his admirable habit, saturated himself in one of his authors, responded with sensitivity to that author's appeal, and used such distinctions between kinds and procedures in vivacious reports, he convinced a great many contemporaries that he was the best of all American critics. What is more, vastly different twentieth-century critics and schools have found—or could have found if they had tried—that he anticipated their approaches, methods, and happiest perceptions.

Richard Altick, a student of historical contexts, for instance, wrote an article, "Was Lowell an Historical Critic?" and presented much evidence of "his awareness of the power exerted by contemporary circumstance upon the literature of a given era." Van Wyck Brooks, after he deserted the iconoclastic party of his youth and rhapsodized over American writers whenever possible, admired Lowell's "felicitous insights and luckier phrases, . . . the tone and texture of his style." He also found that Lowell (like Brooks) was a great appreciator: "Enthusiasm, gusto, relish; it was in these that Lowell excelled. . . . What joy, what shy delights this man revealed when he wrote of the authors he loved! And even, let us add, what judgment!"

Members of the most cohesive critical school of the 1920's, the new humanists, read Lowell with approval and implied or announced that they accepted him as an ancestor. Norman Foerster, for instance, a highly respected new humanist, said he had "the sanest and most comprehensive conception of literature formed in America prior to the twentieth century." Lowell's acceptance of Hellenistic tenets, his stress on reason, grace, and ethical values, and his belief in dualism appealed to Foerster's fellow believers such as Irving Babbitt, Paul Elmer More, Harry H. Clark, Austin Warren, and Stuart Pratt Sherman. Preachments in an 1889 address to the Modern Language Association anticipate those of John Crowe Ransom, Allen Tate, Cleanth Brooks, and Robert Penn Warren. Herbert F. Smith points to still other affiliations:

[Lowell's] feeling for myth, his organicism, his catholicity of taste, align him with other schools of modern criticism. Many of his remarks on myth, tradition, and the artist's need for roots generally precede T. S. Eliot's ideas on these subjects. His organicism and particularly his emphasis on the need for total design in art ally him with R. S. Crane and the Chicago critics generally. Perhaps strangest of all, his insistence on the need to experience a work of art fully and his unwillingness to explicate any part at the expense of total experience, his absolute certainty that matter and manner in art are inextricably combined, find curious echoes in the writings of Susan Sontag and other recent critics who have reacted against the New Criticism and the assumption by the academic world that criticism is their province only.

Smith, who made a fine anthology of some of Lowell's most interesting critical passages, therefore believes that his man is not "entirely dead as a critic."

Despite these acknowledged and unacknowledged kinships, practically nobody reads Lowell's critical volumes nowadays except a few scholars; and even fewer readers think well of them. The same is true of Lowell's other writings. Why?

Both his admirers and the man himself have proffered some answers. Van Wyck Brooks thought he went along too amiably with the establishment, showing himself a master only "when he felt behind him the stream of tradition, when he did not have to judge for himself." Although Lowell now and then was daring enough to praise an unfashionable John Donne or a John Keats, Brooks's claim has merit. Again, Foerster, who greatly admired Lowell's "Poetics," in the end decided that "he leaves an impression of superficiality and futility." The reason—and the point is well taken—is that

. . . it is not his creed that is weak, but the man himself. . . . Lowell stood forth among his contemporaries because of his accomplished versatility rather than because of his high attainment. Once or twice, . . . he was able to fuse most of his powers in adequate expression, but the rest of the time he was a man of parts, a man of shreds. Capable of growth . . . he was unhappily incapable of self-mastery.

Short on inner assurance, he constantly was guided by outside forces. His first wife, Maria White, made him an active reformer. A democratic audience that went for crackerbox satire nudged him into writing *The Biglow Papers.* He responded so well not only to this audience but to others that, at the youthful age of twenty-nine, when the imitation characteristic of a beginner was healthy and a young man's zest might take some of the curse off of it, he did the best creative work of his whole career. Later, Cambridge, Harvard, the Saturday Club, and overawed audiences—some overseas—just led him on.

And some of the qualities that helped Lowell forge ahead in his era have become today's roadblocks. Except in a few lucky instances ("To the Dandelion" and "Auspex" come to mind) his lyrics, lacking the conviction and control of personal emotion to make them memorable, succumbed to banality. What he himself said about his 1869 collection of poems applied to others: "They seem to me just like all the verses I read in the papers—and I suppose they are." Instead of *Under the Willows,* he groaned, perhaps the forthcoming book should be called "Under the Billows or dredgings from the Atlantic." Except for portions (for example, the Lincoln eulogy in "Commemoration Ode"), the longer poems discourage moderns by being too discursive, too topical, or too oratorical. *The Biglow Papers,* the author's finest achievement, suffer because they have similar traits and, in addition, because too much painstaking dialect and too many of Parson Wilbur's erudite maunderings are now considered barriers. And few of today's readers of criticism find it worthwhile to mine page after page of diffuse critical essays for nuggets of insight that once delighted more patient and respectful readers.

For these reasons, this giant that the Victorian era revered as a poet, professor, editor, essayist, critic, and public servant now seems much smaller. Lowell's present reputation offers eloquent evidence that self-discipline, coherence, and economy can help to ensure literary survival.

Selected Bibliography

WORKS OF JAMES RUSSELL LOWELL

The 16-volume Elmwood Edition of *The Complete Writings of James Russell Lowell,* edited by Charles Eliot Norton (Boston: Houghton Mifflin, 1904), is the most comprehensive collection. It includes *Letters* (reedited and expanded to 3 volumes) and Horace E. Scudder's 2-volume biography. It has been supplemented by volumes listed at the end of this section. *The Complete Poetical Works of James Russell Lowell*, edited by Horace E. Scudder (Boston: Houghton Mifflin, 1897, 1917), contains useful headnotes and a chronology.

A Year's Life. Boston: C. C. Little and J. Brown, 1841.

Poems. Cambridge: John Owen, 1844.

Conversations on Some of the Old Poets. Cambridge: John Owen, 1845.

Poems. Second Series. Boston: B. B. Mussey and Company, 1848.

A Fable for Critics. New York: G. P. Putnam, 1848.

Meliboeus-Hipponax. The Biglow Papers. Cambridge: George Nichols, 1848.

The Vision of Sir Launfal. Cambridge: George Nichols, 1848.

Fireside Travels. Boston: Ticknor and Fields, 1864.

Ode Recited at the Commemoration of the Living and Dead Soldiers of Harvard University. Cambridge: Privately printed, 1865.

Meliboeus-Hipponax. The Biglow Papers. Second Series. Boston: Ticknor and Fields, 1867.

Under the Willows and Other Poems. Boston: Fields, Osgood, & Co., 1869.

Among My Books. Boston: Fields, Osgood, & Co., 1870.

The Cathedral. Boston: Fields, Osgood, & Co., 1870.

My Study Windows. Boston: James R. Osgood and Company, 1871.

Among My Books. Second Series. Boston: James R. Osgood and Company, 1876.

Three Memorial Poems. Boston: James R. Osgood and Company, 1877.

Democracy and Other Addresses. Boston: Houghton, Mifflin and Company, 1887.

Political Essays. Boston: Houghton, Mifflin and Company, 1888.

Heartsease and Rue. Boston: Houghton, Mifflin and Company, 1888.

The English Poets: Lessing, Rousseau. London: Walter Scott, 1888.

Latest Literary Essays and Addresses. Cambridge: Riverside Press, 1891.

The Old English Dramatists. Cambridge: Riverside Press, 1892.

Letters, edited by Charles Eliot Norton. 2 vols. New York: Harper & Brothers, 1894. Two volumes and

several articles supplement these. The volumes: *New Letters,* edited by M. A. DeWolfe Howe (New York: Harper & Brothers, 1932), and *The Scholar-Friends,* edited by M. A. DeWolfe Howe and G. W. Cottrell, Jr. (Cambridge: Harvard University Press, 1952). Smaller collections in periodicals are listed in biographies by Duberman and Wagenknecht cited below.

Last Poems. Boston: Houghton, Mifflin and Company, 1895.

Lectures on English Poets [Lowell Institute lectures of 1855]. Cleveland: The Rowfant Club, 1897.

Early Prose Writings. London and New York: John Lane, 1902.

Anti-Slavery Papers. 2 vols. Boston: Houghton, Mifflin and Company, 1902.

The Round Table. Boston: Richard G. Badger, 1913. (Early essays.)

James Russell Lowell, Representative Selections, edited by Harry Hayden Clark and Norman Foerster (New York: American Book Co., 1947).

BIBLIOGRAPHIES

Cooke, G. W. *A Bibliography of James Russell Lowell.* Boston: Houghton, Mifflin and Company, 1906. (Alphabetical and chronological lists of separate works and editions.)

Livingston, Luther S. *A Bibliography of the First Editions in Book Form of James Russell Lowell.* New York: Privately printed, 1914; New York: Burt Franklin, 1968.

Rees, Robert A. "James Russell Lowell," in *Fifteen American Authors Before 1900: Bibliographic Essays on Research and Criticism.* Madison: University of Wisconsin Press, 1971. Pp. 285–305.

[Articles correcting and supplementing these are listed in biographies by Duberman and Wagenknecht cited below.]

BIOGRAPHIES

Beatty, R. C. *James Russell Lowell.* Nashville, Tennessee: Vanderbilt University Press, 1942.

Duberman, Martin. *James Russell Lowell.* Boston: Houghton, Mifflin and Company, 1966.

Hale, Edward Everett. *James Russell Lowell and His Friends.* Boston: Houghton, Mifflin and Company, 1899.

Howard, Leon. *Victorian Knight-Errant: A Study of the Early Literary Career of James Russell Lowell.* Berkeley: University of California Press, 1952.

Scudder, Horace E. *James Russell Lowell.* 2 vols. Boston: Houghton, Mifflin and Company, 1901.

Wagenknecht, Edward. *James Russell Lowell: Portrait of a Many-Sided Man.* New York: Oxford University Press, 1971.

CRITICAL STUDIES

Arms, George. *The Fields Were Green: A New View of Bryant, Whittier, Holmes, Lowell & Longfellow, with a Selection of Their Poems.* Palo Alto, California: Stanford University Press, 1953.

Blair, Walter. "A Brahmin Dons Homespun," in *Horse Sense in American Humor, from Benjamin Franklin to Ogden Nash.* Chicago: University of Chicago Press, 1942. Pp. 77–101.

————. "Down East Humor (1830–1867)," in *Native American Humor.* San Francisco: Chandler, 1960. Pp. 38–62.

Brooks, Van Wyck. *The Flowering of New England.* New York: E. P. Dutton, 1936. Pp. 311–22, 512–25 *et passim*.

Brownell, W. C. "Lowell," in *American Prose Masters.* New York: Charles Scribner's Sons, 1909. Pp. 271–335.

Clark, Harry H., and Norman Foerster. "Introduction" and "Notes" in *James Russell Lowell, Representative Selections.* New York: American Book Company, 1947. Pp. xi–cxxxix, 467–98.

James, Henry. "James Russell Lowell," in *The American Essays of Henry James,* edited by Leon Edel. New York: Charles Scribner's Sons, 1950.

McGlinchee, Claire. *James Russell Lowell.* New York: Twayne, 1967.

Pritchard, J. P. *Return to the Fountains: Some Classical Sources of American Criticism.* Durham, N. C.: Duke University Press, 1942; New York: Octagon, 1966. Pp. 99–118.

————. "Lowell and Longinus," in *Transactions of the American Philological Association,* 1945.

————. "A Glance at Lowell's Classical Reading," *American Literature,* 21:442–55 (1950).

Rivière, Jean. *Le courant abolitioniste dans la littérature américaine de 1808 à 1861.* Lille: Université de Lille III, 1974.

Robertson, J. M. "Lowell as Critic" and "Criticism as Science," *North American Review,* 209:246–62, 690–96 (1919).

Smith, Herbert F. "Introduction" to *Literary Criticism of James Russell Lowell.* Lincoln: University of Nebraska Press, 1969. Pp. ix–xxviii.

Stewart, Charles Oran. *Lowell and France.* Nashville, Tennessee: Vanderbilt University Press, 1951.

Tanselle, G. Thomas. "The Craftsmanship of Lowell: Revisions in 'The Cathedral,'" *Bulletin of the New York Public Library,* 70:60–63 (1966).

Voss, Arthur. "Backgrounds of Lowell's Satire in 'The Biglow Papers,'" *New York Quarterly,* 23:47–64 (1950).

Warren, Austin. "Lowell on Thoreau," *Studies in Philology,* 27:422–62 (1930).

—*WALTER BLAIR*

Bernard Malamud

1914–

THE CLAIM that our spiritual lives are being vitiated by our attachment to material goods and physical comforts is at least as old as the Old Testament. But in America these complaints probably were never so pervasively and variously made as in the late 1950's. To the expected attacks upon the shifts in values, a number of social critics added a line of reasoning that helps to explain the novelists' complaints about the difficulty of getting a fictional hold on post-World War II America. Since one of the primary human realities, if not the dominant one, has been material want, our sense of reality is being diminished to the degree that the new prosperity seems to be lessening our sharp responses to want.

Surely one of the ingredients of the powerful fiction that, with the publication of *The Assistant* in 1957 and *The Magic Barrel* the following year, propelled Bernard Malamud to the foreground of the American fiction scene was his ability to create characters whose privations keep them in dramatically painful contact with their desires and frustrations. Often, material want largely shapes their distressing world. In *The Assistant,* Malamud's second novel, Morris Bober actually feels hopeful when his grocery takes in $150 during a typical workweek of seven days, sixteen hours a day. Pinye Salzman, the marriage broker in the title story *The Magic Barrel,*

is "a skeleton with haunted eyes," whose office, his embittered wife tells us, is " 'in the air . . . in his socks.' " The even more embittered widow in the "graveyard" grocery in "Take Pity" can feed her daughters only from the stock; when that is gone, the bones in their faces show. In "The Bill," a janitor who hates his life of shoveling out ashes and mopping up urine is so overwhelmed by an Italian storekeeper's offer of credit (for "if you were really a human being you gave credit to somebody else and he gave credit to you") that he misuses the new sense of worth that the evaluation gives him and runs up a bill he cannot pay.

If the little businesses in the stories are finally going fairly well, Malamud finds other ways to keep the proprietors from straying very far beyond their painful limits. In "The Loan," for example, "the sweet, the heady smell of Lieb's white bread drew customers in droves." But as the baker, his eyes clouded with cataracts, the button of his truss pressing into his stomach, explains, "For thirty years . . . he was never with a penny to his name. One day, out of misery, he had wept into the dough. Thereafter his bread was such it brought customers in from everywhere."

To an extraordinary degree, then, Malamud's characters are prisoners who are driven to sharp apprehension of the walls that enclose them. Not all of the walls are the metaphorical ones of economic or physical distress. The cells might be the quite literal ones in Kiev in which Yakov Bok (the protagonist of Malamud's fourth novel, *The Fixer*) is for two and a half years beaten, chained, poisoned, isolated, and steadily humiliated. Usually, however, the antecedent for the confinement is not, say, the actual 1911 arrest of Mendel Beiliss on the charge of ritual murder, but the recurrent motif of the prison house of the tormented self that runs through modern literature.

Some of the enclosing walls are built by forces the inmate could not control: an economic depression, the persecution of Jews, illness, unsatisfactory parents, accidents, the death of loved ones, bad luck. But usually the sufferer is driven to the following perceptions: through one failing or another, he has contributed to his immurement; freedom and possibility exist within the painful limits; the need to acknowledge this possibility is as great as the need to acknowledge his complicity in his undoing.

None of this is particularly new. In fact, most literature worth reading dramatizes possibilities within limitations and the relationship of responsibility to both. Even in the god-driven world of *Oedipus Rex,* when the chorus asks the protagonist which god put out his eyes, Oedipus replies, "the god was Apollo. . . . But the blinding hand was mine."

For all of the fervor that Malamud can generate, he never really suggests the literal existence of a God of judgment or salvation: God's in the outhouse during a pogrom, Yakov Bok bitterly observes. There is all the more reason, then, to take full responsibility for the control of our own working out of our human condition: lyrical in its essence, tragic in its fate, and comic in its existence, in George Santayana's haunting words. Bound as Malamud's characters are to their tragic and comic limitations, many of them accept that necessity, which is lyrical in its possibility, of maintaining or finding their way to true, moral identity. We might call this ultimate center the nourishing heart; Tommy Wilhelm, in Saul Bellow's *Seize the Day,* thinks of it as the realm of the "real soul," from which we can say "plain and understandable things to everyone," where "truth for everybody may be found and confusion is only—only temporary."

In his 1959 acceptance speech upon receiving the National Book Award for *The Magic Barrel,* Malamud said:

I am quite tired of the colossally deceitful devaluation of man in this day. . . . Whatever the reason, his fall from grace in his eyes is betrayed by the words he has invented to describe himself as he is now: fragmented, abbreviated, other-directed, organizational. . . . The devaluation exists because he accepts it without protest.

By creating in his best fiction a realm knowable within all of us, where—however fleetingly—truth, beauty, and goodness meet, Malamud has most successfully protested against all of the contemporary assertions of the collapse or disintegration of moral values. To be sure, most of us would, in our lives, flee the apparent fate some of his transformed characters choose. If Frank Alpine is, by the end of *The Assistant,* so transformed that he probably will never rob or rape again, his future is grim. In "The Magic Barrel," the sheltered Leo Finkle finally immerses himself in the actualities of experience, but doing so by falling in love with a prostitute could prove suicidal.

Correspondingly, Malamud's characters sometimes are unable to transcend their limitations. For example, the baker's wife in "The Loan" has had so anguished a past and sees so uncertain a future that she will not permit her husband to lend $200. But the generosity of the baker, hopelessly misguided by "worldly" standards, is powerfully convincing. Malamud's ability to blend grinding actuality with lifting possibility, and concrete detail with sudden emergences of the uncanny, lends such moral urgency to the "optimistic fictions" that we feel Frank's and Finkle's commitments to be both right and necessary, even while part of us rebels against these "solutions."

Malamud was born in Brooklyn on April 26, 1914, and spent most of his first thirty years there. Information about his early years is sparse, but there is enough to suggest that his positive commitment to discipline and community did not develop in an experiential vacuum. In his entry for the 1958 *Current Biography,* Dean Cadle wrote of Malamud:

His mother, who died young, came from a theatrical family. His father was a storekeeper, "a good man" to whom he owes a lot. . . . "My parents worked late and I was allowed to stay out and wander in the neighborhood. We skated, sledded, climbed trees, and played running games. . . . We gypped the 'El' and rode to Coney Island—the ocean, especially at night, moved me. . . . There was adventure and a sense that one was a boy. One got to know people all over the neighborhood. This is important."

As readers of *The Assistant,* "The Cost of Living," and "Take Pity" might suspect, the store was a poor grocery. The neighborhood people Malamud got to know were seldom Jews: as with the grim, nameless milieu of *The Assistant,* the Gravesend area was, in the years Malamud lived there, one of the relatively few in Brooklyn with almost no Jews in it.

Malamud has jokingly said that he was "discovered" at Erasmus Hall High School "where my compositions received high grades and my work appeared in the high school magazine." Although he always wanted to be a writer, he did not commit himself to "sit down . . . in a rooming house in Brooklyn, and . . . write, write,

write and write" until he was twenty-seven. In the intervening years he attended the College of the City of New York, from which he received the B.A. in 1936, and, for the next two years, Columbia University. After writing his thesis on another writer obsessed with determining limitations—Thomas Hardy—Malamud received the M.A. in 1942. From 1940 to 1949 he taught evening classes in high schools, for the first eight years largely to immigrants in Brooklyn and, in the last year, in Harlem. Like S. Levin, the protagonist of his third novel, *A New Life,* he was in his thirties when, in 1949, he accepted a position at Oregon State College, the school after which Cascadia College in that novel is so obviously modeled.

For most of the time at Oregon State, Malamud was, as Richard Astro tells us, "assigned four sections of English Composition in a rigid and closely supervised program." Because "there was a department policy stating that only members of the faculty with Ph.D.'s might teach literature classes . . . Malamud was annually given large doses of composition with only an occasional section of an introductory literature course and a short-story writing class to break the monotony"—even though he published three books and received a number of prestigious awards and grants during his twelve years at Oregon State. In 1961 Malamud gained more agreeable working conditions when he joined the division of language and literature at Bennington College, where he has taught, except for 1966–68, when he was a visiting lecturer at Harvard.

Aside from his resentment of the working conditions at Oregon State, we know little of how much Malamud's studies of hunger and desperation spring from his lived, and not imagined, experience. We do know that while in Oregon he wrote four books and a number of stories by exerting almost as much discipline as he has demanded from any of his characters. His Mondays, Wednesdays, and Fridays were for classes, office hours, paper grading; Tuesdays, Thursdays, Saturdays—"and I sneak parts of Sundays"—for . . . novels and short stories. Malamud said in 1971 of his creative tenacity, "I have a terrifying will that way."

We find the first wholly satisfying fruits of Malamud's creative and moral tenacity in the best stories of his first collection, *The Magic Barrel*. Apart from necessary glimpses at the novels, we would do well to consider a fair number of the stories before turning to the longer works. Taken as a whole, the stories are, more than the novels, cleanly structured around Malamud's abiding moral concerns: the need for and possibilities of love, generosity, understanding, discipline, responsibility, suffering; the damaging power of ignorance, compulsion, hatred, suffering. Many of the locales of these moral dramas are abstracted, so that the struggle to remain or to become "really a human" (to quote from "The Bill") stands out all the more sharply. Of the nine stories in *The Magic Barrel* that are, or could be, set in New York, seven have a strangely timeless, placeless quality. They manifest what is perhaps Malamud's most impressive imaginative achievement: the ability to set down in New York much of the felt world of the *shtetl* (a Jewish village within the tsar's Pale of Settlement), particularly the *shtetl*'s sense of miraculous possibility within the most painful constraints.

To get some sense of the "realistic" ground from which Malamud's more uncanny works will rise, we might begin with "A Summer's Reading." This is the only story in *The Magic Barrel* that takes place in anything like the nourishing, tangible neighborhood in which Malamud grew up. George Stoyonovich, "a neighborhood boy who had quit high school on an impulse when he was sixteen, run out of patience," is, by the time he is almost twenty, ashamed of

not having graduated, but rationalizes in various ways his unwillingness to return to summer or night school. Clearly, he fears both the negative evaluations he might receive in school and the new demands to which completing his education might subject him. Still, he thinks of "a better life for himself," and he wants "people to like and respect him." Consequently he is ashamed simply to tell his kindly neighbor, Mr. Cattanzara, that he is out of work this summer and instead announces that he is reading a lot of books, "maybe around a hundred . . . to pick up my education." Cattanzara spreads the lie around the neighborhood; and George enjoys unearned respect from both neighbors and family, who generously see in his supposed project a disciplined realization of their own desires for a better life. After a superbly rendered scene in which Cattanzara challenges George to name one book he has read, the latter begins, with the anxiety and self-loathing that follow his loose act, his Malamudian education in suffering.

Malamud has listed Sherwood Anderson as one of the short story writers who influenced him. This story, centering on a lie told by a nineteen-year-old who tends to rationalize and has a low opinion of himself, is reminiscent of Anderson's "I'm a Fool." But, unlike Anderson, Malamud ends "A Summer's Reading" happily by bringing a moral development to his protagonist. For, although Cattanzara lets George off the public griddle by spreading the rumor that he has completed his book list, George finally makes the only saving gesture he can: he confronts the frightening possibility of accepting a more elevated conception of himself by running to the library one night; "and though he was struggling to control an inward trembling, he easily counted off a hundred, then sat down at a table to read."

All of this occurs in a neighborhood in which George had, as a boy, played punchball and been given nickels for lemon ices, in which storekeepers and their wives "sat in chairs on the thick, broken sidewalks in front of their shops, fanning themselves,'' and where

Nights, during the hot weather [Cattanzara] sat on his stoop in an undershirt, reading the *New York Times* in the light of the shoemaker's window. . . . And all the time he was reading the paper, his wife, a fat woman with a white face, leaned out of the window, gazing into the street, her thick white arms folded under her loose breast, on the window ledge.

No other locale in all of the Malamud fictions set in the United States provides such communal moral support. In "The Prison," Malamud does render the manners of Greenwich Village, seen by its Italian, not bohemian, inhabitants, with considerable fidelity. The milieu, however, is anything but nourishing. Tommy Castelli's neighborhood involvements lead him to a holdup, to a forced marriage to an unlovable woman, and to working seventeen hours a day in a candy store where "usually the whole day stank and he along with it. Time rotted in him." In this story there is neither the urban poetry of "A Summer's Reading" nor Cattanzara's paternal success: Tommy fails in his attempts to keep a girl from making his own mistake of stealing.

Significantly, the protagonists and settings of these two stories—the only ones in *The Magic Barrel* in which New York neighborhoods are "realistically" rendered—are gentile. The starkly abstracted milieus of the Jewish characters in "The First Seven Years," "The Mourners," "The Loan," "Angel Levine," "The Magic Barrel," and *The Assistant* both invoke the characters' likely *shtetl* origins and lend credence to Philip Roth's claim that Malamud's "people live in a timeless depression and a placeless Lower East Side." That some very close readers have set Morris Bober's store in the Bronx or Manhattan when there are enough hints to place it in Brooklyn merely emphasizes Malamud's characteristic strategy of blending precise details—the way the potato salad is made or the weight of the milk cases—with a strange placelessness.

Roth's observation came in his 1961 essay "Writing American Fiction," in a context surrounding his convincing assertion that "the American writer in the middle of the 20th century has his hands full in trying to understand, and then describe, and then make *credible* much of the American reality." Often Malamud's fictive solution has been to disregard much of this reality: the effects of affluence, the cold war, the struggle for integration, and so on. Thus it is even more irrelevant to try to set the time of *The Assistant* than the place. Morris had installed a new display case a while back, "after the depression." Yet the prices—eight to ten dollars for a good pair of shoes, three cents for a hard roll—are those of the 1930's. In 1958 Malamud said that he writes about Jews because "I know them. But more important, I write about them because the Jews are absolutely the very *stuff* of drama." No headlines, news reports, or radio or television programs intrude to distract Morris, the novel's other characters, or the reader from the theater of the self that they fill with their vivid emotions. (Interestingly, the protagonist of Malamud's first published story, "Benefit Performance" [1943], is an aging actor on the Yiddish stage. The performance he puts on is for himself.)

If the external world intrudes, it does so as a menace that manifests itself in the store or nearby: the opening of a rival grocery; the rape of Morris' daughter Helen in the park. Further, the parties in robbery and rape are Ward Minogue, a neighborhood boy returned, and Frank Alpine, who will become as much of a fixture in store and neighborhood as Morris. We never learn what Morris and Breitbart, the bulb salesman, read in the Yiddish paper; not even Hitler and the death camps are mentioned, although they are, tellingly, in four of the stories in *The*

Magic Barrel. So rigorous is Malamud's selection that, save for a reference in "Angel Levine" to a boy dying "in the war," the rest of contemporary history is silence.

The characters in these works do not have the "conscious sense of being at a distance from history, from history as such and history as a conception in the western world." These words, written by Irving Howe and Eliezer Greenberg in *A Treasury of Yiddish Stories,* refer to the inhabitants of the *shtetl* before such historically insistent forces as Zionism and socialism began to fragment the inhabitants' view of the world. Their historical dislocation followed from the "permanent precariousness" of their condition (for a conclusive pogrom might descend upon them at any time), which bound them all the more firmly to their history,

. . . an almost timeless proximity with the mythical past and the redeeming future, with Abraham's sacrifice of his beloved son to a still more beloved God and the certain appearance of a cleansing Messiah—for heaven was *real*, not a useful myth, and each day that passed brought one nearer to redemption.

Often Malamud has brought to his quasi-timeless, quasi-placeless, quasi-legendary New York much of the *shtetl* situation: the sense of enclosure and limited worldly possibility; the expert knowledge of hunger and suffering but the possibility of transcending both, whether with sudden moral fervor or with prolonged discipline. His characters' recollections of their mythical pasts generally add to their pathos—for example, Morris Bober's memories of running in Polish fields as a boy or of the poem he learned at night school. There is no Messiah, and Malamud's heaven is emphatically unreal, peopled as it might be in "Angel Levine" by Jewish Negroes who, once back on earth, can give way to boozing, wenching, and anti-Semitism. Yet the *shtetl* affinity to the miraculous asserts itself in

what Marcus Klein has called Malamud's "special note . . . a mysticism which compels discrete actualities of life to extremes" and "hurries reality into myth, or into parable or exemplum or allegory, and its typical process has been a sudden transition of particularities."

In 1973, Malamud said, "I don't believe in the supernatural except as I can invent it. . . . I write fantasy because when I do I am imaginative and funny and having a good time." Often much of the imaginative pleasure that comes from his sudden or prolonged surges into the uncanny would seem to follow from his sense that he is capturing with arresting metaphors both the ultimate unknowability of things and the possibilities for moral assertions within that unknowability. For example, Klein offers Salzman's improbable appearances in "The Magic Barrel" as instances of the sudden transition of particularities. But the marriage broker's ultimate mutability derives from a much more complicated blend than, say, the one caused by his explaining an impossibly prompt appearance in Leo Finkle's room with "I hurried." At first reading, Salzman has his complexities but is still the "commercial cupid" who, with the enthusiasm and style of a used-car salesman, overpraises his male clients to his female ones and vice versa. If his eyes are mournful, it may be because, for all his enthusiasm, he does not do well; because his profession is no longer honored; or because his daughter Stella reminds him that he is merely a peddler of flesh when she begins peddling her own. Perhaps he intentionally leaves his daughter's picture with Finkle because the approval he feels for the rabbinical student's face, both ascetically innocent and latently sensual, is his approval of a manageable victim. Whether or not he intentionally leaves the picture, he is in the placement business—and finally places his daughter. Are the prayers for the dead that he chants, while Leo rushes forward to meet Stella, for his own moral self? For Leo's future? Other readings offer themselves but, within this line of reasoning, all lead to Frederick the Great's comment about the sympathy that Catherine II of Russia showed during the third partition of Poland: "She wept but took."

Yet, as Yakov Bok sighs when he learns how he is being framed, "So that's how it is. . . . Behind the world lies another world." Behind the world of Salzman the endearing but scheming pimp lies the world of Salzman the holy spirit, placed on earth to bring Leo Finkle from an arid knowledge of the Law to the perception that he can fulfill the spirit of the Law only by loving in this world. Thus Salzman arranges the meeting between Leo and Lily Hirschorn because he knows it will drive Leo to the shattering admission that "I came to God not because I loved Him but because I did not." As Leo becomes stronger in his resolution to save himself by saving Stella, his need for Salzman grows less. By the time the latter agrees to arrange the meeting, he is "transparent to the point of vanishing," for his work in this world is almost finished. Leo has learned of the universality of suffering, manifested by the terrible pain in the eyes of Salzman and his daughter, and he is determined to do what he can about it. And so, for the first time in the story, Salzman stops eating his fish before he has finished it—one must eat to survive—and it remains only for him to chant the death of the old man and the birth of the new.

With Salzman as spirit, his improbable manifestations become a matter of course. His wife's accusation of her *luftmensch* husband with his office "in the air . . . in his socks" becomes a happy metaphor for the way the spiritual must be grounded in the physical. Correspondingly, the fish that Salzman devours could, as the early Christians believed, symbolize immortality of the spirit. Yet the fishy odors that cling to him and to his pictures of unfulfilled women could, and certainly seem to, come from the magic barrel of life itself, with all its sad experience, desperate innocence, improbable hopes, and teeming, sexual odors.

But, in a way that reminds us of Malamud's frequent mirror images, or optical confusions, or characters whose separate eyes do separate things, each reading keeps swimming back into the other. For example, the story is crowded with biblical allusions or unintentional recastings (for Malamud's imagination is strongly folkloristic), but do these reinforce or ironically undercut Salzman as improbable but intentionally redeeming angel? In the face of irresolvable ambiguity, Leo makes his decision. The reader can choose a "majority reading" of the story; but, like life itself, its "reality" is likely to shift in a way that inspires delight and frustration as we regard it.

Because the fictional terms of "Angel Levine" are more consistently those of fantasy—which is to say they partake somewhat less dizzyingly of the world's ambiguity—the terms of the choice that the afflicted tailor Manischevitz must make are, though complex, much more clear-cut:

> Tears blinded the tailor's eyes. Was ever man so tried? Should he say he believed a half-drunken Negro to be an angel?
>
> . . . a wheel in his mind whirred: believe, do not, yes, no, yes, no. The pointer pointed to yes, to between yes and no, to no, no it was yes. He sighed. It moved but one had still to make a choice.
>
> "I think you are an angel from God." He said it in a broken voice, thinking, If you said it it was said. If you believed it you must say it. If you believed, you believed.
>
> Levine burst into tears. "How you have humiliated me."

Since twice before this climactic scene Manischevitz has been unable to believe that the Negro is an assisting angel, several nodes of meaning cluster here. In terms of interdependency, the tailor's inability to "be human and extend credit" (to reach back to "The Bill") drives Levine into the stereotypes of a *shvarzah* (Negro) joke: from a worried if somewhat sententious correctness to a heavy Negro dialect; from shabbily dressed dignity to lust and drunkenness in a sort of Sporting Life costume. In terms of the workings of faith, the inability to make a difficult assertion only renders it yet more difficult; since Manischevitz cannot accept a sober Levine in his apartment, he has to accept the stage Negro while they are surrounded by anti-Semites in a Harlem dive. But as with the Jews of the *shtetl,* catastrophe may make the impossible possible, the irrational reasonable. With his wife "at death's door," the irrational has spoken as the tailor dreams of Levine preening his wings. From this follows the final trip to Harlem, the leap of faith, Fanny's recovery, and Levine's winged ascension.

The *shtetl* dynamics that inform so much of Malamud's fiction could be described as a simultaneous holding on and letting go. One clings to the possibility of the miraculous, to the value of the morally developed self, to the value of the other. But to make any of these assertions, one might have to relinquish the rational; one might even have to turn one's back on commonsense empiricism. We might better understand the workings of this process if we move beyond the stories of *The Magic Barrel* and turn to "The Silver Crown," a story published in 1972, seventeen years after "Angel Levine" first appeared. Here the petitioner is Albert Gans, a biology teacher whose father is dying of a disease so diversely and unsuccessfully diagnosed and treated that Gans finally goes to a faith healer, Rabbi Jonas Lifshitz. Although Gans has given up on the rational empiricism of the doctors, he still tells the rabbi that his "cast of mind" is "naturally empiric and objective—you might say non-mystical." He therefore wants to know just how his father will be saved by the silver crown (wonderfully priced at $401 or $986) that the rabbi will have cast and then will pray over. Empiricist that he is, Gans demands to see a crown before he pays, and later threatens to go to the police if he does not see the one for which he has paid $986.

Although the story is grounded much more in the tradition of realism than of fantasy, it characteristically swerves toward the allegorical. For Lifshitz and Rifkele, his lumpish, retarded daughter, embody the nonrational or irrational that Gans can only partially embrace. The rabbi cannot permit Gans to see a finished crown because "a miracle is a miracle." Most important to him is not whether Gans doubts, for "doubts we all got," but whether he loves his father. Certainly Gans cares enough to have sorrow, to feel frantic over his father's state, and finally to pay $986. But his strongest emotion toward his father seems to be gratitude—a good distance from consuming, suprarational love—and self-interest undercuts this: he will feel guilty if he does not buy the crown and his father dies. All of this is still further undercut when, near the end of the story, Gans cries out to Lifshitz and Rifkele that he "was mesmerized, suckered" with "freaking fake magic, with an idiot girl for a come-on and hypnotic mirrors."

To suggest that Manischevitz in "Angel Levine" is less than human is, by most standards, unfair. The tailor is most humanly endearing with his complaint to God that suffering is wasted on him, and with his fearful bewilderment as he pushes himself through a Harlem of trousers with a razor slit in the seat or a group of blacks comically, uncannily, engaged in Talmudic exegesis. But the pressure of his need, which in this case derives from his love for his dying wife, drives him to be still more human and give still more credit.

In "Idiots First" Mendel must, on the last night of his life, raise money to send his idiot son to the improbable care of an eighty-one-year-old uncle in California. But the minute that he needs to put his son on the train is denied in the name of "the cosmic universal law, goddamit, the one I got to follow myself." The speaker is Ginzburg, the angel of death, who remains unmoved by Mendel's pleas that his life of suffering has earned him the minute's respite. "You bastard, don't you understand what it means human?" Mendel incongruously cries as he tries to choke Ginzburg. What follows, as each sees himself mirrored in the other's eyes and Ginzburg gives Mendel the minute, is intentionally evasive. But, like the nineteenth-century Russian and Yiddish writers he loves, Malamud seems to be asking us to believe, for an instant, that even universal law must, for an instant, bend and recognize "what means human"—if the petitioner has suffered enough and is desperately enough committed to his just cause. Manischevitz lunges into irrationality, Mendel into violence; but each release is actually a clinging, a heightened commitment to otherness.

"The Silver Crown" also leads to an explosion that is a holding fast; but here the commitment is to love of self, not of other. For it is Gans's concern for his self-image—that he, the rational empiricist, has been tricked—that leads to his cruel accusations. The epiphany comes when Gans responds to the rabbi's pleading "Be kind. . . . Be merciful to an old man. Think of my poor child. Think of your father who loves you" with "He hates me, the son-of-a-bitch, I hope he croaks." The terms of the story are such that we cannot tell whether the elder Gans, who dies an hour later, could have been saved. But Malamud sharply emphasizes how inappropriate in a situation where love is required is any tangle of feeling less than love. In good part, Gans's final outburst follows from his fury over the situation into which he has been led by what positive filial affection he possesses. Malamud also wryly suggests how impractical practicality or half

measures can be in ultimate situations: Gans loses the $986, his self-esteem, and the chance to see whether the crown will work. Ironically, he finally does receive a crown he can feel—the "massive, spike-laden headache" he wears as he rushes out of Lifshitz's.

We have mainly considered stories that emphasize possibility; indeed, with "Idiots First," the farthest extreme of possibility that Malamud can dramatize. However, a large number of fine stories emphasize the need to recognize limits, particularly the limits or compulsions of others. These implacable needs can be assertions of some force, and often the motif expands into another recurrent theme of Yiddish and Russian fiction: the power a victim can exert over his victimizer. So strong is the hold of this interrelationship on Malamud's imagination that it explicitly informs his two best novels, *The Assistant* and *The Fixer,* and some very good stories: "The Mourners," "Take Pity," "A Pimp's Revenge," "An Exorcism," "Rembrandt's Hat," "Talking Horse," and "The Jewbird." In "An Apology" a policeman named Walter unwillingly lets his younger partner arrest a light-bulb peddler who has, instead of a license, a sense of how heavily his misery can bear down upon others. Walter easily convinces the partner to let the peddler go after he breaks out of the police car and tries to jump off the Brooklyn Bridge, but nothing—not the money to replace a carton of bulbs lost in the arrest, not the purchase of new bulbs—can free Walter from the uncanny peddler's accusing presence. The policeman must finally leave his bed in the early morning hours and bend to the peddler's wordless demand that his sense of dignity, stiffened by all he has suffered, be recognized by an apology.

Sometimes one must bow to the imperatives of literal madness. In "The Letter," all of Newman's dutiful attempts to communicate with his insane, institutionalized father fail. Malamud implicitly suggests that he would have more luck if he could, for example, perceive that another inmate and his father (Teddy and Ralph) both recognize as an act of communication the blank pages Teddy repeatedly and unsuccessfully tries to get Newman to mail. In terms of this kind of insight, there is a grain of truth in Ralph's telling Newman that he is crazy and should "come back here and hang around with the rest of us." Gans's total inability to respond sympathetically to Lifshitz' claim that Rifkele is "not perfect, though God who made her in his image is Himself perfection. . . . In her way she is also perfect" emphasizes his shallowness.

With "Take Pity" we move to the dangers of trying to act generously toward someone who could probably pass a clinical test for sanity but is acting out the doctrine of self-reliance with a near-mad vengeance. In a grim, sparsely furnished room in some gray, embittered afterworld (a locale that is a distillation of many of Malamud's already stylized locales), Rosen tells Davidov, a "census-taker," of his attempts to help two orphaned children and their mother. But she will not accept help, out of what combination of twisted pride, self-hatred, death wish, and sense of fatality we can never know. The ambivalent possibilities of the title, with the assertion of "Take" and the sympathetic merging of "Pity," seem to have exhausted themselves by the time Rosen recounts how he said to himself, " 'Here . . . is a very strange thing—a person that you can never give her anything.—*But I will give.*' " He gives his possessions by willing them to the widow and her children, his life by putting his head in the oven. But he only drives her deeper into her compulsion: she kills herself, probably kills her children, and the story ends as they continue their struggle—but with the new twist that she now seeks him out. Davidov writes in "an old-fashioned language that they don't use it nowadays," which is to say that a tale of the amount of damage that two people of strong, conflicting wills can inflict on each other is a very old tale indeed. That one can leave "Take Pity," surely one of Malamud's best stories, thinking of Ugolino and Ruggieri, near the bottom of the Inferno, gnawing each other's heads until Judgment Day, suggests its force.

But disaster can follow from too low a designation of another's moral limits. In "The German Refugee," a superb rendering of the culture shock the educated, previously successful Jews encountered when they fled Hitler to America, we are made to feel that Oskar Gassner is on his way to acculturation, first when he sufficiently overcomes his hatred of the language of the Nazis to write a lecture in German, and then when he apparently demonstrates his acceptance of his new state by so improving his pronunciation that he delivers the lecture successfully in English. But Oskar has not lived, only written and spoken about, his topic—*Brudermensch* (brotherhood) in Whitman. He has threatened to commit suicide if he does not write the lecture. Instead, he takes gas when he learns that his gentile wife, to whom he has been married for twenty-seven years but whom he abandoned in Germany as a part of the hated country, had converted to Judaism and was arrested and shot. She undergoes more of the hideous brotherhood of victimization that characterizes so much of twentieth-century life when she topples "into an open tank ditch, with the naked Jewish men, their wives and children, some Polish soldiers, and a handful of gypsies."

It follows that sometimes the overvaluing of another's inner life can have salutary effects. Toward the end of "The Mourners," Kessler, a disagreeable old man who has been threatened with eviction, sits rocking in his stinking apartment, mourning the hardheartedness of his past. But Gruber, the landlord whose name suggests his apparently intractable physical and psychic grossness, mistakenly thinks that Kessler is mourning his, Gruber's, spiritual death. His distress is followed by the sense that "the room . . . was clean, drenched in [the] daylight and fragrance" of moral rebirth. In a conversion too tricky and hasty to be fully convincing, Gruber suffers "unbearable remorse for the way he had treated the old man" and becomes a mourner himself. It is not too clear whom he is mourning, but Malamud wants us to feel that he has been reborn.

Since Malamud's fiction is so frequently ordered around the moral dispositions of the characters and the directions these dispositions take, we might briefly consider some stories treating these aspects before we turn to the novels. The groupings are admittedly partial and constricting, but they should add to our sense of an overview.

With "Angel Levine," "Idiots First," and "An Apology," we have touched upon stories in which more or less admirable or acceptable men do nothing to diminish before our eyes. We can add to this kind, with all reservations for Arkin's clumsiness and Harvitz's tightness, "Rembrandt's Hat" and "The Man in the Drawer." In the first story, Arkin ends a feud and achieves a new otherness by putting himself in the position of an unhappy sculptor; in "The Man in the Drawer," Harvitz must project a Russian writer's plight upon himself before he will agree to smuggle out stories too "negative" to be published in Russia. Then there are a fair number of understandably painful stories—"The Death of Me," "The Loan," "Take Pity," "My Son, the Murderer," "The Prison," "Black Is My Favorite Color," "In Retirement," and "The Cost of Living"—in which the generous, or at least justifiable, intentions of decent people are frustrated, sometimes by racial or political upheavals, sometimes by the weight of suffering about them, sometimes by cruel business competition. "The Silver Crown" and "The German Refu-

gee" lead toward the revelation of the deficiencies of the protagonist, as does "Behold the Key," in which, with disastrous results, an American studying in Italy refuses to take any responsibility for American involvement there. And in "The Maid's Shoes" a withdrawn American professor makes a few timid attempts to assist his maid, but the chaos of Italian life is finally too much for him and he fires her.

With all of the qualities that make the stories of the preceding groups characteristic Malamud works, most are still in what might be called the tradition of the Joycean epiphanic story, in which everything moves toward the revelation of the essence of the protagonist or his situation. But the attempt to find a new life, truly to change, is a dominant concern in some of the stories as well as in four of the novels. When the protagonist seeks a new life from the outset, the story works to reveal the failings that make true transcendence impossible.

In "The Lady of the Lake," Henry Levin travels under the ironically unsuccessful pseudonym of Freeman in order to escape the limitations of Judaism, only to lose a beautiful and redeeming woman because he cannot accept his Jewish past. Cronin, in "A Choice of Profession," attempts to escape the anguish that follows the discovery that his wife is two-timing him with a friend by leaving Chicago and a well-paying job to become a teacher. However, his inability to put in the past the sexual victimization of a student, abused by a pimping husband and an incestuous brother, forces him to the realization that he has not learned from his experience and that "it's not easy to be moral." But when an older man jars a younger one out of an identity and forces him into a new one, Malamud grants both character and reader intimations of transcendence: Cattanzara forces George, Salzman drives Finkle, and in "The Last Mohican" Susskind torments Fidelman into the kind of emotions and acts that might permit a critic to capture the spirit of Giotto. Of course the tenacity of Malamud's moral imagination has driven him beyond hints of transcendence to full-scale studies of successful or abortive initiations into a new spiritual life. We turn, then, to his first novel, *The Natural*.

The visiting New York Knights are losing to the Cubs by only a run and have a man on second, but there are two outs in the ninth inning. In the stands "Mike Barney, a picture of despair, was doing exercises of grief. He stretched forth his long, hairy arms, his knobby hands clasped, pleading." Down on the field Roy Hobbs, the thirty-four-year-old rookie who has been sent in to pinch-hit, takes the first pitch for a strike, then swings so hard at a bad ball that "the umpire sneezed in the breeze. . . . Wonderboy resembled a sagging baloney. Pop cursed the bat . . . Mike Barney's harrowed puss looked yellow"; Roy feels "sick with remorse that he had traded a kid's life away out of loyalty to a hunk of wood." Then he realizes that the good-looking, dark-haired woman in the stands has stood up to show confidence in him:

At the same time he became aware that the night had spread out in all directions and was filled with an unbelievable fragrance.

A pitch streaked toward him . . . With a sob Roy fell back and swung.

Part of the crowd broke for the exits. Mike Barney wept freely now, and the lady who had stood up for Roy absently pulled on her white gloves and left.

The ball shot through Toomey's [the pitcher's] astounded legs and began to climb. The second baseman, laying back on the grass on a hunch, stabbed high for it but it leaped over his straining fingers, sailed through the light and up into the dark, like a white star seeking an old constellation.

Toomey, shrunk to a pygmy, stared into the vast sky.

Roy circled the bases like a Mississippi steamboat, lights lit, flags fluttering, whistle banging, coming around the bend.

. . . everybody knew it was Roy alone who had saved the boy's life.

All of this happened in Chicago, where, as a nineteen-year-old pitcher of phenomenal promise, Roy had been shot with a silver bullet by the beautiful Harriet Bird. Chicago was also the city where, in what we like to think of as the real world, Eddie Waitkus, a good-looking first baseman, had in 1949 been shot by a girl at the Edgewater Beach Hotel, and where, when asked in 1958 whether he consciously injected the materials of Arthurian romance into *The Natural*, Malamud replied, "I threw *everything* in."

And so it would seem. At the most simple level of plot development Roy, with the assistance of Iris Lemon, breaks out of the slump that has followed his record-breaking hitting streak and fulfills his responsibility to Mike Barney and his dying son Pete. Beneath this, and beneath about a dozen other tales or incidents in the novel, is the popular mythology of baseball history; in this case the account of how Babe Ruth hit a home run to save the life of a boy named Johnny Sylvester. Here the "historical" content is itself an expression of the ability of a hero to rejuvenate life; and appropriately so, for beneath the level of the specific historical allusions, beneath the level of the literary ones to Achilles, Calypso, Thersites, Circe, and Charybdis, and informing the whole of the novel are the medieval legends and romances that incorporate the death and resurrection of the seasons. In these tales a questing knight who is selfless and pure enough to ask or answer correctly certain questions about the lance or the Grail—the male and female reproductive organs, respectively—can cure the ailing, or resurrect the dead, Fisher King and restore fertility to his lands and subjects. Still further beneath, as Jessie Weston argues in

From Ritual to Romance, is "an ancient ritual, having for its ultimate object initiation into the sources of Life, physical and spiritual." This arresting subject is a particularly appropriate one for a writer who has said, as Malamud did in 1958, that "the primal problem is that of man seeking to escape the tragedy of the past."

In his brilliant essay *"The Natural:* Malamud's World Ceres,'' Earl Wasserman observes that Roy "at bat is every quester who has had to shape his own character to fulfill his goal, whether it be the grail or the league pennant.'' So loose and powerful on the mound or at bat, so innately aware when playing left field of the effects of uneven terrain, wind currents, or carom angles off the wall, Roy would seem supremely well qualified to fulfill his quest. As a boy he had fashioned Wonderboy, his animistic bat, from a tree split by lightning, from mana-charged natural life itself. It is with this talisman, the new Excalibur, glittering golden in the sunlight, creating thunder, lightning, and rain, that Roy brings the rejuvenating power of nature to the ailing Knights. To repeat to anyone who has read both *The Natural* and ''The Waste Land'': although the novel spans fifteen years, the dramatized parts begin in early spring and end with winter in the air (the birth and death of the year and the baseball season). The Knights' manager, selflessly committed to the well-being of the team, is Pop Fisher; and the affliction of this Fisher King—athlete's foot of the hands—is eased by Roy's presence in the lineup. Correspondingly, the drought that had reduced Knights Field to dust comes to an end when Roy first comes to bat, and on and on

But Roy needs more than physical gifts to complete his spiritual initiation. Beyond all the wacky collisions of popular culture and medieval romance, then, *The Natural* is not at all the usual sports novel of the rookie who carries his team and their lovable, long-frustrated manager to the championship. Roy would have it that a freak ac-

cident got him shot at nineteen, from which followed his loss of confidence and fifteen years of a "sickening procession of jobs—as cook, well-driller, mechanic, logger, beanpicker.''

But, as Wasserman, with his application of Jungian models, has convincingly argued, the women of the story—Harriet, Iris, and Memo Francis—are all aspects of the dual nature of the psychic mother. The tweaking of Harriet's nipple emphatically suggests Roy's infantilism, and his failure to show through his answers to her questions that he understands the communal responsibilities of his gifts further expresses his immaturity. On the Arthurian level, before the ultimate challenge of the Grail, symbolized by Harriet's hat, Roy proves himself to be an unworthy quester. In the Jungian psychomachy, his immature behavior has turned Harriet into the Terrible Mother (*mater saeva*), who will dam up our energies and engulf us if we do not wean ourselves by propelling ourselves out into the harsh world.

The train on which Roy meets Harriet, and which he hopes is carrying him to his triumph, is also the train of developmental necessity that either brings us from sheltered infantilism to communal commitment, or reminds us of the damage that has followed our inability to make the trip. The opening image of the novel is of Roy on the train: he looks out but, significantly, sees only himself. On the last page, Roy—having tried to throw the last, pennant-deciding game of the season—is fighting overwhelming self-hatred, and thinking, ''I never did learn anything out of my past life, now I have to suffer again.''

Since he has never learned to accept the imperative of the train he feels churning within him (or thinks he hears)—''When will you grow up, Roy?'' Iris asks—he succumbs to the temptation of the other Terrible Mother in the novel, Memo (memory) Francis. Her affinity for stagnant water, her "sick" breast, and her suicidal nature all reinforce her allegorical role as vitiating memory. So does the scene in which the image of her, as the Terrible Mother demanding incest, combines with her Circean overfeeding of Roy until "a rush of dirty water got a good grip and sucked him under"—Memo as *mater saeva* in her Charybdis archetype. Even during his glory months, a regressive infantilism belies the primal appeal of Roy's aggressive domination of the external. For example, "He was like a hunter stalking a bear, a whale. . . . Often, for no accountable reason he hated the pill, which represented more of himself than he was willing to give away."

But the rejection of the mother as engulfment frees us for the other maternal imago, for the mother as the source of all vitality. This acceptance permits our vital energies to flow, unimpeded, into the world. On the Arthurian level she is the Lady of the Lake, who assists worthy knights, just as Memo is an obvious Morgan le Fay figure. In the more literal terms of the novel she is Iris Lemon, who accepts the burdens of motherhood and grandmotherhood and is in general associated with the life-giving fluids that come from accepting one's interpersonal burden. She also embodies a level of mature articulation so different from anything else in the book that its weight is distractingly palpable.

All that has followed the quotation of Roy at bat perhaps makes *The Natural* sound more coherent than it actually is. It might be, as Wasserman claims, that Roy cannot marry Iris because that would make him a grandfather, "which is to say the responsible hero-father who completely possesses his miraculous psychic strength and unselfishly directs it to his human community." But to have Iris tell Roy during intercourse that she is a grandmother or, after she has been felled by a foul ball that has bounced off the head of a heckling dwarf, that she is pregnant with Roy's child is as wacky as a clock at Ebbets Field scattering minutes over the field after one of Roy's drives shatters it.

To return to Roy at bat, he has fallen into a slump the day after succumbing to Memo's unhealthy magic of fog, stagnant water, and sick breasts. Benched because of his unwillingness to try a different bat, he is finally enough moved by Mike Barney's agony to offer to switch bats if Pop will send him in. This is Roy's first moment of otherness. All his goals have smacked of the hubris of selfishness: to break all the records; to be known as the best the game ever saw. Yet most of the community of fans for whom Roy should sacrifice *are* grotesques, and Mike Barney is described here as a gorilla.

Perhaps this will cohere with the emphasis on Roy's responsibility if we remember Rabbi Lifshitz's admonition that even Rifkele is perfect in her own way. And perhaps we can appreciate the descriptions of Mike Barney's "harrowed puss" or Wonderboy, declined from his usual erect puissance into a "sagging baloney," if we see it all as a kind of comic transformation of sportscasterese: banal, matter-of-fact, and fantastic all at once. But the fragrance emanating from Iris and the coolness with which, her miracle done, she calmly pulls on her gloves and departs, belong to much different worlds of emotion and authorial tone. As with what follows—the quick cuts from the cosmic zoom of the ball to Toomey shrunken to a dwarf to Roy as a steamboat out of *Life on the Mississippi*—these colliding worlds can give us the pleasures of comic surrealism, the literary equivalent of the grotesque combinations of food that drive Roy to his Babe Ruth stomachache.

But so much of Malamud's work has given us reason to expect a great deal more. In his discussion of a fully successful fantasy, "Idiots First," Theodore Solotaroff wrote, "A dying man in search of money for his idiot son, the *malach-ha-moves* [angel of death] who pursues and frustrates him, the bitter city streets, and the iron gates of Pennsylvania Station all come to belong, through the sustained unity of writing, to the same order of things.'' The stylistic and referential collisions bring a centrifugal effect to the whole of *The Natural;* but Malamud's failure or unwillingness somehow to unify his tones and viewpoints appears most tellingly at the novel's end, which deals with Roy's decline. From a moral perspective his immaturity pulls him under; from that of the vegetation myths, the decline of the year-god is inevitable. Since Roy would not have thrown the game if he had not known he was washed up, the two levels of motivation are reconcilable. But the comic intrusions of the final game and the behavior of Judge Banner, Gus the Supreme Bookie, and Memo vitiate the considerable emotional leverage Malamud might have gotten from the account of Roy's fall. And on the last page of the book, Malamud explodes the pathos of Roy, feeling old and grimy, realizing that he will have to suffer all over again, by having a boy distractingly ask him what a newsboy was supposed to have asked Shoeless Joe Jackson after that great athlete threw the 1919 World Series.

Malamud's second novel, like his first, is structured around the passage of the seasons; but unlike *The Natural, The Assistant* dramatizes a successful initiation into a new spiritual life. Correspondingly, the movement is from winter to spring. We begin in the dark of a November morning, the wintry wind clawing at Morris Bober's face and blowing his apron up into it as he drags heavy milk cases into the store. We leave the novel eighteen months later, just after Frank Alpine has himself circumcised: ''For a couple of days he dragged himself around with a pain between his legs. The pain enraged and inspired him. After Passover he became a Jew.''

Having entered Morris' store to rob it that November day and having in February more or less raped Helen, Frank stays on to expiate, first as The Assistant and then, after Morris' death early in the first April, as The Grocer himself. For Morris, the *shlimazel* (inept) to whom everything happens, the imminence of the yearly rebirth has been, like so much of his life, a bitterly ironic joke: in this case it kills him. Banished from the store after Morris realized that he had been one of the robbers, Frank views the grocer's death as a chance to continue his atonement—and this gives Malamud twelve more months to convince us of the tenacity of Frank's desire to become a different, better person.

There is no suggestion that the circumcision and conversion mean that Frank will follow the forms of Jewish ritual any more strictly than Morris did. Instead, they serve as symbols of his passage into moral adulthood. In the same way, Malamud generally uses acceptance of one's Jewishness as a metaphor for the acceptance of the responsibilities of the human condition. Or, to put his metaphorical use of Jewishness in a recognizable historical context, when Israel was threatened with extinction in 1966, Malamud said, ''All men are Jews except they don't know it.'' That is, unified as we are by the agonies of the past and the threats of the present and future, we must still struggle to keep in our minds and instill in our acts ''what means human.'' With all of the St. Francis imagery in the novel—from Frank's memories of the appeal the stories of the saint had for him in childhood to the fantasy in the next-to-last paragraph in the book, in which the transformed Frank identifies with the transforming powers of St. Francis—Malamud clearly tries to dispel the notion that saintly ''Jewishness'' is limited to Jews.

Still, there is a good deal of truth in Philip Roth's 1974 claim that while ''the Jew in the post-holocaust decades has been identified in American fiction with righteousness and restraint . . . rather than with those libidinous activities that border on the socially acceptable and may even constitute criminal transgression,'' it is possible to see the transformation of an Italian drifter who robbed and raped not so much as ''a sign of moral improvement but as the cruel realization of Bober's revenge: 'Now suffer, you goy bastard, the way I did.' '' And for Malamud, ''writing out of a fury all his own,'' the pain of the circumcision is a just punishment to the organ with which Frank had attacked Helen.

All of these readings—Judaism as the punishing religion of instinctual restraint, Jewishness as the mystical, saving element in all religions, Frank as the *schlemiel* (well-meaning bungler) who falls into Morris' grave in more ways than one, and Frank as the hero of spiritual rebirth—can be found in the novel. The vitality, which persists after repeated readings, follows from Malamud's ability to hold in balanced tension the poles of his psyche and his literary preferences: the optimism and the pessimism; the sadism and the gentleness, under which are subsumed the beliefs that suffering humanizes and that it deadens; the respect for realistic detail and the fondness for fantasy.

Like Roy Hobbs, come east from Montana to become the greatest baseball player in history, Frank journeys into the rising sun, in this case from San Francisco to Brooklyn (by way of Boston), to become a prince of crime. That this glittering new life should supposedly begin in Morris' poor store serves as an ironic commentary on the hopelessness of that conception of himself. The mirror in the back room shows Frank no glittering czar of lawlessness, but Morris and the bum, Ward Minogue: the two aspects of himself, the two directions his life could take after this act.

In a passage that reverberates through much of the fiction that follows it, Iris Lemon says, ''We have two lives, Roy, the life we learn with and the life we live after that. Suffering is what brings us toward happiness. . . . It teaches us to want the right things.'' Even during the holdup, Frank's partial knowledge of the right things makes itself felt in his fear, his attempts to get Ward out, and, above all, his bringing Morris a

cup of water. The washing and replacing of the cup (an act repeated a few days later with a cup and saucer) serve as more than an anticipation of Frank's eventual transformation into The Grocer. It suggests that even as he is making his ''worst mistake yet,'' he intuitively feels that the store is somehow a place where—not having, as he says about St. Francis, the talent to be born good—he can learn sympathy, generosity, and discipline from Morris, Helen, the nonhuman, inhuman store, and all who come into it. The sometimes cruel irony with which Malamud treats Helen and, particularly, Morris is a crucial component of their successful characterizations, for it keeps them from becoming sentimentalized stereotypes. Still, the weight of their injuries, of Helen's beauty, and of Morris' deadly endurance, proves too much for Frank: he climbs out of Morris' grave, returns to Brooklyn, and reopens the store.

Before this, Malamud has shrewdly kept Frank's objections to Morris from being as telling as Helen's at her father's funeral. Here we know the rabbi's praise of Morris as a good provider to be as false as we know Helen's judgments of his weakness and lack of imagination to be true. But, to take one example, Frank's resistance to Morris' capacity for pity is as psychologically explainable as the relief he experiences when he resumes stealing: as George Stoyonovitch discovered in ''A Summer's Reading,'' accepting a new conception of oneself is frightening. Of course many of Morris' acts have a force of their own, and his most articulate expression of his beliefs has about it the power of mystery and the mystery of power. After Morris says, ''If a Jew don't suffer for the Law, he will suffer for nothing,'' Frank asks:

''What do you suffer for, Morris?''
''I suffer for you,'' Morris said calmly.
Frank laid his knife down on the table. His mouth ached. ''What do you mean?''

"I mean you suffer for me."

The clerk let it go at that.

In part the power is that of a victim over his victimizer, but it still accrues to Morris' moral force. So does Frank's relationship to Helen, for as victims and punishers of Frank, father and daughter flow into each other, as so many of the novel's characters serve in different ways as doubles for each other. But apart from his absolute control of Frank's compulsions, Malamud most convinces us of the rightness and inevitability of his behavior in the latter part of the book through the flat precision with which his purgatorial existence is rendered. Here the narrative authority is so strong that it girds the moral authority. If we look from a highly saturated red surface to a complementary green one, the effect is to rest the eye so that when it returns to the first surface, the red is just as bright as before. In the same way, our minds can wander away from the reading Malamud largely insists upon. We can consider, for instance, Roth's reading. Or we can decide that with a growing rapprochement with Helen, with his youth, and with much more imagination and toughness than Morris ever had, there's no particular reason why Frank should stay in the store. Then we return to face that last paragraph and all that has led up to it.

Something of this strange mixture of rude force and flickering precariousness informs the whole of the novel and strongly contributes to the arresting doubleness of almost every aspect. Malamud said that after *The Natural,* he "wanted to do a more serious, deeper, perhaps realistic piece of work." From the first paragraph, in which Morris' choices are graphically limited to the wind that punishes and the prison of a store, Malamud fuses thought, event, symbol, dialogue, and social detail to command our respect for the reality of the gray Brooklyn block and its inhabitants. It would seem that the lyricism of the novel never really leaves the pavement from which it tries to rise: the rose that Frank carves for Helen ends up in a garbage can.

But it is a "perhaps realism." Through a sudden *trompe l'oeil* the pavement seems to lift or, at least in Frank's vivid fantasy, St. Francis transforms the wood into a true flower and presents it to Helen. The realistic surface is further stretched by the characters' surrealistic dreams, and even the pace of the book has an uncanny doubleness to it. So much of *The Assistant* dramatizes Frank's, Helen's, and Morris' sense of overwhelming stagnation, yet Malamud manages to bring an urgent swiftness to the novel with the ingenious plot complications that propel events forward while so much stays the same, with movements from one center of consciousness to another, with his ability to keep surprising us by showing us new but convincing aspects of the same character, and with his talent for creating characters whose psyches are clearly bounded yet contain aspects of other characters.

Everything that combines to make the novel Malamud's most impressively sustained stylistic achievement brings great energy into the "open grave" of the store. Each voice is distinctive, yet fades into the others through the emotions—the fear, hope, self-hatred, hunger—straining within it; and the most characteristic accents cohere to create a music of pathos: the melodrama of Morris' "I go to my grave!" or the awkwardness belying the assertiveness of "You are afraid of even which it don't exist"; Frank's Lardneresque, earnest clumsiness, "I love you Helen, you are my girl"; Helen's touchingly hopeless attempts to control her life through maxims: "First mutual love, then loving, harder maybe on the nerves but easier in memory." The narrator's range of tones is deceptively wide: from the dislocated, immigrant syntax when he is close to Morris' sensibility, to the colloquial lyricism of Frank spying on the naked Helen.

Almost all of this is gathered into the grocery, the dominant symbol of the book. It is what it is, so convincingly a dying store that we feel in our bones the enervation of entering such a place to face its desperate but resigned proprietor. It is more than what it is. Described as a tomb, an open grave, it is clearly an emblem of the burden of the past, of our existences, of the palpable weight of our bodies, of the nearness of the deaths of these bodies. Appropriately, it is in this tomb that resurrection takes place. That Malamud is able to find a place in its grinding confines for such wraithlike beings as Breitbart, Al Marcus, and, above all, the gnomelike "macher" again testifies to the "perhaps realism" that he has brought off.

A reader of Malamud's first two novels has seen, in one form or another, most of the experiential baggage that S. Levin carries off the train with him at the beginning of *A New Life:* inadequate, damaging parents; the plunge into a derelict's existence; the electrifying perception that lifts him out of sleeping in cellars; the eventual trip across the country to realize that perception, as with Frank Alpine, or to realize true potential, as with Roy Hobbs. Unlike the two earlier protagonists, however, Levin reaches his destination wanting the right things. "Order, value, accomplishment, love," he tells Pauline Gilley, who is the wife of one of his superiors and who will soon become his mistress. Like the older Roy, but unlike the Frank who first enters the store, Levin is usually on frantic guard to keep the destructive patterns of his past from repeating themselves.

With this, Malamud has already excluded from his novel the two moral orderings that largely shaped his preceding ones; he can no longer write a book about a hero who moves or fails to move from anarchic desires to moral discipline. But he has left a good many ingredients for a coherent patterning. Levin's values can be tested and then either deepened or dissolved; or he can either remember, forget, or act in defiance of them as his unconscious or his secret self destroys or nourishes his moral disposition—to varying degrees, for Malamud will never relinquish his insistence upon the force of moral freedom.

To simplify a vast number of possibilities, values can be convincingly tested only in a milieu that is clearly moral and/or immoral enough to serve either as a foil or as a sponge, against which the hero's efforts either stand out in visible relief or are absorbed. Roy fails in a largely "bad" world; Frank succeeds in a paradoxically good one. Although each world has rich associations with the one in which we live, neither immediately derives from quotidian, contemporary reality. Roy's derives much more from the mythology of the present and the past; and in the cloistral store, Malamud has created a quasi-timeless milieu in which the values Morris brought with him from the *shtetl* still obtain, and a unified moral self can survive, however painfully. This is clearly not the case during the horrific day that Morris journeys off his block, into a specifically demarcated New York, to look for a job.

But in *A New Life,* Levin takes his moral baggage off the train at a particular time, the last Sunday in August 1950, in a particular political climate: "the cold war blew on the world like an approaching glacier. . . . Senator McCarthy held in his hairy fist everyone's name." Levin has to add to his own "backlog of personal insecurity his portion of the fear that presently overwhelmed America." Even if we did not know from Malamud's life or the geographic and academic details that Eastchester, Cascadia, "is" Corvallis, Oregon, we can recognize the setting easily enough: a mediocre English department of the state agricultural college, in an attractive small town, in beautiful natural surroundings. We can also quickly recognize the frustrations Malamud experienced as he tried to dramatize his abiding moral concerns in this representative slice of post-World War II America.

In *The Assistant*'s charged, underground

world, the doubling, the coalescence of saint and sinner, and the blending of crime and punishment with salvation through suffering—Frank even identifies with Raskolnikov at one point—the presence of Fëdor Dostoevski is strong indeed. In 1958, during an early stage of writing *A New Life*, Malamud said that the dominant literary influence was much different—Stendhal. This is not the place to begin comparing Julien Sorel or Fabrizio del Dongo with Levin, but we might consider for a moment the world that finally crushes Julien: the aristocratic one of the de La Mole household with all of its historically anointed objects, its lucid cynicism, style, force, self-love, and ambition. And if Mayor de Rênal, Julien's employer and sexual rival in the provinces, lacks aristocratic grace, the bourgeois ideals and rising social force he so perfectly embodies buttress his own gross palpability.

But at Cascadia College, where, by and large, the faculty are so concerned to be thought "normal" and avoid disagreement and demonstration of what education they possess, where their wives are not "without a suggestion of experience in the world and glad to be done with it," and where for both "saving money was a serious entertainment," Malamud has neither assertive force to dramatize, nor the richness of decadence, nor even—in this state that resisted the New Deal and federal aid to education—the sense of decay from a vital past. Since faculty and students seem unaware of the hunger and despair that have served as the lifeblood of so much of Malamud's fiction, and seek above all the contentedness that accompanies normalcy, they are easygoing enough until the contentedness is threatened. Determined as Levin is not to fail again, his ideals, his foolishness, and the consequence of his sexual liaisons drive him from the college and from all college teaching. If the authorities have enough strength to push Levin out, they nevertheless are best characterized by their impotence and inanity.

Inasmuch as Levin has brought his ghetto or *shtetl* economics with him, and is able to think of teaching four sections of composition for $3,000 a year as work with short hours and good pay, he is partaking of the new prosperity. Although he is booted out of the morally flabby culture, Malamud was not so lucky. He decided upon a highly qualified but still morally assertive conclusion: Levin saddles himself with a neurotic woman he no longer loves, her two unlovable children, and a promise never to teach again. The assertion has none of the weight of those in *The Assistant* or *The Fixer*, however. Malamud's attempt to test moral value against the prevailing shallowness of manner and emotion is in large part swallowed by the triviality of the milieu. Levin's fear of failure is supposed to be a real issue in the novel, but it is impossible to visualize significant success in Eastchester.

Of course Malamud chose to create characters and setting in this way, but Richard Astro's detailing of the similarities between the English departments of Cascadia and Oregon State College is telling. For Malamud in the late 1950's, this was the contemporary experience that best lent itself to extended fictionalizing. His decision was, of course, to play the resident academic community for laughs. This part of the book is wholly successful, for Malamud sprinkles wonderfully appropriate epiphanies of the collective banality among his depictions of the smugly earnest mediocrities. For example, the fact that Purtzer, "formerly a track star," distributes the grading curve in the idiotic race to finish marking a departmental exam, sets off the ludicrous inappropriateness of the whole enterprise.

But Malamud also clings to his master theme, moral rebirth from an agonizing past. Since the distance between the imperatives of desperation and the banality of the setting is so great, he in effect creates two Levins: in Theodore Solotaroff's words, " 'Sy' the solemn faculty screwball and radical naif . . . and 'Sam'—the hard case with his 'last chance' who emerges hamstrung but healed at the end." Although most of Malamud's heroes are *schlemiels*—to commit oneself in an imperfect world is to be forced into ludicrous postures—the Sy figure exists only to have one protestation after another punctured. The hostess he is trying to please ladles hot casserole onto his lap; the sight of the smiling, welcoming faces in his first class moves him to eloquence and affection, and only after class does he discover his fly has been open the whole time; his protestations to his sodden colleagues of the value of liberalism achieve nothing. Since the milieu offers so little opportunity for coherent opposition to the Sam figure, usually he surfaces only in his room, where he is plagued by guilt, dread, and loneliness.

Sometimes the puncturings of the academic novel seep into the moral assertions or ponderings. Not long after Levin tells Pauline what he prizes, she falls asleep, her stomach gurgling. And as a part of the need to provide the moral opposition his characters cannot offer, Malamud often parodies what he normally celebrates: the struggle for insight, the importance of freedom and responsibility, the relationship of art, morality, love, and individual rights are sometimes ruminated over for hundreds of words. Malamud's uncertainty about what to do with one of his underground men out there in SuperAmerica sometimes results in a verbosity and repetitiveness unlike anything else in his fiction.

Malamud uses all the possible moral patternings suggested above. Whether or not he intends parody, this is what it amounts to, for Levin "enjoys" deaths and resurrections at least three times in the novel. Yet we are supposed to regard his assumption of his burden at novel's end as a genuine moral triumph. With all of this, *A New Life* has some fine things in addition to the academic parody; in particular, the lyrical evocations of natural beauty, and the humor of Levin, rabbinically bearded and black-hatted, offering a Lifesaver to a balky mule or worrying whether he can fight off nonexistent bears and cougars with his umbrella. Still, what relief Malamud must have experienced during the three years he wrote *The Fixer,* as he immersed himself in the world of pre-World War I Russia, with its color, intensity, and undeniable injustice.

It is a tribute to Malamud's tenacity that after he completed *A New Life,* he was "sniffing for an idea in the direction of injustice on the American scene." Such plights as those of the civil rights workers in the South, Sacco and Vanzetti, and Caryl Chessman had more dramatic potential than Levin in Cascadia; but the novelist rejected these, as he did the Dreyfus affair. Then he remembered the story of Mendel Beiliss, arrested in 1911, on a charge of murdering a Russian boy so that his blood could be used in the making of matzos, by a government eager to renege on liberal concessions and to distract the populace from the country's real problems. After about eight months of intensive research and three drafts, Malamud completed the novel that gained him the Pulitzer Prize and the National Book Award for writing the best novel published in 1966. Here are some of his comments about the process:

I use some of his [Beiliss'] experiences, though not basically the man, partly because his life came to less than he had paid for by his suffering and endurance, and because I had to have room to invent. To his trials in prison I added something of Dreyfus's and Vanzetti's, shaping the whole to suggest the quality of the afflictions of the Jews under Hitler. These I dumped on the head of poor Yakov Bok. . . . So a novel that began as an idea concerned with injustice in America today became one set in Russia fifty years ago, dealing with anti-Semitism. Injustice is injustice.

We never find out what Yakov's life comes to in terms of gaining his literal freedom, for the novel ends with him on his way to trial. Although Beiliss was acquitted, the creator of The Fixer (or handyman) said, "What happens to Yakov Bok after I leave him I don't know." But we follow his path from the *shtetl,* which he left to seek new opportunities for work and education in Kiev, to the opportunities he seizes upon during his ride to court. The most important of these are the fantasized dialogue with Tsar Nicholas II, which concludes with Yakov's shooting the "Little Father" for not being a true father to his people, and The Fixer's ensuing conclusions: injustice inevitably politicizes its victims and forces upon them the imperatives of trying to change history through the attempt to overthrow an unjust government by force.

All of this constitutes the conclusion of Yakov's long movement to symbolic fatherhood, for Malamud the highest expression of moral adulthood. Before history cracks down upon him in the form of a monstrously unjust arrest, prosecution, and incarceration, he has been able to think of himself as outside historical process—even though he has suffered the privations of *shtetl* life and his father has been murdered by a cossack. After his arrest Yakov tells Bibikov, the prosecuting attorney who dies because of his belief in Yakov's innocence, that he is neither a theoretical nor an active revolutionary: "It's not my nature. If I'm anything I'm a peaceful man." Thirty months later, he says in an imaginary conversation with the dead Bibikov the night before his trial, "Something in myself has changed. I'm not the same man I was. I fear less and hate more."

Yakov's changing emotions, perceptions, and commitments are more than the empty gestures of a powerless captive. While in the *shtetl* he sees himself as the victim of his wife's barrenness—as a man without a child he is "alive but dead"—and then of her unfaithfulness: "A black cholera on her!" is his bitter sentence. But when she visits him in prison some eight months

before his trial, he moves from calling her a whore, to admitting that he was as much at fault as she, to attempting to end her ostracism in the *shtetl* by assuming the parenthood of her illegitimate child. He scribbles his claim to fatherhood on an envelope containing a document that, if signed, would presumably give him his freedom by blaming the murder on other Jews. On the document he asserts his protective role to the Jews, as he has to the child, by writing, instead of his signature, "Every word is a lie." As with his other commitments, that is a part of Yakov's covenant with man, not with the redeeming God of Judaism in Whom he cannot believe. Though, as he tells his devout father-in-law, ". . . take my word for it, it's not easy to be a freethinker in this terrible cell."

Before and after the interview with his wife, Yakov must resist offers to set him free if he will confess. He refuses, partly from a sense of communal responsibility, partly from distrust of the authorities, and partly from his unwillingness to grant them any success. The unwillingness follows from his hatred, which constantly increases as he suffers new brutalities; yet he realizes his rights and strengths, and despotism's fears and weaknesses. All of this enables him to fight the temptation to escape his miseries through suicide. With characteristic earthiness he says of the tsar, who would feel relief at his death, "Let him jig on his polished floor. I shit my death on him."

Malamud has said, "If this book isn't about freedom, I don't know what it is about. Every man must be political or where is your freedom?" While celebrating the possibilities of freedom and moral stamina, Malamud preserves enough complexity of attitude to keep the novel from collapsing into simplistic affirmations. Although Yakov's suffering makes him a better man, he tells the tsar in his last fantasy that "suffering has taught me the uselessness of suffering." Here he is referring to misery needlessly inflicted by the state, which should never occur; but the author is also asking if what Yakov has gone through is worth what he has gained. And although one of the great struggles of this largely uneducated man is to make sense of what is happening to him, he says toward the end of the novel that he has learned an extraordinary amount, but "what good will it do me? Will it open the prison doors?" "Still," he finally reflects, with the authority earned by his survival, "it was better than not knowing. A man had to learn, it was his nature."

The many excellences of the writing give Malamud the right to make through Yakov such large generalizations about individual and collective experience. With his vivid, concrete re-creation of the stances and styles of a milieu he has never seen, he achieves his goal and creates imaginatively ordered experience, not the fiction that is "historical fact," or the usual, partially imagined historical novel. That most of what happens to Yakov did not happen to Beiliss testifies to the dominance of the imagined, not of the researched fact. For all of the book's considerable length, more than 130,000 words, we are never in any center of consciousness but Yakov's; and for three-fourths of the novel Yakov is in prison, for half of it in solitary confinement, so that there can be almost no communication with other prisoners. Yet the degrees of desperation, misery, hatred, self-hatred, terror, confusion, perception, and longing that emerge in his conscious moments, dreams, hallucinations, and reveries when he is alone, and in his confrontations with authorities and with his few friendly visitors, are so subtly and variously depicted that Malamud brings powerful narrative movement to the book—even while we are experiencing from the inside a particularly painful wasting away of a life. Perhaps *The Fixer*'s greatest strength is the thoroughness with which this common man is realized. Then, again, as Bok reflects before

his arrest, "few people know who is really common."

About the time *The Fixer* was published, Malamud said to Haskel Frankel:

One of the things I think of now is the Negro, the Negroes who lead lives of second class citizens. Their story is one leading up to a situation that is revolutionary—call it Black Power if you wish. Our country is lucky if this slow bloodletting, these riots that come and disappear, are all we have to pay for what has happened to the Negro. If the Negroes' story today is revolutionary, Yakov's is pre-revolutionary.

With *The Tenants,* which he brought out five years later (1971), Malamud tried to make literary capital from this bloodletting and finally refute the many critics who have argued that he cannot successfully confront contemporary America at novel length. Along with the anti-Semitism that he saw as one of the aspects of Black Power, Malamud wove into the novel another of the dominant concerns of his fiction of the 1960's, the relationship of the artist to his art and to his experience. In a "decaying brown-painted tenement, once a decent house," Harry Lesser sits, as he has for the last nine years, writing his third novel, the one that will redeem him from his poor second one. Late in *The Tenants* we learn that the protagonist of Lesser's book is a novelist who, because he cannot love, is writing a novel about a character who

. . . will in a sense love for him . . . if he brings it off in imagination [he] will extend self and spirit; and so with good fortune may love his real girl as he would like to love her, and whoever else in a mad world is human. . . . Thus Lesser writes his book and his book writes Lesser. That's what's taking so long.

For most of *The Tenants,* Lesser wrestles with the last section, in which he presumably dramatizes the essence and consequences of this love. But, as he tells his landlord, Irving Levenspiel, "something essential is missing that it takes time to find." Clearly the missing ingredient is the kind of largeness that would force Lesser to give in to the pleas of the beleaguered and generally likable landlord by moving out, as all the other tenants have. Then Levenspiel can tear down the building and put up a structure that is both profitable and "comfortable to [his] nature." A fair part of the novel, often couched in Lesser's fantasies, deals with these pleas and Lesser's rejoinders that a change of locale would upset his creative flow—which, to the reader, seems thin enough already.

Even if the protagonist of Lesser's novel is not himself a novelist, the novel about a man who can love, inside a novel by a man who cannot, inside a novel by a man who mistakenly thinks he can, certainly seems claustrophobic enough to be a typical Malamud performance. But its excessively cerebral quality, with all the life driven out by sterile ingenuity, reminds us, by contrast, of the immediateness of Malamud's writing. He tries to drive a steadily widening wedge of conflict into *his* novel by bringing Willie Spearmint into the building to write yet another novel. Willie is a black ex-convict uneasily straddling the gap between his commitments to social revolution and to writing. Malamud can now pit Willie's concern for the "brothers," his fiction of brutality and self-hatred, and his own barely suppressed violence against Lesser's finicky, isolate self, his pallid subject matter, and his sense of the need to subordinate life and subject matter to the demands of form. To Lesser's "If we're talking about art, form demands its rights, or there's no order and maybe no meaning," Malamud can have Willie reply, "Art can kiss my juicy ass. You want to know what's really art? *I* am art. Willie Spearmint, *black man*. My form is *myself*."

Malamud stirs the broth even faster by having Lesser fall in love with Willie's white "bitch," Irene. Their grudging friendship comes to an abrupt end when Lesser idiotically tells Willie that he and Irene are in love and thinking about getting married. Willie's response is to try to heave Lesser out of a fifth-story window, to burn both copies of Lesser's almost completed novel, and to disappear. About eight months later the two are together again: Lesser struggling to rewrite his novel, Willie birthing stories in which blacks kill Jewish landlords and storekeepers. Black and Jew whirl faster in their dance of death until, in a part of the building surrealistically and appropriately transformed into a jungle of monstrous, primal growths, Willie castrates Lesser as the Jew drives a hatchet into the black's brain.

Malamud's cultural conclusion is imbedded within his grim novelistic one. So much damage has been done that we can hope only that one of the adversaries will show extraordinary mercy, the last word of the novel, said 113 consecutive times by Levenspiel. Clearly, Malamud attempts to make the tenement as enveloping a symbolic presence as Morris' grocery. By the time Willie returns, rats, roaches, and new debris from other falling buildings are streaming into the tenement, already defaced by the filth, obscene drawings, and shattered windows that are the gifts of visiting bums—as opposed to the resident fanatics. Lesser can only make a gesture of reconciliation and later fantasize a double wedding in an African village between himself and a black girl, and between Willie and Irene. Total extrication from his "normal" narrowness, symbolized by his obsessions with his novel and Willie, is beyond him. He cannot move out of the house of collapsing race relations; Levenspiel's alternative structure, which would, one hopes, blend black and white as reasonably as it would apartment and store, cannot be built in the world of this novel. Indeed, the landlord's closing plea for mercy is not sufficient proof that he has been cured of his animosity toward blacks.

At one point in *The Tenants,* Willie claims that Lesser cannot understand him or his writing because black and white "feeling chemistry is different." Whether or not Willie is right, his characterization is convincing, with a nice rendering of his different idioms and with his stereotypical militant stances softened by occasional displays of affection and vulnerability (although one does wish that Malamud had occasionally used him instead of Lesser as his reflector).

What most robs the book of the kind of force and inevitability Malamud sought is the unmotivated, flat, and altogether unconvincing way he develops the sexual competition. We first realize that the author has somehow gone wrong when Lesser makes love to a black girl with a group of hostile blacks, including her boyfriend, waiting for them across the hall—an absolutely unbelievable act for a man as guarded and careful as Lesser is until his manuscript is destroyed. In a rather silly scene Willie saves him from a mauling by playing the dozens (exchanging insults) with him. But two pages later, out of nowhere, Lesser—whose life is his writing— "realizes" that he may never write again if he does not tell Irene that he loves her. The affair that develops between the two is as flat as anything Malamud has ever done, in part because Irene is totally unrealized, transparently a convenience for plotting. It was also convenient but ultimately damaging for Malamud that Lesser is so imperceptive of Willie's likely response to the news that a Jew has thrown him out of Irene's bed. Admittedly, Lesser is no giant of insight. But since he has, for example, read a story by Willie in which a black kills a white to eat his heart, it is dizzying to hear this reasonably shrewd man reflect with no irony that Willie "might not want a white man to be in love with Irene."

A much more believable victim of the urge for instant sexual surrender is Arthur Fidelman, Malamud's inept Jew in Italy, "ever a sucker for strange beauty and strange experiences." In the late 1960's Malamud took a holiday from the sense of high social responsibility so evident in *The Fixer* and *The Tenants,* and added three playful Fidelman stories to the three he had already written, all of which were published in 1969 as *Pictures of Fidelman: An Exhibition.* The only Malamud bibliography to include the book lists it both as a novel and as a collection of stories. What makes difficult its classification as a novel, at least in the sense that the gathered stories in William Faulkner's *The Unvanquished* constitute a novel, is the distracting presence of two Fidelmans. The first is the tremulous, fussy art historian of "The Last Mohican," the prisoner of love in "Still Life," the prisoner in a brothel in "Naked Nude," and the pauper who stays alive by charging for piggyback rides over puddles in "Glass Blower of Venice." The second Fidelman is the assured pimp with a sword in his cane in "A Pimp's Revenge" and the con man of art in "Pictures of the Artist," who tells a peasant whom he has swindled, "Tough titty if you can't comprehend Art. . . . Fuck off now."

The gap between the soft passivity of the first Fidelman and the toughness of the second is too great, although Malamud tries in two ways to bridge the distance: the toughness is a shell the second Fidelman has developed to contain the hopeless yearning to recapture mother and sister, both dead; and "Pictures of the Artist" is written in such a fantastic style, a sort of clowning, surrealistic recasting of Giorgio Vasari's *Lives of the Artists,* that it might seem irrelevant to apply any conventional criteria of characterization to it. And if there is no way that the first Fidelman could become the second, the stories are unified by his comic relations to Italians and to art. More important, the level of the stories is generally so high (with ''The Last Mohican'' one of Malamud's best) and the entertainment so substantial that such carpings seem beside the point.

Malamud has said that his 1945 marriage to a gentile, Ann de Chiara, both caused him ''to be concerned with Jewish subject matter,'' for ''it made me ask myself what it is I'm entitled to in Jewish experience,'' and ''through her family . . . opened Italian life to me. Her background is richly Italo-American. When we lived in Rome [in 1956–57], I fell into Italian family life there.''

His Italian connection has proved to be a profitable one. In good part Malamud has been able to work with success the familiar theme of American gullibility and enthusiasm confronting Old World high culture, toughened cynicism, cunning, and opportunism because he has been able, with the Italians, to bring Fidelman into contact with a people who have at least as strong a histrionic impulse as the Jews. Further, a fair number of the Italians in the stories have bizarre, enlivening relations to art: a woman who has drowned her child; the proprietor of a brothel and his majordomo; a pimp; Beppo Fassoli, a glassblower who converts Fidelman from enslavement to women who will not love him and art he cannot create to bisexuality and a useful craft. Thus the book ends happily, with the sentence ''In America he worked as a craftsman in glass and loved men and women.''

Even in a relatively lightweight story like ''A Pimp's Revenge,'' Malamud's need to see Italy with a painter's eye as well as with his sharp, novelist's one produces vivid results. For example:

The painter . . . gazed for a reflective hour at the Tuscan hills in September haze. Otherwise, sunlight on the terraced silver-trunked olive trees, and San Miniato, sparkling, framed in the distance by black cypresses. Make an interesting impressionist oil, green and gold mosaics and those black trees of death, but that's been done. Not to mention Van Gogh's tormented cypresses.

In 1973 Malamud announced that he had begun a difficult novel about a man named William Dubin ''which may not see the light of day.'' Since 1976 came and passed without the book's appearance, Malamud's string of having brought out a novel every four or five years since 1952 came to an end. One long section of ''Dubin's Lives'' (about 17,000 words) appeared in 1977, another section early in 1978. While it is impossible to predict with any confidence the success of the completed novel, what has appeared is in several ways a real advance over anything Malamud has attempted before. With Dubin, a first-rate biographer in his late fifties, the author has a protagonist much less circumscribed by history or his own ineptitude or narrowness, much more like himself. At times one is reminded of Bellow at his best, whether Dubin's sensibility expresses itself in ponderings over transience, incompletion, or death, or in his wonderfully open responses to nature, or in such overflowings of his heart as his apostrophes to the mirror while shaving, or such a lovely attempt to arrest the passage of the seasons as ''Beating his chest, he flails at time. Time dances on. 'Now I am ice, now I am sorrel.' He shakes his useless fist.''

The use of the rich, new stylistic mode reminds us of Malamud's emergence in the 1950's. How new his voice and locale were, with the blendings of realism, fantasy, *shtetl*, New York City, blunt prose, and the gnarled poetry of immigrant syntax and diction; how vivid the sense of life in this and much of the later work has remained. How much works like *The Assistant, The Fixer,* and perhaps fifteen stories have led us to expect. If he has not brought nar rative and moral force to every paragraph he has published—and what writer has?—Bernard Malamud has brought to them enough to justify inclusion among the outstanding writers of fiction of his generation.

Selected Bibliography

WORKS OF BERNARD MALAMUD

NOVELS
The Natural. New York: Harcourt, Brace, 1952.
The Assistant. New York: Farrar, Straus & Cudahy, 1957.
A New Life. New York: Farrar, Straus & Cudahy, 1961.
The Fixer. New York: Farrar, Straus & Giroux, 1966.
Pictures of Fidelman: An Exhibition. New York: Farrar, Straus & Giroux. 1969.
The Tenants. New York: Farrar, Straus & Giroux, 1971.

COLLECTIONS OF SHORT STORIES
The Magic Barrel. New York: Farrar, Straus & Cudahy, 1958. "The First Seven Years," "The Mourners," "The Girl of My Dreams," "Angel Levine," "Behold the Key," "Take Pity," "The Prison," "The Lady of the Lake," "A Summer's Reading," "The Bill," "The Last Mohican," "The Loan," "The Magic Barrel."
Idiots First. New York: Farrar, Straus, 1963. "Idiots First," "Black Is My Favorite Color," "Still Life," "The Death of Me," "A Choice of Profession," "Life Is Better than Death," "The Jewbird," "Naked Nude," "The Cost of Living," "The Maid's Shoes," "Suppose a Wedding," "The German Refugee."
Pictures of Fidelman: An Exhibition. New York: Farrar, Straus & Giroux, 1969. "The Last Mohican," "Still Life," "Naked Nude," "A Pimp's Revenge," "Pictures of the Artist," "Glass Blower of Venice."
Rembrandt's Hat. New York: Farrar, Straus & Giroux, 1973. "The Silver Crown," "Man in the Drawer," "The Letter," "In Retirement," "Rembrandt's Hat," "Notes from a Lady at a Dinner Party," "My Son the Murderer," "Talking Horse."

UNCOLLECTED STORIES
"Benefit Performance," *Threshold*, 3:20–22 (February 1943).
"The Place Is Different Now," *American Preface*, 8:230–42 (Spring 1943).
"A Long Ticket for Isaac," in *Creative Writing and Rewriting: Contemporary American Novelists at Work*, edited by John Kuehl. New York: Appleton, 1967, pp. 71–91.
"An Exorcism," *Harper's*, 237:63–70 (December 1968).
"God's Wrath," *Atlantic*, 229:59–62 (February 1972).
"Dubin's Lives," *New Yorker*, 53:38–50 (April 18, 1977); 53:36–47 (April 25, 1977).
"Home Is the Hero," *Atlantic*, 241, no. 1:42–57 (January 1978).

BIBLIOGRAPHY

Bernard Malamud: A Collection of Critical Essays, edited by Leslie A. and Joyce W. Field. Englewood Cliffs, N.J.: Prentice-Hall, 1974. Pp. 170–79.
Kosofsky, Rita Nathalie. *Bernard Malamud: An Annotated Check List*. Kent, Ohio: Kent State University Press, 1970.

CRITICAL STUDIES, INTERVIEWS, AND BIOGRAPHICAL MATERIAL

Alter, Robert. "Malamud as Jewish Writer," *Commentary*, 42, no. 3:71–76 (September 1966).
Astro, Richard. "In the Heart of the Valley: Bernard Malamud's *A New Life*," in *Bernard Malamud: A Collection of Critical Essays*. Pp. 143–55.
Baumbach, Jonathan. "The Economy of Love: The Novels of Bernard Malamud," *Kenyon Review*, 25:438–57 (Summer 1963).
Cadle, Dean. "Bernard Malamud," *Wilson Library Bulletin*, 32:266 (December 1958).
Dupee, F. W. "Malamud: The Uses and Abuses of

Commitment," in his *The King of the Cats and Other Remarks on Writers and Writing*. New York: Farrar, Straus & Giroux, 1965, Pp. 156–63.

Fiedler, Leslie A. "Malamud: The Commonplace as Absurd," in his *No! in Thunder*. Boston: Beacon Press, 1960. Pp. 101–10.

Field, Leslie A. and Joyce W., eds. *Bernard Malamud and the Critics*. New York: New York University Press, 1970.

———. "An Interview with Bernard Malamud," in *Bernard Malamud: A Collection of Critical Essays*. Pp. 8–17.

Frankel, Haskel. "Interview with Bernard Malamud," *Saturday Review*, 49, no. 37:39–40 (September 10, 1966).

Freedman, William. "From Bernard Malamud, with Discipline and Love," in *The Fifties: Fiction, Poetry, Drama*, edited by Warren French. Deland, Fla.: Everett-Edwards, 1971. Pp. 133–43.

Hicks, Granville. "His Hopes on the Human Heart," *Saturday Review*, 46, no. 41:31–32 (October 12, 1963).

———. "One Man to Stand for Six Million," *Saturday Review*, 49, no. 37:37–39 (September 10, 1966).

Kazin, Alfred. "Bernard Malamud: The Magic and the Dread," in his *Contemporaries*. Boston: Atlantic-Little, Brown, 1962. Pp. 202–07.

Klein, Marcus. "Bernard Malamud: The Sadness of Goodness," in his *After Alienation: American Novels in Mid-Century*. Cleveland: World, 1962. Pp. 247–93.

Podhoretz, Norman. "Achilles in Left Field," *Commentary*, 15, no. 3:321–26 (March 1953).

Richman, Sidney. *Bernard Malamud*. New York: Twayne, 1966.

Roth, Philip, "Writing American Fiction," *Commentary*, 32:223–33 (March 1961).

———. "Imagining Jews," *New York Review of Books*, 21, no. 15:22–28 (October 3, 1974).

Rovit, Earl. "Bernard Malamud and the Jewish Literary Tradition," *Critique*, 3, no. 2:3–10 (Winter–Spring 1960).

Shenker, Israel. "For Malamud It's Story," New York *Times*, October 3, 1971, sec. 7, pp. 20–22.

Solotaroff, Theodore. "Bernard Malamud's Fiction: The Old and the New," *Commentary*, 33, no. 3:197–204 (March 1962).

Tanner, Tony. "Bernard Malamud and the New Life," *Critical Quarterly*, 10:151–68 (Spring–Summer 1968).

Wasserman, Earl R. *"The Natural:* Malamud's World Ceres," *Centennial Review*, 9, no. 4:438–60 (Fall 1965).

Wershba, Joseph. "Not Horror but 'Sadness,' " New York *Post*, September 14, 1958, p. M2.

—ROBERT SOLOTAROFF

Edgar Lee Masters
1868–1950

IN 1915, with the publication of *Spoon River Anthology,* Edgar Lee Masters found himself the center of an American literary controversy. A forty-seven-year-old Illinois lawyer who had longed since boyhood to be a writer, he was delighted: "My strength and my weakness have been that I have lived in the imagination. . . . imagination has been the controlling influence of my life. . . . all the while my heart was on poetry and the literary life." Hailed by John Cowper Powys as "the most original work . . . that American genius had produced since the death of Henry James," *Spoon River Anthology* was not the first of Masters' books nor the most typical. A study of the fifty-two others reveals that instead of exhibiting stylistic originality, Masters was inclined to follow the better popular trends, in whatever genre; and rather than craft and technique (the fascination of many modern writers, particularly poets), he tended to emphasize subject matter and theme. In fact, as Gorham Munson reminisced about the division in writers at a party given for Masters after the collection appeared, "The younger people were as usual discussing the everlasting topic of form, the older people aired their views on anti-religion." If this dichotomy holds, then Masters was in some ways more akin to the "older writers" than to the new writers whose obsession was innovative form.

The pervasive and continuing themes throughout his work would also suggest this kind of categorization. Masters revered poetry and literature because they could better the human condition; they were vehicles to raise the common consciousness. (Many of the wasted lives he depicted in his work could have been improved through some artistic influence.) And the themes that he chose to write about, and from, for the larger part of his life were those of national consciousness—the aims and identity of the American culture—approached from a liberal, altruistic point of view; the middle-class values of honor, beauty, virtue (which might or might not include chastity), personal freedom, industry, and success; and a stubborn insistence on the possibility—even the necessity—of romantic love.

This uneven mixture of popular concepts and ideality is evident throughout Masters' writing and life, and leads—at least so far as his writing is concerned—to unpredictable combinations of bathos and effectiveness, drama and melodrama. John Hallwas and Dennis Reader identify these attitudes with the influence of the American heartland at the turn of the century (and link Masters with Carl Sandburg and Vachel Lindsay in absorbing them): "the midwestern landscape itself, the pioneer history of Illinois, the developing myth of Abraham Lincoln (later rejected by

Masters), the democratic idealism of William Jennings Bryan, the social consciousness of Governor John Peter Altgeld, and the Mississippi River fiction of Mark Twain.'' Masters was thus established in the varied patterns of a strong populist tradition; and even though *Spoon River Anthology* marked the world of contemporary poetry as decidedly as did T. S. Eliot's *The Waste Land* (1922), the two books were speaking for opposing attitudes toward the state of American culture.

In *Across Spoon River*, the 1936 autobiography that describes his life only to 1917 (two years after the publication of the *Anthology*), Masters frequently laments his father's coercing him to study law rather than continue his academic program, which included Greek, literature, and rhetoric. Since his last years in public school, Masters had considered himself a writer; and the influence of a teacher, Mary Fisher, and a supportive friend, Anne, had already given him some appreciation for the great writers. His high school valedictory address was on Robert Burns; later that year he presented a paper on Whitman's poetry for the Scientific Association. The enthusiasm he felt for a literary career is evident years later, when he speaks of his life as lawyer:

I was under heavy living expenses. I was not pursuing the life of a contemplating poet, but the life of a drudging lawyer. I had got into this while doing my best to free myself for what I believed was the exercise of my gifts. I wanted to write, but I had to live.

Although Masters felt himself coerced into a legal career, he did learn important things during his thirty years as a lawyer. At first practicing independently and then, for eight years, as a partner of Clarence Darrow, he gained insight into government, social structures, and, most important, people. The abuses of the legal system gave Masters ammunition for his own progressive social and political attitudes; the people he came to know gave him characters for his writing, especially when dialogue and the approximation of natural speech were important. His legal career did, however, make writing difficult; he describes in detail having to write late at night, at lunch, or early in the morning. His first commercial play, *Althea* (1907), was an attempt to make enough money so that he could retire from the law. Several of his early works (the 1910 and 1912 collections of love poems, *Songs and Sonnets,* and the early single poems of *Spoon River Anthology*) were published under the pseudonym Webster Ford, because he was afraid that people would not do business with a lawyer who wrote about clients.

Reticent as Masters was about his literary leanings, he was adamant that he would not relinquish them; his first collection of essays, *The New Star Chamber and Other Essays* (1904), was one of his first books to be published (in contrast with others, which were only printed but not distributed commercially) under his name. Masters the attorney could write the anti-imperialist essays included here (they had been printed previously in the Chicago *Chronicle* and the pro-Bryan *Jeffersonian Magazine*); they were palatable to his friends and clients, who were also experiencing the enthusiasms of liberal and progressive politics.

The New Star Chamber reflects Masters' insistence that a moral commitment is necessary in whatever career a person pursues. Theodore Roosevelt, in the essay of that title, is an erratic leader because he acts from whim rather than from a firm ethical center; such leaders "lead men into the ways of vulgarity and violence.'' Most of the essays in this collection are wistful; writing on John Marshall, Masters wishes for politicians who will help improve the average person's condition, politicians who are "devoted to the rights of men instead of the powers of government . . . were stirred by the principles of liberty instead of the glory of the state.''

Masters is suspicious of "those thinkers who place the State on a higher plane than men." He is also an anti-imperialist, and his anger about the United States' involvement in the Philippines is evident both in these early essays and poems and in his verse drama *Maximilian* (1902), the theme of which, he said, was chosen to underscore the Philippine travesty. What is most interesting about Masters' use of this political situation is that he consistently imbues it with moralistic implications, as when he insists, in "The Philippine Conquest": "The constitution and the declaration have been duly ravished. . . . The people at large are paying the taxes and undergoing the obvious moral decline which has set in. . . . The whole of society has been shaken. . . ."

In these essays, as in the early poems, Masters' concern, whether he writes about Alexander Hamilton, Thomas Jefferson, William Jennings Bryan, or the whole of democracy, is to maintain the "moral lights" of a culture that had, a hundred years earlier, evinced only promise. In a tone much darker than that of Whitman's *Democratic Vistas*, Masters mourns the country that was so filled with vigor and affirmation during his boyhood. (Corollary themes that become important in his later works are the waste of the Civil War and the duplicity of Abraham Lincoln, and the resulting blight on the United States. Whether it be his own boyhood or the country's pristine state a century past, Masters enjoys lamenting the Eden that he insists on visualizing there.)

Most of Masters' views in *The New Star Chamber* essays are conventional populist expressions and, as such, need little elaboration. What is significant, for his later writing as well, is his tendency to find moral equations in seemingly unrelated social patterns. For example, his censure of Mark Twain, in the 1938 biography of that author, depends on Twain's lack of a firm ethical center: "His principles were vacillating and unheroic. . . . His mind did not rise to issues that concerned measures of historical moment. He had sympathy, he did not have large moral devotions."

Part of Masters' method throughout the portrait is to contrast the real anguish that Whitman experienced at the corruption of his country with Twain's small laughter at the frivolity of nineteenth-century America. His palliative name, meaning "safe water," comes to image his ability—for Masters; and the great promise that surfaced briefly, in *Tom Sawyer* at least, never came to fruition. The cause, according to Masters, lay not in technical weaknesses but, rather, in Twain's self-satisfied, narrow vision. The vision that Masters ascribes to Whitman, of America as "a republic, a great venture in liberty toward a new day, a higher and purer liberty, a better chance for the poor and the oppressed, the cheated, and the wronged," "meant very little to [Twain], certainly nothing compared to what it meant to Whitman."

For Masters, great men—Whitman, Jefferson, Andrew Jackson, William Marion Reedy, himself—had, and maintained, that vision; inferior people, no matter what their public reputation, lacked it. Among the latter would be Mark Twain, Hamilton, Lincoln, Bryan, and Theodore Roosevelt (although once Roosevelt admired *Spoon River,* Masters began to relent in his criticism of him); and one of the major qualities that they held in common was denial of their origin. The greatest people explored and revered their childhood, and especially the country from which they came: Masters wrote nearly a dozen books that emphasized his intrigue with the Sangamon Valley in Illinois, books ranging from the impressionistic novel *Mitch Miller,* to the Petersburg-Lewistown-based Spoon River poems, to the geographic account of the valley itself. His interest in both Lincoln and Stephen A. Douglas, evident in many poems and in the drama *Jack Kelso,* stems also from his fascination with place, for both men lived in that part of Illinois during their formative years. Masters was convinced that moral integrity somehow accompanied a person's acknowledgment of, and pride in, place; and he frequently attributed moral decline to rootlessness: in Twain's case "he lost his home, and in a sense became a wanderer for life."

Somber as Masters' portrait of Twain is, the latter's one redeeming quality is his complete devotion to his wife, Olivia. Fascinated throughout his career with romantic (and usually sexual) relationships, Masters saw a person's capacity for love as an important index of character—or lack of it. His image of the feminine, drawn in part from Arthur Schopenhauer, is that will, passion, and emotion are often at odds with the apparently more masculine faculties of reason, intellect, and control. Often, in Masters' poetry and fiction, woman's will overcomes man's intellect, with disastrous results. But, at its most affirmative, people's willingness to follow their passion is a strength; and in Mark Twain's case, only his love for his wife kept him sane.

Masters' near-obsession with the female principle, the woman as muse, surfaces repeatedly, particularly in his autobiography, where he frequently comments on his early romantic experiences and concludes with several lengthy discussions of "the eternal-womanly." Pointing out the dominance of this figure in every literate culture, Masters emphasizes that

Her image is in every shrine. . . . the mother of all things. She was originally a male saint and became a woman saint. . . . Look how the eternal-womanly emerges to the heightened imagination everywhere: to Faust as Marguerite, to Christians as Mary of Nazareth, to the Chinese as Kuanyin P'usa. . . . to Goethe [in celebrating] love as the all-uplifting and all-redeeming power on earth and in heaven; and to man it is

revealed in its purest and most perfect form through woman.

He continues, candidly:

I dwell upon this subject because I feel that a good deal of my secret is contained in it, and I would be glad if I could fully express it. For myself I divine the operation of the cosmic mind in the love of men and women, and hence I have identified a beloved woman with the mysteries of creative beauty. . . . I have placed all the women in whom I was deeply interested in a role that flesh and blood cannot often fulfill. . . .

The male-female relationship is a dominant theme in most of Masters' writing, both poetry and drama. In *Maximilian: A Play in Five Acts*, he distorts historical events so that the love between Carlotta and her husband can be shown repeatedly. Rather than having Carlotta return to Europe to seek help for Maximilian, he keeps her in Mexico (and borrows much of her mad scene from both *Macbeth* and *Hamlet*) so that she can appear in Maximilian's prison cell just before his execution. The early scenes between them, when they have just arrived in Chapultepec, are drawn with believable love; she enters his room and he says, " 'Tis you, I thought the sun was shining." A few pages later, she speaks in fear as he describes the political chicanery that traps them:

But save me from this shadow, fold me to you—
This ghostly nothing which you pictured so—
Freezes my blood (I would not have you leave—

Once mad, Carlotta continues to lament the fortunes of their brilliant love:

Oh what a love my heart has given you—
All heaven can't contain it.

Maximilian mourns for her sanity, describing her as "some bright planet buffeted with clouds":

Oh, had it been the will of heaven only
To sacrifice my heart, my mind, my life

In this inscrutable struggle. But for her,
This little girl, this princess without fault
To waste her spirit on the barren air. . . .

In this tragedy, Masters does work at presenting political ideas, of course, in keeping with
his insistence that the Philippine situation had
prompted the drama. His interest as dramatist,
however, appears to lie in the personal relationships and in the characterization of Maximilian as hero. Going nobly to his death after he
has refused an escape plan, Maximilian reads to
his cohorts about Socrates and compares himself
to that great figure. The last act of the play
sounds, in fact, as if it might have been written
in 1933, in the midst of the poem "The Serpent
in the Wilderness," in which Masters compares
Jesus Christ with Socrates and finds Socrates far
superior.

The strain of Hellenism that runs through
Masters' writing is partly the result of his interest
in the great figures of Greek culture (countless
references to Aeschylus, for example, or to Socrates or Sappho) but more pervasively of his
belief in the supremacy of the intellect, and in his
character (according to Willis Barnstone) as an
"inconsolable pessimist: not because of facile
skepticism, but because he wanted more; he was
profoundly wounded because life ran out on him,
and, like an arrested adolescent, he was forced to
live with his dreams."

Many of these themes are present in *A Book of
Verses* (1898), a collection that, for all its derivative form and imitative parlor-poetry titles, still
expresses Masters' basic tenets:

> Knowledge, thought, philosophy
> Our attendant angels be. . . .

One of the least formal poems, "An Etching,"
foreshadows some of the characteristics of the
later imagists' work, but its subject is still the abstract duality of intellect-emotion:

> The dull sky and the yellow meads;
> And the stripped trees moaning in the blast.
> The mind that thinks, and the heart that bleeds,
> The unborn day and the buried past,
> And this gray Sphynx called Life.

Many other poems repeat Masters' interest in
this dichotomy, but in traditional forms and language. Their titles suggest their sources: "Ode
to Autumn," "A Dream of Italy," "Ode to
Night," "A Song of Courage," "On Reading
Eckerman's Conversations With Goethe." Romantic and literary models gave Masters his
early education in poetry; it was only after his
experience writing essays and plays, and reading
more widely in other kinds of poetry, that he
began to write more original poems.

There are some traces of that originality in this
early collection, but they are slight. Masters' interest in native country and its fertile environment begins in "Illinois," but his emotion is
quickly lost in clichés: "Illinois, an empire is
thine of billowy fields of glory . . ."; as does
his idea that a person must acknowledge and
explore that environment: "The flower of Art is
the child of the soil and sun." Sappho ("deathless") is one example of that kind of firmly
anchored strength; Whitman, whom he compares
with both Job and Aeschylus, is another. "The
guardian of the land he made divine," Whitman
is remarkable for his soul, his knowledge, and
his "eagle eye." But even though Masters' sentiment is genuine, his choice of figurative language and diction remains embarrassing, not
only in its imitative patterns but also in its
clumsy rhythms. The eulogy "Walt Whitman,"
for example, closes

> He was our truest child,
> Our Western world beguiled
> And heaven bestowed.

Bernard Duffey notes the improvement of
Masters' poetry as early as *The Blood of the*

Prophets (1905), choosing as strong poems "A Ballad of Jesus of Nazareth" and his exploration of love, "Samson and Delilah." Although many readers see the poems in this collection as extensions of the political themes expressed in *The New Star Chamber*—which, to some extent, they are—they also show much evidence that Masters had left certain confining tendencies of formal verse and was moving toward the medium he often chose throughout his career, a long-line stanza resembling blank verse. He used that form for what he called verse drama, poems, plays, and even sections of his fiction. It seemed related in his aesthetic at this time to narrative, regardless of genre; love poems, such as those included in *Songs and Sonnets* (1910), were still written in quatrains, sonnets, or other conventional patterns. These had a lyric identity, as opposed to the storytelling function of much of Masters' other writing. David Perkins writes convincingly of the impact of prose traditions on the new poetry; and Masters' tendency to write narrative verse, using many conventions of prose, is only one of many instances of Perkins' belief.

Masters' greatest opportunity to use prose devices during these early years lay not in poetry but in drama. Although he had high hopes for the commercial success of *Althea,* that play provided only experience. The second of his popular plays, *The Trifler,* was considered by the Harrison Grey Fiskes, who eventually chose not to produce it because it dealt with adultery. Masters was clearly mining the "domestic melodrama" vein—plays descended from *East Lynne* that posed moral problems, rewarded virtue, and often appealed to a feminine audience.

Althea, a study of the "double standard," has as heroine a wife (Althea Hardcastle) whose husband asks her to promise never to remarry if he should die. If she does, she will lose his comparatively large estate. The irony lies in the fact that the husband, Lucian, has had numerous affairs during his marriage; his wife, none. Yet when she asks for time to consider his demand, he grows angry and they separate. Masters complicates the plot needlessly; the play does not, however, gravitate as simply as it might toward sympathy for Althea, because Masters also emphasizes the man's role as breadwinner and its accompanying social pressures. The image of woman "sucking" the man dry is set against the argument for various feminine freedoms. One cannot help but feel that Masters' chafing under financial pressure is reflected in that particular development of his theme.

The Trifler also begins with a sympathetic heroine, the widowed Isabel Sedgwick, but shifts during its three acts to a definite hostility toward her. This is the first of Masters' fictional use of the cousin's wife—also called Isabel in his autobiography—in his work; the plot of the first act parallels his account of their romance as he gives it in other sources. This seems to be an earlier romance than the poignant situation with Deirdre (Tennessee Mitchell, who later became Sherwood Anderson's wife); but there are places where Masters uses the episodes interchangeably: both women are indiscreet, provocative, and challenging. This situation, and the longer involvement with the woman known as Deirdre, dominate such books as *Skeeters Kirby* and *Mirage,* novels from the 1920's; and, as Lois Hartley comments, "one wonders if the effect [of the affair] was ever extirpated, for the episode permeates [all his later writing]."

In the play, as in *Songs and Sonnets,* the theme is unrequited love; the woman is at fault because her love is insincere (she is the trifler). Adding all the elements of melodrama that will fit, Masters includes a suicide pact, an arrest, some debauched characters who try to save Isabel and Laflin (pictured as a harmless romantic, despite his being responsible for his wife's death; his rallying cry is "Nothing is wrong where love is"); Isabel finally cannot marry Laflin even to save him from arrest. He goes off to punishment, and we surmise—from her tears and bowed head—that she has learned how dangerous a flirtation can be.

By the time of *The Leaves of the Tree* (1909), Masters had found a way through his personal dilemma, so that his heroine, Julia McFall, and the idealized stockbroker, Robert Reid, can marry and find equality in the relationship. "I'm for the double code or nothing," swears Reid, and marries Julia although her name has been linked with the wealthy playboy Tracy Bradley. Tracy, in turn, is so brokenhearted by Julia's engagement that he kills himself.

Masters' next two plays, *Eileen* and *The Locket,* return to the Tennessee Mitchell story. The heroine, Eileen, has a lover, Hamilton Townsend, who has been found in her apartment. The character of Carl Crittenden, the male protagonist, is based on Masters himself. *Eileen* once again tells the story of the lovers' visit. *The Locket* is a complicated sequel in which Eileen's husband, a traditional druggist and churchgoer appropriately named John Church, discovers her affair with Carl and forgives her. Carl reappears and wants Eileen to run away with him. The plot is the by-now stale romantic triangle, less melodramatic than the ending of *The Trifler* but no more innovative. As Masters was to emphasize in *The Nuptial Flight,* men and women are driven to marriage, to sexual and social stability; but often such arrangements are wrong.

The Locket studies four marriages, none of which is fulfilling. As Hamilton Townsend says, "Marriage—a citadel of refuge for deserters from the glorious cause of freedom."

The Locket leaves the audience with the dilemma of a passionless society, unhappy because of its passionless relationships. But in *The Bread of Idleness* (1911) Masters attempts to analyze what he sees as the chasm between women and men in the social roles they are forced to play. Still melodramatic and fantastic in places, this play does have sections of convincing dialogue in its four acts; and because it is longer, the changes in character that enable the lovers to reunite seem plausible.

When Herbert Drury goes bankrupt because of the frivolous spending of his young wife Gertrude, his anger causes him to abuse her. Masters builds to this climactic scene by having Gertrude and four of her friends discuss their lives—their spending, pastimes, attitudes toward husbands and society—so that we understand their total ignorance of the business world and adult pressures, and their completely parasitic existence. Gertrude has a sense of her worthlessness and expresses it to her mother: "I am nothing in the scheme of things. . . . I have not fulfilled my mission." She questions the parasitic relationship, even though she is furious when Herbert angrily blames her for his difficulty, by comparing herself with a prostitute:

. . . everything she said was just what I have thought, only she was justifying a life lived against the rules, while I walk in the sunshine of a life lived according to the rules. But we were essentially the same. She made herself attractive; so did I. I got money from a man; so did she. She had no children; neither have I. I took her hand in parting. She was as good as I.

Masters gives enough description of both Herbert and Gertrude so that, as they separate and learn to support themselves through physical labor, their development seems likely. Their final reunion in the new life of personal industry is much less fantastic than the denouements of his other plays.

In drama, as in his other kinds of writing, Masters held out for a realism that he could recognize and work toward. As he wrote in his autobiography, this was the period of a new concept of art, one much less dependent on literary antecedents; and he was soon to be—in the writing of *Spoon River Anthology*—"exhausted. . . . I would experience a sensation of lightness of body. . . . the flame had become so intense that it could not be seen, and I wrote with such ease that I did not realize the sapping of my life forces that was going on.''

The quality and innovation of *Spoon River Anthology* stemmed not only from this great release of Masters' psychic energy, but also from his having found a satisfying poetic model for his interest in narrative. As late as 1910 and 1912, in the two collections *Songs and Sonnets,* his concept of love poetry was conventional. (In his earlier book, *The Blood of the Prophets,* he had already experimented with freer forms; but his innovation occurred largely in poetry that was narrative or political.) While many of the poems in these two books are effective (nearly all of them seem to relate to the Deirdre romance of 1908–09), they suggest that Masters was not easy with the freely measured line that the imagists, Sandburg, and Robert Frost would use a bit later.

In 1913, however, his friend William Marion Reedy (who had never encouraged him to write poetry) gave Masters a copy of J. W. Mackail's *Select Epigrams from the Greek Anthology,* praising its ''ironic, sardonic, epigraphic'' qualities. Earlier that year Masters had become friends with Sandburg and had witnessed the reception of Sandburg's nine ''Chicago Poems'' in *Poetry*—he was, in short, aware that new kinds of poems were afoot. Soon Masters was trying the epitaph form (in free verse) in a poem for Dreiser, ''Theodore the Poet.'' The experiment was a success, and before long his epitaphs were almost writing themselves.

The concentration on present-day and common subject matter was an important change for Masters, but even more important was the parallel between the Greek epitaph and Masters' use of the scene in his drama. The Greek poets' ability to focus on a salient moment or situation, and through that focus to depict essential character,

resembled Masters' own aim in both the early plays and in *Dramatic Duologues* (1934). Each of the four short plays in the latter collection conveys the turning point in a romantic relationship (Henry VIII and Anne Boleyn, Andrew Jackson and Peggy Eaton, Aaron Burr and Mme. Jumel, and Rabelais and the Queen of Whims). They range from tragic to comic, with Masters reaching his poetic best in the first, with the imagery of Anne Boleyn's slender neck.

This selection of the core motivation, with the author pruning description so that nothing remains but that core, is Masters' method in the successful epitaphs. The poems of both *Spoon River Anthology* and the 1924 sequel, *The New Spoon River,* follow one of three general patterns, all of which can be found in the *Greek Anthology.* Of these patterns one is less successful, because it cannot avoid being heavily didactic. The two more vivid forms depend for their impact upon the specific character's revelation of crucial—and often intimate—biographical information early in the poem, and on that character's use of vernacular speech in telling his or her story (many of the poems are spoken by the character presented, in first person). We know the person in the epitaph from both event and speech pattern. Masters, as more than a fledgling dramatist, was comfortable with both of these devices.

The dominant pattern for the best *Spoon River* poems is event-elaboration-meditation, seen in some of the most famous of the poems: ''Lucinda Matlock,'' ''Hannah Armstrong,'' ''Isaiah Beethoven,'' ''Archibald Higbie,'' ''Nancy Knapp,'' ''Nellie Clark,'' ''Julia Miller,'' and ''Benjamin Pantier.'' ''Flossie Cabanis'' shows the pattern clearly, with its informative opening:

> From Bindle's opera house in the village
> To Broadway is a great step.
> But I tried to take it, my ambition fired

This is followed quickly by further detail and event:

When sixteen years of age,
Seeing "East Lynne" played here in the village
By Ralph Barrett, the coming
Romantic actor, who enthralled my soul.
True, I trailed back home, a broken failure,
When Ralph disappeared in New York,
Leaving me alone in the city—
But life broke him also.

"But life broke him also" is the beginning of the last section, the meditation, in which the character makes use of the insight that the sequence of events has provided. The poem closes:

In all this place of silence
There are no kindred spirits.
How I wish Duse could stand amid the pathos
Of these quiet fields
And read these words.

In the case of Lucinda Matlock, Masters' grandmother, the meditation is even more didactic:

What is this I hear of sorrow and weariness,
Anger, discontent and drooping hopes?
Degenerate sons and daughters,
Life is too strong for you—
It takes life to love Life.

It also serves as further "event" in the sequence that Masters has already established, from the opening occasion—"I went to the dances at Chandlerville"—through the rapid recounting of her life's vigorous chronology. Again, as in many of the *Spoon River Anthology* poems, the first-person point of view and the candid subject matter cannot help but be effective.

A second successful pattern for the epitaphs deviates from this basic structure only in that its ending is a kind of reversal; either Masters gives us a surprising event, as did O. Henry, or the character's "meditation" is so ironic, vehement, or violent that its intensity is startling. At its simplest, Masters uses the surprising event to lead to the character's death: Willard Fluke's confession of adultery foiled by his daughter's presence; Eugene Carman's anger at being "Rhodes' slave!" leading to his stroke; Tom Merritt's murder by his wife's lover. Another effective use is to change the reader's opinion of the person, as in the impressive "Elsa Wertman"

I was a peasant girl from Germany,
Blue-eyed, rosy, happy and strong.
And the first place I worked was at Thomas
    Greene's.
On a summer's day when she was away
He stole into the kitchen and took me
Right in his arms and kissed me on my throat,
I turning my head. Then neither of us
Seemed to know what happened.
And I cried for what would become of me.
And cried and cried as my secret began to show.

The "story" and event leave little to the imagination, but Masters begins to vary the expected pattern in the second section:

One day Mrs. Greene said she understood,
And would make no trouble for me,
And, being childless, would adopt it.
(He had given her a farm to be still.)
So she hid in the house and sent out rumors,
As if it were going to happen to her.
And all went well and the child was born—They
    were so kind to me.

The closing section reveals even more of a variance on our expectations:

Later I married Gus Wertman, and years passed.
But—at political rallies when sitters-by thought I
    was crying
At the eloquence of Hamilton Greene—
That was not it.
No! I wanted to say:
That's my son! That's my son!

A dimension not often emphasized in the fiction and drama dealing with this situation is the feeling of the unknown mother. Masters avoids the overt sentimentalism that might easily attach itself to the subject by using the change-of-direction development.

In addition to the surprising event, Masters enjoyed turning the meditation toward irony, often very heavy irony: "Rev. Freemont Deadman" giving up the ministry for public lecturing ("You see I needed money") or the disillusion of Robert Southey Burke over his allegiance to Mayor Blood. These endings are symptomatic of the much greater irony of situation, when a person's acts are consistently misinterpreted, to that person's detriment (the situation of Doctor Meyers and Minerva, "Butch" Weldy, Knowlt Hoheimer, and many of Spoon River's inhabitants).

The sense of great honesty or even impropriety in many of the epitaphs stems from another facet of Masters' surprise-ending device. He frequently uses a sexual or physically violent ending to create fresh impact, as when "Editor Whedon" speaks about abortions or "Belle Dollinger" shouts proudly, "An honest whore's the noblest work of God!" The most striking example of this technique occurs in a poem from *The New Spoon River:* that of Dick Sapper, a liberal outcast jailed for twenty years because of so-called traitorous statements made during World War I. The last section reads:

So they put me in prison for twenty years,
Where my body broke, and my spirit broke,
And where in vain I tried to be pardoned.
And I coughed and cursed to that awful moment
When the blood of my body shot from my mouth
Like a gushing hose, and I was dead.
And some of you call this a republic!
Well, some of you be damned,
And God damned!

Because so few of the epitaphs in *The New Spoon River* are written in the event-elaboration-meditation (or surprise variation on the meditation), this poem is more impressive, by contrast,

than it would have been if it had appeared in *Spoon River Anthology*. The third pattern of epitaphs—occurring in both collections, but much more frequently in *The New Spoon River*—is the least effective because, in it, event has almost disappeared. The heart of the poem is the meditation. While Masters does leave the voice of the poem with its persona, each speaker's identity depends—in some cases, depends entirely—on his or her morality. There is little mention of specific event, place, or person; there is only attitude.

    Marshall Carpenter
Remember not your Creator
In the days of your youth,
But remember your Youth in the days of your
    creator:
Remember how you felt, aspired, loved;
Remember your visions and faiths,
And the beliefs in yourself and others.
Remember whom you chose,
And whom you rejected, and why.
Remember how you looked to others,
And for what you were taken by others.
Remember your house and its trees,
And the village.
Remember the subtle ways of air
Which blew aside intangible curtains,
And showed you what you could not report.
Thus hold to yourself and grow
To yourself as an oak,
Turning never to an alder bush,
Or sand grass!

"Marshall Carpenter" has no memorable self; there is no event with which we may connect his realizations. While a reader may be inclined to follow his advice, as art or as poetry his words mean nothing more than any other platitudinous injunction.

"Bertrand Hume" is another of the many poems that concentrate on message to the near-omission of event and personality:

To recall and revision blue skies;
To imagine the summer's clouds;
To remember mountains and wooded slopes,
And the blue of October water

Moving in this vein, the poem closes with a plea for more life, more chance to live a full life; but that plea is equally bland.

Even in the later poems that attempt to use an event as the substitute for the didactic message, Masters has changed proportion. Meditation is the dominant element. The poem "Ambrose Seyffert" stems from a woman's sacrifice of home and children for love of a man; but the account of that concrete situation occupies only a small section of the poem:

Oh! The years we waste, and the souls we waste
In learning one simple thing—
And what it takes to teach us!
Not until after her lonely sojourn
In Buenos Ayres, leaving her children,
Who had to be left to leave her husband—
All in devotion to me.
Not until after her hopeless return
To the door of dishonor, the roof of remorse,
Did the meaning of that devotion to me
Stare like the blinded eyes of a friend
On my poor heart gifted with vision at last
To know devotion—but when it is lost.
To know devotion! Like one who knows the
    good of a lamp,
When the lamp is out, and he stumbles in
    darkness,
And falls to a fate of endless pain—
Lamenting the absent lamp forever!

This is one of the stronger poems of *New Spoon River*. Masters' increasing turn toward stentorian writing, which taught more openly than it entertained, deadened the lengthy collection of epitaphs to the extent that few readers who had enjoyed *Spoon River Anthology* could feel that this collection was really a sequel. Be-

cause of each character's absorption with making philosophical points, *New Spoon River* is less a connected series of portraits; there are few related plot lines or tangled character relationships. Part of the fun of reading *Spoon River Anthology* lies in sorting through the names and events, and tracing this person to that event in later poems. In *New Spoon River* the narrative sense of discovery is almost completely missing.

Whether or not it was gratuitous self-justification, Masters' own comments about *New Spoon River* indicate that the differences in style were intentional. He wrote to Horace Liveright, his publisher, in 1924 about the new collection, "It cuts deeper philosophically than *Spoon River Anthology* . . . it gets into the skin and flesh of this our America, on religion, politics, sex, everything. It is a son of a bitch, and I want it to be." In somewhat gentler language he explained to Harriet Monroe, "I think it a richer and profounder book than the old one, not so episodical of external things, but as much so as to soul experiences." He continued that it was to deal with "the external evidences of the country's transformation after World War I and a new set of feelings, ideals, and convictions."

For all Masters' personal defense, critical opinion has long held that the second collection is less dynamic and has fewer strong poems. As John T. Flanagan notes summarily, "In 1924 Masters published *The New Spoon River,* admittedly an inferior work which nevertheless added over three hundred individual portraits to his gallery and included occupational types like the miller, barber, cobbler, tailor, and garage mechanic which previously had been omitted." For Lois Hartley, the second collection "has more unity, more purpose." It is, however, 'more speculative, abstract, philosophical, and political. Hatred of industrialism and materialism, hatred of what he considered narrow morality and bigoted religion, and other hatreds that were incidentally evident in the earlier book are now dominant motifs.'' For all Masters' clarity, Hartley concludes that ''Too many voices belong to Masters alone, not to the persons speaking, and there are more shadowy, undefined persons. Few poems from *The New Spoon River* stay in the memory as do 'Lucinda Matlock' and others from *Spoon River Anthology.*''

Masters' career between the 1915 publication of the original *Anthology* and *The New Spoon River* in 1924 was so explosive, so filled with the rewards and problems that followed his becoming an important literary figure, that one can hardly wonder that he seemed to move in half a dozen directions simultaneously. In that period he battled through a divorce to a second marriage, moved from Chicago to New York, and published eleven books—five thick collections of poetry, one novel in poem form (*Domesday Book*), and five substantial novels. None of these publications received either the interest or the praise that *Spoon River Anthology* had provoked; perhaps Masters' return to his Illinois characters and the epitaph method was an appeal for the varied, but at least partly favorable, response of 1915.

Few writers would have been displeased with the kind of attention that the *Anthology* had received. John Flanagan points to a ''vast number of reviews'' in all kinds of publications. Amy Lowell commented in 1917 that ''no book, in the memory of the present generation, has had such a general effect upon the reading community as has this. Every one who reads at all has read it.'' The book went into countless printings and was quickly translated into at least six languages. Decried for its licentiousness, its overt and unnecessary use of sexual material, and its free verse form, *Spoon River Anthology* was just as loudly touted for its candid view of American life (particularly village life) and its psychological reality. Masters was hauled from the populist camp to the realist, from the imagist to the naturalist. *Spoon River Anthology* became a staple in the critical battle over ''the revolt from the village''—even though Masters said repeatedly that the book was an expression of his admiration for the Midwestern town: ''. . . If I had any conscious purpose in writing it and the *New Spoon River* it was to awaken that American vision, that love of liberty which the best men of the Republic strove to win for us, and to bequeath to time.''

Somewhat later, after the critics had coined their phrases, Masters spoke to August Derleth about the matter:

There never was anything to this revolt from the village business. We didn't do any such thing. Maybe Lewis backed away from something that hurt him, but he wasn't rebelling against the American small town any more than I was, and my guess is he'd have stayed there if the people had accepted him as he was. Sure, there's plenty of meanness and narrowness in the American small town; there always was. But there's nobility and courage and comedy, too—I said it all in *Petit*—''Life all around me here in the village: Tragedy, comedy, valor and truth, courage, constancy, heroism, failure—All in the loom. . . .'' We weren't rebelling against the village. We were seeing it without blinders.

Especially since so much of Masters' later work does stress positive elements about the Sangamon Valley and its people, his view of his aims in these Spoon River portrayals should at least be heard; until Reedy dissuaded him, he had planned to title the 1915 collection, innocuously, *Pleasant Plains Anthology.*

That title would have been even less appropriate for any of his next four collections of poetry—*Songs and Satires* and *The Great Valley* (1916), *Toward the Gulf* (1918), and *Starved Rock* (1919)—for, as Herb Russell insists, these are bitter books, many of the poems hardly more than ''personal invective,'' vehicles ''for the poet to revenge himself on his enemies.'' Aside from the love poems in *Songs and Satires,* many of which had been published in *Songs and Sonnets* (1910), over half of the work in the other three collections is in some way a working through of philosophical issues that Masters felt had trapped him in unfulfilling circumstances. Constricted religious views, commonplace attitudes about romantic love, materialism that leads innocent people into war—all the cultural evils readers thought had been suggested in *Spoon River Anthology* are here paraded in full panoply, unfortunately for the artistry of the poems. The apparent depression that followed the exhilarating reception of the *Anthology*—for much about these poems cannot be explained unless Masters was depressed—colored his views about people, locale, and the importance of his art.

By 1917, when he had moved to what was to be his writer's retreat in Spring Lake, Michigan, he was set to write the significant work that his previously harried schedule, with its innumerable interruptions, had never allowed. Instead, at Spring Lake he experienced the antipathy of the local residents, the suspicion of being pro-German, a debilitating romance, and, in September, the end of his nineteen-year marriage. Herb Russell concludes about *Toward the Gulf,* the poetry collection written during that year:

His troubles may have been his own fault, but in his mind he was certain he had been driven out by religious fundamentalists and political conservatives. . . . Put together during these trying circumstances, *Toward the Gulf* is a record of losses. No fewer than fifteen of the forty-six poems discuss a romantic ideal which has in some way failed, and, significantly, the poems are more visibly subjective than in the previous volume.

All the idealistic people in these poems suffer a loss of hope. . . .

Masters' own despair during this period is suggested by the fact that he ends his autobiography, *Across Spoon River* (1936), at the year

1917 with his recognition that "the world had become insane, and Chicago was insane." While he admitted that many of his problems "were the spawn of my own nature in part," his defensiveness about the events of these years—and his genuine anger that the poems in these four books had been ignored—is clearly revealed in his choice of poems for a selected volume in 1925; more than two-thirds of all the works were from these four neglected collections.

Perhaps the most interesting aspect of Masters' debacle during the period beginning in 1917—when, he writes, "I lost everything except my health and my concentration of mind" —was that he continued his prodigious production and published two of his best-written books in 1920. *Domesday Book* is a psychological novel in poem form, proving Amy Lowell right in her description of Masters as "Dostoevsky in *vers libre*"; and *Mitch Miller* is a boys' novel that manages to convey Masters' overwhelming nostalgia and reverence for his Illinois past, with some very well-handled touches of humor and literary satire.

The technical challenge of *Domesday Book* was partially responsible for Masters' fondness for it (and for his choosing to write a long sequel to it nine years later, *The Fate of the Jury*). In his 1933 essay about *Spoon River,* he stated, "I think . . . that I have written many poems better than anything in either Spoon River, and that both 'Domesday Book' and its epilogue, 'The Fate of the Jury,' surpass them." But in his description of that technical challenge, Masters also allows that the attempt he was making in the novel-in-poetry form, to show all facets of a character who might otherwise be misjudged, was personally important to him. Had he not been, in his view, misjudged and misinterpreted throughout his life?

Quite deliberately I set out to tell the story of a life from as many angles as possible. . . . every one has many sides to his nature, and that perhaps when the eyes of many are used to appraise him that a completer judgment is arrived at. . . . I have felt urged to show in my poems that it is the understanding of any character that leads to compassion, and that it is almost fated to do so.

Masters' use of the masculine pronoun here may be more than a grammatical convention, for even though the heroine of *Domesday Book* is Elenor Murray, her life has many correspondences to that of Masters—her asking her grandfather for money for college and his refusal, for example. As he often did with those of his feminine characters whom he considered admirable, Masters placed his traits in their characters, thereby achieving a partial disguise while still expressing themes that were personally interesting to him.

The themes of *Domesday Book* are the familiar ones of illusion/reality, morality/evil, and the differences in the male and female psyches, themes with which Masters had worked for the past twenty years. In telling the story of Elenor Murray, Masters was able to show all the social prejudices he hated so vehemently: judging on appearance; convicting on circumstantial evidence; making decisions from rigid and often irrelevant moral concepts, with no understanding of the individual circumstances; acting only from self-interest and, often, financial self-interest.

Elenor is a typical Masters heroine. Careless of her sexual purity, she has followed great loves and shaped her life without self-interest around them. The cultural reaction to her is censure, condemnation; even her family is relieved when she dies. As he did in so many of his plays, Masters uses the highly visible moral dilemma of the heroine as a focus for varying responses by others in the drama—not only principal characters but also some that are very remotely connected with Elenor and her life (the chief flaw of the 400-page poem is that it includes too many characters about whom we care little). Masters'

thematic point is that the "riffles" from one person's life, as well as death itself, are countless; and that, rather than each life being a discrete entity, it is a part of the common soul, the common national complex. For even though *Domesday Book* is primarily about a woman's existence in turn-of-the-century America, Masters insisted that it is also about that America: "a census spiritual/ Taken of our America . . . . For William Merivale, the coroner,/ Who probed the death of Elenor Murray goes/ As far as may be, and beyond his power,/ In diagnosis of America,/ While finding out the cause of death."

Domesday Book thus becomes a continuation of Masters' understanding in *Spoon River,* in which he had realized that the passions and attitudes of people in his small Illinois towns are no different from those of the people in Chicago; for all the attention given to urban and rural differences, the human heart is everywhere the same. Similarly, Elenor Murray's life, for all its origin in a rural area, touches people all over the country, as well as abroad (through her wartime experiences). If Masters' blank verse contained some pretentious echoes of John Donne's sentiments, it was more than accidental.

Coroner Merivale is also a character who interested Masters. His need to investigate the death—and life—of the woman so as to understand the culture surrounding her, and himself, is commendatory. Masters uses all his knowledge of law, all his feeling for altruistic ventures, to make Merivale more than a dull man whom life has passed by. Merivale is the key character of the group that Masters had conceived years before, men gathered in his father's law office in Lewistown discussing logic and philosophy, trying to find truth, knowledge, and understanding through intelligent comradeship. As Masters planned to use the characters, one of the group was to commit suicide, and the others were to report their recollections as witnesses; the variance in testimony intrigued Masters but on more than a simple recollection-of-detail level.

The kinds of details that people emphasize tell much about their own characters:

They also gave varying and contradictory analyses of the suicide's character, and even of his physical appearance. I have observed that few people can remember the color of the eyes of their friends and acquaintances, something that I always take note of with particular care.

John Flanagan points out similarities between Masters' *Domesday Book* and Robert Browning's *The Ring and the Book,* the long poetic narrative about a Roman murder case. Perhaps a more natural source (or complex of sources) for the story would be Masters' desire to tackle the men in discussion (as his sequel, *The Fate of the Jury,* finally does); the somewhat autobiographical characters of both Merivale (for at this stage in his life, Masters felt bereft of romantic love) and Elenor (who had, in essence, sacrificed her life to the pursuit of the perfect relationship); and an event from his father's law practice, the death of Cora Peters. Masters helped to prepare the brief for his father (the defense attorney), so in some ways, even in 1899, he was involved in the case.

Cora Peters, a twenty-four-year-old prostitute, was found dead on Christmas Day, 1899, beneath a train trestle at the Spoon River crossing. She had left a tavern the previous night with John Hellyer, a sixty-year-old farmer. Hellyer claimed that Cora had been struck by a train, and her injuries were consistent with that explanation; but he was charged with murder. He was convicted and sentenced to twenty-five years in prison; but Hardin Masters won an appeal freeing him. Masters had already used some of the details of the case in the poems "Jennie M'Grew" and "Steam Shovel Cut," so the case had stayed in his mind.

Only in basic respects is Elenor Murray's situation similar: the kind of reputation the women carry threatens to influence the "justice" that their deaths warrant (and the opinion of the town, and the jury, as influenced by this "reputation"); the responsibility of the man involved with the woman—should he be charged with murder because she meets her death after a tryst with him? (in *Domesday Book,* Elenor's death from syncope is much more directly caused by her lover's charge that she is a whore); what becomes of the woman's "name" as a result of her scandalous death? They are important respects, however, especially when one considers that Masters' primary interest in choosing the incident and its connecting themes was not to write an American tragedy—Dreiser was to begin work on that a few years later—but to record those endless riffles spreading to "the utmost shores." Implicit in this purpose is the definition of "Domesday Book," which Masters makes clear early in the poem:

A word now on the Domesday book of old:
Remember not a book of doom, but a book
Of houses; domus, house, so domus book.
And this book of the death of Elenor Murray
Is not a book of doom, though showing too
How fate was woven round her, and the souls
That touched her soul; but is a house book too
Of riches, poverty, and weakness, strength
Of this our country.

Many of the stylistic peculiarities of the book, for which Masters was criticized, relate to this purpose. The ostensible story could have been told much more quickly, but he thought it important, whenever a new witness or speaker was introduced, to explain that person's background as well; judging his or her reaction was impossible unless more than the immediate facts were known. The story is not only that of Elenor Murray, but also that of everyone touched in any way by her life and death. The chief quality in which Masters was interested was somewhat difficult to depict—that of spirit, soul, the presence of which sometimes had to be written about very indirectly. As Merivale mourned, the culture needed to create a system "For saving and for using wasting spirits,/ So wasted in the chaos, in the senseless/ Turmoil and madness of this reckless life,/ Which treats the spirit as the cheapest thing."

Elenor is emblematic of that spirit, not only in the descriptions of her and her life throughout the poem, but also in her use of the words from Joan of Arc, "To be brave and not to flinch." Caught in the stifling social conventions of which her mother speaks so bitterly at the inquest, Elenor has little choice, once she discovers that the men to whom she looks for love are as frail and narrow as the people she had known in her childhood. Mrs. Murray demands:

Then make the main thing inner growth, take
    rules,
Conventions and religion (save it be
The worship of God in spirit without hands
And without temples sacraments) the babble
Of moralists, the rant and flummery
Of preachers and of priests, and chuck them out.
These things produce your waste and suffering.
You tell a soul it sins and make it suffer,
Spend years in impotence and twilight thought.
You punish where no punishment should be,
Weaken and break the soul. You weight the soul
With idols and with symbols meaningless,
When God gave but three things: the earth and
    air
And mind to know them, live in freedom by
    them.
Well, I would have America become
As free as any soul has ever dreamed her,
And if America does not get strength
To free herself, now that the war is over,
Then Elenor Murray's spirit has not won
The thing she died for.

Mrs. Murray's overstatement of purpose in the death of her daughter does not undercut the intensity of her earlier words, and Masters returns once more to his theme of personal freedom and conscience—usually imaged in a romantic relationship—but in a narrative that, because of its speed and reach, remains interesting throughout its extreme length and, in places, verbosity. The character of Elenor Murray is not sacrificed to his message, and she remains a vivid, complex persona to the end of the book. (The same statement cannot be made about Coroner Merivale, who becomes much more clearly the hero in *The Fate of the Jury* [1927].)

Masters works very hard at the end of the novel/poem to return to his theme of America as feminine, maternal. In the concluding testimony of Elenor's final lover, Barrett Bays, she is cursed precisely because she is America:

Corrupt, deceived, deceiving, self-deceived,
Half-disciplined, half-lettered, crude and smart,
Enslaved yet wanting freedom, brave and coarse

. . .

This leads to Merivale's "defense" of Elenor by reading her hundred unanswered letters to Bays, in which she explains her love with great clarity. Her letters exonerate her; the jury plans a park and monument to her and her experience; and Merivale concludes that Elenor is, like America, the pearl to be found only after the decay and mud have been pierced: "the soul maternal, out of which/ All goodness, beauty, and benevolence/ . . . Mother Mary of all tenderness." His last words are surely Masters':

                The tragedy
Is that this Elenor for her mother gift
Is cursed and tortured, sent a wanderer;
And in her death must find much clinging mud
Around the pearl of her.

Perhaps it is the intensity of Masters' feeling about the needless deaths of both Elenor Murray and Mitch Miller that makes *Domesday Book* and *Mitch Miller* parallel, for all their obvious differences. The poison of social opinion leads each to an unexpected death; each represents the waste that Masters lamented throughout his career.

Mitch Miller is ostensibly a boys' book, a nostalgic adventure on sunny summer days that leads to the sharp reality not only of adulthood, as in most initiation stories, but also of death. Its plot is so derivative that many critics have noticed its resemblances to *Tom Sawyer:* the rural setting near a major river; the dual protagonists, Mitch and the narrator, Skeeters Kirby (a Tom and Huck Finn parallel); the story told in a first-person voice with a strangely vernacular diction; the treasure hunt and courtroom scenes; and the running warfare with adults and their authority. Yet Masters' means of telling his ordinary story is so effective that one reviewer said the novel comes close to being a masterpiece.

In *Mitch Miller*, Masters establishes and maintains a rolling narrative pace that continues throughout the story (except for the poignant scenes of Billie's and Mitch's deaths and mourning). Skeeters' idiom, with its unexpected contractions and elisions, re-creates the events from the participants' perspective—and does so succinctly. There is no time for the moralizing or digressing so common in Masters' poetry. The opening section is an intimate, open monologue:

And then supposin' one day all the things in the house was loaded on a wagon and you rode with your ma up the hill to a better house and a bigger yard with oak trees, and the things were put in the house and you began to live here, . . . and then supposin' you began to hear your pa and ma talk of Mr. Miller and what a wonderful man he was, and Mrs. Miller and what a good woman she was, and about the Miller girls, how funny and smart they was, and about Mitch Miller, the wonderfulest boy in town. . . .

It not only establishes the place of veneration that Mitch Miller holds in everyone's eyes; it also—in its entirety—plays on the theme of illusion/reality by having Skeeters cast his reminiscence as if he had just awakened ("you kind of knew things was goin' on around you, but still you was way off in your sleep and belonged to yourself as a sleeper"). Once into the monologue, Masters uses Shakespeare's "Our little life is rounded by a sleep," both as repetition of imagery and as foreshadowing. Spoken in Skeeters' idiom, even though the sleep/illusion image occurs repeatedly, it seems natural rather than literary.

Mitch and Skeeters' life is an illusion, a believable and innocent one, as they pattern their fun on Tom Sawyer's and long for the romance of the Mississippi River. The climax of their boyish adventure comes when Mitch writes to Tom Sawyer and receives an answer (from the butcher so named). But the reality of the hard rural life begins to break through: people lose jobs, Mitch is separated from his sweetheart, Little Billie dies, and Skeeters is ill. The search for adventure, which is also the search for a hero—if not Tom Sawyer, then "Linkern"—modulates into the search for understanding. That Skeeters finds this quality only after Mitch's death in a train accident is the price that Masters asks from the sentient person who lives in the modern world. "No book that I have written is closer to my heart, or pleases me more," Masters said, not only because *Mitch Miller* did re-create boyhood events and atmosphere, but also because his writing itself carried that re-creation.

This novel was the first of what Masters termed his "trilogy" of semiautobiographical prose; the second and third were *Skeeters Kirby* and *Mirage*. The novel is important for that reason, and also because it marks the beginning of Masters' career as novelist. Even though he was fifty-one when *Mitch Miller* was published, he wrote six others (and six verse dramas almost simultaneously) between 1922 and 1937. His interest had turned increasingly toward the narrative; and since critics had complained so loudly about the blank-verse form of *Domesday Book,* Masters had little choice but to write in prose.

Besides *Mitch Miller* three other novels are set in the Sangamon Valley and are drawn heavily from Masters' own experiences. *Skeeters Kirby* (1923), *Mirage* (1924), and *Kit O'Brien* (1927) continue the Miller story in various ways, the two earlier novels completing Skeeters' life to his forties and focusing more intently than is interesting on his later love affair, the disappointing romance with Becky Norris (Pamela). *Kit O'Brien* is a thin Huck Finn kind of story about a sadistic religious fanatic and Kit's part in righting the wrongs he has created.

The other three of Masters' seven novels are historical; and while they all are set in Illinois, they are, to a certain extent, thesis novels. *The Nuptial Flight* (1923) and *The Tide of Time* (1937) both question the validity of love and marriage, as does *Children of the Market Place* (1922), which has Stephen A. Douglas as hero.

While it is unreasonable to dismiss everything Masters wrote after the Spoon River collections, *Domesday Book,* and *Mitch Miller* as worthless, many of his later books are either thesis-ridden or repeat materials and characters presented more successfully earlier. Bernard Duffey goes so far as to say:

The general level of those books [written from 1915 to 1942] did not vary widely. Until his last three collections of verse, where he turned to sentimental recollection of the Spoon River country, his argument remained what it had been in *Spoon River* itself—the evils of inhibition, the virtues of freedom and self-fulfillment, and the villainous roles of banker and preacher in American life. But with the exception of a few individual poems, perhaps a dozen in all, Masters' work was dull, tremendously garrulous, and wholly

unenlightened by the imaginative and dramatic resilience which had marked *Spoon River*.

While Masters could have used a good editor, particularly during his later years, there are clear patterns and interests during this late writing that deserve to be described. In keeping with his constant fascination with America and its people, Masters turned increasingly to studies of national heroes, both present and past. Lincoln and Stephen A. Douglas are important because of their origin in his section of Illinois; Robert E. Lee because he too is a victim of a cultural catastrophe, the Civil War. Nearly all of Masters' books written during the 1920's deal in some way with one or another of these men: *The Open Sea* (1921) parallels Brutus with Lincoln; *Children of the Market Place* (1922) emphasizes Douglas but also touches on Lincoln; *Lee* (1926) is a verse drama depicting Lee as Hamletlike (and foreshadows *Gettysburg, Manila, Ácoma* [1930] and *Richmond* [1934]); *Jack Kelso* (1928) is Lincoln's companion, and in that verse drama Masters features the romance of Anne Rutledge and Lincoln. By exploring the Lincoln legend—first through the sensibility of the boys' novel and then through more intimate psychological accounts—Masters arrived at the 1931 biography, *Lincoln: The Man.*

So pervasive is Masters' interest in locale, however, in his last books as well as in all his work after 1920 (when he had moved to New York), that it seems almost as if he chose the Illinois heroes as a way of understanding place rather than through having been in search of heroes per se. He said of *Kit O'Brien,* "I love the town of my boyhood, its people and its ways too deeply to disparage them." More important, the understanding of locale was a means to fathom the American character. For instance, he spoke of the verse drama *Jack Kelso* as being

an appraisal of the theories and beliefs which are the enemies of the American programs. My work

. . . which began with the *Spoon River Anthology* . . . enlarges and more profoundly defines its interpretations in . . . this comprehensive study of America through the eyes of Jack Kelso, who in real life was the chum of Lincoln.

In 1931 Masters completed the Kelso story in a strange dramatic poem titled *Godbey,* which has as refrain "One's youth again and yet again is ended. . . ." Whether one views Masters' repeated return to the subjects of boyhood experience, or the re-creation of boyhood heroes and legends, as simple nostalgia or as poverty of subject matter, its presence is striking and a little frightening. It is as if those sweeping aims that he chanted so gleefully had dwindled to the kind of study a small-bodied old lady would undertake at the county records office—even though in 1933 he proclaimed:

There is a vast task for the singer of America,
And it will be the work of a great singer to find
　　the soul of America . . .

One can only set against them these more somber lines from "Brutus and Antony":

Wine, weariness, much living, early age
Made fall for Antony. October's clouds
In man's life, like October, have no sun
To lift the mists of doubt, distortion, fear.

　Aside from his dramatic verse, much of Masters' late poetry mines the same themes. Of the eight collections published between 1930 and 1942, nearly all include many poems about Illinois, Michigan, rural themes and characters; the last two books, in fact, *Illinois Poems* (1941) and *Along the Illinois* (1942), have these focuses exclusively in their largely reprinted selections. Masters' tone is that of lament: "All the good, beloved people, those/ Who drove the plow near the ford of Mussel Shells,/ Are gone. . . ." Or, as he had written earlier, "All the old hotels are vanished from America,/ All the frame hotels

in a white-housed town. . . ." His blatant oversimplification leads Masters from one exaggeration to another, blaming cities for modern evil ("Give Us Back Our Country") or blaming steamboats and railroads for America's misunderstanding of its heroes ("Andrew Jackson"). His 1936 poem "The House Where Mark Twain Was Born" clearly illustrates his simplification of ideas and of the poetry expressing them:

Are there any more old villages
Like Florida anywhere
In Missouri or Illinois,
As when Mark Twain was a boy,
And life was purest bliss, . . .
For now that we are rich in
Cities and sculptured squares
Is there now no Mark Twain kitchen
With its three or four old chairs,
Its table and cooking stove,
Where patience, laughter and love
In the humble family throve,
Where poverty had no pride,
And hence was without a fear;
Where the heart was fortified
By eyes that were calm and clear?

There are souls, if they knew enough,
Who would barter their country seat
For a cottage with such a roof,
For a hearth so humble and sweet;
Where a wonder boy might sleep,
Or dream by the kitchen stove,
And grow and laugh and keep
A simple heart through youth
For earth and life and love,
For people and for truth.

　Masters' return to end rhyme and conventional form may have been symptomatic of his need to establish firm control: the dichotomy of black/white, urban/rural, good/bad is undeniable. His angry retort to August Derleth that "Anderson can't write, never could" because

"He's always groping for what he wants to say" suggests that by the last years of his life, he needed those clear directions and that any natural ambivalence or ambiguity—the basis for most of the great writing of history—was threatening to him. This was a different stance from Masters' attitude while writing the Spoon River works and *Domesday Book,* when he was curious to see whether he could present those ambivalences. In the late poems, as in his memoirs of the Sangamon Valley and Chicago, his only desire was to return; by then his only means of returning was through memory. He says in "River Towns," in comparatively effective verse:

Far from New York by the ship-traveled sea
Stand the river-towns I knew
Changeless as memory. . . .
They speak but quiet words around the
    square. . . .

The town is memory longing for the places
Far up the river, never found
By the river's winding spaces
Which the heart forever follows.

Before his turn to retrospection was complete, Masters devoted much of his energy during the last decade of his writing career to biography. At his most cantankerous was *Lincoln: The Man* (1931); at his most worshipful, *Whitman* (1937). In 1935 he undertook a biography of Vachel Lindsay as a personal favor to Lindsay's widow; the portrait of Mark Twain (1938) he saw as an opportunity to "diagnose and cauterize . . . the American diseases which attack writers and idealists."

Masters brought to biography an ability to locate character in salient and economical details; to express character in relation to larger concerns—national well-being and promise, philosophical satisfactions; and to tell an interesting story. Sections of all four biographies show his abilities to good advantage (his first bi-

ography, *Levy Mayer and the New Industrial Era* [1927], is not included here because Masters dictated the book rather than writing it himself). On the whole, however, Masters' biographies are marred by the idiosyncratic convictions evident in his later poems. As he slants his accounts (unfavorably in the cases of Lincoln and Twain), his narratives suffer from lack of proportion and continuity. Masters emphasizes some traits, and scenes that illustrate them, and omits others. At their most critical, reviewers accused him of outright misrepresentation of evidence, intense prejudice, and diatribe.

Historians who reviewed the biographies were consistently troubled by Masters' incomplete research. He wrote without documentation, so there was no way of knowing the factual bases for his assumptions. Often, evidence that had been available for years was not included. Masters also tended to be inaccurate about dates and chronology, relying on his impressionistic prose to be convincing. In the books about Whitman and Twain, he quoted at length from material that was already accessible, and he evidently had not read any prior scholarship. The result was very little new insight, and reviewers often questioned the need for the biography.

The need for a particular book was, of course, Masters' own, and his turn to biography was part of the search for America's heroes that had dominated his fiction and verse drama during the 1920's and early 1930's. (In addition to the published work, he also wrote a verse drama about Andrew Jackson, which was performed in 1934 at the University of Chicago, and another about the Mormons, performed in 1936 at Schenectady, New York.) He had written in *American Mercury* in 1935 that it was essential "that there should be an understanding of the country's principal heroes. Not otherwise can a country have its true character."

The biography of Lincoln, coming after the many novels touching on his life and legend, is the only one of Masters' four biographies that deals with a person who is important historically rather than literarily. Written from April 29 to June 14, 1930, in Room 312 of the Chelsea Hotel in New York City, the 520-page book again illustrates Masters' prodigious ability to concentrate on the project at hand and devote himself to days of sheer physical work in completing it. One might suggest that such application may not have resulted in superior quality, but the Spoon River poems were also written in this way; it seemed to be Masters' habitual pattern.

The first sign that *Lincoln: The Man* was not intended to be complimentary was its dedication to "the memory of Thomas Jefferson, the preëminent philosopher-statesman of the United States, and their greatest president; whose universal genius through a long life was devoted to the peace, enlightenment and liberty of the union created by the Constitution of 1787." Masters is already maligning Lincoln for his unconstitutional assumption of powers, his power-seeking, as he does on page 5 of the text, where he compares him negatively with both Jefferson and Andrew Jackson (and, later, with Ralph Waldo Emerson and Whitman). The person Lincoln *can* be compared with, unfortunately, is Woodrow Wilson:

Our greatest Americans are Jefferson, Whitman and Emerson; and the praise that has been bestowed on Lincoln is a robbery of these, his superiors. Armed with the theology of a rural Methodist, Lincoln crushed the principles of free government.

Masters, in his return to the prairie years and his adolescent values, seems also to have returned to his grandfather's views of Lincoln; but the biography lays Lincoln's faults to his "neverchanging mind" and a "lack of a real passional nature." Lincoln's quiet romantic life—whether or not relevant to his performance as president—puzzled and even angered his biographer.

That Masters' last biographies—and his last major writings—were about America's great writers is indicative of a further change in direction. Just as his comparisons of Lincoln with Emerson and Whitman had indicated, Masters' hierarchies of greatness knew no categorical boundaries—Lincoln became president partly because of his ability with language; as a thinker and a writer he (like Jefferson) should therefore be judged with other men of that profession. For, Masters had finally decided, it was not military acumen or public interest that identified the American hero. He wrote in 1936, "It is possible that this life veils something deeper and truer. Poetry can penetrate this veil if any human expression can; for poetry is the most articulate, it is the profoundest, art of man."

Following this conviction, Masters wrote *Vachel Lindsay: A Poet in America,* "one of his best books." Masters' emphasis on Lindsay's search for truly American "traditions and stories of wonder" and his understanding of his friend's background made the book an important study of the development of an American poet. An emphasis new to Masters was his interest in Lindsay's mysticism (an interest that colors his subsequent biography of Whitman), the search for a "deeper reality." Whether or not this was sufficient reason to consider Lindsay a greater poet than Edgar Allan Poe, as Masters does, the book does describe the problems that the non-Eastern American writer faces in the established literary community.

In 1936 Masters wrote perhaps his most important life story, his own, filled with almost successful rationalizations presented in a blend of simple narrative and philosophical bombast that tends to disarm the reader through its candor. *Across Spoon River* has the same kind of charm that carried *Mitch Miller*. Whether or not the book establishes many truths, it conveys the author's conviction that it does. Even Carl Van Doren, who noted that Masters failed to reconcile the most apparent intellectual contradictions, praised its vitality as being "the blunt, ardent story of a troubled man finding out he was a poet."

In 1937 Masters published his most sympathetic biography, *Whitman*. Partly because Whitman echoed Jefferson's principles, partly because he was compassionate, partly because he "put into his long lines the rise and fall of his own spiritual diaphragm," partly because he revered the Greek dramatists—and there seems to be no division among those qualities in Masters' judgment—Whitman was perhaps the greatest of America's poets. Not that he reached the highest kind of poetry, for he "sang the seen—not the unseen." Although he did make "a spiritual survey of America" and saw the direction American poetry had to take, "The distinctive American poetry which Whitman wanted sung required a genius that he did not possess." Whitman's greatness, for Masters in the 1930's, rested in his being "a lover," "a prophet of democracy," "a voice raising itself in behalf of comradeship and against that spirit which withdraws, stands aside, is ashamed of tenderness, communion, fellowship."

After *Whitman* the Twain biography—which Masters was careful to distinguish as "portrait," no doubt to protect himself legally—seems anticlimactic. It is Masters at his petulant worst, comparing Twain, criticizing him solipsistically. The Twain portrait was discussed in the opening pages of this essay; and perhaps it is appropriate to come full circle, as Masters' own sympathies and interests did near the end of his career. In his biographies, instead of Spoon River characters Masters was creating the heroes of America for his readers—but he was still *creating* them; he was locating their greatness, giving them the life spark through anecdote and detail so that a reader would remember, learn, and follow. No less the moralist at the end of his career than at the beginning, Masters was still the writer as teacher more than he was the writer as craftsman, as artist.

Judged as craftsman, Masters should be praised for his characterization, especially his ability to draw people who are believable psychologically. He should be praised for his attempts to capture speech idioms, although his frequent tendency to write in blank verse made successful patterning difficult (the freshness in the language of *Mitch Miller,* as in many of the Spoon River portraits, is an example of Masters at his best). Masters was seldom content to be a miniaturist: his range was wide and, like Pieter Brueghel, he created many memorable characters. He was a willing artist—willing to try, perhaps too much; to innovate; and, repeatedly, to risk failure.

Some of these same points must also appear in a debit column, especially Masters' great self-confidence that led him to write so much—the prolix, the undistinguished, the repetitious. His tendency toward pretension paralleled his fondness for overt literary references—Masters seemed always conscious of his role as writer, which to him seemed to mean authority, on matters historical, legal, and moral. And, as authority, he gave his views with an aura of positive knowing that was, however offensively, inarguable. Roy Harvey Pearce, in *The Continuity of American Poetry,* dismisses all of Masters' work summarily because even the best of it is marked by reductionary sentimentality. More recently David Perkins, in *A History of Modern Poetry,* considers Masters as a part of the important current in the twentieth century that saw poetry as being "accessible, sympathetic, and deliberately popular."

The line between "sentimentality" and "accessibility" has shifted with patterns of literary taste for the past 2,000 years. Generally, however, the use of the word "sentimentality" as derogation suggests an excess of appeal to popular taste and—when applied to the writer's craft—the manipulation of readers by the writer. All writing offers opportunities to sentimentalize, but the great artists are those who reject the easy option, who, as Joseph Waldmeir put it, maintain

> the pattern which the story [or poem] itself dictates, leading the reader into no emotional dead ends or sloughs. And as a consequence, the emotion one feels at its end is honest and earned; for one is convinced that the story has gone exactly where it had to go in the only way possible for it to get there.

While one could say this about many of the Spoon River portraits, and about parts of *Domesday Book* and *Mitch Miller,* there is little other of Masters' work that maintains its own integrity.

Masters' late themes unfortunately led him easily into unthinking sentiment—nostalgia for the past is an almost surefire trap, partly because the characters and scenes are gauzed over with a memory that softens any dichotomies that did exist; partly because relatively simple answers did exist half a century earlier, at least in Masters' culture. Masters was increasingly the product of the Protestant, middle-class work ethic of the prairies. In 1936, even returning to that location and culture would not have brought back their viability.

During his last twenty years, however, Masters wrote and thought of very little besides that return. In the mid-1930's he wrote in his autobiography, "The prairies are in my blood for all time, and are closer to my heart than the most beautiful part of the Maine coast, or the hills of Columbia County or the mountains of Vermont, all so much more beautiful than anything in Illinois." At about the same time, in a characteristically "literary" statement, he wrote to John Cowper Powys:

> I just HONE for the prairies, and want to go there with my heart, but my mind wont [sic] let me. I know that everything I loved is gone, and much that I cannot stand has taken its place. The result is I stay here [in New York], growing more and more at the top, and less and less at the

roots, and more and more a mere voice fleeting and unlocatable. Maybe I'm Tithonus.

Tithonus, Aurora's mortal lover, enjoyed the privilege of loving the goddess of dawn; but he enjoyed his privilege too long. Aurora had asked that he be granted immortality, but she neglected to request eternal youth. When Tithonus had begun to age, she left him; and finally, when there was little left of him but a whisper of voice, she changed him into a grasshopper.

Maybe. Except that *Spoon River Anthology* remains more than a whisper; and so, perhaps, do *Mitch Miller, Domesday Book,* and, in other ways, *Whitman* and *Across Spoon River.* The rest, the nearly fifty other books that Masters gave his career to producing, can best be described as popular, as was the aesthetic from which Masters lived and wrote; and, as popular books, they will meet their timely, natural end.

Selected Bibliography

WORKS OF EDGAR LEE MASTERS

A Book of Verses. Chicago: Way & Williams, 1898.
Maximilian: A Play in Five Acts. Boston: Richard G. Badger, 1902.
The New Star Chamber and Other Essays. Chicago: Hammersmark, 1904.
The Blood of the Prophets. Chicago: Rooks Press, 1905. (Written under pseudonym Dexter Wallace.)
Althea: A Play in Four Acts. Chicago: Rooks Press, 1907.
The Trifler: A Play. Chicago: Rooks Press, 1908.
The Leaves of the Tree: A Play. Chicago: Rooks Press, 1909.
Eileen: A Play in Three Acts. Chicago: Rooks Press, 1910.
Songs and Sonnets. Chicago: Rooks Press, 1910. (Written under pseudonym Webster Ford.)

The Locket: A Play in Three Acts. Chicago: Rooks Press, 1910.

The Bread of Idleness: A Play in Four Acts. Chicago: Rooks Press, 1911.

Songs and Sonnets: Second Series. Chicago: Rooks Press, 1912. (Written under pseudonym Webster Ford.)

Spoon River Anthology. New York: Macmillan, 1915; augmented edition, 1916.

Songs and Satires. New York: Macmillan, 1916.

The Great Valley. New York: Macmillan, 1916.

Toward the Gulf. New York: Macmillan, 1918.

Starved Rock. New York: Macmillan, 1919.

Mitch Miller. New York: Macmillan, 1920.

Domesday Book. New York: Macmillan, 1920.

The Open Sea. New York: Macmillan, 1921.

Children of the Market Place. New York: Macmillan, 1922.

Skeeters Kirby. New York: Macmillan, 1923.

The Nuptial Flight. New York: Boni and Liveright, 1923.

Mirage. New York: Boni and Liveright, 1924.

The New Spoon River. New York: Boni and Liveright, 1924; with introduction by Willis Barnstone, New York: Macmillan, 1968.

Selected Poems. New York: Macmillan, 1925.

Lee: A Dramatic Poem. New York: Macmillan, 1926.

Kit O'Brien. New York: Boni and Liveright, 1927.

Levy Mayer and the New Industrial Era. New Haven: Yale University Press, 1927.

Jack Kelso: A Dramatic Poem. New York: Appleton, 1928.

The Fate of the Jury: An Epilogue to Domesday Book. New York: Appleton, 1929.

Gettysburg, Manila, Ácoma. New York: Horace Liveright, 1930.

Lichee Nuts. New York: Horace Liveright, 1930.

Lincoln: The Man. New York: Dodd, Mead, 1931.

Godbey: A Dramatic Poem. New York: Dodd, Mead, 1931.

The Serpent in the Wilderness. New York: Sheldon Dick, 1933.

The Tale of Chicago. New York: G. P. Putnam's Sons, 1933.

Dramatic Duologues: Four Short Plays in Verse. New York: Samuel French, 1934.

Richmond: A Dramatic Poem. New York: Samuel French, 1934.

Invisible Landscapes. New York: Macmillan, 1935.

Vachel Lindsay: A Poet in America. New York: Charles Scribner's Sons, 1935.

Poems of People. New York: Appleton-Century, 1936.

The Golden Fleece of California. Weston, Vermont: Countryman Press, 1936.

Across Spoon River: An Autobiography. New York: Farrar & Rinehart, 1936.

Whitman. New York: Charles Scribner's Sons, 1937.

The Tide of Time. New York: Farrar & Rinehart, 1937.

The New World. New York: Appleton-Century, 1937.

Mark Twain: A Portrait. New York: Charles Scribner's Sons, 1938.

More People. New York: Appleton-Century, 1939.

The Living Thoughts of Emerson. New York: Longmans, Green, 1940.

Illinois Poems. Prairie City, Illinois: James A. Decker, 1941.

The Sangamon. New York: Farrar & Rinehart, 1942.

Along the Illinois. Prairie City, Illinois: James A. Decker, 1942.

Posthumous Poems of Edgar Lee Masters. Austin: Humanities Research Center, University of Texas, 1969. (Selected and edited, with introduction, by Frank Kee Robinson; preface by Padraic Colum.)

CRITICAL AND BIOGRAPHICAL STUDIES

For relatively complete listings, see the chapter-end notes in Flanagan (see below) and William White, "Lindsay/Masters/Sandburg: Criticism From 1950–1975" in Hallwas and Reader (see below), pp. 114–28.

Barnstone, Willis. "Introduction" to *The New Spoon River.* New York: Macmillan, 1968.

Berthoff, Warner. *The Ferment of Realism.* New York: Free Press, 1965.

Bridgman, Richard. *The Colloquial Style in America.* New York: Oxford University Press, 1966.

Brown, Clarence. "Walt Whitman and the 'New Poetry,' " *American Literature,* 33:33–45 (1961).

Burgess, Charles E. "Masters and Whitman: A Second Look," *Walt Whitman Review,* 17:25–27 (March 1971).

Derleth, August. *Three Literary Men: A Memoir of Sinclair Lewis, Sherwood Anderson, and Edgar Lee Masters.* New York: Candlelight Press, 1963.

Duffey, Bernard. *The Chicago Renaissance in American Letters: A Critical History.* East Lansing: Michigan State College Press, 1954.

Flanagan, John T. "The Novels of Edgar Lee Masters," *South Atlantic Quarterly.* 49:82–95 (1950).

———. *Edgar Lee Masters: The Spoon River Poet and His Critics.* Metuchen, New Jersey: Scarecrow Press, 1974.

Greasley, Philip. *American Vernacular Poetry: Studies in Whitman, Sandburg, Anderson, Masters and Lindsay.* Ph.D. dissertation, Michigan State University, 1975.

Hallwas, John E., and Dennis J. Reader, eds. *The Vision of This Land.* Macomb: Western Illinois University Press, 1976. (Includes Charles E. Burgess, "Edgar Lee Masters: The Lawyer as Writer," pp. 55–73; Herb Russell, "After *Spoon River:* Masters' Poetic Development 1916–1919," pp. 74–81; and William White, "Lindsay/Masters/Sandburg: Criticism from 1950–1975," pp. 114–28.)

Hartley, Lois. "Edgar Lee Masters—Biographer and Historian," *Illinois State Historical Society. Journal,* 54:56–83 (1961).

———. *Spoon River Revisited.* Muncie, Indiana: Ball State University Press, 1963.

———. "Edgar Lee Masters—Political Essayist," *Illinois State Historical Society. Journal,* 57:249–60 (1964).

———. "The Early Plays of Edgar Lee Masters," *Ball State University Forum,* 7:26–38 (1966).

———. "Edgar Lee Masters and the Chinese," *Literature East & West,* 10:302–05 (1966).

Havighurst, Walter. *The Heartland: Ohio, Indiana, Illinois.* New York: Harper, 1956; 1974.

Herron, Ima Honaker. *The Small Town in American Literature.* Durham, North Carolina: Duke University Press, 1939.

———. *The Small Town in American Drama.* Dallas: Southern Methodist University Press, 1969.

Kramer, Dale. *Chicago Renaissance: The Literary Life in the Midwest 1900–1930.* New York: Appleton-Century, 1966.

Lowell, Amy. *Tendencies in Modern American Poetry.* Boston: Houghton Mifflin, 1917.

Masters, Ellen Coyne. "Those People of Spoon River," New York *Times Book Review,* February 12, 1950, pp. 5, 25.

Masters, Hardin W. *Edgar Lee Masters: A Centenary Memoir-Anthology.* South Brunswick, New Jersey: Barnes, for the Poetry Society of America, 1972.

Munson, Gorham. "A Comedy of Exiles," *Literary Review,* 12, no. 1:47, 49, 56 (Autumn 1968).

Nye, Russel B. *The Unembarrassed Muse.* New York: Dial Press, 1970.

Pavese, Cesare. *American Literature: Essays and Opinions,* translated by Edwin Fussell. Berkeley: University of California Press, 1970.

Pearce, Roy Harvey. *The Continuity of American Poetry.* Princeton, New Jersey: Princeton University Press, 1961.

Perkins, David. *A History of Modern Poetry.* Vol. I. Cambridge, Massachusetts: Harvard University Press, 1976.

Pizer, Donald. *Novels of Theodore Dreiser.* Minneapolis: University of Minnesota Press, 1976.

Powys, John Cowper. "Edgar Lee Masters," *Bookman,* 69:650 (August 1929).

Putzel, Max. *The Man in the Mirror, William Marion Reedy and His Magazine.* Cambridge, Massachusetts: Harvard University Press, 1963.

Robinson, Frank Kee. The Edgar Lee Masters Collection: Sixty Years of Literary History," *Library Chronicle* (University of Texas), 8:42–50 (1968).

———. "Edgar Lee Masters Centenary Exhibition: Catalogue and Checklist of Books," *Texas Quarterly,* 12, no. 1:4–69 (1969).

———. *"The New Spoon River:* Fifteen Facsimile Pages," *ibid.,* pp. 116–43.

———. "Posthumous Poems of Edgar Lee Masters," *ibid.,* pp. 70–115.

Schreiber, Georges, ed. *Portraits and Self-Portraits.* Boston: Houghton Mifflin, 1936.

Simone, Salvatore. *E. L. Masters.* Bari: Tipografia Adriatica, 1973.

Stauffer, Donald Barlow. *A Short History of American Poetry.* New York: E. P. Dutton, 1974.

Thomas, Dylan. "Dylan Thomas on Edgar Lee Masters," *Harper's Bazaar,* June 1963, pp. 68–69, 115.

Van Doren, Carl. "Behind Spoon River," *Nation,* 143:580 (November 14, 1936).

Waggoner, Hyatt. *American Poetry from the Puritans to the Present.* Boston: Houghton Mifflin, 1968.

Waldmeir, Joseph J. "John Steinbeck: No *Grapes of Wrath,*" in *A Question of Quality,* edited by Louis Filler. Bowling Green, Ohio: Popular Press, 1976. Pp. 219–28.

Yatron, Michael. *America's Literary Revolt.* New York: Philosophical Library, 1959.

—*LINDA W. WAGNER*

Samuel Eliot Morison

1887–1976

*T*HE writings of twentieth-century American historians have not matched the literary achievements of the nineteenth-century Boston gentleman-historians: George Bancroft, John Lothrop Motley, William Hickling Prescott, and Francis Parkman. These historians seized upon grand, romantic themes and developed them in multivolume works that reached a wide public. This method has been extended into the professionalized historical scholarship of the twentieth century in the long and productive career of the naval historian Samuel Eliot Morison.

"I have stuck to the antique methods of writing but also the modern idea of trying to get to the bottom of things," he said late in his career, emphasizing that "history means primarily story." Three themes clearly emerge from his more than fifty books. He wrote, first of all, with a regional interest, about the New England of his ancestors. Second, he combined his lifelong love of the sea with scholarship to write about maritime commerce and naval battles, exploration and discovery—books with the ocean always as subject and as backdrop for the human drama. Third, he wrote of great and successful men in the nation's past: of Christopher Columbus and the discovery of America, of the Puritan founders, and of naval heroes from John Paul Jones down to Admiral Raymond Spruance and the battle of Midway in World War II.

Morison was born on July 9, 1887, into one of Boston's old families, four generations removed from the famous Federalist political leader Harrison Gray Otis. He was raised in the house at the foot of Beacon Hill built by his maternal grandfather; number 44 Brimmer Street would be his residence, except during periods of travel, until his death in 1976. As a boy he took the penny ferry with other boys to nearby East Boston, to climb over the full-rigged sailing ships from distant ports. His parents vacationed each summer at Northeast Harbor, Maine. In his well-traveled life that was nevertheless rooted in New England, Morison made Northeast Harbor his summer home, and wrote that "it was there that I acquired my almost passionate love for the sea and for Mount Desert Island."

He was schooled in Greek and Latin at Noble's School in Boston and St. Paul's in Concord, New Hampshire, and grew up in surroundings rich in history. He found manuscript letter books of his great-great-grandfather, who traded in the South Seas and Hawaii, in the library of his grandfather, Samuel Eliot. This side of the family, which included Charles W. Eliot, president of Harvard, and Charles Eliot Norton, had established a place in education and literature.

Morison entered Harvard with the intention of becoming a mathematician, but foundered on calculus and was attracted instead to the distinguished history faculty, which included Albert Bushnell Hart, whose assistant he became; Edward Channing, the last historian to write a history of the United States from the original sources; and Frederick Jackson Turner, historian of the West. In Channing, Morison observed an impatience with the ideals and idealists associated with the Concord school and New England's favorite "isms"; a clear business head and the skill to get on in the academic and literary worlds; and the ability as a historian to dismiss preconceived interpretations and to study periods anew, reaching fresh conclusions. These traits were passed on to Morison, as was Channing's course on American history in the colonial period, which Morison began teaching in 1916.

Morison's association with Harvard was long. He entered in 1904, received the B.A. in 1908 and the M.A. in 1909, and was awarded the Ph.D. in history in 1913. While an assistant to Hart, he rode to and from the campus on horseback, carrying in saddlebags the papers to be graded. After forty years (1915–55) as lecturer and professor he retired from active teaching as Jonathan Trumbull professor of American history, emeritus. Into the 1970's, as he researched and wrote about the early exploration of the Americas, he retained Channing's old office, number 417 in the Widener Library.

Morison's dissertation, *The Life and Letters of Harrison Gray Otis, Federalist, 1765–1848*, a biography of his famous ancestor, was published in 1913. It was a two-volume biography of the life-and-times variety commonly associated with nineteenth-century letters, except that in addition to detailing political life, it reflected what was then a new interest of the professional historian: social history, the details of how people lived. Thus, there are accounts of society life in Boston, in Philadelphia, and in Washington during the early years, when the capital of the new democratic nation resembled an aristocratic court. (For this Morison was criticized by reviewers, for having chronicled "small beer.") Household family life, real estate speculation, political oratory, literary trends, and the taste for and means

by which wealthy Bostonians acquired Madeira wines are described and blended with accounts from family tradition.

The Federalist party declined in influence throughout Harrison Gray Otis' life, and the principal event of his political career was the ill-fated Hartford Convention at which New England states considered their right to secede during the unpopular War of 1812. Although Otis' political career was not marked by success, Morison wrote of his life:

The personality of Harrison Gray Otis was singularly well rounded and attractive. In him were blended all the qualities that make up a man beloved by men; and he was indeed beloved, during and after his lifetime, as few men have been. Sociable without dissipation, clever without affectation, brilliant without hypocrisy, he retained through years of political disappointment and domestic misfortune a genial, sunny nature that shed happiness.

The use of antithesis in this assessment is a characteristic of Morison's prose style that appears throughout his works. Normally his emphasis is on the successful—his subsequent biographies were of men of the stamp of Columbus and naval heroes like John Paul Jones. Other traits that appear in this first work are Morison's readiness to enter third-person narrative through personal observations, and his regional loyalty, combined with the ability to state strong opinions forcefully. Thus, he concluded his relation of the Hartford Convention by stating that among the New Englanders of the early nineteenth century, love of Union was stronger than in the South at midcentury, for they endured wrongs "far more real" than those of the eleven states that attempted to break up the Union.

Years later, when writing about the theories of pre-Columbian discoveries of America, Morison stated that he was not interested in "dead-end" explorers. His account of the aristocratic tendencies of the New England Federalists, a blind alley in the development of American democracy, thus was out of the mainstream of Morison's historical interest. He was no doubt attracted to his ancestor as a subject because of family and regional loyalties. But the biography is also marked with judgment and criticism. Morison was raised in the Brahmin traditions that extended from the values of the aristocratic Federalists, but he was also trained to enter a historical guild that celebrated the dual rise of nationalism and democracy. Whereas Harrison Gray Otis believed democracy would bring the leveling downward of society, and social revolution, Morison, student of Frederick Jackson Turner, who had described the development of democratic institutions on the American frontier, wrote that his ancestor would never have imagined the "self-sacrifice, endurance, and devotion to the Union that the American democracy showed fifteen years after his death." Yet Morison, in light of the corruption and anti-intellectualism of Massachusetts administrations following the passing of the Federalists, argued that although Federalist efforts may have ended in futility, they did not end in dishonor. The characteristic here that appears elsewhere in Morison's treatment of American history is that despite his rejection of the narrow view of democracy held by his ancestors, he did not abandon their aristocratic values.

Identifiable in this first work of Morison's is a personal code of sociability and compromise. Later he would select balance or *mesure* as the quality most requisite in a historian. And he would look for humor, entertainment, and satisfaction in achievement in the lives of the people about whom he wrote. He was credited with having some of the traits he admired in his ancestor. Described as a sociable man who shared his pleasures, Morison involved his friends in his sailing and entertained them at his summer home in Maine. It is told that at one dinner, wines from three different centuries were served. This example of the continuity between past and present

in Morison's life was also evident in 1906 when Professor Hart allowed him to build a course around a case of old Federalist correspondence he had found in his grandfather's wine cellar. His tastes, his attitudes, and even the documents of his first book were passed down to him through his family.

Morison revised his biography of Harrison Gray Otis for republication in 1969, omitting some of the political matter and footnotes and adding to the chapters describing the social life of the period. However, the scholarship of the fifty-six years intervening between the two editions—including treatment of the Federalists by James Truslow Adams and Charles and Mary Beard—did not lead him to change any of his original conclusions.

"The impulse for all my books has come from within myself," Morison wrote, arguing that "you cannot fascinate your readers unless you yourself are in love with the subject." In his second book, *The Maritime History of Massachusetts, 1783–1860*, Morison turned to the sea for the subject and theme of an economic-social history. Although the greatest economic-social historian, in his opinion, was Richard Henry Tawney, Morison credited Guglielmo Ferrco with teaching him the importance of social history.

But since he wished to be a historian of America and the modern age, Morison found inspiration in the career of his grandfather's friend Francis Parkman, who had written a monumental history chronicling the struggle between France and England for the possession of North America. This contest, set against the backdrop of the American wilderness, remains forever young in Parkman's work, Morison wrote:

". . . with the immortal youth of art"; his men and women are alive; they feel, think and act within the framework of a living nature. In Parkman's prose the forests ever murmur, the rapids perpetually foam and roar; the people have parts and passions. Like that "sylvan historian" on the Grecian urn, he caught the spirit of an age and fixed it for all time, "forever panting and forever young."

Parkman's grand theme was the American forest; he was not interested in the sea. Here Morison saw his opportunity. He conceived the idea of writing the maritime history of Massachusetts in 1910, and a decade later it was written in "one swoop on a wave of euphoria." The book is an exuberant presentation of life in the era of sail, and romantic in its evocation of scenes long past.

Within the framework of a flourishing maritime trade marked by cycles of depression and doomed to eventual decline, Morison presented the ports of Salem and Boston, tied by commerce to the Sandwich Islands, China, and the East Indies, and the communities of Nantucket and Gloucester, tied to the whale and the cod. Commerce, interrupted by the naval battles of the Revolution and the War of 1812, and by Jefferson's embargo, was revived by venturesome merchants opening new markets, by the ingenuity of ship designers and craftsmen, and by the fortuitous discovery of gold in California that drew the clipper ships of Massachusetts around Cape Horn to link a continental nation.

Morison described diverse customs and social issues ranging from the practice of ships' captains taking their wives to sea and the prosperous building mansions in their home ports to the punishments for common sailors, impressment, and exploitation of the foreign proletariat of the sea who manned Yankee ships when the native sons turned to manufacturing or the West for a place in life without economic enslavement. "Was Cape Cod democratic?" Morison asked a Barnstable man who had gone west before the Civil War. "Why, yes; it wasn't like Boston— everyone *spoke* to everybody else." "But was it democratic like Wisconsin?" Morison asked. "No! by no means!"

What the seamen ate and wore, how they navigated and rigged their ships, and when changes occurred in catching the cod and designing the boats and ships—such topics, many of them technical in definition and difficult to explain simply, are presented effectively, with the research and scholarly apparatus suppressed.

The technical and practical achievements that Morison highlighted reflect his bias for the study of the physical world, the verities of the senses over the ideal and the philosophical. This is best expressed where he points out that it was by virtue of the Mediterranean trade of Boston that Ralph Waldo Emerson was transported to his meeting with Thomas Carlyle and other English transcendentalists, and that a Boston merchant selling shiploads of Massachusetts ice in Asia had built a bridge between "Concord anarchy and Indian philosophy."

The heroes of *The Maritime History of Massachusetts* are practical men. One is Nathaniel Bowditch, author of one of the internationally recognized books written early in the American national history, *The Practical Navigator*. Foremost is Donald McKay, builder of the *Stag Hound, Flying Cloud, Lightning, Westward Ho!, Romance of the Seas,* and *Great Republic*—clipper ships that placed America ahead of all other nations in ship design.

The period of the clipper ship, which concluded the maritime history of Massachusetts as unique in the United States, was short-lived economically. "Far better had the brains and energy that produced the clipper ships been put into the iron screw steamer," Morison observed, for Massachusetts maritime preeminence succumbed to changes on the national scene. (But parenthetically he questioned whether Phidias would have been better employed in sanitation or Euripides in discovering the printing press.) With the triumph of the clipper ship, Morison capped his history of the maritime development and decline of his native state, for in the clipper ship he saw the finest expression of a particular culture—"the long-suppressed artistic impulse of a practical, hard-working race burst into flower." He continued: "The *Flying Cloud* was our Rheims, the *Sovereign of the Seas* our Parthenon, the *Lightning* our Amiens; but they were monuments carved in snow. For a brief moment of time they flashed their splendor around the world, then disappeared with the sudden completeness of the passenger pigeon."

The Maritime History of Massachusetts is filled with the action of the whaling chase and vessels scudding before the wind on record runs, with salty language, snatches from ballads, and sea anecdotes. It contains panoramic word pictures of ports from Salem to Canton. This book was the first Morison wrote with the ocean as his subject, the theme he would develop over a lifetime. For energy and vividness it is an effort he would not surpass.

At age thirty-four Morison obtained a leave of absence from Harvard to become Harmsworth professor of American history at Oxford University. With his family (he had married Elizabeth Shaw Greene in 1910) he spent 1922–25 abroad. In England he sought out the villages of Ipswich, Dedham, Groton, and Braintree, whose people had settled Massachusetts Bay Colony. On his return journey to the United States, Morison acquainted himself with the archive materials on Christopher Columbus, and in Toledo he was impressed with the age and continuity of the institutions of Spain. In the United States, where all institutions are relatively young, his alma mater, Harvard College, was the oldest corporation and would shortly celebrate its tercentenary. Why not be the historian of Harvard, he asked; proposed the same to President Abbott Lowell of Harvard; and was forthwith appointed official historian.

Morison also contracted to write a history of the United States for a British audience. *The Oxford History of the United States, 1783–1917*, published in 1927, was history written as past politics—primarily a political history of the nation, but with considerable emphasis on naval matters. It details American geography, features of the Constitution, and such political institutions as the Supreme Court with which his audience would not be familiar. One of the virtues of this history is the effective use of quotations; Morison blends the general with the particular by assessing the character of statesmen through the words of their contemporaries, drawn from personal letters, and presenting partisan viewpoints from the mouths of their authors.

As in all Morison's histories, candid views directly stated are in evidence; for instance, he describes the Federalists, about whom he had written sympathetically before, as being an "oligarchy of wealth and talent" that was not sufficiently "broad or deep" and that "passed into a minority party which contained more talent and virtue, with less practical common sense, than any of their successors." Writing about John Adams, who lacked social grace in almost the same proportion that Harrison Gray Otis possessed it, Morison said: "The Adams family have generally been right, but they are uncommonly disagreeable about it."

The history also emphasized political oratory, the Senate debates, and the inaugural addresses that gave definition to the politics of the nineteenth century. And it cast in dramatic form particular episodes in the nation's past. One was the duel between Alexander Hamilton and Aaron Burr, which in dramatic miniature marked the death of an aristocratic concept of what would become, instead, a democratic America. "So perished one of the greatest men of the age, for his little faith in the government he had formed and in the people he had served so well," Morison wrote of Hamilton. The scene at Appomattox is told in dramatically sketched phrases. Lincoln's assassination breaks upon the pages in numbed passages drawn from the secret diary of

Gideon Welles, who served as Lincoln's secretary of the navy.

The material in Morison's *Oxford History* was the basis for his contribution to a successful collaboration with Henry Steele Commager on a textbook of American history, *The Growth of the American Republic*. Published in 1930, this book has been read by generations of college students in its six editions. Morison was responsible for the material up to the Civil War; and in later editions, which included more sympathetic pictures of Indians, Mormons, and other minorities, he assumed responsibility for the chapters on World War II.

In 1930–36, Morison's scholarship focused on the Puritans of the seventeenth century. In the decade following World War I, it had become fashionable to denigrate the Puritans. Amid changing manners and mores, and liberalized attitudes toward sex and entertainment, the term "puritan" was used as a symbol of the repressive elements in American culture. H. L. Mencken defined puritanism as "the haunting fear that someone, somewhere, may be happy." In literary circles it became fashionable to view colonial American literature as particularly barren and to condemn puritanism as the explanation of why particular American artists had been stymied in their careers and why American literature generally had not developed to its potential. James Truslow Adams, then considered the foremost scholar of New England, Brooks Adams, and others accepted the label "glacial period" to describe a century of New England's cultural history. This label was derived from a book by Charles Francis Adams, *Massachusetts, Its Historians and Its History* (1893), in which he wrote that following the banishment of Anne Hutchinson, "a theological glacier . . . slowly settled down upon Massachusetts."

Almost as though he had set out to demonstrate that for once the Adamses were wrong, Morison's study of the Puritan leaders, Harvard College, and the education and culture of the colonial period argues that whatever the sins that may be laid to puritanism as a cultural force in the nineteenth century, the seventeenth-century Puritans were courageous people who, within the framework of a theological view of the world that is no longer shared in the twentieth century, lived intellectually stimulating lives and developed institutions that sustained science and literature. Along with Vernon L. Parrington, whose *Main Currents in American Thought: The Colonial Mind, 1620–1800* (1927) reassessed the development of political thought through the letters of colonial America, Morison shared a renewed appreciation of the Puritan mind that scholars such as Perry Miller, Edmund Morgan, and Bernard Bailyn have sustained down to the present.

Builders of the Bay Colony, published in 1930, treats biographically a selection of people in the first generation of the Massachusetts Bay Colony whose lives appealed most to Morison. They represented various aspects of life: adventurers, an artist, a lawyer and wit, an educator, the evangelical John Eliot, and the poet Anne Bradstreet. Seeking to describe the Puritans truthfully, yet in modern terms, he defined their moral preciseness and recognized their high sincerity of purpose and integrity in life. Even as he did not often find among them "breadth of mind," Morison did find "a spiritual depth that belongs only to the great ages of religious experience." He recorded an account in John Winthrop's journal in which a man who spoke ill of the colony left it, and was followed by the Lord, whose justice was visited upon him when madness overtook one daughter and two of his children were abused sexually. "That is the kind of statement which flies up in your face when you are beginning to think the Puritans were pretty good fellows," Morison wrote, showing "us what a chasm separates the thoughts of even the best men of that time and persuasion, from ourselves."

As for the allegation that Puritans took a morbid interest in sex, Morison discussed the sexual outbreaks, which Puritan chroniclers frankly detailed and ascribed to the influence of the devil, in terms of the coarse origins of the indentured servants, their hard labor, and the late marriages their indentures necessitated. He concluded that the same troubles occurred in Virginia, and for the same reasons; and with respect to superstition and coarseness, the New England Puritan "was no better nor worse than the average educated Englishman of the time."

The emphasis of *Builders of the Bay Colony*, however, is on those who were not coarsened by the harsh conditions of a frontier colony and were not confined by narrowness of thought. John Winthrop and John Eliot lived long, full lives; and Henry Dunster founded Harvard College, an institution that would grow with New England although he, for the independence of his religious beliefs, was severed from the school. Anne Bradstreet, a housewife and mother, employed the adversity of a new land to her spiritual advantage and in her religion furthered creative art.

In 1935 *The Founding of Harvard College* was published, followed a year later by the two-volume *Harvard College in the Seventeenth Century*. Unlike the brick-and-mortar variety of institutional history common with universities, Morison attempted to blend social and intellectual history, describing the development of curricula and inaugural pageantry, and the relationship of town and gown, as well as the board and lodging of undergraduates, their spring pranks, and their sports. A separate volume, published in 1936, *Three Centuries of Harvard* (1636–1936), also was written for Harvard's tercentenary celebration and intended not as a reference book but, rather, to be read and enjoyed by a larger audience, especially the returning alumni. This book emphasizes the role of the great presidents in Harvard's development and traces the early and faithful adherence of the institution to the principle of academic freedom as one of the reasons for Harvard's twentieth-century attainments and stature. These three books were Morison's first experience in blending three different types of history: official, academic, and popular.

Also in 1936 Morison published *The Puritan Pronaos: Studies in the Intellectual Life of New England in the Seventeenth Century,* a more explicit rebuttal than he had written before to the critics of early Puritanism. Examining the schools, printing, libraries, sermons, histories, and verse of New England Puritans, and specifically excluding the works of those born or schooled in England, Morison asserted that there is evidence of an "early flowering" of New England in the seventeenth century.

The attack on Puritanism in the post-World War I period was but one of the literary fashions to which Morison was impervious. Another was the biographical debunking of great men. Historians had long since rejected the "great man" theory of history, as had such nineteenth-century champions as Thomas Carlyle, thus clearing the way for what they took to be the scientific study of economic and social forces. Lytton Strachey set the tone for postwar disillusionment in leadership with his short and brilliant *Eminent Victorians* and his *Queen Victoria*. These works, emphasizing brevity of expression and insight into the psychological motivations of their subjects, were the models for a host of American books that more ponderously removed the mother of George Washington from the saintly ranks and distinguished between the "man and the myth" in treatments of Washington and other early national heroes. Morison's view of the debunkers and the dialectical materialists also writing in the 1920's and 1930's was that they would "admit of no high-mindedness, no virtue, no nobility of character . . . ," and that "by robbing the people of their heroes, by insulting their folk-memory of great figures," they drove people away from written history.

There were, however, other trends in biography that developed in the 1930's. Morison contributed more than two dozen pieces, some of them lengthy ones on important figures, to the *Dictionary of American Biography*. Although he felt he was given a choice of secondary New Englanders with whom James Truslow Adams did not choose to bother, some of the interesting figures he did do are Elbridge Gerry (Harrison Gray Otis' counterpart in the Democratic politics of Massachusetts), Fisher Ames, James Otis, William Bradford, and Squanto.

Also indicative of the rising interest in the study of American subjects were a number of long biographies published in this period. Douglas Southall Freeman's biography of Robert E. Lee, Carl Van Doren's *Benjamin Franklin*, and Allan Nevins' biographies of Grover Cleveland, John Charles Frémont, and John D. Rockefeller were examples of a return to a type of biography very much like the life-and-times variety of the nineteenth century, yet combined scholarly diligence with a celebration of important and successful Americans. Morison, researching the voyages of Christopher Columbus in the late 1930's, participated in this nationalistic trend in American letters that extended from the Great Depression through the Cold War of the 1950's.

Morison's biography of Columbus, *Admiral of the Ocean Sea: A Life of Christopher Columbus*, was published in 1942; but as far back as 1916 he had decided that he would sail to the West Indies and check Columbus' landfalls and coastings. Twenty years later he did so, cruising on a racer to the Windward and Leeward Islands. In 1939 Morison organized the Harvard Columbus Expedition, which sailed on the *Capitania*, a three-masted schooner yacht, and the *Mary Otis*, a ketch, to Spain and then retraced Columbus' route across the Atlantic to the West Indies. Again in the summer of 1940 he sailed in the *Mary Otis* to the Bahamas and around Cuba.

In this activity Morison was following the practice of the historian he so much admired, Francis Parkman. Parkman, fighting against a bodily constitution subject to nervous collapse and the bookish routine of a scholar's life, sought to live a life of action like that of the soldiers and explorers about whom he wrote. Thus, as a historian he made a practice of personally visiting the North American sites—forts, battlegrounds, encampments, and points of discovery—where history was made by the people about whom he would write. His sojourn among the Sioux in 1846, which is described in *The California and Oregon Trail*, was his attempt personally to realize, among Indians west of the line of settlement, the experience of the Jesuit missionaries whose relations with the Great Lakes tribes he would record in two volumes. Parkman also made expeditions into the New England forests, visited the ruins of Fort Ticonderoga, and lived briefly among the Passionist monks of Rome. As a result the pages of his histories are enriched by vivid scenes and a sense of personal experience, qualities that have made his work endure. Such visits are a romantic activity that bespeaks a strong identification between the historian and the subject upon whose footprints he stands while contemplating the dramatic past. But they are also a practical activity, for the terrain is one of the primary documents on which are etched clues to the campaigns of generals, the routes of explorers.

Morison admired Parkman's going into the wilderness before writing about it. The sea was a subject that had not received much attention from American historians. Much land surface, because of growth and technology, was unrecognizable, greatly changed from what it was a century before. The one thing unchanged since Columbus' day was the ocean, and, Morison observed, "I was willing to ask questions of it." On the Harvard Columbus Expedition 10,000 miles were logged, and all the European ports and islands Columbus visited were examined.

More than thirty places in the New World touched by Columbus were identified. Rough waters in a section of ocean described in the abstract of Columbus' journal were confirmed when the rudder of one of the vessels of the expedition was disengaged; Columbus' sighting of a mourning dove far out at sea was similarly matched on the expedition, though Morison had previously been told that Columbus was in error.

The work of the expedition allowed Morison to make a reevaluation of Columbus as a seaman and navigator. Columbus not only showed the way to the New World; but in his four voyages to the West Indies he located, for those who would follow him, the fastest seasonal routes. He successfully navigated the uncharted shallow waters of the Caribbean, where he read and avoided the hurricane winds of the region. The second, third, and fourth voyages "even more than the first," Morison concluded, "proved him to be the greatest navigator of his age."

This determination was the directly practical yield of Morison's site visits; and just as Parkman identified with the active life of the forest heroes, Morison identified with Columbus. (He wrote that the "*Nina* was the Admiral's favorite and so mine.") The result is an exposition of Columbus' character that is as interesting as his examination of the man as a navigator. Morison looked in vain for reminiscent passages in Columbus' writings; Columbus was too much the man of action. He checked the admiral's few celestial observations, found them cockeyed, and concluded that "Columbus was not conscious of the stars."

Unlike most sailors—and indeed, like most men until the eighteenth-century Romantic shift in aesthetic sensibilities—Columbus did have an aesthetic appreciation for the landscape around him. Morison celebrated those few remarks that come down to us, such as Columbus' comments on the "savor of the mornings" or fine weather "like April in Andalusia." Columbus was not a celestial navigator, but a dead-reckoning naviga-

tor, sailing with log and line, his eyes trained to messages in the clouds and on the surface of the sea. And so Morison, in tracing Columbus' routes and landfalls, traced also vivid pictorial scenes: for instance, at dawn, approaching an island in the West Indies, the island is a vague shadow, a dark shape against the celestial sphere, that takes substance, form, and color— gray, green, and finally a blue lighter than the sea.

Defects in Columbus' character were his pride, strong will, and stubborn persistence, qualities that made him a poor administrator; but he was without defect in his most important quality, his seamanship. A man of vast ambition who was assailed by circumstance both early and late in life, he nonetheless, Morison concluded, had a happy life.

In this biography Morison generally removed from the reader's view the scholarship that stands behind his account, except in two respects. At points of unresolved controversy he often presented the contending sides and let the reader judge for himself, or asserted an unequivocal argument of his own based on an appeal to common sense. There is, for instance, the famous anecdote of the egg that Columbus, in a playful contest, stood on end (by crushing it slightly), demonstrating to the critical nobility there assembled that *after* a discovery is made, such as Columbus' discovery of the New World, people think how easy it is and that anyone might have done it. It is too good a story to pass up; but whereas Washington Irving in his biography of Columbus claimed that "the universal popularity of this anecdote is proof of its merit," Morison noted that "unfortunately the egg story had already done duty in several Italian biographies." Morison also let the "seagoing scholarship," the insights resulting from extensive nautical experience and from the experience of sailing the same waters Columbus sailed, intrude in the narrative. This lends an authenticating stamp, as if to say: "I know; I was there." These intrusions keep the biography personal in tone, as does an informality of organization that admits digressions to reconcile accounts, weave in stories and sea traditions, and describe the routines on a sailing ship.

Admiral of the Ocean Sea was one of the two central works of Morison's career. It was preceded by two books that came out of the preliminary research: *The Second Voyage of Columbus* (1939) and *Portuguese Voyages to America in the Fifteenth Century* (1940). A scholarly two-volume edition, containing citations and a thorough review of such questions as whether syphilis was of New World or Old World origin, was issued along with the trade edition of *Admiral of the Ocean Sea,* which has been translated into five European languages. Morison returned to his Columbus material in 1955 to write a simplified life of Columbus for young readers, *Christopher Columbus, Mariner;* and in 1964, after a photographic reconnaissance flight over the islands discovered by Columbus, he published with Mauricio Obregon an illustrated book, *The Caribbean as Columbus Saw It.* In 1942 Morison received his first Pulitzer Prize, for his life of Columbus. As his biography of Harrison Gray Otis had served as his introduction into academic circles early in his career, his biography of Columbus opened doors for him during World War II, when he sailed with the United States Navy, taking notes and holding interviews for his multivolume history of the Navy at war. Though to ship commanders, from the point of view of fighting effectiveness, Morison was merely an extra body on the bridge, they welcomed this middle-aged lieutenant commander on their ships; he was the biographer of Columbus.

The first door opened by the Columbus biography was that of President Franklin Delano Roosevelt. Morison enjoyed telling of how he came to be appointed "historian of naval operations." As with his previous appointment as official historian of Harvard, the idea originated with him.

He could point out that the Navy history of World War I was not begun until after the fighting ended and that it was still not completed as the country, more than twenty years later, was again at war. He was fifty-four years old and in good health, possessed the requisite historical and practical maritime training, and was anxious to apply his "Columbus technique" to naval warfare. He had been an undergraduate at Harvard when Roosevelt was there, though not in the same class, and had served on a committee giving advice on presidential papers.

In an interview it took but ten minutes to get the approval of the president; and Morison, who had served for a few months as an Army private during World War I, was commissioned a lieutenant commander in the Naval Reserve attached to the secretary of the navy, Frank Knox. This relatively low rank, linked with high connections, gave him access to records and reports he desired, permitted him to sail in the naval operations of his choice, and allowed him to work with a staff of his own choosing. He extracted from the Navy the agreement that, apart from security regulations, he was not to be censored, nor was he required to publish until the war was over, when the records of the enemy navies would be available. Thus the war years found Morison sailing on the Atlantic and the Pacific, gathering impressions and checking reports, conscious that like Thucydides, the historian of the Peloponnesian War, he was participating in, and would write the history of, a war greater and more memorable than any previous one.

Morison crossed the Atlantic on the U.S.S. *Buck* in the summer of 1942, returned to an antisubmarine patrol out of Boston, and crossed the Atlantic again in October on the U.S.S. *Brooklyn* for an eyewitness view of the landings in North Africa. Twice more during the war he crossed to Europe, including a reconnaissance, shortly after they had been secured, of the landing beachheads of Provence. In the Pacific he coasted Papua in a torpedo boat. Morison participated in the Solomons campaign, ran "up the slot" at Rabaul, and was present at operations in Guadalcanal, the Gilberts and the Marshalls, the Marianas, Leyte Gulf, and Okinawa. He was on board a vessel struck by a torpedo and eyewitness to night battles at sea, island bombardments, and kamikaze attacks.

The model for Morison's historical method during this time was Thucydides, who had written: "Of the events of the war, I have not ventured to speak from any chance information, nor according to any notion of my own; I have described nothing but what I either saw myself, or learned from others of whom I made the most careful and particular inquiry." Operations in which Morison was unable to participate were covered by several assistants (ensigns, for the most part, who had been his students at Harvard). "My method was to participate in an operation," he wrote, "then settle down at some naval base, read all the action reports I could obtain, write a preliminary draft, file it for future use, and then shove off on another operation." Thucydides observed that "eyewitnesses of the same occurrence gave different accounts of them as they remembered." Morison learned from his experience the importance of oral testimony as opposed to official reports, and the value of visual observation, even though the eye is not always infallible. In a night battle, for instance, he had seen two burning enemy ships where Japanese records available after the war demonstrated that it was one ship blown in half.

Thucydides feared that "the strictly historical character" of his narrative "may be disappointing to the ear." Morison, concluding his account of the battles of Savo, Guadalcanal, and Tassafaronga, addresses the reader with the explanation that "if this tale has seemed repetitious with shock and gore, exploding magazines, burning and sinking ships and plummeting planes—that is simply how it was." Thucydides believed that

a "true picture of events which have happened" would prove useful, since similar events "may be expected to happen hereafter in the order of human things." Similarly, Morison believed in the utility of his enterprise and found in it military lessons and examples of the significance of sea power that would remain valid even in a nuclear age.

His participation in the war gave him insight, Morison believed, into the military mind, and an appreciation and perspective from which to judge the personalities of naval leaders. There were "fewer duds in the U.S. Navy," he said, "than on the Harvard faculty." Observing the near miss of many torpedoes and the unsought opportunities and problems that presented themselves to commanders at sea, he was impressed with the role that chance played in warfare. A corollary of this was his belief that experienced commanders who suffered defeat in battle would often prove able if given a second chance.

Three times during the war Morison had interviews with President Roosevelt, who continued to be interested in the history project. Morison sent his preliminary drafts of the operation against French Morocco and "The Battle of the Atlantic" to the president and Secretary Knox for their comments. In June 1944, Roosevelt wrote to the new secretary of the navy, James Forrestal, suggesting that "the performances of the P.T. squadrons should be made subject of a separate chapter of U.S. Naval history." Forrestal replied that he could not learn of Morison's plans because Morison was in the Pacific for the next month, but told the president that he had instructed Morison to comply with the president's request. Morison's reply to this order to do what he probably had already intended was written with the complaint attitude of a naval officer to his superior ("I am fully prepared," he wrote), but also with the chary independence of a professional historian ("to give them [P.T. squadrons] their due place in Naval History.").

Believing a large staff would sap his energies, Morison kept his to a minimum during the war. After the war, as the fifteen volumes of the *History of United States Naval Operations in World War II* came out at the rate of better than one a year from 1947 to 1962, his staff numbered an average of two clerical and two professional assistants. The German and Japanese records were made available in 1946. Officers of enemy navies were interviewed, as were those of the French navy, with whom Morison examined the coast of Normandy in 1951. The beachheads of Sicily and Tokyo Harbor were among the overseas sites that Morison visited after the war; in the United States he divided his time between Boston; the naval station in Newport, Rhode Island; Washington, D.C.; and Northeast Harbor, Maine.

The first two volumes, *The Battle of the Atlantic* and *Operations in North African Waters,* which came out in 1947, included a description of the jurisdictional rivalry between the Army and Navy in the conduct of antisubmarine warfare. In the subsequent volumes that appeared during the 1950's, the services, including the Air Force, were depicted as engaged in a rivalry sometimes called "the battle of the budget." The lessons shown in Morison's history could be used to support the Navy's push for the construction of an expensive carrier fleet; and the image of the Navy was further enhanced as the result of the production, by Morison's foremost wartime assistant, Henry Solomon, Jr., of the successful documentary television series "Victory at Sea." The official Army history, *United States Army in World War II,* which has run to more than threescore volumes, and shorter multivolume series by the Air Force and Marines, appeared during this period; but they were written by groups of historians for a professional audience and did not rival Morison's work in popularity.

The publication of the third volume, *The Rising Sun in the Pacific,* describing the attack on Pearl Harbor, drew Morison into a vituperative debate over the responsibility for this defeat. He wrote that a few days before the attack, the Chicago *Tribune* "had 'patriotically' published to the world" the United States' basic war plan, "as evidence of the 'duplicity' and 'war mongering' of the Roosevelt Administration." The *Tribune* responded with an editorial headlined "A Hired Liar," in which it argued that Roosevelt maneuvered the Japanese into firing the first shot. The editorial concluded with this comment on Morison: "He is doing his job as his patrons would want it done. A hired liar knows what's expected for his pay." The Navy's response was that Morison's history was not an "official" history. Morison, no longer on active duty, was writing it under contract, with the royalties going to the Navy for the research and writing of United States naval history.

Morison insisted that the opinions and judgments expressed in the history were his own and, unlike the histories of the other armed services, it did not pass before a board of review. He stood by his account of the Pearl Harbor disaster, relying on the massive testimony and findings of the congressional investigation. Moreover, he carried the argument into the ranks of the professional historians, challenging, in an article in the *Atlantic Monthly* titled "History Through a Beard," Charles A. Beard, the foremost of the revisionist historians who argued that Pearl Harbor was the result of a conscious and deliberate design on the part of the Roosevelt administration. Morison's naval history was, as he claimed, not an official history in the usual sense of the word; but charges that he was writing as a "court historian" were not unfounded either. His characteristic view and sympathies were closely allied with those of the administration.

Morison was not indifferent to the perils of writing contemporary history. Each new printing of his Navy volumes included corrections of errors, notice of which he sought from his readers.

He was, however, proud of those narratives, such as that of Savo Island, which remained virtually unchanged. Morison was aware that he shared in the emotions as well as the scenes of the war. Of Guadalcanal he wrote that he could not "pretend to write of that stinking island" with "detachment and objectivity." Having had a part in the "torment and the passion," he sometimes felt he was "writing not for the present or for posterity" but for the ghosts of those who died on the island.

This sense of involvement, although it detracts from Morison's attempt to give a detached assessment of the war leaders, permeates the history and is one of its chief virtues. Battles are viewed from the perspective of the grand strategy, but also through the eyes of a seaman, a submarine skipper on patrol, sailors on deck anticipating the enemy as battle nears. In addition to using point of view to dramatic advantage, Morison employed his descriptive sense, giving the reader grand scenes of the wartime Atlantic and Pacific, as well as night gunfire actions of a kind "that we may never see again." Some of the best of the writing, such as the fast-paced battles he describes in volume XII, *Leyte,* may simply be described as sea action.

The heroes of the series are the principal strategists on the American side, Adm. Ernest King ("best naval strategist and organizer in our history") and Adm. Chester Nimitz. In the early volumes the commander of the German U-boats, Adm. Karl Doenitz, emerges as the most significant personality, and Adm. Isoroku Yamamoto is rated as the most competent adversary. Of the sea admirals Morison found no equal to Raymond Spruance. The completed series was dedicated to Franklin Roosevelt, who gave inspired leadership, in Morison's opinion, and, unlike Winston Churchill, "never imagined himself to be a strategist."

Morison regarded his fifteen volumes on the U.S. Navy as his greatest challenge as a historian, and believed that they were regarded as his most important work. Except for research delegated to his assistants on minor operations such as submarine patrols, and much exacting correspondence and checking of data, he did all the research himself, going directly to the sources. And the writing was his own. His decision, contrary to the practice of the other armed services, to keep a small staff, and the decision of the Navy to commit its history to one man rather than committees of historians, was vindicated by the result. Morison's favorite narratives from these volumes, it is said, were those operations in which he participated. He later chose the action-filled chapter "The Battle off Samar" to be included in a volume of writings selected from his career.

As with his history of Harvard and his biography of Columbus, Morison followed his multivolume history of the Navy in World War II with a single-volume condensation in 1963, in order to make his scholarship available to an even wider audience. *The Two-Ocean War,* as befitted a popular history, was dedicated not to the war leaders, but to the wartime shipmates with whom Morison had sailed on eight different vessels. A naval history containing allusions to the great naval strategist Albert Thayer Mahan, but also to Ossian, John Milton, and Sophocles, it strives, even more than the multivolume version, to include the personalized sentiments of wartime.

Morison's history of the U.S. Navy, a labor of twenty years, gave him the opportunity to realize the injunction of Polybius, that a historian should be a man of action. Of all his works it drew the greatest comment and criticism. It confounds the categories into which the separate varieties of history have been divided within the professionalized history writing of the twentieth century. It is an official history that escaped committee authorship and the imprimatur of a review board, and came to command professional respect and have a wide audience. It is contemporary history that draws together official, scholarly, and popular history.

While Morison was engaged in writing his Navy volumes, he was author or editor of eight other books. The period following his retirement from teaching in 1955 was especially productive, and was also a time in which he gathered honors. In 1951 he was placed on the Navy's honorary retired list with the rank of rear admiral. The year before, he had been elected president of the American Historical Association. In 1960 he received a second Pulitzer Prize; he traveled to Rome in 1963 to receive, along with Pope John XXIII, the Balzan Award; and he was awarded the Presidential Medal of Freedom in 1964.

Morison's presidential address before the American Historical Association, "Faith of an Historian," was included in *By Land and by Sea,* a volume of his selected essays (1953). And his receipt of the Balzan Award occasioned a similar volume, *Vistas of History* (1964), containing an essay titled "The Experiences and Principles of an Historian." These two works clarify his attitude toward twentieth-century trends in historical writing.

Morison claimed to have observed early in his career the frustration of Henry Adams in his search for a law of history, and therefore concentrated on human experience as a historian, not concerning himself overly with a philosophy of history. He relied on Thucydides' definition of history as being without romance, a "true picture of events which have happened," and the dictum of the nineteenth-century German historian Leopold von Ranke, that history should simply explain an event "exactly as it happened." Armed with this intention, he believed, the historian, in his desire to instruct and please, could maintain his professional integrity, giving his work artistic form without falsifying in the manner of popularizers and amateurs determined to prove a thesis or write a best-seller.

Holding to this view of history writing, Morison spoke out against the progressive thinking among professional historians that reasoned that history writing, reflecting as it does the needs and aspirations of the time in which it is produced, should be consciously enlisted in the struggle for social progress. The relativist view of history, recognized as the "new history" of James Harvey Robinson at the turn of the century and brilliantly articulated by Carl Becker, became dangerous, in Morison's opinion, as practiced by Charles A. Beard. Beard's earlier presidential address to the same body of historians, "Written History as an Act of Faith," argued that a historian should write history with a "frame of reference" consistent with the sort of future America he wanted. Admitting that a historian's own values enter into his selection of facts, and that there is no such thing in history as scientific objectivity, Morison nevertheless insisted that it was the historian's prime duty to present, to the best of his ability, a body of ascertained fact.

Morison believed that the historian was obliged to give advice when the past gave insight to which statesmen and the public were blind. In this vein he admonished his fellow historians for ignoring the significance of war in the nation's past, claiming that through the pacifism and disillusionment they reflected in the period after World War I, they shared in responsibility for the country's unpreparedness at the outbreak of World War II. "War does accomplish something . . . is better than servitude," and has been "an inescapable aspect of the human story," he said; and historians should have known this.

Historians, Morison felt, were losing their influence with the public. He ascribed this in part to the abandonment and flouting of tradition by the debunkers, followed by historians attracted to dialectical materialism, with the result that there was "the mass murder of historical characters" by those who would acknowledge no great men capable of high-mindedness, nobility, or virtue. Though he saw debunking and Marxism as enthusiasms in the profession that reached the greatest influence in the two decades between the wars, Morison counseled historians to pay respect to traditions and to folk memory, "to deal gently with your people's traditions." And though his commitment to biography remained strong from the 1950's to the 1970's, the fashionable interest in psychohistory did not touch him. Neither did the catchwords that indicated shifts in historiographic interest during this period—"ambiguity," "complexity," "paradox," "ambivalence," "irony"—enter his writings significantly.

The relationship of historians to the reading public concerned Morison. During the 1930's, Allan Nevins led a discussion about the status of historical writing, which appeared to him as polarized between books by popularizers and books by pedants. Concerned that good historical scholarship was failing to reach a wide public, Nevins, Carl Becker, Douglas Southall Freeman, and others lent support to the creation of a popular, illustrated history magazine, an effort that resulted in *American Heritage* magazine. Morison's support of this view was largely by example. He conceded that modern history writing, especially social history, placed additional demands of form and style on the historian. Moreover, he believed it was all the more necessary to write well because the classical education one could once expect of the reading public was gone. "The common knowledge that one could assume in 1901, has slipped away," he wrote, "driven out by the internal-combustion engine, nuclear fission, and Dr. Freud."

In the 1940's Morison wrote for the students in his graduate seminar an essay, *History as a Literary Art,* which was published as an Old South pamphlet and as part of his contribution to the *Harvard Guide to American History*. Clarity, vigor, and objectivity were defined as the three

prime qualities of historical composition. He admitted there were no special rules for writing history, and warned against the fallacy of thinking that facts speak for themselves. "Most of the facts that you excavate from the archives, like all relics of past human activity, are dumb things," Morison counseled, requiring "proper selection, arrangement, and emphasis." His advice was to "assume that you are writing for intelligent people who know nothing about your particular subject but whom you wish to interest and attract." This was his own practice in the postwar period, following the death of his first wife and his remarriage: he read aloud the drafts of his work to Priscilla Barton Morison, his second wife, who was a generation younger than himself, and relied on her comments and criticism.

Morison's advice to young historians was to read the Greek and Latin classics. Better than the science of psychology, he thought, they give insight into the ways of men, and they dispel provincialism. The great historical stylists, such as Parkman, Prescott, and John Fiske, benefited from the study of Latin and Greek as "superb instruments of thought" that enabled them to develop clear and forceful styles in English. The moral laws of ancient Greece are "the creative forces in our own civilization," Morison believed; and education should strive for a vision of excellence instead of conforming to the values of the average. He described the educational philosophy of John Dewey as the ugly duckling "which continues to befoul American education to this day," and said it was hatched out of the anti-intellectualism of Jacksonian democracy—a society "contemptuous of the artist and the scholar." Morison advised historians, in addition to writing on subjects of national and international interest, to write local history, for it served to integrate the historian with the community, so that he would not be viewed as just another professor.

In the postwar period three short books by

Morison were of local interest. *The Ropemakers of Plymouth* (1950) surveyed the 125-year history of the Plymouth Cordage Company. *The Story of Mount Desert Island, Maine* (1960) was an affectionate account of the history and people of the island. *One Boy's Boston: 1887–1901,* published in 1962, describes late nineteenth-century Boston. It contains Morison's favorite stories from childhood, with anecdotes of old-rip relatives, the Otises (who "did nothing in particular. And did it very well"), Eliots, and personalities from Boston society and Boston streets.

During the postwar period Morison edited several books: *The Parkman Reader* (1955), Prescott's *History of the Conquest of Peru* (1957), and *Journals and Other Documents on the Life and Voyages of Christopher Columbus* (1963). Most important of his edited books was William Bradford's *Of Plymouth Plantation* (1952), which Morison introduced to a much wider audience than had read the previously available editions containing the abbreviations and variant spellings of the original manuscript. Treating Bradford as a modern editor would the plays of Shakespeare or the King James Bible, Morison made the work conform to modern practices of spelling and capitalization, but omitted nothing and gave scrupulous respect to Bradford's actual language.

Morison published a small volume of essays titled *Spring Tides* in 1965. Describing his feeling for the sea, he wrote, was "almost as embarrassing as making a confession of religious faith." The subjects of these discursive essays are the tides, yacht design, people, a summer cruise, and the sea literature of the ancients. Morison brought a unique appreciation to the classical poets of Greece and Rome. Their works were accurate in nautical technique, he argued, in contrast with modern sea poetry, which invariably contains landlubberly mistakes. He rated Aeschylus' description of the battle of Salamis—a battle in which Aeschylus took part—as the finest narrative of a naval battle in all literature. Aeschylus knew the sea firsthand better than any Greek poet but Homer, in Morison's opinion. Homer's power to set an ocean scene in a few words was improved on by Virgil, who, with Dante, wrote the best maritime poetry. In contrasting the modern sentiments of the sea life, including his own recreational sailing, with that of the ancients, Morison identified the central motif of the ancients as "the waves of the sea, laden with suffering."

In the postwar period Morison wrote two biographies of naval heroes, *John Paul Jones: A Sailor's Biography* (1959) and *Old Bruin: Commodore Matthew C. Perry, 1794–1858* (1967). They make an interesting contrast. On-site research for both was conducted while collecting materials for his World War II Navy history, his travels taking him to London, Scotland, France, Mexico, and twice to Japan and the Far East. As a result both books are scenic, as usual, but are especially rich in dramatic and exotic settings: John Paul Jones's *Bonhomme Richard* engaging the H.M.S. *Serapis* within sight of the chalk cliffs of Flamborough Head, Commodore Perry's black-hulled ships anchored in Tokyo Harbor as the commodore negotiates with officials of the imperial court. These biographies contain comments on personalities and events by use of aphorisms (La Rochefoucauld and Poor Richard), sayings borrowed from sea lore, and terse comments of Morison's own: "The government of the Dutch Republic was a peculiar one which seems to have been devised for the purpose of avoiding decisions." In both biographies there are chapters composed mainly of sea action, told with the tense shifted to the present; and both biographies, near the close, contain an impressionistic summation of past scenes from the hero's life, in the manner of Lytton Strachey's *Queen Victoria*.

In the character of the hero, these two biographies differed greatly. Whereas Perry's life had not generated great enthusiasm or controversy, the life of John Paul Jones had inspired fiction by James Fenimore Cooper, Herman Melville, Sarah Orne Jewett, William Thackeray, and a host of biographers who provided Morison with a challenge similar to that of his Columbus biography—approaching freshly a subject that in previous books had assumed conventional forms and the accumulations of legend. At one point in the Jones biography, Morison, using a convention of nineteenth-century history writers, describes and studies the two life portraits of Jones, inferring from them the manner of the man. Elsewhere he declines to look to psychological explanations of the man's character, insisting instead that like many men of action, Jones was not much given to reflection and regretted nothing he had done, only what others had done to him.

Morison found Jones a less than amiable character; traced with a historian's care, but also with a bemused interest, Jones's numerous intrigues with the women he attracted; and asserted that Jones was a lonely man. Morison ascribed this to Jones's colossal egotism that put off friendships, and observed it also in Jones's letters written during his travels in Russia and two years in Paris during the French Revolution—letters that are poor in observation of all but himself. Morison assessed the quality of Jones's seamanship by stating only one qualification. A brilliant tactician, Jones never had proper scope for his talents; and although he may have proven himself a great strategist, he was given only opportunities at the tactical level.

As if to balance out the qualities of the complete naval leader, Morison's life of Matthew Calbraith Perry is one of an officer who demonstrated sound seamanship but whose achievements were in planning, strategy, and development of the Navy. Whereas the life of Jones was short, dramatic, and romantic, and his legacy to the United States Navy the example of his indomitable will to victory, the most dramatic incident in the Navy during Perry's long, successful career was the *Somers* mutiny, a tragic affair in which Perry was not centrally concerned. Perry was a family man. His accomplishments were in organization, such as giving logistic support to the Army during the Mexican War. The triumph of his career was his diplomatic mission to Japan, which resulted in the opening of that country to Western trade and culture.

For his biography of Jones, Morison received the Pulitzer Prize for 1960. Although he had earlier criticized pacifist historians and lectured the profession not to ignore the significance of war, it is interesting to note that Morison, who believed a historian had an obligation to share with his country what the past can teach about present policy, was writing, during the country's Vietnam involvement, the life of a naval officer who distinguished himself in a peacetime navy and in diplomacy. Morison also shared authorship with two other historians in 1970 of the book *Dissent in Three American Wars,* an account drawing on history to show that dissent is not necessarily unpatriotic. In it Morison chronicled the War of 1812 as the United States' most unpopular war.

At one time Morison planned to write a textbook of American history for high school students. Instead, in 1965 he again published a general history of the United States. *The Oxford History of the American People* was intended to be his legacy to his fellow citizens of the half-century in which he studied, taught, and wrote history; lived through critical times; took part in both world wars; and met and spoke with most of the American presidents in the twentieth century. In this one volume, which begins with pre-Columbian America and extends down to the 1960's, Morison attempted to give readers a sense of American ways of living in bygone times—the social place of horses, ships, sports, and eating, drinking, and smoking habits. Political history was not ignored; and to his previous treatments of the Civil War and the War of Independence, Morison brought fresh material. He wrote that he was impressed with the continuity, over three centuries, of American habits and institutions.

This work was given a popular reception, and also the critical appraisal by Carl Degler that though "brilliantly written" and "clearly organized," Morison's legacy was "written without a philosophy of historical significance" and was, as a result, "arbitrary" and "irrelevant," failing to be "a powerful tool of contemporary thought." Indeed, Morison did not find it worthwhile to concern himself much with a philosophy of history, and *The Oxford History of the American People* does close somewhat inconclusively with an enthusiastic appraisal of the "Camelot" years of President John Kennedy. But there are assumptions underlying Morison's view of history even though no theory of progress is evidenced, no guiding hand directs the fortunes of the nation as in the nationalistic histories of the nineteenth century, and there is no anticipated inevitability of a socialist future or a decline of the West.

In all of Morison's histories, the actions of man have standing alongside the forces of history. In times of stress, leadership counts for something, history assuming the directions it does as the result of the actions of great men. It is almost as though, in the words of Edmund Burke, "The means by which providence raises a nation to greatness are the virtues infused into its great men," except that in the corpus of Morison's work there is no providence or certain destiny in the affairs of men. Rather, there is the occasional flowering of what is truly fine in a culture. Anne Bradstreet's poetry is an example from Puritan America. And the clipper ships, Morison had written, were America's Rheims, its Amiens. The greatest flowering of culture, in his opinion, occurred in the politics, art, and literature of ancient Greece. He saw the Allied victory in World War II, beyond changing the balance of power, as meaning "that eternal values and immutable principles, which had come down to us from ancient Hellas, had been reaffirmed and reëstablished." Morison invariably measured Western culture, which stemmed from the ancients of Greece and Rome, by the extent to which it carried on and preserved the classical ideals.

The 1950's and 1960's were undoubtedly satisfying for Morison. In his global travels of historical reconnaissance during these years he was always accompanied by his wife, who was fondly mentioned in the dedications of the books from this period. He was assisted in his correspondence, editing, and other tasks by Antha E. Card, formerly a member of his small, loyal Navy staff. Until World War II he never taught during the summers, preferring to vacation with his children. But after age seventy time was more precious, and he wrote: "Knowing that death will break my pen, I now work almost the year around, praying to be spared to write what is still in me to write."

At this time Morison resolved on an ambitious project. Turning once again, and for the last time, to the sea, he undertook a trilogy of the pre-Columbian and post-Columbian discoveries in the New World. *The European Discovery of America: The Northern Voyages* appeared in 1971. This subject took him once again into the thicket of contending scholarship of "first discoveries" along the coast of the Americas, causing him to read, he complained, "some of the most tiresome literature in existence." With age his visiting of sites was altered. Unable to retrace under sail the coasts described by John Cabot, Jacques Cartier, and Giovanni da Verrazano, he arranged to view them from an airplane. His intention also to write a volume on the northern voyages of later explorers in the seventeenth century was realized only in part with the publication of *Samuel de Champlain: Father of New France* in 1972. Again he flew over the terrain explored by his subject.

In these two books Morison expanded a theme

that appeared earlier in his praise of the dead-reckoning navigation of Columbus. He extolled the skills of practical seamen who relied on their common sense and feel for the sea, and who were not dependent, as seamen in modern days were, on complex navigational devices. He claimed that the lore passed on to him by fishermen and Maine sailors added greatly to what he had learned from his personal experience; and he repeated the example of Capt. Joshua Slocum, who sailed around the world with only a dollar alarm clock, a sextant, a farmer's almanac, and a copy of Bowditch for navigational aids. The sea, Morison reasoned, "still delights us and fortifies us against a mechanized culture which reduces man to a moron." He saw little comparison between the qualities and achievements of discoverers like Columbus, Cabot, Verrazano, and Cartier, and the achievements of the astronauts who landed on the moon. Amid the events of the early 1970's, Morison was aware that he was writing in times of social upheaval. In the Champlain biography he compared the promiscuity of the Huron Indians with the 1972 life in college dormitories. He hoped his tales of boldness, faith, and resourcefulness illustrated in the stories of the early explorers would serve as models in an apprehensive age.

The European Discovery of America: The Southern Voyages (1974) was dedicated to the memory of his wife. This book relates principally the voyages of Columbus, Sir Francis Drake, and Ferdinand Magellan, who stand supreme, among the navigators of the Age of Discovery, in Morison's opinion. As part of the research for the book he flew over coasts of South America and California, and was lent the services of a U.S. Coast Guard cutter to check on one of Drake's landings. Like the sea narratives that preceded it, *The Southern Voyages* blends scholarship from the libraries of several continents and is an honest attempt to shed light on an early period. Exuberantly told, it was Morison's final history.

"I need rest. Age makes it easy to want to retire," Morison said in 1972, at age eighty-four. Of the four remaining years of his life, much time was spent at his home in Northeast Harbor, Maine, with his wife's garden outside the door, the ocean coast beyond.

Morison lived the role of a gentleman-historian, an aristocrat amid the mass society of twentieth-century America. Rear Adm. Ernest Eller, in whose command Morison worked during World War II, described him on board ship "with his crooked London coronas, his Colombo songs, his Scottish thrift, his Boston charm or haughtiness as the mood served, and his indefatigable application." His aristocratic manner was evidenced in his cultivation of social graces and society, including the old ladies of Boston. His haughtiness appeared in the disdain with which he spoke of "armchair navigators" or of historians who entered the profession without the requisite command of the European languages. Democratic society does not admit of the virtue of condescension; but Morison practiced this as well, cultivating the society of Maine fishermen, masters of the Lisbon banker fleet, and others from whom he could learn about the sea. Condescension reflected in the world of scholarship is simply expressed in Morison's statement that it was the duty of scholars and scientists to produce *oeuvres de vulgarisation,* to impart their knowledge to the public in the simplest terms.

In 1977 the American Heritage Publishing Company posthumously established an annual prize in Morison's name for the "best book on American history by an American author that sustains the tradition that good history is literature as well as high scholarship." It is ironic that for all the democratic trends in the historical profession, including recent groupings such as the New Left historians, it was the aristocratic Morison, the "court historian," who was recognized as successful in reaching a large public.

He attributed his success as a writer to industry, the "painstaking cultivation of moderate abilities.'' He said he could write anywhere, but that historical research such as that on Columbus and other explorers, and on the United States Navy, required access to records, maps, and libraries in Boston, Washington, Europe, and elsewhere, so that a careful use of his time was necessary. Morison normally had several projects going at once. As a writer his style did not change with age, nor did he pioneer new forms in historical literature; but his works always evidenced romantic enthusiasms: for the scenic, the deeds of the great and daring.

According to Samuel Johnson, history writing requires application, but "great parts [are] not requisite for a historian" and "imagination is not required in any high degree." Good workmanship was the only quality to which Morison laid claim, and he did not rate himself with the great historians of the past. The three qualities that he recognized in Francis Parkman's work making for good historical literature—research, evaluation, and literary presentation—are apparent in his own writing. And he earned the right to say, as Parkman wrote in his history of Montcalm and Wolfe, "The subject has been studied as much from life and in the open air as at the library table." Morison, believing that "all your experience in life can get into your work one way or another," lived an active life and produced a substantial literature over a long career. He concentrated his energies on his vocation as a historian; and in his commitment to history as literature, he paid respect to a tradition in American letters that has had no more faithful advocate in the twentieth century.

Selected Bibliography

WORKS OF SAMUEL ELIOT MORISON

BIOGRAPHY

The Life and Letters of Harrison Gray Otis, Federalist, 1765–1848. 2 vols. Boston: Houghton Mifflin, 1913.

Builders of the Bay Colony. Boston: Houghton Mifflin, 1930. London: Heinemann, 1931. Sentry ed., with supp. ch. on William Pynchon, Boston: Houghton Mifflin, 1964.

The Second Voyage of Columbus. Oxford: Clarendon Press, 1939.

Admiral of the Ocean Sea: A Life of Christopher Columbus. 2 vols. Boston: Atlantic–Little, Brown, 1942. 1-vol. ed., Boston: Little, Brown, 1942. Paperback ed., 2 vols., New York: Time, Inc., 1962; Mentor, 1962.

Christopher Columbus, Mariner. Boston: Atlantic–Little, Brown, 1955 (juvenile). British ed., enl. and ill., London: Faber & Faber, 1955. Paperback ed., New York: Mentor, 1956.

John Paul Jones: A Sailor's Biography. Boston: Atlantic–Little, Brown, 1959. Paperback ed., London: Faber & Faber, 1959; New York: Time, Inc., 1964.

Old Bruin: Commodore Matthew C. Perry, 1794–1858. Boston: Little, Brown, 1967.

Harrison Gray Otis, 1765–1848; The Urbane Federalist. Boston: Houghton Mifflin, 1969.

Samuel de Champlain, Father of New France. Boston: Little, Brown, 1972.

HISTORY

The Maritime History of Massachusetts. Boston: Houghton Mifflin, 1921; rev. ed. with supp., 1941. London: Heinemann, 1923. Sentry ed., 1961.

The Oxford History of the United States, 1783–1917. 2 vols. London and New York: Oxford University Press, 1927.

With Henry Steele Commager. *The Growth of the American Republic*. New York: Oxford University Press, 1930; 1936. 2nd ed., 2 vols., 1937. 3rd ed., 2 vols., 1942. 4th ed., 2 vols., 1950. 5th ed., 2 vols., 1962. 6th ed., with Henry Steele Commager and William E. Leuchtenburg, 2 vols., 1969.

The Founding of Harvard College. Cambridge, Mass.: Harvard University Press, 1935.

Harvard College in the Seventeenth Century. 2 vols. Cambridge, Mass.: Harvard University Press, 1936.

Three Centuries of Harvard. Cambridge, Mass.: Harvard University Press, 1936; 1963.

The Puritan Pronaos: Studies in the Intellectual Life of New England in the Seventeenth Century. New York: New York University Press, 1936. 2nd ed., *The Intellectual Life of Colonial New England*. New York: New York University Press, 1956. Paperback ed., Ithaca, N.Y.: Great Seal Books, 1960.

Portuguese Voyages to America in the Fifteenth Century. Cambridge, Mass.: Harvard University Press, 1940. New York: Octagon, 1965.

The History of United States Naval Operations in World War II. 15 vols. Boston: Atlantic–Little, Brown.

    I *The Battle of the Atlantic*. 1947. Rev. ed., 1964.

    II *Operations in North African Waters*. 1947. Rev. ed., 1962.

    III *The Rising Sun in the Pacific*. 1948. Rev. ed., 1963.

    IV *Coral Sea, Midway, and Submarine Actions*. 1949. Rev. ed., 1962.

    V *The Struggle for Guadalcanal*. 1949. Rev. ed., 1964.

    VI *Breaking the Bismarck's Barrier*. 1950. Rev. ed., 1962.

    VII *Aleutians, Gilberts, and Marshalls*. 1951. Rev. ed., 1962.

    VIII *New Guinea and the Marianas*. 1953. Rev. ed., 1962.

    IX *Sicily–Salerno–Anzio*. 1954. Rev. ed., 1964.

    X *The Atlantic Battle Won*. 1956. Rev. ed., 1964.

    XI *The Invasion of France and Germany*. 1957. Rev. ed., 1964.

    XII *Leyte, June 1944–January 1945*. 1958. Rev. ed., 1963.

    XIII *The Liberation of the Philippines*. 1963.

    XIV *Victory in the Pacific*. 1961.

    XV *Supplement and General Index*. 1962.

The Ropemakers of Plymouth. Boston: Houghton Mifflin, 1950. New York: Arno, 1976.

The Story of the "Old Colony" of New Plymouth, 1620–1692. New York: Knopf, 1956 (juvenile).

Strategy and Compromise. Boston: Atlantic–Little, Brown, 1958. British ed., *American Contributions to Strategy of World War II*. London: Faber & Faber, 1958.

The Story of Mount Desert Island, Maine. Boston: Atlantic–Little, Brown, 1960.

The Two-Ocean War, a Short History of the U.S. Navy in the Second World War. Boston: Atlantic–Little, Brown, 1963.

The Oxford History of the American People. New York: Oxford University Press, 1965.

With Frederick Merk and Frank Freidel. *Dissent in Three American Wars*. Cambridge, Mass.: Harvard University Press, 1970.

The European Discovery of America: The Northern Voyages. New York: Oxford University Press, 1971.

The European Discovery of America: The Southern Voyages. New York: Oxford University Press, 1974.

ESSAYS AND MISCELLANEOUS WORKS

History as a Literary Art: An Appeal to Young Historians. Boston: Old South Association, n.d.

By Land and by Sea. New York: Knopf, 1953.

Freedom in Contemporary Society. Boston: Atlantic–Little, Brown, 1956.

The Scholar in America. New York: Oxford University Press, 1961 (address delivered at Rockhurst College, Kansas City, Mo., 1960).

One Boy's Boston, 1887–1901. Boston: Houghton Mifflin, 1962.

Vistas of History. New York: Knopf, 1964.

With Maurice Obregon. *The Caribbean as Columbus Saw It*. Boston: Little, Brown, 1964.

Spring Tides. Boston: Houghton Mifflin, 1965.

Vita Nuova: A Memoir of Priscilla Barton Morison. Northeast Harbor, Me.: Samuel Eliot Morison, 1975.

Sailor Historian: A Samuel Eliot Morison Reader, edited by Emily Morison Beck. Boston: Houghton Mifflin, 1977.

BOOKS EDITED

The Key of Libberty [sic], *Written in the Year 1798 by William Manning*. Billerica, Mass.: The Manning Association, 1922. Repr. in *William and Mary Quarterly*, 3rd ser., 13:202–54 (1956).

Sources and Documents Illustrating the American Revolution and Formation of the Federal Constitu-

tion. Oxford: Clarendon Press, 1923. Rev. eds. to 1960.

The Development of Harvard University, 1869–1929. Cambridge, Mass.: Harvard University Press, 1929.

The Log Cabin Myth, a Study of the Early Dwellings of the English Colonists in North America, by Harold R. Shurtleff. Cambridge, Mass.: Harvard University Press, 1939.

Of Plymouth Plantation, by William Bradford. New York: Knopf, 1952. Parts repr. in *Major Writers of America*, edited by Perry Miller. New York: Harcourt, Brace and World, 1963.

The Parkman Reader. Boston: Atlantic–Little, Brown, 1955. British ed., *France and England in North America*. London: Faber & Faber, 1955.

History of the Conquest of Peru, by William H. Prescott. New York: Limited Editions Club, 1957; Heritage Press ed., 1957.

Journals and Other Documents on the Life and Voyages of Christopher Columbus. New York: Limited Editions Club, 1963; Heritage Press ed., 1964.

CRITICAL STUDIES

Degler, Carl N. "History Without a Beard." *Tri-Quarterly*, 6:144–50 (Spring 1966).

Herold, David. "Samuel Eliot Morison and the Ocean Sea." *Dalhousie Review*, 54:741–48 (Winter 1974–75).

—*DAVID HEROLD*

Thomas Paine

1737–1809

ONE pictures Thomas Paine, the quintessential American, shuttling between London and Paris in the early days of the French Revolution, his radical pamphlets in one hand and plans for his iron bridge—with its promise of financial success—in the other. Already famous by 1790 as the author of one of the most brilliant political pamphlets ever written, he refused in his early fifties to settle for a placid and well-deserved fame; instead, after supporting rebellion in America, he turned to France, where he became a central figure in that later revolution. Continuing to publish his radical sentiments in a torrent of political writing to the end of his life, he infuriated almost everyone he knew by his loyalty to libertarian principle and his cavalier attitude toward those in power.

Maligned by his contemporaries, often difficult to tolerate personally, but generous to the poor and skeptical toward all tradition, Paine remains a fascinating and problematic figure, a much celebrated but curiously neglected writer. His own description of himself as "citizen of the world" rings true through two centuries of harsh criticism by those opposed to his ideas and uncritical admiration by those devoted to his political and religious teachings. Although English by birth and residence for most of his life, he was the author of several all-time best-sellers in America and our first professional pamphle-

teer—two reasons for his prominent place in American literary history. "It was the cause of America that made me a writer," Paine wrote at the close of the Revolution. But it was the causes of common people—political freedom and economic justice—that determined his career as a literary radical. To an extraordinary degree, Paine's life and writings are one; each is best understood in relationship to the other and to the revolutionary era in which he played a vital part.

From the time of his contemporaries until now, Paine's appearance and behavior, as well as his politics, have influenced attitudes toward him. Certain ugly features—the crimson cheeks and nose, the latter drooping and somewhat bulbous—were taken as outward manifestations of his soul's condition, and accounts of his personal behavior were used to justify indictments of his political and religious teachings. Paine's politics, like Milton's, have prejudiced commentators either for or against him to an inordinate degree, and the portrait of the man is often strongly colored by the ideological paintbrush of the artist.

Most portraits of Paine, verbal or otherwise, are based upon physical descriptions of him at the end of his life, usually as he appeared in the painting, bust, and death mask by John Wesley Jarvis, a young artist who lived with Paine, in New York City, until shortly before his death.

But these must not be taken as the only views of him or obscure the apparent charm and popularity of the younger Paine.

In his early years, Paine is usually remembered for his lively, radiant, blue eyes, and for his uncommonly interesting talk, humorous and full of anecdote. Five feet, nine inches tall, he was described as having a "lofty and unfurrowed" forehead and a ruddy, "thoroughly English" complexion. Regarded initially as shy, even moody, he did not make a strong first impression, but quickly warmed to the company at hand and, with his knowledge of many subjects, delighted everyone. He fancied himself as something of a ladies man, although the testimony of women suggests that they did not regard him as highly as he regarded himself (vanity remained a persistent flaw in his character). Everyone agreed, however, about his powers of conversation, even those who saw him as something of a rascal. By all accounts, he never depended upon vulgar or indecent stories to entertain his audience, and no one spoke derogatorily of his brandy drinking until after he became a famous revolutionary.

Even late in life, Paine was remembered as an attractive personality—his eyes "full, brilliant, and singularly piercing." His memory preserved its capacity to recall events and arguments from years before, his mind irresistible in its "obdurate determination to pursue whatever object it embraces." Sometimes, when his reputation for drink and vanity had preceded him, his charm overwhelmed new acquaintances. "In spite of his surprising ugliness, the expression of his countenance is luminous, his manners easy and benevolent, and his conversation remarkably entertaining." Those who expected to find a raving maniac, as the Federalist and Calvinist press described him, found Paine "unaffected, guileless, and good-natured."

As a man who moved quickly from obscurity to fame, and almost as quickly back to obscurity, Paine suffered from periodic anxiety about the future, even when his financial state appeared reasonably secure. "I have sustained so much loss, by disinterestedness and inattention to money matters, and by accidents, that I am obliged to look closer to my affairs than I have done," he wrote in his late sixties. And his fears increased during the next decade. To some degree, Paine's last escape from England came to be symbolic of his life: people hissing him as he boarded the boat to leave his homeland; people cheering him as he disembarked from the same boat in France. From the very beginning his was neither an easy nor a simple existence.

Thomas Pain (he added the "e" only after coming to America) was born in the village of Thetford, seventy miles northeast of London, on January 29, 1737, the only son of Joseph Pain, a staymaker and small farmer who worshipped with the Society of Friends, and Frances Cocke, an attorney's daughter who belonged to the Church of England. In his actions and writing the religious background retained its significance, especially his father's association with the Quakers. Paine's being called an atheist is simply one of several charges by which hostile critics, including Theodore Roosevelt, libeled him.

During seven years of formal education in the local schools, Thomas Paine proved to be an intelligent—if unsettled—student, and was taken from his studies at thirteen to serve as an apprentice in his father's shop. He remained there for about three years, helping in the manufacture of whalebone stays for corsets, developing a mechanical skill and dexterity that remained with him throughout his life.

At about sixteen, a love of adventure and independence got the better of him, and he left his father's shop. After various attempts at making it on his own, first at sea, as a privateer on the *Terrible* and the *King of Prussia,* and then as a staymaker himself, at Sandwich, he returned to

Thetford in April 1759. His first wife, Mary Lambert, a lady's maid and daughter of an excise officer, died in 1760, within a year after their marriage at Sandwich on September 27, 1759. Having taken the examination for a post in the excise service himself, Paine received an appointment to that office on August 8, 1764, in Alford, Lincolnshire. After being discharged from this job for a minor neglect of duty, he went on to several other temporary assignments as teacher and perhaps as preacher, also unsuccessfully.

Eventually reinstated as an excise officer in 1768, at Lewes, a city of 10,000 people in Sussex, he remained there for six years. On March 26, 1771, he married a second time, to Elizabeth Ollive, daughter of Samuel Ollive, a Quaker who owned a tobacco shop where Paine worked after the owner's death. His experience as a merchant and his marriage, never consummated, ended somewhat disastrously. His time in Lewes, a center for disaffection, contributed not only to his immediate fortune but also to his later life as a political journalist. John Wilkes, a radical member of Parliament, was popular in the town and elaborate Guy Fawkes celebrations, with antipopery pageantry, gave evidence of a general discontent with traditional politics and religion, a sentiment that was to characterize much of Paine's later writings.

In Lewes, Paine also began an association with several influential persons, including George Lewis Scott—a friend of Edward Gibbon, Samuel Johnson, and Benjamin Franklin—and in 1772 Paine wrote his first important public statement, *Case of the Officers of Excise,* a plea for better wages. A modest but well-argued case for a salary increase for overworked and underpaid civil employees, it was written in a vigorous plain style, with a sociological sense that contributed to Paine's popularity among workers and farmers in prerevolutionary America and in England. "The rich, in ease and affluence," he said, "may think I have drawn an unnatural portrait," but could they "descend to the cold regions of want, the circle of polar poverty, they would find their opinions changing with the climate. There are habits of thinking peculiar to different conditions, and to find them out is truly to study mankind."

The pamphlet, which he forwarded to Oliver Goldsmith with a letter of introduction, brought Paine's talent as a writer to the attention of many people; 4,000 copies were printed and privately distributed among members of Parliament, government officials, and the general public. The publication also earned Paine some money, and gave him an entree into London coffeehouses, where he continued his campaign on behalf of his fellow workers and where he eventually met Benjamin Franklin. Through his earlier associations with other "natural philosophers," such as Dr. John Bevis, a distinguished astronomer and later a fellow of the Royal Society; Benjamin Martin, a mathematician; and James Ferguson, an astronomer and an inventor; Paine gathered information about the practical sciences that informed his political and religious pamphlets. Subsequently, he conducted scientific experiments on the causes of yellow fever and developed designs for engines, smokeless candles, and an iron bridge. Although publicly loyal to the Church of England, Paine had begun to breathe the liberating air of the deists, and found it healthful, even invigorating. Twenty years later, in *The Age of Reason,* the pamphlet that provoked more personal hostility than any other he wrote, Paine would become deism's best-known proselytizer.

In the various English towns where he lived, Paine experienced the inequities of the English social system, which was dominated by the landed aristocracy, the object of numerous attacks in his writings. His first pamphlet suggests his hatred of the rich, whose wealth, he argued, caused the ill fortune of others. In London, food riots, industrial disputes, and desperate poverty dramatized the failure of the constitutional monarchy. All of these matters provided fuel for his later fiery denunciations of what the English usually regarded as an imperfect but satisfactory system.

Paine's campaign for increased salaries for the excise officers ended, like most of his projects during his first forty years, in failure, and in April 1774 he was discharged from his own job in Lewes. Both of these humiliations he associated with the person of George III, that "hardened, sullen-tempered Pharaoh of the English," as he later described him, who "with pretended title Father of his People can unfeelingly hear of their slaughter, and composedly sleep with their blood upon his soul."

Although his fortunes were limited, Thomas Paine's life appears not to have been totally unhappy. The separation from his second wife, agreed to on June 4, 1774, was amicable. Each continued to speak well of the other, and although he never married again, he wrote respectfully of the institution of marriage, and apparently helped his second wife in old age—as he did many people—when she needed money.

Near the time of the separation, he began to make plans for events that would change not only his own life but also the course of history. With letters of introduction from Benjamin Franklin to his son-in-law Richard Bache in Philadelphia, and to his son William, royal governor of New Jersey, Paine set sail for the American colonies, with tentative plans for several occupations, including the establishment of an academy for young women. Among his various associates in England, only Franklin, who called him "an ingenious, worthy young man," and George Lewis Scott saw the thirty-seven-year-old "failure" as a man of promise. But their opinion was more important politically than most, and Paine was to fulfill that promise in ways that they could hardly have anticipated. Almost from the mo-

ment he arrived in Philadelphia, on November 30, 1774, as a cabin passenger on the *London Packet,* he began to take a central role as an American journalist and man of letters.

Despite his former failures, Paine came to the New World enjoying several advantages over other immigrants of the 1770's, most of whom arrived as indentured servants. Almost immediately he joined the staff of a magazine that was to become, with his help, the most popular periodical thus far published in the colonies (over 1,500 subscribers). The editor, a Scot named Robert Aitken, was determined to make the *Pennsylvania Magazine; or, American Monthly Museum* a distinctly American magazine, and with the help of Paine, John Witherspoon, president of the College of New Jersey (Princeton), and Francis Hopkinson, a lawyer, he eventually succeeded in doing so.

An incident at the beginning of Paine's new career in the colonies suggests not only the energy of the man, but also his immediate sympathy with America's move toward independence. Sick abed on arrival, probably from typhus, he had to be carried from the ship and nursed back to health during his first six weeks in Philadelphia. Illness failed to keep him down, however, and by January 1775 local citizens were already reading "A Dialogue Between General Wolfe and General Gage in a Wood near Boston," a brief essay that talked about Parliament's unjust treatment of the colonists, the rightful inheritors of British liberty.

Two months later, his poem "The Death of General Wolfe," later set to music, celebrated the exploits of America's first continental hero, describing contemporary events with references to classical mythology. Although predictable in manner, its execution was competent. Paine took considerable pride in his skill as a poet, and his poems, which he enjoyed declaiming, were among his most popular writings in the colonies. (At the same time, as an eighteenth-century rationalist, he remained somewhat skeptical about poetry, repressing rather than encouraging his talent for it, for fear that it might lead "too much into the field of imagination.")

Paine's essays for the *Pennsylvania Magazine* indicated his interest in people's struggles for freedom and independence around the world, particularly against the English. In "Reflections on the Life and Death of Lord Clive," he portrayed Clive in old age, anguished and repentant over his hard rule of India, implying a resemblance between him and the royal governors in America. Contemporary readers could easily substitute "America" for "India," and "General Gage" for "Lord Clive."

The magazine's policy of not publishing controversial writings ended with the American and British confrontation at Concord and Lexington in April 1775, and in the next issue Paine spoke directly to the matter of independence. His song "Liberty Tree," printed in the *Pennsylvania Evening Post* and set to music, attacked "all the tyrannical powers,/ Kings, Commons, and Lords," responsible for the mercantile restrictions imposed on the colonies. In an article signed "Humanus" (October 1775), Paine wrote, "I hesitate not for a moment to believe that the Almighty will finally separate America from Britain. Call it independence or what you will, if it is the cause of God and humanity, it will go on."

Earlier that same year, Paine published a blistering attack on slavery, following the example of his distinguished friend and admirer Benjamin Rush, physician and scientist, who had circulated a similar polemic in 1772. Through the efforts of these two men, Pennsylvania was one of the first states to emancipate slaves in the early years of the Revolutionary War.

The arguments favoring independence, which he so powerfully presented in *Common Sense,* appeared in many of Paine's writings during his first year in America, as if he had immediately

assimilated the American ethos and the native mythology from birth. But perhaps the most prophetic statement, relating to imagery and theme in his later American writings, is "The Dream Interpreted." Appearing in the May 1775 issue of the *Pennsylvania Magazine,* the essay tells of a traveler who, on a journey through Virginia, falls asleep and dreams about a pleasing landscape that is transformed, by a night storm, from a scene of beauty and tranquillity to one of horror and destruction. Morning, however, brings a new vision lovelier and more felicitous than that of the previous day. After he awakens, the narrator meets another traveler, who interprets his dream: "That beautiful country which you saw is America. The sickly state you beheld her in has been coming on her for these few years past . . . which nothing but a storm can purify. The tempest is the present context, and the event will be the same."

In this essay Paine—like many of the Puritan writers before and several Romantic historians after him—implied that the struggle for America's future carried supernatural implications and that, as God's people, Americans had a special destiny:

He who guides the natural tempest will regulate the political one, and bring good out of evil. . . . The cause is now before a higher court, the court of Providence, before whom the arrogance of kings, the infidelity of ministers, the general corruption of government, and all the cobweb artifice of courts will fall confounded and ashamed.

Like so many of Paine's early essays, "The Dream Interpreted" combined political argument and poetic imagery in a style that brought together the best in eighteenth-century rationalism and nineteenth-century romanticism— a realistic view of the injustices of the past and present and a utopian vision of the future. Thus did Paine's writings promote a hopeful image of the New World; a place where individual merit, not social position or inherited wealth, established the limit of one's achievement. For Paine, as for so many later immigrants, America spelled future success. His essays embellished the American dream and showed a deep trust in the democratic process, as represented by the colonial experiment. It showed a firm belief in a new age, free of the burdens of the past. "We have it in our power to begin the world over again," he wrote in *Common Sense*. "A situation similar to the present has not happened since the days of Noah until now."

Through these early journalistic pieces, as well as through his scientific experiments and his witty, polemical conversation, Paine soon became well known among Philadelphia artisans, merchants, and members of the Continental Congress, in session there since September 1774. Congress had sent a number of statements to George III and to Parliament—all ignored—about the deteriorating state of the colonies' relationship with the mother country. Franklin, John Adams, and others had talked about independence, and among several groups of Philadelphians there was warm support for Paine's sentiments.

In a city whose fate rested more on the demands of the crowd than it did on the actions of political leaders, his writing had come to exert considerable influence, and it was only natural, in this revolutionary context, that he began to think of a more ambitious literary project. Despite all that went before, *Common Sense,* slapdash, rambling, and crude, as historian Bernard Bailyn has said, is hardly explainable without explaining genius itself.

"My motive and object of all my political works, beginning with *Common Sense*," Paine wrote in 1803, "have been to rescue man from tyranny and false systems and false principles of government; and enable him to be free." Thus,

later in life, he recognized that his basic beliefs and principles remained the same, even as the location varied. In general, Paine regarded all political questions as moral questions, directly related to how people lived. He believed in a universal moral order sanctioned and supported by nature; in the equality of people; and in the desirability of establishing that equality by political means. Paine saw no need for ruling aristocracies, traditions, and institutions, trusting that people could bring about a just society on their own and that progress would come through the application of reason to all areas of life, philosophical and practical. Although his hatred of England eventually became something of an obsession, he usually viewed conflicts from an internationalist perspective, as "a citizen of the world." He thought that American independence benefited this general ideal, the colonies being, as he said in the introduction to *Common Sense,* "the cause of all mankind."

His first major contribution to American journalism also revealed his skill in sizing up, after only a brief residence in this country, the political situation in the colonies. As late as 1776, the movement for independence was still multivarious and confused, proceeding on several fronts at once and exceeding the grasp of almost anyone native to a particular region. In *Common Sense* Paine managed to appeal to many different and conflicting groups at once: to Quakers and Germans in one section; to the economic self-interest of farmers and merchants in another; to radicals and artisans in another; to conservative merchants and landowners in another. Standing midway between the crowd and the Founding Fathers, he made the most of the alienation that colonists sometimes felt toward one another and united them, in common cause, against a previously ill-defined foe. He brought everyone together, in theory at least, against England. In the colonies, from Massachusetts to North Carolina, the lower classes had shown a growing sophistication, through boycotts and demonstrations, in defying upper-class rule. They came to recognize in Paine a spokesman for the distress, confusion, and uncertainty they felt in the New World. As a popular writer, he explained away the past and, in a pseudo-scientific language, elucidated the new politics, the new religion, and the secular city, which they came to recognize as their own.

According to Paine, he began forming the outline of *Common Sense* in October 1775 at Franklin's suggestion. Benjamin Rush and David Rittenhouse saw the first draft, but the author is rightfully credited with the overall scheme. Published anonymously, with Rush's title, rather than Paine's "Plain Talk," it appeared on January 10, 1776, the same day as George III's bellicose and intransigent speech to Parliament on the American question.

The first thousand copies of *Common Sense* sold out within two weeks, and by the end of the first year, 150,000 copies, in twenty-five editions, were circulating among three million people in the colonies. According to the *American Annual Register for the Year 1796*, "the greatest orators of antiquity did not more tyrannically command the conviction of their hearers than the writer of *Common Sense*." Translated into several languages, it fanned the fires of revolution in France and Spain, as well as in Latin America. "I know not," John Adams later observed, somewhat grudgingly, "whether any man in the world has had more influence on its inhabitants or affairs for the last thirty years than Thomas Paine."

Although the power of the document rests not so much in its logic as in its vigorous language, Paine's reasoning deserves more than casual attention. After a brief introduction describing the natural conflict between nature and the people, as against custom and king—between America and the oppressed, as against Parliament and the usurpers—Paine argued the "common sense" of the colonies' separation from England by reference to four general topics.

Part One, "On the Origin and Design of Government in General, With Concise Remarks on the English Constitution," questions the validity of the English constitution and contrasts the naturalness of society and the unnaturalness of government in a way that Henry David Thoreau did seventy years later in *Civil Disobedience*. Speaking to the people's old suspicion of those in power, it distinguishes between the people and their rulers and sets in motion an argument by which the ruling monarch could be deposed.

Paine defines government as that peculiar institution whereby "the palaces of kings are built upon the ruins of the bowers of paradise." In a spirited enumeration of the abuses of power by monarch and Parliament, Paine forced his American readers to confront a set of charges that were crucial to their education as revolutionists and that anticipated Jefferson's list of abuses in the Declaration of Independence six months later. The English system of government, long regarded as workable and generally humane, is in truth, he said, ineffectual and oppressive.

Part Two, "Of Monarchy and Hereditary Succession," mercilessly denigrates the concept of the divine right of kings as being both unreasonable and antireligious (this argument appealed especially to religious dissenters). Paine described William the Conqueror, George III's ancestor, as a French bastard, "a very paltry rascally original," who landed with armed banditti and established himself as king against the consent of the natives. Such ancestry "certainly hath no divinity in it."

Part Three, "Thoughts on the Present State of American Affairs," reviews the arguments for and against separation from Britain, skillfully undermining Britain's claim as parent country by identifying Americans as "the persecuted lovers of civil and religious liberty from every part of Europe." Reconciliation with Britain, after the long period of harassment during the 1760's, "is now a fallacious dream." The American movement for independence and a constitution is not only reasonable, but natural, in the light of recent events. Nature and Nature's God call for it.

Finally, reflecting briefly in Part Four, "On the Present Civility of Americans, With Some Miscellaneous Reflections," and giving a brief outline of structures and programs for the independent country, Paine made this universal plea:

O ye that love mankind! Ye that dare oppose not only the tyranny but the tyrant, stand forth! Every spot of the old world is overrun with oppression. Freedom hath been hunted round the globe. Asia and Africa have long expelled her. Europe regards her like a stranger, and England hath given her warning to depart. O receive the fugitive, and prepare in time an asylum for mankind.

Paine enjoyed the sudden popularity of his pamphlet and was drawn more and more deeply into the American cause once his authorship became widely known. The frequently reprinted *Forester's Letters,* replies to an Anglican clergyman who opposed "independence and republicanism," further popularized Paine's revolutionary ideas and arguments. He donated the early profits of *Common Sense* to the American troops in Quebec, and soon after the adoption of the Declaration of Independence by the Continental Congress he volunteered his services to the army, first at Perth Amboy, New Jersey, and later at Fort Lee, as General Nathanael Greene's aide-de-camp. In an effort to rally the people of Pennsylvania particularly, and to encourage the Continental Army generally, he soon returned to writing, and each of the *Crisis* papers, signed simply "Common Sense," addressed a particular subject or event in the long war for independence.

"These are times that try men's souls." Thus began *American Crisis I,* published on December 19, 1776, followed by twelve other numbered papers and three supplements, appearing at various intervals over the next seven years. Printed in a variety of forms, often at Paine's own expense, and widely distributed, they were written to inspire a people at war. The following statement, from *American Crisis II,* accurately describes the extended enterprise, even though Paine did eventually seek payment from Congress after the war: "My writing I have always given away, reserving only the expense of printing and paper, and sometimes not even that. I never courted fame or interest, and my manner of life, to those who know it, will justify what I say. My study is to be useful."

The *Crisis* papers included: extended attacks on American Tories, on Quakers who refused to bear arms, and on those endeavoring to negotiate an early peace with Britain; sympathetic reports about Washington's defeat at the Battle of Brandywine and about the troops at Valley Forge; appeals to the citizens of England and France for support of the American cause and to the people of the colonies for the acceptance of war taxes imposed during the Revolution.

In addition to rallying the soldiers and the people at critical times, the *Crisis* papers exhibited Paine's changing attitude toward government. Although still bitterly opposed to the English system and the monarchy—an attitude more fully developed in *Rights of Man*—he became less hostile toward bicameralism than he had been in earlier pamphlets. He also moved gradually toward a justification of centralized government and made every effort to win the support of wealthy merchants for the revolutionary cause through his arguments supporting the Bank of North America and the power of the federal government to levy taxes.

American Crisis XIII (April 1783), for example, urged a stronger union among the states: the kind of centralized government that Paine had criticized earlier. But as he said at the beginning of the paper, "The times that tried men's souls are over—and the greatest and completest revolution the world ever knew, gloriously and happily accomplished." During the next few years, before going to France, he entered his most conservative phase, withdrawing from active support of the radical and reform movements that characterized most of his life. In the 1780's, Paine spent much of his time attending to his own and the country's commercial interests.

George Washington was only one of the many people who acknowledged the "utility of the common cause" of Paine's publications during the *Crisis* period, and in 1782 Washington suggested a salary of $800 for Paine's help in "informing the people and rousing them to action." In 1777 he had been elected secretary of the Committee for Foreign Affairs by the Continental Congress, a tribute about which he remained very proud; but within two years he was obliged to resign as a result of the furious tempers that boiled up over the infamous Deane affair. Prudence seldom guided Paine in any of his actions or writings on public affairs, and the controversy surrounding Silas Deane, the American commissioner to France, was only one of several instances of his throwing himself into a political fray with vehemence and abandon, alienating powerful politicians and potential allies in the process.

France's policy of surreptitiously supplying funds to the American rebels was a scheme providing every opportunity for double-dealing on all sides. Paine regarded Deane as a scoundrel and a schemer, and was one of the few people to say so publicly; but in exposing Deane's crooked dealings, Paine revealed confidential data, betraying the secrecy of his office and endangering the delicate relationship between France and the colonies. Later revelations—in papers discovered a century after his death—proved Paine right, but the immediate harm had been done, and enemies made as a result of the Deane affair hurt Paine for the rest of his life. Like his attack on traditional religion, his involvement in this conflict seriously prejudiced some early commentators against him. In an age of scurrilous journalism, he was both victim and, occasionally, perpetrator of savage personal attacks. In the case of his contemporaries (Thomas Jefferson, John Adams, even Alexander Hamilton), history often ignored the most outrageous slanders; but with Paine, the libelous remarks became, for over a century, a significant part of his "official" biography.

Despite some political difficulties, however, the ten years following the publication of *Common Sense* were profitable for Paine and brought some recognition for his services to his adopted country. On July 4, 1780, he was awarded an honorary master of arts degree from the University of Pennsylvania and about the same time served as clerk of the Pennsylvania assembly. In 1781 he made a successful trip to France, with Colonel John Laurens, in search of aid for the new country. In 1783 George Washington, as one who entertained "a lively sense" of the importance of Paine's work, invited him to visit his home at Rocky Hill, near Princeton, New Jersey. In 1784 the New York legislature voted to give Paine a 227-acre farm, sequestered from a Tory resident of New Rochelle, for his contributions "to the freedom, sovereignty and independence of the United States." In 1785 Congress, with the direct encouragement of Washington and James Madison and the indirect support of Thomas Jefferson, then in France, paid him $3,000.

Paine's writing in this period included *Public Good* (1780), a pamphlet arguing that the lands to the west claimed by Virginia belonged not to one colony but to the whole country (this pamphlet probably cost him a pension from this state, after the war); "Letter to Abbé Raynal" (1782), a defense of America against the popular French author's suspicions in regard to the new republic; and *Dissertations on Government; the Affairs of the Bank; and Paper Money* (1786), an argument favoring Robert Morris' plans for the Bank of North America. In addition he sent numerous letters to his friends in politics on matters relating to public policy; they valued his services as an ally, but frequently wished to avoid too close an association with him, and certain people, including John Adams, regarded him as vain, impetuous, and rowdy.

Although still much admired as an author and a patriot, Paine, by 1785, had alienated a number of his old friends by attacking or defending almost every controversial cause during the early days of the republic. One widely circulated verse satire called him Janus-faced, and the response of his political adversaries during his appeals for financial assistance was often less than enthusiastic. But, as before, he remained relatively content, and in semiretirement near Bordentown, New Jersey, he focused his attention on less political matters, giving himself over to a typically American scheme, that of making a fast buck by skillfully applying his scientific knowledge to a couple of practical questions.

The return of Benjamin Franklin to America, after almost a decade as minister to France, coincided with Paine's return to various scientific experiments. An interest in natural philosophy, as the physical sciences were called in the eighteenth century, had brought the two men together initially, and Paine now wanted to know what Franklin thought of his smokeless candle and to get his endorsement for an iron bridge he had designed. Christened "a child of Common Sense" and constructed of a single arch uniting thirteen sections—in tribute to the American colonies—the model for the bridge went on display first in Franklin's garden in Philadelphia and, on New Year's Day 1787, in the State House yard there. A price tag of $330,330, among other things, kept the iron bridge from being approved by the Pennsylvania Assembly and from being built across the Schuylkill River, near Philadelphia. So Paine decided to return to the Old World in pursuit of endorsements by the Royal Society of London and the Royal Academy of Sciences in Paris.

Armed with numerous letters of introduction from Franklin to French politicians and nobles, and a particularly lengthy one to Thomas Jefferson, who had replaced Franklin as the minister to France, Paine left New York on April 26, 1787, planning to return before the end of the year. In twelve and a half years as an American he had gathered some money, numerous friends (and enemies), property, and international fame—considerably more than he had arrived with from England in 1774 and more than he would return with from Europe in 1802.

Paine arrived in Paris in May 1787, more interested in getting an endorsement for his iron bridge—from influential scientists and rich noblemen—than in political causes. Lafayette and Rochefoucauld paid tribute to his achievement, and the Royal Academy of Sciences gave its approval. Soon after his arrival he did write one brief pamphlet, *Prospects on the Rubicon* (1787), criticizing William Pitt's alliance with the king of Prussia against the republican forces in the Netherlands. The pamphlet, addressed to the people of England, called for democratic reform in his native country and for changes that would render war less central to British policy, particularly in responding to democratic reforms in Europe.

In addition to showing a precise knowledge of contemporary European affairs, *Prospects on the Rubicon* contained an eloquent plea against war. Although capable of championing people's wars on behalf of his favorite cause—as in the *Crisis* papers—Paine lamented, in this essay, the "unforseen and unsupposed circumstances that war provokes.'' Despite the fact that ''the calamities of war and the miseries it inflicts upon the human species, the thousands and tens of thousands of every age and sex who are rendered wretched by the event,'' any rumor of war is often greeted enthusiastically in London. ''There are thousands who live by it; it is their harvest; and the clamor which these people keep up in newspapers and conversations passes unsuspiciously for the voices of the people.'' Yet it is governments, not people, that foster wars, the latter learning of the deception only after the mischief has been done.

Following three eventful months in France, Paine traveled to England (where *Prospects of the Rubicon* was already circulating) to seek the Royal Society's endorsement for his bridge. There he met Edmund Burke, later his antagonist. On first meeting and in several subsequent conversations, they talked, however, as loyal friends of the American Revolution. While in his homeland, Paine took time to arrange a suitable pension for his ninety-year-old mother, who still lived in Thetford; to visit the friends of his youth; and to spend pleasant hours with Benjamin West, American painter and sculptor living in England, and Joel Barlow, American poet and pamphleteer, with whom he associated frequently until Paine's imprisonment in 1793.

From 1787 to 1789 Paine remained in England most of the time, serving as an unofficial American envoy (John Adams had returned home by this time), sending important information about the British scene in numerous, lengthy letters to Thomas Jefferson in Paris and to friends in America. He and Jefferson debated the issues raised by news from the Constitutional Convention in Philadelphia, exchanging letters on the distinction between civil and natural rights, in language that was to influence Jefferson's political philosophy and, in time, the American government.

In a letter to Jefferson the day before the fall of the Bastille, Paine said that he looked forward to his iron bridge being built across the Thames in London. His major preoccupation is further revealed in Edmund Burke's description of him at this time as a person who was ''not without some attention to politics, but more deeply concerned about mechanical projects.''

The events in Paris in the fall of 1789—the bread riots, and the forced movement of the king and the National Assembly to Paris during the October Days—convinced Paine that he must return to France, which he did in November. From Paris he wrote Burke enthusiastic letters about the consequences of the Revolution, comparing it to the one in America; but Burke responded coldly. In the words of David Freeman Hawke, ''Burke feared that the turbulence in France would contaminate England. Paine hoped it would.'' The fundamental disagreement between the two men eventually spilled over into public debate, in two of the most popular books of the century, Burke's *Reflections on the Revolution in France* (1790), written essentially to encourage the English to value things as they were, and Paine's *Rights of Man,* written expressly to provoke the English to follow France's lead and to revolt.

Paine's attitude toward the French Revolution was optimistic from the beginning, since he regarded it as a harbinger of radical social change throughout Europe. Moving back and forth between Paris and London, he became increasingly involved in the affairs of France. Lafayette had honored him by entrusting him with the key to the Bastille, to be sent to George Washington; Paine called the key ''an early trophy of the spoils of despotism, and the first ripe fruit of American principles transplanted into Europe.'' With the help of two aristocrats, Condorcet and Du Castelet, Paine and Brissot, a journalist and member of the National Assembly, founded the Société Republicain and started a journal, published by Nicolas de Bonneville, to circulate their writings among other intellectuals. Paine's ''A Republican Manifesto,'' published in 1791, spoke of Louis XVI for the first time as ''simply Louis Capet,'' and his *Declaration of Universal Peace and Liberty* urged the French king to join the republican side.

In the early 1790's, anxious to further the cause of revolution in England, Paine met frequently with English dissenters friendly to France—William Godwin, Mary Wollstonecraft, Thomas Hardy, and other radicals who made up the Society for Constitutional Information in London and the Corresponding Society for the Unrepresented Part of the People of Britain. He visited frequently with Gouverneur Morris, United States representative to England and later the official envoy to France. But in the midst of all these activities, Paine devoted his fullest energy to making arrangements for erecting his bridge.

The experimental arch in Paine's bridge design, eventually incorporated in a structure built to span the River Ware, at Sunderland in northern England, created something of a stir, as he had predicted. It came to be regarded, in fact, as one of the greatest triumphs of bridge architecture, admired and imitated by many people. It brought him fame, a place in the history of bridge construction, but no money. Thus his financial state—always precarious, since he gave money away when he had it—was little improved.

In the midst of promoting his bridge during the fall of 1790, he sent an essay, ''Thoughts on the Establishment of a Mint in the United States,'' to Jefferson, who had it published in America. Finally, after months of waiting, Burke's long-announced publication, *Reflections on the Revolution in France,* appeared in November of that year.

Although the two men had agreed previously, if superficially, in supporting the American cause, Burke's attack against the revolution in France challenged everything Paine stood for, and several phrases in *Reflections* appeared to be written with him in mind. Justifiably criticized by Paine (and others) as ill-informed, prejudiced, and even unhistorical, Burke's treatise nevertheless did contest successfully the theoretical basis of the natural rights philosophy and, thus, the foundation of Paine's political writings. Burke argued that all rights are social, rather than universal, inherited from the past and embodied in constitutional precedents and traditional institutions. The implications of his argument were profoundly conservative, calling not only for a reinterpretation of the tradition of the Glorious Revolution of 1688 in England, but also for a vigorous denunciation of the present revolution in France. The basic thrust of Burke's argument was suggested by his general lament about the consequences of the French Revolution when he wrote that ''the age of chivalry is gone. That of sophisters, economists, and calculators has succeeded.'' He saw the Revolution as a force whereby learning was ''trodden under the hoofs of a swinish multitude.'' In extolling the glories of the past, in the person of the embattled aristocracy, Burke—Paine said—''pities the plumage but forgets the dying bird.''

Paine understood Burke's pamphlet for what it was: an attack not only on the French Revolution, but also on the radical tradition in England. It threatened the movement for parliamentary reform that the Revolution had encouraged. Having made some arrangements already for the publication of a response, Paine went to work immediately, and within three months, in February 1791, Part I of *Rights of Man* appeared in England and, shortly afterward, in France. An ode to Paine in a New York newspaper summarized the book's theme in a couplet: ''From reason's source a bold reform, he brings./ By raising up mankind he pulls down kings.''

Rights of Man combined personal indictments of Burke, point-by-point refutations of his criticisms of the new French constitution, historical notes on the sequence of events leading to the

French *Declaration of the Rights of Man and the Citizen* and the storming of the Bastille, and—particularly in Part II—extended lectures on political theory. In arguing for a written constitution and a popularly elected legislative body, it was, as Paine suggested in his dedication to George Washington, a kind of prayer that the natural rights of man might become universal and that the Old World might be regenerated by the New. Years later, Paine accurately described the principles informing it as "the same as those in *Common Sense*," and mentioned that the effects would have been the same in England as they had been in America, "could the vote of the nation be quickly taken."

The preface to the French edition of *Rights of Man* begins in the manner of *Common Sense*, making a distinction between the people and the government, between those in England who favored the French Revolution and those in government, represented by Burke, who opposed it. In words and phrases similar to those of his earlier statements, Paine argued the right of every age and generation to act for itself: "I am contending for the right of the *living*, and against their being willed away, and controlled and contracted for, by the manuscript-assessed authority of the dead." In Part I, Paine resorted to direct personal attack, accusing Burke of accepting pay from the crown and of relying on artifice rather than truth in maligning the Revolution. "Accustomed to kiss the aristocratical hand that hath purloined him from himself, he degenerates into a composition of art, and the genuine soul of nature forsakes him." In each case, Paine's charges were partly true.

Burke had advocated a constitution, in the English manner, based upon a monarch and determined by tradition. Paine advocated a constitution, in the American manner, based upon the sovereignty of the people and determined by natural rights—those inherited from the original condition of mankind. Burke's *Reflections* de-

pended upon eloquence as well as logic to defend the glories of the past. Paine's *Rights*, although not as consistently skillful as a literary work, used passion as well as reason to justify the revolutionary present:

When we survey the wretched condition of man under the monarchical and hereditary systems of government, dragged from their homes by one power, or driven by another, and impoverished by taxes more than enemies, it becomes evident that those systems are bad, and that a general revolution in the principle and construction of governments is necessary.

Without fully realizing it, Burke and Paine were waging, in theory, the great political battle of the century, and the outcome would influence English politics for decades to come. The fact that neither author was particularly knowledgeable about the subject that provoked the controversy—the French and their history—troubled them only slightly. The second half of Burke's title, . . . *On the Proceedings in Certain Societies in London Relative to That Event*, indicated the principal concerns of, and audience for, both books. Future events connected with the Revolution—regicide, terror, war—determined who "won" the argument. Once the Revolution turned to chaos, Paine lost much of his middle-class support in England and even radical Whigs were frightened into conformity. English politics, with the political theories of Burke as a base and the Tories in power, took a different direction from the one Paine advocated, declaring ideological war on him and his friends and imprisoning or arresting those who circulated his books.

A personal argument, the controversial nature of Paine's pamphlet, and perhaps government pressure led its original publisher to cancel the initial agreement for printing *Rights of Man*. Paine turned it over to his friends William Godwin, Thomas Brand Hollis, and Thomas Holcroft, who fitted it for the press; Part I appearing in England in February 1791, and two months later in Paris, with a new preface. Income from sales, as with several of Paine's other best-sellers, went to support a libertarian cause, the Society for Constitutional Information, an organization of tradesmen, shopkeepers, and mechanics; their principles were consistent with his, and their steady increase in this period is directly attributable to Paine's popularity. He had discovered an audience for inexpensive political literature, and with his writings, working-class politics in England came of age.

But his effectiveness in dispersing democratic ideas among the people provoked a strong reaction from his opponents. His popularity, one might say, added to his difficulties. A scurrilous biography by "Francis Oldys" (George Chalmers), commissioned by the English government and entitled *Life of Thomas Pain, author of Rights of Men. With a Defence of his Writings,* did much to discredit its subject, by now a national celebrity. Chalmers, a lawyer, had lived in Maryland and hated all friends of the colonies. Well-read and writing on a government subsidy, he brought to light, in a vicious but well-researched study, all the failures of Paine's early years in England as shopkeeper, husband, and general ne'er-do-well. The biography, which ran through ten editions in two years, exposed him to public ridicule for the rest of his life and helped his political enemies, especially members of the upper class, in their efforts to undermine Paine's influence and integrity.

A month after the publication of Part II of *Rights of Man,* in March 1792, the government ordered Paine into court on charges of sedition. The trial date of June 8 was postponed until December, but he continued to say in speeches what he had already said in print. In danger of being arrested, he decided, on the advice of William Blake, to flee the country—just twenty minutes ahead of the arresting authorities, as it turned out—on September 13, 1792.

He never saw his homeland again. Just after his escape he was tried *in absentia,* found guilty, and permanently banished. Prosecutions for publishing or circulating *Rights of Man* continued for years. Ironically, the author was jeered in public and burned in effigy, even as his book was becoming the greatest best-seller in English history.

The hostility and confusion that attended Paine's escape from one side of the Channel contrasted sharply with the enthusiasm with which he was met on the other. "We arrived at Calais," said one observer, "and as soon as he was known to be on the shore, the people flocked to see him." Having been designated a French citizen by the National Assembly four months earlier, Paine was greeted officially with a salute from the guards. That night his election to the National Convention representing Calais was announced to the townspeople amid shouts of "Vive la Nation! Vive Thomas Paine!" Similar crowds greeted him along the road to Paris.

The celebrations ended, however, once he arrived in Paris, just two weeks after the September massacres; he got caught up in the political turmoil that raised a man up one day and brought him down the next. Paine, given to speaking his mind under any circumstances, was not meant for such treacherous political waters; and within months he came near to drowning, with the Jacobins—especially Marat and Robespierre—contributing to his misfortune.

One of only two foreigners among the 748 members of the National Convention, Paine was named to a committee of eight to draw up a new constitution. After the trial of Louis XVI, however, Paine risked his reputation as a friend of the Revolution and, in a very real sense, his life, by a courageous speech before the Convention favoring exile, rather than death, for the king. As Bancal, philosopher and secretary of the Convention said later, Paine's vote against execution anticipated the vote of posterity. His final defense of this position, during a second vote, was challenged and then shouted down by Marat. "Paine voted against the punishment of death because he is a Quaker," Marat screamed. The king was put to death, and potential allies, horrified by such treachery, declared war on the French regicides.

From this time on, Paine lost influence in and commitment to the Convention's deliberations; although continuing to support it he relinquished much of his hope in the Revolution. When Robespierre gained control of the Convention, he and his allies accused "moderates," such as Paine and his associates, the Girondins, of being traitors. Aware of his danger, but remaining in France and writing as usual, Paine turned his full attention to *The Age of Reason, Being an Investigation of True and Fabulous Theology.* He completed Part I of the book on the eve of his arrest, December 23, 1793, leaving the manuscript with Joel Barlow as soldiers carried him off to Luxembourg prison.

Robespierre regarded foreigners and journalists as enemies, so Paine remained in prison during the duration of his reign, expecting to be guillotined any day. Even in those difficult days, with no outside word for months, he impressed those around him by his cheerful philosophy, "his sensibility of heart" and his powers of conversation, as "confidant of the unhappy" and "counselor of the perplexed," as one of his companions described him.

In prison he wrote "Essay on Aristocracy," "Essay on the Character of Robespierre," and other essays and poems; he revised and read aloud from *The Age of Reason,* and expressed his firm belief in its principles to inmates he expected not to see the following day. In the summer of 1794 he lay five weeks in a fever, of which he remembered little. On the day that Robespierre fell and was brought to the same

prison for execution, Paine began to improve. Finally, after ten months, nine days, and numerous pleas for help, he was released, through the intervention of the new American minister to France, James Monroe.

Even before Paine got out of jail, *The Age of Reason,* published in a French edition, with the help of his French translator, François Lanthenas, had created something of a stir and provoked several published responses. Part I, prompted by his fear that unless superstition were abolished, people would turn to atheism, was a generalized attack on the Bible, which Paine said could more consistently be called "the word of a demon than the Word of God." Its principal arguments deal with the unreliability of any word of God, because of the mutability of language; the reliability of creation as a guide, because of its availability and truth; the moral duty of human beings, as manifest in God's beneficence toward His creation.

The book is characteristically deist in its commentary on mysteries, miracles, revelations, and stories associated with the Old Testament and with Jesus. Paine believed in "one God, and no more," as he said in the preface, and in "doing justice, loving mercy, and endeavoring to make our fellow creatures happy." He thought these reasonable beliefs needed no support from authority or tradition. These were self-evident truths, while most of the commentary associated with the Bible was unnecessary, idolatrous, and untrue.

Paine began writing Part II of *The Age of Reason,* with a brief note in the preface on his imprisonment, as soon as he took "temporary" residence with Monroe and his wife (he stayed there a year and a half). Part I had been a general indictment of scripture without benefit of a text, Paine said. Part II examined "the authenticity of the Bible" and cited specific books, by chapter and verse. "Moses is not the author of the books ascribed to him." The book of Joshua is "horrid

. . . a military history of rapine and murder, as savage and brutal as those records of his predecessor in villainy and hypocrisy, Moses.'' The book of Ruth is ''an idle, bungling story.'' The book of Isaiah is ''prose run mad.'' As history, he said, the Bible is contradictory, disorderly, spurious, erroneous, and obscure. Time spent reading it is better spent on natural philosophy, mathematical and mechanical sciences—''a continual source of tranquil pleasure, and in spite of the gloomy dogmas of priests and of superstition, the study of these things is the study of true theology.'' Benjamin Franklin—his mind ever young, ''his temper ever serene''—rather than Solomon, teaches us how to live.

What does one learn from ''the pretended thing called revealed religion?'' Nothing that is useful to human beings, and everything that is dishonorable to their Maker. The scheme of the Christian Church is ''to hold man in ignorance of the Creator, as it is of Governments to hold man in ignorance of rights.'' What audacity of the church and priestly ignorance to impose such writings upon the world, Paine said of the Old Testament; and the New Testament, ''founded upon the prophecies of the old,'' followed the fate of its foundation.

Combining the skepticism of the encyclopedists and the enthusiasm of the dissenters, he shook the foundations of traditional religion, writing in a style that everyone previously excluded from such theological discussions could read. Perhaps no other writer of his time could have performed such a task so successfully, and certainly no person who valued his reputation or his life would have risked doing so in this way. ''His awful reverence for God unnerved those who took their religion lightly,'' wrote Hawke, and neither the elite nor the conventionally religious ever forgave him.

For Paine, *The Age of Reason* followed *Rights of Man* as naturally as the latter had followed *Common Sense*. In religion, as in politics, he sought what was ''natural'' as opposed to what was ''artificial.'' He regarded his book as constructive, rather than destructive, to religion, written to purge, rather than to abuse, ''lest in the general wreck of superstition, of false systems of government, and false theology, we lose sight of morality, of humanity, and of the theology that is true.'' Paine made a similar statement in a letter he wrote to Samuel Adams in 1803. He told Adams that he wrote the book because, living continually in a state of danger, he saw the people of France ''running headlong into Atheism'' and wanted ''to stop them in that career.''

Clergymen, indeed most religious people, failed to understand Paine's objective, and many of them, including Dr. Richard Watson in England and the Reverend Uzal Ogden in America, wrote replies. The Federalists, including Timothy Dwight, president of Yale, argued that atheists and anarchists were, with Paine's help, endeavoring to undermine American morality. *The Age of Reason,* in fact, prompted more responses and more vigorous denunciation than any of Paine's previous writings and helped to confirm the opinion of those who had regarded him as dangerous all along. It was partially because of the response to this book that many of his American friends kept him at a distance for the rest of his life. Thomas Jefferson, for example, who generally agreed with Paine's religious teachings, carefully avoided saying so in print. As late as 1813, four years after Paine's death, Jefferson would not allow his letters to Paine to be published, lest they draw on him ''renewed molestations from the irreconcilable enemies of republican government.''

Deism had, of course, been a gentleman's religion at least since the time of Alexander Pope's *Essay on Man* (1733). Paine's major fault lay in making such beliefs available to everyone. Writing them down only stirred up the people. The controversy over Part I of *The Age of Reason* had already gathered steam by 1795, and the publication of Part II, in the fall of that year, brought the controversy in England to a steady boil.

Paine had been very ill in early 1796, but through the help of Monroe and his wife, who cared for him faithfully through periods of difficulty and occasional ingratitude, he regained his health. The prison experience had greatly embittered Paine. He blamed his illness partly on Robespierre and partly on George Washington, whom he suspected of treachery in not working for his release from Luxembourg prison but who apparently knew little about his distress. Gouverneur Morris, the American minister prior to Monroe, had not worked as arduously as he might have in order to seek Paine's release (Paine had been made an American citizen some years before).

Whether conscious or unconscious, Washington's neglect led to Paine's seventy-page angry list of specific grievances, "Letter to George Washington." The "Letter" reflected also Paine's deep resentment of Jay's Treaty (1796) for being conciliatory to England and unfriendly toward France. But the principal vendetta was aimed at Washington, a man who was "treacherous in private friendship" and "a hypocrite in public life," for abandoning the author of *Common Sense*. In passing, Paine also settled accounts with his old antagonist, John Adams, and the "prating," pompous Gouverneur Morris. The only thing Paine accomplished by circulating such a letter was to revive interest in himself in America. If attacking the Bible was outrageous, attacking George Washington was worse, prompting William Cobbett, Paine's American biographer, to write, in *The Life of Thomas Paine* (1797), that "Men will learn to express all that is base, malignant, treacherous, unnatural, and blasphemous by one single monosyllable—Paine."

Those wishing to villify the author of *The Age of Reason* and "Letter to George Washington" got some help from the man himself, who occasionally horrified observers by his vanity and drinking, perhaps brought on by loneliness, boredom, and neglect. Exaggerated reports of his behavior were encouraged, but Paine, who had no desire to conform to anyone's idea of good or conventional behavior, either ignored them or, by attacking the originators of these tales, spurred them on to further harassment.

During this period, Paine periodically made plans to return to America and devoted his attention to religion, joining the Society of Theophilanthropists (a name made up of three Greek words meaning God, love, and man), attending the French National Convention, to which he had been readmitted in 1794, and writing *Atheism Refuted: in a Discourse to Prove the Existence of God*. The greatest work of these years is, however, *Agrarian Justice* (1795–1796), written in France as a response to a sermon by the bishop of Llandaff, Dr. Richard Watson, on "The Wisdom and Goodness of God in having made both rich and poor." Paine's response to this thesis was "It is wrong to say that God made Rich and Poor; he made only Male and Female, and He gave them the earth for their inheritance." William Blake, in comparing biblical commentaries by the two men, wrote later, "It appears to me now that Tom Paine is a better Christian than the Bishop."

The central argument of *Agrarian Justice* has to do with land distribution, a system that "while it preserves one part of society from wretchedness, shall secure the other from depredation." Seeing land as "the free gift of the Creator in common to the human race," Paine proposed a system whereby the government, as an agency of social welfare, would use taxes to pay pensions of aged persons and to aid unpropertied people according to their need. In doing so he steered a middle course between the position of the anarchists and the traditional aristocrats or, in his terms, between the French communists, led by François Babeuf, and the royalists.

Paine's moderate stand in regard to the redistribution of property, like his earlier position favoring a national bank and a centralized government, indicated his limitations as a radical theorist. Writing before the industrial revolution and in the early years of state capitalism, he failed to understand the conflict between his position here (earlier he had included the right to property among the inalienable rights) and the rest of his ideology. It was a dilemma that would haunt American radicals and weaken their position for generations to come, leaving them open to ridicule by later socialists, particularly Marxists, who seized upon this inconsistency in order to dismiss their radicalism as reformist rather than revolutionary.

As long as inalienable rights excluded the right to property, the poor lived at the mercy of inherited or accumulated wealth, and the practical implications of Paine's radical politics remained vulnerable. Anticipating Karl Marx, Paine wrote in *Agrarian Justice* that "the accumulation of personal property is, in many instances, the effect of paying too little for the labor that produced it; the consequences of which is that the working hand perishes in old age, and the employer abounds in affluence." A society based upon profit and accumulated property proved to be a more serious threat to the rights of man than Paine realized, and Thomas Spence, an English radical who called Paine's pamphlet "a dire disappointment," exposed its weaknesses in economic theory almost immediately.

Nonetheless, *Agrarian Justice* provided the groundwork for land reforms in language similar to that of Franklin and Jefferson, with an ideological perspective that looked forward to the Chartists and socialists of the nineteenth century rather than backward to the agrarians. And its arguments in favor of a socially responsible government were borrowed and expanded by later reformers, particularly Theodore Parker and Henry George.

By 1797 Paine, at sixty, had few reasons to remain in France, but unfriendly relations between that country and the United States, as a result of Jay's Treaty, and the possibility of his falling into the hands of the English, who persistently stopped American ships on the high seas, caused him to postpone or cancel plans for returning to the United States. Under John Adams, the Federalists, who had reacted against the French Revolution somewhat as the Tories did under William Pitt, initiated a rather repressive era, with the passage of alien and sedition laws and the use of scare tactics limiting traditional liberties.

Paine's hatred for the Federalists led him to write numerous attacks on Washington, Adams, and Gouverneur Morris in *le Bien Informé*, a newspaper edited by Paine's friend Nicolas de Bonneville, with whose family he stayed during his last five years in Paris, 1797–1802. He continued to involve himself with various revolutionary schemes, particularly those aimed at England. He befriended Irish radicals in Paris, wrote a widely circulated pamphlet on *The Decline and Fall of the English System of Finance* (1796), and encouraged Napoleon in his plans to invade Great Britain. "When this monster of national fraud and maritime oppression, the government of England, shall be overthrown, the world will be freed from a common enemy," he had written earlier. These and similar sentiments appeared in essays published in America, as well as in France and England, and suggested, particularly to the Federalists and occasionally to the French, that his resentment against his native country had unhinged his reason. By the turn of the century, he had few influential allies in England, France, or the United States.

With the election of Jefferson in the fall of 1800, the Republicans gained the advantage over the Federalists, and Paine now had a friend in power. He encouraged Jefferson's efforts to establish better relations between the United States and France, and his pamphlet, *Maritime Compact* (1801), sent to Jefferson earlier, received a favorable hearing. When word leaked out that Jefferson might actually provide passage to the United States for Paine on a public vessel, the president's antagonists, the Federalists, reacted indignantly. But Paine had friends among the common people, both those who visited the Bonneville home, in Paris, and those who supported Jefferson's decision, in the United States.

Waiting patiently for the necessary arrangements to be completed for his return, he devoted his final days in France to plans for a system of canals and iron bridges that would encourage unity among the French people and further development of their industries. His other preoccupations—politics, religion, and the applied sciences—are reflected in his personal associations at this time. Among the most frequent visitors were Robert Fulton, whose enthusiasm for mechanical inventions, including the steamboat, provided a basis for an immediate friendship with Paine, and Clio Rickman, whom he had lived with in England and who had printed Paine's later work there. Napoleon, who claimed to have been influenced by *Rights of Man,* visited the author and talked of his plan to invade England. "Common Sense" subsequently wrote two articles for Bonneville's journal which included descriptions of and plans for the use of gunboats. He also sent similar descriptions to Jefferson, in letters to whom he frequently included construction plans and designs for buildings and gadgets. On April 20, 1805, he wrote to Jefferson commenting on his activities at this time: "When I was in France and in England since the year 1787, I carried on my political productions, religious publications, and mechanical operations, without permitting one to disturb or interfere with the others." Obviously, however, in his friendships and political associations, as well as in his publications, Paine's enthusiasms often overlapped.

As his long stay in France came to an end, Paine must have realized that much of what he had devoted his extraordinary energies to in Europe had failed. The constitution ratified by the French resembled only slightly the one based upon *The Declaration of the Rights of Man and the Citizen,* which he advocated; the industrial revolution and a political "counter-revolution," as he called it, made life worse for workers in England than it had been previously, when the party of Wilkes and the writings of Paine signified a move for substantial social change. His iron bridge, though influential, brought no financial rewards. He had become somewhat irascible and physically weaker because of two serious illnesses. Rumors of his death had circulated in the late 1790's, with strong hints of a deathbed conversion (apocryphal stories that continue to circulate to the present day). In this somewhat confused state of affairs, Paine embarked for the United States from Le Havre, on September 1, 1802, and his loyal friend Clio Rickman wrote this valedictory poem about the event: "Thus smooth be the waves, and thus gentle the breeze/ As thou bearest my Paine far away."

Arriving in Baltimore on October 30, Paine went to Washington, D.C., to visit the president, bridge models in hand and political advice in tow. Jefferson, to his lasting credit, received Paine courteously, even as the Federalist press ranted about his consorting with a rancorous, obscene old sinner. Paine responded to them in an open letter, "To the Citizens of the United States," saying that Providence, not "the prayers of priests" or the "piety of hypocrites," carried him through the dangers of the French Revolution and would take care of him still. Regarding the behavior of the Federalists, he said, "those who abuse liberty when they possess it, would abuse power could they attain it." His wit had lost none of its bite; his style none of its vigor.

He wrote seven additional public letters "To the Citizens of the United States," repeating his criticisms of Washington and Adams (he attacked the latter man's "consummate vanity" and "shallowness of judgment"); supporting the Louisiana Purchase ("Were I twenty years younger . . . I would contract for a quantity of land . . . and go to Europe and bring over settlers"); encouraging a closer alliance with France; exposing the dangers of a large standing army ("It was for the purpose of destroying the representative system, for it could be employed for no other"); and defending Jefferson's presidency, often anonymously, against his numerous enemies.

During this second American period, the last seven years of his life, Paine lived variously in Bordentown, New Jersey, in New York City, and finally on his farm at New Rochelle. In 1804–1805 he began to assemble his writings for a collected edition. In 1806 he published a popular essay on the causes of yellow fever—not wholly accurate in its diagnosis, but reasonably close for a man only periodically engaged in scientific research or study. Occasionally, Paine was asked to speak at public events, and he continued his correspondence with his friends in power, particularly Jefferson.

All his life Paine had had friends who looked after him in time of need and during his last days, when he needed care, friends came to assist him. John Fellows, American publisher of *The Age of Reason;* Elihu Palmer, a deist and publisher of *The Prospect,* a journal that had published Paine's essays; and John Wesley Jarvis, an artist, all stayed with him at various times. But Mme. Marguerite Bonneville, wife of his French publisher, and her children—one of whom was his namesake—were particularly loyal to the very end.

Even in his final days, a brief period when he was very ill, Paine was badgered by religious militants bent on his conversion. On at least two occasions they pushed their way into his bedroom and proposed his reconciliation with traditional religion. To one person, who claimed to be God's messenger and threatened him with damnation, Paine reportedly had the strength and wit to respond: "Pshaw, He would not send such a foolish, ugly old woman as you about with His message. Go away." To another set of visitors, two ministers on a similar mission, he was quoted as saying: "Let me have none of your popish stuff. Get away with you. Good morning, good morning."

One June 8, 1809, shortly after expressing a firm commitment to his religious beliefs, Thomas Paine died, at 59 Grove Street, in Greenwich Village, New York City. He was buried at his farm in New Rochelle, because the Quakers would not admit him to their burial ground. Before a small group of mourners, Mme. Bonneville gave this final tribute: "O! Mr. Paine! My son stands here as testimony of the gratitude of America, and I, for France." His last will, written six months before his death, began with a brief review of his writings. He bequeathed his principal inheritances to his loyal friends, particularly the Bonnevilles and their children, so that they might "bring them well up, give them good and useful learning, and instruct them in their duty to God, and the practice of morality." His judgment on himself Paine pronounced with calm authority: "I have lived an honest and useful life to mankind; my time has been spent in doing good, and I die in perfect composure and resignation to the will of my Creator, God."

The political and religious controversies surrounding Paine during his lifetime did not subside after his death. His obituaries, in fact, raised them anew, and early biographies exploited the exaggerated accounts of his drinking habits and sensational stories about his "blasphemies" and "licentiousness." Since the time of the Puritans any critic of the political and religious establishment might expect to be accused of sexual excesses, and Paine had that charge thrown at him as well.

Comments by Joel Barlow, published at the time of Paine's death, combined eloquent tribute with the harsh personal judgment of a former friend. Barlow talked of Paine's low, vulgar, and disgusting habits, as well as of his exceptional writings, saying that "the most rational thing he could have done would have been to have died the instant he had finished *Common Sense.*" James Cheetham, a libertarian in England who turned reactionary in America, had the last word on his political enemy, in a revengeful biography. Cheetham's work was so scandalous that Mme. Bonneville sued him for libel and won. Yet Cheetham's work and the earlier biography by George Chalmers fixed an image in the popular mind of Paine as profligate, if not lecherous. That kind of impression dies slowly.

Nonetheless, a clear picture of Paine as man and writer begins to emerge as recent biographers and historians make fruitful use of new information about Paine's later years in France and America, about the early days of the industrial revolution and its popular literature, about founding fathers and members of the crowd. Such historical and sociological background is crucial to understanding a figure like Paine, since it helps to explain not only his idiosyncrasies as a person but also his style as a writer. As a pamphleteer he often had to write without benefit of subsidy or of a reliable patron. The fact that his service to the United States brought him little adulation angered him; his letters and statements to public officials after 1802 are characterized by a bravado best understood as the hurt feelings and disappointment of one once celebrated.

Paine's detractors have argued that he invited or enjoyed personal harassment and isolation, but nothing in his writing—either his published works or his extensive correspondence—supports this judgment. He was simply too preoccupied with public affairs and events to give much attention to his own. From his letters he appears to have been a man for whom people and circumstance remained somewhat distant. Although he moved in society among the merchants and political leaders of Philadelphia and among the intellectuals in France, he never gave up certain working class habits, refusing to adopt the manners necessary for easy movement in middle-class society. Accounts of his slovenly living quarters, irregular hours, and occasional rowdiness indicate only that he was as indifferent to social convention as he was to traditional political and religious customs.

Rationalist, utilitarian, and humanist in the eighteenth-century tradition, Paine was nonetheless a profoundly religious person, for whom moral questions were the questions of ultimate concern. Although never a member of the Society of Friends and often critical of its pacifism, he revealed in his writings on church and state an indebtedness to that religious persuasion. It provided a point of reference for judging other institutions. His pamphlet, "Worship and Church Bells," published in France in 1797, recommended, for example, that French Catholics do "as the Quakers do": worship without priests, inquire into the truth, value education, and alleviate the deplorable state of the poor.

In his impetuous denunciation of Paine during the French Convention, Marat, another kind of radical, claimed that Paine had voted against Louis XVI's execution because of his Quaker background. Marat's accusation was a cynical political trick calculated to confuse the issue and to win a political argument, but the incident calls attention to an important aspect of Paine's life and character: the persistent effect of his religious roots. Quakers, he said, were "deists without knowing it." Paine was at times a Quaker without admitting it; his father's religion influenced him directly and indirectly, and one of his last requests was to be buried in Quaker ground.

Three years before his death, Paine said that the motive of his religious writing was "to bring man to right reason . . . and to excite in him a spirit of trust, confidence and consolation in his Creator, unshackled by the fable and fiction of books, by whatever invented name they may be called." His teachings, influential among a small group after his death, survive principally among free thinkers, and the value systems of later humanists—Bertrand Russell in "A Free Man's Worship" and *Why I Am Not a Christian,* for example—are consistent with Paine's.

The humanitarian values Paine espoused were evident in the affairs of his daily life, according to witnesses during his time in prison and through his last days. Although he justified wars of independence, he was generally appalled by violence, opposing it philosophically and acting practically to protect others against it. "Peace, which costs nothing," he said, "is attended with infinitely more advantage than any victory with all its expense." An early American essay of his attacked the "gothic and absurd" custom of dueling. The effort to end capital punishment, he wrote, "must find its advocates in every corner where enlightened politicians and lovers of humanity exist." During the French Revolution he intervened to protect an Englishman who struck him (a capital offense, since Paine was a member of the Convention) and even provided money for the man's escape. He acted on behalf of Francisco de Miranda, adventurer and soldier, who narrowly escaped execution at the time of the Terror. Late in life, Paine refused to bring charges against a person who shot out a window in his house and endangered his own life.

Jefferson compared the literary style of Paine with that of Benjamin Franklin, but he might more profitably have compared them in personality. Paine had Franklin's wit, intelligence, and gregarious nature, but not his natural tolerance and wily political skill. He provoked his enemies, while Franklin charmed them into neutrality or won them to his side. Paine was, like Franklin, a true child of the Enlightenment—deist, skeptic, gadgeteer. It is no wonder that the two men got on famously. Jefferson's loyalty to Paine, even in the face of political harassment, grew from a similar appreciation of their common interests and beliefs.

As a writer and thinker, Paine built upon two intellectual traditions and one new social development. The first is the radical political tradition, dating from the time of Milton and the arguments justifying the Commonwealth, the Glorious Revolution of 1688, and the political upheavals in England and America in the later eighteenth century. Paine knew the radical Whigs, his principal allies in England, many of whom remained loyal to him through a period of repression and imprisonment under the Pitt government. By their lives and writings, James Burgh, Joseph Priestley, John Wilkes, Catherine Macaulay, Richard Price, and William Godwin—all pamphleteers of the late eighteenth century—are justifiably linked with Paine.

The second is the prophetic and dissenting religious tradition extending from the Puritans of the early seventeenth century and especially from the Quakers of the late seventeenth century. Since the time of their refusal to bear arms under Charles II, the Quakers had maintained a jealous guardianship of the militant nonconformist tradition, risking imprisonment and death in their resistance to any unjust law and enduring the fiercest religious persecution in the private and public fulfillment of their duty to conscience. Paine's persistence in the face of imprisonment, exile, and near death resembles the zeal of these dissenting radicals.

To these two major influences, Paine added—or perhaps one should say incorporated—a third: his experience as a worker and his association with people lingering on the fringes of society, unsuccessful by most standards, dispossessed, even hopeless. Like Moll Flanders or the figures in Hogarth's engravings on city life, they lived out their lives under the threat of debtor's prison, which Paine himself experienced at least once and escaped another time. With this background he gave to his writing a strong sense of "the other England," previously excluded from formal political, religious, and literary debate. In the writings of Daniel Defoe, in John Gay's *The Beggar's Opera,* and in Samuel Johnson's *Life of Savage,* poor people played a central role, but in Paine's essays, a writer speaks for them and voices their discontent.

In his furious, moralistic attacks on church and state, Paine spoke in the voice of a person victimized by traditional institutions. His vehement denunciation of the rich reflects his close association with poverty before he came to America, when life seemed to promise little. He made out of this anger a literary style—not, like Swift, by transforming anger into cutting irony, but by applying it directly, in order to surround and annihilate his foe. In response, for example, to a royal proclamation issued for the purpose of suppressing *Rights of Man* and to a charge of libel brought against the book's publishers, Paine said:

If, to expose the fraud and imposition of monarchy, and every species of hereditary government—to lessen the oppression of taxes—to propose plans for the education of helpless infancy, and the comfortable support of the aged and distressed—to endeavor to conciliate nations to each other—to extirpate the horrid practise of war—to promote universal peace, and civilization, and the commerce—and to break the chains of political superstition, and raise degraded man to his proper rank—if these things be libellous, let me live the life of a Libeller, and let the name of LIBELLER be engraved on my tomb.

Paine's is the focused rage that one associates with all great revolutionary writers, expressed in language that is outrageous and penetrating.

He helped to create, in fact, a language for revolution in which, as Eric Foner has said, "timeless discontents, millennial aspirations and popular traditions were expressed in a strikingly new vocabulary"; and Paine's rhetoric—simple and direct, "his arguments rooted in the common experience of a mass readership"—suggests a great deal about the changing nature of the popular audience for literature in the late eighteenth century. He became for the lower classes what Locke had been for the merchant class in the English revolution of the previous century. Paine regarded himself, however, as a different kind of writer, calling Locke's writings "speculative" rather than "practical," and describing his style as "heavy and tedious." Traditionalists like Burke accurately recognized Paine, popular journalist and Grub Street rabble-rouser, as being—in some insidious way—the wave of the future.

Although he possessed an incisive mind and is legitimately called a rationalist, Paine operated as much by intuition and feeling as he did by logic. He picked up the political scent in any situation with the skill of a novelist, assuming, rather than demonstrating, the viability of the principles upon which his argument was based. His understanding of the evils of poverty and the perpetual disgrace of hardship give his writings a strong resemblance to Charles Dickens' or George Orwell's in their later descriptions of the urban poor. But Paine had a faulty ear for detail and a poor sense of narrative—one reason, perhaps, why he gave up his plans for writing a history of the American Revolution. He lacked the patience of the careful observer, his mind running quickly toward an abstract concept or a moral truth implicit in a situation rather than toward a detail or image that might recreate it immediately in the mind of the reader.

Randolph Bourne, who first used the term "American literary radical" in 1918, rightfully looked to Paine as progenitor. His unique and lasting contribution to American culture was as a literary radical, being at once its embodiment and a sign of later developments in that tradition. Although Paine's life and ideas were firmly rooted in a preindustrial society, he lived according to the values of and spoke a language similar to later radicals: William Lloyd Garrison, Margaret Fuller, and Wendell Phillips in the nineteenth century; Emma Goldman, Eugene Victor Debs, and Dorothy Day in the twentieth century. Under the pressure of other injustices, they directed themselves to similar libertarian causes: the abolition of slavery, the rights of workers, the emancipation of women. All, as editors and agitators, raised their voices against the established order, advocating a more open society, with something of Paine's anger, frustration, and persistence. Like him, they eventually came to an indictment of the whole social system.

Revolutionaries, rather than reformers, working, by choice or accident, outside the centers of political power, they affirmed similar radical principles: that the basis of a just society is a universal good, often self-evident to everyone; that each person has a right to direct his or her own life, as Paul Goodman said, "without being pushed around"; that the purpose of society is to serve people, not property—the living, not the dead; that good citizens have a right to revolt and, in the face of unjust laws, as Mulford Q. Sibley said, an "obligation to disobey"; that people owe allegiance not to one nation, but to all people. Paine's motto, "My country is the world," called attention to the limitations of nationalism just as it gathered strength in Europe as an ideology; Garrison and Debs repeated Paine's saying, and saw internationalism as central to their own radical program.

Commentators emphasizing Paine's limita-

tions as a political theorist often ignore the value of his perspective on public matters; they criticize his failure to influence the established order and to commit himself to conventional political action. Although it is often essential in any movement for social change, compromise does tend to dilute an issue. Discontent among the lower classes and injustice in government, not the structural means for correcting abuses, constituted Paine's lifework. It was characteristic of him that an injudicious disclosure of fact, in the indictment of Silas Deane, led to Paine's dismissal from a major political office. A different mode of behavior is easily defensible on political grounds, but he assumed, like many literary radicals, that a principal means of correcting injustice is to publicize it.

Paine never defined himself within the context of legislative politics, and had trouble maintaining his composure during extended parliamentary debate. Franklin and Madison could carry on the tasks of practical politics. As a writer, Paine spoke to a different, but equally important, public need, identifying grievances and clarifying relationships in a time of change. In a malleable society he gave people a libertarian vision of the future and raised their level of expectation about how they might govern themselves. Although he suffered from a common fault of writers—assuming that social change could be carried on through exhortation, rather than by action and reconciliation—he helped to establish a tradition that, in the lives and writings of later literary radicals, continues to inform American culture.

During his thirty years as a public figure, Paine repeatedly affirmed his loyalty, in theory and practice, to the lower classes, rather than to the upwardly mobile merchant classes that came to dominate the American scene after the Revolution and the ratification of the Constitution. Many of his contemporaries and compatriots—including John Adams, John Hancock,

Charles Carroll, and Samuel Adams—were "revolutionary" in regard to American independence, but increasingly "conservative" in regard to the policies of the new nation. Paine, for all his inconsistencies, remained "revolutionary" to the end. Writing forcefully and originally about fundamental social change, he left, in Walt Whitman's words, "a deep, clear-cut impression on the public mind."

Selected Bibliography

WORKS OF THOMAS PAINE

An authoritative collected edition of Paine's public and private writings is badly needed, but two previous collections are useful. *The Complete Writings of Thomas Paine*, edited by Philip S. Foner, 2 vols. (New York: The Citadel Press, 1945), is the latest and best. *The Writings of Thomas Paine*, edited by Moncure Daniel Conway, 4 vols. (New York: G. P. Putnam's Sons, 1894–1896), is standard.

Common Sense, 1776.
The American Crisis, 1776–1783.
Rights of Man: Being an Answer to Mr. Burke's Attack on the French Revolution, 1791–1792.
The Age of Reason: Being an Investigation of True and of Fabulous Theology, 1794–1796.
Agrarian Justice, 1797.

CURRENT EDITIONS
Rights of Man. New York: E. P. Dutton, 1935.
Common Sense and Other Political Writings, edited by Nelson F. Adkins. Indianapolis: Bobbs-Merrill, 1953.
Age of Reason, Part 1, edited by Alburey Castell. Indianapolis: Bobbs-Merrill, 1957.
Thomas Paine: Representative Selections, edited by Harry Hayden Clark. Rev. ed. New York: Hill and Wang, 1961.
Common Sense and the Crisis. New York: Doubleday, 1970.
Rights of Man, edited by Henry Collins. Baltimore: Pelican, 1970.

BIOGRAPHIES

Aldridge, Alfred Owen. *Man of Reason: The Life of Thomas Paine*. Philadelphia: J. B. Lippincott, 1959.
Conway, Moncure Daniel. *The Life of Thomas Paine*. 2 vols. New York: G. P. Putnam's Sons, 1892.
Foner, Eric. *Tom Paine and Revolutionary America*. New York: Oxford University Press, 1976.
Hawke, David Freeman. *Paine*. New York: Harper and Row, 1974.
Williamson, Audrey. *Thomas Paine: His Life, Work and Times*. London: George Allen & Unwin, 1973; New York: St. Martin's Press, 1973.

CRITICAL STUDIES

Bailyn, Bernard. "Common Sense," in *Fundamental Testaments of the American Revolution*. Washington: Library of Congress, 1973. Pp. 7–22.
Clark, Harry Hayden. "Thomas Paine—Introduction," in *Thomas Paine: Representative Selections, with Introduction, Bibliography, and Notes*. Rev. ed. New York: Hill and Wang, 1961.
Derry, John. *The Radical Tradition: From Tom Paine to Lloyd George*. New York: St. Martin's Press, 1967.
Fennessy, R. R. *Burke, Paine, and the Rights of Man: A Difference of Political Opinions*. The Hague, 1963.
Gimbel, Richard. *Thomas Paine: A Bibliographical Check List of Common Sense, with an Account of Its Publication*. New Haven: Yale University Press, 1956.
———. "Thomas Paine Fights for Freedom in Three Worlds: The New, The Old, The Next . . . Catalog of an Exhibition Commemorating the 150th Anniversary of His Death," *Proceedings of the American Antiquarian Society*, 70, Part II, 397–492 (1960).
Lynd, Staughton. *Intellectual Origins of American Radicalism*. New York: Pantheon Books, 1968.
Thompson, E. P. *The Making of the English Working Class*. New York: Pantheon, 1963.
Young, Alfred F., ed. *The American Revolution: Explorations in the History of American Radicalism*. DeKalb: Northern Illinois University Press, 1976.

—MICHAEL TRUE

Sylvia Plath

1932–1963

*T*HE publication of *Ariel,* the volume of poetry that Sylvia Plath completed in the week before she committed suicide, precipitated a uniquely intense critical reaction, in part because it is a uniquely intense poetry, strikingly original and deeply troubling to any reader. It is a poetry that shocks by virtue of some of its more sensational thematic concerns: injury, victimization, parasitism, alienation, brutality, war, cannibalism, death in all forms, torture, murder, suicide, patricide, genocide, holocaust, angst, fate, mental illness, paralysis, and anger. They are all there, and in such intensity, embodied in such startling images, that it has taken some time for the discussion to calm. The later publication of both *Winter Trees* and *Crossing the Water,* which made some poems available for the first time and reprinted many others that had been scattered in periodicals, has aided in bringing about a more evenhanded approach to this difficult poet. These volumes made more visible the existence in Plath's work of contrasting thematic concerns: of love, of motherhood, of spiritual search, of intense life, of transcendent moment, of tenderness, and, albeit on narrow grounds, of affirmation. This recognition in turn produced a reevaluation of similar themes as they occur, if not so emphatically or sensationally, in *Ariel* itself.

Initial reactions were precipitated at least as much by the fact of her suicide as by the nature and concerns of the poetry itself. *The Bell Jar,* Plath's autobiographical novel, also contributed to the view, first presented and later affirmed further by A. Alvarez (who knew Plath), that the poetry and the suicide were inextricably intertwined, that one was essentially the cause of the other. Such observations probably made inevitable the dominance of psychoanalytic criticisms of Plath's work. The debate among the psychoanalytic critics revolves around reconstructing the poetry and interpreting it as the case history of a woman with severe mental illness. These interpretations have produced a variety of diagnoses: exogenous depression; manic depression; schizoidschizophrenia. The strong oedipal themes of some of the works provide added impetus to this style of criticism, a style that persists in David Holbrook's *Sylvia Plath: Poetry and Existence* and, in a more heavy-handed way, informs Edward Butscher's *Sylvia Plath: Method and Madness.*

Holbrook's study is the most careful and comprehensive, attempting a full explication of the text from this point of view, an explication of great value. Yet the book also illustrates some of the weaknesses of this approach. First, it collapses too completely the distinction between Sylvia Plath, human being and poet, and the personae of the poems that she constructed. To be sure, Plath's extensive use of the autobiographical in her writing irresistibly invites such a collapse. Yet she had very strong notions about the poet's responsibility to move beyond the autobiographical. Second, Plath had read Freud; and one is often uneasy with the feeling that to analyze in this way is to accept at face value a Freudian myth of self that Plath calculatedly constructed. One wonders if such an approach is not closer to paraphrase than to analysis. Finally, the criticism itself raises questions about what need we have to read Plath's poetry as pathological: why do we, who share the twentieth-century culture from which she sprang and to which she addressed her work, feel so powerful a need to see her as deviant?

The last question is central when it is recognized that Holbrook's quarrel with Alvarez and, for that matter, with the critics whose essays are collected in Charles Newman's *The Art of Sylvia Plath,* is fundamentally a quarrel about social responsibility in literary criticism. Holbrook argues that critics must negatively evaluate a poem like "Edge," despite its technical brilliance, because it is an example of moral inversion, of "Evil be thou my good." Thus, too, what he calls the poems of hate and of self-destruction. The fact that these urges are genuine is not sufficient to praise their embodiment in art. Holbrook's argument is also clearly directed at R. D. Laing's view that the schizoid condition is a normal one in our world, that since civilization is schizoid, a schizoid personality formation is a predictable survival strategy and suicide is an expectable and often a warranted act. We are involved, then, in the classic "art for art's sake" versus "art for life's sake" argument, and Plath seems to raise this issue in a particularly pressing way.

Sylvia Plath, even if discussed only from the psychoanalytic framework that has dominated comment on her work, is an extremely controversial poet. Her work as a whole is courageously honest, surrealistically associational, and, in the individual poems, as concentrated as that of any contemporary poet. Yet Barbara Hardy may be right in suggesting that Plath simply does not have typical poems. Rather, she seems to have fulfilled the desire of Esther Greenwood, the heroine in *The Bell Jar,* to be an arrow shooting off in all directions. This is not to say that the poetry is random or uncontrolled, although it is certainly obscure at times. Quite the contrary. Plath's poetry is experiential, and takes many directions in the eternal search for human identity and meaning. To enter into this search with Plath is to do so in the company of a poet of great technical skill and original personal voice, a voice forged through a sustained and difficult apprenticeship. Hers is the unmistakable idiom of a midtwentieth-century American woman. And critics have agreed on one thing: at their best, Plath's poetic hooks are as sharp as the experiential "hooks" of which she writes.

Sylvia Plath was born in Boston, Massachusetts, on October 27, 1932, to Otto and Aurelia Plath. Otto had emigrated to America from Germany at the age of sixteen to study for the ministry at Northwestern College, a small Lutheran school. By Aurelia's report, Otto's ambitions changed because he did not feel a genuine "call," and after receiving the master of arts from Washington University and the doctor of science from Harvard, he became a professor of biology at Boston University in 1928. Aurelia taught German and English at Brookline High School until January 1932, when she and Otto married, and she "yielded to my husband's wish that I become a full-time homemaker." The Plaths then settled in Winthrop, a seaside town near Boston, where Aurelia's Austrian immigrant parents lived and where Sylvia spent her early childhood.

The Plath household, Aurelia reports, was a patriarchal one in the traditional, Old World sense. And she was consistently and heavily involved in her husband's career: they had planned cooperative scholarly projects before their marriage, and afterward she prepared and updated lecture notes, reviewed current scholarly literature, and jointly researched, wrote, and edited the monographs published by her husband. Indeed, Otto's work was central to the household, which was organized and scheduled, including the routines of Sylvia and her brother Warren, around the needs of a scholar for privacy and work space. The Plaths did not lead active social lives, and Sylvia's earliest associations were largely limited to her parents, her brother, her maternal grandparents, and a few friendly neighbors.

These early years in Winthrop were personally and artistically crucial to Plath's development; she came to regard them as "beautiful, inaccessible, obsolete, a fine, white, flying myth." "My childhood landscape," she says in a reminiscence titled "Ocean 1212-W" (her grandmother's phone number at Point Shirley), "was not land but the end of land—the cold, salt, running hills of the Atlantic." She continues:

I sometimes think my vision of the sea is the clearest thing I own. I pick it up, exile that I am, like the purple "lucky stones" I used to collect . . . and in one wash of memory, the colors deepen and gleam, the early world draws breath.

Plath summons here a nostalgic reminiscence of a childhood Eden, but the memory is structured by the adult consciousness it informs. Like all "flying" myths, this one contains an element of tragedy.

For Plath, the sea is ambiguous, mysterious, impenetrable: "Like a deep woman, it hid a good deal; it had many faces, many delicate terrible veils . . . if it could court, it could also kill." She associated the sea with her early life, referring to her "ocean-childhood," and she regarded this childhood as "probably the foundation of [her] consciousness." There are, therefore, sources for Plath's ambiguity about the sea: her experience of the sea as a changeful and unpredictable natural phenomenon in its own right, as an objective entity, was concrete, and this became, for her, a model of the experience of the self in nature. Her experiences of the sea also are tied subjectively to her mother, father, and grandmother, and to feelings of powerlessness, vulnerability, betrayal, and loss, as well as to "bright mirrors," days of play at the beach and the warmth of her grandmother's home at Point Shirley.

"One day," she reports, "the textures of the beach burned themselves on the lens of my eye forever." She discovered, on that day, that her mother had "deserted" her for three weeks in order to return with a baby brother.

I, who . . . had been the center of a tender universe felt that axis wrench and a polar chill immobilize my bones. . . . As from a star I saw, coldly and soberly, the separateness of everything. I felt the wall of my skin: I am I. That stone is a stone. My beautiful fusion with the things of this world was over.

Plath sought solace from the sea that day, looking for a "sign. . . . A sign of election and specialness. A sign I was not forever to be cast out." Clearly, this is the classic birth of self-consciousness, coupled with a child's powerful need for affirmation, for continuity, for community, and, above all, for specialness; in the language of a historic New England, for "election." The tension between the desire for fusion and the desire for specialness in face of inevitable otherness, which was stimulated first by the birth of her brother, eventually became one of the major themes Plath explored in her later works.

She sought in her early childhood to assuage this sense of otherness by establishing a strong relationship with her father. He took pride in her childhood accomplishments, and Sylvia, apparently, idolized him. But in 1940 he became ill from a neglected case of diabetes, and died in November, of complications from the disease. This second loss, also associated with early childhood, as another traumatic demonstration of separateness, became a major turning point in Plath's life, and later she wrote of it, in "Lady Lazarus," as her own first death. It was certainly one of the events in her life that continued to haunt her. After her first suicide attempt, at the age of nineteen, she reported to her friend Nancy Steiner one of her reactions to her father's death: "He was an autocrat . . . I adored and despised him, and I probably wished many times that he were dead. When he obliged me and died, I imagined that I had killed him."

The personae of many of her poems, including perhaps the most famous, "Daddy," work through the effects and implications of the father-daughter relationship; and in *The Bell Jar* Esther Greenwood's visit to her father's grave is an important event. In dealing with these matters artistically, water imagery, most often sea imagery, is employed either for purposes of thematic development and enrichment or as the direct means of thematic expression. For Plath, then, the seascape is fused with memories of her father, more so because his death occasioned the family's move inland to Wellesley, "whereon," she says, "those nine years of my life sealed themselves off like a ship in a bottle."

Her last memories of the sea, Plath states, were memories of violence, "a still unhealthy day in 1939, the sea molten, steely slick, heaving at its leash like a broody animal." A hurricane was due, and when it came, it spread all the devastation a child "might wish." "The only sound was a howl, jazzed up by the bangs, slams, groans, and splintering of objects tossed like crockery in a giant's quarrel. The house rocked on its root." Land's end is, for Plath, the tangled bank of "Point Shirley," the scene of

the eternal natural drama of life and death, as in "Suicide off Egg Rock," and a primary symbol of alienation from nature, as in "Mussel Hunter at Rock Harbor."

Yet this early experience was not quite as "sealed off" as Plath suggests, for the seascape became one of the major metaphoric resources of her poetry; and it was a sea poem that introduced her to poetry itself. She recalls her mother reading to her and her brother from Matthew Arnold's "Forsaken Merman." Her response, she says, was immediate: "I saw the gooseflesh on my skin. I did not know what made it. I was not cold. . . . It was the poetry. A spark flew off Arnold and shook me, like a chill. I wanted to cry; I felt very odd. I had fallen into a new way of being happy."

At the age of eight, Sylvia Plath had her first poem published, in the Boston *Sunday Herald:*

> Hear the cricket chirping
> In the dewy grass.
> Bright little fireflies
> Twinkle as they pass.

With this Plath began an apprenticeship that culminated in the publication of her first collection of poems, *The Colossus* (1960), by William Heinemann, Ltd., in England. For nearly twenty years she worked at poetry, developing and honing a technique, moving toward a mature voice and style that were unmistakably hers, a voice that has since been much imitated but never duplicated. Writing became one route to the specialness she sought—to "election." As she put it, she wanted to become "a woman poet . . . the world will gape at."

It was not, however, the only route. Those who admire the figure of the alienated writer look with considerable astonishment at the normalcy of Plath's girlhood; at least it was normal for a very bright, highly motivated middle-class girl in post-World War II America. As a student, Plath was consistently a high achiever. She was recognized by her teachers as especially gifted in writing; she served as editor of the school newspaper, participated in student theatrical productions, and persistently submitted her writing for commercial publication, finally placing a story in *Seventeen* after forty-five rejections. She was elected to the National Honor Society, and among the many other honors she received was a scholarship to Smith College. She listed her intended profession as "writer," but during her college years she vacillated between writing and the graphic arts as professional concerns. In each case, she thought of both commercial and artistic success, the "slick" and the serious, as compatible pursuits, seeing one as possible support for the other. Long after her decisive turn toward poetry and serious fiction, Plath continued to work on fiction slanted toward the slick magazine, describing publication in the *Ladies' Home Journal* as an aim even during the last year of her life.

In the fall of 1950 Plath entered Smith College, supported by money from the Olive Higgins Prouty Fund, the Nielson Scholarship, and the Wellesley Smith Club. Her letters home are full of the typical concerns of a Smith coed in the 1950's: clothes, Ivy League men, cream-colored convertibles, friends, blind dates, grades, and the need to be "versatile." She became well known at Smith through the stories she had published, and won third place in *Seventeen*'s writing contest during her freshman year.

Plath's first three years at Smith were, with few exceptions, the logical extension of her high school career. She was known as a brilliant, energetic, and highly motivated student. Her essential intellectuality extended to active involvement in the cultural events of the college; especially, she sought out visiting writers, often commenting critically on their personalities and presentations. During this time, too, she wrote almost constantly, producing a large volume of poetry (often reflecting the influence of poets she was reading in her classes) and persisting in her efforts to be published. Some of the poems and short stories of this period are still available in back issues of such periodicals as *Seventeen, Christian Science Monitor, Mademoiselle, The National Poetry Association Anthology,* and *Harper's.* (Some have also appeared in limited editions published after her death by Rainbow Press.) Along with commercial publication, contribution to Smith College periodicals brought Plath wider recognition both at school and in a wider literary world. Eventually she received all of Smith's poetry prizes and was elected to Alpha, the Smith honorary society for the arts. In 1953 she was one of two national winners of the *Mademoiselle* fiction contest and was selected as managing editor for the August issue. She commented that the *Atlantic* and the *New Yorker* remained her "unclimbed Annapurnas."

Plath's activity as a student, an aspiring writer, and a "versatile" coed must have been frenetic. And there were signs, especially during her third year, that the intense pressure of such activity was beginning to have its effect: she had periodic bouts with sinus colds that physically and mentally exhausted her, and she chafed at any academic difficulty. She was a perfectionist, and could not abide the fact that she was receiving B's in German. She resented, to an irrational degree, the science requirement of the college. She wrote to her mother in the fall of 1952:

. . . I have practically considered committing suicide to get out of it [a science course]. . . . It just seems that I am running on a purposeless treadmill . . . dreading every day of the horrible year ahead. . . . I have become really frantic: small choices and events seem insurmountable obstacles, the core of life has fallen apart. I am obsessed by wanting to escape from that course. . . . When one feels like leaving college and killing oneself over one course . . . it is a rather serious thing. . . .

. . . I have built it up to a devouring, malicious monster. . . . I know I am driving myself to distraction. Everything is empty, meaningless. This is not education. It is hell. . . .

Clearly, Plath had fixated on this particular course as the focus of frustrations and anxieties that were much deeper than a single course could possibly engender. The letter in its entirety (dated November 19, 1952) is an indicator of things to come. Still, at this time Plath recognized the problem as stemming from her own psychological state, recognized that she herself had made the course a "monster." To the credit of her advisers at Smith, Plath was able to resolve her problems with science in a scheduling compromise, but the larger anxieties so evident here surfaced in extremely destructive ways in the summer of 1953.

Three days after the completion of her final examinations, Plath found herself in New York at the editorial offices of *Mademoiselle,* engaged in a nonstop series of activities planned for the group of college students chosen to edit the August issue of the magazine. At first hand, she saw the world of slick publication and flashy commercial fashion. Plath worked hard at her magazine assignments and, on the surface at least, enthusiastically engaged in even the most superficial of the activities. Her letters indicate very unstable attitudes toward her experience: "I have been very ecstatic, horribly depressed, shocked, elated, enlightened, and enervated—. . . I want to come home and vegetate in peace . . . with the people I love around me for a change." New York apparently came as a shock to her, and she desired retreat from "these slick admen, these hucksters" and the "breathless wasteland of the cliffdwellers."

Her retreat was to be far more complete than her letters suggest, for other bad news awaited her at home. Plath had not been accepted for Frank O'Connor's short story class, which she had planned to attend that summer. Her mother

was surprised at the intensity of her daughter's reaction to this news. Disillusionment in New York and rejection for a chance at serious work under respected guidance struck at Plath's twin professional ambitions and psychologically combined to invoke the earlier and unresolved losses of "specialness" and her father to produce the downward spiral of clinical depression.

On August 24, 1953, she nearly succeeded in a carefully planned and executed suicide attempt. Plath later spoke of this period as the blackest in her life, and says in "A Birthday Present": "I would have killed myself gladly that time any possible way."

Yet the most significant testimony we have about Plath's condition at this time is embodied in her most significant work of fiction, *The Bell Jar.* Probably written prior to the publication of *The Colossus* (but published only a month before her death), *The Bell Jar* is a work of imaginative transformation of experience. The temptation to read it as straight autobiography is great, for its details are taken so literally from Plath's life. But the book was written by a woman a full decade older, one who had matured enormously as an artist and whose artistic aim was directly to make use of personal experience in a larger and more encompassing mission—a mission of relevance. The testimony here is significant in a twofold way: as it fixes in perusable form the life experience that partly lies behind the driving force of Plath's poetic vision, and as it represents the more mature Plath assessing that experience and connecting it to themes that personally, socially, and culturally transcend "cries from the heart that are informed by nothing except the needle or the knife."

The novel is presented from the single point of view of its central character, Esther Greenwood. Esther, like Plath, is a college student who has been selected to be a guest editor of a major New York-based women's magazine for part of a summer. The narrative opens with a set of associations of both public and private "historical" significance:

It was a queer, sultry summer, the summer they electrocuted the Rosenbergs, and I didn't know what I was doing in New York. I'm stupid about executions. . . . but I couldn't help wondering what it would be like, being burned alive all along your nerves.

I thought it must be the worst thing in the world. . . .

I kept hearing about the Rosenbergs. . . . It was like the first time I saw a cadaver. . . . pretty soon I felt as though I were carrying that cadaver's head around with me on a string, like some black, noseless balloon stinking of vinegar. . . .

I was supposed to be having the time of my life.

From the opening lines of the novel, the reader is aware that there is something wrong with Esther. And very shortly the narrator reveals that she, too, is aware that there is something wrong: "I felt very still and very empty, the way the eye of a tornado must feel, moving dully along in the middle of the surrounding hullabaloo." The novel is designed to convey a psychological frame of mind, the mental condition to which the novel's title gives metaphoric embodiment. Events are not reported chronologically, but associationally, as the narrative present gives way to the narrative past in a modified stream-of-consciousness structure. Esther's consciousness is characterized by increasing patterns of dissociation, fragmentation, alienation and, finally, psychological paralysis. Plath provides relief for the reader only by means of the narrator's apparent objectivity, technically achieved through a strong sense of irony, in this context an irony amounting to black humor.

Esther Greenwood's essential problem is one of choice, of identity. Up to this point in her life,

like Plath herself, Esther has steered a relatively straight course, winning scholarships and prizes, preparing herself for success in the standard middle-class way. She has arrived at a turning point, sees an "era coming to an end," and finds herself unable to choose a future:

I saw my life branching out before me like [a] green fig tree.

From the tip of every branch, like a fat purple fig, a wonderful future beckoned and winked. One fig was a husband and a happy home and children, and another fig was a famous poet and another fig was a brilliant professor, and another fig was Ee Gee, the amazing editor, and another fig was Europe and Africa and South America, and another fig was Constantin and Socrates and Attila and a pack of other lovers with queer names and offbeat professions, and another fig was an Olympic lady crew champion, and beyond and above these figs were many more figs . . .

I saw myself sitting in the crotch of this fig tree, starving to death, just because I couldn't make up my mind. . . . I wanted each and every one of them, but choosing meant losing all the rest, and, as I sat there, unable to decide, the figs began to wrinkle and go black. . . .

Esther's inability to choose results largely from her own perception of the choices as mutually exclusive, a perception that finds its source in the internalized cultural expectations of her society, coupled with her own distorted vision of her abilities and experience. Indeed, she is greenwood, and she is about to face "realities" that she can neither imagine as escapable nor deal with realistically.

Esther's severest conflicts revolve around her identity as a woman, or, rather, her evolving identity as an autonomous person, clashing directly with the socially defined ideals of womanhood. She sees no way in which she can manage to achieve social acceptance, which she badly wants, as well as pursue the other things she judges valuable and important. She observes and imaginatively (not actually) tries out a variety of female identity types. Indeed, that is the function of the other female characters in the novel: they remain flat products of Esther's projections and do not take on individually compelling characters, precisely because they are hypothetical models, personae in an internal drama.

Esther explores the culturally standard varieties of the wife-mother combination through three characters: Dodo Conway, Mrs. Willard, and her own mother. In no case do the clichéd versions of happy wife and mother seem to fit the realities of the lives of these three women as Esther sees them. Dodo Conway is woman as reproductive machine, with six children and the "sprawling paraphernalia of suburban childhood." Assured by religious conviction (Dodo is Catholic), she wades through Rice Krispies and peanut butter, daily walking her "smudgy" children with cowlike serenity. Esther is interested in Dodo "in spite of" herself, but it is a perverse fascination with something that disgusts her, for children "make her sick." Dodo is the exaggeration of the suburban mother-wife, and her children represent for Esther the mindlessness of such a life.

Both Mrs. Willard and Mrs. Greenwood represent older and less exaggerated versions of the selflessness (not unselfishness) of Dodo Conway. Mrs. Willard, the mother of one of Esther's boyfriends, cooks, cleans, and washes from morning to night; her life is dedicated to Mr. Willard, a sentimental middle-aged man who cannot deal with his son, and to Buddy, a shallow young man who comes to represent male hypocrisy for Esther. Esther sees some sign of selfhood in Mrs. Willard's rug-making, yet she notes that "instead of hanging the rug on the wall the way I would have done, she put it down in place of her kitchen mat" and it became "undistinguishable from any mat." Esther sees this

as precisely analogous to Mrs. Willard's position in marriage:

And I knew that in spite of all the roses and kisses and restaurant dinners a man showered on a woman before he married her, what he secretly wanted when the wedding service ended was for her to flatten out underneath his feet like Mrs. Willard's kitchen mat.

Like Mrs. Willard, Esther's mother soon had confronted the realities of marriage when, shortly after the ceremony, Mr. Greenwood remarked: "Whew, that's a relief, now we can stop pretending and be ourselves." "From that day on," Esther comments, "my mother never had a minute's peace." Like Plath's own father, Esther's father died when she was nine ("I had never been happy since I was nine"), and Mrs. Greenwood was faced with the prospect of raising a family and providing an income. Esther remembers that her mother never grieved over her father's death and never forgave him for not having had enough insurance. Both Mrs. Willard and Mrs. Greenwood have continuous, sentimental, moralistic, and prosaic advice to offer about relations between men and women (women should keep themselves pure) and about the future (get secretarial skills; even the apostles had to have a trade). Neither offers Esther any alternative that might prove hopeful.

Esther's considerable anxiety about sex roles in conflict with identity is explored as well through her relationships with a series of men: Buddy Willard, Constantin, Marco, and Irwin. Her relationship with Buddy is one of long standing but little reward. He becomes the means through which she discovers male refusal to take female aspirations seriously, her own deep fears about motherhood, and the hypocrisy of the double standard. Fully taken with his own mother's pronouncements about the nature of men and women, Buddy is smug: he tells Esther, in a "sinister and knowing way," that after she has children, she won't want to write poems anymore. "So I began to think," reports Esther, "maybe it was true that when you were married and had children it was like being brainwashed, and afterward you went about numb as a slave in some private, totalitarian state." At one point Buddy, who is a medical student, takes her to see the birth of a baby in the hospital where he works. Although she comments casually that she could "see something like that every day," it is clear that she has been deeply affected by the "torture" chamber atmosphere, the drugging of the women ("just like the sort of drug a man would invent"), the pain of the birth, and the impersonality of the event.

Esther confronts the double standard when Buddy confesses that he had an affair with a waitress. Buddy's hypocrisy is complete for Esther; and she later wonders, as she considers the *Reader's Digest* article "In Defense of Chastity," given to her by her mother, whether it might be worth considering "how a girl felt." Purity was a big issue for her generation; she thought her whole life would change with the loss of her virginity. But it seemed intolerable to her that women should be pure while men could "have a double life, one pure and one not." Esther's efforts to lose her virginity are sparked by this insight, and she seeks sexual encounter, first with Constantin, a United Nations interpreter she meets during her month in New York. She romanticizes this relationship, imagining after just meeting him what it would be like to be married to him. Ironically, she has met Constantin through Mrs. Willard, and although they enjoy an evening together, none of Esther's obvious efforts bring about the desired seduction. Even Marco, a sadistic misogynist who violently threatens Esther as the representative of all hated womanhood and accomplishes her total effacement before men, leaves her a virgin. She waits until after her attempted suicide and consequent hospitalization to discover, in the company of an unscrupulous visiting professor named Irwin, that the loss of her virginity does not transform her into a being of some other order.

There are, then, no positive male figures in the novel, with the possible exception of Esther's father, who is dead. Even Dr. Gordon, a psychiatrist to whom Esther is initially referred when her mental and physical condition noticeably deteriorates, is a negative figure—smug, self-satisfied, and uncaring rather than vicious. Esther is not so much fearful of relationships, however, as she is fearful that relationships are, or necessarily become, empty and meaningless ("I wondered if as soon as he came to like me, he would sink into ordinariness. . . . I would find fault after fault"). She is not so much afraid of being a woman as she is resentful of the role that threatened to wipe out all other aspects of her identity, reducing her to a mere biological function or social and sexual object: "the trouble was, I hated the idea of serving men in any way."

After Esther's self-esteem has been eroded in other ways as well, she comes to mistrust her own intellectual ability and her ability to function in the day-to-day world: "there were so many things I couldn't do." And she feels that she is a sham, that she will be discovered for the stupid and shallow person she "really" is. This is, of course, life in the bell jar. She fears all those to whom she might turn, because they are potentially the penetrators of her mask, the discoverers of her vile and unworthy nature. It is crucial to point out that her guilt and anxiety are not so much the result of her own behavior or the application of the standards of others to it, as of her own perfectionism, which produces a distorted view of her "sins" and incompetencies. She takes wishes or possibilities as behaviors. For example, she wishes that she could be like Doreen, "a secret voice speaking out of her bones," confronting the male world as a shallow, predatory, and cynically manipulative woman; then, for merely imagining herself as Doreen, she feels "dirty" and bathes in ritual purification. Periodically, she wistfully turns toward religion, thinking she should become a Catholic so that she might confess her own despicable nature.

Esther can imagine no future in the world and perceives herself as split, disassociated. When asked about her future plans: " 'I don't really know,' I heard myself say. I felt a deep shock, hearing myself say that, because the minute I said it, I knew it was true."

Like Plath, Esther returns home to discover her rejection from a summer writing seminar. Thereafter she is almost totally sleepless, falling into the patterns of extreme depression. She sees "the years of [her] life spaced along a road in the form of telephone poles, threaded together by wires. . . . [and can't] see a single pole beyond the nineteenth." She concludes that she wants "to do everything once and for all and be through with it." She wanders aimlessly, contemplating various methods of suicide. She makes a ritual visit to her father's grave, howling her "loss to the cold salt rain." She then, after carefully deceiving her mother, takes an overdose of sleeping pills and secrets herself in a crawl space underneath her house.

Esther's next awareness finds her in a hospital, in terrible physical and mental condition, and it is here that her recovery begins. She is subjected to most of the standard therapeutic devices: electroshock, drug treatment, and psychoanalysis. She develops a good relationship with her psychiatrist, a woman with compassion and skill. As she grows stronger, as the bell jar lifts, she is gradually moved outward from the institution into the world from which she fled. Her competence is tested by the suicide of an acquaintance (regarded as another double), which leads her eventually to affirm her freedom and "the old brag of [her] heart. I am. I am. I am." She leaves the sanatorium for an uncertain future,

feeling the need of some kind of ritual "for being born twice—patched, retreaded and approved for the road."

The novel is so consistently autobiographical that Esther's fear that the bell jar eventually might lower again must be read as Plath's own. Moreover, the basic themes of the novel are to be seen time and again in the stronger voice of Plath the poet, directly in poems like "The Stones," "Lady Lazarus," and "The Applicant," more subtly in others. Plath herself is said to have referred to the novel as a "pot-boiler," and she first published it in England under the pseudonym of Victoria Lucas. The pseudonym is itself a revealing one. Victoria is an obvious reference, given the nature of the novel, to the repressed sexuality attributed to Victorian England; Lucas is a variant on Luke, the disciple-physician. The name, then, contains reference to the specific illness and to the writer as self-healer; Plath also later saw the novel as an exercise in psychological catharsis. Given its autobiographical qualities, however, there was clearly more than one reason for the pseudonym; indeed, after Plath's death her mother attempted to prevent American publication of the novel, believing it would cause unnecessary pain to many who had been Plath's friends.

The Bell Jar is not a great novel. Yet it is a better novel than Plath herself recognized. It is technically sound, if not in the forefront of narrative technique or of style. It is a comic, if painful, comment on American life during what one critic has called the Tranquilized Fifties, a female version of *The Catcher in The Rye*. The degree to which the personal and idiosyncratic have been transcended in the novel is directly to be measured by the ironic social comment represented in Esther Greenwood's internalized cultural landscape. Her dilemmas are plausible precisely because, through Esther, Plath has connected her private history to the relevant social history of her time. And no amount of literary or philosophical sophistication had prepared her for the experiences that led her to the isolation of the bell jar, most particularly those experiences connected with a specifically female identity search.

For reasons that are by now obvious, the novel has become a staple in the study of women's fiction. More interesting, perhaps, is the fact that it is read outside academic circles, beyond the tight world where literature is an all-encompassing professional concern. Such popularity will not serve the novel well in certain critical circles. It surely would not have bothered Plath, however, who sought vindication of her work from both quarters. In any case, *The Bell Jar* is certainly the best of Plath's fiction and an invaluable key to an examination of her far more difficult and aesthetically superior poetry, for in the novel Plath employed an approach to reality and style that prepared her for the poetic achievement of the last two years of her life.

Sylvia Plath's own return from "symbolic death and . . . the agony of slow rebirth" was to Smith College, in February 1954, where she rapidly reestablished her academic and creative reputation. During the year and a half following her illness, she studied German on a scholarship at Harvard; worked on creative writing with Alfred Kazin; published a number of poems, including "Two Lovers and a Beachcomber by the Real Sea" and "Circus in Three Rings"; and, in addition to the Academy of American Poets and Christopher's prizes, won at least two more Smith poetry prizes. During this time, too, she completed her honors thesis, "The Magic Mirror: A Study of the Double in Two of Does-toevsky's Novels," and earned the bachelor of arts *summa cum laude* in June 1955. And in the spring of that year, Plath was notified that she had won a Fulbright Fellowship to Newnham College, Cambridge.

While at Cambridge, Plath met and admired a number of British and American poets and intel-lectuals, including T. S. Eliot, David Daiches, C. P. Snow, F. R. Leavis, Stephen Spender, and Philip Larkin. If her letters home are any indication, she faced the intellectual rigor of Cambridge with confidence and skill. Her tutors, while at times amused and baffled by her "all-American girl" demeanor, found her to be a gifted student; and it is clear that Plath matured significantly during her two years of graduate work. Her association with older women scholars apparently prompted further exploration of her own female identity; this exploration is recorded in letters to her mother, and it provided the material for at least two of the poems Plath included in *The Colossus,* "Spinster" and "Strumpet Song." Together the poems reject a withdrawn and orderly life of "discipline/ Exact as a snowflake" without love and sexuality, as well as a life of mere sexuality that might be dictated by the lustful self looking "out from black tarn, ditch and cup/ Into my most chaste own eyes."

In February 1956, Plath met Ted Hughes, who was becoming known as a promising young British poet, and on June 16 they were "secretly" married in London. After their marriage they spent time in the town of Benidorm, Spain, where they each did some writing and studied languages. Plath began to serve as literary agent for both of them, which she apparently did for as long as they were married. In the fall they moved into a flat near Grantchester; Plath returned for her second year at Newnham (her Fulbright having been renewed); and Hughes took a teaching position at a day school in Cambridge. For Plath the combination of emotional and professional life in marriage seemed ideal. Her letters to her mother during this first year with Hughes are full of hope and joy. She saw him as her ideal male counterpart, "always just that many steps ahead of me intellectually and creatively so that I feel very feminine and admiring." According to Hughes, the year produced, in addition to

"Wreath for a Bridal" and "Epitaph for Fire and Flower," several poems that Plath later retained for inclusion in her first collection.

In all of these poems, the predominant themes lay down fundamental attitudes toward nature and the individual's role in natural drama. Nature is seen as alternately overwhelming, hostile, and indifferent in "Hardcastle Crags" and "Departure"; as bizarre and unruly in "Faun" and "Sow"; as deceptive, even crafty, in "Watercolor of Grantchester Meadows." Individuals are seen as unwilling and often unwitting or naive participants in nature's patterns, as for example in "All the Dead Dears" and "Faun." That Plath's model for nature is taken from her earlier intimacy with the sea is metaphorically clear in "Hardcastle Crags"; and death as the ultimate fact of nature and the controlling feature of human destiny emerges strongly in "All the Dead Dears." For Plath, death combines with urges for survival and rebirth to produce the "gross eating game." "All the Dead Dears" addresses itself to themes of kinship within the human condition, placing the individual within a long continuum of past and future deaths that ultimately assert the poet's own relation to the fourth-century woman whose coffin, on display at a museum, occasioned the poem. The poem also presents a first glimpse of what becomes a major concern in the late poetry, the father-daughter relationship.

During the first half of 1957, a number of events prepared the way for Plath's return and Hughes's first visit to the United States. Hughes's first volume, *The Hawk in the Rain,* was published simultaneously in England and America and was subsequently awarded the Poetry Center Award. Plath completed her degree at Cambridge and accepted a position at Smith for the next school year. In June the Hugheses arrived at Wellesley and within days were settled at Cape Cod, where Plath prepared for fall classes and wrote.

She apparently retained only one poem from this period, but it is a fine one. "Mussel Hunter at Rock Harbor" was, according to Hughes, her first exploration in syllabics; and, as such, it marks the beginning of a transition to a poetic style that is distinctively Plath's. The poem also represents an imaginative effort by the persona to take on the identities of other sentient beings. In the poem, the mussel hunter meets with a microcosmic universe, the universe of the tide pool, which is wholly foreign to her. In the fourth stanza, the inhabitants of this universe have become available for observation. The mussel hunter is particularly attracted by one of them, the fiddler crab, who wears a "Claw swollen to a shield large/As itself—no fiddlers arm/Grown Gargantuan by trade,/But grown grimly, and grimly/Borne, for use beyond my/Guessing of it." Speculation proves futile; the worlds of the mussel hunter and the sea are "absolutely alien." Yet in a single "strayed" crab rivets the hunter's attention: "There was no telling if he'd/Died recluse or suicide/Or headstrong Columbus crab." Yet this crab signifies possible postures toward nature and establishes, if not kinship, at least analogy, for "this relic saved/Face, to face the bald-faced sun."

In this poem, too, the colloquial voice that characterizes the late poetry begins to emerge, although some of the academic qualities of the earlier poems remain. The view of nature remains consistent, characterized by cycles of life and death, hostility and wars of survival, and a stoic beauty and fundamental mystery. But here it is observed in less grand and panoramic terms. Nature has become less a gross landscape and more a metaphoric microcosm, in this case a microcosm of alienation.

Plath continued to write throughout the year, while teaching at Smith, but found academic life in deep conflict with her writing. Not only did she find high-quality teaching (which she certainly did) demanding of time and emotional energy, but she also realized that the posture of teacher and analyst of literature was inimical to her as yet embryonic method of composition. Nonetheless, the poems from this period included in *The Colossus* exhibit not only technical development but also a more clear focusing on the thematic material that recurs in the later works. "Full Fathom Five" (as well as "Electra on Azalea Path," which was not included) confronts the Electra theme more directly than anything previous and, along with "Lorelei," begins the panoply of poems dedicated to the direct exploration of the faces of death, here seen as a desirable pursuit of peace. The role of the artist is taken up in "Snakecharmer" and "Sculptor"; both poems offer the artist a priestly role, as mediator between society, self, and forces essentially spiritual and irrational. "The Disquieting Muses" declares a new poetic voice to come as imminent, severing it from the patterns of artistic development fostered by a genteel and well-intentioned upbringing, an upbringing informed by a world "never, never found anywhere."

Two other poems from this period are important in that they signal the emergence of a social-critical dimension of the poetry. In "Night Shift," Plath first uses the machine as a metaphor for modern life, a machine that "stunned the marrow" and was accepted as matter-of-factly as the beating of a heart. Modern man is reduced to "Tending, without stop, the blunt/Indefatigable fact." In "The Thin People," Plath first turns to the Holocaust as a central event of the modern world. The poem is restrained, still dominated by an objective and public persona; but the significance of this monumental victimization, despite the strategies employed to repress it ("It was only in a movie, it was only/In a war making evil headlines when we/Were small"), is asserted as blighting all life force, the victims' "withering kingship. . . . Making the world go thin as a wasp's nest."

Apparently Plath experienced a rather fallow period after her decision to leave teaching so that she could write less hindered by intellectual obligations. Yet she did continue to explore death themes and Oedipal themes in such poems as "Man in Black," "Two Views of a Cadaver Room," "Suicide off Egg Rock," and "Point Shirley" (a poem that Hughes says was a deliberate exercise in Robert Lowell's early style). She worked part-time at Massachusetts General Hospital writing case histories, which in part may explain the metaphors of physical injury, violation, and modern medicine that take on greater significance in the later works. She also attended Robert Lowell's poetry seminar at Boston University, and there met Anne Sexton and George Starbuck. Lowell's influence was decisive; and later in an interview with Peter Orr, she cited both Lowell's and Sexton's work:

Robert Lowell's poems about his experience in a mental hospital . . . interested me very much. These peculiar, private and taboo subjects, I feel, have been explored in recent American poetry. I think particularly the poetess Anne Sexton who writes about her experiences as a mother . . . who has had a nervous breakdown, is an extremely emotional and feeling young woman and her poems are wonderfully craftsman-like poems and yet they have a kind of emotional and psychological depth which I think is perhaps quite new, quite exciting.

In summer 1959, Plath and Hughes toured the Western United States; none of the poems occasioned by the trip were included in *The Colossus,* but some were published posthumously in *Crossing the Water,* a collection described by the publishers as transitional poems. Plath became pregnant, a condition Hughes says (and the later poetry confirms) she regarded "in a deeply symbolic way." When they returned from the trip, they were invited as writers-in-residence to Yaddo, in Saratoga Springs, where they lived and worked for approximately two months. It was here that Plath completed the poems collected in *The Colossus,* taking decisive steps toward the poetic voice and exploratory method of the poems in *Ariel* and *Winter Trees.* At the time, she was reading both Paul Radin's collection of African folktales and Theodore Roethke's poems. Hughes reports that at this time she deliberately began to improvise.

As she worked at Yaddo, a number of simultaneous changes occurred. In a series of poems jointly titled "Poem for a Birthday" (published in its entirety only in the British edition of *The Colossus),* she draws directly on her experience of mental illness for the first time. In the total sequence, the reader is drawn into the disintegration and reintegration of a personality (the same process recorded in *The Bell Jar*), and here the process takes on both archetypal and social dimensions. In the final poem of the series, "The Stones," the persona finds herself emerging (purged and purified by fire in "Witch Burning") from what can only be called the dark night of the soul. Yet she emerges not to ecstatic life affirmation, but into the mechanistic institutional setting of a modern hospital, "the city of spare parts." Ironies abound as her "pebble" self is worked upon: she lies on "a great anvil"; is worked over by "pincers," "delicate hammers"; her eyes opened as the "jewel-master drives his chisel"; "Volt upon volt" is applied; and "catgut stitches [her] fissures." This is the city where they can doctor "heads or any limb," even provide new hearts. Despite all of this, reintegration occurs, "the vase" is reconstructed and again "houses the elusive rose." "Love is the bone and sinew of [her] curse," the fact that will not permit her to remain a "still pebble." Certainly the "elusive rose" is a reference to her own life force, as well as to the child she was carrying at the time the poem was written. But the triumph is a qualified one: "My mendings itch. There is nothing to do./I shall be good as new." Society and institutions play their roles here, but certainly they are seen as mechanistic and effective virtually despite themselves. Re-

generation comes through identification with love, with the life force.

In addition to tapping the most painful and personal of experience, the poems from Yaddo signal a new strategy and posture toward nature. "The Stones" makes use of the rose in an emblematic way, while "Mushrooms" and "Blue Moles" move the persona toward a complete identification with the subjects. This poetic stance is the equivalent of Keats's "negative capability" and clearly shows the influence of Theodore Roethke. This is the imaginative projection of self that Marjorie Perloff, working with Northrop Frye's taxonomy, sees as animism and that, coupled with angst, places Plath within the oracular tradition of William Cowper, Christopher Smart, and William Blake. Perloff also suggests that this indentification with nature characterizes the best of the later poems and contrasts them to others centered primarily on human consciousness.

Yet it seems clear that the basic projection of self into other holds as well for poems such as "Mystic," "Insomniac," "Three Women," and "Getting There"; and to suggest that these poems are just Plath herself speaking directly is to violate her careful construction of persona, even when Plath speaks, as she always does in the *Ariel* poems, in the first person. This view also deemphasizes the other common technique of using objects of nature in an emblematic way. Plath's approach often has been misread as a drive to turn everything into an aspect of herself, to create a universe that is embraced wholly by her own sensibility, rather than as a search to understand other in order to define self.

Actually Plath's technique is linked to a change in the way she experienced herself as a poet. Hughes reports that her method of composition changed dramatically between the completion of the *Colossus* poems and the writing of those in *Ariel.* Throughout her apprenticeship (she regarded everything prior to "The Stones" as juvenilia) she composed laboriously, working always with a thesaurus, "as if she were working out a mathematical problem." However, by the time she wrote "Tulips" (1961), the thesaurus was discarded and she wrote "at top speed, as one might write an urgent letter." She spoke interestingly about the experience of composition itself in the Orr interview:

I don't think I could live without it. It's like water or bread, or something absolutely essential to me. I find myself absolutely fulfilled when I've written a poem, when I'm writing one. Having written one, then you fall away very rapidly from having been a poet to becoming a sort of poet at rest, which isn't the same thing at all . . . the actual experience of writing a poem is a magnificent one.

The act of composition itself, then, becomes a kind of epiphany, similar to what Abraham Maslow has called a "peak" experience. For Plath, the writing of poems became a means of empathetically experiencing alternate identities and modes of consciousness, a means of vicarious experience. There is a quality of experience here that is simply not embraced by the notion of the creation of a persona, one that seems to resemble more what "method" actors must experience, and one that at least in part accounts for the peculiar intensity of her late work.

Finally, the last of the poems in *The Colossus* represent a shift to a poetic voice that embraces, almost entirely, the colloquial. In diction, rhythm, and sound, Plath began to move to the patterns of oral discourse, of natural, even casual, speech. Plath herself emphasized the importance of this change, noting in 1962 that she had not been so attentive to the sound of the poems she wrote until after *The Colossus:*

These ones [poems] that I have just read, the ones that are very recent, I've got to say them, I speak them to myself, and I think this in my own writing development is quite a new thing with

me, and whatever lucidity they may have comes from the fact that I say them to myself, I say them aloud.

This move into the colloquial, as Alicia Ostriker has observed, places her squarely in the American tradition of Walt Whitman and Henry David Thoreau. And with the inclusion of private and taboo materials, it has also placed her, perhaps mistakenly, in the so-called "confessional school."

In December 1959, Plath and Hughes returned to England and settled in a flat in London, awaiting the birth of their first child. Each of them was receiving small but regular payment for poems published in periodicals. (That winter *Lupercal,* Hughes's second book of poems, was published; he later received the Somerset Maugham Award for *Hawk in the Rain.*) In February 1960 Plath signed a contract with William Heinemann, Ltd., for the publication of *The Colossus.* Apparently, she also was at work on *The Bell Jar.* On April 1, 1960, Plath gave birth at home, with the help of a midwife, to their first child, Frieda. It was not long until a comfortable routine permitted Plath to continue with her writing. Her letters home at this time indicate that she and Hughes were regularly involved in the social life of London's literary circle and that she had taken a heightened interest in the political issues of the time, an interest markedly absent from her earlier correspondence.

Early in 1961 Plath had a miscarriage, which was shortly followed by an appendectomy. Her hospitalization was the occasion that brought forth two of her best-known and most controversial poems, "Tulips" and "In Plaster." While still in the hospital, Plath received a first-reading contract from Alfred A. Knopf in New York, a clear recognition of her rising reputation; in May, the formal agreement was made for the American publication of *The Colossus.* At about the same time, clearly recovered from her health crises, Plath described herself to her mother as "working fiendishly." In early summer Plath discovered that she was pregnant again; she and Hughes looked for and purchased a house in Devon. That summer, too, Plath was awarded first prize in the Cheltenham Festival Poetry Contest. In November she received a Eugene F. Saxton Fellowship to work on her novel, although it appears from a letter to her mother that *The Bell Jar* probably was already completed. After moving to Devon, Hughes and Plath resumed their habit of splitting the day between writing and work on the house and in the garden, each caring for Frieda while the other wrote.

On January 17, 1962, their second child, Nicholas, was born, and for a period of time Plath's writing became a matter of secondary importance. In letters home she had begun to report a renewed interest in religion (reflected, too, in some of the late poems: "Mary's Song"; "Mystic"; "Lyonnesse"), and in March, despite some reservations about rural Anglicanism, the Hugheses had both of their children baptized. In June the adjustment of the new baby seemed well accomplished, and, according to Lois Ames, Plath told a friend that she was "writing again. Really writing." Undoubtedly these are the poems that eventually were published in *Ariel* and *Winter Trees,* described by Hughes as roughly contemporaneous. In addition, "Three Women" already had been accepted for broadcast early that summer by the British Broadcasting Company. By the end of July, however, it became evident that the marriage was in serious difficulty. Hughes had been seeing another woman; and at the end of August, Plath wrote her mother that they were seeking a legal separation. Hughes moved to London immediately; Plath remained in Devon until December, when she, too, moved to London with the children. The letters to her mother at this time, although heavily edited, do indicate a high level of emotional stress related to the breakup of the marriage; yet they also indicate a strong determination to put her life back together as an independent person.

Despite difficulties of physical health and persistent problems in obtaining adequate help with the care of the children, Plath continued to work. In *London Magazine* she said of this work:

These new poems of mine have one thing in common. They were all written at about four in the morning—that still blue, almost eternal hour before cockcrow, before the baby's cry, before the glassy music of the milkman settling his bottles.

Of course they do have more in common, yet it is important to understand that the late poetry was written under extreme personal stress. Probably the best-researched work on this to date is Judith Kroll's *Chapters in a Mythology: The Poetry of Sylvia Plath.* Kroll, too, emphasizes that the poem as experience itself is a chief characteristic of this late work. More importantly, however, she established Robert Graves and Sir James Frazier as primary sources for Plath.

Following out a statement made by Hughes that the poems should be viewed mythically, Kroll delineates a system of myth that serves as the ground of meaning in Plath's late work. She argues that to understand these poems, one must understand that within Plath's system there coexists a paradox of true and false selves. The true self, often associated with childhood, is loyal to Graves's White Goddess (moon goddess), who is Plath's mythic muse. The true self is also genuinely powerful and free. The false self, on the other hand, is helpless and trapped, but it coexists with the true self to form the persona of the poems. The false self, however, has the power to be reborn as the true self by means of suicide, reunion by proxy, and exorcism by ritual killing. Life is promised through "transcendence, purgation, and purification," as in "Stings" and "Fever 103°." For Plath, then,

"Dionysian or muse-inspired poetry and not Apollonian poetry is true poetry."

Kroll gives an explication from this point of view of many of the most puzzling and previously obscure images of these poems. The moon muse is not a smiling one, but is demanding of perfection unto death. The heroine-persona of the poems resolves her status as a life force with her loyalty to the moon muse by becoming a "dying and reviving goddess" who mourns or celebrates "the death of her god" (husband, father), which is necessary to her resurrection, to the rebirth of the true self. All of this, Kroll argues, is summarized in "Daddy" and "Lady Lazarus." And "Ariel" stands as the poem of mystic transcendence. Plath's real search, then, is not for death but, rather, first for the death of the false self, and finally for a state of transcendent selflessness.

Kroll's approach to Plath's work is remarkably compatible with that of Marjorie Perloff: both emphasize the qualities of Plath's poetry that stem from a view of the artist as a kind of priest or oracle. A mythic sensibility, moreover, is quite often accompanied by an animistic view of nature. Yet each, for different reasons, underestimates the importance of a social vision that is also present in the late poems. Kroll seeks to rescue Plath from the critical view that constructs the poems as case history; Perloff seeks to rescue the work from those who would reduce it to political ideology.

Perloff, in her discussion of "Tulips," insists on divorcing that poem from anything that resembles an intention to critique agreed-upon American values. In fact, she states that she fails to see such a critique "anywhere in her . . . poems." She cites a statement of Plath's in support of her contention:

For me, the real issues of our time are the issues of everytime—the hurt and wonder of loving; making in all its forms, children, loaves of bread, paintings, building; and the conservation of life of all people in all places. . . . Surely the great use of poetry is its pleasure—not its influence as religious or political propaganda.

Yet the phrase omitted from the quotation is significant indeed: "the jeopardizing of which no abstract double-talk of 'peace' or 'implacable foes' can excuse." As Margaret D. Uroff has noted, Plath was quite "aware that making in all its forms was an imperilled issue in our time."

The mistake in emphasis seems to be a result of Perloff's own formalist stance, which tends to regard any taint of social criticism as somehow disqualifying a poem as art. And Perloff certainly means to defend Plath as artist, in her discussion of the poems and of *The Bell Jar*. Yet this is to misunderstand the social and cultural roots of art, to turn such roots into ideology or to construe comment that has to do with negatively evaluated cultural assumptions as crass didacticism. No poet—certainly not Plath—stands pristine and removed from the culture that informs and is embodied in the very language each seeks to transform. Most good poets are in fact subversive of those assumptions, and it was clearly Plath's intention to be so, to offer her own alternative construction of reality both through the poems that Kroll shows us are directly concerned in the presentation of a mythology, and in the others that explore the human identity as it is formed in and related to nature and civilization. However Plath might have wished it, and Kroll's work suggests that at least in part she did, she could not be a poet and at the same time be that pure selfless baby stepping from the "black car of Lethe" at the end of "Getting There." Isn't that, in the end, why words fail her?

Kroll's work, on the other hand, does not so much deny as fail to emphasize the social vision, primarily because her aim is to get at a grounded explication of some of those most difficult and apparently obscure late poems. Yet the construction of a mythology has a purpose that goes far beyond the presentation of a fantasy. It is a fiction in the sense of a making, but its urge is to create an explanation and to connect the human being in some meaningful way to nature and society, which seem so overwhelming. It is informed by the desire that Henry Adams recognized when he stated, "Chaos is the law of nature, order is the dream of man." Adams is more relevant here than it might at first seem, for he had made it the task of his life to find the truth through science, a search that he regarded as a failure. And it is science, the most encompassing contemporary myth of Western civilization, that Plath rejects so totally in constructing her own myth.

In an interview with Peter Orr four months before her suicide, Plath talked of her poetic aims. Recall that in that interview she began by asserting that Robert Lowell's *Life Studies* and Anne Sexton's poems were important to her because Lowell and Sexton had moved into an exploration of very private and taboo subjects, and had managed to achieve a new kind of emotional and psychological depth. The exploration of the taboo is in its very nature a critique of the common understandings of reality, and Plath's own poetry seeks the same end. She goes on to say:

I think my poems immediately come out of the sensuous and emotional experiences I have, but I must say I cannot sympathize with these cries from the heart that are informed by nothing except a needle or a knife, or whatever it is. I believe that one should be able to control and manipulate experiences, even the most terrifying, like madness, being tortured, this sort of experience . . . with an informed and intelligent mind. I think that personal experience is very important, but certainly it shouldn't be a kind of shut-box and mirror-looking, narcissistic experi

ence. I believe it should be *relevant,* and relevant to the larger things, the bigger things such as Hiroshima and Dachau and so on.

Addressed directly on the question of her poems that use thematic material derived from the Holocaust, she responds:

My background is, may I say, German and Austrian . . . and so my concern with concentration camps . . . is uniquely intense. And then again, I'm rather a political person as well, so I suppose that's what part of it comes from . . . and I think that as I age I am becoming more and more historical.

Indeed, Plath takes for herself a considerable task: to create poems in which the microcosm and the macrocosm become one. Perhaps that is why she regarded poetry as a "tyrannical discipline." "You've got to go so far, so fast, in such a small space that you've just got to turn away all the peripherals," she said.

In the poems written between 1960 and her death, Plath is still shooting off in all directions. But the emphasis and the landscape in which these poems are set have changed dramatically. As we have seen, nature in its broad and panoramic aspect has dropped away; it remains in the late poems in an animistic or emblematic way. In large, Plath seems to have resolved her view of nature as the eating game. But in microcosm there is the affirmation that one finds in the earlier "Black Rook in Rainy Weather:"

> . . . I only know that a rook
> Ordering its black feathers can so shine
> As to seize my senses, haul
> My eyelids up, and grant
>
> A brief respite from fear
> Of total neutrality. . . .
>
> The wait's begun again,
> The long wait for the angel,
> For that rare, random descent.

Carried over into poems like "Tulips," "Poppies in July," and "Poppies in October," nature in microcosm becomes a life force as well as a death force, the attitude of the personae alternating situationally.

Nature now appears more strongly embodied in the biological ground of sexual identity and procreative activity, as in "Three Women" and the bee poems. Both in the poems mythically grounded and in others, Plath's clear concern is an exploration of female identity, no longer cast so strictly in the terms of conflicting social role dominant in *The Bell Jar* (although there is some remnant of this in "The Applicant" and "Three Women"), but now embracing the total reality of female biological existence. From the mythic point of view delineated by Kroll, this exploration has implications that increasingly place women in absolute opposition, if not to individual men then to the male principle that is determined by a different biology and a different relation to both nature and society.

Women are seen as the true creators of life. Yet they are forever subject to the psychological tragedy inherent in the biological cycle; they are continuously subject to loss: of blood and potential life in menstruation and spontaneous abortion; of self-realization through infertility; of vitality by virtue of the demands of pregnancy and childbirth. Should the biological cycle complete itself, they do have the rewards of creation, yet these are threatened by society by virtue of the severence of the mother-child relation that civilization demands ("Three Women," "Childless Woman," "Brasília"). Over this seeming squandering of life force presides the moon muse and it is, therefore, no accident that Plath refers to poetry as "the blood jet," and an earlier poem, "Stillborn," is about poems that lack life despite their apparent technical quality. As in the more generalized nature poems, the ground for affirmation is narrow and threatened always by the forces of nature and civilization, which are not seen as life enhancing. Yet affirmation is there, and the poems of motherhood often embody the "rare random descent" of "Black Rook." In "Nick and the Candlestick":

> The blood blooms clean
>
> In you, ruby. . . .
>
> Love, love,
> I have hung our cave with roses. . . .
>
> You are the one
> Solid the spaces lean on, envious.
> You are the baby in the barn.

In "Child:"

Your clear eye is the one absolutely beautiful
    thing.
I want to fill it with colors and ducks,
The zoo of the new

Whose names you meditate—

In "The Night Dances:"

> Surely they travel
>
> The world forever, I shall not entirely
> Sit emptied of beauties, the gift
>
> Of your small breath, the drenched grass
> Smell of your sleeps, lilies, lilies.

Others of the poems on children lead directly to the examination of the forces that Plath sees as threatening this fundamental relation. In "Nick and the Candlestick" the persona asks, "And how will your night dances lose themselves. In mathematics?" And in "Magi" the significance of "mathematics" is made clear:

The abstracts hover like dull angels:
Nothing so vulgar as a nose or an eye
Bossing the ethereal blanks of their face-ovals.

Their whiteness bears no relation to laundry,
Snow, chalk or suchlike. They're
The real thing, all right: the Good, the
    True— . . .

Loveless as the multiplication table. . . .
They want the crib of some lampheaded
    Plato. . . .
What girl ever flourished in such company?

Mathematics and abstractions are the enemy, and they are invariably associated with civilization and the male principle. The secretary (second voice) in "Three Women" makes the connections when she realizes that she has just lost a baby:

I watched the men walk around me in the office.
    They were so flat!
There was something about them like cardboard,
    and now I had caught it,
That flat, flat flatness from which ideas,
    destructions,
Bulldozers, guillotines, white chambers of
    shrieks proceed,
Endlessly proceed—and the cold angels, the
    abstractions.

Later in the poem she returns to make larger connections; she has tried, she says, to be natural and not to think too hard, not to see other "faces." But the faces were still there:

. . . The faces of nations,
Governments, parliaments, societies,
The faceless faces of important men.

It is these men I mind:
They are so jealous of anything that is not flat!
They are jealous gods
That would have the whole world flat because
    they are.
I see the Father conversing with the Son.
Such flatness cannot but be holy.
"Let us make a heaven," they say.
"Let us flatten and launder the grossness from
    these souls."

Flatness, mathematics, abstraction, ideas, mechanism, perfection, "the cold light of the mind," and the male principle become conjoined in Plath's work (such as "Brasília") and appear simultaneously in a poem set in the institution of "health" that "civilization" has created. In "The Surgeon at 2 A.M." we see the principles perfectly conjoined to produce a persona who, although in awe of the organic garden in which he works, sees his patients as things, "statues," which he perfects with "pink plastic" limbs. The surgeon walks through the ward at the end of the poem:

I am the sun, in my white coat,
Grey faces, shuttered by drugs, follow me like
    flowers.

Nathaniel Hawthorne would certainly have appreciated the deep sense of violation that Plath places at the heart of modern science. But Plath does not stop here. She comes to condemn even self-consciousness itself ("Brasília"), and asks that her child be left "mirror safe, unredeemed." For it is only by virtue of self-consciousness (remember her early perception of her otherness precipitated by the birth of her brother) that it becomes possible to speak of truth as divorced from point of view, as being beyond situation, context, or time. The subject-object dichotomy, which is the essence of Western science, is also seen as the principle that attacks the proper balance of the male and female principles. "The Applicant" joins mechanistic images directly to the ironic vision of the female as

A living doll everywhere you look.
It can sew, it can cook,
It can talk, talk, talk.
It works, there is nothing wrong with it. . . .
Will you marry it, marry it, marry it?

In "Daddy" and "Lady Lazarus" the principle is seen to underlie the fascism and monumental victimization of modern war, for it is possible to perpetrate mass annihilation on the scale of Hiroshima only by regarding people as objects. Viewed in this light, our fiction or myth of the objective and of science is rationality to the point of madness. Plath recognizes that the cooperation of the victim is part of the pattern ("every woman loves a fascist"), but these poems promise that there is another dynamic at work as well: victims will remain victims for only so long and, then, as in both "Daddy" and "Purdah," they will turn to revenge. The male figures in these poems are not persons, autobiographical or otherwise. They are types, and the female persona has turned to the very viciousness (of abstraction) decried in order to find freedom, to find what Kroll has called the true self.

Total transformation of being, death and rebirth, seems to be the only answer, since "every little word [is] hooked into every little word, and act to act" ("Three Women"). And death and transfiguration are the central themes of at least a dozen of Plath's poems, and recurrent lesser themes or motifs in many more. This is one of the features of Plath's poetry that is so troubling to readers. Yet as Charles Newman has pointed out, other poets have insisted that "the imaginative realization of dying is the determining, climactic experience of living." In this, her kinship with New England is clear, for such a view informed the work of Anne Bradstreet, Edward Taylor, and Emily Dickinson as well. But, we respond, this is a twentieth-century woman.

In saying that, we reveal our problem. The poetry somehow seems so atavistic, especially in its mythic preoccupation with death. Death and dying are taboo in our society; they are un-American activities. And suicide is worst of all, for it, by choice, denies the future, and we are a future-oriented people if we are anything. Even when the imaginative face of death that Plath presents can only be seen as a triumphant achievement of transcendent wholeness, as in "Ariel," we feel the need to see the poet as mentally ill. Here Plath confronts our greatest taboo, and her view is coupled with a view of modern medicine and science (surely doctors are the priests of America) that denies its ability to transcend death and attacks our fundamental myths.

It is probably the power of these myths that assured that poets would emerge who would face our denial.

As D. H. Lawrence, James Joyce, and Henry Miller spoke to the repressed sexuality of their time, Plath, Sexton, and Berryman speak to the repressed voice of death in ours. But to admit that her poetic voice is often more sane than mad is to be forced to admit that we may need to face the irrational in ourselves. This is not to say that we should follow Plath's example and seek suicide. Surely, as Holbrook has argued, Plath is at her best when she manages to see that life in the here and now offers a kind of transcendence. And she has left us her work, a creative and communicative achievement that affirms human community and stands witness to her own creative life.

Plath has also left us a poetry that specifically explores female identity in a thoroughly courageous way. This particular aspect of her work has led to interpretation that makes use of her search in specifically political ways. Yet it has also led to a misevaluation of her work as dismissable because it comes from a hysterical woman. Plath herself was not an ideologue, but the evaluation of her work does challenge canons of literary evaluation that have tended to regard the female experience and the forms of its embodiment in art as inferior versions of the male. Since the late 1960's women artists and critics have moved toward a critique of those canons and have begun a reevaluation not only of the art that explores women's experience but also of the art that women have produced, much of which has suffered in evaluation because the male experience has been taken as the "universal" in our culture.

The work of Adrienne Rich, in particular, is of great significance here, since Rich is steadily creating a body of poetry, as well as a body of criticism, directly aimed at forging an art that comprehends and includes women's experience in all of its complexities. Moreover, this effort will, in the long run, have significant effect on what we have taken to be "objective" standards of criticism. Art itself is not objective; neither is criticism. Both are in culture, and therefore require us to move with considerable caution when we claim some transcendent set of evaluative standards, for more often than we would like to admit, those standards are culturally solipsistic.

Sylvia Plath did, indeed, find herself in the middle of a paradox, for as a poet she had to work, and even loved to work, in abstractions; yet it was abstraction she opposed. She was, however, capable of making words work against the tendency of language to reduce and distort experience by abstraction. Some of the poems are clearly poems of derangement. Yet we need not suggest that derangement is justified or desirable in a poet or in a society in order to insist that it may well be produced in part by the conditions of alienation and brutality of the modern world that, if not different from the past in kind, surely at times seem different in degree. How does one actually come to grips with the human meaning of Hiroshima and Dachau? Plath's answer was to project the poetic persona empathetically into the victim's role and to take us with her. With her, we also see the dynamic that eventually transforms the victim into the persecutor. "The Thin People" indeed continue to haunt our own lives, but Plath's search for identity in poetry, which was experience for her, testifies to an honesty and courage that is called for in the search for meaning in our time.

Sylvia Plath, having left out milk and bread for her children, who were still asleep, committed suicide on February 11, 1963. Lois Ames reports that she had, at the time, sought medical help both for her recurrent sinus infection and for a depression that threatened to produce again the descent of the bell jar "with its stifling distortions." The very late poetry is dominated by a feeling of meaninglessness, to be sure. Yet what is thought to be her last poem is a testimony to the power of "Words":

Axes
After whose stroke the wood rings,
And the echoes!
Echoes travelling
Off from the center like horses.

The sap
Wells like tears, like the
Water striving
To re-establish its mirror
Over the rock

That drops and turns,
A white skull,
Eaten by weedy greens.
Years later I
Encounter them on the road—

Words dry and riderless,
The indefatigable hoof-taps.
While
From the bottom of the pool, fixed stars
Govern a life.

Plath herself succumbed to what she called the "illusion of a Greek necessity" ("Edge"). Words, the most sustaining feature of Plath's life, had failed her. Yet there is that "I" encountering the "indefatigable hoof-taps" that continue to break through the "mirror," the narcissism that she so clearly escapes in the best of her work. Certainly, although encounter with her work is nearly always painful, it accomplishes what all good poetry does: it subverts our commonsensical stabilities, confronts our social and cultural complacencies, reminds us that we are irrational beings and that rationality is both hard-won and humanly costly, whatever its gains. Sylvia Plath calls us back to the universal in the particular, and reorders and renames that we may see.

Selected Bibliography

WORKS OF SYLVIA PLATH

The Colossus. London: William Heineman, Ltd., 1960; New York: Alfred A. Knopf, 1962; London: Faber and Faber, 1967.

The Bell Jar. London: Faber and Faber, 1963; New York: Harper and Row, 1971.

"Ocean 1212-W." *Listener,* 70:312–13 (August 29, 1963).

Ariel. London: Faber and Faber, 1965; New York: Harper and Row, 1966.

Three Women: A Monologue for Three Voices. London: Turret Press, 1968.

Crossing the Water. London: Faber and Faber, 1971; New York: Harper and Row, 1971.

Crystal Gazer and Other Poems. London: Rainbow Press, 1971.

Lyonnesse: Poems by Sylvia Plath. London: Rainbow Press, 1971.

Pursuit. London: Rainbow Press, 1973.

Letters Home: Correspondence 1950–1963, edited by Aurelia Schober Plath. New York: Harper and Row, 1975.

BIBLIOGRAPHY

Hornberger, Eric. *A Chronological Checklist of the Periodical Publications of Sylvia Plath.* Exeter: University of Exeter, 1970.

Northouse, Cameron and Thomas P. Walsh. *Sylvia Plath and Anne Sexton: A Reference Guide.* Boston: G. K. Hall and Co., 1974.

BIOGRAPHY AND CRITICISM

Aird, Eileen M. *Sylvia Plath: Her Life and Work.* New York: Barnes and Noble, 1973.

Alvarez, A. *The Savage God: A Study of Suicide.* New York: Random House, 1971.

Ashford, Deborah. "Sylvia Plath's Poetry: A Complex of Irreconcilable Antagonisms," *Concerning Poetry,* 7:62–69 (Spring 1974).

Butscher, Edward. *Sylvia Plath: Method and Madness.* New York: Seabury Press, 1976.

Cox, C. B. and A. R. Jones, "After the Tranquilized Fifties: Notes on Sylvia Plath and James Baldwin," *Critical Quarterly,* 6:107–22 (Summer 1964).

Hardy, Barbara. "The Poetry of Sylvia Plath: Enlargement and Derangement," in *The Survival of Poetry: A Contemporary Survey,* edited by Martha Dodsworth. London: Faber and Faber, 1970. Pp. 164–87.

Holbrook, David. *Sylvia Plath: Poetry and Existence.* London: Athlone Press, 1976.

Hoyle, James F. "Sylvia Plath: A Poetry of Suicidal Mania," *Literature and Psychology,* 18:187–203 (1968).

Hughes, Ted. "Sylvia Plath's Crossing the Water: Some Reflections," *Critical Quarterly,* 13: 165–72 (Summer 1971).

Jones, A. R. "Necessity and Freedom: The Poetry of Robert Lowell, Sylvia Plath and Anne Sexton," *Critical Quarterly,* 7:11–30 (1965).

Kroll, Judith. *Chapters in a Mythology: The Poetry of Sylvia Plath.* New York: Harper and Row, 1976.

Melander, Ingrid. *The Poetry of Sylvia Plath: A Study of Themes.* Stockholm: Almqvist and Wiksell, 1972.

Newman, Charles, ed. *The Art of Sylvia Plath: A Symposium.* Bloomington: Indiana University Press, 1970.

Oates, Joyce Carol. "The Death Throes of Romanticism: The Poetry of Sylvia Plath," in *New Heaven, New Earth: The Visionary Experience in Literature.* New York: The Vanguard Press. Pp. 113–40.

Ostriker, Alicia. " 'Fact' as Style: The Americanization of Sylvia," *Language and Style,* 1:201–12 (Summer 1968).

Perloff, Marjorie, "Angst and Animism in the Poetry of Sylvia Plath," *Journal of Modern Literature,* 1, no. 1:57–74 (1970).

——— " 'A Ritual for Being Born Twice,': Sylvia Plath's *The Bell Jar,*" *Contemporary Literature,* 13:507–22 (Autumn 1973).

Phillips, Robert. *The Confessional Poets.* Carbondale: Southern Illinois University Press, 1973.

———. "The Dark Funnel: A Reading of Sylvia Plath," *Modern Poetry Studies,* 3 (1972), pp. 49–74.

Rosenthal, M. L. *The New Poets: American and Brit-*

ish Poetry Since World War Two. New York: Oxford University Press, 1967.

Steiner, Nancy. *A Closer Look at Ariel*. New York: Harper's Magazine Press, 1973.

"Sylvia Plath's 'Tulips': A Festival." *Paunch*, 42–43 (December 1975), pp. 65–122.

Uroff, Margaret D. "Sylvia Plath on Motherhood," *Midwest Quarterly*, 15:70–90 (October 1973).

———. "Sylvia Plath's Women," *Concerning Poetry*, 7:45–56 (Spring 1974).

INTERVIEWS

In Peter Orr, *The Poet Speaks*. London: Routledge and Kegan Paul, 1966.

—LONNA M. MALMSHEIMER

Adrienne Rich

1929–

ADRIENNE RICH's poetry provides a chronicle of the evolving consciousness of the modern woman. Written in a period of rapid and dramatic social change, her work explores the experience of women who reject patriarchal definitions of femininity by separating themselves from the political and social reality that trivializes and subordinates females. As Rich observes in her *New York Review of Books* essay "The Anti-Feminist Woman," published on November 3, 1972, a patriarchal society is one in "which males are dominant and determine what part females shall and shall not play, and in which capabilities assigned to women are relegated generally to the mystic and aesthetic and excluded from the practical and political realms." As a feminist poet Rich insists on the importance of the "imaginative identification with all women (and with the ghostly woman in all men)" and commits herself to the re-creation of a female community that is dedicated to a nurturing ethos and a reverence for life.

In a statement written with Audre Lorde and Alice Walker, which Rich read at the ceremony when she was presented the National Book Award for *Diving into the Wreck* (April 18, 1974), she dedicated the occasion to the community of women that transcends race and class: "the poet, the housewife, the lesbian, the mathematician, the mother, the dishwasher, the preg-

nant teenager, the teacher, the grandmother, the prostitute, the philosopher, the waitress. . . ." This community of women, Rich hopes, will not only resist the damaging and crippling effects of patriarchy but will also create a culture in which women have equal economic, social, and political rights with men. In a concluding prophetic stanza of *Snapshots of a Daughter-in-Law*, her first volume of poems about herself as a twentieth-century woman, Rich envisions a heroine who will emerge from the collective feminist struggle:

>   Well,
> she's long about her coming, who must be
> more merciless to herself than history.
> Her mind full to the wind, I see her plunge
> breasted and glancing through the currents,
> taking the light upon her
> at least as beautiful as any boy
> or helicopter,
>   poised, still coming,
> her fine blades making the air wince
>
> but her cargo
> no promise then:
> delivered
> palpable
> ours

Rich's heroine celebrates the ancient chthonic mysteries of blood and birth, but no longer will she be defined solely by her reproductive functions; her understanding and experience of life will give her vision as effective and as commanding as history has known. Here is a generative vision that transcends the imperatives of biology; the future heroine will be in command of her body, her erotic and creative energies, and she will celebrate life, not death. No longer will she be an ornamental servant but autonomous, self-directing, and free from the patriarchal edict that anatomy is destiny. This new woman will not spring full-grown from the head of Zeus, or from Adam's side; she must pass through the dangers of this life: she must survive and transcend a culture that can wound or kill her. Her strength and commanding power will depend on her capacity successfully to pass through or turn away from patriarchal domination.

Rich's poetry weaves a cultural and emotional tapestry that is bold, sometimes uneven, but always innovative and profoundly original and powerful. Certain strands persist throughout—a commitment to lucidity, authentic communication, community and social change; other threads —revolutionary anger, political activism—are more obvious in her later volumes, such as *Leaflets* (1969) and *The Will to Change* (1971), than in the early volumes, *A Change of World* (1951), *The Diamond Cutters* (1955), and *Snapshots of a Daughter-in-Law* (1963).

The increasing political urgency of Rich's recent volumes has disturbed some critics and readers because they fear that activism destroys art. However, Rich's poetry has been galvanized by her commitment to re-visioning our lives. Poetry, for her, has become more than an aesthetic rendering of experience; it is a way of changing the world. Her work has immense power because it crystallizes the perceptions of modern American women and, by naming their experience, gives shape to their lives. Rich is a major American poet because the breadth of her vision and the range of her experience are compellingly

expressed in carefully crafted language and original forms.

The centrality of female experience and the collective struggle of women have become increasingly important in Rich's poetry. From *Snapshots of a Daughter-in-Law* to *The Dream of a Common Language,* her poetry has evolved from the perceptions of a woman dependent on men for social and sexual identity, as well as economic support, to the discoveries and difficulties of a woman who has taken hold of her own life. The language and form of her poems have changed from the traditional rhymed stanzas of the reflective, meditative earlier verse of *A Change of World* and *The Diamond Cutters* to intense, lyrical, searching lines that are punctuated by silences as weighted as her words. In the later poems the forms are stretched, altered to convey the intensity of her struggle to understand her own life. The language of the later poems is less cautiously precise than that of the early work, as her powerful words name our deepest emotions and her commanding images ring with the intensity of feeling that results from describing the discovered rather than the known. In these poems even familiar objects and events are seen with new vision:

these rusted screws, this empty vial

useless, this box of watercolor paints
dried to insolubility—

but this—
this pack of cards with no card missing

still playable
and three good fuses

and this toy: a little truck
scarred red, yet all its wheels still turn

The humble tenacity of things
waiting for people, waiting for months, for years
("From an Old House in America," 1974)

Much of the time Rich's language blazes a trail, sears the darkness of repressed experience and possibilities denied:

The fugue   Blood in my eyes   The careful sutures

ripped-open   The   hands   that   touch
    me   Shall it be said
I am not alone
    ("Not Somewhere Else, but Here," 1974)

Adrienne Rich was born in Baltimore, Maryland, on May 16, 1929. As a child she was encouraged to write poetry by her father, Dr. Arnold Rich. Under his tutelage she read mostly Victorian writers: "Tennyson, Keats, Arnold, Blake, Rossetti, Swinburne, Carlyle, and Pater." In 1951 she graduated Phi Beta Kappa from Radcliffe College and published *A Change of World,* which was chosen by W. H. Auden for the Yale Younger Poets series. In his foreword to this volume, Auden wrote:

Miss Rich, who is, I understand, twenty-one years old, displays a modesty not so common at that age, which disclaims any extraordinary vision, and love for her medium, a determination to ensure that whatever she writes shall, at least, at last, not be shoddily made.

He goes on to praise her "talent for versification," her "ear and an intuitive grasp of much subtler and more difficult matters like proportion, consistency of diction and tone, and the matching these with the subject at hand." He is pleased by her modesty: "The poems . . . are neatly and modestly dressed, speak quietly but do not mumble, respect their elders but are not cowed by them, and do not tell fibs."

Thus, her first poems are, according to Auden, noteworthy for their competent craftsmanship, elegant order, exquisite proportion, and good manners. Rich herself observed, years later, that being praised for meeting traditional standards

gave her the courage to be innovative and to break the rules in her mature work. However, as Albert Gelpi points out in his essay on Rich, her first poems do contain the seeds of her later work: the relationship between men and women, the difficulty of and necessity for communication. Instead of the retiring modesty praised by Auden, Gelpi understands that Rich "sees shelter as self-preservation," and wonders if "the artifice no matter how skillfully wrought, may serve as a partial evasion of . . . conflicts." Perhaps her artifice is not an evasion but, rather, a quiet, persistent building of her own vision while mastering her craft.

In 1952–53, Rich traveled in Europe and England on a Guggenheim fellowship. In the latter year she married Alfred H. Conrad, a Harvard economist; and they lived in Cambridge, Massachusetts, until 1966. Her first son, David, was born in 1955; in the same year *The Diamond Cutters and Other Poems* was published and received the Ridgely Torrence Memorial Award of the Poetry Society of America. In an essay praising this volume, Randall Jarrell calls her "an enchanting poet," "a sort of princess in a fairy tale." Like Jonathan Edwards commending the virtuous and lovely Sarah Pierpont, Randall Jarrell approves of Rich's feminine, graceful style. Describing her scansion as "easy, limpid, close to water, close to air," he exclaims that "she lives nearer to perfection . . . than ordinary poets do." Again she is praised for poetic decorum and captivating style.

In 1957 and 1959, Rich gave birth to her sons Paul and Jacob. Describing these years of childbearing and child rearing in her essay "When We Dead Awaken: Writing as Re-Vision" (1971), Rich wrote that she felt that she had "either to consider myself a failed woman or a failed poet, or to try to find some synthesis by which to understand what was happening to me." She was frightened by the sense that she had lost touch with her own energy and was passively drifting "on a current which called itself my destiny." Later, in her fourth volume of poems, *Necessities of Life* (1966), which was nominated for the National Book Award, she included "Halfway," a poem that was partly a lament for the death of her active self: "A young girl, thought sleeping, is certified dead." Rich observed that she was writing very little in these years of child rearing, "partly from fatigue, that female fatigue of suppressed anger and the loss of contact with her own being; partly from the discontinuity of female life with its attention to small chores, errands, work that others constantly undo, small children's constant needs." Nevertheless, her experiences during these years provided the foundation for later work; the pain and deprivation of her life as a young mother gave her the basis for understanding the lives of a wide range of women.

It was eight years from the publication of *The Diamond Cutters* to that of *Snapshots of a Daughter-in-Law,* which won the Hokin Prize of *Poetry Magazine,* in 1963. During these years awards continued to come in recognition of her work: in 1960 she was Phi Beta Kappa poet at the College of William and Mary; in 1961 she received the National Institute of Arts and Letters award for poetry; she lived in the Netherlands while on a Guggenheim fellowship in 1961–62; in 1962 she won a Bolligen Foundation grant for the translation of Dutch poetry; in 1962–63 she received an Amy Lowell traveling fellowship. During these years she was "reading in fierce snatches, scribbling in notebooks, writing poetry in fragments." A section from her notebook of these years is included in "When We Dead Awaken" (1971):

Paralyzed by the sense that there exists a mesh of relationships—e.g. between my anger at the children, my sensual life, pacifism, (I mean sex in its broadest sense, not merely sexual desire)—an inter-connectedness which if I could see it, make it valid, would give me back myself, make it possible to function lucidly and passionately. Yet I grope in and out among these dark webs.

Snapshots of a Daughter-in-Law was the first volume of poetry in which Rich wrote consistently about her experiences as a woman whose energy was directed to meeting the needs of other people, especially men. Rich observes that until this volume she "tried *not* to identify myself as a female poet." These poems are written from the perspective of Virginia Woolf's self-sacrificing "angel in the house," and the title poem explores the legacy of self-hate and wasted energy experienced by a woman in a society that demands her subordination to men. Trapped in the feminine ethic of selflessness, the woman in these poems is a midwife to men: "Nursing your nerves / to rest, I've roused my own; well, / now for a few bad hours!" ("The Afterwake," 1961). The energy of this woman has been mobilized to meet the demands of her man: she has succeeded in soothing him by absorbing his anxiety and pain; he is asleep, and she is alone, too tense and exhausted to sleep.

The title poem, "Snapshots of a Daughter-in-Law," written during 1958–60, explores the depression of many middle-class women in the 1950's for whom success was defined by the feminine mystique, the "sweetly laughing; sweetly singing" woman who must attract and hold a man who cares for her, that is, "takes care" of her. Rich laments the waste of energy in a society that values women not for experience but for beauty: "Sigh no more, ladies / Time is male / and in his cups drinks to the fair." Time, which should enrich by adding fullness and complexity to life, becomes an enemy: "has Nature shown /her household books to you, daughter-in-law, / that her sons never saw?" The middle-aged and older woman is mired in anxiety, just as the independent woman is hounded by guilt or the fear of being unfeminine; anger is denied, converted into despair and even madness or suicide: ''A thinking woman sleeps with monsters. / The beak that grips her, she becomes.'' The poet struggles with these cultural traps, insisting on the primacy of her perceptions as did Mary Wollstonecraft, in spite of being labeled ''harpy, shrew and whore''; but for many women authentic selfhood is impossible in a culture that holds them captive to male needs.

Rich observes that this

. . . poem was written in a longer, looser mode than I'd ever trusted myself with before. . . . it strikes me now as too literary, too dependent on illusion; I hadn't found the courage yet to do without authorities, or even to use the pronoun ''I''—the woman in the poem always says ''she.''

However, the gentle cadences and carefully rhymed stanzas of her earlier poems disappear in Snapshots, and the modern use of language and form connects her to the tradition of Sylvia Plath, Robert Lowell, and T. S. Eliot.

Other poems in Snapshots of a Daughter-in-Law protest the pragmatic basis for relationships that define men as providers and women as nurturers. In ''Merely to Know'' (1959) Rich articulates a desire to relinquish economic and psychological dependency, to know the man for his own sake rather than to use him: ''I'll give you back / yourself at last to the last part. / I take nothing, only look. / Change nothing. Have no need to change. / Merely to know and let you go.'' In 1961, Rich appended a third section to the poem in which she spurns cultural norms and resolves to follow her inner direction:

> spirit like water
> molded by unseen stone
> and sandbar, pleats and funnels
> according to its own
> submerged necessity—

This resolution to follow her own path, to understand her own experience in her own terms, is articulated again and again in Rich's poetry: the commitment to spiritual autonomy and psychological authenticity—to lucidity—is renewed in each phase of her development.

Albert Gelpi observed in his essay ''Adrienne Rich: The Poetics of Change'' that this volume marks her ''penetration into experience that makes for a distinguishing style. Her themes . . . begin to find their clarifying focus and center.'' In Snapshots, Rich makes the transition from dependence to independence, and rejects the traditional dichotomy between private and public, domestic and political, agency and passivity. This refusal to bifurcate experience becomes increasingly evident in her later work, especially in the prose work Of Woman Born (1976) and in the volume of poems The Dream of a Common Language. ''I too have lived in history,'' she writes in ''Readings of History'' (1960). When the poet takes responsibility for her own life, she confronts the existential loneliness that replaces the illusions of romantic love:

> Two strangers, thrust for life upon a rock,
> may have at last the perfect hour of talk
> that language aches for; still—
> two minds, two messages.
>
> (''A Marriage in the 'Sixties,'' 1961)

With this poem, Rich embarks on a modern path that eschews Cartesian dualisms that divide the world into active and passive spheres; instead of passively orbiting her mate, she accepts her intrinsic energy and begins to interact with the world on her own terms. The Cartesian bifurcations that were the basis for the social roles of the traditional couple—''I knew beyond all doubt how dead that couple was''—give way to Alfred North Whitehead's process in which relationships are governed by laws of mutual appreciation and bonding is based on responsiveness to others as individuals rather than as actors in social and economic roles. This is a new journey involving change and frightening risks; there are no guides, no certainties, no rules to subdue the terror of the unknown, and no guarantees to ward off the risks. The poet begins to understand that she must accept risk and anxiety as part of discovery, that she must be strong to survive and to make sense of the ambiguity and confusion that are inherent in her journey. She is in uncharted territory: "Things look at you doubly / and you must look back / and let them happen" ("Prospective Immigrants Please Note," 1962).

In *Necessities of Life* (*Poems 1962–65*) Rich explores the fundamental truths of her own life. In the title poem, history threatens to consume her—"whole biographies swam up and / swallowed me like Jonah"—but she resists its influence and forms: "I used myself, let nothing use me. . . . What life was there, was mine." Her experience is unmediated by cultural edicts; and as she separates herself from the sociohistorical context, her own personal reality emerges: "now and again to name / over the bare necessities." Many of the poems of this volume articulate physical sensations, the truths of the body; and the central images reveal a psyche stripped bare of social encrustation.

> Is it in the sun that truth begins?
> Lying under that battering light
> the first few hours of summer
> I felt scraped clean, washed down
> to ignorance.
>
> ("The Corpse Plant," 1963)

The poet affirms her connection to nature—"The night is fresh, the whole moon shines / in a sky still open" ("The Trees," 1963)—but avoids romantic escapism. Nature is not a pastoral idyll, but is intertwined with her deepest feelings and perceptions: "In the heart of the queen anne's lace, a knot of blood. / For years I never saw it" ("The Knot," 1965). The arbitrary separation of mind and body, spirit and matter, subject and object that results in the loss of reso-

nance in language, metaphoric richness, and personal identification with the cosmos is one of the themes of this book of poems. Throughout the volume Rich laments the loss of the capacity for fusion with nature that is the result of the need to objectify, dominate, and control the environment. The price of mastery is alienation; the natural world that is suffused with radiance for the poet is threatened by the man who must objectify it in order to control it. She asks:

> how save the eggshell world from his
> reaching hands, how shield
>
> ourselves from the disintegrating
> blaze of his wide pure eye?
>
> ("The Stranger," 1964)

Necessities of Life was published in 1966 and nominated for a National Book Award; in the same year Rich was Phi Beta Kappa poet at Harvard and then moved to New York City, where her husband taught at the City College of New York. In 1966–68 she taught at Swarthmore College, at the graduate school of Columbia University (1967–69), and then in the SEEK and open admissions program at the City College of the City University of New York (1968–72). She subsequently taught at Brandeis University (1972–73), and the City College of the City University of New York (1974–75). The range of institutions at which Rich has taught reflects the breadth of her concerns and abilities; she has been able to function effectively in the elite educational institutions of Harvard and Columbia and also to be deeply involved with complex educational and social needs of working-class students at City College. Perhaps the contrasting environments of Harvard and City College, Cambridge and New York City, gave her a more personal and complete understanding of the need for social reform. During these years she was also increasingly active in the protest against the Vietnam War. Her activism has had a profound effect on her poetry, which has become increasingly concerned with social and political issues.

In 1969, *Leaflets* was published. Written from 1965 to 1968, these poems represent another major shift in Rich's vision. No longer does she differentiate her personal experiences from political reality; her life is part of a larger social reality, and the poems in this volume explore the possibilities for reweaving the fabric of our private and public lives. "A new / era is coming in," she writes, "Gauche as we are, it seems / we have to play our part" ("The Demon Lover," 1966). Since culture is created by people, and social reality is an elaborate network of agreed-upon perceptions, it is time for *her* to try to shape the world, even if the monolithic patriarchy threatens to render such efforts futile. In the same poem, the ambiguity of the phrase "we have to make it" conveys the sense of possibility coupled with precariousness of survival:

> *The world, we have to make it,*
> my coexistent friend said, leaning
> back in his cell.
> Siberia vastly hulks
> behind him, which he did not make.

Rich has developed from being a sensitive observer of her life to a woman intent on coming to grips with the political sources of her pain: her mission as a poet is to break down existing social reality to create, or re-create, a new world. Her poetry becomes a record of this transforming process, and for this reason it is intensely political; for Rich poetic language does not simply involve reflections about cultural experience, but can be a means for changing consciousness and for creating social change.

In *Leaflets* Rich again blurs the traditional distinction between art and life, aesthetics and politics. She is writing poetry with the intention of changing people's lives: "I wanted to choose words that even you / would have to be changed by" ("Implosions," 1968). In the title poem she writes:

> I want this to reach you
> who told me once that poetry is nothing sacred
> —no more sacred that is
> than other things in your life—

For Rich poetry reconnects the personal and the political, permitting a reintegration of feeling in order to re-create the forms of civilization. The impulse to write poetry, then, is linked to the desire to create a good civilization. Art and life are not distinct—aesthetics and politics are intertwined. In these poems there is openly expressed rage that comes from having to live in a world in which she does not have a voice, as well as a refusal to be a victim of history. Insisting on the fundamental connection between all people, Rich makes it clear that she no longer writes as an isolated individual, but as part of the human family:

> In the bed the pieces fly together
> and the rifts fill   or else
> my body is a list   of wounds
> symmetrically placed
> a village
> blown open   by planes
> that did not   finish the job
> ("Nightbreak," 1968)

The gaps between the words of this poem suggest a groping for understanding; the contrapuntal lines and tension between phrases reveal the intensity of effort required to overcome the arbitrary cultural barriers that divide human consciousness from itself. *Leaflets* documents the political upheavals of the 1960's: the turmoil of the Vietnam War, Algeria, the student revolution in France. At this time Rich feels sympathy toward the revolutionary male because theirs is a common struggle: "I am thinking how we can use what we have / to invent what we need"; later she separates herself from his vision and begins to create a female community with priorities and goals that reflect the needs of women.

In part 3 of *Leaflets,* "Ghazals: Homage to Ghalib," Rich chooses a poetic form that is sufficiently flexible and experimental to permit her to capture the texture of social dislocation. A ghazal contains five couplets; and in her introduction to this section, Rich says, "each couplet [is] autonomous and independent of the others. The continuity and unity flow from the associations and images playing back and forth among the couplets in any single ghazal." The couplets evoke a disordered and discordant world:

In Central Park we talked of our own cowardice.
How many times a day, in this city, are those
    words spoken?

      .   .   .

Did you think I was talking about my life?
I was trying to drive a tradition up against the
    wall.

      .   .   .

I can't live at the hems of that tradition—
will I last to try the beginning of the next?

Although the ghazals evoke the fragmentation and isolation of modern life, connections, however subjective or tenuous, can be made: "How frail we are, and yet, dispersed, always returning, / the barnacles they keep scraping from the warship's hull." And there is always continuity in simple biological existence: "The hairs on your breast curl so lightly as you lie there, / while the strong heart goes on pounding in its sleep."

In general, in many of the poems in *Leaflets,* Rich projects the active, forceful part of herself onto the man:

Today again   the hair streams
to his shoulders
the eyes reflect   something
like a lost country   or so I think . . .
    he *isn't giving*
or taking any shit

                    ("Gabriel," 1968)

Her vision is entwined in his; he is at the center of her political dream, but soon there will be a parting of their lives:

I get your message Gabriel
just   will you stay looking
straight at me
awhile longer

A few years earlier Rich had tried to reclaim the active part of herself, her animus:

A man reaches behind my eyes
and finds them empty
a woman's head turns away
from my head in the mirror
children are dying my death
and eating the crumbs of my life.

                    ("Orion," 1965)

However, the poet is uneasy with the resolution. In her essay "When We Dead Awaken," Rich says that the choice for her at the time of writing "Orion" still seemed to be between love and ambition, nurturing and work; given this duality, she wanted to claim her right to be as "cold and egotistical"—as self-centered and creative—as any man. Nevertheless, she adds that these dichotomies, these rigid and exclusive alternatives, are false and unnecessary. Three years later she tried to fuse the need to love and work in "Planetarium" (1968), which appears in *The Will to Change, Poems 1968–70:*

        I am an instrument in the shape
of a woman trying to translate pulsations
into images   for the relief of the body
and the reconstruction of the mind.

In *The Will to Change* Rich once again protests the culture of greed and repression in which she lives, and her rage about this waste of human resources, especially the energies of women, increases:

I am a woman in the prime of life, with certain
    powers

and those powers severely limited
by authorities whose faces I rarely see.

. . .

a woman feeling the fullness of her powers
at the precise moment when she must not use
them
a woman sworn to lucidity

("I Dream I'm the Death of Orpheus," 1968)

Her pursuit of lucidity is made more difficult by the fact that the modes of thought, the habits of communication, the language she uses are not her own: "This is the oppressor's language / yet I need it to talk to you." But the poet has no choice but to try to express herself in the language that has no names for her experience; and, in doing so, perhaps she will find a new language. She must have courage and determination to repair the failures of communication: "The fracture of order / the repair of speech / to overcome this suffering." Rich's concern about the need for authentic communication becomes increasingly central in her poetry.

The failure of communication between women and men, between oppressors and the oppressed, is, in part, the consequence of the consistent denial of human feeling:

Some of the suffering are: it is hard to tell the
truth; this is America; I cannot touch you
now. In America we have only the present
tense.
I am in danger. You are in danger. The burning
of a book arouses no sensation in me. I
know it hurts to burn.

("The Burning of Paper Instead of Children,"
1968)

The lines of this poem, set as prose, are unusually long for Rich; the phrases within each line are fragmentary, expressing the confusion and dislocation of political and emotional upheaval.

The task of the poet is to reclaim feeling, to forge poems in which language and feeling are fused. As Rich explores the possibilities for the transformation of language, she experiments with cinematic techniques and uses a series of visual images in "Images for Godard." Like Jean-Luc Godard she is committed to capturing the reality behind the official image, but she discovers that poetry is perhaps more effective as a medium for creating social change than are cinematic images in photography or film: "In a flash I understand / how poems are unlike photographs / (the one saying *This could be* / the other *This was*" ("Photograph of the Unmade Bed," 1969).

In 1970 Adrienne Rich left her marriage, and perhaps fragmentary lines of "Shooting Script" reflect the splintered emotions following her separation: in a montage of images capturing a series of interrelated feelings that are not logically connected, the poem reflects a shattered life:

Now to give up the temptations of the projector;
to see instead the web of cracks filtering
across the plaster.
To read there the map of the future, the roads
radiating from the initial split, the filaments
thrown out from that impasse.
To reread the instructions on your palm; to find
there how the lifeline, broken, keeps its
direction.
To read the etched rays of the bullet-hole left
years ago in the glass; to know in every
distortion of the light what fracture is.
To put the prism in your pocket, the thin glass
lens, the map of the inner city, the little
book with gridded pages.
To pull yourself up by your own roots; to eat the
last meal in your old neighborhood.

The tension between cracks, split, broken lifeline, fracture, and web, filaments, directions, and rays conveys the need for repair of the torn fabric of a life—but not before the damage is analyzed and understood. As the old patterns change, new ones emerge. In subsequent volumes of poetry, new combinations of chance, necessity, and free will in the poet's life are expressed in new poetic forms.

In *The Will to Change,* Rich for the first time asserts herself and expresses her vision in language and forms that are stretched to reach the perimeter of her broadened experience. This volume marks the beginning of a major phase of bold experimentation and testing of the limits of her life and art. The poetic journey in this book has required great courage. The poems demonstrate Rich's capacity for risk-taking as well as her exceptional artistry.

In the early 1970's feminism became increasingly significant as a force for social change; and Rich became more and more active as a radical feminist. *Diving into the Wreck: Poems 1971–1972,* published in 1973, reveals the depth of her commitment to getting to the root of personal and political pain; she chooses George Eliot's observation "There is no private life which is not determined by a wider public life" as one of the quotations to preface part I of the volume. The first poem in the volume, "Trying to Talk with a Man" (1971), explores the consequences of the blind need for dominance, the thoughtless drive for mastery, the reflexive effort to control that results in the breakdown of communication between men and women. The mechanistic, objective perspective of the patriarchal male, based on the repression of feeling, makes emotional or true intellectual exchange impossible: "Out here I feel more helpless / with you than without you." In "Waking in the Dark" (1971) she laments: "The tragedy of sex / lies around us, a woodlot / the axes are sharpened for." The rape of the earth by industrial society, the oppression of women and children by men are part of this tragedy: "A man's world. But finished. / They themselves have sold it to the machines." And she wonders "what on earth it all might have become."

The poet begins to spin her own web of experience, her own version of reality:

> to know the composing of the thread
> inside the spider's body
> first atoms of the web
> visible tomorrow
>
> ("Incipience," 1971)

The internal resonances of assonance and consonance signal a new beginning, an emerging life. In the second part of the poem, the women separate themselves from a man who fears their independence and who turns them into monsters rather than face his own fears:

> We are his dreams
> We have the heads and breasts of women
> the bodies of birds of prey
> Sometimes we turn into silver serpents

His terror of the power of women must be resolutely ignored; the poet must step out of the limitations of his vision, out of his social and emotional myopia:

> Outside the frame of his dream we are stumbling
> up the hill
> hand in hand, stumbling and guiding each
> other
> over the scarred volcanic rock

Now it is necessary for women to return to the origins of social and psychic life, haltingly to traverse the primordial obstacles, and to help each other find their original power, which lies submerged like the volcano dormant beneath the lava.

In this volume Rich emphasizes the need for sisterhood, for a community of women to counteract the isolation of women's lives, and she marvels at the possibilities of collective female energy:

> It is strange to be so many women,
> eating and drinking at the same table,

those who bathed their children in the same basin
who kept their secrets from each other
walked the floors of their lives in separate rooms
and flow into history now as the woman of their
    time

> ("After Twenty Years," 1971)

In order to correct the patriarchal distortions in the cultural lens, women must return to prehistory, to the shrouded early matriarchy of which J. J. Bachofen and Robert Briffault write:

even you, fellow-creature, sister,
sitting across from me, dark with love,
working like me to pick apart
working with me to remake
this trailing knitted thing, this cloth of darkness,
this women's garment, trying to save the skein.

> ("When We Dead Awaken," 1971)

Here is an intricate pattern of interlocking assonance and consonance; the letter "k" appears eight times, for example. The skein of language is as tangled as the task.

Anger and the tenderness that follows its release become sources of energy indicating the direction in which she must go:

my visionary anger cleansing my sight
and detailed perceptions of mercy
flowering from that anger

> ("The Stranger," 1972)

As Rich observed in a conversation with Albert and Barbara Gelpi, "I think anger can be a kind of genius if it's acted on." In this volume Rich's anger ignites her imagination and frees her from social bonds she does not respect. Anger is an energizing force releasing the poet from forms that no longer fit her experience.

The purifying rage sustains the effort to create an independent reality, allowing the poet to proceed and to face the loneliness of her solitary journey and her search for a community:

If I'm lonely
it's with the rowboat ice-fast on the shore
in the last red light of the year
that knows what it is, that knows it's neither
ice nor mud nor winter light
but wood, with a gift for burning

> ("Song," 1971)

The taut, terse diction of the poem moves the reader swiftly from the last light of winter to the prosaic wood with its potential for transformation into a blazing fire. The image of wood or logs occurs frequently in Rich's poetry; in her early poems the logs are "half rotten" or dead, while in her later work, as she comes to understand and act on her anger, the logs burn with a fierce, illuminating intensity. Sometimes anger makes lucid vision possible, as Rich observed in her conversations with the Gelpis:

Women's survival and self-respect have been so terribly dependent on male approval, I almost think that we have a history of centuries of women in depression: really angry women who could have been using their anger converted into creation. . . . And therefore it's not only that there are unwritten books, but many of the books that were written were subdued, they're like banked fires—they're not what they might have been.

The commitment to use this anger as a guide requires that the past be reviewed—re-visioned—which often throws doubt on the meaning of basic experiences—marriage, motherhood, love, and sex:

I do not know
who I was when I did those things
or who I said I was
or whether I willed to feel
what I had read about
or who in fact was there with me
or whether I knew, even then
that there was doubt about these things

> ("Dialogue," 1972)

Not only must the poet confront the meaning of experiences she thought she understood, she must finally return to the primal origins of psychic and cultural life. "Diving into the Wreck" is the poem that most graphically imagines the undertaking: diving into the sea, the origin of life, Rich explores the wreck, the remnants of Western culture. She brings with her the artifacts of this civilization that might help her survive and understand her journey: the "book of myths," or cultural constructs commonly used to mediate experience, to give structure to what is essentially a miasma of perceptions; the loaded camera to record what she sees; the sharpened knife blade to defend herself from dangers of the sea—sharks, seaweed; the diving suit, "armor of black rubber," and "the grave and awkward mask," the protective physical and psychic layer shielding her from terrors of the primal deep.

This is an extraordinary visual poem; the clearly elaborated metaphor of the diver gives shape to an otherwise amorphous experience. As she descends alone, like an "insect down the ladder," there is no one to make distinctions for the poet, to tell her where the land ends and water begins: "there is no one / to tell me when the ocean / will begin." There is no one to categorize her experience, to separate day from night, dawn from dusk, order from chaos, love from hate. Because she is alone, she need not make the arbitrary separations that characterize the Western psyche. "I have to learn alone / to turn my body without force / in the deep element." She makes this journey in order to see for herself, to make up her own mind, "the thing I came for: / the wreck and not the story of the wreck / the thing itself and not the myth."

Returning to the center, to these primal beginnings, the poet recovers the wholeness, the circle of life before dualities, distinctions, divisions occurred. In the sea the tensions between subject and object, mind and matter, male and female are dissolved:

This is the place.
And I am here, the mermaid whose dark hair
streams black, the merman in his armored body
We circle silently
about the wreck
we dive into the hold.
I am she: I am he

Finding the cargo of the wrecked ship—rotting barrels of "silver, copper, vermeil," "half-destroyed" instruments, "water-eaten log," the "fouled compass"—the poet ironically observes that she returns to this scene "by cowardice or courage," bearing the artifacts and implements of her culture that she did not invent or devise and "a book of myths / in which / our names do not appear." There is no historical connection between women and this civilization or its wreck; nevertheless, the poet has made the journey, to reclaim her energy and to begin again—this time as the namer of her own experience.

In addition to the striking visual imagery in the poem, the rhythms of the short declarative sentences describe the matter-of-fact procedures of preparing for the dive as well as the actual dive itself: "I put on / the body-armor of black rubber," and "I go down. / Rung after rung." These abrupt, almost utilitarian phrases are a dramatic contrast to the more lyrical cadences and flowing rhythms of the second half of the poem, which describes what she actually sees, "the wreck and not the story of the wreck":

the drowned face always staring toward the sun
the evidence of damage
worn by salt and spray into this threadbare
    beauty

So Rich discovers where "the split began" in our Judeo-Christian heritage of a world divided, a world in which light is separated from darkness, earth from water, the creatures of air, land, and water from each other. Often there are elaborate hierarchies that further divide forms of life, as in the Western cosmologies that separate cherubim, seraphim, powers and dominions, virtues, archangels, planets, elements from each other and from human life. These divisions breed other divisions between subconscious and conscious, sacred and profane, being and nothing, inside and outside. These arbitrary splits diminish the metaphoric resonance of our lives, and the loss of ambiguity and multivalence reduces the mythic dimensions of our experience. In this desiccated, objectified, externalized world, the world within is lost.

Parts II and III of *Diving into the Wreck* excavate emotions that are often repressed; because they are not experienced or understood, these submerged feelings are expressed in distorted, destructive ways. Anger, hate, despair denied become madness, murderous rage, or suicidal self-hate. The complex interrelationships of these feelings are traced out in detail; no simplistic resolutions are permitted as the poet insists on comprehending the origins and effects of feelings that are the source and antithesis of humanity. "The Phenomenology of Anger" (1972), a ten-part poem, creates the textures and tonality of rage—the poet's own barely controlled anger and its effects on herself as well as collective anger and its effects on civilization. Rich does not retreat into sentimental solutions or escape into utopian visions; she is not afraid to face her own anger and, unlike the patriarchal male, does not project it onto others in the name of courage. She realizes, finally, that in order to love, she must be able to feel and understand hate, that hatred repressed causes aridity, a numbness that creates a deadness at the center.

The first two sections of the poem explore the differences between confinement and freedom, measured boundaries and limitlessness, letting go and holding back: "The freedom of the wholly mad / to smear & play with her madness" is contrasted with the damage done by a functional, utilitarian approach to life: "How does a pile of rags the machinist wiped his hands on / feel in its cupboard, hour upon hour?" She experiences the loss of eros resulting from feeling denied: "I huddled fugitive / in the warm sweet simmer of the hay / muttering: *Come*."

The next three sections connect the consequences of rage denied—numbness, emotional aridity, loss of sensuality—with geopolitical events: "The moonmen come back from the moon / the firemen come out of the fire." In public form, repressed emotion is expressed as the masculine attempt to dominate the elements, to colonize the moon. The poet asks, "Madness. Suicide. Murder. / Is there no way out but these?"

In the declarative fragments of section 7, Rich acknowledges her hatred for the death carrier, this man who feels nothing, who destroys everything around him, including himself, in the name of mastery. She shouts:

I hate you.
I hate the mask you wear, your eyes
assuming a depth
they do not possess, drawing me
into the grotto of your skull
into the landscape of bone

Metaphorically using his own weapons on him, not to kill but to transform him, the poet becomes the modern Amazon doing battle with the monster "gunning down the babies at My Lai / vanishing in the face of confrontation," and "burning the crops with some new sublimate."

When I dream of meeting
the enemy, this is my dream:

white acetylene
ripples from my body
effortlessly released
perfectly trained
on the true enemy

raking his body down to the thread
of existence

burning away his lie
leaving him in a new
world; a changed
man

There is longing for community in harmony with
nature in this poem, for the possibility of a diverse and many-aspected world:

I would have loved to live in a world
of women and men gaily
in collusion with green leaves, stalks,
building mineral cities, transparent domes,
little huts of woven grass
each with its own pattern—
a conspiracy to coexist
with the Crab Nebula, the exploding
universe, the Mind—

But this is a fantasy in a technological society
that levels forests, paves over the plains and
wetlands, erects monolithic buildings of concrete
and steel, where the roar of machines is heard
everywhere—in the sky, on the ground, under
the ground. The last part of the poem documents
this reality in fierce, driving phrases. The reader
is hurled into the inferno of the grinding everyday lives of the captives of technological / industrial society:

10. how we are burning up our lives
testimony:
          the subway
          hurtling to Brooklyn
          her head on her knees
          asleep or drugged
    la vía del tren subterráneo
    es peligrosa

Italics and colons, alternating assertions and evidence, convey the force of Rich's observations,
her sense of apocalypse:

many sleep
the whole way

others sit
starring holes of fire into the air

others plan rebellion:
night after night
awake in prison, my mind
licked at the mattress like a flame
till the cellblock went up roaring

Part III of *Diving into the Wreck* continues to
explore anger that fuels the poet's drive to re-
create the denatured world: "For weeks now a
rage / has possessed my body, driving / now out
upon men and women / now inward upon myself" ("Merced," 1972). In contrast with the
fragrant pine forest and "cold quick river Merced," Rich rails against the prefabricated, chem-
ically flavored world "masculinity made / unfit
for women or men."

Again, in "A Primary Ground" (1972) Rich
maps the psychic ground of many male/female
relationships in our society: "And this is how
you live: a woman, children / protect you from
the abyss." And in "Translations" (1972) she
observes, "she's a woman of my time / obsessed / with Love, our subject: / we've trained
it like ivy to our walls." She laments the loss of
mutuality, of love that transcends the barriers of
individuality, possessiveness, jealousy, and
competitiveness:

The pact that we made was the ordinary pact
of men & women in those days

I don't know who we thought we were
that our personalities
could resist the failures of the race
                    ("From a Survivor," 1972)

With this acknowledgment of the distortions of
romantic love, and the impossibility of effortless
fusion of two psyches, she mourns her dead husband and the mutuality based on genuine independence they might have created:

Next year it would have been 20 years
and you are wastefully dead
who might have made the leap
we talked, too late, of making

In "August" (1972) Rich turns from past failures to face her powers and their destructive potential. In a series of fluid, coupled lines, she spins out the inevitable question:

If I am flesh sunning on rock
If I am brain burning in fluorescent light

if I am dream like a wire with fire
throbbing along it

if I am death to man
I have to know it

In the same poem she gropes toward the understanding of the chthonic mysteries of prehistory, when mother-right yielded to father-right. The poem concludes with an emphasis on the destruction resulting from male possessiveness and territoriality:

His mind is too simple, I cannot go on
sharing his nightmares

My own are becoming clearer, they open
into prehistory

which looks like a village lit with blood
where all the fathers are crying: *My son is mine!*

In "Mediations for a Savage Child" (part IV of *Diving into the Wreck*), a series of poetic reflections based on *The Wild Boy of Aveyron* (*De l'éducation d'un homme sauvage*) by Jean-Marc Gaspard Itard, Rich deplores the hubris of scientists who focus so excessively on a limited range of logical behavior that they ignore truths of the body; their efforts to extinguish or subdue deep-rooted responses to nature that humans share with other creatures is the kind of narrow masculinity that has poisoned our civilization. *De l'éducation d'un homme sauvage* is a record of the efforts of Itard, an eighteenth-century rationalist, to socialize a child who was discovered in 1799 wandering naked in the woods, looking for acorns and roots to eat. Although the child had never lived in society and spoke no human language, Itard was convinced that he could stamp out all primitive habits through systematic training.

Itard's account of the training of the child reveals the profound depth of the connection between people and the natural world. In her poem Rich expresses horror at Itard's relentless efforts to stamp out the child's extraordinary vitality and sensitivity to nature. For example, Itard is distressed because the child does not readily adopt "our sober and measured gait . . . because of his constant tendency to trot and gallop." Rich deplores Itard's ethnocentricity as he tries to teach the boy "names / for things / you did not need." The child does not care about the artifacts of European society: "muslin shirred against the sun / linen on a sack of feathers / locks, keys / boxes with coins inside." Instead, Itard's account makes it clear that the boy longed to be outdoors:

If . . . a stormy wind chanced to blow, if the sun behind the clouds showed itself suddenly illuminating the atmosphere more brightly, there were loud bursts of laughter, an almost convulsive joy, during which all his movements backwards and forwards very much resembled a kind of leap he would like to take, in order to break through the window and dash into the garden.

Observing that Itard never saw the child weep until one day, while trying to discipline him, he

drew near him with every appearance of anger and seizing him forcibly by the haunches held him out the window, his head directly turned towards the bottom of the chasm . . . afterwards he went and threw himself on his bed and wept copiously.

Rich asks, "why should the wild child / weep / weep for the scientists / why." For the poet there is a parallel between Itard's efforts to subdue and discipline the boy from the woods and the efforts of men to control women:

At the end of the distinguished doctor's lecture

a young woman raised her hand:

You have the power
in your hands, you control our lives—
why do you want our pity too?

With this question Rich underscores her conviction that it is self-destructive for women to feel sympathy for the men who control their lives, often by physical coercion, who deny them even the freedom of their bodies.

The emotional and artistic power of *Diving into the Wreck* has been recognized by critics and readers. In "Ghostlier Demarcations, Keener Sounds," Helen Vendler observes:

"The forcefulness of *Diving into the Wreck* comes from the wish not to huddle wounded, but to explore the caverns, scars, and depths of the wreckage. At first these explorations must reactivate all the old wounds, inflame the old scar tissue, awaken all the suppressed anger, and inactivate the old language invented for dealing with the older self. But I find no betrayal of continuity in these later books, only courage in the refusal to write in forms felt to be outgrown."

The volume received the National Book Award, and marks Rich's command over her voice and material.

"From an Old House in America" (1974) is a sixteen-part poem in which Rich scans the past in search of lost women whose traces can still be discerned in an old country house. The house is a metaphor for history itself, and the poet wonders about its former inhabitants: the woman whose flowerbeds still grow; the woman who gazed at postcards from distant lands—Norway, Corsica. She ponders the complexities of their relationships with their men: "wife and husband em-

battled." When their relationship was based on necessity, the nineteenth-century couple represented an economic paradigm; their respective spheres, public and private, professional and domestic, were carefully mapped-out areas of activity that were required for survival. The poet reaches back in time and thinks about the first women who came to America, across the Bering Strait, and later with the Massachusetts Bay Company. The New World mission was not theirs: "I never chose this place / yet I am of it now." Rich recalls the African women brought to the American South as enslaved laborers and child breeders, and the women of the mining camps and frontier settlements of the West, isolated from each other. These women were not without power, but it was "brief and local"; their influence was very real, but not far-reaching—their vision did not shape the world in which they were forced to live and in which they somehow survived.

The dreams of these captive women—"her hand unconscious on the cradle, her mind with the wild geese"—create a counterpoint to the harsh edicts of the fathers. Rich contrasts the generative, nurturing, holistic ethos of these women with the divisive, rigid, legalistic systems of the men: "It was made over-simple all along / the separation of powers / the allotment of sufferings." The male drive for mastery, to clear and cultivate the forests of the New World, to consecrate their settlements to God, was sustained by women's sacrifices. While the men focused on their goals—perceived as divine calling—the women lived with the harsh realities: "her spine cracking in labor / his plow driving across the Indian graves."

In the final sections of the poem, Rich goes beyond American or Western European history, to prehistory, to the time when men's fear of women's reproductive capacity drove them to suppress female power: "their lust and fear of our deep places." The poet returns to primal scenes of fear of females, of mother-hatred:

"their terror of blinding / by the look of her who bore them"; she sees "the fathers in their ceremonies / the genital contests," and comprehends the ancient contest between female fecundity and the sterile order of masculine systems, between the gift of life and the compulsion to dominate experience. She understands that this struggle continues. In section 14 of the poem the old dialogue is given modern form:

> *will you punish me for history*
> he said
>
> *what will you undertake*
> she said

The italicized exchanges are blunt, direct. There is no evasion as the woman in the poem makes it clear that this time she will not join him in his destructive mission; this time he must join forces with the women.

Section 15 of the poem declares that the time has come for judgment—not the judgment of the patriarchal fathers but of "The Erinyes," the female Furies who punished crimes against kin in ancient Greek society. The angry God is superseded by "the Mother of reparations," who does not punish wantonly, but corrects imbalances in an attempt to reverse the destructive direction of patriarchal culture. This Mother calls out from ancient recesses of civilization to women to recognize and honor the ancient female powers:

> if you have not come to terms
> with the inscription
>
> the terms of the ordeal
> the discipline   the verdict
>
> if still you are on your way
> still She awaits your coming

The insistent, driving rhythm of the lines impels the reader toward the inevitable confrontation with the great Mother. The chthonic mysteries of birth and blood replace patriarchal law.

Section 16 of the poem explains the need for female community: to undo the old order, "groping through spines of nightmare," to find and mark out "the line dividing / lucidity from darkness." The experience of all women is needed for this mission; they must resist the temptations of isolation and have faith in their collective resources. The network of sisterhood must be preserved so that women can name and create their experience and their future: "Any woman's death diminishes me."

This poem blends a variety of styles from portraiture ("in my decent collar, in the daguerrotype") to historical documentary ("I am an American woman: / I turn that over") to fragments of monologue ("*I will live for others, asking nothing / I will ask nothing, ever, for myself*"). From this patchwork of American women's faces, voices, stories a pattern can be discerned:

> yet something hangs between us
> older and stranger than ourselves
>
> like a translucent curtain, a sheet of water
> a dusty window
>
> the irreducible, incomplete connection
> between the dead and the living
>
> or between man and woman in this
> savagely fathered and unmothered world

The images in the poem are vivid and concrete, creating a highly textured surface; the language is often clear and musical, a lyrical mesh of assonance and consonance:

> Tonight in this northeast kingdom
> striated iris stand in a jar with daisies
>
> the porcupine gnaws in the shed
> fireflies beat and simmer
>
> caterpillars begin again
> their long, innocent climb
>
> the length of leaves of burdock
> or webbing of a garden chair

This complex network of images gives depth to the historical narratives and individual portraits unifying the separate stories in a tapestry that encompasses prehistory as well as the present moment. Weaving back and forth between past and present, the poem binds opposites together: lucidity and darkness, isolation and community, suffering and reparations, primal power and terrors, finally forging "the irreducible, incomplete connection / between the dead and living." This weaving together of disparate parts of personal and historical experience creates the new ground on which women will recreate their lives.

Of Woman Born: Motherhood as Experience and Institution (1976) is a historical and political analysis and personal exploration of some of the themes expressed in lyrical form in "From An Old House in America." This book considers the ways in which patriarchal social institutions deny women control over their lives (as Rich implies in her chapter headings), a world in which "the Kingdom of the Fathers" eclipses "The Primacy of the Mother." Rich summarizes the archaeological, anthropological, and mythical theories of James Mellaart, Erich Neumann, Robert Briffault, and J. J. Bachofen as well as of G. Rachel Levy and Elizabeth Gould Davis, which suggest that women were of primary importance in these early societies; the "Neolithic, pre-Columbian, Cypriot, Cycladic Minoan, predynastic Egyptian" goddess cults placed women at the center of experience as bearers and nourishers of life. The great Mother had magical powers—her ability to conceive and give birth to children was viewed as a magical phenomenon—as having mana. Linguistic evidence of the female power exists in many languages. The words for mother and matter are close in many languages: "mutter, madre, mater, materia, moeder, modder." Rich explores the associations regarding women and nature: the connection of the menstrual cycle with the lunar cycle, and the fertility cults. She emphasizes the transformative power of childbearing; menstrual blood and mother's milk are physical proof of the female power to create and sustain life.

Rich also reviews archaeological and anthropological evidence that suggests the existence of a considerable male fear of female power, resulting in the splitting of the "good," nurturing mother from the terrible mother. This division is the genesis of the devaluation of the mother by the monolithic, patriarchal cultures.

The ancient desire to control female reproduction is traced through time to the eighteenth and nineteenth centuries, where it is expressed in the usurpation by the doctors of the midwife's role in child delivery. The elaborate skills of the midwife, based on centuries of tradition and experience, are acquired by the obstetrician, a male medical specialist in childbearing. Rich observes that the invention of the forceps, a tool that replaced the midwife's hands, reinforced male hegemony in the field of midwifery. In the eighteenth century the Chamberlen forceps generally were not available to women; and since women were not admitted to medical school, they were replaced by doctors in the maternity wards.

In a chapter titled "Alienated Labor," Rich explores the gradual control of all phases of female reproduction by male doctors. Pregnant women were expected to wait passively for directions from doctors, and to suffer in silence. Pain in childbirth was the curse of Eve, and considered to be the lot of women. Since maternity wards were now located in hospitals rather than at home or a lying-in hospital, puerperal fever was a great danger; physicians, failing to wash their hands after operating on patients with infectious diseases, often went directly to the delivery room. Midwives did not dissect corpses or perform other operations, so the infection rate among their patients was much lower. Rich observes that the current controversy about abortion and contraception focuses on the issue of control of body, and she notes that women are still cut off from their sexual and procreative process and powers.

Rich explores the contemporary bifurcation of women into good and bad, normal and deviant, self-sacrificing and self-centered, which is an extension of the ancient split between the nurturing and terrible mothers. She postulates that deep fear and resentment of mothers by their sons sustains modern patriarchy; that is, these sons oppress women out of the need to contain the power of their mothers. At the same time the sons long to be comforted and nurtured by women. Patriarchy ensures maternal benevolence while eliminating the aspects of female power that men fear. Feminism is threatening because it reintroduces the fear of abandonment by their mothers.

In her chapter "Motherhood and Daughterhood," Rich traces the legacy of self-hate and repression that is passed down from mother to daughter: "This cathexis between mother and daughter—essential, distorted, misused—is the great unwritten story." Exploring the maternal legacy of self-hatred and the subsequent matrophobia, she says:

Matrophobia can be seen as a womanly splitting of the self, in the desire to become purged once and for all of our mothers' bondage, to become individuated and free. The mother stands for the victim in ourselves, the unfree woman, the martyr. Our personalities seem dangerously to blur and overlap with our mothers'; and, in a desperate attempt to know where mother ends and daughter begins, we perform radical surgery.

Rich suggests that an antidote to this damaging separation of mother and daughter is found in the Eleusinian mysteries, which celebrate the reunion of Demeter with her daughter Kore (Persephone). The initiates to this cult are depicted as carrying an ear of corn, a symbol of the fertility and growth with which Demeter blesses the earth in celebration of the return of her daughter. Pointing out the necessity of "courageous mothering," Rich emphasizes the importance of a mother's "struggle to create livable space around her, demonstrating to her daughter that these possibilities exist," and calls for a female bonding that will recognize the strength and diversity of women's abilities and powers. Neither self-sacrificial nor terrible, neither a madonna nor a whore, a woman has emotions and capacities that are many and varied; and Rich wants a community that permits women to break free of confining, even crippling, dualisms.

Rich's concluding chapter explores the violence frequently experienced by women who bear children in a culture that curtails their sexuality and places the burden of caretaking primarily on them. Since the mother/child dyad is a central relationship—even the essential core—of society, it is tragic that our culture makes it so difficult for good parenting to occur in this context.

In her "Afterword," Rich observes, "The repossession by women of our bodies will bring far more essential change to human society than the seizing of the means of production by workers." She urges women to honor the truths of their bodies, to resist the "death-culture of quantification, abstraction," to create "a new relationship to the universe." Like much of her recent poetry, this is a visionary book that outlines future possibilities.

Throughout *Of Woman Born* Rich refers to her own experience as a daughter and a mother. She cites specific events in her own life, and she talks openly of her complicated feelings about her own mother and children. Sometimes she quotes from her diaries and journals: "I write this as the early rays of the sun light up our hillside and eastern windows. Rose with [the baby] at 5:30

A.M. and have fed him and breakfasted. This is one of the few mornings on which I haven't felt terrible mental depression and physical exhaustion."

Although these observations from her personal experience create an unusual blend of subjective insights and objective analysis, some critics felt that the book lacked scholarly rigor; others, that it was inappropriate for a poet to write on a political subject. By using the pronoun "I" in a straightforward manner rather than veiling her personal experience with the impersonal "it," Rich frankly admits that value-free scholarship is an illusion; that all her analysis depends on a subjective response. At present the issue of value-free scholarship is controversial; but many scholars insist that all theory is based on the perceptions and feelings of individuals, that all interpretations of the past require imaginative leaps. By writing a book on a historical and political topic, Rich brings her power and sensitivity to bear on one of the most crucial problems of our time.

In a conversation with Robin Morgan about poetry and women's culture that appeared in *The New Woman's Survival Sourcebook* (1975), Rich observes that the women's movement has had a profound effect on modern art: "What is happening here is not only a feminist renaissance, but because of that . . . a renaissance of art. Art has the possibility of becoming alive again, relevant to people's needs, to suffering, to human emotion and possibility." She also says that her life as a twentieth-century American woman and feminist is inseparable from her poetry. Much of her work through *Diving into the Wreck* explores the pain and anger of a creative, thinking woman in a culture that denies the most essential aspects of her experience. As she becomes increasingly conscious of this pain and the need to understand its psychic and historical origins, her poetry reflects the need to name her own experience for

herself and to reweave the fabric of her life; this personal perspective is broadened in *Of Woman Born,* which concludes with a discussion of the need for women collectively to re-vision their lives. Rich says, in her conversation with Robin Morgan, "It is not as interesting to me to explore the condition of alienation as a woman as it is to explore the connectedness as a woman."

The Dream of a Common Language, Poems 1974–77 reflects this interest in exploring and expressing the "connectedness" Rich feels with other women. Part I of this volume is called "Power"; and many of the poems in it, written in 1974–75, parallel the material in *Of Woman Born:* the suffering of women separated from community, the joys of collective effort, the need for mutual understanding among women, the desire to name her own experience and to share this knowledge, the danger of permitting cultural myths to obscure personality.

The title poem, "Power," explores the paradox of the woman who fails to understand the truths of her experience as Marie Curie's life becomes a metaphor for women's lives in patriarchal society:

Today I was reading about Marie Curie:
she must have known she suffered   from
     radiation sickness
her body bombarded for years   by the
     element
she had purified

.   .   .

She died   a famous woman   denying
her wounds
denying
her wounds   came   from the same source
     as her power

The long caesuras between phrases underscore the difficulty of Marie Curie's alienated struggle to isolate radium, which, paradoxically, kills her.

This implosion of female energy exists in

direct contrast with the joyful explosion in "Phantasia for Elvira Shatayev," the next poem in this section. Elvira Shatayev was the leader of the women's team that climbed Lenin Peak in August 1974; all of the women were killed in a storm. Although, like Marie Curie, these women die in their effort to understand the elements, there is exhilaration in the collective struggle, the communal effort:

> we stream
> into the unfinished   the unbegun
> the possible

In this poem there is commitment to struggle, to process, to collective effort; this time the caesuras signal not rigid isolation but possibility. The phrases are not isolated from each other, indicative of resistance to be overcome. Instead, the silences play back and forth between phrases, permitting sharing of syntactic resources and meanings. The pauses are meditative, indicating possibilities, not limitations: "We could have stitched that blueness together like a quilt." Together the women confront the sky and the mountain, simultaneously bringing their separate experience to each other to be stitched into a common fabric.

"Origins and History of Consciousness," written over a two-year period (1972–74), again focuses on a common language that is the title for the desire to be related, connected but not dependent, to another human. The desire for relatedness and for genuine communication is the genesis of the human community:

> yet the warm animal dreams on
> of another animal

> .   .   .

> No one sleeps in this room without
> the dream of a common language

Rich explores the difficulty of relationships in which there are no roles signaling the limits of awareness, or that mark out boundaries of rit-ualized consciousness; she describes the terror and exhilaration of the meshed and validating awareness of two autonomous beings:

> Trusting, untrusting
> we lowered ourselves into this, let ourselves
> downward hand over hand as on a rope that
> quivered
> over the unsearched. . . . We did this.
> Conceived
> of each other, conceived each other in a darkness
> I remember as drenched in light
> I want to call this, life.

No longer is Rich diving into the wreck of civilization, but into the psychic abyss that is illuminated by recognition of another human being—a recognition that is mutual. Hannah Arendt writes, in *Reflections: Thinking Part I,* that human beings exist to display or reveal themselves to each other and to receive impressions from each other—to impress and be impressed by. Rich expresses this need for lovers to recognize each other and to be recognized by others, by the large community:

> But I can't call it life until we start to move
> beyond this secret circle of fire
> where our bodies are giant shadows flung on a
> wall
> where the night becomes our inner darkness, and
> sleeps
> like a dumb beast, head on her paws, in the
> corner.

"Splittings" (1974) is a three-part poem exploring isolation and intimacy, the pain of being separated from a lover and the consequences of separation. The poet recognizes that, in many respects, her pain is self-generated, that absence of a loved one does not necessarily mean loss. Pain stalks her as a predatory animal would:

> *It is not separation calls me forth but I*
> *who am separation   And remember*
> *I have no existence   apart from you*

The poet struggles with loss, a sense of forlorn helplessness, and commits herself to do battle with it:

I choose not to suffer uselessly
to detect primordial pain as it stalks towards me
flashing its bleak torch in my eyes

She vows to be courageous, "not to suffer uselessly": "I choose to love   this time   for once / with all my intelligence." This poem is a personal record of the refusal to be a victim of masochistic self-torture, to internalize norms of feminine helplessness. The poet is thrown back on herself, her own resources, and vows to do her best to combat the regressive and potentially annihilating forces that rage within. The internal monologue that takes the form of dialogue with a personified form of pain underscores the poet's conflict, the sense of being divided from within, as well as the need to struggle with a self-generated pain so powerful that it is experienced as an external assault.

"Hunger. . . ." (1974–75), dedicated to the black poet Audre Lorde, takes the personal suffering and struggle expressed in "Splittings" and extends its scope to include the division of one nation from another, of men from women and women from women:

huts strung across a drought-stretched land
not mine, dried breasts, mine and not mine, a
    mother
watching my children shrink with hunger . . .
Quantify suffering, you could rule the world

In the concluding lines of this poem, Rich imagines what it would be like if a community of women vowed to live intelligently—this is the transformative power of the great goddess who represents the energy of collective commitment:

of what it could be
      to take and use our love,
hose it on a city, on a world,
to wield and guide its spray, destroying

poisons, parasites, rats, viruses—
like the terrible mothers we long and dread to be.

The image of love as a force to be used has appeared in earlier poems, such as "The Phenomenology of Anger"; in this poem, however, revolutionary love is not envisioned as the resolute heroic effort of one woman, but as a collective commitment.

"To a Poet" (1974) is concerned with the institutional failures of modern domestic life and with the agony of a deeply suffering woman, mother, and poet—probably Sylvia Plath—who is trapped and wounded by the domestic scenario:

Scraping eggcrust from the child's
dried dish   skimming the skin
from cooled milk   wringing diapers
Language floats at the vanishing-point

"Cartographies of Silence" (1975) is a phenomenological map of communication and its failures. It is an eight-part poem composed of couplets that create a montage of impressions and feelings. Silences true and false are explored: the first four sections include silences of omission, manipulation, lies that obscure or destroy truth; the following section, silences that leave space for truth, for richer possibilities, more complex truths. The isolating, fragmenting effects of silence affect all of us:

A conversation begins
with a lie. And each

speaker of the so-called common language feels
the ice-floe split, the drift apart

This alienated separation exists in direct contrast with the shared quiet after talking all night:

If there were a poetry where this could happen
not as blank spaces or as words

stretched like a skin over meanings
but as silence falls at the end

of a night through which two people
have talked until dawn

But, finally, it is words that give authentic shape
to the silences:

what in fact I keep choosing

are these words, these whispers, conversations
from which time after time the truth breaks moist
    and green

In "Part II: Twenty-one Love Poems," love is
not hidden, but made visible in lines that are
declarative, often flat and unadorned. The tone
of these poems is sometimes conversational,
even colloquial; the images focus on simple details of everyday experience:

I wake up in your bed. I know I have been
    dreaming.
Much earlier, the alarm broke us from each
    other,
You've been at your desk for hours.

The mood is often lyrical, but there is no yearning
for escape. Instead, there is an affirmation of the
here and now. Even the garbage-strewn streets
celebrate ordinary, daily life. These are sonnets
of ecstasy, but not of flight. But behind the
simple, proselike stanzas is Rich's courageous
commitment to reveal her erotic relationship
with another woman. These poems represent a
leap of faith, a desire to trust her love enough to
affirm it publicly:

I dreamed you were a poem
I say, *a poem I wanted to show someone* . . .
and I laugh and fall dreaming again
of the desire to show you to everyone I love,
to move openly together
in the pull of gravity, which is not simple,
Which carries the feathered grass a long way
    down the upbreathing air

Moving "openly together" is complicated and
dangerous in a culture that, in spite of its pen-

chant for social experimentation, is not fundamentally accepting of nontraditional sexual involvements. In publishing these poems, Rich
risks the irrational response of her readers and
critics. By making herself vulnerable to their
homophobic fears, she asserts the primacy of her
experience.

The poet marvels at the power of her love for
someone very much like her, yet different:
"Your small hands, precisely equal to my
own— / only the thumb is larger, longer"
(poem VI). There is no need to construct a myth
of the mysterious other, an inaccessible stranger.
Instead, she finds deep pleasure and joy in the
similarities and differences of herself and her
lover:

But we have different voices, even in sleep,
and our bodies, so alike, are yet so different
and the past echoing through our bloodstreams
is freighted with different language, different
    meanings—
though in any chronicle of the world we share
it could be written with new meaning
we were two lovers of one gender,
we were two women of one generation.
                    (poem XII)

The unadorned statement "we were two lovers
of one gender, / we were two women of one generation" is not obscured by an opaque metaphor
or image; instead, its direct simplicity is an unflinching declaration.

The eros that suffuses all of the poems is concentrated in "The Floating Poem, Unnumbered,"
a lyrical celebration of their lovemaking:

    Your travelled, generous thighs
between which my whole face has come and
    come—
the innocence and wisdom of the place my
    tongue has found there—
the live, insatiate dance of your nipples in my
    mouth—

your touch on me, firm, protective, searching
me out, your strong tongue and slender fingers
reaching where I had been waiting years for you
in my rose-wet cave—whatever happens, this is.

The play on "travelled, generous thighs" and
"come" conveys the physical and emotional
power of their passion.

This is not an easy love—few loves are; there
are obstacles both external and self-generated,
particularly for two people who are committed to
equality. Authentic human relationships require
work and careful attention. The poet does not indulge in the illusion that her passionate involvement will eliminate the need for struggle in daily
life. Here is no romantic escapism, but the acceptance of ordinary life.

> If I could let you know—
> two women together is a work
> nothing in civilization has made simple,
> two people together is a work
> heroic in its ordinariness.
>
> (poem XIX)

The intricacy of two sets of feelings, two sets of
responses, requires "fierce attention" in order to
make possible mutuality without sacrificing independence. And there is inevitably pain and
loneliness that even the most powerful love cannot eradicate:

> and I discern a woman
> I loved, drowning in secrets, fear wound round
> her throat
> and choking her like hair. And this is she
> with whom I tried to speak, whose hurt,
> expressive head
> turning aside from pain, is dragged down deeper
> where it cannot hear me,
> and soon I shall know I was talking to my own
> soul.
>
> (poem XX)

The poet's lover cannot "move / beyond this
secret circle of fire"; mired in her fears, she is
unable publicly to acknowledge the relationship.
Nevertheless, the poems are an affirmation of the
will to live and an acceptance of the fact that
pain, anger, and fear cannot be escaped, but
must be lived with as part of the circle of human
emotions. In the final poem in the series, Rich
acknowledges that she lives in this circle, and as
a poet she will continue to trace the intricate
and variegated emotional patterns within it: "I
choose to walk here. And to draw this circle." In
this poem the circle is literally Stonehenge, an
ancient site of religious and magical rituals. For
the poet the circle keeps power concentrated,
permitting her to pull her energies back into herself. The ancient site of Stonehenge, then, provides a metaphor for the centering of her energies.

"Part III: Not Somewhere Else, but Here"
also contains poems written over the three-year
period 1974–77. It is interesting to note that Rich
does not organize the material in this volume
chronologically or even thematically. In each
section the same concerns, themes, images appear and reappear; and the effect of this repetition is to create ever-widening spirals of intensified meaning. As in other poems, caesuras are
used in this section to indicate resistance and to
underscore the difficulty of communication. In
the title poem Rich writes:

> Spilt love   seeking its level   flooding
> other   lives   that must be lived   not
> somewhere else   but here   seeing through
> blood   nothing is lost

The form of historical monologue and portrait
is used again in "Paula Becker to Clara Westhoff"; these two women met at an artists' colony
near Bremen, Germany, in 1899. Becker was a
painter and Westhoff a sculptor. In 1901, Clara
Westhoff married Rainer Maria Rilke and Paula
Becker married Otto Modersohn; the women
continued to be close friends until Paula Becker
died in childbirth. She is said to have murmured:

"What a pity!" In the poem Becker speaks of their pledge "to create according to our plan / that we'd bring against all odds, our full power / to every subject. Hold back nothing / because we were women." Using fragments of Paula Modersohn's diaries, Rich creates a portrait of two women artists who have been largely ignored until their recent rediscovery by feminist art historians.

"Nights and Days" centers on the friendship of two twentieth-century women who are also lovers; like Westhoff and Becker, their lives are conditioned by everyday truths: "We have been together so many nights and days / this day is not unusual." But in addition to friendship and shared commitment, there is the added dimension of sexual desire and love:

someone who saw us far-off would say we were
    two old women
Norns, perhaps, or sisters of the spray
but our breasts are beginning to sing together
your eyes are on my mouth.

In many respects this poem begins where "Paula Becker to Clara Westhoff" ends: it is concerned with the shared lives of two women and the possibilities that emerge from their commitment to each other.

"Sibling Mysteries" (1976) is a six-part tour de force using themes that have deepening importance for Rich: chthonic mysteries, the primordial power of the great Mother, denial by patriarchs of this power, the longing to return to the mother; these mythic elements are intertwined in the lives of two sisters who live today. The first section of the poem calls up ancient rituals:

Remind me how the stream
wetted the clay between our palms
and how the flame

licked it to mineral colors
how we traced our signs by torchlight
in the deep chambers of the caves

In section 2 these memories of the primitive landscape are associated with their mother's body and her healing powers:

our faces dreaming hour on hour
in the salt smell of her lap   Remind me
how her touch melted childgrief

The two sisters share the common bond of their connection of their mother, and their mutual gaze reaches "through mirrored pupils / back to the mother."

The daughters never were
true brides of the father

the daughters were to begin with
brides of the mother

then brides of each other
under a different law

The emphasis in this poem is on shared understanding as sisters that transcends the limitations of their experiences as individuals; a shared effort to penetrate mysteries, familial and primordial, replaces the competition of rivalrous siblings. In this beautiful and powerful poem the rhythms move easily; the lines are graceful and controlled: "Remind me how we loved our mother's body/ our mouths drawing the first / thin sweetness from her nipples." The images are vivid and resonant, appealing to sight and touch: "smelling the rains before they came / feeling the fullness of the moon / before moonrise." The rich blend of assonance and consonance creates a complex texture of sound and sense: "and how we drew the quills / or porcupines between our teeth / to a keen thinness." This is a poem that stands out as a landmark in an often obscure and treacherous psychological landscape.

"A Woman Dead in Her Forties," an eight-part poem written in 1974–77, focuses on the evolution of a friendship; the friend's influence touches all aspects of the poet's life, and the death of this woman from breast cancer is a tragic loss. The poem is both a tribute to the friend and a statement of unspoken love—"In plain language: I never told you how I loved you"—as well as an acceptance of death unacknowledged: "We never talked at your death-bed of your death."

"Natural Resources" (1977) recapitulates all of the themes and controlling images of the poems in this volume. Yonic images such as "The core of the strong hill: not understood: the mulch-heat of the underwood" suggest the still unexcavated terrain of the female landscape; the insistent repetition of the vowel "o" sounds the depth of the unexplored caverns. The metaphor of the miner is used to describe the effort of a woman exploring the crevices of her mind; this psychological excavation is likened to the physical tasks that confront a mountain laborer. There is much work yet to be done, and the poet expresses anger about those men who threaten to interfere with the process of female discovery—men who misuse words like "humanism" and "androgyny" to conceal smoldering violence: "children picking up guns / for that is what it is to be a man." She warns against "a passivity we mistake / —in the desperation of our search— / for gentleness," and calls forth the active nurturing power in women to "help the earth deliver." This is a visionary poem that reaffirms the poet's desire to remake the world. The energy for this recreation comes from generations of women who bring forth and sustain life.

> My heart is moved by all I cannot save:
> so much has been destroyed
>
> I have to cast my lot with those
> who age after age, perversely,
>
> with no extraordinary power,
> reconstitute the world.

If "Natural Resources" extends our horizons by reaching out for meaning, "Toward the Sol-stice" compresses our vision by focusing on the past: "I am trying to hold in one steady glance/ all the parts of my life." The poet looks back, reviewing the past before letting it go—"to ease the hold of the past / upon the rest of my life/ and ease my hold on the past." She searches for the rite of separation that will finally set her free, and she longs for some external validation of her desire to leave the past behind. At the same time, she realizes that freedom must come from within herself:

> It seems I am still waiting
> for them to make some clear demand
> some articulate sound or gesture,
> for release to come from anywhere
> but from inside myself.

Reviewing the textures and patterns of her life, Rich sees a parallel between her efforts to understand her experience and

> the loving humdrum acts
> of attention to this house
> transplanting lilac suckers,
> washing the panes, scrubbing
> wood-smoke from splitting paint,
> sweeping stairs, brushing the thread
> of the spider aside,
> and so much yet undone
> a woman's work

Again, an internal physical space represents her psychic life; the effort she expends in caring for the house parallels her efforts to understand and heal her emotional wounds:

> A decade of cutting away
> dead flesh, cauterizing
> old scars ripped open over and over
> and still it is not enough.

The play on the phrase "a woman's work is never done" and the cataloging of household tasks convey the understanding and acceptance of life as process, as effort repeated and renewed as the spider's web that she uses as a metaphor for history in this poem: "If history is a spider-thread / spun over and over though brushed away."

"Transcendental Etude," the final poem in this volume, is a sustained vision of a woman whose energies are balanced between the self and the world around her. There is immense strength in this poem—strength based on the capacity for quiet observation as well as for sensitive responsiveness: "Later I stood in the dooryard, / my nerves singing the immense fragility of all this sweetness." The poet has come to a physical and emotional space that permits her to absorb life's varied forms, to appreciate and respond to the plenitude of nature:

I've sat on a stone fence above a great, soft,
     sloping field
of musing heifers, a farmstead
slanting its planes calmly in the calm light,
a dead elm raising bleached arms
above a green so dense with life,
minute, momentary life—slugs, moles, pheas-
     ants, gnats,
spiders, moths, hummingbirds, groundhogs,
     butterflies—
a lifetime is too narrow
to understand it all, beginning with the huge
rockshelves that underlie all that life.

This long poem is not broken into sections or parts; the language is lyrical and flows without pause or interruption. Here Rich expresses the intensity of her feelings with her full voice: "a whole new poetry beginning here / Vision begins to happen in such a life."

The poem focuses on the experiences of daily life, and Rich uses the example of a woman sitting in the kitchen, making patterns out of "bits of yarn, calico, and velvet scraps," to underscore, once again, her commitment to the commonplace circumstances of ordinary existence. In "Transcendental Etude" Rich is not concerned with mastery or product, "the striving for greatness, brilliance," but "only with the musing of a mind/ one with her body." In this poem she does not separate herself from her actual experience, but finds a fusion of mind and body in everyday events. Like many of her other poems, "Etude" uses the metaphor of spinning and weaving:

          experienced fingers quietly pushing
dark against bright, silk against roughness,
pulling the tenets of a life together
with no more will to mastery,
only care for the many-lived, unending
forms in which she finds herself

For more than twenty years, Adrienne Rich's poetry has spun the tapestry of her experience as an American woman, tracing the intricate pattern of our lives.

Selected Bibliography

WORKS OF ADRIENNE RICH

POEMS

A Change of World. New Haven: Yale University Press, 1951.

The Diamond Cutters and Other Poems. New York: Harper, 1955.

Snapshots of a Daughter-in-Law. New York: Harper and Row, 1963; reissued, New York: W. W. Norton, 1967; London: Chatto and Windus, 1971.

Necessities of Life. New York: W. W. Norton, 1966.

Selected Poems. London: Chatto and Windus, 1967.

Leaflets. New York: W. W. Norton, 1969: Chatto and Windus, 1972.

The Will to Change. New York: W. W. Norton, 1971. London: Chatto and Windus, 1973.

Diving into the Wreck. New York: W. W. Norton, 1973.

Poems: Selected and New. New York: W. W. Norton, 1975.

The Dream of a Common Language. New York: W. W. Norton, 1978.

BOOKS

Of Woman Born: Motherhood as Experience and Institution. New York: W. W. Norton, 1976.

ESSAYS, REVIEWS, INTRODUCTIONS, FOREWORDS

"Review of *The Lordly Hudson* by Paul Goodman," *New York Review of Books*, 1, no. 1:27 (undated, 1963).

"Beyond the Heirlooms of Tradition: Review of *Found Objects* by Louis Zukofsky," *Poetry*, 105, no. 2: 128–29 (November 1964).

"Mr. Bones, He Lives: Review of *77 Dream Songs* by John Berryman," *Nation*, 198, no. 22:538 (May 25, 1964).

"On Karl Shapiro's *The Bourgeois Poet*," in *The Contemporary Poet as Artist and Critic*, edited by Anthony Ostroff. Boston: Little, Brown, 1964. Pp. 192–94.

"Reflections on Lawrence: Review of *The Complete Poems of D. H. Lawrence*," *Poetry*, 106, no. 3: 218–25 (June 1965).

"For Randall Jarrell," in *Randall Jarrell 1914–1965*, edited by Robert Lowell, Peter Taylor, and Robert Penn Warren. New York: Farrar, Straus & Giroux, 1967. Pp. 182–83.

"Foreword: Anne Bradstreet and Her Poetry," in *The Works of Anne Bradstreet*, edited by Jeannine Hensley. Cambridge, Massachusetts: Harvard University Press, 1967. Pp. ix–xx.

"Living with Henry: Review of *His Toy, His Dream, His Rest* by John Berryman," *Harvard Advocate* (John Berryman Issue), 103, no. 1: 10–11 (Spring 1969).

"Review of *Pilgrims* by Jean Valentine," *Chicago Review*, 22, no. 1: 128–30 (Autumn 1970).

"Introduction to 'Poems from Prison' by Luis Talamantez," *Liberation*, 16, no. 16: 10 (November 1971).

"A Tool or a Weapon: Review of *For You* and *The Clay Hill Anthology* by Hayden Carruth," *Nation*, 213, no. 13: 408–10 (October 25, 1971).

"The Anti-Feminist Woman: Review Essay on *The New Chastity and Other Arguments Against Women's Liberation* by Midge Decter," *New York Review of Books*, 19, no. 9: 34–40 (November 30, 1972).

"Poetry, Personality, and Wholeness: A Response to Galway Kinnell," *Field: Contemporary Poetry and Poetics*, 7: 11–18 (Fall 1972).

"Review of *Welcome Eumenides* by Eleanor Ross Taylor," New York *Times Book Review*, July 2, 1972, p. 3.

"Review of *Women and Madness* by Phyllis Chesler," New York *Times Book Review*, December 31, 1972, pp. 1, 20–21.

"Voices in the Wilderness: Review of *Monster* by Robin Morgan," Washington *Post Book World*, December 31, 1972, p. 3.

"Caryatid: A Column," *American Poetry Review*, 2, no. 1: 16–17 (January–February 1973); 2, no. 3: 10–11 (May–June 1973); 2, no. 5: 42–43 (September–October 1973).

"Jane Eyre: The Temptations of a Motherless Woman," *Ms*, 2, no. 4: 68–72, 98, 106–07 (October 1973).

"Review of *The Women Poets in English: An Anthology* edited by Ann Stanford," New York *Times Book Review*, April 15, 1973, p. 6.

"The Sisterhood of Man: Review of *Beyond God the Father: Toward a Philosophy of Women's Liberation* by Mary Daly," Washington *Post Book World*, November 11, 1973, pp. 2–3.

"Teaching Language in Open Admissions: A Look at the Context," in *The Uses of Literature*, edited by Monroe Engel (Harvard English Studies, 4). Cambridge, Massachusetts: Harvard University Press, 1973.

Adrienne Rich's Poetry, edited by Barbara and Albert Gelpi. New York: W. W. Norton, 1975. In addition to a selection of poetry and essays by Rich, this Norton Critical Edition contains the following essays on Rich's work: W. H. Auden, "Foreword to *A Change of World*"; Randall Jarrell, "Review of *The Diamond Cutters and Other Poems*"; Albert Gelpi, "Adrienne Rich: The Poetics of Change"; Robert Boyers, "On Adrienne Rich: Intelligence and Will"; Helen Vendler, "Ghostlier Demarcations, Keener Sounds"; Erica Jong, "Visionary Anger"; Wendy Martin, "From Patriarchy to the Female Principle: A Chronological Reading of Adrienne Rich's Poems"; and Nancy Milford, "This Woman's Movement."

"Susan Sontag and Adrienne Rich: Exchange on Feminism," *New York Review of Books*, 22, no. 4: 31–32 (March 20, 1975).

"Toward a Woman-Centered University," in *Women and the Power to Change*, edited by Florence Howe. New York: McGraw-Hill, 1975. Pp. 15–46.

"Vesuvius at Home: The Power of Emily Dickinson," *Parnassus*, 5, no. 1: 49–74 (Fall–Winter 1976).

"When We Dead Awaken: Writing as Re-Vision," in *American Poets in 1976,* edited by William Heyen. Indianapolis: Bobbs-Merrill, 1976. Pp. 278–83.

"Women's Studies—Renaissance or Revolution," *Women's Studies,* 3: 121–26 (1976).

Foreword to *The Other Voice,* edited by Joanna Bankier *et al.* New York: W. W. Norton, 1976.

Foreword to *Working It Out,* edited by Sara Ruddick and Pamela Daniels. New York: Pantheon, 1977.

INTERVIEWS WITH ADRIENNE RICH

"Adrienne Rich and Robin Morgan Talk About Poetry and Women's Culture," in *The New Woman's Survival Sourcebook,* edited by Susan Rennie and Karen Grimstead. New York: Alfred A. Knopf, 1975. Pp. 106–11.

Boyd, Blanche. "An Interview with Adrienne Rich," *Christopher Street,* 1, no. 7: 9–16 (January 1977).

Bulkin, Elly, "An Interview with Adrienne Rich," *Conditions,* 1, no. 1: 50–65 (Spring 1977).

Kalstone, David. "Talking with Adrienne Rich," *Saturday Review: The Arts,* 4, no. 17: 56–59 (April 22, 1972).

Plumly, Stanley, Wayne Dodd, and Walter Tevis. "Talking with Adrienne Rich," *Ohio Review,* 13, no. 1: 29–46 (1971).

Shaw, Robert, and Joan Plotz. "An Interview with Adrienne Rich," *Island,* 1, no. 3: 2–8 (May 1966).

—*WENDY MARTIN*

Harriet Beecher Stowe

1811–1896

*A*T one point during the Civil War, Abraham Lincoln is supposed to have greeted the diminutive, bird-like Mrs. Stowe, who was visiting him in the White House, with the words, "So this is the little lady whose book started this big war." Lincoln was referring to her size, not to her remarkable sensibility, which had impressed him. Fundamentally, she was a broadminded religious writer who was able to unite conservative religious thinking with progressive social action. She believed and helped her countrymen to believe that in blacks, in women, and in certain regional characteristics and aesthetic sensibilities there were ways of being and feeling that an expansive and aggressive nation badly needed to incorporate into its spiritual identity, if it were to survive the nineteenth century with its soul intact. In her writing she unconsciously transformed Sir Walter Scott's dialectic sense of history as a struggle between religious, social, and political forces into a Christian drama in which her characters struggle in ambiguous circumstances with cosmic issues. And she wrote in a language that sparkles with the tension of the issues and the immediacy of the characters.

In the development of American realism, she is a key figure between James Fenimore Cooper and Mark Twain, loosening plot structure in favor of character development and dialogue. She is also an American humorist. When Haley,

the slavetrader in *Uncle Tom's Cabin,* talks about his respectability, we know that his speech belongs in the same tradition as Ben Franklin's justification for eating cod and Huck and Jim's debate over the morality of stealing watermelons. She was also a sentimentalist, but she knew how to use sentimentalism in her novels to show how others could find in their feelings patterns for their lives.

Born in Litchfield, Connecticut on June 14, 1811, Harriet Beecher was a contemporary of a group of authors who published much of their best work during the "American Renaissance" (1850–55). She was seven years younger than Nathaniel Hawthorne and six years older than Henry David Thoreau, and she outlived Herman Melville and Walt Whitman. *Uncle Tom's Cabin,* her most famous but not her only good book, began to appear serially in 1851—the same year that saw publication of *Moby Dick* and *House of the Seven Gables.* Her story became a best seller in book form the next year, while Melville's *Pierre* and Hawthorne's *Blithedale Romance* were setting unsold on bookstore shelves. *Walden* and *Leaves of Grass* were only two and three years away.

She may seem to have more in common with her British contemporaries: with the humor and dialogue of Dickens or the breadth of Thackeray; with the moralistic George Eliot, whom she deeply admired and to whom she frequently wrote; and even with the reformist realism of Mrs. Elizabeth Gaskell and Charles Reade, who used the documentary method of Mrs. Stowe's *A Key to Uncle Tom's Cabin* for his own novels. But a second look at the patterns by which her characters move reveals a strikingly orthodox version of her fellow American transcendentalists' beliefs. With Ralph Waldo Emerson, Whitman, and Hawthorne, she shares a strong sense of the transcendent qualities of historical forces—forces that she sees as a Christian order realizing itself in the secular world. She came to agree with Emerson, Hawthorne, and Thoreau that it is an order that is resisted, not so much because of original sin but because one generation passed on to the next its own social systems and ways of being, acting, and feeling, legacies that blocked God's unfolding plan by insisting that the future follow the past. Hawthorne's magnetic chain of humanity has an orthodox counterpart in her sense of a community transcending racial, sexual, and regional boundaries and centered in a brotherhood and sisterhood of the heart deeper than any bond of the mind. She changed the old Calvinist demand that the believer be willing to be damned for the glory of God into a prescription for acting and suffering with Christ on behalf of the oppressed. She preached, thereby, a harder gospel of social action than most of her fellow American romantics. She felt, with Melville, that the self realizes itself only by confronting the world; with Hawthorne, that sin can be educative; and with Emerson, Thoreau, and Whitman, that the individual is not a sleepwalker between two worlds but a nexus of history—of God's plan—and that waking to this fact transforms the individual's relation to his world.

Her family first taught her to see the connections between the imminent and the transcendent. The daughter of the Reverend Lyman Beecher and Roxanna Foote, she was the seventh of nine children in a remarkable theological family. Later, there would be two stepmothers and more children. Lyman Beecher, a Presbyterian, lived intensely with his children and his God. His mother had died in giving him birth, and his father, a blacksmith, shipped him off to be brought up by relatives. Later, Beecher went to Timothy Dwight's conservative Yale to fight liberalism, unitarianism, and republicanism. Perhaps his early disappointment with his earthly father later led him to modify his ideas of the believer's relationship with his heavenly one. Through the influence of a more liberal friend, the clergyman Nathaniel W. Taylor, he came to believe that freedom of choice was compatible with God's purposes. His stress on man's possibilities later brought upon him a series of heresy trials from old-school Presbyterians. At Yale he also learned the revival methods that orthodox ministers were using to harvest souls and to fight the "blight" of notional and ethical Christianity sweeping Harvard. Later, Lyman's doctrinal tinkering to widen the gates for church members helped his children in further tinkering of their own, to broaden and apply orthodox doctrine.

Lyman Beecher was colorful. Craving intimate family relationships, he shared his exaltations and depressions freely. When he was wound up from worship or duties, he could relax in the middle of the family playing a violin—badly—and dancing. Harriet Beecher later remembered one tune, "Go to the Devil and Shake Yourself." He loved reading Byron and wished the poet had swept his harp for Christ. He came to approve of Scott's tales and lightened kitchen chores by urging the children to retell the plots. He had a good sense of humor and a lively sense of the ridiculous, even when he was its object. While he was leading a temperance crusade in Boston, his church caught fire. The church basement was leased to a liquor dealer, and when the firemen brought the hoses they howled with delight as they saw the blue flames licking up from the building, which they promptly nicknamed Beecher's Jug. The next morning, Beecher broke the austerity of his church council by announcing "My jug is broke!" His congregation got him a new one.

Harriet Beecher's mother was more polished and more retiring. She came from a "better" family, read widely, and spoke French—at that time the language of atheism and republicanism. She was Episcopalian, but she permitted her husband to bring her—as he was later to bring many of his own children—to a lively sense of her inadequacy and to a hope for grace. Harriet Beecher recalled her mother as "one of those strong, restful, yet widely sympathetic natures in whom all around seem to find comfort and repose." Her death when Harriet was five left an enormous emotional vacuum in both Harriet and her younger brother Henry Ward. Shortly before Roxanna Beecher died, she told her husband of premonitions and visions of heavenly splendor, adding, while shivering lightly, that she would not be much longer for this world. Shortly afterward, she died of galloping consumption, her devoted family standing by. Lyman said he felt like a child, terrified and shut out in the dark. We can imagine what Harriet felt. Her older sister Catharine, her father's favorite, replaced her mother in the household, serving Harriet as surrogate mother and later, with Harriet's older brother Edward, as spiritual midwife.

A life is shaped by the pattern of responses to events that are chosen as significant. The death of Harriet's mother, her separation from her childhood home at the age of thirteen, and her subsequent need to accept and give mothering play a central part in her books and life. In these events lie the beginnings of her emotional strategy to remake the world around her to yield her the mothering—the emotional support—she needed. Still later, her background gave her insight into the consequences of the lack of social

mothering—of feminine nurture—in American culture.

Harriet Beecher was born to a religious generation that stressed the differences between the individual and the godhead and that bred strong, torturing doubts about the individual's acceptability as a person. Her own life at first confirmed this sense of cosmic separation, which became the framework upon which subsequent losses would weave themselves into her life. In later years, she made her son Charles begin his biography of her with the account of her mother's death—a memory that stayed with her through her life "as the tenderest, saddest, and most sacred memory of her childhood." Henry Ward Beecher later improved upon this idealization by analogizing their mother's role in their family with that of the Virgin Mary for Catholics.

Harriet's sensitivity to death was sharpened throughout her life. Her parents had given her the name, room, crib, and bedding of another little girl who had died three years before Harriet was born. Her sense of vicarious participation in death was severe. When she was nine her little stepbrother Freddy died from scarlet fever. She also came down with the disease and nearly died. Later, she was to lose two of her own sons.

In *Poganuc People,* a rather thinly veiled autobiography of her youth, we see some of Harriet's childhood through the eyes of Dolly Cushing, whose girlhood lot it was "to enter the family at a period when babies were no longer a novelty" and consequently to be "disposed of as she grew up in all those short-hand methods by which children were taught to be the least possible trouble to their elders." Lively at times, at times abstracted, Harriet seemed to those around her melancholy, even depressed. In 1824 Catharine brought her to live in Hartford, where she had set up a woman's seminary. She hoped that meeting girls her own age would lighten Harriet's depression.

It is possible to make both too much and too little out of Harriet Beecher's childhood. The death of her mother, which awakened her spiritually; the physical separation from her childhood home; and, later, the regional separation from her native New England were experiences personal to her yet widely shared by a whole generation of Americans and American writers. (Consider how different the work of Emerson, and Hawthorne, Melville, and Whitman might have been had any of them experienced paternal continuity. What would have happened to Hawthorne's preoccupation with the theme of filial disloyalty? to Emerson's gently iconoclastic transcendentalism? to Melville's concern with capricious deities, and to Whitman's trying on of male masks?) Harriet's spiritual solution, her sentimentalism, is one complemental and feminine response to a dilemma that we have been more trained to recognize in our male authors as furnishing much of the energy behind their Romantic iconoclasm. A sense of exile from the parent's world (often underscored by the absence in the writer's family of one parent) is a feeling that occurs repeatedly in nineteenth-century literature and finds expression in that standard figure of fiction, the orphan or bachelor who must make his world anew. Luckily for Harriet, she had older brothers and sisters, and it was Catharine and Edward who bridged for her the gaps between her parents' world and her own. Catharine and Edward, the two older children, were, according to her son, Charles, her closest spiritual advisors and, significantly, they were present while she wrote *Uncle Tom's Cabin*. Their own adjustments to their father's world helped Harriet's own development.

Temperamentally and spiritually closest to her father, Catharine was curious and energetic, but she was precluded by her sex from training for the ministry. Unable, perhaps, to accept her exclusion from a cultural role that claimed all her younger brothers, she resisted the conversion experience—the first stage of which usually demanded that the believer express a strong conviction of personal depravity. When Lyman Beecher brought in his sons to help his favorite child through this stage, he only frightened Catharine, making her more resistant. While she struggled, she became engaged to Alexander Metcalf Fisher, a brilliant young Yale mathematician who had taught her brother Edward. After their engagement, in 1822, Fisher sailed for Europe to gather books and equipment for a promising career. But his boat foundered off the Irish coast, and he was drowned.

Grief-stricken, Catharine fled the home where her father and brothers lost no time in urging her to see in Fisher's untimely death a warning for her own spiritual estate. She spent the next year living with Fisher's parents where, reading her fiancé's diary, she found to her horror that he too had remained technically unconverted because, much like herself, he had not experienced lively feelings of his own depravity. At the end of this trying period, Catharine opened a new spiritual ledger with her God and started a new system of accounting. She could not imagine that God had cast out Fisher and her from heaven; this would be to imagine a cruel and vengeful deity utterly incompatible with the spirit of suffering love revealed in Jesus Christ. Since the path of conversion seemed closed to her as a means of salvation, she decided to make a life of sacrifice her path to sanctification. She would remain single and devote herself to the spiritual uplift of American women. She began the project by setting up the Hartford Female Academy, which drew upon the daughters of the prominent and taught them to become not just ornaments in the drawing room but useful in society.

Under Edward Beecher's spiritual guidance Catharine Beecher shifted her intellectual and emotional allegiance from God the Father to God the Son, in whose life of redemptive suffering she found values that spoke particularly to women. She took those values of self-sacrifice and submission and made them the cornerstone of a new religion of feminine domesticity that elevated the home and the school into secular churches, with the woman ministering a still center of spiritual and cultural uplift to her family. Eventually, her feminine ideal modeled on the compassion and sufferings of Christ, the Man of Sorrows, became one pole of the nineteenth-century feminist movement to help heal the growing social, racial, and geographic antagonisms in an aggressive and expansive male-dominated culture. She spent her life with the help of others—Harriet included—putting her ideals to work by setting up normal schools to train women to educate the rising generations in the Midwest. Catharine's role let Harriet identify her unresolved grief for her mother with the grief expressed by Christ and led her to see the tie between her own lack of mothering and a general lack of social mothering in a masculine culture. Through Catharine's presence and thinking, Harriet found her needs confirmed and her talents legitimized, first in her role as a teacher at Catharine's school and later as a fiercely devoted mother and as the harassed wife of an intelligent but impractical and underpaid seminary professor.

The summer that Catharine began to resolve her conversion struggles found Harriet still unregenerate. A year later, at the age of fourteen, Harriet Beecher felt sad during a sermon preached by her father as she thought "that when all the good people should take the sanctified bread and wine I should be left out. . . ." Lyman Beecher had abandoned his usual notes and was speaking from his heart about God's patience and love in the figure of Christ. Harriet, who called her father's usual preaching "as intelligible as Choctaw," felt at that moment warm and accepted, and when she related her feelings to her father after the service he tearfully (perhaps overeagerly) accepted her as the latest flower sprung forth in the Kingdom of God.

The experience did not last, however, and it did not change her ideas of God or of herself.

Her God quickly regained old-fashioned proportions, and a year later she was still dreamy, peevish, and depressed. When she came to Hartford, Catharine pressed her to write Edward, who urged her to see in Christ the primary revelation in history of God and to take him as a friend. Depressed, she could not at first frame for herself a god other than a judging Jehovah. But Edward urged her to draw closer and to address God as a familiar friend. Still, to the girl who was not yet friends with herself, to use "easy and familiar expressions of attachment and that sort of confidential communication which I should address to papa or you would be improper for a subject to address to a King, much less for us to address the King of Kings. The language of prayer is of necessity stately and formal, and we cannot clothe all the little minutiae of our wants and troubles in it." But Edward's steady urging to find in Christ's acceptance of her, her own acceptance of herself wins through, and her resistance dissolves into playfulness. A year later she shared her excitement of their mutual feelings about Jesus:

Oh, Edward, you can feel as I do; you can speak of Him! There are few, very few who can. Christians in general [and Harriet, for most of her youth] do not seem to look to him as their best friend, or realize anything of His unutterable love. They speak with a cold, vague, reverential awe, but do not speak as if in the habit of close and near communion; as if they confided to Him every joy and sorrow and constantly looked to Him for direction and guidance. . . .

Edward helped Harriet find an accepting savior in the figure of a suffering and compassionate Christ, and Harriet went on to connect her brother's figure of the biblical Christ with her sister Catharine's feminine ideal of a motherly, self-sacrificing teacher. In the same letter to Edward she writes: "I love most to look on Christ as my teacher, as one who, knowing the utmost of my sinfulness, my waywardness, my failing, can still have patience; can reform; purify and daily make me more like myself.'' Her new insight was not won without backsliding, but by 1832 we find her writing a close friend: "Well, there is a heaven, —a heaven, —a world of love, and love after all is the lifeblood, the existence, the all in all of mind.''

Edward helped mediate for her a new kind of God and also a new sense that God was making history all around her. The opening of Western lands that promised economic growth brought with it a feeling of national expansiveness. Lyman and Edward Beecher, too canny to shut up their God in their Bibles, saw in the great national movement West and in the accompanying ferment of spiritual uplift, God visibly writing history all about them. They decided to move West as a vanguard, reaping for orthodoxy and their God a harvest of souls in the Mississippi River valley, which would counter their waning cultural influence back East. Edward went first, and when Lyman was offered the presidency of the newly founded Lane Theological Seminary at Walnut Hills, near Cincinnati, he came back with a glowing report of the city and its possibilities.

In 1832 the Beechers set out overland. They liked to recall themselves as a noisy hymn-singing caravan, passing out tracts and preaching in pulpits along the way. Perhaps they were whistling in the dark for courage. When they finally arrived in Cincinnati, they congratulated themselves on their decision by admiring the city's elegance and prosperity, its religious tone, and the number of settlers from New England. Harriet helped Catharine set up the Western Female Institute, modeled upon the Hartford seminary, and she assisted her father and stepmother with the household.

There were pleasures as well as duties. On Monday nights, she visited the literary Semi-Colon Club in the company of Cincinnati's cul-tural spokesmen. Here she and other family members would hear the news and listen to essays, stories, and poetry being read and discussed. Guiding spirits at the club were Samuel Foote, her mother's brother and a former captain; the prominent Cincinnatians Dr. Daniel Drake and his brother Benjamin, who had published accounts of the city; the lawyer Salmon P. Chase; Caroline Lee Hentz, a nationally recognized author; and the enterprising Judge James Hall, who had founded the West's first literary periodical, *The Western Monthly Magazine*. With his program of cheerfulness, uplift, and regionalism, he gave direction to the literary soirées.

As a child, Harriet Beecher had read most of the literary figures of the seventeenth and eighteenth centuries as well as childhood favorites such as nursery tales, *The Arabian Nights,* and even Cotton Mather's fascinatingly repellent *Magnalia.* But, for her, reading and writing were not only pastimes but a separate world both visited and created. Edward Wagenknecht's biography has rescued for us Edward Everett Hale's memory of her engrossment as an adult:

I have seen her come into the house to make a friendly visit, and take up a book within the first half-hour of that visit and interest herself in it, and then sit absorbed in nothing else, till it was time for her to go home in the evening. I have known her, simply because she had an interesting book in her hand . . . take a streetcar going out of town and ride three or four miles without observing that she should have been going in the other direction.

She never lost the child's habit of visualizing the scenes on the page. As a writer, she drew upon her talent for visualization to guide her composition. She would not write until she had a clear and living picture in her mind from which she could literally sketch. This made her art seem like a succession of tableaux, but it gave both characters and dialogue a reality missing from the pages of James Fenimore Cooper, who built his characters slowly and laboriously by amassing external details. Harriet Beecher, supported by the reality of the picture she visualized while she wrote, dispensed with Cooper-like long narrative introductions. With a few bold strokes, she set her characters talking in the parlor, knowing that their life was confirmed every step of the way in the next move she had visualized for them.

"You don't know," Harriet Beecher wrote to her childhood friend Georgiana Day back East, "how coming away from New England has sentimentalized us all." Harriet discovered her past after she had broken with it, sensing for the first time the human geography of her native region across the gulf of intervening states. At the Semi-Colon Club she shared her recollections with other New England members just as Washington Irving had shared, scarcely ten years earlier, an older New York and a lost England.

In the spring of 1834, she won first prize for her story "Uncle Lot" in a competition to exemplify Judge Hall's literary program. It is a New England sketch that Hall had probably heard read at the club in another version the previous fall. "Uncle Lot" and another early story, "Love *versus* Law," were printed together with other stories arguing for temperance, charity, and uplift in her first collection, *The Mayflower,* in 1843. "Uncle Lot" and "Love *versus* Law" are especially interesting because they illustrate the typical way that she sizes up and resolves human dilemmas, and because she catches a regional consciousness with the eye and the ear. They show her to be a sentimental realist.

Uncle Lot is a "chestnut burr, abounding with briers without and with substantial goodness within. . . ." He has, too, "a kindly heart; but all the strata of his character were crossed by a vein of surly petulance, that, half way between joke and earnest, colored every thing that he said and did." He is father to Grace, the heroine, who is being courted by young James. But James has "too much of the boy and the rogue in his composition" to please Uncle Lot. At meeting, James leads the singing with a flute rather than a pitchpipe. His freedom, energy, and amplitude of spirit anger Uncle Lot, who marches more to the dead beat of convention. It takes George Griswold, Uncle Lot's son who has come home from seminary, to mediate their differences. Around George, all wrangling seems out of place. Even the disputatious congregation "dispersed with the air of people who had *felt* rather than *heard.*" James makes George's acquaintance, which deepens with time and with George's failing health. When George lies bedridden, Uncle Lot, who dismissed James as a callow youth, is moved by his care. When George dies, the bereft Uncle Lot adopts James and gives him money for college. So sentimental a death is yet touched with the comic pathos of Uncle Lot's petulant agony in a corner of the death room: "I suppose the Lord's will must be done, but it'll *kill* me."

Harriet Beecher's concern with the sensibility of her region extends into the setting. The relationship of the houses to each other—each has a different color and is planted every which way— tells us about the inhabitants. They in turn are described in terms of their houses: "The natives grew old till they could not grow any older, and then they stood still, and *lasted* from generation to generation." Character is sketched dramatically and with an ear cocked to regional dialect. A boy comes to borrow Uncle Lot's hoe:

"Why don't your father use his own hoe?"
"Ours is broke."
"Broke! How came it broke?"
"I broke it yesterday, trying to hit a squirrel."

"What business had you to be hittin' squirrels with a hoe? say!"

"But father wants to borrow yours."

"Why don't you have that mended? It's a great pester to have every body usin' a body's things."

"Well, I can borrow one some where else, I suppose," says the suppliant. After the boy has stumbled across the ploughed ground, and is fairly over the fence, Uncle Lot calls,— "Halloo, there, you little rascal! what are you goin' off without the hoe for?"

"I didn't know as you meant to lend it."

"I didn't say I wouldn't, did I? Here, come and take it—stay, I'll bring it; and do tell your father not to be a lettin' you hunt squirrels with his hoes next time."

In "Love *versus* Law" Deacon Enos mediates between the quarreling factions. "That God was great and good, and that we were all sinners, were truths that seemed to have melted into the heart of Deacon Enos, so that his very soul and spirit were bowed down with them." It is Uncle Jaw, Deacon Enos' neighbor, who is the problem in this story. He is "tall and hard-favored, with an expression of countenance much resembling a northeast rain storm—a drizzling, settled sulkiness, that seemed to defy all prospect of clearing off, and to take comfort in its own disagreeableness." Jaw has a long-standing dispute with Jones over an old rail fence that might have set his property lines "*a leetle* more to the left hand. . . ." When Jones dies he tries to prosecute his case on the elder daughter, Silence Jones—a "tall, strong, black-eyed, hard-featured woman, verging upon forty, with a good, loud, resolute voice, and what the Irishman would call 'a dacent notion of using it.' " Since the Deacon has been cheated by Jones in another matter, Jaw tries to pull him into his case, but the good Deacon refuses—with good reason. He is quietly matchmaking between Uncle Jaw's son,

Joseph, and Jones's youngest daughter, Susan. He marries off the couple and settles his own disputed portion of the land on the newlyweds. Jaw, who always judges things by their price, is so staggered by this act of magnanimity as to be "materially changed for the better." He is heard to declare at the funeral of the old Deacon: "after all, a man got as much, and may be more, to go along as the deacon did, than to be all the time fisting and jawing; though I tell you what it is," he said afterward, " 'tain't every one that has the deacon's *faculty,* any how."

What surprises in these stories is the amplitude of Harriet Beecher's religious vision. Jaw and Lot are genuine sensibilities seen with a sharp but accepting eye. After their conversion, they still have streaks of their former selves. Sin is not the usual array of melodramatic vices—cards, rum, truancy—but is reinterpreted as spiritual repression. Grace says of her father, Uncle Lot: "He is the kindest man that ever was . . . and he always acts as if he was ashamed of it." Conversion is to be freed from repression and to experience a greater freedom in living out one's better impulses, rather than to demonstrate obsessively pious behavior. Deacon Enos and George Griswold work their cures through acceptance rather than by playing on guilt.

The stories published in *The Mayflower* are examples of Harriet Beecher's apprenticeship work; "The Old Meeting House" and "Old Father Morris" also explore New England's religious sensibilities. The largest group of stories has women and children and their roles as its focus. "Earthly Care a Heavenly Discipline" shows in womanly suffering the same kind of road to salvation that Longfellow was painting in *Evangeline,* while "Christmas, or the Good Fairy" and "The Coral Ring" rouse the daughters of the wealthy from their vapors on the ottoman and send them scampering down the streets on errands of mercy. These exhibit Catharine's spell on her younger sister. "The Ministration of Our Departed Friends'' depicts a dead mother's influence over the living, and ''A Scene in Jerusalem'' forges an emotional connection between the suffering of Jesus and maternal suffering. ''Children,'' ''The New Year's Gift,'' ''Little Fred, the Canal Boy,'' ''Aunt Mary,'' and ''Little Edward'' deal in sentimental fashion with children; while ''The Sabbath'' and ''Conversation on Conversation'' take up the role of Sunday schools for debate.

Harriet Beecher's life in Cincinnati from 1832 to 1850 was drab, punctuated by poverty and illness in the home, violence and pestilence in the city, and dissension and controversy in the seminary. Eventually problems with health and financial security drove Harriet and her family back to New England. In 1836—only four years after leaving New England—she had married Calvin Stowe, a seminary professor whose wife Eliza—a close friend of Harriet's—had died in 1833. Stocky and gregarious, Calvin had been a class ahead of Hawthorne and Longfellow at Bowdoin. He was trusted and liked by his peers; and he enjoyed posing, as did Lyman, as a yankee hick, telling stories in dialect that his wife would later use in *Oldtown Folks* and *Sam Lawson's Oldtown Fireside Stories*. An eminent Biblical historian, he adjusted to his wife's subsequent fame, taking advantage of the financial freedom it offered to do research. Their letters show much exasperated cameraderie, exhortations, consolations, teasings, pleadings, and humor.

With marriage came shabby gentility, bearing and rearing of children, and supervision of the household—with its close, hard, mean work leading to overwork, exhaustion, depression, and breakdowns. If in an occasional letter Harriet Beecher Stowe strikes the pose of the harried housewife who wouldn't give it up for the world, a letter to Calvin in 1845 reveals: ''I'm sick of the smell of sour milk, and sour meat, and sour everything, and then the clothes will not dry, and no wet thing does, and everything smells mouldy . . . I feel no life, no energy, no appetite.'' In following years both she and Calvin took yearlong rests and water cures at Brattleborough, Vermont; yet back in Cincinnati, psychosomatic illnesses would recur.

Meanwhile, Cincinnati, the Queen City of the West, was showing an uglier side. When James G. Birney brought out the *Philanthropist,* an abolitionist newspaper, in 1836, prominent citizens had their sons lead a mob against him and his assistant, Dr. Gamaliel Bailey. Not content with dumping Birney's press in the Ohio, the mob ''lost control'' and burned down the black district. Another, bloodier race riot broke out in 1841; and the mob ravaged in 1842, 1843, 1844, and 1845. Then, cholera struck—lightly in 1848 and severely in the summer of 1849 when, during the Fourth of July weekend alone, more than a thousand people died. On July 20 Harriet Beecher Stowe's son Samuel Charles succumbed. To Calvin, who was back East, Harriet Stowe wrote: ''Many an anxious night have I held him to my bosom and felt the sorrow and loneliness pass out of me with the touch of his little warm hands. Yet I have just seen him in his death agony, looked on his imploring face when I could not help nor soothe nor do one thing, not one, to mitigate his cruel suffering, do nothing but pray in my anguish that he might die soon.'' Impoverished, with one child dead, several others to be tended, and Harriet pregnant again, Calvin returned to Cincinnati. The offer he had received of the most poorly paid post at Bowdoin must have felt to both of them like a deliverance out of Egypt.

Looking back, the Beechers barely endured. Conservative trustees at Lane Seminary brought upon Lyman a series of heresy trials to discredit him and regain control of the seminary. Between trials, Lane was besieged by liberals as well. Theodore Weld, an older evangelical student who had recruited other students to Lane, had been converted to William Lloyd Garrison's brand of abolitionism and tried to focus the seminarians' religious energies by holding debates on abolition—a delicate matter in 1834 in the border town of Cincinnati with its commercial ties to the South.

Lyman Beecher, a gradualist at best, resisted the idea of the debates; but while he was off East, the acting president forbade the discussion, and the angry students held their debate and scandalized the citizens by fraternizing with blacks on the streets. Weld wrote to Arthur Tappan, a wealthy New York philanthropist whom he had converted to Garrisonism and who was also Lane's financial backer, asking for Tappan's support. Weld then took a good part of Lane's student body and enrolled himself and them at Oberlin with Tappan's backing. In 1835, Garrison's *Liberator* issued a statement from the seceding students calling Lane "a Bastille of oppression." Lyman, who disliked Garrison's denunciatory tactics, denounced the abolitionists as "a mixture of vinegar, aqua fortis, and oil of vitriol, with brimstone, saltpetre, and charcoal to explode and scatter the corrosive matter." But Weld's successful coup debilitated the seminary, and Lyman Beecher lived to see Oberlin rather than Lane fill Western pastorates.

"It may not be clear why slavery and theology should go hand in hand," Charles Beecher wrote to explain his older brother Edward's commitment to antislavery—a commitment that was to engage all the family members—

But if we reflect that theology is but another name for the politics of the universe, or the kingdom of God, the problem becomes simple. Two systems or schools of theology were contending at that time Old School and New School. The former enthrones absolutism, the latter constitutionalism. According to the one things are right because God wills them, according to others, God wills them because they are right. The Old School theology enthrones a Great Slaveholder over the Universe; New School enthrones a Great Emancipator.

The Beechers simply applied consistently for their democratic times the social consequences of their theological stance. Having found in Christ's suffering love the historical pattern for human relationships in God's universe, they saw that the old master-slave relationship had to be discarded along with other signs of an outworn dispensation: God's arbitrary Lordship, which propped up the absolute monarchies and kept the people servile.

Contrary to popular belief, the Beechers' familiarity with abolition was of long standing. William Lloyd Garrison had been a member of Lyman's Boston congregation in 1829, and James G. Birney had heard Lyman preach in Boston in 1830 while he visited Catharine Beecher's Hartford seminary. Birney later reprinted several stories by Harriet Beecher Stowe. In November 1837, Edward's friend and former congregational member, Elijah P. Lovejoy, who had helped Edward form the Illinois Anti-Slavery Society, was killed and his press destroyed by a mob at Alton, Illinois. Edward wrote the nationally distributed *Narrative* of the scandal in 1838, while Calvin preached the sermon at Lane on Lovejoy's death. By 1837 all of Lyman's sons by Roxanna had become committed to the antislavery movement with the exception of young Henry Ward, who later electrified the country by introducing black women during services in his elegant Plymouth Church in Brooklyn and making his congregation buy the women's freedom by passing the plate.

One more event in Cincinnati deserves mention. In 1837 and 1838 Alexander Kinmont, a midwestern proponent of Swedenborgianism, gave a series of twelve lectures "on the natural history of man," which spun a new racial mythology about blacks and whites. Pointing out intellectual development and material expansion as dominant characteristics of an evolving white race, Kinmont urged that blacks also had a role in the progress of mankind perhaps more important than whites: to illustrate the Christian ideal of service and to create in Africa a far nobler civilization than the hardheaded and aggressive Anglo-Saxon race had achieved in America—a civilization that would show the divine attributes of Christianity: compassion and mercy. It is quite probable that Harriet Beecher Stowe attended the series or read Kinmont's lectures, which were published in 1839, or later came in touch with his widely propagated ideas through William Ellery Channing. George M. Fredrickson suggests a meeting of minds in *The Black Image in the White Mind* and shows that she drew on his ideas for *Uncle Tom's Cabin*. His ideas would be all the more attractive to her because blacks assumed in Kinmont's thinking the same countercultural function as women did in Catharine Beecher's feminism. Both Kinmont and Catharine Beecher saw as the dominant threat to a Christian civilization a ruthlessly hardheaded and aggressively expansionist culture. American culture, Harriet believed, would need to be complemented by softer qualities—black and female—in order to be spiritually fulfilled.

Strictly speaking, it is the public, not the author, that makes a best seller. *Uncle Tom's Cabin* did not so much cause a sensation as confirm the existence of it and focus it so dramatically that many generations have found it impossible to think about slavery outside the pictures it created. The inspiration for the book came, Harriet Stowe later liked to recall, during a Sunday communion service in Brunswick as she tried to imagine the death of a pious black man at the hands of a white master. We may only guess that what happened during this mo-

ment was that her perception of her black victim fused with her prior thinking about feminine and Christian self-sacrifice and that she saw suddenly that she could treat the issue of race in the same way that she and Catharine had celebrated women: as a redemptive, countercultural, and Christian force. She rushed home in tears and wrote the incident down before it faded away.

The white master in her reverie took the shape of a burly white whom her brother Charles had met years back in New Orleans. He had flexed his muscles and bragged that he got them from "knocking down niggers." In her fiction, he became a transplanted Vermont yankee running a plantation as if it were a northern factory. Hardhearted as well as hardheaded, he has rejected the social graces of the plantation way of life to pursue his lonely profit. He is the son of a drunkard and has spurned his mother and suppressed his softer side in order to conquer the world. He is calculating and brutal, but not stupid. He stands for the darker side of a "go-ahead" ideology and has sensed in Tom qualities that would fit him for a spot in his hierarchy—if only he'd forget that nonsense about the Bible:

"Come, Tom, don't you think you'd better be reasonable?—heave that 'ar old pack of trash in the fire, and join my church!"

"The Lord forbid!" said Tom fervently.

"You see the Lord an't going to help you: if he had been, he wouldn't have let *me* get you! This yer religion is all a mess of lying trumpery, Tom. I know all about it. Ye'd better hold to me I'm somebody, and can do something!"

"Father" Josiah Henson, a well-known, pious, fugitive slave whom Stowe knew, filled out the dim figure of Uncle Tom. In this black figure, who was to be torn from his family and sold down the Mississippi to meet a martyr's death, she invested her accumulated feelings about separation, victimization, and motherly self-sacrifice. At the opening of the novel, he is stroking young George Shelby's hair and speaking to him in a voice "gentle as a woman's."

When Calvin Stowe read his wife's description of Uncle Tom's death, he wept over it much as readers had wept over the passing of Dickens' Little Nell a decade earlier. Most of all, he urged her to continue it, and with his encouragement Harriet Stowe committed herself to a serial for Gamaliel Bailey's antislavery weekly, the *National Era*. The book simply "grew up" around the scene that occurs late in the finished novel. Here, the characters step out of their naturalistic roles to become, momentarily, figures in a cosmic drama and a cultural debate:

Legree drew in a long breath; and, suppressing his rage, took Tom by the arm, and, approaching his face almost to his, said in a terrible voice, "Hark 'e, Tom!—ye think, 'cause I've let you off before, I don't mean what I say; but, this time, I've *made up my mind,* and counted the cost. You've always stood it out agin' me: now I'll *conquer ye or kill ye!*—one or t'other. I'll count every drop of blood there is in you, and take 'em, one by one, till ye give up!"

Tom looked up to his master, and answered, "Mas'r, if you was sick, or in trouble, or dying, and I could save ye, I'd *give* ye my heart's blood; and, if taking every drop of blood in this poor old body would save your precious soul, I'd give 'em freely, as the Lord gave his for me. O, Mas'r! don't bring this great sin on your soul! It will hurt you more than 't will me! Do the worst you can, my troubles'll be over soon; but, if ye don't repent, yours won't *ever* end!"

Like a strange snatch of heavenly music, heard in the lull of a tempest, this burst of feeling made a moment's blank pause. Legree stood aghast, and looked at Tom; and there was such a silence that the tick of the old clock could be heard, measuring, with silent touch, the last moments of mercy and probation to that hardened heart.

It was but a moment. There was one hesitating pause,—one irresolute, relenting thrill,—and the spirit of evil came back, with sevenfold vehemence; and Legree, foaming with rage, smote his victim to the ground.

Legree overreacts because Tom reminds him of the side of himself that he has suppressed. Tom's offer of a qualitatively new life has caught Legree off guard by the sheer genius of its insight into his condition. The blank pause during which the clock ticks off those last minutes of grace extended to a hardened sinner captures those moments of self-despair in which a figure from a dominant and aggressive culture is tempted by the vision of a better way in the culture he has just subjugated—only to follow up his insight with an even more desperate betrayal.

What amazes about the dramatic climax is that Legree is damned to hell, not just that Tom is sent to heaven. It is Legree, then, and not the South who is the national demon. Twenty years of thinking about the repressed and calculating Uncle Jaw led Harriet Stowe to sense the connection between her regional stereotype and a national characteristic: the pursuit of profit without a motive. It is natural for Legree to "make up his mind" and "to conquer." That he has "counted the cost" to "count every drop of blood" is simply an extreme case of business as usual in an economic system that transforms human beings into property. As a representative of the system that gave him birth, Legree is as American as apple pie, and Harriet Stowe saw that the American sin was his state of mind. He is the symptom of a fundamental cultural malaise in what she saw as the Anglo-Saxon race. The contours of earlier debates between the head and the heart, and between law and grace, yield her, tentatively, to a racial conflict between a hard, masculine Anglo-Saxon race bent upon domination and the values represented by women, children, and blacks acting out visibly God's love in history.

This conflict of values touches nearly every character and relationship in the novel. It splits the personality of George Harris, a mulatto modeled upon Frederick Douglass, whose character and career counterpoint Uncle Tom's. From a white father he inherits allegedly white qualities—an excellent mind and a proud and independent spirit; but from his black mother, his legacy is that of bondage and sensitivity. His militancy and atheism (alienated "white" values) must be redeemed by complemental feminine and "black" values in the Quaker home of Rachel Halliday, who presides over a domestic life centered around Christian charity.

Harriet Stowe shared with her brother Edward the perception that slavery was an organic sin, a state of society into which one was born, and not the personal sin that Garrison was denouncing. This insight allowed her to create a rich and complex group of characters, neither very wicked nor very good, whose efforts to struggle with the issues are undercut by the economic system in which they are trapped. The cultured and kindhearted Mrs. Shelby could have graduated from Catharine Beecher's Hartford seminary. When her husband's finances require him to sell Uncle Tom and Eliza's son, she sees their economic base turning into a moral abyss: "How," she asks her husband—who will absent himself on the day of the sale to spare his feelings—"can I bear to have this open acknowledgement that we care for no tie, no duty, no relation, however sacred, compared with money?" Worse, she realizes her false position: "It is a sin to hold a slave under laws like ours . . . but I thought I could gild it over,—I thought, by kindness, and care, and instruction, I could make the condition of mine better than freedom,—fool that I was!"

Tom's next master is already so demoralized that he has refused to play any role at all. Augustine St. Clare is a Byronic figure alienated from his slave-holding father, brother, and society.

From his willful and autocratic father he has inherited all the perquisites of *noblesse,* but from his mother, a deeply sensitive nature, an abhorrence of slavery, and a frustrated sense of *oblige.* Pursuing a course of indulgent anarchy, he cannot bring himself to discipline the servants—they have not been taught better—nor to free them—they would simply be outcasts in a society that has not taught them anything useful. "Some how or other," he explains to his northern Aunt Ophelia, "instead of being actor and regenerator in society, I became a piece of driftwood, and have been floating and eddying about, ever since." But Ophelia has herself lost her soul. She is a bondslave to her sense of moral obligation; for her the word *love* has been transmuted by a New England alembic into *duty.* Her energetic determination to set things right doesn't fool Topsy, who spots the truth about her chill virtue: "she can't bar me, 'cause I'm a nigger!—she'd 's soon have a toad touch her!''

For these broken figures Harriet Beecher Stowe affirms a possible cosmic destiny: of awakening to the power of God's transforming love in history, a love represented by Little Eva, trailing clouds of glory with her; in the suffering sacrifice of women such as Rachel Halliday and Mrs. Bird; and in the racial character of Uncle Tom, who is the culminating example of a new Christian consciousness to which Africa is the key:

If ever Africa shall show an elevated and cultivated race,—and come it must, some time, her turn to figure in the great drama of human improvement—life will awaken there with a gorgeousness and splendor of which our cold western tribes faintly have conceived. In that far-off mystic land of gold, and gems, and spices, and waving palms, and wondrous flowers, and miraculous fertility, will awake new forms of art . . . and the negro race . . . will, perhaps, show forth some of the latest and most magnificent revelations of human life. Certainly they will in their gentleness, their lowly docility of heart, their aptitude to repose on a superior mind and to rest on a higher power, their childlike simplicity of affection, and facility of forgiveness . . . they will exhibit the highest form of the peculiarly *Christian life.* . . .

Readers who reject this pastoral racial mythology should realize the needs that it satisfied and the cultural functions that it served: to awaken whites to the necessity of recovering their humanity. In this function, American attitudes toward race have not significantly advanced beyond that of Mrs. Stowe. For the figure of Uncle Tom, our times have unfairly substituted the figure of the black hipster, or performer, or radical to carry the burden of our own liberation.

In *Dred: A Tale of the Great Dismal Swamp* (1856), Mrs. Stowe tried to develop a further scenario: what might happen to a religious black figure tortured beyond endurance? The result is the character of Dred, an impressive achievement. He is a full black of magnificent stature and high intellectual demeanor modeled upon Denmark Vesey. He is a biblical prophet of wrath and judgment, who has assembled a group of fugitives in a swamp retreat to strike out in vengeance when God shall give the sign:

The large eyes had that peculiar and solemn effect of unfathomable blackness and darkness which is often a striking characteristic of the African eye. But there burned in them, like tongues of flame in a black pool of naphtha a subtle and restless fire that betokened habitual excitement to the verge of insanity. If any organs were predominant in the head, they were those of ideality, wonder, veneration, and firmness; and the whole combination was such as might have formed one of the wild old warrior prophets of the heroic ages.

Dred's counterpoint is Milly, a black woman who warns the wavering mulatto hero, Harry Gordon, away from Dred: "He han't come to de heavenly Jerusalem. Oh! Oh! honey! dere's a blood of sprinkling dat speaketh better things dan dat of Abel. Jerusalem above is *free,*—is *free,* honey; so don't you mind, now, what happens in *dis* yer time."

But Harriet Stowe was unable to reconcile Milly's gospel of grace with Dred's gospel of judgment. Horrified by the possibility of race war, she uses the female figure of Milly to head it off. As the fugitives wait for the signal to strike at the community, a wild and mournful tune is warbled through the trees, and Milly steps forth singing "Alas! and Did My Savior Bleed." "When Dred saw her, he gave a kind of groan, and said, putting his hand out before his face:— 'Woman, thy prayers withstand me!' " The pie remains in the sky; the chief characters flee North; and religious femininity rather than racial solidarity wins the hour. In the end, Mrs. Stowe came to focus on gender rather than race to help balance her cultural equation.

Three succeeding novels explore the feminine sensibility suggested by Milly more thoroughly and with a greater understanding of its limitations. *The Minister's Wooing* (1859), *The Pearl of Orr's Island* (1862), and *Agnes of Sorrento* (1862) show through the differing cultural restraints of New England and Italy the limitations placed on feminine development. Although the religious motive remains a central factor, Stowe focuses on the imaginative qualities necessary for religious empathy and forges a bond between the aesthetic and the religious that gave a Christian legitimacy to her function as artist and redirected her ideas of her mission in the world.

The Pearl of Orr's Island, begun in 1853, is a study in contrasting male and female sensibilities. The story of the two orphans, Mara and Moses, is framed by two New England "fates": the hardnosed, realistic Aunt Roxy and the softhearted, sentimental Aunt Ruey, who both superintend at the births and deaths on the island.

The physical settings repeat the opposing sensibilities. The rocky island is a bastion against a deep and mysterious sea; the outcropping granite headlands confront sandy inlets that invite to play; and the outdoors calls to action and adventure, while the indoors suggests a hoped-for sociality that yields as often to withdrawal and reverie. And so the children. We catch Moses shinnying up a tree to steal eagles' eggs, while Mara sits below copying a cluster of scarlet rock columbine:

All that there was developed of him, at present, was a fund of energy, self-esteem, hope, courage, and daring, the love of action, life, and adventure; his life was in the outward and present, not in the inward and reflective . . . she was, the small pearl with the golden hair, with her frail and high-strung organization, her sensitive nerves, her half-spiritual fibres, her ponderings, and marvels, and dreams, her power of love, and yearning for self-devotion. . . .

Mara is hemmed in and wants to expand her world; Moses himself comes to realize his limitations and senses in Mara a different kind of strength won through suffering, experience, and insight. After long periods of studied neglect he proposes to her, but it is too late and she dies slowly from consumption. Her insight, "I may have more power over you, when I seem to be gone, than I should have had living," is confirmed in Moses' marriage to Sally Kittridge, a robust flirt and Mara's friend. "We have been trained in another life,—educated by a great sorrow,—is it not so?" Moses asks Sally as they recall Mara. Sally replies: "I know it."

The Minister's Wooing, published in installments in 1859 to help out Oliver Wendell Holmes's financially beleaguered *Atlantic Monthly,* deepens Harriet Beecher Stowe's study of the captive sensibility by exploring the repressive effect of late eighteenth-century High Calvinism on Mary Scudder's and Mrs. Marvyn's human needs.

We are looking at New England character and society at a time when Puritan fervor has congealed into dogma and ritual piety. Mrs. Stowe's metaphor for the culture is the crystal. James Marvyn's father has "one of the clearly cut minds which New England forms among her farmers, as she forms quartz crystals in her mountains. . . ." The sensibility of the culture is locked in granite and ice, emerging sporadically in congregational song, "those wild, pleading tunes" born in "the rocky hollows of its mountains, and whose notes have a kind of grand and mournful triumph in their warbling wail. . . ." At the center of the religious sensibility is the Reverend Hopkins' crystalline Calvinism, which presents salvation in the famous image of the ladder, at the very top of which:

. . . blazes dazzling and crystalline that celestial grade where the soul knows self no more . . . this Ultima Thule of virtue had been seized upon by our sage as the all of religion. He knocked out every rung of the ladder but the highest, and then, pointing to its hopeless splendor, said to the world, "Go up thither and be saved!"

The spiritual carnage is visible all around in the worst as well as in the best. It is reflected in Aaron Burr's recoil, which turns Hopkins' icy dogmatics upside down into a chill and opportunistic hedonism. And it is implicit in the plain-spoken cynicism of Cerinthy Ann, who "come out, declarin' . . . that the best folk never had no comfort in religion; and for her part she didn't mean to trouble her head about it, but have jest as good a time as she could while she's young, 'cause if she was 'lected to be saved she should be, and if she wa'n't she couldn't help it, anyhow." At the teas, everything is admired but little is enjoyed. The china, the silver, the linen, hopes for husbands and hopes for heaven—each has to be picked over, fingered, and laid aside only after the cost has been calculated. Life amidst the spotless linens is a little thin.

Mary Scudder's is the predicament of a heartfelt obligation to a New England past that cannot satisfy her needs, while she yearns inarticulately for a future represented by a group of "outsiders" who understand her far better than she does herself. Her predicament sums up the plot. She loves the dashing but unconverted James Marvyn, and he manages to extract a marriage vow before disappearing on an ocean voyage. He is thought drowned, and Mary's mother makes her give herself to the Reverend Hopkins, a benign man whose personality contradicts his theology, and who is old enough to be her father. When James does return—and freshly regenerate at that—he is eager for Mary, who refuses to break her vow to the good Hopkins.

Those who come to her aid by interceding with the minister are more worldly, or exotic: Miss Prissy, the milliner, who knows about Parisian fashions; Mme. de Frontignac, who is pursuing an affair with Aaron Burr behind the back of her French diplomat husband; and Candace, Mrs. Marvyn's black cook. They manage the minister and he releases her from her vow and blesses her marriage with James.

Neither Hopkins nor his theology is meant for the human heart. When Mrs. Marvyn thinks that James has drowned unconverted, Hopkins urges her to submit and affirm her horrified vision of her son's eternal damnation. This is too much for Candace, who brushes aside the emotional cripples standing around:

"Come, ye poor little lamb," she said, walking straight up to Mrs. Marvyn, "come to ole Candace!" and with that she gathered the pale form to her bosom, and sat down and began rocking her, as if she had been a babe. "Honey, darlin', ye ain't right,—dar's a drefful mistake somewhar," she said. "Why, de Lord ain't what ye tink,—He *loves* ye, honey! Why, jes' feel how *I* loves ye,—poor old black Candace,—an' I ain't bettern' Him as made me! Who was it wore de crown of thorns, lamb? —who was it sweat great drops o' blood?—who was it said, 'Father, forgive dem'? . . . Dar, dar, now ye'r crying'! —cry away, and ease yer poor little heart! He died for Mass'r Jim, —loved him and died for him, —jes' give up his sweet, precious body and soul for him on de cross! Laws, jes' leave him in Jesus's hands!"

Candace's gospel of the heart suggests a new religious sensibility in the book; while Prissy, Mme. de Frontignac, and James Marvyn, through their greater experience in the world and the broader sweep and livelier play of their imaginations, introduce an aesthetic sensibility that balances the sad earnestness of Mary Scudder. James sees in Mary "a picture he had once seen in a European cathedral, where the youthful Mother of Sorrows is represented." Aboard ship he has had a vision of a ladder, not Hopkins' but Jacobs':

Well, there [Jacob] was as lonesome as I upon the deck of my ship. And so, lying with the stone under his head, he saw a ladder in his sleep between him and heaven, and angels going up and down. . . . He saw that there was a way between him and God, and that there were those above who did care for him, and who could come to him to help him.

James's trust in a descent from above, in incarnation, gives him his ability to see God's presence in the things of this world, to see where God's light is playing and to see what Hopkins has forgotten: that the base of the ladder to God is planted "in human affections, tender instincts, symbolic feelings" and "sacraments of love."

Such vision, Jonathan Edwards had pointed out a generation earlier, was religious. Harriet Beecher Stowe did not lose the chance to appropriate the insight to her conception of the artist's vocation. To find romance in a prose world was both a way of redeeming it and a way of tracing the hand of the Creator in His works:

All prosaic, and all bitter, disenchanted people talk as if poets and novelists *made* romance. They do,—just as much as craters make volcanoes,—no more. What is romance? whence comes it? Plato spoke to the subject wisely . . . when he said, Man's soul, in a former state, was winged and soared among the gods; and so it comes to pass that, in this life, when the soul, by the power of music or poetry, or the sight of beauty, hath her remembrance quickened, forthwith there is a struggling and a pricking pain as of wings trying to come forth. . . .

The Reverend Theophilus Sewall, with the skeleton of romance in his closet, and story-telling Captain Kittridge are the two figures in *The Pearl of Orr's Island* whose sensibilities can comprehend both Mara's and Moses'. In *The Minister's Wooing* this function is performed by Candace, Prissy, Mme. de Frontignac and by Mary's lover, James. In *Agnes of Sorrento,* which she began in 1859 as an entertainment for her own daughters while traveling in Italy, Harriet Beecher Stowe continued exploring the aesthetic dimension in the figure of the Italian artist monk, Father Antonio. It is he who brings about a marriage between the saintly Agnes and the proud and atheistic Agostino Sarelli (note the resemblance to Augustine St. Clare). An Italian nobleman whose patrimony has been robbed by a corrupt Catholic church, Sarelli is led to a state of grace by Father Antonio.

The scenery of *Agnes of Sorrento* is the antithesis of rocky New England. The fertile Italian landscape suggests overripe human development; an abundance of brilliant flowers, lush foliage, and colorful birds veil black charnel chasms and smoldering volcanoes. Italy suggests a garden much like that of Hawthorne's Rappaccini, but one where decay and hidden passion are the poisons.

Agnes shrinks from contact with this world. Her mother has been debauched and abandoned by an Italian nobleman, and she has left Agnes in the hands of her own mother, Elsie, who seems like a New England import with a strongly practical streak. She wants to marry off Agnes to a rough but honest tradesman. And when Sarelli spots Agnes in the marketplace and falls in love with her, Agnes and her grandmother see little before them but the melodramatic alternatives of Giulietta's whoredom or Mother Theresa's nunnery. The church is sunk in sloth and sin and proves wholly incapable of dealing with her problem. Her confessor, Father Francesco, is a voluptuary who frightens her away from Sarelli by persuading her she will accomplish her own and his eternal perdition if she encourages him. Mother Theresa is ignorant not only of the times and of the church, but of a young girl's heart as well.

Father Antonio steps in to untangle these motives. He is Elsie's brother and has been searching for a pure original from which to paint a saint's portrait and is thrilled when he sees that Sarelli's motives for a portrait of Agnes match his own. In Sarelli's aesthetic sensibility, Father Antonio discovers veiled religious feelings, and he sets about to win Sarelli over for Savonarola and his God, while assuring Agnes that her lover's impulses are honorable. Agnes' faith in her church is finally shaken when she is kidnapped by church officials eager for some fun during her pilgrimage to Rome.

Through Father Antonio's sensibility, then, Agnes forges a relationship with the world. When she exclaims to Antonio how happy he must be, he replies: "Happy! . . . Do I not walk the earth in a dream of bliss, and see the footsteps of my blessed Lord and his dear Mother on every rock and hill?" In him, Harriet Beecher Stowe justifies the creation of artistic symbols. It is "one of the first offices of every saint whose preaching stirred the heart of the people, to devise symbolic forms, signs, and observances, by which the mobile and fluid heart of the multitude might crystalize into habits of devout remembrance.'' Here, she is thinking not only of rosaries, crucifixes, shrines, banners, and processions but also of the artist's task of fitting rungs in the ladder that will lead believers to their God. Even Agnes, who is often as severe as Hilda in Hawthorne's *The Marble Faun,* cannot help but exclaim as Father Antonio delineates the death of a saint: ''How great a grace must come from such pictures! It seems to me that the making of such holy things is one of the most blessed of good works.''

Each novel in this group marks a development in the heroine by showing her fascination with a progressively more worldly male figure: the robust Moses; the dashing, wealthy James; and finally Agostino Sarelli, a worldly prince. Most important, however, is the reformist Father Antonio, whose religious aesthetics sum up Mara's devotional sketching of flowers and James Marvyn's habit of seeing Mary Scudder in terms of old-world religious portraits. Father Antonio's capacity for seeing is matched by his ability to turn his vision into art. The artist's involvement with the world does not mean to surrender to its values but to consecrate its moments of love and suffering. Through Mara Lincoln, Mary Scudder, and Agnes, Harriet Beecher Stowe wrote herself out of her fascination with girlish martyrs and into the figure of the artist. It is through these eyes that she takes a final, broader look at New England.

Harriet Beecher Stowe continued to write of New England—*Oldtown Folks* (1869), *Sam Lawson's Oldtown Fireside Stories* (1872), and *Poganuc People* (1878)—not because of a narrow interest in regionalism, but because she rediscovered her region's significance for the growth of the nation, and because she found a fresh perspective. In this, her final group of novels, the New England story becomes an opening chapter in an unwritten book about the national character. New England is seen as a cradle of the republic disclosing the problems and possibilities of life in America. Looking closer, she also discovered a new perspective from which to tell her story—the perspective offered by native, Down East humor. It is a dry, comic point of view that allows her to tell grimmer truths than before about the weight of her region's past while dissipating the anguish of some of that past in humor. In *Oldtown Folks,* we listen to the story of a generation of children through whose sensibilities a New England town is able to recover its capacity for enjoyment. In *Sam Lawson's Oldtown Fireside Stories,* the village do-nothing, mentor to the children in *Oldtown Folks,* tells humorous stories that unlock the grim incidents and frozen personalities that Harriet Beecher Stowe saw as typical of her region. Perhaps by telling these stories first through the medium of her husband's personality (Calvin is Horace Holyoke in *Oldtown Folks*) and then through the comic perspective offered by Sam Lawson, she found the breathing space that she needed before she put herself on stage as Dolly Cushing in *Poganuc People* to tell about her own growth.

Mrs. Stowe based the theme of *Oldtown Folks* on the tale of Hansel and Gretel, children cast out in the world by their impoverished parents and who must free themselves from the spell of a witch. In her New England version of Grimm, the witch is a Calvinist hag who lives in the granite mountains and her spell is melancholy. She has crippled the children's parents and threatens the children as well. There are, in other words, strong gothic shadows in a book otherwise noted for its sunlight. Oldtown with a relative sufficiency of grace is contrasted with the town of Needmore, where joy shivers at the door; the benign grandparents who first take in Horace, then Harry and Tina, are the pleasant aspect of a regional character that includes Crab Smith and his sister Miss Asphyxia, witches themselves who have squeezed grace dry and turned life into a tortuous round of work. Against the strong, melancholy groundswell of High Calvinism, Parson Lothrup's Arminianism and Lady Widgery's Episcopalianism ripple ineffectually.

In the parents' generation, Horace's father has died in poverty as a broken-down schoolmaster; and his mother, once a pert socialite, has been worn down to a shadow and later disappears under the merciless wing of her sister Lois, a scolding old maid. Uncle Fly and Aunt Keziah are more softhearted—but also quite softheaded. Harry and Tina's father is the alcoholic son of a minor British nobleman and has abandoned his consumptive wife. The Rossiters, a third major family group, carry the psychic scars of a Calvinism against which their hearts rebel. Outwardly wise, they inwardly bleed. Parson Avery's family dilemma derives from his inability to widen the Calvinist sheepfold fast enough to prevent the spiritual ulceration of his daughter, Esther, of whom we are told "her body thought." Finally, we have those whose nerves have snapped: the brilliant lost ones, Ellery Davenport and Emily Rossiter, who skim life's surface, hoping by speed to escape the terror that drives them on and, in the end, claims them.

Horace, Harry, and Tina, the central characters in *Oldtown Folks,* are spiritual as well as literal orphans to the world of their parents and find more comfortable guardians in their grandparents. Harriet Beecher Stowe took the main features of Horace's story from her husband's childhood. Calvin Stowe had been orphaned under similar circumstances; he was adopted by his grandparents; and he experienced the same spiritualist longings for the alter ego playmate that Harry becomes in the story. Horace's nighttime vision of a boy like Harry standing before him in his bedroom matches exactly Calvin Stowe's own account of a childhood reverie. Horace's tale may, then, be twice-told: first, literally, in his adoption and his achieving his father's lost dream of an education; then, symbolically, through the figure of Harry, whose story seems to develop the darker side of Horace's own.

Harry and his sister, Tina, have been abandoned by their father and brought by their dying mother to the village of Needmore where they are taken in by Crab and Sphyxy Smith who act out in New England fashion the witch's role in *Hansel and Gretel.* The children are fattened— not for eating (there is no joy in food in Needmore), but for work. Fleeing from a house in which Calvinist grace has been debased in work, the children take refuge in an abandoned mansion the former notoriety of which suggests the degeneracy of a British heritage. Here the children are found by Sam Lawson and he brings them to Oldtown, where they come as if in response to the starved hearts of Horace and Mehitable Rossiter and where they win the affection of the town.

Tina's spirit is elemental fizz. She is bubbly and irrepressible, and her effervescence takes the grandparents by storm. A natural mimic, she sends the adults into stitches with her comic renditions of themselves and their neighbors. Her adoption by Mehitable Rossiter brings joy to the life of the childless old widow and her drab maid. Tina's brother, Harry, is more serious, but equally resistant to attempts, such as Parson Avery's, to scare him into orthodoxy. In short, the children subvert the overly serious adult world through humor and play, and in their presence the village of Oldtown recovers its youth.

Before graduating from school at Cloudland, the children put on two plays for the adults, "Jephtha's Daughter," and a New England farce, which further displace the values of the parents' orthodox world. The central scene in their version of "Jephtha's Daughter" is a procession of the town's young men and women who carry out and bury the corpses of Jephtha's daughter (played by Tina) and her lover (Harry) under the remorseful eyes of Jephtha (Horace). What we are seeing is a mock-tragic representation of New England sacrificing her best sons and daughters on the altar of the past. In the farce that follows, the children exorcise the twin community demons: workaholism and do-nothingism. Tina becomes Hepzibah, the scold; Harry, the ineffectual Uncle Fliakim. These comic performances, which invite the community's symbolic participation and elicit its laughter, break the spell of the hag. And, as the community joins them in laughing at itself, we know at least that Horace, Tina, and Harry will be able to leave those roles behind and escape the fate of their parents' generation.

Tracing the theme of comic displacement brings us to Sam Lawson, the talented village do-nothing who is married, like Rip Van Winkle, to a nagging wife. He spreads Aunt Lois' clock over her kitchen floor while fixing it but walks quite calmly away from the pieces—and Aunt Lois' rage—to return when another fit of work shall strike him. In a community of overwork, Sam Lawson is dangerous and badly needed. Only he can take time out to find and comfort Horace after his father's death and to discover Harry and Tina and bring them to Oldtown. His leisure allows him to father the children on expeditions to the countryside. He is the village's source of knowledge about the entire country, and he is given the central place at the family fireside to tell his stories. *Oldtown Folks* closes with his hoping for an easy missionary job in the South Seas. Luckily, Harriet Beecher Stowe brought him back as the central figure in his own book, *Sam Lawson's Fireside Stories,* where his comedy transfigures both the people in his tales and his listeners.

In *Fireside Stories,* Sam Lawson says to Horace, ''. . . you look at the folks that's allus tellin' you what they don't believe,—they don't believe this, and they don't believe that,—and what sort o' folks is they? Why, like yer Aunt Lois, sort o' stringy and dry. There ain't no 'sorbtion got out o' not belivin' nothin'.'' Whether his stories are told at the winter hearth-

side, in a Thanksgiving kitchen, or (as they mostly are) on rambles for berries and on trout-fishing expeditions, his tales always manage to hook the children and yield their own wild fruits. In this no-nonsense world, they supply more than community and continuity between the generations: they are the antidote to Aunt Lois' terrible rationalism. They offer the thirsting soul homegrown marvels capable of rousing its capacity for imagination and wonder.

We relax in the company of Sam Lawson, who has made success out of failure. He has seen the world on ship; he has had a love affair; and he likes to leave us with the impression that, had he wanted to, he could have done better for himself. But, he concludes with unselfconscious irony, after telling the tales of other people's misbegotten wealth, ''this 'ere hastenin' to be rich is sich a drefful temptation.''

Sam Lawson tells us about people suffering the agonies of a haunting, or caught in the spell of greed, or gripped by the dead hand of formalism—and they become transfigured through his dry, gothic humor. Humor unlocks the parson, for example, whose Sunday meeting is broken up by a sheep that spots a wig and knocks down the deacon wearing it. His shocked parishioners report him to the session for laughing in church; but the session itself dissolves with laughter when he tells the story. A groom working for another parson runs his master's horse in races behind his back during meeting. When the parson gathers a group of his parishioners to put an end to Sabbath racing, his own horse abandons caution and plunges into a race with the parson on his back. A third parson marries his chambermaid after his wife's death despite the town's rumors. Ghost stories, spiritualist tales, folk tales, tales from the Revolution, and funny stories alike are told in leisurely fashion: ''He would take his time for it and proceed by easy stages. It was like the course of a dreamy, slow-moving river through a tangled meadowflat,—not a rush nor a bush but was reflected in it; in short, Sam gave his philosophy of matters and things in general as he went along, and was especially careful to impress an edifying moral.''

The yearning to escape the routines of Old-town is satisfied through more direct means than stories in Harriet Beecher Stowe's last novel, *Poganuc People*. Here, the central character falls for a world of pearls, purples, and Episcopalians. Her book pays tribute to her father's orthodox world but leaves it behind. We may see in Dolly Cushing's flight from the Presbyterians to the Episcopalians a justification for Harriet Beecher Stowe's own return to her mother's and grandmother's childhood religion. She cut her religious ties with her father's church when she left ''dour'' Andover in 1867. Now, she was a nationally recognized figure with a fine home in Hartford, Connecticut, a pew in the local Episcopalian church, and a winter home in Florida. From this vantage point, she came to see that her bleak childhood world had nourished a fugitive beauty but that it had also vexed the soul. Her memories of her father's austere world set her to create the childhood that she might have had had her mother lived.

Poganuc People opens on little Dolly Cushing standing outside the newly built Episcopalian meeting house, which is being decorated with greens and gilt for a Christmas illumination. Longing for its promise of beauty and glory, Dolly tiptoes out of her empty house at night and enters. There she discovers some of her brothers, as well, drinking in the Episcopalian splendors while their own meeting house is shut up in darkness.

Dolly's growing up, Nabby's love affair with Hiel, and Zepheniah's reconciliation with his God and his church come, as did the Christmas illumination, as treasured moments of transcendence in an otherwise tedious life. Colonel Davenport recalls the moment when George Washington broke propriety and swore furiously at officers and troops for disobeying an order. Zepheniah Higgins shocks and delights his town

when he pulls a schoolhouse down from the top of a hill into the village. Even Dolly's father breaks the routine of parish duties to organize nutting expeditions. Inside the Cushing house, small surprises vary the monotony. The children delight in exploring the basement with its possibility of terror. Dolly finds a copy of *The Arabian Nights*. Atop the kitchen stairs is an alcove that opens into a smokehouse. Young eyes transform the smokehouse into the byway to hell in *A Pilgrim's Progress*. The Parson's attic study with its copy of Mather's ''Magnilly'' and its bins of old sermons serves as home for several generations of theological kittens. New England abhors a holiday as nature abhors a vacuum, yet the citizens turn out and transform the Fourth of July into a festive display.

Much of the description is from Harriet Beecher Stowe's childhood home. The capable Mrs. Cushing resembles Catharine, and Harriet's mother reappears as the wife of Zepheniah. Her father is sympathetically sketched in the figure of Parson Cushing, whose fine words to Dolly after her conversion match Lyman Beecher's own words to his daughter on the same occasion. At times obtuse, at times sensitive, he gains a literal truth at the expense of an imaginative one when he warns Dolly that celebrating Christmas without a firm date is unscriptural, popish, and heathenish; but his refusal to meddle during Zepheniah Higgins' mental crisis is a study in pastoral tact.

Her father's world, though, offers little for her development. It seems to turn in on itself, to become ingrown. Again she finds its typical expression in church song:

The wild warble of St. Martins, the appointed tune whose wings bore these words, swelled and billowed and reverberated through the house, carrying with it that indefineable thrill which always fills the house when deep emotions are touched—deepest among people habitually reserved and reticent of outward demonstration. It was a solemn undertone, this mysterious, throbbing subbass of repressed emotion, which gave the power and effect to the Puritan music.

But it is precisely "outward demonstration" that Dolly wants. She wants to be able to show her feelings and to find in the world around her such images of beauty, love, excitement, and surprise as she yearns for. The austerity of her father's faith simply demands too great a sacrifice. Perhaps Parson Cushing has sensed this, for when he readies Dolly, at the end of the novel, for a visit to her Episcopalian relatives in Boston, he urges her kindly to attend the Episcopalian services. Her visit fulfills even extravagantly the wishes of this daughter of the Puritans. It brings her the gift of a beautiful prayerbook bound in purple velvet, a pearl necklace from Uncle Israel, a scarlet cloak trimmed with lace from an aunt, and the offer of marriage from an Episcopalian Englishman who shares her evangelical piety.

Later, more toughminded generations would dismiss such endings—indeed most of Harriet Beecher Stowe's work—as sentimental. But she would probably have found material for comedy in knowing that a generation trained on existentialism and Marxism should so despise the dialectics of the bittersweet. Tenderminded as she was, she would probably have told us that ours are, as hers proved to be, historical attitudes.

Selected Bibliography

WORKS OF HARRIET BEECHER STOWE

SEPARATE WORKS

Prize Tale. A New England Sketch ["Uncle Lot"]. Lowell, Mass.: Alfred Gilman, 1834.

The Mayflower; or, Sketches of Scenes and Characters Among the Descendants of the Pilgrims. New York: Harper, 1843.

Uncle Tom's Cabin; or, Life Among the Lowly. 2 vols. Boston: John P. Jewett, 1852. Kenneth S. Lynn in the 1962 Harvard University Press edition and Russel B. Nye in the 1963 Washington Square Press edition have written excellent introductions.

A Key to Uncle Tom's Cabin. Boston: John P. Jewett, 1853.

Uncle Sam's Emancipation . . . and Other Sketches. Philadelphia: Willis P. Hazard, 1853.

Sunny Memories of Foreign Lands. 2 vols. Boston: Phillips, Sampson, 1854.

Dred: A Tale of the Great Dismal Swamp. 2 vols. Boston: Phillips, Sampson, 1856.

Our Charley and What to Do With Him. Boston: Phillips, Sampson, 1858.

The Minister's Wooing. New York: Derby and Jackson, 1859.

The Pearl of Orr's Island: A Story of the Coast of Maine. Boston: Ticknor and Fields, 1862.

Agnes of Sorrento. Boston: Ticknor and Fields, 1862.

A Reply . . . of American Women. London: S. Low, 1863.

House and Home Papers. By Christopher Crowfield [pseud.]. Boston: Ticknor and Fields, 1865.

Little Foxes. By Christopher Crowfield [pseud.]. Boston: Ticknor and Fields, 1866.

Religious Poems. Boston: Ticknor and Fields, 1867.

Queer Little People. Boston: Ticknor and Fields, 1867.

Daisy's First Winter and Other Stories. Boston: Fields, Osgood, 1867.

The Chimney-Corner. By Christopher Crowfield [pseud.]. Boston: Ticknor and Fields, 1868.

Men of Our Times; or, Leading Patriots of the Day. Hartford: Hartford Publishing, 1868.

Oldtown Folks. Boston: Fields, Osgood, 1869.

The American Woman's Home. New York: J. B. Ford, 1869.

Lady Byron Vindicated: A History of the Byron Controversy. Boston: Fields, Osgood, 1870.

Little Pussy Willow. Boston: Fields, Osgood, 1870.

My Wife and I; or, Harry Henderson's History. New York: J. B. Ford, 1871.

Pink and White Tyranny: A Society Novel. Boston: Roberts Brothers, 1871.

Sam Lawson's Oldtown Fireside Stories. Boston: James R. Osgood, 1872.

Palmetto-Leaves. Boston: James R. Osgood, 1873.

Woman in Sacred History. New York: J. B. Ford, 1873.

We and Our Neighbors; or, The Records of an Unfashionable Street. New York: J. B. Ford, 1875.

Betty's Bright Idea and Other Stories. New York: J. B. Ford, 1876.

Footsteps of the Master. New York: J. B. Ford, 1877.

Poganuc People: Their Loves and Lives. New York: Fords, Howard, and Hulbert, 1878.

Our Famous Women. Hartford: A. D. Worthington, 1884.

COLLECTED EDITIONS

The Writings of Harriet Beecher Stowe. Riverside Edition. 16 vols. Boston and New York: Houghton, Mifflin, 1896.

BIBLIOGRAPHY

John R. Adams. *Harriet Beecher Stowe*. New York: Twayne, 1963. Lists uncollected writings.

Joseph Sabin. *Bibliotheca Americana*. 29 vols. New York: Bibliographical Society of America, 1868–1936. Volume 24 lists works published up to 1860.

Robert E. Spiller, *et al. Literary History of the United States*. 4th ed., rev. New York: Macmillan, 1974. The bibliography volume has the most generally useful list of primary and secondary sources.

BIOGRAPHIES

Annie Fields. *Life and Letters of Harriet Beecher Stowe*. Boston: Houghton, Mifflin, 1897.

Charles Edward Stowe. *The Life of Harriet Beecher Stowe*. Boston: Houghton, Mifflin, 1889. Good for establishing emphases.

Charles Edward Stowe and Lyman Beecher Stowe. *Harriet Beecher Stowe: The Story of Her Life*. Boston: Houghton, Mifflin, 1911.

Edward Wagenknecht. *Harriet Beecher Stowe: The Known and the Unknown*. New York: Oxford University Press, 1965.

Forrest Wilson. *Crusader in Crinoline: The Life of Harriet Beecher Stowe*. Philadelphia: J. B. Lippincott, 1941. The best and most comprehensive.

CRITICAL STUDIES

John R. Adams. *Harriet Beecher Stowe*. New York: Twayne, 1963. Emphasizes magazine fiction.

Harry Birdoff. *The World's Greatest Hit: Uncle Tom's Cabin*. New York: S. F. Vanni, 1947. The fascinating story of *Uncle Tom's Cabin* on stage.

Herbert Ross Brown. *The Sentimental Novel in America, 1789–1860*. Durham, N.C.: Duke University Press, 1940. Good for understanding sentimentalism.

Alice C. Crozier. *The Novels of Harriet Beecher Stowe*. New York: Oxford University Press, 1969. Emphasizes her two slavery novels.

Leslie Fiedler. *Love and Death in the American Novel*. Meridian Books. New York: Criterion Books, 1960; rev. ed., New York: Stein and Day, 1966. The cultural psychology behind the sentimental tradition.

Charles H. Foster. *The Rungless Ladder: Harriet Beecher Stowe and New England Puritanism*. Durham, N.C.: Duke University Press, 1954. The best study and excellent intellectual and cultural history.

George M. Fredrickson. *The Black Image in the White Mind: The Debate on Afro-American Character and Destiny, 1817–1914*. New York: Harper and Row, 1971. Excellent study of the development of and changes in American racial thinking.

Edwin Bruce Kirkham. *The Building of Uncle Tom's Cabin*. Knoxville: University of Tennessee Press, 1977. Traces the Beechers' involvement with antislavery and tracks down the origins in life of the incidents in *Uncle Tom's Cabin*.

Robert Merideth. *The Politics of the Universe: Edward Beecher, Abolition, and Orthodoxy*. Nashville: Vanderbilt University Press, 1968. Excellent cultural and intellectual history of her brother's thought which clarifies much of Harriet Beecher Stowe's intellectual origins.

Kathryn Kish Sklar. *Catharine Beecher: A Study in American Domesticity*. New Haven: Yale University Press, 1973. An excellent cultural and intellectual study of Catharine Beecher's evolving feminism, a strong influence upon Harriet Beecher Stowe.

Lyman Beecher Stowe. *Saints, Sinners, and Beechers*. Indianapolis: Bobbs-Merrill, 1934. Colorful anecdotes about the Beecher clan.

William Robert Taylor. *Cavalier and Yankee: The Old South and American National Character*. New York: G. Braziller, 1961. Places regional typologies such as Mrs. Stowe's in a cultural perspective.

—PAUL DAVID JOHNSON

James Thurber

1894–1961

WHEN *Punch* invited James Thurber to attend its Wednesday lunch and carve his initials on the table, he was the first American to be so honored since Mark Twain. He has been universally acclaimed as the greatest American humorist since Twain; indeed, E. B. White says he prefers Thurber. Yet just as Twain had to contend with the attitude that he was merely a "phunny phellow," not meriting serious consideration as an equal of Whittier, Longfellow, or Emerson, so Thurber has tended to get short shrift in American literature, at least in the groves of academe, where he usually is passed over in favor of more ponderous and pretentious writers who have what Matthew Arnold called "high seriousness." Humor also is handicapped by the fact that it soon becomes dated if it reflects only passing fads or follies, and the work of any prolific humorist is bound to contain a fair amount of forgettable trivia. Yet the great humorists are not merely amusing; they use laughter to expose the deeper predicaments and perplexities of mankind. In this sense, Thurber has diagnosed the twentieth-century condition more perceptively and memorably than many of his contemporaries have.

Born in Columbus, Ohio, in 1894, Thurber grew up in the twilight of the Victorian era; his narratives of Columbus life and the colorful characters of his boyhood retain the exuberance of nineteenth-century frontier humor. But as he moved farther into the twentieth century, his work became increasingly inspired by "the damp hand of melancholy"; and his writing, he explained, was "not a joyous form of self expression but the manifestation of a twitchiness at once cosmic and mundane." The twitchiness was partly personal, partly philosophical. Thurber's innate nervousness and high-strung temperament were intensified by blindness. When he was six years old, his older brother William accidentally shot him in the left eye with an arrow during a game of William Tell. Following the faulty advice of a local doctor, his parents failed to have the injured eye removed promptly. By the time they got around to it, sympathetic ophthalmia attacked the right eye. Miraculously, the disease arrested itself, giving him nearly forty more years of sight; but his vision started to blur in the late 1930's, and in 1940–41 he underwent five operations, after which he was legally blind. During his boyhood the eye injury made Thurber feel inferior at sports, turned him into a spectator, and drove him deeper into fantasy. After he lost the sight in his remaining eye, he reacted to the frustration with sporadic fits of depression or outbursts of rage.

The cosmic aspect of Thurber's melancholy was an acute perception of human weakness and perversity. Despite the tragic awareness of most of its artists, the official nineteenth-century ideology was optimism, a bland faith in progress and human perfectibility. Thurber rediscovered mankind's fallibility and would have agreed with Herman Melville that "in certain moods, no man can weigh this world without throwing in something, somehow like Original Sin, to strike the uneven balance." Maintaining that "The closest thing to humor is tragedy," Thurber portrayed people distressed by domestic discord, humiliated by the hazards of technology, and made to feel impotent under the complex pressures of modern times.

In his revolt against the gospel of reason and the glorification of man, Thurber resembles many modern thinkers, for the psychological discovery of the unconscious, the nightmare of total war, the spread of dictatorship, the unnerving growth of technological and bureaucratic complexities, and the widespread loss of faith in religious or moral certainties have undermined the facile optimism that reason is sufficient to keep man from acting irrationally. In "Interview With a Lemming" (1941), a lemming being interviewed by a scientist calls mankind "murderous, maladjusted, maleficent, malicious and muffle-headed. . . . You kill, you mangle, you torture, you imprison, you starve each other. I know that you are cruel, cunning and carnivorous, sly, sensual and selfish, greedy, gullible and guileful—" The scientist agrees with the catalogue of "our sins and our shames." He has been studying lemmings and knows all about them, except why they rush to the sea and drown themselves. "How curious," the lemming replies. "The one thing I don't understand is why you humans don't." Similarly, a Thurber dinosaur who is sneered at by a supposedly superior human responds, "There are worse things than being extinct, and one of them is being you."

Two centuries earlier, Jonathan Swift wrote that our exaltation of ourselves as reasoning beings is unjustified, since we use reason primarily "to aggravate our natural corruptions, and to acquire new ones which nature had not given us." Thurber agreed. In his words, "Abstract reasoning, in itself, has not benefited Man so much as instinct has benefited the lower animals. In moving into the alien and complicated sphere of Thought and Imagination he has become the least well-adjusted of all creatures on the earth, and, hence, the most bewildered." At the beginning of World War II, Thurber said that no human power has

. . . ever moved naturally and inevitably in the direction of the benign. It has, as a matter of fact, almost always tended in the direction of the malignant. . . . This tendency, it seems to me, would be especially true of the power of the mind, since it is that very power which is behind all the deviltry Man is now up to and always has been up to. . . . Man, as pacifist and economist, has gone steadily from bad to worse with the development of his brain power through the ages.

Yet Thurber was far from being anti-intellectual; deploring mindless conformity and the unreasoning appeal of demagoguery, he championed learning and called art "the one achievement of Man which has made the long trip up from all fours seem well advised."

In contrast with man's folly and cruelty, Thurber admired the instinctive wisdom of animals:

It may be that the finer mysteries of life and death can be comprehended only through pure instinct; the cat, for example, appears to Know. . . . Man, on the other hand, is surely further away from the Answer than any other animal this side of the ladybug. His mistaken selection of reasoning as an instrument of perception has put him into a fine quandary.

Thurber's animals, particularly the ubiquitous dogs in his drawings, have a placid innocence and a harmony with the world that his more alarming humans have long since lost. In Thurber's art, nature has not fallen along with man; and his whimsical wildlife often appear in a still Edenic garden. In 1961, the year of his death, Thurber hoped that with their superior mental powers, dolphins, "all gaiety, charm, and intelligence . . . might one day come out of the boundless deep and show us how a world can be run by creatures dedicated not to the destruction of their species but to its preservation." Three years earlier he told Henry Brandon, "I often think it would be fine if the French poodles would take over the world because they've certainly been more intelligent in the last few years than the human being." The domesticated dog, which Thurber worked into his drawings "as a sound creature in a crazy world," has found life with man laughable; but "His sensitive nose . . . has caught at one and the same time the bewildering smells of the hospitals and the munitions factory. He has seen men raise up great cities to heaven and then blow them to hell." By contrast, the amusing implausibility of many birds and beasts helped Thurber to believe in a divine creative force; there must be, he said, an amiable God to make such a creature as Bosman's potto.

Although not doctrinal, Thurber retained a religious attitude, a sense of reverence, which he found too often lacking in his fellow humans. In 1935 he stated: "If I have any beliefs at all about immortality, it is that certain dogs I have known will go to heaven, and very, very few persons will be there. I am pretty sure that heaven will be densely populated with bloodhounds, for one thing."

For all his insistence on the thin line between humor and tragedy, Thurber insisted that he was an optimist; and despite his rages, he was not a misanthrope. Like Mark Twain, who in his later years denounced "the damned human race," Thurber had a great capacity for friendship. His anger came from an awareness of man's inhu-

manity to man; British cartoonist Ronald Searle noted that Thurber's "exasperation and occasional bitterness arose more out of concern for humans than out of his dislike for them." When in his cups, Thurber was often vituperative; but everyone agreed with Wolcott Gibbs that he "was the nicest guy in the world up to five o'clock in the afternoon," and some, like Peter De Vries, would draw the line at a much later hour, if at all.

Mark Van Doren, a friend and neighbor, thought that Thurber's explosions of irritability were attributable partly to his drinking and partly to "his rage at everyone who could see— because he was *not* a malevolent man, God knows." Following his eye surgery, Thurber asked Van Doren whether his blindness

. . . was not a punishment for the kind of writing he had done. "I have done nothing," he said, "but make fun of weakness and folly; wisdom, strength, goodness have never been my subjects as they ought to be for anybody—as they are for you. I have been pitiless, trivial, destructive. And now this trouble comes."

Van Doren replied that Thurber's satire was motivated by concern, not scorn, for the human condition. He observed that Thurber

. . . has never pitied himself for being blind, though his rages—terrible, fantastic—could be traced to that condition. In my own opinion they are a satirist's indignations: savage, like Swift's, and with as deep a source. These rages end as suddenly as they begin, and a great sweetness follows. Thurber is tiger, then is turtle dove.

Despite Thurber's explosive temper, many writers praised his intense interest in people and his sympathy and help during times of trouble. John Duncan Miller, an English friend, admitted that Thurber drank too much and liked to monopolize the conversation, but called him "An utterly charming man—witty, refreshing, generous. His one consistency was his loyalty to his best friends.'' As Ronald Searle put it, ''Thurber was no kindly old charmer, and his exasperation and occasional bitterness arose more out of concern for humans than out of dislike for them.'' Thurber summed it up by observing:

The human species is both horrible and wonderful. Occasionally, I get very mad at human beings, but there's nothing you can do about it. I like people and hate them at the same time. I wouldn't draw them in cartoons, if I didn't think they were horrible, and I wouldn't write about them if I didn't think they were wonderful.

This statement is too simple; the cartoon figures are often amiable, and the prose portraits are sometimes savage. But as he said when dedicating Denney Hall at Ohio State University to his former English professor, Joseph Villiers Denney, ''The heart in which there is no fighting is as barren as the soul without conflict or the mind without anxiety or the spirit without struggle.''

Thurber struggled a good deal in his own life. Lonely as a boy, he was gangling, gawky, shy, and disheveled. His eyesight kept him from participating in athletics, which he enjoyed as a spectator; despite his portraits of dumb football stars in ''University Days'' (1933) and *The Male Animal* (1940), he was a sports enthusiast and football fan, and wrote a good deal about tennis under the pseudonym ''Foot Fault.'' That he was a teacher's pet did not endear him to his classmates—or to himself, for that matter. These tensions surfaced more than forty years later in a harrowing short story, ''Teacher's Pet'' (1949). Its protagonist is Willber Kelby, a middle-aged scholar forced to endure a lifetime of abuse by bullies. As the smartest boy in grade school, he had become the unwilling but official teacher's pet and accordingly was hated by his dim-witted but brawny classmates, such as Zeke Leonard, a boy with ''the brains of a pole vaulter,'' who resented Willber ''for his intelligence, his name,

his frail body, and his inability, according to Zeke, to do anything except study.'' Thirty-seven years later, Kelby still suffers from the memory of the day when Zeke trapped him after school and slapped him around while the other boys jeered at his impotent attempts to defend himself. When a woman at a cocktail party asks him why he is brooding, Kelby tells her about the incident. She is incredulous and asks, ''What had you done?''

''A teacher's pet doesn't have to do anything,'' Kelby said. ''It is the mere fact of his existence that makes the stupid and the strong want to beat him up. There is a type of man that wants to destroy the weaker, the more sensitive, the more intelligent.''

The woman replies that her son Elbert has similar problems and is constantly bullied by the arrogant athletes in his class; the chief tormentor is Bob Stevenson, son of their host. Nursing his trauma, Kelby is bitter; he hates the bullies but also despises the weakness of their victims.

''But they are not cowards,'' said the woman defensively. . . . ''At least I know Elbert is not a coward.''
. . . ''There are a lot of comforting euphemisms,'' he [Kelby] said. ''Hypersensitive, nonaggressive, peace-loving, introverted—take your choice.''

Two days later, Kelby comes across the two boys and sees a reenactment of his childhood, for Bob is making cruel fun of Elbert and insolently roughing him up. In a fury, Kelby intervenes and orders Bob to leave his victim alone. But when the rescued Elbert sniffles and whimpers, Kelby turns on him with self-hatred, slaps him, and calls him a coward and a crybaby. At this crucial point, Elbert's father comes on the scene. Thurber's concluding irony is devastating. '' 'I've seen some bullies in my time,' Mr. Reynolds told the elder Stevenson later, 'but I never saw anything to match that.' '' Stevenson replies that Kelby has threatened his son too. " 'You never know about a man, Reynolds,' he said. 'You just never know.' ''

Thurber was never a sissy, but he was vulnerable to attack until defended by one of the toughest boys in the class. Willber Kelby and Elbert Reynolds fail, not because they are ineffectual at fistfights but because they lack fortitude, break down, and snivel under attack. By equating weakness with cowardice, Kelby comes to accept the values of the bullies he resents; and his anger is not so much against aggression itself as against the fact that he has been on the receiving end. His defeat is not that he has lost the fight with others, but that he has lost it with himself.

Thurber, on the other hand, always denounced aggression; and in his fairy tales, the heroes are not warriors but seemingly unheroic toymakers, jesters, poets, and musicians. As an old man tells Prince Jorn in *The White Deer* (1945), "The peril and the labor, Prince, lie not in dreadful monsters or in mighty deeds, but in the keeping of the heart a man has won." This is the difficulty confronting the spouses in Thurber's stories of marital stress. In *The Male Animal,* when the protagonist, a thin, nervous professor, finds his marriage endangered by his wife's flirtation with a former football star, he challenges his rival to a fistfight and is knocked out. He wins his wife back not by pugilism, but by his quixotic courage in standing up for his principles and defying a tyrannical trustee.

In high school Thurber overcame his initial unpopularity and ended up as president of the senior class. But at Ohio State University he was again out of step. He could never pass the obligatory military drill and infuriated Captain Converse with his seemingly perverse ineptness; and he exasperated his science teachers by his inability to see through a microscope. Socially, he seemed an outcast. Thurber felt so forlorn that he unofficially dropped out of school for a year, not telling his parents that he was spending his days drifting around town. Reinstated, he impressed a fellow student, Elliott Nugent, with his literary skills. Nugent was a big man on campus—an athlete, dramatic star, fraternity man, and president of the junior class. Under his tutelage Thurber spruced himself up, joined The Strollers (the dramatic society), wrote for the campus newspaper, and became editor of it and of the *Sundial,* Ohio State's humor and literary magazine.

When World War I broke out, Thurber left college without a degree and became a code clerk for the United States embassy in Paris. On his return home, he got a job as reporter for the Columbus *Dispatch;* but his ambition was to be a creative writer rather than a journalist. He found an outlet in writing a Sunday column called "Credos and Curios" and in creating the libretto and lyrics for some musical productions of The Strollers and of Columbus' Scarlet Mask Club. But little of this work gives promise of the artist to come; Thurber later called it "practice and spadework by a man of 28 who sometimes sounds 19. . . ." A late bloomer, Thurber did not publish his first story, "Josephine Has Her Day," until 1926, when he was thirty-one. He resigned from the *Dispatch* in the summer of 1924 and made an unsuccessful attempt to support himself by writing fiction on a free-lance basis. After another brief stint in Columbus, the thirty-year-old writer manqué went to France in the spring of 1925 to complete a novel about Ohio college life. As with several subsequent attempts at novels, he aborted it as a hopeless failure. Instead, he got a job as translator and rewrite man for the Paris, and later the Riviera, editions of the Chicago *Tribune*. Back in New York in 1926, he was again unsuccessful at selling stories and a satiric book called *Why We Behave Like Microbe Hunters*.

Once more Thurber turned to journalism, as a reporter for the New York *Evening Post*. He began sending short pieces to the newly founded *New Yorker,* but not until 1927 was one of them accepted. In February of that year he met E. B. White; White introduced Thurber to the *New Yorker*'s editor, Harold Ross, who instantly hired him as an editor. It took Thurber several months to get "demoted" to writer; but once he succeeded, he had found his niche. The *New Yorker* "casual" was the ideal form for a humorist who was unable to sustain a long work. As Thurber put it:

I am afraid all of my novels would be complete in one chapter, from force of habit in writing short pieces and also from a natural incapability of what Billy Graves [one of his Ohio State English professors] would call "Larger flight." . . . Of course I could never do a novel seriously; it would slowly begin to kid itself, and God knows what it would turn out to be like.

He seems to have assumed that a novel must have high seriousness, although two of his favorites were Evelyn Waugh's bizarre satires *Vile Bodies* and *Decline and Fall.*

With the publication of his illustrations for *Is Sex Necessary?* in 1929, Thurber's second career as a cartoonist was launched; and he found himself, in his mid-thirties, belatedly acclaimed as a visual and verbal artist. The subject of his art was the predicaments and perplexities of *Domesticus americanus.* Echoing Wordsworth's definition of poetry, Thurber called his humor "emotional chaos told about calmly and quietly in retrospect." His characters (some of them a persona of Thurber himself) are not engaged in heroic conflicts but are preoccupied with "the smaller enormities of life"; they are badgered by bureaucrats and are unable to master machinery or to cope with technological trivia. The gestures of such a humorist, he explained, "are the ludicrous reflexes of the maladjusted; his repose is the momentary inertia of the nonplussed."

Thurber's burlesque autobiography, *My Life and Hard Times* (1933), is a mock-heroic account of the chaos caused by imaginary disasters. The Thurbers and their neighbors are prone to panic when they think the dam has broken in the 1913 Ohio flood, when they believe Father has been killed by a falling bed, when they imagine a ghost is haunting the house. Their comic anxieties are caused by nonexistent menaces: Briggs Beall, a visiting cousin, fears that he will suffocate in his sleep, Aunt Sarah Shoaf has a nightly dread that a burglar will blow chloroform under her door; Mother worries that the Victrola will blow up; and the servants are invariably paranoid—Dora Gedd shoots at her lover, Vashti thinks she is desired by an imaginary stepfather, Mrs. Doody believes Mr. Thurber is the Antichrist and attacks him with a bread knife, and Edda Millmoss accuses Mr. Thurber of having swindled her out of her rights to the land under Trinity Church in New York.

Elsewhere in his fiction, people worry about electricity leaking through the house from empty wall sockets and about causing a short circuit by dropping needles down a sink drain. "I know nothing about electricity and I don't want to have it explained to me," Thurber wrote. His men are menaced by the innate malignancy of automobiles. "Every person," wrote Thurber, "carries on his consciousness the old scar, or the fresh wound, of some harrowing misadventure with a contraption of some sort"; and people must practice " a natural caution in a world made up of gadgets that whir and whine and whiz and shriek and sometimes explode."

Most of the great film comedians from Charlie Chaplin, Buster Keaton, and Stan Laurel and Oliver Hardy down to Woody Allen specialize, like Thurber, in humiliation; and often the visual humor comes from their inability to cope with machinery run amok. Audiences are amused, not because of sadism but because of the absurd implausibility of the situations that, though outlandish, are still close enough to the familiar for empathy; they can imagine themselves being equally flabbergasted and frustrated. Moreover, Thurber felt that the dilemmas his characters encounter help the reader to endure his own problems through "the comfortable feeling that one has had, after all, a pretty sensible and peaceful life, by comparison." Furthermore, the perspective his art gives to past moments of ineffectuality provides a comic catharsis. As Thurber put it, "The things we laugh at are awful while they are going on, but get funny when we look back. And other people laugh because they've been through it too."

Thurber's first book came out in 1929; and his characteristic accounts of failure and frustration were written during the Great Depression, under the threat of an impending world war. Although his characters, like those of his favorite novelist, Henry James, seem to have no financial worries, they are not aggressive businessmen; and whatever ambition they may have had has been replaced by apprehension. An unconscious irony of the success books that Thurber satirized in *Let Your Mind Alone!* (1937) is the fact that they ignored the economic realities of the 1930's, when victims of the Great Depression could not pull themselves out of the economic quagmire by means of inspirational slogans. As the wife says in one Thurber cartoon, "We're all disenchanted." Thurber wrote to E. B. White in 1938:

Our lives become, right after college, as unworkable as a Ford in a vat of molasses, but nobody is giving this frightful problem any thought. Everybody is monkeying with the superstructure of economics, politics, distribution, etc. which stick up out of the vat also covered with molasses. I know damn well, of course, that nobody will ever get the superstructure cleaned off, let alone the Ford out of the vat. A world in which there are millions of people, hundreds of millions, can have no possible chance of working. If you get more than six people together in a room, it won't work.

Certainly he had no faith in the "strive and succeed" philosophy that flourished during the 1930's in such books as Dale Carnegie's *How to Win Friends and Influence People* and Dorothea Brande's *Wake Up and Live!* Irritated by their facile psychic panaceas and concerned about their exhortations to conformity, Thurber immersed himself in the genre and came up with an antidote in *Let Your Mind Alone!* Besides Carnegie and Brande, he read "the most incredible crap" (as he put it to a friend), "but filled with such a walking into my spider trap as you wouldn't believe." Among them were David Seabury's *How to Worry Successfully*, Dr. James L. Mursell's *Streamline Your Mind*, Sadie Myers Shellow's *How to Develop Your Personality*, and Dr. Louis E. Bisch's *Be Glad You're Neurotic.* Thurber found that these mental disciplinarians and advocates of masterful adjustment would ignore or suppress personal idiosyncrasies that, if they often result in confusion, also enhance life by keeping the imagination free and the individual irrepressible. He maintained that "The undisciplined mind runs far less chance of having its purposes thwarted, its plans distorted, its whole scheme and system wrenched out of line. The undisciplined mind, in short, is far better adapted to the confused world in which we live today than the streamlined mind." Thurber preferred the free association of thoughts and fought against minds "of the guardian type."

Another group that will not let your mind alone are political extremists, the most sinister of all, because their way of streamlining your mind is to brainwash, censor, straitjacket, and regiment it—to perform, in effect, an ideological lobotomy. Thurber was almost entirely detached from politics; his main political interest was in being left alone, and he contended "that my stories and my pictures were about relationships between men and women which are entirely apart from any consideration of economics, politics, or anything of the sort." To E. B. White he wrote: "It's the personal and intimate that really affect one's life. All this concern about political forms is nonsense. No government in the world is as big as a man's liver.'' In the preface to *My Life and Hard Times,* he observed:

Your short-piece writer's time is not Walter Lippmann's time, or Stuart Chase's time, or Professor Einstein's time. It is his own personal time, circumscribed by the short boundaries of his pain and his embarrassment, in which what happens to his digestion, the rear axle of his car, and the confused flow of his relationships with six or eight persons and two or three buildings is of greater importance than what goes on in the nation or in the universe.

Accordingly, Thurber was enraged when, at a party given by Malcolm Cowley, the militant Communist critic Mike Gold called him and his fellow *New Yorker* writers a bunch of ''college punks'' who had lost their virility. Thurber practically came to blows with Gold; later, he responded with a fifteen-page letter to Cowley in which he stated his reasons for disliking ''literary communists.'' One of his objections was that the proletariat literati are not members of the proletariat but are middle-class intellectuals who show a pathetic ignorance of real working people: ''I have never yet seen one of them quote, directly, a worker or a leader of workers.'' Thurber could find no clear statement of what the Communists wanted in order to save the working class; they merely expressed their hatreds. Thurber was annoyed by their ''warnings, threats, and ominous announcements and prophecies.'' One of their hatreds was artists who did not share their dogmas and dialectic. Gold had denounced Ring Lardner and had called traditionalists like Willa Cather (a Thurber favorite) and Thornton Wilder cowards. Granville Hicks earned Thurber's ire for condemning Emily Dickinson and Henry James as failures for not coming to grips with social evils. ''It's incredible in this so-called enlightened age,'' said Thurber. ''Am I to believe that before Commu-

nism can get anywhere all writers must cease to write anything that isn't proletarian?'' The specter of thought control loomed behind the intellectual arrogance, intolerance, and self-righteousness that Thurber found characteristic of the Communists, whose inference was that the sort of writing published in the *New Yorker*

. . . no matter how funny or well done or, in its way, right—should be stopped. If these men, who write such attacks, should ever get in control, do you think there wouldn't be a commissar of literature who would be appointed and commissioned to stop it, who would set us at work writing either poems in praise of the American Lenin or getting up time tables for work trains? If you do, [he wrote to Cowley] you're missing a low, faint, distant rumbling.

Thurber's response was a thoughtful one, not the hysteria of a Red-baiter. He was well aware that in the Great Depression capitalism was sick and might need drastic cures. He wanted to engage in dialogue with the Communists in order to learn more about them, but he found that they turned a deaf ear to anyone not subscribing to their orthodoxy. ''They won't compromise, they won't debate, they won't listen, they just annoy and disturb people. . . . Does no Communist writer listen to any other?'' he asked. ''Don't they give advice, don't they ever come out with 'horse's ass' and 'god damn fool' [to each other]? Well, they should. In mere unthinking solidarity . . . there is nothing but the grain of ruin.'' He predicted that if they should take over, they would not bring freedom, but would ''subject the individual to the political body, to the economic structure,'' and would ''put the artist in a uniform. . . . It is this desire to regiment and discipline art—the art of writing and the art of living—that some of us are afraid of. . . .''

Cowley responded by inviting Thurber to review Granville Hicks' anthology, *Proletarian Literature in the United States* (1936) for the *New Republic.* Thurber took the assignment conscientiously and slaved for weeks to produce a fair and objective analysis. He praised some selections but protested that too many degenerated into irrelevant invective against "bourgeois" writers. (To Cowley, he wrote that "bourgeois" is "a hell of a goddam loose word to apply to all Americans who are not proletarians.") He was particularly incensed by Joseph Freeman's sweeping generalization that love is confined to the proletariat and that the middle class consists entirely of lechers and narcissists. Thurber demanded evidence for this and asked, "Just what . . . makes the proletarian unlecherous, fine, spiritual . . . ?" On artistic grounds he did not object to the subject matter of the book, but to their predominantly poor style and syntax; "I grant the importance of the scenes on which all these stories are based, but they cannot have reality, they cannot be literature, if they are slovenly done. . . . Art does not rush to the barricades." The ultimate and fatal weakness was the anthology's total lack of humor.

In the late 1930's, Thurber was convinced that the real menace came neither from Communism nor from capitalism, but from fascism. "I also firmly believe," he wrote to Cowley, "that it is the clumsy and whining and arrogant attitude of the proletarian writers which is making that menace bigger and bigger every day."

Thurber saw something of this menace at close range when he and his wife went to Europe in 1937–38. His casuals from France, later collected as Part 2 of *My World—and Welcome to It* (1942), contain a wistful sense that its Gallic charm is threatened, that war looming over the horizon may black out the city of light. Feeling that artists, as well as art, should not rush to the barricades, he forebore to cross the Pyrenees into Spain. "I decided I would only get in Spain's way," he confessed to Katharine White. "I am somewhat convinced that Spain-politics-war, etc. is not Precisely My Field."

Thurber's way of attacking fascism was through fables and parables. *The Last Flower* (1939) shows the mindless destruction of civilization in a war brought about by "liberators," militarists, and their legions of goose-stepping soldiers. Only when love returns to the world is there some hope for rebirth. As W. H. Auden, who reviewed Thurber's book, wrote in the same year, "We must love one another or die." In 1940, Thurber published *Fables for Our Time,* several of which deal with fascist oppression. "The Rabbits Who Caused All the Trouble," according to the devouring wolves, is an allegory of the Nazis' anti-Semitism; and "The Owl Who Was God," although himself innocent, is an emblem of the blind worship of a blind leader, a führer who leads his followers to destruction. On the other hand, "The Very Proper Gander," in which the barnyard creatures persecute a harmless gander when they mistake the praise "a very proper gander" for rumors about "propaganda," is a fable about witch-hunting that could apply equally well to homegrown fascism of the radical right. At that time the Dies Committee, allegedly investigating subversion, was harassing liberals on the assumption that liberalism was Communism; and right-wingers were denouncing the New Deal as treasonable.

Thurber responded with a play, *The Male Animal,* a defense of intellectual and academic freedom. The work has two interacting plots: a comedy of domestic discord in the tradition of Thurber's stories of matrimonial misunderstandings, and a conflict over academic freedom. The latter occurs when Tommy Turner, a professor of English at Midwestern University, plans to read a passage by Bartolomeo Vanzetti as one of several examples of ungrammatical eloquence. Somehow, word of his intention reaches Ed Keller, a boorish right-wing trustee, who has been directing the university's inquisition into faculty politics in order to purge alleged Communists. Described as a Neanderthal man who "rolls like the juggernaut over the careers of young professors," Keller is intolerant of any opinion differing from his own. In conjuring up a wave of anti-Red paranoia, he has not uncovered any authentic Communists but has fired several perfectly loyal liberals in an ordeal by slander. Turner, a mild-mannered scholar, wants to avoid trouble; but a radical student journalist publishes an editorial in the campus magazine calling the trustees fascists and praising Turner's integrity. Keller demands that Turner not read the Vanzetti letter and that he denounce the editorial. Turner's wife wants him to back down; and Dean Damon, head of the English department, advises appeasement but indicates that he will be disappointed if Turner does not stand up for academic freedom.

"We don't want anything Red—or even Pink—taught here," insists Keller. When Turner asks, "But who's to decide what is Red and what is Pink?" Keller snarls that the trustees are to judge. The faculty are a bunch of weaklings who insist on weighing all the evidence and are thus unfit to determine curriculum. Nothing but Americanism should be taught, insists Keller, who cannot define it except in terms of his own prejudices. Turner, driven to the wall, maintains "that a college should be concerned with ideas. Not just your ideas or my ideas, but all ideas."

Threatened with the loss of his job, Turner finds that he must take a stand if he is to retain his self-respect. "If I can't read this letter today, tomorrow none of us will be able to teach anything except what Mr. Keller here and the Legislature permit us to teach. . . . We're holding the last fortress of free thought, and if we surrender to prejudice and dictation, we're cowards." Maintaining his integrity costs Turner his job but wins back his wife, who had been tempted to leave him for an old flame and former football star back in town for the homecoming weekend.

Thurber wrote *The Male Animal* in collaboration with his Ohio State friend Elliott Nugent, who had become a successful playwright, stage and screen actor, and film director. Originally

the matrimonial comedy was Thurber's idea, and Nugent added the issue of academic freedom; but by the time the play was finished, it was impossible to separate the elements of the collaboration. Ironically, Nugent, a friend of the militantly conservative actor Robert Montgomery, later turned right-wing during the early 1950's; and it was Thurber who continued the fight for freedom of thought and expression. Several times that fight involved combating attempts at censorship by Ohio State University. As the Cold War paranoia persisted, Ohio State caught the contagion and in 1951 passed a gag rule for visiting speakers, requiring them and their speeches to be screened for possible subversion. It was *The Male Animal* come to life. Just as Tommy Turner sacrificed his job for his principles, so Thurber declined an honorary Litt.D. from Ohio State, writing to President Howard L. Bevis:

I have faith that Ohio State will restore freedom of speech and freedom of research, but until it does I do not want to seem to approve of its recent action. The acceptance of an honorary degree right now would certainly be construed as such approval, or as indifference to the situation.

As an antidote to McCarthyism, Thurber turned back to the placid years of his childhood, "the age of innocence, when trust flowered as readily as suspicion does today. . . ." The result was *The Thurber Album* (1952), a collection of idealized prose portraits of his family and friends in turn-of-the-century Columbus

. . . when there wasn't this fear and hysteria. I wanted to write the story of some solid American characters, more or less as an example of how Americans started out and what they should go back to. To sanity and soundness and away from this jumpiness. It's hard to write humor in the mental weather we've had, and that's likely to take you into reminiscence.

As early as 1948, Thurber had pointed out the pitfalls of political witch-hunts, "In the present Era of Suspicion, it is a wise citizen who disproves any dark rumors and reports of his secret thoughts and activities before they can be twisted into charges of disloyalty by the alert and skillful minds now dedicated to that high-minded and patriotic practice." His deepest outrage was directed at the fact that the inquisitors were particularly suspicious of artists. "If we don't stop suspecting all writers," he said in 1952, "it will be a severe blow to our culture. I think all writers, even the innocent ones, are scared. There's guilt by association, guilt by excoriation, there's guilt by everything the politicians invent." Thurber counterattacked with *Further Fables for Our Time* (1956), which won the American Library Association's Liberty and Justice Award, and with an adult fantasy, *The Wonderful O* (1957), an elaborate piece of wordplay in which a pirate tries to ban the letter *o* because his mother had been pushed through a porthole; the moral is that words with *o* are essential to civilization, and the most indispensable one is "freedom."

Looking back in 1958, when McCarthy had been discredited, Thurber told Henry Brandon:

The six or eight years that went by—those terrible years—when all the American Congress seemed to do was to investigate writers, artists, and painters—to me were the dreadful years. All this time Russia was getting ahead of us, all this time we were fighting a new cold civil war—suspecting neighbors, suspecting the very nature of writing, of academic intellectualism, anything—that was a very bad moment in our history—perhaps the darkest we've ever had.

In the last decade of his life, Thurber became increasingly pessimistic, preoccupied with what he thought was the decline of comedy and of civilized values in general. A major reason was his concern with the oppressive political atmosphere; and he lost no opportunity to strike back at the heresy hunters, insisting: "Our comedy should deal, in its own immemorial manner, with the American scene and the American people, without fear or favor, without guilt or grovelling." Despite his discontent, he remained ultimately hopeful that reason would prevail, largely through the saving sanity of humor. He wrote in his reply to receiving the Sesquicentennial Medal of the Ohioana Library Association in 1953:

As a matter of fact, comedy, in all of its forms, including the rusty art of political satire, is used to surviving eras of stress and strain, even of fear and trembling, but it sickens in the weather of intimidation and suppression, and such a sickness could infect a whole nation. The only rules comedy should tolerate are those of taste and the only limitations those of libel.

A major reason for the melancholy of Thurber's males is the dominant nature of the Thurberian female. The war between men and women was declared in his first book, *Is Sex Necessary?*, written in collaboration with E. B. White. In its satire of the inhibitions and false delicacy of the genteel tradition, and of the Victorian veneration of women as mysterious creatures made of finer substance than man's coarse clay (burlesqued in such mock misconceptions as the belief that pregnancy is induced by bringing bluebirds into a room filled with lilies), Thurber was declaring independence from his own upbringing. One thinks of the typical Thurber woman as a dowdy nag oppressing an intimidated spouse. In his drawings her shapeless figure is sheathed in a long gown resembling a gunnysack; she is endowed with stringy hair, a receding chin, and a sharply pointed nose. Her expression shows either a manic gleam in her eyes or a look of frowning disapproval or grim determination. Often larger than the male, she is as physically formidable as a runaway rhinoceros. Yet the youthful Thurber was steeped in the romantic attitude toward women and liked to visualize them as Henry

James heroines. Although later, until his second marriage, he had a reputation as a womanizer, he was a prudish young man whose sexual initiation came comparatively late. Not until after Elliott Nugent introduced him to college social life did Thurber start dating in earnest; he was then twenty-two years old.

From Paris during and after World War I, he wrote interminable adolescent letters gushing about the glory of the American girl:

Nugey, she is a Princess of Youth, and the Apotheosis of the American Beauty. . . . And there is nowhere in all the world their equal. . . . The A.E.F. in France has learned to respect American womanhood, to revere,—to worship the clean, fine morals of American womanhood, and to idealize American girls,—and to worship them with a fire that burns brighter and steadier than ever before,—and that will never die down.

In the spring of 1919, he wrote Nugent a prudish testament about the purity of American sexual morality and the wholesomeness of the American girl, worship of whom keeps the American soldier free from the seductions of Parisiennes. But in that same year he lost his virginity to a Folies Bergères dancer named Ninette. Trying to talk himself out of a consequent nervous collapse, he wrote to Nugent, "I have no regrets, fortunately, but I will say that I can't see it except as a passing experience once in—or twice in—a life-time, providing there is no One Girl."

The One Girl seemed to him to be Althea Adams, an Ohio State "Rosebud," whom he married on May 20, 1922. He wrote to Nugent that she was not only "more beautiful than new snow with the light of stars upon it, or than cool flowers in the soft of dawning" but also was "ravishingly intelligent, with characteristics so much like mine in many directions you would of course find her fetching." But later, he admitted, "She always scared me." His friends described her as Amazonian, "both physically and mentally," and noted that she did her best to domi-nate her husband. Thurber's second wife later said, "Althea was strong, like her father, the Army officer. Jamie ended up marrying Captain Converse in drag." Thurber's brother Robert called her "the domineering type, bossy and pushy, always wanting her own way"; and she and Thurber's mother instantly disliked each other. The forbidding Thurber woman of the cartoons and stories is a blend of the two. Thurber's family was matriarchal; his father was mild and comparatively passive, while his mother was strong-willed, an antic comedienne, and addicted to practical jokes. She is the model for the more manic women in her son's art. Although he later made much of her, Thurber was not very close to his mother when young and spent considerable time living away from home with "Aunt" Margery Albright (no relative), whom he idolized.

Despite the unsuitability of his marriage, Thurber continued to idealize women and love in his "Credos and Curios" column for the Columbus *Dispatch*, denouncing the "sordid" treatment of sex in the works of James Joyce, Sinclair Lewis, Sherwood Anderson, and D. H. Lawrence, and complaining of "Jurgen's endless, sly and sneaking philanderings" in the works of James Branch Cabell. He preferred Zona Gale's *Faint Perfume* for "its note of idealistic love . . . flung like a fresh rose among the sordid sex stuff that prevails in present day novels," and for its "fine fragrance of a sensitive, clean love which permeates and changes everything."

In view of the frumpy long gowns of his cartoon women, it is curious to find the romantic young Thurber objecting to the short skirts of 1923:

There was no loveliness in them, no rhythmic music, nothing to suggest a lady in a garden or a girl on a river when it is summer and afternoon. They suggested, rather, stout ladies bowling duck pins. . . . The long dress breathes of muted harpsichord music, of old colonnades under the moon, of lilacs at twilight, of romance on wide shining stairways, of figures posed in tall palace windows, of lovers' heads against the blue night.

Within six years Thurber was demolishing this sort of mooning in *Is Sex Necessary?* But that volume, a lighthearted spoof of the sex books then current, is merely an opening skirmish in the war between the sexes. The first major battle occurs in the eight stories about Mr. and Mrs. Monroe in *The Owl in the Attic* (1931). His most extended character studies, they present marriage at its most maddening. Thurber wrote to his friend Herman Miller, "The Monroe stories were transcripts, one or two of them varying less than an inch from the actual happenings." This may be true of the basic situations, but Thurber gives them a sardonic twist. Certainly he would not claim that Mr. Monroe is a self-portrait, for he is Thurber's extreme example of the helpless, ineffectual male. In Thurber's description, "Mr. Monroe didn't really have any character. He had a certain charm, yes; but not character. He evaded difficult situations; he had no talent for firm resolution; he immolated badly; and he wasn't even very good at renunciation, except when he was tired or a little sick."

Like Walter Mitty, Monroe daydreamed of himself as a masterful individual, "giving the impression of a strong, silent man wrapped in meditation." But we never see his dreams, nor do they offer anything comparable to Mitty's world of derring-do. Instead, we find him afraid of customs inspectors, terrified by a bat, fearful of imaginary burglars, and perpetually indecisive. His wife is forceful and (from his frustrated point of view) infuriatingly competent. To an extent they represent Thurber and his wife; he was inept with machinery and had a tendency to stumble over things, while, according to his agent, John Gude, "Althea had the bad habit of

doing everything as well as a man could, which infuriated Jim." But whereas Mr. Monroe was cowed to the point of tears by his nervous inability to cope, Thurber never lacked aggressiveness. Quite the contrary. Mr. Monroe's "helpless despair" was not that of his creator, who had formidable powers of survival.

Mr. Monroe is Thurber's contribution to the several portraits of impotent modern man in the literature of the 1920's and early 1930's; and the fact that his is a domesticated situation in which anyone might occasionally find himself brings him closer to home than the remote Fisher King of *The Waste Land,* the perverted Popeye of *Sanctuary,* or the expatriate Jake Barnes of *The Sun Also Rises.* They are enveloped in legend, Gothic horror, or Continental glamour, whereas Monroe is uncomfortably familiar.

A comparable but more whimsical relationship between the sexes appeared a year later in Thurber's picture parable, "The Race of Life" (1932). At the outset of this journey, in which a man, woman, and child traverse a varied landscape to reach a heavenly gate on a high hill, the woman sets out with a hopeful look in her eye, while her mate slumps behind her looking perplexed and the child grimly carries a banner on which is written "Excelsior." For a while they travel neck and neck; but after the man trips over a rock and the woman takes the lead in leaping over a stream, she consistently sets the pace. Her look is always cheerful or resolute, while he appears hesitant or apprehensive. When he becomes winded, she carries him under her arm. She dashes boldly downhill, while he timidly descends backward. While he cowers behind, sheltering the child, she advances to fight an eerie figure labeled "Menace" and an angry bear. She sits guard at night while the others sleep, and at the climax she dashes toward the celestial gate, exhorting the man, who collapses behind her in a rainstorm.

The satiric situation of Thurber's drawings

was taken seriously in many radio soap operas. In a lengthy study of soap opera included in *The Beast in Me* (1948), Thurber observed that the men were regularly stricken with such melodramatic afflictions as amnesia, temporary blindness, and paralysis, thus becoming "symbols that the listening women demand." When their men are incapacitated, "the good women become nobler than ever." Even when the men of soapland are not crippled by disease, the heroines try to keep them subordinate and emotionally dependent:

Suitors in Soapland are usually weak and Helen [Trent]'s frustration of them is aimed to gratify the listening housewives, brought up in the great American tradition of female domination. . . . The weak men continually confess their weaknesses to the good women, who usually manage to turn them into stable citizens by some vague and soapy magic. The weak men and the good men often confess to one another their dependence on the good woman.

In the era of women's liberation, one might conclude that soap opera situations were a compensation for the dependent, bored-housewife syndrome, that they were the women's version of Walter Mitty's wish projections.

Thurber revolted against female domination, but he had a grudging admiration for women's vitality and exuberance, shown more often among his Ohio eccentrics than among his New York sophisticates. Although he wrote a satiric obituary that "Socially, economically, physically and intellectually, Man is slowly going . . . to hell. . . . Man's day is indeed done; the epoch of Woman is upon us," he was amiably amused by the spectacle of women going on forever, singing, dancing, playing kettledrums, and chinning themselves at 114 years of age, while their men are prematurely played out. His cartoon men are usually diminutive, bald, flabby, and myopic (wearing pince-nez), whereas the women are physically formidable and quite capable of outwrestling their mates. ("Two Best Falls Out of Three—Okay, Mr. Montague?" says an oversized woman in one cartoon.) They wield Ping-Pong paddles and tennis rackets like battle-axes, swing croquet mallets like scythes, have a vicious backhand at polo, and hurl bowling balls as if they were anarchist bombs. Uninhibited, they make love to other women's husbands, pick fights in bars, and pass out drunk at parties. At the same time, they continually deflate their husbands when the latter try to imagine themselves as heroic. "Who are you today—Ronald Colman?" sneers a wife as her husband, imitating the dueling scene of *The Prisoner of Zenda,* lunges with a cane at a floor lamp. Mrs. Malcolm Cowley said that Althea Thurber had no sense of fantasy; and that is a fatal defect in Thurber's women, who are unable to acknowledge unicorns in their gardens.

Overwhelmed by domineering wives, Thurber's men, like Walter Mitty, seek escape in their imaginations, where they are adventurers and swashbucklers; but their spoilsport spouses try to correct even their fantasy lives. As for home, it is seen by an apprehensive husband in one cartoon as the personification of a glowering wife. When the situation reaches the breaking point, some of the men attempt to do their wives in. A number of cartoons feature an enraged male trying to strangle a female. In "Mr. Preble Gets Rid of His Wife" (July 8, 1933), Mr. Preble attempts to lure his wife into the cellar so that he can bash her over the head with a coal shovel and bury her. In "The War Between Men and Women" (1934), it is a man who commits the overt act, tossing a highball in a woman's face. On the other hand, the spouses of numerous Thurber women have died mysteriously or gone out of their minds; and when one husband asks, "Have you seen my pistol, Honeybun?" she is holding it behind a newspaper and aimed at him. None of this violence is to be taken seriously; it is no more deadly than the feud between Tom and Jerry or the roadrunner and the coyote in animated cartoons. One story, "The Whip-poor-will" (1941), is grimly realistic, proceeding by gradual steps from matrimonial quarreling to madness and murder as the irritable Mr. Kinstrey, writhing under his wife's smug superiority, his frayed nerves tortured by the incessant shrieking of a whippoorwill, kills his wife, servants, and himself with a carving knife. Thurber wrote this story (along with two other macabre ones, "A Friend to Alexander" [1942] and "The Cane in the Corridor" [1943]) to work off his pain and frustration after five eye operations had left him blind; but he was thoroughly in control of his material and was not indulging in Freudian wish fulfillment.

Aside from the fairy tales, none of Thurber's stories deals with courtship; and sex is rarely a factor in his accounts of marital antagonisms. In "The Interview" (1950), Mrs. Lockhorn repeatedly corrects her husband and tries to restrain his drinking, while he sneers sarcasms at her; we see only negative emotions, and Lockhorn complains to the interviewer that sexual intercourse is only for holidays. In "Smashup" (1935), Tommy Trinway, belittled by his bossy wife because of his fear of driving the family car, regains his confidence by skillfully avoiding an accident when her sprained wrist forces him to drive through a metropolis, and then asserts his newfound independence by ordering separate bedrooms at their hotel. But ordinarily Thurber concentrates on the repartee between a high-strung couple whose conversation consists almost entirely of verbal thrusts, parries, and ripostes. (It is significant that many of Thurber's drawings are of fencers crossing blades or of sparring partners.) Thurber usually presents marriage in medias res, showing neither the courtship nor the conclusion but some point at which the constant friction of minute irritants is wearing the relationship through. "It is a com-

monplace that the small annoyances of the marriage relationship slowly build up its insupportabilities, as particles of sediment build up great deltas," Thurber observed. Often the source of friction is trivial or absurd. "The Breaking Up of the Winships" (January 11, 1936) is caused by a quarrel over the comparative acting abilities of Greta Garbo and Donald Duck; the unnamed couple in "A Couple of Hamburgers" (1935) reach the combustible stage over a disagreement on where to stop for a meal; and Mrs. Bidwell divorces her husband because he amused himself by seeing how long he could hold his breath.

Clearly, the surface tension is only the tip of the iceberg; the stories imply that a great deal has gone on before. "Take more'n a whip-poor-will to cause a mess like that," comments a state trooper on observing the bodies of Mr. Kinstrey and his victims in "The Whip-poor-will."

After numerous separations and attempts at reconciliation (during one of which Thurber's only child, Rosemary, was born), Thurber's first marriage ended in May 1935. At that time he published two serious stories about the emptiness of solitude. In "The Evening's at Seven" (1932), the protagonist finds that an attempt to relieve the monotony of a loveless marriage by a visit to an old flame is merely frustrating. Yet divorce is no better, as the autobiographical story "One Is a Wanderer" (1935) shows. Rejecting the idea of visiting his married friends, Mr. Kirk realizes that he would only be an intruder. "It isn't because I'm so damned unhappy—I'm not so damned unhappy—It's because they're so damned happy, damn them. Why don't they know that? Why don't they do something about it?"

If marriage was difficult, solitude was worse. To a friend Thurber wrote: "Life alone to me is a barren and selfish and pointless thing." He had been alone for some time before his divorce; shortly afterward (June 25, 1935) he married again, this time very happily. If he continued to have periods of cantankerousness and depression, it was not the fault of his second wife, Helen Muriel Wismer. She had edited several minor magazines and possessed great intelligence, charm, and a wit to match Thurber's own. His friends and family instantly liked her; and his agent said, "Helen was the best possible woman for him in the whole world." Robert Thurber added, "She couldn't have been a better wife for Jamie. . . . My parents loved her, especially as compared to Althea." Thurber observed that Helen delighted Herman Miller "because he saw she was made to order for me—and a tough order that is." After Thurber's blindness and other illnesses, friends observed that although he had to endure a good deal of suffering, he was at least spared the ordeal of marriage to a "Thurber woman." His English publisher, Hamish Hamilton, wrote: "For many years Helen took the place of his eyes. His writing was made possible by her infinite patience in copying, reading, and re-reading and helped by her critical comments. His burden was lightened by her stimulating company and her affectionate teasing. . . . Helen turned Jamie's night into day." Thurber fondly called her his seeing-eye wife.

Although Harold Ross instantly liked Helen Thurber, he worried that a happy marriage would defuse Thurber's battle of the sexes; he was relieved to see that the antagonism did not abate in Thurber's cartoons and prose. But after 1935 the shrews appear much less frequently, and the quarrels are more often touched off by an irascible husband. In the first-person pieces the second Mrs. Thurber is not a nagger, but the voice of moderation and reason.

From the perspective of women's liberation, what is the reader to make of Thurber's prolonged war between men and women? Is it merely a more literary version of the comic-strip spats between Jiggs and Maggie or Blondie and Dagwood, or does it have more meaningful sub-stance? Was Thurber a misogynist, or was he making some valid interpretations of personal relationships? There is, of course, an ancient literary tradition of antifeminism, as seen in the "book of wikked wyves" owned by one of the husbands of Chaucer's Wife of Bath (who by her sheer vitality overwhelms any antifeminism in her own portrait), and of sexual skirmishing (the essence of Restoration comedy); but the existence of a tradition is not enough to validate it. Some of Thurber's acquaintances thought he really did dislike women; he was nasty to most of them on occasion. But he also raged at most of his friends, and many of his closest friends were women. "Women have always come to my rescue," he admitted.

Those who fare badly in Thurber's work are the insensitive and intolerant ones like Mrs. Bidwell, Mrs. Mitty, and Mrs. Lockhorn. Thurber particularly objected to women's supposed intellectual inadequacy and limited powers of imagination. To the extent that there is any truth in this, it may be the result of sexual chauvinism, the pressures that told girls not to get good grades and that kept most women away from careers and confined to "Kinder, Kirche, Küchen." Thurber's women compensate by domineering their spouses, repressing their romantic and creative instincts, and trying to mold the men into conformists. Like the female hares and guinea pigs in the fable "The Bragdowdy and the Busybody" and the female chipmunk in the fable "The Shrike and the Chipmunks," they often pressure their men to produce more, to get ahead by applying themselves more diligently. Denied careers, they show all the aggression of businessmen and try to advance themselves vicariously through their husbands. But as Henry Bamford Parkes points out in *The American Experience,* "Insofar as the American people were committed to the American ideology of personal success, they were attempting something that for most of them was impossible. Judged by the prevalent standards of American society, most Americans were compelled to regard themselves as having failed and to attribute their failure to some shortcoming within themselves.'' Thus the man of the industrial age felt vulnerable to impotent failure and was ''apt to have a neurotic dependence, first upon his mother and afterwards upon his wife, owing to his own insecurity and lack of masculine self-assurance.'' Thurber's healthiest males, whether human or animal, tell their spouses to let their minds alone; and his most vital females are the exuberant eccentrics.

At heart, Thurber wanted both sexes to be liberated. He objected to sexual stereotyping and observed, ''The wife who keeps saying, 'Isn't that just like a man?' and the husband who keeps saying, 'Oh, well, you know how women are,' are likely to grow farther and farther apart through the years. These famous generalizations have the effect of reducing an individual to the anonymous status of a mere unit in a mass.'' He preferred the reciprocal respect of Henry James's men and women, who ''were capable of friendship.'' Thurber liked intelligent women and told Eddy Gilmore, ''When I get mad at women it's usually because they fall below my standard.'' Wives should, he insisted, be helpmates to their husbands; and he praised Helen Thurber as a Mount Holyoke graduate and a great proofreader and editor. He frequently observed that American women did not care much about knowledge, and stated that they would not become less feminine from studying science, history, or politics. Considering man's political perversions and warlike aggressions, Thurber came increasingly to see woman as the sane hope for peace:

The most frightening study of mankind is man. I think he has failed to run the world, and that Woman must take over if the species is to survive. Almost any century now Woman may lose her patience with black politics and red war and let fly. I wish I could be on earth then to witness the saving of our self-destructive species by its greatest creative force. If I have sometimes seemed to make fun of Woman, I assure you it has only been for the purpose of egging her on.

Thurber often presented himself as the protagonist of his casuals, but the characterization is far from authentic autobiography. Although he was indeed high-strung and nervous, he was anything but the timorous, ineffectual character of his fiction. The literary character is a persona, like the imbecilic role that Samuel Clemens sometimes assumed. Among Thurber's drawings are a few self-portraits; but he bore no resemblance to the quintessential male of his cartoons, even those for casuals in which Thurber is the central character. In the drawings the adult male is diminutive and bald, and wears a pince-nez; the real Thurber was six feet, one and a half inches tall, with a short, trimmed moustache and a thick head of often disheveled hair. Although handicapped by blindness in his later years, he was by no means the incompetent and intimidated figure of his art that some critics found comparable to J. Alfred Prufrock.

Rather, Henry Brandon found that ''Thurber's gaunt figure and his flat, commanding voice were a little intimidating at first. This was not the 'little-man-what-now' type trapped between the 'hard covers' of life, this was a man who knew what he wanted, who had learned and obviously succeeded in overcoming many vicissitudes of life.'' The *Paris Review* interviewers expected to find in person ''the shy, trapped little man in the Thurber cartoons'' and the ''confused and bewildered'' fumbler of his fiction; they were surprised to meet an assured and confident individual. Wolcott Gibbs, who knew Thurber for more than a generation, was vastly amused by

. . . the idea that he would be helpless in the face of any known social situation. . . . There have been times when I thought that he dealt a little more erratically with life than most of the men I know, but I have certainly never seen him defeated, or even perceptibly disconcerted by it. The essence of Mitty and Monroe is that they are, so to speak, driven underground by more confident personalities; the essence of Thurber is such that in any real contest of personalities, everybody else would be well advised to take to the hills.

Thurber did have bouts of depression and suffered a nervous breakdown after he became blind. As he put it, "I went into a tailspin, crashed, and burst into flames." But with the help of his wife and of two women doctors, he made a quick recovery. "God knows I have been down in the bowels of terror," he wrote to E. B. White, "but I have climbed out of it with what Dr. [Ruth] Fox thinks is remarkable speed." Blindness, of course, forced him to find new techniques for writing and drawing. Although legally blind, he could still perceive shapes and colors for a number of years anad managed, through magnification, to see sufficiently to scrawl about twenty words, in large writing, on a page of yellow copy paper. With the aid of a Zeiss loop—a magnifying helmet used by precision craftsmen in defense plants that made him look "like a welder from Mars"—Thurber was able to resume drawing in 1943, although doctors set a daily limit of five minutes apiece on two drawings. From then until 1947, when he did his last original drawing for the *New Yorker,* he produced some of his best sketches, particularly the quite realistic if whimsical animals in "A Gallery of Real Creatures" (1948) and the fantastic birds, beasts, and bugs of "A New Natural History," in which he fused his interest in animals with his addiction to wordplay and created a series of such zoological puns as "A Garble with an Utter in its claws," "A Trochee encountering a Spondee," "The Whited Sepulchre," "The Common Blackguard," and "a female Volt with all her Ergs in one Gasket."

Thurber objected to having his cartoons taken as seriously as his writing. Although he was a meticulous prose stylist who rewrote most of his work a dozen times or more, he dashed off his drawings in a few minutes. He always claimed that his drawing was mere doodling and meant little more than "tossing cards in a hat," yet he was gratified, if surprised, at the success that his pictures had in gallery exhibitions at home and abroad, and he was pleasantly amused to find himself compared to Henri Matisse. They probably meant more to him than he admitted, and he lost some of his zest when he had to give them up.

The blind writer turned to dictation, aided by the possession of nearly total recall that enabled him to hold several complete versions of a piccc in his mind at once. "Soapland" (1948), *The Thurber Album* (1952), and *The Years with Ross* (1959) required extensive research; but although he had assistants to do the legwork, Thurber had to synthesize all the details. He found that "the imagination doesn't go blind," and in fact all of the fairy tales came after his blindness; but the loss of his sight did make his subsequent work more aural. Increasingly he turned away from the visual humor of eccentric catastrophes and toward conversation pieces, in which the narrator engages in verbal fencing with fellow partygoers or with nuisances harassing him with unwelcome visits, bad jokes, unwanted accounts of their lives, or reflections on the state of the world. In this work Thurber ceased writing about his bewildered little man of the 1930's; instead, his protagonist was a witty cosmopolitan, no longer frustrated by gadgetry or a domineering spouse, but badgered by social and political imbecilities against which he defended himself with caustic repartee. The humor does not depend upon situation but comes from Thurber's verbal wit and dazzling wordplay with puns, palindromes, literary allusions, coinages, alliteration and assonance, and often startling metaphors.

The prose of Thurber's earlier work relied upon the carefully polished simplicity characteristic of the best *New Yorker* writing. Before joining the magazine, Thurber had perpetrated a mixture of journalese, echoes of his favorite novelist Henry James, and a touch of the lush style of Joseph Hergesheimer. He credited E. B. White with teaching him discipline: "The precision and clarity of White's writing helped me a lot, slowed me down from the dogtrot of newspaper tempo and made me realize a writer turns on his mind, not a faucet." To Malcolm Cowley he wrote: "Humor cannot afford the ornaments and indulgences of fine writing. . . ." Yet although he never lost his clarity, the fairy tales, word-game essays, and conversation pieces are full of linguistic innovations that at times resemble the jabberwocky of *Finnegan's Wake* by James Joyce, another nearly blind writer.

Part of this verbal virtuosity was Thurber's way of turning the tables on what he called "carcinomenclature," the debasement of the language into jargon, gobbledygook, or slovenly garble. As a psychosemanticist, Thurber made many of the points that George Orwell stressed in "Politics and the English Language." He satirized the moribund diction of political terminologists, "smoke-screen" euphemisms, the linguistic muddle of Madison Avenue, "the tendency of tired American businessmen and statesmen to use slang and slogan," and the degeneration of meaning through perverse pejorations. "My most intense dedication," he stated, "is the defense of the English language against the decline it has suffered in this century and particularly since the end of the last war." As a blind man's main contact with the world, language became for Thurber a symbol of integrity; and he increasingly complained of "the awful price of continuous cacophony." His answer at times was to turn the tables by inventing even madder garblings.

During his final years Thurber became progressively more disturbed at what he considered the growing morbidity and degenerate subject matter of writers "more interested in the sordid corners of life than in the human heart" and at "The trend of the modern temper . . . toward gloom, resignation, and even surrender. . . ." He lamented the decline of humor and considered that even comedy was going crazy, identifying itself "with the very tension and terror it once did so much to alleviate." As the menace of the machine and the nagging wife were replaced by the H-bomb, McCarthyism, and a ubiquitous *Angst,* Thurber caught the fallout. Although he hated the decline of comedy into "terror, horror, morbidity, ghastliness, and decadence," he conceded that "it fits the Zeitgeist" and harped upon it or parodied it so much that some of his own work communicated the very quality he wished to exorcise. In interview after interview, he protested too much; and the comedy of such late (1961–62) pieces as "The Manic in the Moon," "The Future, if Any, of Comedy," "Afternoon of a Playwright," and "Carpe Noctem, if You Can" is more depressing than amusing.

The gloom that Thurber fought, although internal as well as external, was not an ingrained pessimism but the sorrow of a disillusioned idealist who still held to his ideals. Although he frequently found it impossible to accept "The Dignity of Man and the Divine Destiny of Man . . . with whole-hearted enthusiasm," he had an intense zest for life that was not diminished by blindness; he continued to travel, maintained an active social life, and even acted on Broadway in *A Thurber Carnival* for three months in 1960. "I salute any man who can carry into his middle years, untarnished and undiminished, those first fine affections of his youth," he wrote; and he was not about to abandon them. Although they were dreams and illusions—"The fine brave fragile stuff that men live by . . . go[es] to pieces so easily"—he still believed in them and continued to yearn, like the moth, for the star. Cried a querulous conversationalist to him:

Great God! Are you looking for the bluebird of happiness? Do you think there are actually hinges on chimneys so the stars can get by? Do you believe Love will slay the dragon and live happily ever after?

"I believe in the sudden deep greenness of summer," I said. In the fifteen years I have known Charles, his skepticism has always shattered against my affirmation, and he knows it.

Like William Faulkner, who in his Nobel Prize acceptance speech said that man must rise above fear by lifting his heart, by relearning the old verities of pity, pride, compassion, sacrifice, and endurance, Thurber maintained at the end of his life that we can overcome *Angst* "By the lifting of the spirit. . . . It takes guts to be happy, make no mistake about it; and I don't mean slap-happy, or drink-happy, or drug-happy." If he did not always succeed in his final years, it was in part because, unknown to himself, he had a series of undiagnosed minor strokes in the twenty-four months prior to the major one that led to his death on November 8, 1961.

Although Thurber's tragic awareness could be as deep as Faulkner's, he also (like Faulkner and such writers as Joseph Conrad, Ernest Hemingway, and Albert Camus) would not have us capitulate to despair but, rather, counter it with courage. He recognized that "The sentimental pure heart of Galahad is gone with the knightly years, but I still believe in the heart of the George Meredith character that was not made of the stuff that breaks."

However, his characters often need a temporary escape, for "Who flies afar from the sphere of our sorrow is here today and here tomorrow." Just as today's readers turn to heroic fantasy or period romance as a refuge from the pressures of reality, so Thurber stressed the need for the free flight of the romantic imagination, whether in his fairy tales or through his delight in the idiosyncratic speech of his hired man Barney Haller or his maid Della, whose mispronunciations in such statements as "They are here with the reeves" enabled him to conjure up a world of fantastic images. "I share with Della a form of escapism that is the most mystic and satisfying flight from actuality I have ever known," he wrote. When Barney Haller spoke of hunting grotches in the woods or announced, "We go to the garrick now and become warbs," his imagination was ignited. "If you are susceptible to such things, it is not difficult to visualize grotches. They fluttered into my mind: ugly little creatures about the size of whippoorwills, only covered with blood and honey and the scrapings of church bells." Thurber found his spirit enriched by such "cherished transfiguring of meanings" as "Our Father, who are in Heaven, Halloween by thy Name," which provided "a thrill, a delight, and an exaltation that the exact sense of the line could not possibly have created."

Like many Romantics, Thurber often found his imagination stimulated by what Wordsworth called "the ministry of fear," which arouses a sense of mystery and the capacity for wonder. "Both my poodles and I myself believed . . . in fiends, and still do," Thurber wrote. "Fiends who materialize out of nothing and nowhere, like winged pigweed or Russian thistle." Among his other alleged fears he listed "the bears under the bed, the green men from Mars, the cats sealed up in the walls, the hearts beating under the floor boards, the faces of laughing girls that recede, float past, and come back again." If his characters often feel stalked by menace and wait for some lurking, unknown doom, they are at least liberated from dullness. In an essay on the Oz books, Thurber faulted L. Frank Baum's intention of keeping heartaches and nightmares out of his fantasies—and was glad he failed to do so.

Thurber was impatient with the militant realists who, like the mind controllers in Ray Bradbury's "Usher II," would prohibit fantasy. When Dr. Paul Schilder diagnosed *Alice in Wonderland* as full of "cruelty, destruction, and annihilation," Thurber was incensed, for such views were hostile to the very nature of imaginative literature.

Dr. Schilder's work . . . is cut out for him. He has the evil nature of Charles Perrault to dip into, surely as black and devious and unwholesome as Lewis Carroll's. He has the Grimms and Hans Christian Andersen. He has Mother Goose, or much of it. He can spend at least a year on the Legend of Childe Rowland, which is filled with perfectly swell sexual symbols. . . . This one piece of research will lead him into the myth of Proserpine and into Browning and Shakespeare and Milton's *Comus* and even into the dark and perilous kingdom of Arthurian legend. . . . When he is through with all this, Dr. Schilder should be pretty well persuaded that behind the imaginative works of all the cruel writing men . . . lies the destructive and unstable, the fearful and unwholesome. . . .

Thurber would have agreed with Bruno Bettelheim that the element of enchantment in fairy tales and fantasy, fables and parables, is therapeutic in reaching for truth on a deeper, mythic level than is offered by didactic realism, and in intimating "that a rewarding, good life is within one's reach despite adversity."

A Romantic at heart, Thurber scoffed at "scientists, statisticians, actuaries, all those men who place numbers above hunches, figures above feelings, facts above possibilities, the normal above the phenomenal. . . . with their eyes on the average, they fail to discern the significant." From Wordsworth to F. Scott Fitzgerald and E. E. Cummings, Romantics have disliked the analytical reasoning of scientists, who insist upon verifiable fact. Just as Wordsworth argued that "All science which waged war with and wished to extinguish Imagination in the mind of man, and to leave it nothing of any kind but the naked knowledge of facts, was . . . much worse than useless," Thurber satirized those scientists, the heirs of Dickens' Gradgrind, who would have us "get a precise and dogmatic meaning out of everything they read, thus leaving nothing to the fantasy and the imagination." As Cummings put it, "I'd rather learn from one bird how to sing/ than teach ten thousand stars how not to dance." Thurber recalled that when he was eight, he thought that " 'Post No Bills' meant that the walls on which it appeared belonged to one Post No Bill, a man of the same heroic proportions as Buffalo Bill. Some suspicious-minded investigator cleared this up for me, and a part of the glamour of life was gone."

"It is respectable to have no illusions—and safe—and profitable—and dull," wrote Joseph Conrad. "Yet you, too, in your time must have known the intensity of life, that light of glamour in the shock of trifles, as amazing as the glow of sparks struck from a cold stone—and as short-lived, alas!"

For Thurber, Lord Jim was the recurring symbol of romantic escapism; and in self-mockery he often compared himself to Conrad's hero, finding himself unable to achieve a comparable high adventure. Harassed by the demands of humdrum living, he thought of wandering around the South Seas

like a character out of Conrad, silent and inscrutable. But the necessity for frequent visits to my oculist and dentist has prevented this. . . . Furthermore, my horn-rimmed glasses and my Ohio accent betray me, even when I sit on the terrasses of little tropical cafes, wearing a pith helmet, staring straight ahead, and twitching a muscle in my jaw.

His own adventures were anticlimactic, for when he spent a summer in the West Indies, no exotic girl like Tondelaya in *White Cargo* offered to go to pieces with him; instead, the native women tried to sell him trinkets, and someone stole the pants to his dinner jacket. He realized that

There was, of course, even for Conrad's Lord Jim, no running away. . . . In the pathways between office and home and the houses of settled people there are always, ready to snap at you, the little perils of routine living, but there is no escape in the unplanned tangent, the sudden turn.

Many of Thurber's men find at least a temporary escape in the realms of imagination, but none does so as triumphantly as Walter Mitty. First published in 1939, "The Secret Life of Walter Mitty" has become one of the best-known stories of the century. The name has entered the language in endless allusions to him, and *Lancet*'s nomenclature includes the "Walter Mitty syndrome." Like many of Thurber's henpecked husbands, Mitty represents the modern male's sense of inadequacy, of being superfluous in a complex world with which he is unable to cope. Mitty is tyrannized by the trivia of shopping lists and the incomprehensibility of automobiles. But unlike Mr. Monroe, Mr. Preble, Mr. Pendley, Mr. Bidwell, and Thurber's other hapless antiheroes, Mitty transcends his frustrations by daydreaming himself into the regions of heroic romance. As a supremely cool daredevil, he commands a Navy hydroplane through a hurricane, performs miracles of surgery, is the dashing hero of courtroom drama, and flies on a suicide mission as a dauntless member of the Dawn Patrol, whistling "Auprès de ma blonde" as he jauntily prepares to take off for "forty kilometers through hell." At the end, in a close parallel to *Lord Jim,* he faces the firing squad without flinching, "proud and disdainful."

Among other things, "Mitty" is a masterpiece of popular culture; just as the humor in "The Catbird Seat" (1942) derives in part from the clichés of gangster fiction, in which Mr. Martin, a prissy and proper clerk, formulates his plans to do in the braying Mrs. Ulgine Barrows, who threatens his orderly routine, so Mitty's daydreams are full of clichés from popular melodrama. As a boy, Thurber was addicted to nickel novels and was always a great movie fan; and he incorporated the spirit of Hollywood heroics into Mitty's secret life. During World War II the troops found in Mitty a kindred spirit and formed fan clubs in honor of the daredevil who was not afraid of hell.

Mitty is both timely and timeless, with literary antecedents at least as old as Don Quixote. He has the panache of Cyrano and d'Artagnan. Tom Sawyer's adventurous fantasies of playing Robin Hood, pirate, and the hero of a Dumas novel are in Mitty's ancestry; and his progeny include Snoopy in his Sopwith Camel fighting the Red Baron and Woody Allen wishing he were Humphrey Bogart. He is also, of course, the James Thurber who wrote the eighth-grade class prophecy in which he rescues his classmates from possible disaster as their Seairoplane approaches Mars. "Unless that rope is gotten out of the curobator we will all be killed," cried one of the students; but he need not have feared, for James Thurber, who had been a tightrope walker for Barnsell's and Ringbailey's circus, nonchalantly walked out on the beam and extricated the rope. Mitty is, in fact, a universal figure; and his wistful gallantry elevates him above the forlorn and frustrated figures in Thurber's art whom he otherwise resembles. Our ultimate impression of him is not of the browbeaten spouse but of the dashing and undaunted swashbuckler—"Walter Mitty the Undefeated, inscrutable to the last."

Like the work of other humorists, a good deal of Thurber's art consists of trivia—word games, clever but forgettable conversation pieces, minor skirmishes in the war between men and women—but in the best of his stories, essays, and drawings, he laid a finger upon a nerve and touched something basic. The menace of modernity, the anxiety of being overwhelmed by baffling complexities, the threat of technology out of control, the feeling of futility, the sense of individual impotence have intensified since Thurber's death. From our perspective the Thurber years were comparatively tranquil; they now nurture nostalgia. The reasons for despair in the 1930's, 1940's, and 1950's have deepened in the 1970's; we are now afflicted with social, economic, political, and environmental turmoils. Thurber's birds and beasts are now an endangered species, and so are we. Things are doom-shaped with a vengeance, and humor is far more of the gallows variety. Urban alienation has become more extreme; New York is no longer "the Big Apple" but closer to "The City of Dreadful Night," as the cocktail party and the lonely crowd have given way to the multi-lock door and the fear of muggers. We are all far more disenchanted as we try to avoid being paralyzed by future shock. The "ministry of fear" finds expression in disaster epics, an obsession with the occult, and fictions of Satanic possession.

In its more innocent way, Thurber's art anticipates these tensions and terrors. We can recognize ourselves in his baffled and bewildered protagonists, and can appreciate their predicaments and perplexities. Thurber not only has diagnosed our diseases but also has offered a remedy—the innocence of animals, the lessons of love, the creative force and discipline of art, and the saving grace of humor. His humor, noted T. S. Eliot, contains

. . . a criticism of life at the bottom of it. It is serious and even somber. Unlike so much humor, it is not merely a criticism of manners—that is, of the superficial aspects of society at a given moment—but something more profound. His writings and also his illustrations are capable of surviving the immediate environment and time out of which they spring. To some extent they will be a document of the age they belong to.

Selected Bibliography

WORKS OF JAMES THURBER

BOOKS

Is Sex Necessary? or Why You Feel the Way You Do. New York: Harper and Brothers, 1929. (Written with E. B. White.)

The Owl in the Attic and Other Perplexities. New York: Harper and Brothers, 1931.

The Seal in the Bedroom and Other Predicaments. New York: Harper and Brothers, 1932.

The Middle-Aged Man on the Flying Trapeze. New York: Harper and Brothers, 1935.

Let Your Mind Alone! New York: Harper and Brothers, 1937.

Cream of Thurber. London: Hamish Hamilton, 1939.

The Last Flower. New York: Harper and Brothers, 1939.

The Male Animal. New York: Random House, 1940. (Written with Elliott Nugent.)

Fables for Our Time and Famous Poems Illustrated. New York: Harper and Brothers, 1940.

My World—and Welcome to It. New York: Harcourt, Brace, 1942.

Many Moons. New York: Harcourt, Brace, 1943.

Men, Women and Dogs. New York: Harcourt, Brace, 1943.

The Great Quillow. New York: Harcourt, Brace, 1944.

The Thurber Carnival. New York: Harper and Brothers, 1945.

The White Deer. New York: Harcourt, Brace, 1945.

The Beast in Me and Other Animals. New York: Harcourt, Brace, 1948.

The 13 Clocks. New York: Simon and Schuster, 1950.

The Thurber Album. New York: Simon and Schuster, 1952.

Thurber Country. New York: Simon and Schuster, 1953.

Thurber's Dogs. New York: Simon and Schuster, 1955.

A Thurber Garland. London: Hamish Hamilton, 1955.

Further Fables for Our Time. New York: Simon and Schuster, 1956.

Alarms and Diversions. New York: Harper and Brothers, 1957.

The Wonderful O. New York: Simon and Schuster, 1957.

The Years With Ross. Boston–Toronto: Atlantic, Little, Brown, 1959.

Lanterns and Lances. New York: Harper and Brothers, 1961.

Credos and Curios. New York: Harper and Row, 1962.

A Thurber Carnival. New York: Samuel French, 1962.

Vintage Thurber. 2 vols. London: Hamish Hamilton, 1963.

Thurber and Company. New York: Harper and Row, 1966.

BOOKS ILLUSTRATED OR INTRODUCED BY THURBER

Hawes, Elizabeth. *Men Can Take It.* New York: Random House, 1939. (Illustrated by Thurber.)

Kinney, James R., V.M.D., and Ann Honeycutt. *How to Raise a Dog in the City and in the Suburbs.* New York: Simon and Schuster, 1938; 2nd edition, revised, New York: Simon and Schuster, 1953. (Illustrated by Thurber.)

Mian, Mary. *My Country-in-Law.* Boston: Houghton Mifflin, 1946. (Introduction by Thurber.)

Moates, Alice Leone. *No Nice Girl Swears.* New York: Alfred A. Knopf, 1933. (Illustrated by Thurber.)

Petty, Mary. *This Petty Pace, a Book of Drawings.* New York: Alfred A. Knopf, 1945. (Preface by Thurber.)

Samuels, Margaret. *In a Word.* New York: Alfred A. Knopf, 1933. (Illustrated by Thurber.)

Sayre, Joel. *Persian Gulf Command.* New York: Random House, 1945. (Introduction by Thurber.)

INTERVIEWS

Interview with Harvey Breit, "Mr. Thurber Observes a Serene Birthday," *New York Times Magazine,* December 4, 1949, p. 17.

Interview with R. T. Allen, "Women Have No Sense of Humor, but They Don't Seem to Know It," *MacLean's Magazine,* 64:18, 19 ff. (June 1, 1951).

Interview with Harvey Breit, "Talk with James Thurber," *New York Times Book Review,* June 29, 1952, p. 19. Reprinted in Harvey Breit, *The Writer*

Observed. Cleveland–New York: World, 1956. Pp. 255–57.

Interview, "Says Superwoman Will Force Peace," AP News, August 22, 1953. Reprinted in Columbus *Dispatch,* August 23, 1953, p. 7.

Interview with George Plimpton and Max Steele, "The Art of Fiction," *Paris Review,* 10:35–49 (Fall 1955). Reprinted in *Writers at Work,* edited by Malcolm Cowley. New York: Viking Press, 1959. Pp. 82–98.

"James Thurber in Conversation with Alistair Cooke," *Atlantic,* 198:36–40 (August 1956).

Interview with Maurice Dolbier, "A Sunday Afternoon with Mr. Thurber," *New York Herald Tribune Book Review,* November 3, 1957, p. 2.

Interview with Henry Brandon, "Everybody Is Getting Very Serious," *New Republic,* 138:11–16 (May 26, 1958). Reprinted more fully as "The Tulle and Taffeta Rut" in Henry Brandon, *As We Are.* Garden City, New York: Doubleday, 1961. Pp. 257–82.

Interview with Eddy Gilmore, "James Thurber Isn't Sure He's Funny." (London, August 2, 1958). Reprinted as AP News in Cincinnati *Enquirer,* August 3, 1958, p. 47 (and in other papers that day).

Interview with Carol Illig, "Hear Your Heroes," *Seventeen,* January, 1960, pp. 88–89.

Interview with Arthur Gelb, "Thurber Intends to Relax Till '61," *New York Times,* March 28, 1960, p. 35.

Interview with Virginia Haufe, "Thurber Gives Advice to American Women," *Ohioana,* 3:34–36 (Summer 1960).

Interview with J. B. Weatherby, "A Man of Words," *Manchester Guardian Weekly,* February 9, 1961, p. 13.

Interview with Eddy Gilmore, "American Male No Panther, He's a Pouncer" (London, May 6, 1961). Reprinted as AP News in the Salt Lake *Tribune,* May 7, 1961, p. W-19 (and in other papers that day).

UNCOLLECTED PIECES

It is impractical to list the hundreds of uncollected stories, essays, drawings, and cartoons. Most of the uncollected prose is listed in Robert E. Morsberger, *James Thurber* (New York: Twayne, 1964); all of the prose and drawings are listed in the definitive bibliography by Edwin T. Bowden, *James Thurber: A Bibli-*

ography (Columbus: Ohio State University Press, 1968).

CRITICAL AND BIOGRAPHICAL STUDIES

BOOKS

Baker, Samuel Bernard. "James Thurber: The Columbus Years." (Unpublished M.A. thesis, Ohio State University, 1962.)

Bernstein, Burton. *Thurber: A Biography.* New York: Dodd, Mead, 1975.

Black, Stephen A. *James Thurber: His Masquerades, a Critical Study.* The Hague: Mouton, 1970.

Blair, Walter. *Horse Sense in American Humor.* Chicago: University of Chicago Press, 1942.

———. "The Urbanization of Humor," *A Time of Harvest,* edited by Robert E. Spiller. New York: Hill and Wang, 1962.

Bohn, William E. *I Remember America.* New York: Macmillan, 1962.

Cowley, Malcolm. *The Literary Situation.* New York: Viking, 1954.

Eastman, Max. *Enjoyment of Laughter.* New York: Simon and Schuster, 1936.

Gill, Brendan. *Here at the New Yorker.* New York: Random House, 1975.

Hackett, Francis. *On Judging Books in General and Particular.* New York: John Day, 1947.

Holmes, Charles. *The Clocks of Columbus.* New York: Atheneum, 1972.

———, ed. *Thurber, a Collection of Critical Essays.* Englewood Cliffs, N.J.: Prentice-Hall, 1974.

Kramer, Dale. *Ross and The New Yorker.* New York: Doubleday, 1952.

Morsberger, Robert E. *James Thurber.* New York: Twayne, 1964.

Murrell, William. *A History of American Graphic Humor (1865–1938).* 2 vols. New York: Whitney Museum of American Art, 1934; New York: Macmillan, 1938.

Nugent, Elliott. *Events Leading up to the Comedy.* New York: Trident, 1965.

Pollard, James E. "James Thurber," *Ohio Authors and Their Books, 1796–1950,* edited by William Coyle. Cleveland–New York: World, 1962.

Stone, Edward. *The Battle and the Books.* Athens: Ohio University Press, 1964.

Tobias, Richard C. *The Art of James Thurber.* Athens: Ohio University Press, 1970.

Updike, John. *Picked-up Pieces.* New York: Alfred A. Knopf, 1975.

Van Doren, Mark. *The Autobiography of Mark Van Doren.* New York: Harcourt, Brace, 1958.

Yates, Norris W. *The American Humorist.* Ames: Iowa State University Press, 1964.

PERIODICALS AND NEWSPAPERS

Albertini, V. R. "James Thurber and the Short Story," *Northwest Missouri State College Studies,* 28:3–15 (1964).

Arnold, Olga. "James Thurber, Humorist," *Amerika,* 7:1–18 (December 4, 1956).

Auden, W. H. "The Icon and the Portrait," *Nation,* 150:48 (January 13, 1940).

Baldwin, Alice. "James Thurber's Compounds," *Language and Style,* 3:185–96 (1970).

Benchley, Nathaniel. "If There Is No Human Comedy, It Will Be Necessary to Create One," *New York Herald Tribune Book Review,* November 25, 1962, p. 3.

Benét, Stephen Vincent, and Rosemary Benét, "Thurber: As Unmistakable as a Kangaroo," *New York Herald Tribune Book Review,* December 29, 1940, p. 6.

Benét, William Rose. "Carnival with Spectres," *Saturday Review of Literature,* 28:9 (February 3, 1945).

Bernard, F. V. "A Thurber Letter," *English Language Notes,* 8:300–01 (1971).

Black, Stephen A. "The Claw of the Sea-Puss: James Thurber's Sense of Experience," *Wisconsin Studies in Contemporary Literature,* 5:222–36 (August 1964).

Brady, Charles. "What Thurber Saw," *Commonweal,* 75:274–76 (December 8, 1961).

Brandon, Henry. "Thurber Used Humor to Camouflage His Exasperations with the Human Race," *Washington Post,* November 3, 1961, p. B-4.

Branscomb, Lewis. "James Thurber and Oral History at Ohio State University," *Lost Generation Journal,* 3:16–19 (1975).

Braunlich, Phyllis. "Hot Times in the Catbird Seat," *Lost Generation Journal,* 3:10–11 (1975).

Budd, Nelson H. "Personal Reminiscences of James Thurber," *Ohio State University Monthly,* 54:12–14 (January 1962).

Coates, Robert M. "Thurber, Inc.," *Saturday Review of Literature,* 21:10–11 ff. (December 2, 1939).

Cowley, Malcolm. "James Thurber's Dream Book," *New Republic,* 112:262–63 (March 12, 1945).

————. "Lions and Lemmings, Toads and Tigers," *Reporter,* 15:42–44 (December 13, 1956).

De Vries, Peter. "James Thurber: The Comic Prufrock," *Poetry,* 63:150–59 (December 1943).

Eckler, A. Ross. "The Wordplay of James Thurber," *Word Ways,* 6:241–47 (1973).

Elias, Robert H. "James Thurber: The Primitive, the Innocent, and the Individual," *American Scholar,* 27:355–63 (Summer 1958).

Friedrich, Otto. "James Thurber: A Critical Study," *Discovery* (New York), 5:158–92 (January 1955).

Geddes, Virgil. "Not Everyone Liked Thurber," *Lost Generation Journal,* 3:7 (1975).

Gilder, Rosamund. "Brain and Brawn, Broadway in Review," *Theatre Arts,* 24:158–62 (March 1940).

Hasley, Louis. "James Thurber: Artist in Humor," *South Atlantic Quarterly,* 73:404–15 (1974).

Hawley, Michael. "Quintet Honors Thurber Fables," *Lost Generation Journal,* 3:21–22 (1975).

"James Thurber, Aphorist for an Anxious Age," *Time,* November 10, 1961, p. 81.

Krutch, Joseph Wood. Review of *The Male Animal, Nation,* 150:81–82 (January 20, 1940).

Lindner, Carl M. "Thurber's Walter Mitty—the Underground American Hero," *Georgia Review,* 28:283–89 (1974).

MacLean, Kenneth. "James Thurber—a Portrait of the Dog-Artist," *Acta Victoriana,* 68:5–6 (Spring 1944).

————. "The Imagination of James Thurber," *Canadian Forum,* 33:193, 200–01 (December 1953).

"Men, Women, and Thurber," *Time,* November 15, 1943, p. 38.

Moynihan, Julian. "No Nonsense," *New Statesman,* 64:872 (December 14, 1962).

Nugent, Elliott. "Notes on James Thurber the Man or Men," New York *Times,* February 25, 1940, p. 10-3.

————. "James Thurber of Columbus," *Ohio Valley Folk Publications,* new series, no. 95 (April 1962).

"Priceless Gift of Laughter," *Time,* July 9, 1951, pp. 88–90 ff.

"Salute to Thurber," *Saturday Review,* 44:14–18 ff. (November 25, 1961).

Schlamm, William S. "The Secret Lives of James Thurber," *Freeman,* 2:736–38 (July 28, 1952).

School, Peter A. "Thurber's Walter Ego: The Little Man Hero," *Lost Generation Journal,* 3:8–9 (1975).

Soellner, Rolf. "James Thurber as a Shakespeare Critic," *Kansas Quarterly,* 7:55–65 (1975).

Sundell, Carl. "The Architecture of Walter Mitty's Secret Life," *English Journal,* 56:1284–87 (December 1967).

"That Thurber Woman," *Newsweek,* November 22, 1943, pp. 84–86.

"Thurber Amuses People by Making Them Squirm," *Life,* February 19, 1945, pp. 12–14.

"Thurber—an Old Hand at Humor with Two Hits on Hand," *Life,* March 14, 1960, pp. 103–08.

"Thurber and His Humor. . . . Up with the Chuckle, Down with the Yuk," *Newsweek,* February 4, 1957, pp. 52–56.

Updike, John. "Indignations of a Senior Citizen," *New York Times Book Review,* November 25, 1962, p. 5.

Walker, C. L. "The Legendary Mr. Thurber," *Ladies Home Journal,* 53:26–27 ff. (July 1946).

Weales, Gerald. "The World in Thurber's Fables," *Commonweal,* 55:409–11 (January 18, 1957).

White, E. B. "James Thurber," *New Yorker,* 37:247 (November 11, 1961).

White, Ruth Y. "Early Thurber," *Life,* April 22, 1940, pp. 108–09.

Wilson, Edmund. Review of *The White Deer, New Yorker,* 21:91–94 (October 27, 1945).

—*ROBERT E. MORSBERGER*

Thorstein Veblen

1857–1929

THORSTEIN VEBLEN may well be described as the first social theorist to give the "dismal science" of economics a long-needed comic relief. After Veblen the idea of "economic man" became something more than a creature of rational interests and something less than an agent of social virtue. Against the prevalent interpretations of his day, including the Marxist as well as the conservative neoclassical, Veblen depicted capitalism as irrational and essentially hedonistic; an atavistic phenomenon that could be grasped not by studying charts and statistics but by probing the behavior of archaic men and women living in primitive, tribal communities. The genius of Veblen lies in his combining an anthropologist's sensitivity to the noneconomic motives of human behavior and a literary artist's sensitivity to the strategy of irony and satire. He remains, above all, a masterful parodist of playful solemnity. Is human labor, as both Marx and Ricardo insisted, the source of value? Veblen, despite his own belief in the "instinct of workmanship," explains, in an observation that can be appreciated for its wit as well as its wisdom, why the idea of the "nobility of labor" is a fiction:

In persons of delicate sensibility, who have long been habituated to gentle manners, the sense of the shamefulness of manual labor may become so strong that, at a critical juncture, it will even set aside the instinct of self-preservation. So, for instance, we are told of certain Polynesian chiefs, who, under the stress of good form, preferred to starve rather than carry food to their mouths with their own hands. It is true, this conduct may have been due, at least in part, to an excessive sanctity or tabu attaching to the chief's person. The tabu would have been communicated by the contact of his hands, and so would have made anything touched by him unfit for human food. But the tabu is itself a derivative of the unworthiness or moral incompatibility of labor; so that even when construed in this sense the conduct of the Polynesian chiefs is truer to the canon of honorific leisure than would at first appear. A better illustration, or at least a more unmistakable one, is afforded by a certain king of France, who is said to have lost his life through an excess of moral stamina in the observance of good form. In the absence of the functionary whose office it was to shift his master's seat, the king sat uncomplaining before the fire and suffered his royal person to be toasted beyond recovery. But in so doing he saved his Most Christian Majesty from mental contamination.

Summum crede nefas animam praeferre pudori,
Et propter vitam vivendi perdere causas.

628

The passage is from *The Theory of the Leisure Class,* Veblen's best-known work. This classic may be read as social satire (in this instance the inanities of status and social roles that render rational consumer behavior a quaint fixation of orthodox economic theory). But Veblen could be equally sardonic in his numerous scholarly papers that appeared in such academic publications as the *Journal of American Sociology* and the *Journal of Political Economy*. In these articles, which were later collected and reprinted in his two most theoretical works, *The Place of Science in Modern Civilization and Other Essays* and *Essays in Our Changing Order,* Veblen often could not resist letting slip a sardonic aside that drove home his point far more effectively than had he used the traditional mode of scholarly discourse.

Criticizing neoclassical theorists for treating economic phenomena as a static exercise in taxonomy, and for building abstract models in order to invoke the "normal case" and thereby ignore the abnormalities of real, everyday behavior, Veblen questioned whether the mystique of a "hypothetically perfect competitive system" could actually explain what it purported to describe. He also suggested, in his playfully exaggerated prose, that the very vocabulary of orthodox theory cannot represent reality realistically and, therefore, may be linguistically bankrupt:

But what does all this signify? If we are getting restless under the taxonomy of a monocotyledonous wage-system and cryptogamic theory of interest, with involute loculicidal, tomentous and monoloform variants, what is the cytoplasm, centrosome, or karyokinetic process to which we may turn, and in which we may find surcease from the metaphysics of normality and controlling principles?

The passage is a specimen, albeit an exaggerated one, of Veblenese. Veblen was as unique a literary artist as he was an economist. He wrote by indirection, in a style designed to disguise his own thoughts. His humor could often be deadpan, reminiscent of the comic spirit of writers like Mark Twain; the slow, dense, and repetitive manner of his writing reflects the apparent stolid impassivity of his outlook.

Veblen's prose style has been the subject of considerable discussion and much debate among social scientists, literary scholars, and even analytic philosophers. The continuing interest in his expository style is further indication that much of Veblen's appeal lies in his power as a writer and rhetorician. While his economic ideas have long been assimilated by social scientists, his literary craftsmanship cannot be fully appropriated or imitated. One remains fascinated as well as occasionally frustrated by an overlabored prose that combines ponderous academic solemnity with witty and arresting epigrams as well as brilliant insights that are often relegated to asides or footnotes.

Some scholars are upset by Veblen's long, convoluted descriptions that leave one with the sense, as Max Lerner put it, "of endlessly chugging polysyllables, as if his sentences were a long string of freight cars rolling on forever." Others complain of Veblen's masking his own moral stance behind a coldly objective prose that purports to be scientifically neutral. Still others are put off by Veblen's use of the mode of the academic monograph and the scholarly treatise to poke fun at the "higher learning" of the brain merchants of the status quo.

Above all, it is Veblen's repetitiveness, his weakness for tautologies and circumlocution, that leaves many readers weary. H. L. Mencken, Veblen's ideological nemesis and severest literary critic, believed that Veblen's writings should be excommunicated from the English language:

It is as if the practice of that incredibly obscure and malodorous style were a relentless disease, a sort of progressive intellectual diabetes, a leprosy of the horse sense. Words are flung upon words until all recollection that there must be a meaning in them, a ground and excuse for them, is lost. One wanders in a labyrinth of nouns, adjectives, verbs, pronouns, adverbs, prepositions, conjunctions and participles, most of them swollen and nearly all of them unable to walk. It is difficult to imagine worse English within the limits of intelligible grammar. It is clumsy, affected, opaque, bombastic, windy, empty. It is without grace or distinction and it is often without the most elementary order. The learned professor gets himself enmeshed in his gnarled sentences like a bull trapped by barbed wire, and his efforts to extricate himself are quite as furious and quite as spectacular.

Before one fully accepts Mencken's critique, two things must be kept in mind. First, Mencken's essay in *Prejudices* on "Professor Veblen" (1919) was directed more at the substance than at the style of his adversary's thought, especially at Veblen's satires on capitalist behavior, his defense of women, and his treatment of the rugged American male individual as the finest flower of primitive barbarism. Second, Mencken would not allow himself to perceive that Veblen's ponderous style may have been deliberate, not so much a failure of proportion as an artful attempt to engage the serious feelings of people in order better to expose the silliness of conventional wisdom. In the "invisible world" of sociology, in which the implications of customs, habits, and values remain hidden from the ordinary reaches of consciousness, what better style could be employed to sensitize human awareness? In his perceptive introduction to *The Portable Veblen* (1948), Max Lerner explains why there is an ingenious method behind Veblen's seemingly maddening redundancy.

There is about this early style an air of quaintness, but it is a controlled quaintness. It never becomes eccentric or hopelessly obscure or turgid. Nor does the irony . . . become a frozen attitude of ill-humor and indignation. Veblen uses here the long probing approach, followed by the quick turn of the knife. His manner is outwardly academic, and he invests the analysis with the appearance of a deliberate and detached gravity which is intended to put the reader off his guard. Then suddenly the coupling of competitive sports with "lower-class delinquents" and "atavistic elements," and you get the juxtaposition that Kenneth Burke has well called the method of "perspective by incongruity." But Veblen is never content to achieve his effect and let it go at that. He keeps turning the knife in the wound. Affecting a sustained gravity throughout, he works out a protracted parallel between leisure-class sportsmen and lower-class delinquents, introducing a running sequence of phrases whittled down to dagger effectiveness which impale his meaning forever in the reader's memory. Then, at the end of the paragraph, the clinching sentence, with the sudden stripping away of the academic ornateness he has affected, and the introduction of a homegrown phrase from the common speech.

It would perhaps be facile to suggest that how one responds to Veblen's style depends upon how one responds to his analysis of modern American society. Yet Veblen's liberal and radical champions do tend to see in his prose further evidence for the dictum that truth is approximated by satiric technique, by unmasking cant and debunking reigning misconceptions. In this enterprise Veblen employed various literary devices of satire and irony and in the process created some of his own. One example is his creation of symbolic types, like the hapless university president parodied in *The Higher Learning in America;* another is his use of invented phrases that have a cunning twist—such memorable expressions as "conspicuous consumption," "trained inability," "resolute conviviality," "pecuniary emulation," "imbecile institutions," "conscientious withdrawal of efficiency," "naive brutality," "honorific waste," "invidious distinction," and "gifted with ferocity."

Veblen's prose is weighed down with cumbersome sentence structures and heavy lines that often sag from sheer erudition. But his diffuse style is always relieved by a touch of playfulness, a casual insight, an ironic twist, or a wicked sense of humor that occasionally rises to epigrammatic brilliance. "Plato's scheme of folly," wrote Veblen in *The Higher Learning,* "which would have the philosophers take over the management of affairs, has been turned on its head; the men of affairs have taken over the direction of the pursuit of knowledge." Despite the criticisms of conservatives like Mencken, and even the reservations of liberal admirers like Lerner and Alfred Kazin, Veblen remains one of the great writers in American social thought. A keen observer of manners and morals, he elevated social science to the level of literary art; and if he tended to conceal his own purposes behind a dense prose style, he also illuminated the deeper meaning of social behavior with imperishable perceptions.

Veblen's strangely esoteric prose reflected an author who was himself a stranger to Victorian America and its genteel manners. Indeed, Veblen stands out as one of the most baffling writers in American cultural history. Eccentric, reticent, detached, unfathomable, he struggled to sustain personal obscurity even as he gained academic notoriety. To the frustration of all those who have attempted to study his mind and career, Veblen requested in his will that all letters and remaining materials pertaining to his life be destroyed. Fortunately his contemporaries were willing to tell what they knew of him to Joseph Dorfman, who published the definitive biography, *Thorstein Veblen and His America* (1934).

Veblen had the physical appearance of a Norwegian peasant. A stolid, lean face with shrewd eyes, a shaggy beard and bristling mustache, long limbs and large hands, and a lethargic and seemingly slow-moving body that led some of his students to believe he was half asleep—such is the image remembered by contemporaries. His clothes were generally rumpled, his collars usually several sizes too large, his trousers baggy, and his thick woolen stockings invariably supported by pins clipped to his pant legs. Scornful of ostentation—and this should not surprise us—he wore no jewelry or any kind of mark of status; he carried his watch on a piece of black ribbon hooked to his vest by a large safety pin.

Veblen led a bizarre life that scandalized the academic world of his time. Much of his continuing troubles stemmed from his blatant philandering, which led to his dismissal from the University of Chicago and from Stanford. Although his love life is one of the most discussed and least documented aspects of his career, there can be no doubt that he was involved in one affair after another—once with a colleague's wife who later became the mistress of Anatole France. Veblen made no attempt to conceal his life-style, and no doubt he delighted in shocking the sensibilities of Victorian America. When the chancellor at the University of Chicago, William Rainey Harper, expressed to Veblen his paternal concern for the "moral health" of his colleagues' wives, Veblen readily obliged. Legend has it that he replied slowly, in a low voice, slouching before the chancellor's desk, "I've tried them all. They are no good."

If Veblen's erotic exploits were intolerable to authorities, his teaching methods were no less insulting. He gave all his students the grade *C,* regardless of their work. To a student who complained that his mark was the lowest he had ever received, Veblen explained: "My grades are like lightning. They are liable to strike anywhere." But when another student needed a higher score to qualify for a scholarship, Veblen raised the evaluation from "medium" to "superior," and when that failed to do the trick, to "excellent," leaving the dean's office utterly bewildered.

Veblen might be described as a failure as a teacher and a genius as an educator. His lectures were delivered in a low monotone, so mumbled that his sly humor and learned insights were often lost to the audience. One pupil, sedulously taking notes, requested that a sentence be repeated, only to be told that it was not worth repeating. Sarcastic, Veblen once asked a devout student of religion to explain to him the value of her church in terms of beer kegs. Yet he was also reticent, and replied to a student who asked him if he ever took anything seriously: "Yes, but don't tell anyone."

It is almost painful to contemplate what ratings Veblen might have received had student evaluations been used in his era. Enrollments in his classes continued to dwindle as he continued to ramble. His very erudition and vastness of knowledge—economics, philosophy, anthropology, sociology, history, Cretan archaeology, Norse literature, and Icelandic mythology—handicapped him as an instructor, even though students could not help but be impressed.

Yet the genius of Veblen as an educator was in his ability to excite the minds of those select few who understood him—such former students and disciples as Wesley C. Mitchell, James Hayden Tufts, C. E. Ayres, Walton Hamilton, Isidor Lubin, and Lewis Mumford, all of whom became distinguished scholars and public servants. If a teacher's contribution is measured more by lasting impact than by ephemeral popularity, Veblen certainly deserves to be ranked among the outstanding educators in American social science. Harold Laski, the British political scientist and colleague of Veblen at the New School for Social Research, explains why his intellectual mentor deserved to be so judged:

I first met Professor Veblen shortly after the opening of the New School. . . . He was very shy, and, in the first weeks of our acquaintance, it was difficult to get on intimate terms with him. But, once the initial barriers had been overcome, he was an entrancing companion. He delivered himself, in a half-oracular, half-ironical way, of extraordinary pungent judgments upon men and things. I remember particularly his admiration for Marx . . . his praise of F. J. Turner and Charles Beard. . . . He used to insist that we had entered upon an epoch of revolution and he doubted whether any American of his time would see again the kind of social peace characteristic of America in his youth. . . . He impressed me greatly both by his sudden flashes of insight—a streak of lightning which revealed unexpected vistas—and the amazing range both of his general knowledge and his memory for almost esoteric facts. It would have been easy to describe much of his talk as cynical; but one saw quite early that this was in fact merely a protective colouring beneath which he concealed deep emotions he did not like to bring to the surface. I was moved by his patience, his willingness to consider difficulties, his tenacity in discussion, and his anxiety, in matters he regarded as important, to discover common ground. When I first met him, he was beginning to get the recognition he deserved; and it was profoundly moving to watch his shy delight in realising that his long struggle was at last beginning to bear fruit. . . . I do not remember discussing anything with him without receiving illumination; and his kindness to a much younger teacher remains one of the abiding memories of my years in America.

What did Veblen have to say about modern society that made him so compelling an intellect to Laski and numerous other contemporaries? One of the problems in answering this question is that Veblen's writings did not usher in a distinct school of thought—although "institutional economics" has often been associated with his name—nor did his ideas add up to a systematic social theory or a definite methodology of social inquiry. Another difficulty in ascertaining the ultimate significance of his thought is the ambiguous nature of his own ideological legacy. Marxists, for example, praise his critique of capitalist ideology but are upset by his rejection of Hegel and dialectical materialism. Liberals admire his attack on big business but are troubled by his skepticism about historical progress. Conservatives may rejoice in his exposure of the foibles of mass society but are shocked by his disrespect for the rich and the powerful. And feminists esteem his understanding of the archaic basis of masculine domination but are puzzled by his own relationships with women. Veblen seems to delight everyone and satisfy no one.

Although Veblen remains an ideological enigma, one can note briefly the main features of his writings that have done so much to influence our understanding not only of the world of economics in particular but also of social relations in general.

Veblen was perhaps the first professionally trained economist to draw upon the findings of contemporary anthropology in order to illuminate better not only past experience but also present realities. Indeed, he was convinced that in the study of archaic society lies the key to the structure of human relationships in modern industrial life. Veblen quoted M. G. Lapouge: "Anthropology is destined to revolutionize the political and social sciences as radically as bacteriology has revolutionized the science of medicine." Like Marx, Veblen came to the study of economics by way of an early training in classical philosophy; but Veblen extended his analysis of economic behavior into the relatively pioneering disciplines of ethnology and sociology. By rediscovering the ways in which men and women related to one another in early archaic communities, he uncovered new ways of looking at contemporary social relations.

Thus Veblen focused on such modern rituals as competitive sports, extravagant dress, and wasteful feasts to draw parallels between archaic traits and contemporary customs. The rituals of potlatch and kula discussed so much today by anthropologists, the symbolic practice among primitive tribes of exchanging gifts to demonstrate through ceremony the superiority of the giver to the receiver, were perceived by Veblen as a form of conspicuous consumption with its roots in archaic man and extending to the prodigal habits of the affluent in modern industrial society. For the tribal chief as well as for the modern business tycoon, a common behavior could be found in the dictum "What is wasteful is reputable." "Costly entertainments, such as the potlatch or ball," wrote Veblen in the *Leisure Class,*

are peculiarly adapted to serve this end [ostentation]. The competitor with whom the entertainer wishes to institute a comparison is, by this method, made to serve as a means to an end. He consumes vicariously for his host at the same time he is a witness to the consumption of that excess of good things which his host is unable to dispose of singlehanded, and he is also made to witness his host's facility in etiquette.

Before Veblen gained a reputation as a satirist of leisure-class habits, he had already become well known, at least in academic circles, as the bête noire of neoclassical economics. This late nineteenth-century school of thought had its roots in the laissez-faire doctrines of Adam Smith and his disciples. In America, classical economic theory found one of its staunchest defenders in John Bates Clark, whose writings Veblen mercilessly criticized. Orthodox economics assumed that competition was the rule of life and reflected man's "natural" tendency toward self-assertion. Accordingly, the economy operated within the laws of supply and demand, a self-regulating mechanism that governed price and wage levels to the benefits of the buyer and the seller. And since self-interest was and always would be the mainspring of human action, the behavior of "economic man" was rational, and thus capable of empirical analysis and, perhaps eventually, scientific predictability.

Veblen addressed his early writings to the reigning orthodox system of economics in three specific articles: "The Preconceptions of Economic Science"; "Why Is Economics Not an Evolutionary Science?"; and "Professor Clark's Economics." In an attempt to expose the shaky foundations of neoclassical thought, Veblen pointed out that orthodox economists were mired in the "metaphysics of normality." That is, they constructed models based on unreal hypotheses ("if perfect competition prevailed," "if consumers and sellers were guided by one motive," and so on) that at best could yield only logically consistent propositions but could tell us little about the real forces at work in everyday economic behavior.

Consider, for example, the issue of money, which orthodox economists had treated as a medium of exchange, a standard of value, and a store of wealth. To Veblen this approach seemed too rational, confined as it was to the psychology of self-interest and economic calculation that prevailed in neoclassical theory. Veblen was more interested in exploring the context in which money circulates, a social-cultural dimension that enables us to perceive money not primarily as a means of exchange but as an expression of power in its conspicuous display. The real motive behind the acquisition of money is seen as a deeper desire to achieve power over men and women by possessing the symbols of wealth. Hence Veblen attempted to demystify the authority of wealth by exposing an economic system that runs on noneconomic motives. Although Adam Smith would not have been disturbed by such subjective explorations, which he himself had probed in *The Theory of Moral Sentiments,* Veblen wanted to expand the scope of neoclassical thought to take into account the new data of anthropology and sociology, and thereby view economic behavior in more than one dimension.

So expanded, Veblen's perspective enabled him to question a traditional body of economic theory that focused on land, labor, and capital on the one side, and on rent, wages, and profits on the other. Among the preconceptions that Veblen questioned was the "theorem of equivalence," the presumed equity between aggregate output and individual reward. This implied that workers get as much as they produce, and produce as much as they earn; and that consumers pay as much as the commodity is worth and give what they are willing to pay. Veblen observed that such a theorem presupposed free competition, when in reality the absence of even a measure of consumer sovereignty and worker's control points up not the beauties of competition but the power of coercion that characterizes the marketplace.

It should not be assumed that because Veblen was critical of the theoretical foundations of capitalism, he remained favorably disposed to the philosophical foundations of socialism. Indeed, he tended to see the economic theories of socialism and capitalism as both having grown out of the background of Ricardian economics, which stressed the factors of production and the role of labor as essential to the creation of value. Such objective considerations did not fully analyze the subjective attitudes of individual consumers toward commodities that satisfied human desires. Although Veblen remained critical of Marx's labor theory of value (he himself never worked out a persuasive theory of value), he was quick to defend Marx against critics who accused him of identifying the concept of value solely with "exchange value." Veblen also admired the "boldness of conception" and "great logical consistency" in Marx's writings. He tried to distinguish Ricardo's view of human labor as an "irksome" necessity from Marx's *homo faber,* a principle of labor based on the intrinsic value of work, "surplus" value that becomes the quantum of congealed labor in the commodity produced for exchange. Beyond that, however, Veblen took his departure from Marx.

He could not accept the "law of capitalist accumulation," in which Marx insisted that profits would be jeopardized to the extent that capitalists introduced labor-saving technology. Nor could he accept the "law of increasing misery," the assumption of progressive distress of the working class, an assumption that fits into the scheme of the Hegelian dialectic, in which the proletariat arises to "negate" capitalism. It is, however, a scheme of history that has no basis in the actual facts of human experience. Veblen believed that Marx's theories were faulty primarily because they derived from two incompatible sources: Hegelian philosophy and its materialist interpretation by Marx and the English system of natural rights from which Marx supposedly derived his notion that the worker was entitled to the full product of his labor. The former source postulates historical development as self-actualizing— a teleological movement unfolding by "inner-necessity." The latter proceeds on the "motives of interests" and on the basis of "class struggle," and not on metaphysical ideals. Indeed, the doctrine of class is of "utilitarian origin and of English pedigree, and it belongs to Marx by virtue of his having borrowed its elements from the system of self-interest. It is in fact a piece of hedonism, and it is related to Bentham rather than to Hegel." Thus stripped of the spell of Hegelian dialectics—a logic of contradiction that assumes that a historical tendency in one direction will produce its own negation— the idea of class struggle could not, Veblen argued, produce the historical reality of a classless society.

Whereas Marxists generally looked to the working class for the solution to modern capitalism, Veblen saw that class as part of the prob-lem. Much of Veblen's work focused on the life-style of the affluent leisure classes and on the behavioral traits that related the activities of modern capitalists to their forebears. But in "Some Neglected Points in the Theory of Socialism" (1892), Veblen addressed himself to the issue of the working class. He questioned both Herbert Spencer's claim that the discontent of the workers lies in "ennui" and the liberal reformer's belief that workers were dissatisfied because they realized that the rich were getting richer and the poor poorer.

The true source of labor's restlessness, Veblen observed, may be found in a sense of envy and injured dignity—what present-day sociologists would call "relative deprivation." The existing economic system may not necessarily make the poor poorer in absolute terms, but it evokes feelings of "slighted manhood" and other status anxieties. Desiring to climb into the middle class, and influenced by the culture of the nouveaux riches, the worker seeks the elusive respect of those classes above him. And to the extent that the worker compares himself to his image of the people in upper-class strata, he concedes the right of his "superiors" to judge him. Veblen was less interested in the "exploitation" of the working class than in its gradual integration and socializing through the process of "invidious comparison." Where Marxists were inspired by the radical potential of the labor movement, Veblen was appalled by its conservative direction.

Why does the working class seemingly collaborate in its own subordination? To answer this question one must consider a Veblenian insight that was rare in late nineteenth-century America. Whereas the dominant Victorian culture preached the "gospel of work" and the Protestant virtues of industry and thrift, Veblen was the first social scientist to point out that work was actually held in disesteem and that leisure, not labor, represented the goal of those who identified the "pursuit of happiness" with the acquisition of commodities. Again Veblen traced this attitude to the activities of early archaic societies; the advent of hunting and warfare as the dominant economic mode of life elevated predation and exploit to an honorable status as it brought about the dishonor of productive and socially useful employments. What is admired in advanced societies, no less than in ancient communities, is not so much the productions of the leisure class as its possessions. Such goods can be appropriated with the full approval of the community because the skills of the hunter and warrior, often the techniques of "force and fraud," are esteemed as evidence of "preeminent force." The masses in modern society, including the working class (which Veblen called the "underlying populations"), crave the symbols of success displayed by the leisure class—items of consumption that advertise the relative freedom of the possessor from the mundane demands of work.

The stigma of work in modern society can best be seen in the situation of the contemporary woman. In the 1890's, when the feminist movement in America was beginning to assert itself, Veblen published two illuminating essays, "The Barbarian Status of Women" and "The Economic Theory of Women's Dress." A half-century before the anthropologist Claude Lévi-Strauss described women as the first form of "currency," Veblen not only had depicted them in similar terms of economic exchange, but had gone so far as to suggest that private property originated in the capture of women; that marriage evolved from a system of "coercion-ownership" that had been sustained by the ritual of "mock seizure"; and that the status of the modern woman remained almost what it was when her forebears were being abducted—that of a "chattel." Veblen's anthropological specula-

tions are difficult to verify—though present writings on such phenomena as "bride-price" transactions among African tribes seem to bear out some of his insights—but his observations on the status of women in contemporary America are still worth pondering.

Veblen traced the stigma attached to women's domestic work to the early advent of property and male prowess, which marked the passing of "peaceable savagery" and the emergence of the "barbarian" era of predatory activity. Now women, who were once esteemed as the source of knowledge about the soil and seasons and the rhythms of growth and fertility, were relegated to a subordinate status as they were forced to labor relentlessly, digging roots, drawing water, milking cattle, and doing other household chores that seemed to men so "ceremoniously unclean." Similarly, middle- and upper-class wives and daughters in contemporary America are influenced by the leisure-class scheme of values, which has become stronger with each generation that inherits the habit of conspicuous idleness. Thus, modern industrial work, like earlier agricultural and manual labor, is seen as degrading; and even professional work related to the useful production of goods and services becomes "vulgar" and "unwomanly." Married women especially are excluded from the industrial work force by those husbands who have fallen under the influence of the canons of reputability. The wife remains an appendage to the husband, whose interests she serves and whose image of the good life she replicates in her role as consumer.

That the wife remains a victim of the ceremony of consumption may be seen in her dress habits. Her attire, Veblen noted, is designed not only to advertise wasteful expenditure but also to dramatize her freedom from productive employment. The dangerously high "French heel," the ankle-length skirt, and the tight-squeezing corset indicate that the wives have incapacitated themselves for work, demonstrating in their social lives the same disdain for productive occupations that their husbands display in their white-collar professions. In Veblen's analysis of the "barbarian status of women," the affluent wife, the debutante, and the young girl at finishing school are culturally conditioned to believe that they are the objects upon which husbands, suitors, and fathers should lavish their wealth. Their "calling" in life is "to honor, love, and obey"; not to produce, but to consume (as Charlotte Perkins Gilman wrote in *Women and Economics* [1898]: "She is forbidden to make, but encouraged to take."). Veblen may have exaggerated the social motive (in contrast with the sexual) in changing dress styles; one wonders what he would have made of the mini-skirt as evidence of women's physical incapacity!); and he may have exaggerated the continuity between primitive and modern patterns of apparel. Yet Veblen shrewdly demonstrated the element of class emulation in the sociology of clothing styles, and thus cultural critics like Quentin Bell, author of *On Human Finery* (1949), can develop a whole treatise on fashion based in large part on Veblen's enduring insights.

Veblen's perception of the social foundations of economics has many ramifications—the vicissitudes of fashion and the status of women, the esteem of wealth and leisure, the fate of workmanship and the Protestant ethic, and so on. But the most revealing aspect of Veblen's analysis of the cultural hegemony of capitalism and the cultural stigma of labor is his sensitivity to the sociological dimension of human existence. Like Emile Durkheim and Max Weber, Veblen saw society as a power that stands over and against the individual, whose every thought and gesture is shaped by the external forces of social interaction.

Thus, in seizing upon the idea of "emulation" as a key to motivation, Veblen proved to be an early student of what came to be known in social science as "role-playing." In Veblen's economic writings, the portrait of the atomistic, self-reliant individual, so prevalent in British utilitarian thought, disappears from the picture. Instead, Veblen depicts the completely socialized man whose entire life is absorbed in his social role; a life that is driven, if not determined, by the instinct of "emulation." The desire for esteem and approbation, a part of human nature as described by many Enlightenment philosophers, Veblen saw as a universal trait having its roots in archaic society (there are similarities here between Veblen and Rousseau). And the craving for respect and social acceptance characterizes all classes, a tendency that may help explain why "class consciousness" is deflected in a social order where there is a measure of upward mobility, or the appearance of such possibility.

The crucial feature of Veblen's theory of emulation is its conservative implications. Although an uncompromising radical himself, Veblen conceded what most other social critics were reluctant to acknowledge: that the hegemony of capitalism is perpetuated by the masses' emulating the culture and life-styles of the classes immediately above them. Thus, the norms that organize and provide cohesion to a society's value system originate at the top of the social structure and permeate downward, affecting or "contaminating" the populations of the various strata below. And this is true however repugnant or fallacious may be the values of the upper classes, particularly those of the leisure class.

In Veblen's sociological insights one may find a key to a problem that has troubled many social scientists: how does a ruling class in a democratic society legitimate itself if not by force? Veblen was able to see America as a class society without a class conflict precisely because of his appreciation of the conservative function of emulation. In a mass democratic society, the phenomenon of power, the ability to command obedience by the threat of coercion, gives way to the phenomenon of influence, the ability to command respect by the tendency to emulation. And it is this persuasive tendency that explains why men and women seemingly consent to their own domination. In contrast with Marx, who was too quick to dismiss all ideologies as a form of "false consciousness," Veblen was closer to Durkheim and other twentieth-century scholars who stressed the ways in which consciousness is conditioned by the ideas that society, and not only the marketplace, imposes on its members; the "invisible" values and attitudes that arise from the inexorable socializing processes of human existence.

Against the power of culture and the relentless force of society that repress the individual, Veblen looked to science as the source of enlightenment and liberation. Veblen believed that science would eventually extirpate animism and anthropomorphism, those psychological tendencies that led man to attribute human qualities to natural phenomena and thereby to see in nature the fetish of an "invisible hand," the presumed sanctity of existing institutions, and the lawful character of a social order supposedly ordained as an unalterable fact of the structure of the natural universe or of God's inscrutable will. Science, in short, could penetrate the phenomenon of reification. The emphasis in scientific analysis on cause-and-effect relationships could eliminate animism and reification. Thus modern science, especially a mode of inquiry inspired by "idle curiosity" and wonder, emancipated historical man from superstition, myth, lore, magic, and all the animistic forces of authority and tradition that render what is natural and changeable sacred and immutable.

With Veblen's faith in the liberating power of science, it is not difficult to understand why he looked to the engineers and technicians as the last hope for radical social change. This theme, implicit in *The Theory of Business Enterprise* (1904), is fully articulated in *The Engineers and the Price System* (1921). Disciplined by "the machine process," the scientifically trained engineers were the one class that would see things in terms of cause and effect rather than of good and evil; of "weight, tale, and measure" rather than of merit or demerit; of evolving natural processes rather than of unchangeable precedent and convention. Veblen's hope that the scientists and technicians would be the political redeemers of modern industrial society is easy to ridicule (as his critics are well aware); and it is hardly necessary to remind oneself that the first professionally trained engineer to reach the pinnacle of power, President Herbert Hoover, proved something less than a revolutionary, or that the present chief executive, Jimmy Carter, can combine his background in nuclear engineering with his devotion to Protestant theology.

But one must ask what other force in modern society can bring about that objectivization of human relationships that will eliminate the subjective factors of status and prestige, the "invidious comparisons" of wealth and power? What, after all, is more threatening to false social distinctions than a "machine process" that makes no cultural distinctions and has as its goal the practical and useful? Science may have turned out to be an instrument of domination instead of liberation, but it contained the potential for being an agency of human emancipation, as Lewis Mumford, one of Veblen's admiring disciples, has persuasively argued in *Technics and Civilization* (1934) and in *Technics and Human Development* (1967).

However misplaced Veblen's faith in science and engineering may have been, it enabled him to perceive a truth of modern economic theory that seems to have escaped generations of social scientists: that there is a profound distinction between business and industry and that the respective aims of each activity are so different that these two dimensions of economic life may be incompatible. According to capitalist ideology, or at least its popular expression under the rubric of Andrew Carnegie's "gospel of wealth" or Ben Franklin's alleged "Protestant ethic," possession of goods was somehow related to the moral worth of the possessor, the assumption being that capitalist man had created wealth by virtue of his labor and superior intelligence and character.

Thus, to appreciate fully Veblen's efforts, one must keep in mind that he was writing against a dense background of tendentious economic theory that placed the businessman at the forefront of historical progress. Every major economist from the time of Adam Smith had regarded the capitalist as the driving force in the process of industrialization; even Marx hailed the capitalist as the demiurge of history. The businessman was the prime mover, the entrepreneurial genius who sensed the right opportunities, applied his great organizational talents, drew upon his imagination and vision, and thereby initiated the various processes of modernization that created the "wealth of nations." Veblen, the masterful ironist, completely reversed this picture.

It was not businessmen, much less "pure" capitalists, Veblen argued, but men of industry—inventors, engineers, technical experts—who did the actual intellectual work, devised the blueprints, developed the techniques, and even provided the expectations for economic gain that made the modern industrial system possible. The scientist and technician must first create the mechanical possibility of new and more efficient methods of producing before the businessman's eyes are opened to new investment opportunities. But is the businessman at all interested in productivity? Not always. Veblen drew a sharp distinction between the engineer and the capitalist, between those engaged in what he called the "industrial and the pecuniary employments," between those who made goods and those who made money. The engineer, according to Veblen, is primarily concerned with productivity, serviceability, and efficiency; and his calling differs from that of the businessman, whose chief interest is in optimum prices and maximum profits. At certain junctures in history, particularly during the early stages of industrialization, the two activities may coincide.

But as the craftsman and merchant allow themselves to become absorbed solely in trade, commerce, and investment, and relegate the technical aspects of production to subordinates, the respective activities come into conflict and the interests of capital take precedence over the interests of science. Whenever there is a cleavage, the businessman may curtail supply in order to maintain high prices, transfer funds from productive operations to speculative investment, deceive consumers as well as competitors, and generally engage in a number of unconscionable activities that Veblen described, with characteristic irony, as a "conscientious withdrawal of efficiency." Accordingly, the profit system had little or nothing to do with achieving and sustaining maximum industrial productivity in the interests of getting the largest amount of goods to the greatest number of people at the lowest possible price. In a pecuniary culture devoted to the rule of commodities, the power of money triumphs over the logic of machinery.

It should be obvious by now that only an intellectual as eccentric as Veblen, an outsider who observed the normal habits of American society as an anthropologist studies the strange customs of a tribal village, would be able to discern the incongruities, not to say the "contradictions," of capitalism. Veblen remains one of the great critics of capitalism, but not because he foretold its decline and fall. On the contrary, he perceived that the culture and ideology of capitalism, insofar as it represented a modified continuation of, and not a definitive break with, the feudal tradition of status and glory and the "barbarian" survivals of prowess and esteem, would continue to enjoy hegemony in the twentieth century. The brilliance of Veblen's critique lies in the fact that he assaulted capitalism on its own terms: efficiency, productivity, and utility. Who was this odd figure whose writings trouble capitalists as much as they puzzle socialists?

Thorstein Bunde Veblen was born on a frontier farm in Wisconsin in 1857. He came from the same Midwest border region that produced such giant contemporaries as Charles Beard, Vernon L. Parrington, Simon Patten, Frederick Jackson Turner, and Lester Ward—historians and sociologists who would mount a far-reaching assault on the economic and cultural values of the East. Veblen, however, was a stranger not merely to the Eastern establishment but to the country as a whole; and this more profound alienation was mirrored in his harsher and more thoroughgoing critique of American society.

Veblen was the fourth son and sixth child of an immigrant Norwegian family. His parents had arrived in the United States ten years before his birth, bringing with them bitter memories of the old country, where they had suffered the loss of family land and with it the loss of status as property owners. In Minnesota the Veblens encountered similar troubles with land speculators and moneylenders. Yet Veblen's animus against capitalism cannot simply be traced to the deprivations of his childhood. Although his household was characterized by austerity in the early years, by the time he was a teenager, his father had managed to become a relatively prosperous farmer; and he expected his sons to enter a profession and surpass his own status in an American society that rewarded the industrious. Thus one day in 1874, young Veblen was simply called from the field, put on the family buggy along with his packed bags, and sent to Carleton College, a Congregational oasis of New England culture on the Minnesota prairies. Although sent to Carleton in the hope that he would enter the Lutheran ministry, Veblen proved to be too irreverent, impish, and even lazy to benefit from the pious atmosphere there. After shocking the missionary-oriented faculty by writing essays on the virtues of alcohol and cannibalism, Veblen graduated in 1880.

Veblen tried teaching for a year at a small college and then decided to follow his brother Andrew (father of the mathematician Oswald Veblen) to Johns Hopkins to study philosophy. He took courses from the Hegelian philosopher George Sylvester Morris and from the liberal political economist Richard T. Ely. He also audited the lectures in logic given by Charles Sanders Peirce; and it is possible that Veblen's interest in semeiology, the study of signs and the symbolic aspects of communication (gesture, manners, and so on), derived from Peirce's early explorations in this field. Veblen maintained an interest in the epistemological dimensions of social knowledge, and he later wrote his doctoral dissertation on Kant. But at Hopkins, Veblen's application for a scholarship was rejected, despite glowing recommendations from former teachers.

Veblen then transferred to Yale and continued his study of philosophy under its president, Rev. Noah Porter. He soon became drawn to the Olympian figure of William Graham Sumner, the conservative Social Darwinist who was struggling to radicalize the religious-centered curriculum by introducing more courses on modern society. Veblen could accept the biological foundations of Darwinism, but not its spurious political conclusions formed by conservative apologists. The "survival of the fittest" proved not that "the best" survived in the course of evolutionary development but that the more brutish species triumphed, and did so possibly because each preceding extinct species was less aggressive; hence, at the dawn of human history man may have indeed been a "peaceable savage."

Veblen left Yale with a Ph.D. in philosophy in 1884, but without any prospects of academic employment. He returned home to Minnesota depressed and lethargic, and less inclined than ever to hard farm work. He insisted he was not well; his family suspected laziness. "He read and loafed," wrote a brother, "and then the next day he loafed and read." Actually, the seven years spent on the farm were a period of great reflection for Veblen, who steeped himself in a curious selection of reading materials: political tracts, botanical studies, treatises on anthropology, economics, and sociology, and even Lutheran hymnbooks.

In the meantime Veblen married Ellen Rolfe, the niece of the president of Carleton College and the daughter of one of the leading families in the Middle West. Despite his Ph.D., his wife's connections, and his letters of recommendation, Veblen remained unsuccessful in obtaining an academic post or even employment as a railroad bookkeeper. Meanwhile he and his wife read about the Populist movement that was sweeping through the Middle West and pored over Edward Bellamy's *Looking Backward,* "the turning point of our lives," Ellen later wrote. Stirred by the wave of agrarian unrest, Veblen began to study economics seriously and to consider resuming his graduate studies. At the age of 34, after seven years of premature retirement, he was encouraged by his family to return to school and to make one more attempt to break into the academic world.

In 1891, Veblen entered Cornell University to study economics. There the radical and irreverent misfit somehow impressed J. Laurence Laughlin, a pillar of conservative economic doctrine. Laughlin immediately secured Veblen a fellowship and encouraged him to write theoretical articles for the *Quarterly Journal of Economics.* When the University of Chicago opened the following year and hired Laughlin to head the economics department, he invited Veblen to join him. Thus, in his thirty-fifth year, Veblen finally acquired his first job, at a salary of $520 a year.

Veblen stayed at the University of Chicago for fourteen years, a difficult period for both the school and the scholar. His unorthodox manners and ideas, his uninspired teaching, and his inspired love life led to frequent clashes with university officials. But notwithstanding his bouts with administrative bureaucrats and entrepreneurs—which he later satirized in *The Higher Learning in America*—Veblen was fortunate in having a stimulating intellectual environment peopled by such distinguished scholars as John Dewey in philosophy, William I. Thomas and George Herbert Mead in sociology, Jacques Loeb in psychology, and Franz Boas in anthropology. When *The Theory of the Leisure Class* appeared in 1898, Veblen suddenly became famous and such phrases as "conspicuous consumption" became the topic of conversation as "Veblenism" came to connote wickedly sardonic observations on all that had once been safe and sacred. Veblen's second book, *The Theory of Business Enterprise* (1904), failed to arouse the popular reception enjoyed by his first. Although a skillful dissection of the structural flaws in capitalism, the work pleased neither radicals expecting a recipe for revolution nor conservatives hoping for a refutation of socialism.

Officials at the University of Chicago could take pride in Veblen's scholarly achievements, but his unconcealed private life was another matter. When pressure was exerted on him to conform to academic propriety, Veblen chose to look for another position. In 1906 he went to Stanford University; but his libertine habits confirmed the notorious reputation he had brought with him, and within three years he was asked to resign. Veblen applied for posts at a number of schools and finally was offered a job at the University of Missouri in 1911, owing to the support of Herbert J. Davenport, a former student and an enduring friend and admirer.

Veblen felt isolated in the town of Columbia, where he lived as a recluse among the Rotarians and philistines. Lonely (his wife divorced him in 1911), seemingly dejected, a bitter man writing in Davenport's cellar, Veblen nevertheless had a productive period at Missouri. He finished two of his most important books, *The Instinct of Workmanship and the State of the Industrial Arts* (1914) and *Imperial Germany and the Industrial Revolution* (1915). By 1918 he had published two more books, *An Inquiry into the Nature of Peace* and *The Higher Learning in America,* the latter having been conceived and partially written during his Chicago years. His subsequent books were either collections of previous essays, such as *The Vested Interests and the Common Man* (1919) and *The Place of Science in Modern Civilization* (1919); restatements of previous theses, as in *The Engineers and the Price System* (1921) and *Absentee Ownership* (1923); or posthumous publications like *Essays in Our Changing Order* (1934). He wrote, in all, 11 books and more than 150 articles and essays.

When America entered the war in 1917, Veblen decided to leave Missouri for Washington, D.C., to offer his service to the American cause. His support of the war offended many of his radical admirers; but a few years later, when he moved to New York and wrote favorably on the Bolshevik Revolution in the *Dial,* he once again became something of a celebrity intellectual among liberals, pacifists, and radicals. Yet Veblen's book *The Nature of Peace* and his essays on the Russian Revolution have not worn well. In the former work he underestimated the power of patriotism, and in the latter he completely misperceived the nature of Bolshevism, likening the "soviet" to a New England town meeting. Veblen also referred to a "soviet of engineers" emerging in the industrial West to overthrow the old order, but his skepticism of the technical intelligentsia posing a radical counterforce was too strong for him to entertain the illusion for long. By the time he wrote *Absentee Ownership* in 1923, Veblen was certain that the forces of order in the West had survived both war and revolution.

The single document of Veblen's war writings that has enduring value is *Imperial Germany and the Industrial Revolution.* In this work, which is often cited by social scientists who are coming to grips with the problem of modernization, Veblen explained why Germany was able to overtake England in industrialization, and suggested why Japan would do likewise, vis-à-vis Western nations, in the near future: England, where the industrial revolution began, suffers "the penalty for taking the lead" as its technological equipment deteriorates, while Germany and Japan, unencumbered by democratic institutions, can move rapidly through the stages of industrialization because machine technology can more easily be harnessed to a dynastic state steeped in authoritarian traditions. Because Veblen foresaw the danger of a nation combining technical efficiency with national power, and assimilating a modern economy with a medieval mentality, he supported the Allied nations, to the consternation of the noninterventionist Left, against the threat of German militarism.

Veblen's writings go far toward explaining why England has fallen behind in the twentieth century; other "latecomers" like Germany, Russia, and Japan have become leading industrial powers because their "take-off" began at a later, and therefore higher, technological level. Veblen may have underestimated the real benefits gained by the German working class under the imperial regime; but scholars have remained impressed by his pioneering efforts to explain Germany's history in terms of objective forces rather than the variables of personality, national character, or realpolitik. Indeed, Veblen was the first scholar, in Europe as well as America, to play down the role of Otto von Bismarck and to approach modern German history from what today would be called a "structuralist" point of view, stressing not the dramatic actions of statesmen but the inexorable processes of industrialization.

Although *Imperial Germany* has come to be esteemed as a minor classic, it had little impact during the war years and was, in fact, banned from the mails, possibly because it appeared to a zealous postmaster general as insufficiently pro-British. During the war Veblen worked for the government in Washington. His duties included preparing several memoranda for Col. Edward House's "Inquiry," a study group of intellectuals that President Woodrow Wilson had asked to explore the terms of a possible peace settlement. Walter Lippmann, who headed the committee, requested a report from Veblen advising what steps might be taken in the aftermath of war to prevent the exploitation of underdeveloped countries in Asia and Africa by the victorious powers. However, most of Veblen's reports were lost in the Washington labyrinth.

Toward the end of the war, when Veblen moved to New York, he became a star among the luminaries associated with the *Dial*. In the aftermath of the war, his cynical writings found sympathy among liberal intellectuals disillusioned with Wilsonianism, while his positive response to the Bolshevik Revolution pleased the Marxist Left. But interest in Veblen rapidly declined once the war was over and the intellectual community concerned itself more with cultural matters and less with political causes. For a few years he taught at the New School for Social Research, where he was in the company of such eminent colleagues as Charles Beard, Harold Laski, Wesley Mitchell, and Horace Kallen. But Veblen was also a tired man; and his lectures, at first packed with curious students, turned out to be boring ordeals.

By the mid-1920's, Veblen was nearly seventy; and the years had begun to take their toll.

He felt increasingly lonely in New York. His second wife, whom he married in 1914, had suffered a mental breakdown and had been committed. Yet Veblen still had many admirers, and a number of academic economists signed a petition recommending him for president of the American Economic Association. But Veblen declined, commenting, "They didn't offer it to me when I needed it." He returned to Palo Alto and settled in his small cabin on the outskirts of town, living in almost total isolation yet hungering for companionship and conversation. In the two years before his death (on August 3, 1929), he lived in his shack, where, according to a neighbor, he settled himself on a handmade chair, dressed in Sears Roebuck work clothes, and sat passively, lost in distant thoughts, while a wood rat explored the cabin or a skunk brushed up against his pants.

The British social scientist Graham Wallas once pleaded for someone to write "a 'Secret of Veblen,' summoning up (with an index!)" his mischievous books and possibly his mysterious mind and personality as well. Actually, Veblen himself provided the best clue to his character in a curiously revealing essay written in 1918, "The Intellectual Pre-Eminence of Jews in Modern Europe."

In this essay, which may be regarded as a self-portrait, Veblen expressed great admiration for the Jewish intellectuals and, indeed, envied their alienated status in modern culture. Like such Jewish savants as Spinoza, Marx, Freud, and Einstein (who greatly admired Veblen's writings on Germany and Japan), he hailed science as the benign destroyer of pernicious illusions and the harbinger of modern consciousness. Like the Jews, with whom he identified, Veblen felt himself a marginal man, an eternal outsider with no firm ties to the existing culture or to prevalent institutions, a stranger in the land. But while some Jewish writers might lament this rootless, lonely existence, Veblen saw in it certain advantages. For one thing, estrangement created a questioning frame of mind that kept the Jew in the "vanguard of modern inquiry"; and Veblen was convinced that new knowledge arises from the independent intellectual who is exempt from preconceptions, endowed with a "skeptical animus, *Unbefangenheit,* released from the dead hand of finality."

In a certain sense Veblen's portrait of the Jew resembles Georg Simmel's description of "The Stranger" and Karl Mannheim's treatment of the "free-floating" intelligentsia. All three social scientists believed that the deracinated intellectual enjoyed a privileged "objectivity" because he remained uncommitted to values that would prejudice his perceptions. But Veblen seemed to enjoy his unassimilated status perhaps even more than the Jew, and in spite of the fact that it meant eternal ostracism. "The intellectually gifted Jew," wrote Veblen,

is in a peculiarly fortunate position in respect of this requisite immunity from the inhibitions of intellectual quietism. But he can come in for such immunity only at the cost of losing his secure place in the scheme of conventions into which he has been born, and at the cost, also, of finding no similarly secure place in that scheme of gentile conventions into which he is thrown. For him as for other men in the like case, the skepticism that goes to make him an effectual factor in the increase and diffusion of knowledge among men involves a loss of that peace of mind that is the birthright of the safe and sane pietist. He becomes a disturber of the intellectual peace, but only at the cost of becoming an intellectual wayfaring man, a wanderer in the intellectual no-man's land, seeking another place to rest, farther along the road, somewhere over the horizon. They are neither a complaisant nor a contented lot, these aliens of uneasy feet.

Thorstein Veblen remains an important figure in American intellectual history; and while some of his ideas are relevant to life in advanced in-

dustrial society, others may be quietly forgotten—the fate that awaits all great minds who are at once influential and controversial. Consider his two major contributions to modern social theory: his rejection of the popular assumption that wealth and virtue go hand in hand, and his denial of the constructive role assigned to the capitalist in the march of industrial progress. Had these negations been nothing more than fanciful assaults, one might dismiss Veblen as a utopian daydreamer or a malcontent ideologue. Actually there was some substance to Veblen's attacks on capitalist ideology. His *Theory of Business Enterprise* drew upon the nineteen-volume *Report of the Industrial Commission,* the result of a government investigation into illegal business practices designed to eliminate competition. Charles and Henry Adams' *Chapters on Erie* offered ample evidence that financiers did indeed conspire against the interests of production, a pattern of sabotage against railroad engineering that repeated itself in the building of the great transcontinentals.

No doubt there were some production-minded capitalists who might have agreed with Veblen—James J. Hill and Andrew Carnegie, and later, Henry Ford and Henry Kaiser, proved themselves honest spokesmen for hard work and industrial efficiency. But the Goulds, Fisks, Drews, Morgans, Rockefellers, Vanderbilts, and Stanfords were more interested in the exciting maneuver of huge piles of intangible wealth than in the boring task of turning out useful goods—a point effectively made in Robert Heilbroner's brilliant chapter on Veblen in *The Worldly Philosophers.*

It was Veblen's desire to bring science to the service of industry that attracted his small following around the turn of the century. It is unclear whether Frederick Winslow Taylor, the so-called father of "scientific management," was influenced directly by Veblen; but both shared a disgust for the waste and inefficiency of the industrial system. Around 1901 the phrase "efficiency expert" became increasingly common, and a few groups emerged to echo Veblen's critiques and even to call upon the engineer to prepare to take the place of the businessman. Nothing came of these plans during the war years; but in the 1920's, Howard Scott organized the Technical Alliance, which went unnoticed until the depression, when Scott's name appeared in the news as the leader of what was now called "technocracy." This organization continues to exist in our time, and it claims Veblen as one of its patron saints.

Another group influenced by Veblen's writings were the "institutional economists." Established at the University of Wisconsin in the late nineteenth century, the institutionalists followed Veblen's mode of analysis; but some, such as John Commons and Richard T. Ely, departed from his anarcho-syndicalist suspicion of the state when they looked to government as a positive agency of social reform. Several scholars influenced by both Veblen and the institutionalists—Rexford Guy Tugwell, Thurman Arnold, Jerome Frank, Henry Wallace, and Mordecai Ezekiel—were important in the administration of Franklin D. Roosevelt and saw in the New Deal the possibility of experimenting with the Veblenian idea of production-for-use.

American Marxists have also been influenced by Veblen's writings. Although they tend to overlook his criticisms of dialectical materialism and the doctrine of class struggle, they are impressed by his trenchant analysis of economic orthodoxy and his mordant satire of the capitalist ethic of rugged individualism. In 1905, in the midst of the "golden era" of American socialism, William English Walling informed readers of the *International Socialist Review* that Veblen's analysis of business enterprise was not only more evolutionary, but also more "revolutionary," than that of Karl Marx. Three decades later, during the depression, another generation

of radicals could read the sophisticated *Marxist Quarterly* and find reassurance in Lewis Corey's exhortation: "All that is vital in Thorstein Veblen may fulfill itself in Marxism and socialism."

During this era of the "Old Left," only the German emigrés in America—philosophers and sociologists like Herbert Marcuse, Theodor Adorno, and Max Horkheimer—seemed to be aware of the difficulties of assimilating Veblen into the Hegelian tradition that had shaped Marx's thought. Impressed by the richness of his cultural criticism, they nonetheless lamented Veblen's alleged "positivism," his capitulation to the factual as the normative, and his yearning for the restoration of the wholesomeness of primitive man. After World War II, American Marxist economists such as Douglas Dowd and Paul Sweezy continued the effort to incorporate Veblen, while in Europe radical scholars like Georges Friedmann still appear to be seeking ways to reconcile his ideas with the Left and to regard him as a socialist *malgré lui*. Such efforts at assimilation created more problems than they solved, as this writer has pointed out.

In the field of American literature, Veblen's writings have had some influence. After the turn of the century, the vocabulary and witticisms of *The Theory of the Leisure Class* entered the idiom of social criticism. When William Dean Howells reviewed Veblen's book in 1899, he titled his two-part essay "An Opportunity for American Fiction." Although Howells doubted that an "aristocraticisation of society" can take place in America, he believed that the writer could find a promising subject in the dilemmas of a leisure class whose destiny is problematic in a native culture without monarchical conditions and aristocratic traditions. "It is," Howells observed in reference to what he believed would be the increasing displacement of the leisure class, "the most dramatic social fact of our time, and if some man of creative imagination were to seize upon it, he would find in it the material of that great American novel which after so much travail has not yet seen the light.''

In America, Howells continued, interest in the social culture of the elite is widespread among democratic citizens, for ''our appetite for everything that relates to the life removed from the life of work, from the simple republican ideal, is almost insatiable.'' Any attempt to deal with the life of fashion, luxury, and leisure can be done successfully, Howells advised, only by one who takes it seriously but remains outside its milieu. Veblen offers such a perspective, and it is now time for a novelist to translate into dramatic terms his account of the evolution of a European leisure class in America's democratic society. ''Is not this a phenomenon worthy of the highest fiction?''

One might think that Howells had in mind Henry James; but there is no evidence that James, who was deeply concerned about the fate of social elites, ever read Veblen. It is doubtful that American writers followed Howells' advice, though there are Veblenian (as well as Nietzschean) overtones in the Chicago-based novels of Robert Herrick and Ben Hecht. Indeed, the one important American novelist deeply influenced by Veblen, John Dos Passos, chose to dramatize not the plight of a moneyed aristocracy but an even more telling subject: the conflict between science and business, and the defeat of the industrialist at the hands of the capitalist.

In the 1920's, Dos Passos became interested in the technocrats, and while working on his great trilogy, USA, he compiled a folder of ''Vebleniana.'' After reading several of Veblen's works, Dos Passos became convinced that this eccentric social scientist was ''the only man of genius who put his mind critically to work on American capitalism.'' ''I admire his delicate surgical analysis more and more,'' Dos Passos wrote to Edmund Wilson in 1934. ''I shouldn't wonder if he were the only American economist whose work had any lasting value. His work is a sort of anthropological footnote to Marx.'' Dos Passos never reconsidered his high estimate of Veblen even as he underwent a political conversion to conservatism and capitalism in his later years. Thus in both the radical and pro-socialist *The Big Money* (1936) and in the conservative and pro-free enterprise *Midcentury* (1961), Dos Passos revealed his admiration for the technician and craftsman and his scorn for the men of money and power, the ''saboteurs'' of the economy. As the grandson of a Portuguese immigrant, Dos Passos also identified with the Norwegian immigrant's son, the thinker who asked ''too many questions'' and ''couldn't get his mouth around the essential yes,'' the estranged scholar who

established a new diagram of a
society dominated
by monopoly capital,
etched in irony
the sabotage of production by business
the sabotage of life by blind need
for money profits,
pointed out the alternatives: a warlike society
strangled by the bureaucracies of the monopolies forced by the law of diminishing returns to
grind down more and more the common man
for profits, or a new matter-of-fact commonsense society dominated

by the needs of the men and women who did the work and the incredibly vast possibilities for peace and plenty offered by the progress of technology.

The vogue of Veblen has fluctuated throughout the twentieth century, reflecting, no doubt, the shifting political moods of different generations of intellectuals. Veblen's disdain for gradual, piecemeal reform found little sympathy among the liberals and humanitarians who forged the Progressive movement around the turn of the century. Not until the years immediately before the war did he become a cultural hero. The rebels of Greenwich Village looked to Veblen as an intellectual ally. His theory of the "instinct of workmanship" struck a response in their own value system, conditioned, as it was, by their various Protestant backgrounds; and in turn they could use his anthropology of "tribal customs" to attack the respectability of the starched-collar class represented by their parents' values.

As a critic of the pretensions of class society, Veblen became a valuable resource in intergenerational conflicts. No one was more aware of this than H. L. Mencken. "All over the *Nation,* the *Dial,* the *New Republic,*" complained Mencken, Veblen's "books and pamphlets began to pour from the presses, and the newspapers reported his every wink and whisper, and everybody who was anybody began gabbling about him." Throughout 1918, Veblen virtually "dominated the American scene," moaned Mencken:

All the reviews were full of his ideas. A hundred lesser sages reflected them. Everyone of intellectual pretensions read his books. Veblenism was shining in full brilliance. There were Veblenists, Veblen clubs, Veblen remedies for the sorrows of the world. There were even, in Chicago, Veblen girls—perhaps Gibson girls grown middle-aged and despairing.

Veblen's reputation suffered an eclipse during the 1920's, when the "New Era" economics of Calvin Coolidge promised increasing prosperity for the flappers as well as the financiers. In the following decade Veblen reemerged as the sage who presumably had foretold Wall Street's crash and the world depression. The once-forgotten Veblen "now . . . shines like a star of the first magnitude," wrote John Chamberlain in *Farewell to Reform.* To writers like Chamberlain,

Max Lerner, and Alfred Kazin, Veblen was the anatomist as well as the satirist of the vested interests; and to a young radical student of literature like Harry Levin, who was looking for a non-Marxist perspective, Veblen could be read as the Balzac of sociology.

It was during this period that some of Veblen's uncollected essays were published by admiring students, as was Joseph Dorfman's biography, a monumental study that caused even the jaded Mencken to have second thoughts about Veblen. When Mencken wrote on Veblen in 1919, he claimed that his nemesis had briefly overtaken philosopher John Dewey as the leading intellectual of the generation. In the late 1930's, Malcolm Cowley conducted a survey for the *New Republic* on "Books That Changed Our Minds." Veblen came in way ahead with 16 mentions, followed by Charles Beard (11), John Dewey (10), Sigmund Freud (9), Oswald Spengler and Alfred North Whitehead (7 each), and V. I. Lenin and I. A. Richards (6 each). Yet in the desperate years of the depression, Veblen's social criticism seemed only to negate everything and affirm nothing. Even so admiring a disciple as Dos Passos titled his portrait of Veblen in *The Big Money* "The Bitter Drink."

After World War II, Veblen's reputation suffered another decline, partly due to the spectacular performance of the American economy during the war and the positive reappraisal of American society in the "silent" 1950's. Yet his legacy remained vital to Max Lerner, who regarded Veblen as "America's greatest social scientist," a nearly forgotten cultural critic whose writings presaged not only the collapse of Wall Street but also the rise of Fascism. Veblen's melancholy wisdom also appealed to a number of academic scholars during the postwar years. Intellectual historians like Daniel Aaron, Henry Steele Commager, and Morton White assessed Veblen's thought in the light of

America's liberal tradition, while the economists Robert Heilbroner and Robert Lekachman praised his devastating critiques of neoclassical orthodoxy (now enjoying a revival in the writings of Milton Friedman), and sociologist C. Wright Mills resurrected Veblen as the "comic" thorn in the side of the complacency of the 1950's.

Of all the postwar scholars who participated in the effort to revive Veblen's stature, economist John Kenneth Galbraith deserves special mention. Galbraith found himself personally attracted to Veblen; he too was raised by hardworking immigrants (Scottish Canadians) who derided, not with envy but with "amiable contempt," the haughty manners of the wealthy classes. He also shared Veblen's conviction that the study of economics is as much a matter of literary persuasion as of statistics; hence he too became the rhetorician, coining new phrases like "conventional wisdom" to update what Veblen once described as the "ceremonial adequacy" of orthodox economic ideas. In *The Affluent Society* and *The New Industrial State,* Galbraith continued his Veblenian critique of America's culture of consumption, stressing the priority of socially useful production and calling for the recognition of the "technostructure," a new economic order run by an empirical intelligentsia interested in maximum output and technical virtuosity.

By no means was there unanimity about Veblen in the postwar era. Talcott Parsons, one of the most influential social scientists of that period, maintained that Veblen's social theory was "essentially very simple" and that a "quite adequate comprehension of all Veblen's real contributions could be found in Max Weber's work." Parson's dismissal completely misses Veblen's and Weber's profoundly different attitudes toward religion, capitalism, bourgeois culture, and the work ethic. Parsons, for example, likened Veblen's "instinct of workmanship" to Weber's Protestant idea of "the calling," thereby equating a biological endowment with a religious imperative.

If Veblen could be dismissed for being intellectually derivative, he could also be falsely attacked for being morally devious, the charge made by the conservative Catholic Lev Dobriansky, whose *Veblenism: A New Critique* (1957) indicted the social scientist for his ethical nihilism. For a more balanced treatment, one should consult Morton White's chapter on Veblen in *Social Thought in America* (1949), revealingly titled "The Amoral Moralist." Similarly, Veblen could be attacked for his alleged political naïveté and irresponsibility regarding the nature of power. Thus Daniel Bell, in his introduction to *The Engineers and the Price System* (1952), claimed that Veblen's ultimate aim, like that of all technoauthoritarians from Saint-Simon to James Burnham, was to become the "active political force" of a "new class" capable of overthrowing the existing order. Bell's argument that Veblen "must be ranked on the side of the elitists" should be qualified. It may be true that Veblen's syndicalist dream leaves unresolved the dilemma confronting all technocrats—the autonomy of the producing organizations.

Yet it does not follow that because Veblen's faith in the engineering class contained elitist implications, he must be judged a closet elitist who secretly sought power as a result of the frustrations in his own personal and professional life. Such an interpretation ignores Veblen's own maverick personality, which functioned incompatibly with the demands of any organized movement. Surely a man who sympathized with the Wobblies, scorned academic entrepreneurship, and declined an offer to become president of the American Economic Association was not simply lusting after power. Nor did Veblen's sarcastic disposition give much encouragement to the technicians and engineers, the one class possessing the expertise that would enable it to control the productive operations of society. Indeed, the history of the engineering profession in America, and its subordination to corporate capitalism, suggests that the power of knowledge does not necessarily lead to the knowledge of power.

If Veblen was not an elitist with an urge for social control, what then motivated him? It is revealing that this question was raised in the early 1950's during the period of "consensus" scholarship. In the context of a school of thought that stresses the wholesome stability and continuity of American values, it was natural that some scholars would be inclined to dismiss Veblen as something of an intellectual deviant. The state of his mental health was discussed not only in the *American Quarterly,* the leading journal of American studies; it also became the central question of David Riesman's *Thorstein Veblen: A Critical Interpretation* (1953). Here the Harvard sociologist presented a provocative but impressionistic Freudian analysis of the childhood determinants that supposedly influenced Veblen's antipathy toward class society. Riesman's book helps us better understand Veblen; but it also helps us understand why "consensus" scholars were puzzled by Veblen's hostility to capitalism, and why they were inclined to trace his ideas to individual pathology rather than to social reality.

Although Veblen may have had his share of "neuroses," not all neurotics shared his insights. Veblen was an idiosyncratic personality, to be sure; but in intellectual history, if not in psychohistory, it is the man's work, and not his life, that poses the most compelling questions for social philosophy. And Veblen, more than any other modern social scientist, proved himself an uncanny genius in showing why a culture supposedly devoted to the ethic of work and the value of efficiency actually esteems unearned wealth and wasteful consumption. In so doing, he uncovered two problems that remain with us in contemporary social thought—the cultural hegemony of capitalism and the social stigma of labor.

Selected Bibliography

WORKS OF THORSTEIN VEBLEN

The Theory of the Leisure Class: An Economic Study of Institutions. New York, 1898; Mentor ed: New York, 1953.

The Theory of Business Enterprise. New York, 1904; Augustus Kelley ed: Clifton, N.J., 1964.

The Instinct of Workmanship and the State of the Industrial Arts. New York, 1914; Norton ed: New York, 1964.

Imperial Germany and the Industrial Revolution. New York, 1915; University of Michigan Press ed: Ann Arbor, 1966.

An Inquiry into the Nature of Peace and the Terms of Its Perpetuation. New York, 1917.

The Higher Learning in America: A Memorandum on the Conduct of Universities by Business Men. New York, 1918; Hill & Wang ed: New York, 1957.

The Place of Science in Modern Civilization and Other Essays. New York, 1919; Capricorn ed: New York, 1969. (Capricorn ed. bears the new title, *Veblen on Marx, Race, Science and Economics.*)

The Vested Interests and the Common Man. New York, 1919; Capricorn ed: New York, 1969.

The Engineers and the Price System. New York, 1921; Harcourt ed: New York, 1963.

Absentee Ownership and Business Enterprise in Recent Times. New York, 1923; Beacon ed: Boston, 1967.

Essays in Our Changing Order. New York, 1934; Augustus Kelley ed: Clifton, N.J., 1964.

CRITICAL AND BIOGRAPHICAL STUDIES

Daugert, Stanley. *The Philosophy of Thorstein Veblen.* New York, 1950.

Dobriansky, Lev E. *Veblenism: A New Critique.* Washington, D.C., 1957.

Dorfman, Joseph. *Thorstein Veblen and His America.* New York, 1934; Augustus Kelley ed: Clifton, N.J., 1972.

Dorfman, Joseph. "New Light on Veblen" in *Thorstein Veblen: Essays, Reviews and Reports: Previously Uncollected Writings.* Clifton, N.J., 1973.

Dowd, Douglas. *Thorstein Veblen.* New York, 1964.

Dowd, Douglas, ed. *Thorstein Veblen: A Critical Reappraisal.* Ithaca, N.Y., 1958.

Duffus, R. L. *The Innocents at Cedro: A Memoir of Thorstein Veblen and Some Others.* New York, 1944.

Hobson, John A. *Veblen.* New York, 1937.

Qualey, Carlton C., ed. *Thorstein Veblen.* New York, 1968.

Riesman, David. *Thorstein Veblen: A Critical Interpretation.* New York, 1953.

Rosenberg, Bernard. *The Values of Veblen: A Critical Appraisal.* Washington, D.C., 1956.

Schneider, Louis. *The Freudian Psychology and Veblen's Social Theory.* New York, 1948.

Seckler, David. *Thorstein Veblen and the Institutionalists: A Study in the Social Philosophy of Economics.* Boulder, Colo., 1975.

Teggart, Richard. *Thorstein Veblen: A Chapter in American Economic Thought.* Berkeley, Calif., 1932.

Some of the best writing on Veblen has appeared in the form of articles or introductions to his works. Among the most illuminating commentaries are the following:

Adorno, Theodor. "Veblen's Attack on Culture," *Studies in Philosophy and Social Science* 9, no. 3 (1941), 389–413. This brilliant essay has been reprinted in Adorno's *Prisms.*

Galbraith, John Kenneth. "A New Theory of Thorstein Veblen," *American Heritage* 24 (1973), 32–40. Galbraith's essay also appears as the introduction to the Houghton Mifflin ed. of *The Theory of the Leisure Class* (Boston, 1973).

Lerner, Max. Introduction to *The Portable Veblen.* New York, 1948.

Mills, C. Wright. Introduction to Thorstein Veblen, *The Theory of the Leisure Class.* New York, 1953.

BACKGROUND READING

Aaron, Daniel. *Men of Good Hope: A Story of American Progressives.* New York, 1951.

Brooks, Van Wyck. *The Confident Years: 1885–1915.* New York, 1957.

Commager, Henry Steele. *The American Mind.* New Haven, 1950.

Coser, Lewis. *Masters of Sociological Thought.* New York, 1971.

Diggins, John P. *The Bard of Savagery: Thorstein Veblen and Modern Social Theory.* New York, 1977.

Heilbroner, Robert. *The Worldly Philosophers.* New York, 1961.

Kazin, Alfred. *On Native Grounds: An Interpretation of Modern American Prose Literature.* New York, 1942.

Noble, David. *The Paradox of Progressive Thought.* Minneapolis, Minn., 1958.

White, Morton. *Social Thought in America: The Revolt Against Formalism.* New York, 1949.

—JOHN P. DIGGINS

E. B. White

1899–

E. B. WHITE's life is almost coextensive with the twentieth century, a significant coincidence in view of his role as an interpreter of American experience. Throughout his literary career, White has been a spokesman for freedom of the press and privacy of the individual. Like Mark Twain and H. L. Mencken, he is a smiling moralist, the most endurable kind. The moralism perhaps sprang from the middle-class, turn-of-the-century culture in which he grew up; but the smile was his own. Although his childhood in Mt. Vernon, New York, was so happy that he feared it might disqualify him as a serious writer, it had enough bad moments that it cannot of itself explain the good humor and optimism that later became characteristic of his tone.

The youngest of six children, Elwyn Brooks White was born after his family's early years of financial insecurity; and he was able to enjoy such benefits as regular summer vacations in the Maine woods. He regarded himself as lucky from the day of his birth, July 11, 1899, in Mt. Vernon, N.Y., and with good reason. His parents were well-to-do and loving; his brother Stanley taught him to read and fish; his sister Lillian, concerned about his bashfulness, tried to teach him the one-step. His sister's help came too late to forestall a moment of awkwardness in his mid-teens when he invited a girl to a tea dance in New York City. In the languor of day-

dreaming about the arrangements and the frenzy of making them, he had forgotten that he could not dance. It was this pattern of expectation and disappointment that became the mark of White's self-deprecating anecdotes for the *New Yorker*.

As a child, White was a brooder, responding with all he had to the ordinary troubles of childhood. One reason that he began to write was his loneliness in being the youngest of a large family. He suffered for years from the fear of having to speak in the school assembly, although he was saved by the terminal alphabetic position of his name from having to speak more than once. His self-consciousness later was the subject of several widely anthologized pieces—"The Door" and "Second Tree From the Corner"—and the need to overcome it was perhaps the source and end of his offhand, self-mocking humor.

For a man who regarded himself as lucky, White went through his share of failures. Throughout his high school years he admired girls, but he felt that his accomplishments—playing the piano, writing poems, and riding his bicycle while sitting backward—were not what it took to win them. His only romantic triumph during these years was ice-skating "hundreds of miles" with a girl who said nothing but had strong ankles. Of that event he wrote in the introduction to his *Letters:* "I remember what it was like to be in love before any of love's complexities or realities or disturbances had entered in, to dilute its splendor and challenge its perfection." This vein of idealistic melancholy, which he later remarked was an essential of good clowning, opened up in him early. To Alice Burchfield, whom he courted, lost, won, and finally broke off with, White wrote in April 1922: "I'm a born idealist, Alice, and when I sometimes seem blue it's because the pictures that I paint in my mind are often disappointing when they appear in the bald cold colors of everyday life."

At Cornell University, White belonged to the Manuscript Club, guided by Professor Martin Sampson, who gave the members the following motto: "To be frank, to use one's brains, to write what is in one to write, and never to take oneself too damned seriously or too damned lightly." It was some time before White managed to balance his style or his life between these two poles.

White's misadventures in seeking and holding jobs could not have added to his self-esteem. Although he studied English under Professor William Strunk, whose textbook on writing style White later revised, and was editor in chief of the Cornell *Sun,* he had the usual hard time breaking into the newspaper business after college. He wrote to his friend Luella Adams in December 1921: "I am the person at whom the city editors shy their paper weights and other missiles. I sneak into their office when the desk-boy isn't looking and hand them stories that they don't like."

Apparently the stories were thrown away, swept up from the floor by the janitors: "If it wasn't for me there would be thousands of janitors out of work in New York City." White gave it more of his time than he liked. After failing to establish himself in the aggressive world of New York newspapers, White tried doing publicity work, despite his distaste for it. An editor of his acquaintance was shocked to find such an idealist in a "tainted profession." White wrote to Alice Burchfield: ". . . nice pleasant way to start the day having a person like that inform you that you're tainted. I had a mental picture of Mother sniffing me when I came home at night, the way she does butter to see if it is all right. . . ." At this point in a career that was going nowhere, White made the first of several abrupt and risky changes in the way he was managing his affairs. In his life as well as in his prose, his greatest asset was his ability to imagine the unexpected and then to do it.

Uncomfortable with publicity writing, White set off in March 1922 with Howard Cushman, a college friend, on a car trip west, a journey he described in his essay "Years of Wonder." The American pattern of striking out for the frontier when discontented with the civilization and commercialism of the East is as old as James Fenimore Cooper's Natty Bumppo and as rich in possibilities as the unwritten life of Huckleberry Finn after he lit "out for the Territories." White's Model T was romantically named Hotspur, as if to underscore the young man's intention to live the spontaneous, insouciant life. (Significantly, when he settled for a while in Seattle to write for the *Times,* he sold Hotspur and bought a coupe.)

Traveling on poorly mapped roads that were even more poorly constructed, White and Cushman intended to confront life and to assert their mobility and capacity for change, much as the American entrepreneur of the 1920's was risking investment in business and the stock market.

After the end of World War I, America was itself in a mobile and restless state, of which the continuing rise and spread of the automobile emerged as an appropriate metaphor. Social changes were in the air; and radio was just beginning to obsess Americans, shortening distances between them with its disembodied voices. As space was being challenged by the automobile and the radio, so was the sense of rootedness in old places and old pieties. Moral experiment, economic speculation, and radical changes in the worn-out imperatives of work and family were the order of the day. White found it difficult to be a rebel in America, where there was nothing to rebel against except one's own stupidity in electing incompetent public officers and paying taxes on a standard of living far above the simple needs of life. Still, rebellion was part of the American tradition, as was self-reliance, and White, now in his mid-twenties, embraced them both.

After a short and financially marginal existence working for the Seattle *Times*—a destiny to which he felt "doomed" in view of his inability to do anything else—White was laid off in June 1923. He was sure that the discharge occurred because he was "almost useless" as a reporter, yet he was relieved that he was once again his own man. Instead of using his savings for a trip home, he bought a first-class ticket on a boat bound for Alaska and Siberia, although he had only enough money to travel to Skagway.

He envied the successful businessmen with whom he was traveling, even while he despised them from behind his Menckenesque pose. His descent from first-class passenger to mess boy, when he ran out of money at Skagway, was a shock to the comfortable Babbitts who had taken him for one of their own, and White enjoyed their consternation. He appreciated the metaphoric fitness of his situation: a writer in a floating world of capitalists, in appearance and manner like them, but in fact a card-carrying member of the working poor. He saw that they were bored and that they wanted what he knew he had—the capacity to live at firsthand, to risk exposure to the unfamiliar.

Describing the voyage in his essay "Years of Wonder," he wrote that he was then at that youthful point in life "when he has little to cling to except his unmanageable dream, little to support him except good health, and nowhere to go but all over the place." It was a state of mind he seemed determined to preserve long past the delirious decade that was its initial context and justification.

Through his "exalted footlessness" he observed what went on around him without partici-

pating in it, imitating other writers rather than speaking in his own voice: "My prose style at this time was a stomach-twisting blend of the Bible, Carl Sandburg, H. L. Mencken, Jeffrey Farnol, Christopher Morley, Samuel Pepys, and Franklin Pierce Adams imitating Samuel Pepys." Indeed, his style was as unsettled as his life, for he had not yet discovered "the eloquence of facts" or faced their consequences as a grown man.

After returning to New York in the fall of 1923, White lived first with family, then with friends, while working in the advertising business. By 1926 he had sold some pieces to the recently founded *New Yorker* and was invited by the editor, Harold Ross, to join the staff. White recounted, in the introduction to chapter 3 of his *Letters*, how he sat in Katharine Sergeant Angell's office, ". . . gazing at the classic features of my future wife without, as usual, knowing what I was doing." Before making a commitment to the magazine, White drifted for another year, to Washington, D.C., Ithaca, N.Y., and Europe, and was absorbed in a largely literary love affair with a southern girl who eventually married someone else. Even after he went to work full time for the magazine in 1927, he put in erratic hours, disappearing from the office while other writers worked from morning until night; but wherever he went, he met his deadline, and Ross had no reason to complain.

In 1929 White was busy publishing his first two books, *The Lady Is Cold,* a collection of poems, and *Is Sex Necessary?* (written with James Thurber), marrying Katharine Angell, and again trying to decide whether or not to quit his job. The *New Yorker* did not force him to write against the grain; and White admitted that he was not rebelling against excessive interference with his style or matter. Still, something was wrong. He went to the Canadian woods on an unauthorized vacation and wrote to Ross that good as his life was at the *New Yorker,* it was not complete. He preferred the life at an Ontario camp where he had worked as a young man, and found it a place that did not change, one "door" that did not close and lock on him. The birth of his son Joel, in December 1930, brought him satisfaction enough to put aside for a few years the idea of giving up New York and his job, for he was now engaged in "peopling the earth." He and his wife shared the prosperity of the *New Yorker;* and they survived the Great Depression well enough to purchase a Maine farmhouse in 1934.

Offered the editorship of the *Saturday Review* early in 1936, White preferred to stay clear of offices, commitments, and power and to be an "office boy de-luxe" at the *New Yorker*. He added that he was a "literary defective," reading "so slowly & so infrequently that it causes talk even here in my own family. . . ." The idea that the *Saturday Review*, "casting about for someone who wasn't 'literary,' " had chosen him, gave White obvious pleasure. But he had already become enamored of broody hens, sailboats, and the absence of deadlines; and two years later, he persuaded his wife to leave New York and live the year round in North Brooklin, Maine.

The move was preceded by a nervous crisis that sent White on a vacation from both work and marriage—"sort of a delayed sabbatical." He hoped to write a long autobiographical poem during this year of freedom, in a last resurgence of self-concern, but the poem never got off the ground. (Fragments of it are embedded in "Zoo Revisited," in *Second Tree From the Corner*.) "A person afflicted with poetic longings of one sort or another," he wrote to his wife (May 31, 1937), "searches for a kind of intellectual and spiritual privacy in which to indulge his strange excesses." To do so, one has "to forswear certain easy rituals, such as earning a living and running the world's errands. . . ." and to escape the increasingly artificial atmosphere of the city.

. . . I long to recapture something which everyone loses when he agrees to perform certain creative miracles on specified dates for a particular sum.

I realize, too, that the whole plan [of dropping out] sounds selfish and not much fun for you; but that's the way art goes.

He will probably be irregular about meals, he warns her, for he means to take up "a new allegiance—to a routine of my own spirit rather than to a fixed household & office routine." After a little experience of the free life, White gave up even the restrictions of his nine-to-one writing schedule, remembering that he "had never written anything between nine and one anyway." Instead, he went fishing, made an ax handle, raised vegetables, and talked to the locals, describing himself to Thurber (October 1937) as "the second most inactive writer living, and the third most discouraged." When the year's sabbatical was up, White wrote again to Thurber (January 8, 1938) that he had made a mess of his experiment, his wife's health, and his "own spirit." Despite his complaints White continued to produce the half-comic, half-melancholy essays for *Harper's* that were later collected in *One Man's Meat* (1942).

During World War II, White turned down an offer to cover the events in Europe for the *New Yorker*. "The war is so damn near," he wrote Harold Ross in June 1941, "that it is no longer possible to use printer's ink in place of blood in a man's circulatory system . . ." But White returned to the magazine when the general mobilization left it understaffed. Caught up in the spirit of patriotism and unity, White turned to serious essays on world government, which were collected in *The Wild Flag* (1946).

Another project engaged him during these years: with Malcolm Cowley, Reinhold Niebuhr, Max Lerner, and Archibald MacLeish, White wrote a pamphlet based on Roosevelt's "Four Freedoms" speech. Soon after he arrived in Washington, White was given the job of rewriting the whole pamphlet. But the prospect of writing a book divorced from facts and ordinary human experience disturbed him. He felt that the committee was preoccupied with abstractions and paralyzed with talk, and he had a hard time getting the members to put anything down on paper. He wrote to his wife (February 4, 1942): "I always write a thing first and think about it afterward, . . . because the easiest way to have consecutive thoughts is to start putting them down." White also felt that the best way to find out what President Roosevelt meant by his "Four Freedoms" speech was to ask him—and no one would. After the project was finished, he continued to wonder what it had all been about.

He suffered another spell of restlessness in 1943, perhaps because he was dissatisfied with his role as no more than a publicity agent for America; at the age of forty-four, he had even less respect for advertising than he had had at twenty-five. After the peak of enthusiasm had been reached in the middle of the war, White felt depressed and wrote to Ross that the war was making him "lose my perspective, or grip. Writing any sort of editorial stuff about this universal jam that everyone is in, is for me a gruelling and rather frightening job." He spent his time collecting brown eggs, conducting local air raid drills, and waiting to be drafted.

Despite the gift of a new Underwood typewriter from his wife some months before, White again wrote Ross that he had ". . . not been able to make it spell out a single god damn word." By March 1943, he had to write Frederick Lewis Allen, his editor at *Harper's*, that he could no longer do the "One Man's Meat" column: "The desire is very strong in me to rid myself of any writing commitment. It is not simply that I want a vacation or a rest . . . but rather that I want to change my state of mind, and there is no other way to do it." His doctor, he explained, ". . . is feeding me strychnine, which is what I always thought they fed dogs when they didn't want the dogs." A month later he was in the midst of a "nervous crack-up," and the final installment of "One Man's Meat" was published in the May 1943 issue. White re-

turned to the *New Yorker*, believing he could do the most good for the war effort from his "old editorial perch."

By 1945 the end of the war was suddenly in sight. Instead of gloomy letters on his stuffed sinuses, which he called the "Bronx Concourse of the head," White wrote light complaints to Ross asking that the *New Yorker* stop sending stapled "Newsbreaks" to him, because removal of the staples bloodied the fingers. He was also making light of his own depression, caused by the "mice in the subconscious. . . . The whole key to the neurotic life is simple," he wrote to his brother Stanley in January 1945, "in fact the simplicity of it is the greatest hurdle, because it tends to make it impossible or unacceptable to highly complex natures, who insist on meeting their troubles with suitably devious devices and cures." After a year and a half of falling apart, he reminded himself of the goal he had drawn from Thoreau's *Walden* and his own experience, "simplicity, simplicity, simplicity," and he began to work and sleep again. When the war was over, White and his wife settled into a duplex apartment at Turtle Bay Gardens, on East 48th Street, and resumed steady work at the *New Yorker*.

White had begun his first children's book, *Stuart Little*, in the early 1930's, but he continued to rework it for nine years, and it was finally published in 1945. Discussing it in the context of White's work, Annie Parson wrote with more insight than tact: "It is quite possible to believe that Stuart Little *is* E. B. White. Indeed in real life, Mr. White physically resembles a mouse. He is about five feet six inches tall, with a little pointed face and sharp ears." This analysis, White wrote to Carol and Roger Angell on July 15, 1968, "puts a new light on my passion for cheese." Autobiographical or not, *Stuart Little*, like the later *Charlotte's Web*, contains themes consistent with those of all of White's work.

Both children's books could be called miniaturizations in the manner of *Gulliver's Travels.* Having first postulated something beyond the bounds of reason—that a mouse can be born to a human mother, or that a girl can talk to a pig—White proceeds to treat these absurd situations with delicate realism, as Swift might be said to have treated the Gulliver stories with indelicate realism. The charm in both cases lies in the cleverness with which the writers solve the problems posed by their initial postulates. What kind of life can a talking mouse have in a middle-class Manhattan household in the 1930's? He must, of course, learn to make himself useful and pleasing to those around him, like any member of a family. The socialization of Stuart, not the protection of his individual uniqueness, is the chief concern of his parents. Like the reader, the Littles accept the fantastic given, as they do the realistic details of their lives. Stuart has ice skates made from paper clips. He must offer a tiny foil coin to the trolley conductor, as if he took up a seat just like anyone else. And in *Charlotte's Web,* White employs a realistic style to portray a fantastic, talking spider.

The style of both stories echoes that of "Dick Whittington and His Cat," *Gulliver's Travels,* and the *Life of Samuel Johnson.* The formality of Stuart's speech is that of the Anglo-Saxon young man of history and legend going out into the world to seek his fortune. Stuart's letter to Harriet Ames could have been written by the amorous James Boswell: "Yesterday the keeper of your local store, who has an honest face and an open manner, gave me a most favorable report of your character and appearance." The gentle humor here could not exist without the tradition of formal exposition and diction preserved through Samuel Johnson, Henry Fielding, and Jane Austen. Clearly, White regards himself as part of that tradition, even while he mocks it lightly by incorporating it into the genre of the English "dressed animal tale," as it was developed by Lewis Carroll and Beatrix Potter. Such stories were largely the creation of Victorian

writers and were concerned with teaching children about adult motives and conduct while satisfying their need to people the universe with congenial and surprising figures of fantasy.

Stuart Little is a novel of growing up, as is *Charlotte's Web.* In one case, it is the animal hero who outgrows his home, senses his differentness, and moves on. In the other, it is the girl Fern who grows away from life in the barnyard and toward adulthood. Why, in writing the only extended fiction of his long career, did he choose the form of the children's novel? For one thing, it allowed him to explore the natural world, which had always fascinated him, from the fresh and immediate viewpoint of a child. For another, he was not being held to the serious and self-conscious standards proper to the novelist writing for adults. His novels were written as play, not as art, and for love, not for money, as White always wished he could have been free to do. It is characteristic of him to have couched the tragic themes of lost love, alienation, and ultimate frustration of desire in the comic, lighthearted terms of animal stories, distancing his own pain through the lens of innocent laughter. Perhaps the librarian to whom Katharine White submitted *Stuart Little* was more right than she or the Whites knew, when she distrusted the suitability of the book for children. It is a tale of loss and sorrow, and does not attempt to decorate life with a hope that ignores sadness.

The story begins with an outrageous untruth, under which lies a truth too awful to bear: "When Mrs. Frederick C. Little's second son was born, everybody noticed that he was not much bigger than a mouse." Although his older brother has reservations about the new "child," "his parents preferred to keep him rather than send him away. . . ." The pathos of Stuart's condition is balanced by its humor. White writes crisply and unsentimentally about Stuart's usefulness in finding small, lost objects and unsticking piano keys. On each occasion, however, Stuart must suffer miseries that his family cannot imagine: he is covered with slime in a trip down a drain to retrieve a lost ring and is temporarily deafened after a session inside the piano. His parents are worried about Stuart's identifying himself as a mouse instead of as a human being, and they take steps to draw him into their world long before he is aware of what or who he is. He must, for instance, use a tiny hammer to turn the faucet so he can brush his teeth. In such an episode, White captures the strangeness that he and all sensitive children have felt when obliged to carry out the alien rituals of those who launch us into life—a life defined and maintained independently of the child's needs or wishes.

From his earliest days, Stuart is threatened by tight places: drains, a rolled-up shade, a pounding piano hammer. Relief is offered only by solitary flight. He is entranced by a modest ship on the Central Park pond, and his joy in the adventure of sailing is expressed in terms too large for the occasion: Stuart ". . . loved the feel of the breeze in his face and the cry of the gulls overhead and the heave of the great swell under him." Characteristically, White connects the trivial to the grand without giving the reader time to adjust himself to the discrepancy between subject and language. The technique establishes Stuart's dual role as the animal hero of a picaresque frolic and White's own projection of himself as an unsettled, lonely drifter, mysterious even to his family. After the triumphant sailboat race, when his brother asks him where he was, Stuart answers only, "Oh, knocking around town." His parents have such trouble locating him that he must wear a hunter's cap, an ironic touch in view of the fact that it is Stuart who is hunted by the Littles' vicious house cat. From the start, Stuart seems on the verge of disappearance. The coming of the bird Margalo, halfway through the book, only confirms what Stuart has always sensed: a longing for freedom and a belief that he is different from everyone around him.

Margalo is a mystery, just as Stuart is. No one knows what kind of bird she is, although Stuart's brother tries to assign her a scientific name. She appears when Stuart is very sick, and she herself is almost dead when the family finds her. Together the two regain their health and find that they share a world beyond that of Stuart's family. Their intimacy is sealed by Stuart's rescue of Margalo from the Littles' cat and her rescue of him from a garbage scow, which he has gloomily observed will probably bear him out of this world. After the adventure, Mr. Little, who has never been outside of New York, wants to know what the sea is like..When he hears, he sighs that someday he may get away from his business long enough to find out for himself. His is the sort of life that Stuart, like White, had to reject.

During his search for Margalo, who has disappeared after being threatened by the cat, Stuart goes through the motions of the life that he has been taught. He gets a car, takes a job as a substitute teacher, and even tries to court Harriet, who is as tiny as he. But Harriet has been completely assimilated into human society, and she leaves him lonelier than before. And so, Stuart heads north, alone, without prospects or leads, but sure, somehow, that he is headed in the right direction. As he had instructed the schoolchildren in his charge, the only thing worth doing or even worth talking about is "what's important." For Stuart, this means breaking the rules of the world that has been made for him, because that world does not fit with what he is or what he suspects he might become.

Stuart quickly forgets Harriet. He invites her to go for a paddle and makes elaborate plans, but his one great romantic occasion is ruined by the wreck of his canoe. He does not renew his suit, for he is a young mouse on the move. He is a wayfarer, for whom romance is only an interlude—and not a very happy one at that. What he does well is to explore, defend the weak, and pursue the plenitude of nature. What lures him on is partially expressed by the telephone lineman at the end of the book: " 'Swamps where cedars grow and turtles wait on logs but not for anything in particular; fields bordered by crooked fences broken by years of standing still; orchards so old they have forgotten where the farmhouse is.' '' He and Stuart agree that north is the direction, if, like White himself, one wants to go home to Eden, to the farm.

In *Charlotte's Web,* White gives a classic description of what he saw, or rather experienced, in life on the farm.

The barn was very large. It was very old. It smelled of hay and it smelled of manure. It smelled of the perspiration of tired horses and the wonderful sweet breath of patient cows. It often had a sort of peaceful smell—as though nothing bad could happen ever again in the world.

White describing a barn sounds like Hemingway describing a woman. Their common delight in the repetition of human patterns suggests that the life we have always known does not end. When Fern Arable is more interested in sitting in a ferris wheel with a boy than in talking to Wilbur, her pet pig, we need not be told explicitly that only children talk to animals, and that love makes men and women of us. When Charlotte the spider dies accepting death, as Wilbur must accept it, we are reading a sermon on the continuity of the generations, preached, as Sir Philip Sidney would have it preached, through an engaging fiction. When Mr. Arable wants to sell the pig because it will be expensive to feed, and Fern's desire to mother it prevails, we know that he is being practical, as is his responsibility, and she is being motherly, as is hers.

Charlotte's Web, also, has a hero who is almost too small to survive, who is born, threatened, and saved. Initially Wilbur, the runt of his litter, is saved by the farmer's little girl Fern; ultimately, when Fern has grown up too much to care about him anymore, Wilbur is saved by the motherly spider, who has taken Fern's place in his lonely life. The saving of a pig, as White well knew, was a larger issue than merely preserving the barnyard economy. When Fern saves Wilbur, her father acknowledges that she was "trying to rid the world of injustice." She acts out of childish love and nourishes Wilbur in that spirit. But Fern is only playing at love, pushing Wilbur in a carriage, as he lies beside her doll. In time, when Wilbur is moved to a neighboring farm, she loses interest in him. Wilbur, like Stuart, becomes lonely. He craves freedom and tries to escape the confines of the barnyard, only to return ignominiously for the treasures of the trough. Despite his security, he lacks companionship, and only Charlotte's kindness brightens his life.

As Margalo was of a different species from Stuart, so is Charlotte from Wilbur. He is at first horrified by her sucking of blood, but learns that life is a matter both of construction and destruction, finding and losing. The lesson is confirmed for him at the end when Charlotte saves him, only to die herself after laying her eggs. Wilbur befriends her children, seeing her in them, as White later described, in "Once More to the Lake," seeing himself in his son. The generations continue without a break, although individuals are lost between them.

Perhaps *Charlotte's Web* has less appeal than *Stuart Little* because in the later novel White has two foci: Fern's growth to young womanhood and Wilbur's relationship with the wise old spider. Stuart, on the other hand, with his adventures, suffering, and maturity, is the only focus of the first novel, and his small, restless consciousness dominates the book in a way that neither Fern's nor Wilbur's is strong enough to do. Wilbur is too dependent and Fern is too fickle to unify the later novel as Stuart did the earlier one. If Charlotte had been the "reflector" of the action, as Stuart was, White might have given the second novel more depth and significance.

Although White objected to symbolic interpretations of his work, he acknowledged that in looking for the lost bird Margalo, Stuart Little was looking for what he could not find or even give a name to—the beautiful and the good. To Dorothy Nielson he wrote in April 1946: "I think many readers find the end inconclusive but I have always found life inconclusive, and I guess it shows up in my work." Stuart did not find the bird; and White, resisting the demands of his young readers, did not write a sequel.

It is a curious paradox that White's deliberate and classical effacement of himself from his work has resulted in a distinctly personal voice in his writing. He is more powerfully and unmistakably present in his work than are contemporary confessional poets, who pride themselves on their tragic uniqueness. T. S. Eliot explained this intersection of personal and impersonal in modern literature: "Poetry is not the expression of personality but an escape from personality. But, of course, only those who have personality and emotion know what it means to want to escape from these things."

Brendan Gill has given a sensitive description of White as he knew him later in life:

At seventy-five, White is small and wiry, with an unexpectedly large nose, speckled eyes, and an air of being just about to turn away, not on an errand of any importance but as a means of remaining free to cut and run without the nuisance of prolonged goodbyes . . . what he achieves must cost him a considerable effort and appears to cost him very little. His speaking voice, like his writing voice, is clear, resonant, and wary. He wanders over the pastures of his Maine farm, or, for that matter, along the labyrinthine corridors of *The New Yorker* with the offhand grace of a dancer making up a sequence of steps that the eye follows with delight and that defies any but his own notation. Clues to the bold and delicate nature of those steps are to be discovered in every line he writes, but the man and his work are so closely mingled that try as we will, we cannot tell the dancer from the dance.

What appears to be romantic individualism in White should be viewed against the tradition in American literature to see the individual self as a member of the collective democratic body. In his withdrawal to the Maine farm, White does not break his connection with the American democratic process; he affirms it. He does not set himself up as a misanthrope, rebuking the sins of society in isolation, like Rousseau or Mencken; he joins the farmers, lobster fishermen, and attenders of town meetings as a man no different from them. "The self he sought was not only his, but America's," Sacvan Bercovitch writes, "or rather his *as* America's and America as his." White joked, for instance, that his allergic cough was like the pollinosis of Daniel Webster, which was important enough to influence the Compromise of 1850. He rejected the collective of the socialists for the one he shares with Emerson and Thoreau, convinced, as he explained in his essay "Freedom" (1940), of the "vitally important pact which a man has with himself, to be all things to himself, and to be identified with all things. . . ." He declares that his love of freedom began in childhood, with a sense of "mystical inner life; of God in man; of nature publishing herself through the 'I.' " Freedom for him does not exist independently from the selves of others but rather in voluntary cooperation with them; and the inspiration for that union is the land itself.

White treats the individual as a microcosm of the whole country. He is concerned as much with the moral life of America as with the details of his immediate surroundings. Tocqueville once remarked that Americans are interested in either the grand abstraction or the petty detail. It might be fairer to say that they are concerned with the relationship between the grand and the petty, and are establishing correspondences between them. For White, as for Emerson and Thoreau, the individual is the microcosmic laboratory in which public events can be personally investigated and understood. As Thoreau put it, ''I should not talk so much about myself if there were anybody else whom I knew as well.'' The view that self and America are mystically one entity vindicates the American principle that individualism is the proper basis for a national order, and even, White felt, for a world order. He wrote to Alison Marks (April 20, 1956) that the ''problem is to establish communication with one's self, and, that being done, everyone else is tuned in.'' Indeed, White's style has a quality that Richard Poirier describes as ''the speaker's capacity to relinquish his particular identity and assume an ever more inclusively general one.''

The individual in a democracy, if he intends to stay free, must have discipline from within, a condition also necessary, in White's view, for writing literature. He objected to the free-thinking, innovative ''descriptivists'' in college English departments, and years later he complained about verbal and written expression to Kellogg Smith (February 3, 1961), that ''. . . what is lacking today is discipline. . . .'' It might appear from White's own desire to leave journalism for freelance writing, and his pain at having to order his words on a page, on time, and for money, that he was a careless rhapsodist who wrote only from his heart when the wind stirred his strings. But his success at the *New Yorker* indicates that he was an attentive craftsman who drove himself hard. Passed under Harold Ross's editorial eye, White's work had to withstand the scrutinizing of every phrase for factual and grammatical accuracy, logic, clarity, grace, and wit. Ross was much struck by Mark Twain's attack on Cooper's diction: ''Use the right word, never its second cousin, never omit a necessary detail. Employ a simple and straightforward style.'' According to Brendan Gill, Ross's attention to the details of his writers' prose might ''prompt as many as one hundred and fifty . . . ruminations and challenges'' on a single ''Profile'' piece. Ross armed himself for his

editorial labors with Webster's dictionary in one hand and Fowler's *English Usage* in the other, apparently in the belief that if the Lord had wanted him to read any other book, He would have given him more than two hands. Although Ross himself played the English language only by ear, having had little formal instruction, he evidently possessed the literary equivalent of perfect pitch, and White's style profited from his guidance. Ross did not so much tell him what to write as help him say what he wanted in the most natural way. Whatever was left of the extravagances and posturings of the adolescent prose of White's early letters and ''Journal'' seems to have been pruned by Ross's sharp critiques.

White became impatient with the *New Yorker* policy of boiling every word before it was presumed safe for consumption. He wrote Ross on July 10, 1945: ''I am not as sure of myself as I used to be, and write rather timidly, staring at each word as it comes out, and wondering what is wrong with *it*.'' It was characteristic of him to resist situations that made him self-conscious, a state of mind that he found destructive both of personal happiness and creative effort. When as a college student he was rejected by Alice Burchfield, he wrote to her in April 1922, ''I suppose you wonder why I don't act like a normal person. I wonder too. Instead, I wait on bridges for people and when they don't come, I pack up and go on to Geneva. I hope I may get over it someday.'' The classical style that distances and controls his romantic content was the chief means he chose toward that end. As he sought to retain the initial freshness and power of his personal relationships in the face of time's corrosive effect, White sought in his prose to relay immediate experience in a form that would give it a classical permanence. His concern for permanence in a world of flux also informs his social and political values.

Like Tocqueville, White often pointed out the dangers of mediocrity and apathy to which democracies are especially liable and which can lead them into tyranny if they are not vigilant in guarding their liberty. People who had come to tolerate a car inferior to the original Model T, he feared, might in time come to tolerate a government inferior to the one they began with. In the essay "The Motor Car," White describes his fascination with "the anatomy of decline, by the spectacle of a people passively accepting a degenerating process which is against their own interests." His essay "Farewell, My Lovely!" (1936) links the simple, responsive Model T to nature by means of an organic metaphor: the driver "broods the engine," as a hen would brood her eggs. His car was as personal and living a thing to him as a horse. To break such an organic bond between man and what he uses seems to White a sign of decline, a slipping into mechanical, cold, inhuman manipulation of nature and of other men.

"Farewell, My Lovely!" combines the language of conversation with the language of elegy. The initial sentences establish this improbable conjunction: "I see by the new Sears Roebuck catalogue that it is still possible to buy an axle for a 1909 Model T Ford, but I am not deceived. The great days have faded, the end is in sight." White's continual lament over our fall from some original, half-remembered state of grace is both the theme and the structural principle of the essay. "Everyone remembers springtimes," he writes in the next line, remembering his own springtime as the young owner of a Model T. Two time lines, past and present, run simultaneously through the narrative, converging in the mind of the narrator, who obliges us to live in both by an implicit comparison of the Model T's machinery to our own contemporary state of mind. At the same time, he makes the Ford and our relationship to it a metaphor of a lost America ("the old Ford practically *was* the American scene") and of ourselves, trying to find our place in a world traveling at a frighten-

ing velocity toward an unknown destination. For White, the destination is always unknown, and he must resist aloud the impulse to expect the worst. This reluctance to pin down the future one way or another is in accord with his refusal to write an essay on the metaphysical problem of human identity or security in the midst of unstoppable process. He refuses to talk of significant matters except in terms of insignificant ones.

The creation of the Ford is rhetorically linked with the creation of man: "It was the miracle God had wrought. And it was patently the sort of thing that could happen only once. Mechanically uncanny, it was like nothing that had ever come to the world before." The machine is indistinguishable from its owner and becomes, in White's carefully constructed series of comparisons, an extension of man's spirit into the world: "A Ford was born naked as a baby," "My own generation identifies it with youth," a reflector was bought so "your posterior would glow in another car's brilliance." He does not have to make the linkage between man and machine explicit, nor does he ever do so. As always, his method is to speak of the concrete without reference to the metaphysical. The Model T is itself and no more, unless we choose to make it so. White does not insist on the connection.

The Ford's engine is also a metaphor of the earth's movement through space, its transmission being "half metaphysics, half sheer fiction." White assigns the engineer's adjective "planetary" to the Ford's transmission, meaning it in both the epicyclic or mechanical sense as well as in the sense of "wandering" and "erratic." It is characteristic of White to give both a commonplace, literal meaning to a word and at the same time to imply a moral or metaphysical significance beyond anything he would be willing to state by itself, apart from the concrete instance. After suggesting a link between the car and its owner, for instance, White writes: "It was hard-working, commonplace, heroic. . . .

Its most remarkable quality was its rate of acceleration.'' He does not mean only the Ford but the driver, the twentieth-century man who is himself driven by forces he cannot control except when ''enthroned'' in his Model T. In a new car, White writes, ''Letting in a clutch is a negative, hesitant motion,'' while ''pushing down the Ford pedal was a simple, country motion—an expansive act, which came as natural as kicking an old door to make it budge.'' In this sentence, White forgets Strunk's grammar and reverts to country diction, as he does to a country simile: not ''naturally'' but ''natural.'' In the same spirit, White is not making a point about the machine as an extension of the modern psyche, but demonstrating the union of the ''commonplace and heroic.'' The very ignition of the Ford is made a significant action; typically White dramatizes the central noun, ''abruptness'': ''the car, possessed of only two forward speeds, catapulted directly into high with a series of ugly jerks and was off on its glorious errand. The abruptness of this departure was never equalled in other cars of the period.''

Like the irregularity of its response, another feature of the Ford revealed a relationship to the nature of the men who operated it: the car began its career in an incomplete form. When White says the Model T was ''a vibrant, spirited framework to which could be screwed an almost limitless assortment of decorative and functional hardware,'' he is describing one thing with the intention of describing another, leaving the reader to link a concrete material object to an abstraction. The car, and by extension the men it represents, are for White more curious and beautiful than they are useful. Both defy the laws of physics; the Pegasus attached to the hood does ''something godlike to the owner.''

Ultimately the Model T is not an object owned but a state of mind; to refuel it ''the driver had to unbend, whether he wanted to or not.'' What a man was in his heart could be determined by his attitude toward his Model T. Some men were suspicious enough to buy a rearview mirror; others bought a newfangled foot accelerator. There were those who wanted luxuries like lavender perfume dispensed in their cars; these esthetes, White writes, echoing the scriptures, ''builded along different lines.'' If you wanted your touring car turned into a sedan, Sears Roebuck would do it and ''you went forth renewed.'' As in all accounts of conversion, the landscape of the senses becomes that of the imagination. The soft, collapsible fenders of the Ford ''wilted with the years and permitted the driver to squeeze in and out of tight places.'' The metal took on the malleability of skin and the adaptability of the vulnerable and physically threatened men who owned them.

The Ford machine was no mere distanced object to be used and discarded but an emblem of the universe's mystery, not to be controlled or solved. White joins the mechanical problems of the Ford to the lore and legend of the way ''old women discuss rheumatism.'' He associates the operation of this erratic and mysterious machine with a life of faith, of dependence on the unexpected and random element in human life. Here, as nowhere else, White acknowledges mystery and spontaneity where modern men ordinarily endorse only common sense and rationality. He claims the new Ford models are ''effete'' emblems of a declining civilization. Their owners rely on instruments for success, while White remembers the failed timers on his ''sick Ford'' (a locution that suggests that he is as closely identified with it as he was with his dying pig in another essay), and his need for ''showing off before God'' by setting matters right. Repairing the car, then, was rhetorically transformed into a metaphysical gesture.

White treated the car as an animist does his totem: ''I remember once spitting into a timer; not in anger, but in a spirit of research. You see, the Model T driver moved in the realm of metaphysics. He believed his car could be hexed." For White, a strong and precise connection existed between an inanimate object and the man engaged in manipulating it: "The oil used to recede and leave Number One dry as a clam flat; you had to watch that bearing like a hawk. It was like a weak heart—you could hear it start knocking, and that was when you stopped and let her cool off." No amount of good will or mechanical ingenuity would keep Number One alive. Her survival depended on continual acts of faith, as do the connections between White's sentences, where the unsaid must be imagined. Both created a hunger in the eyes that distinguished the "fixers" from all other men. The "fixers" were White's metaphor for modern artists; they knew the Model T's were "conceived in madness."

The machine was "bound to be a mighty challenging thing to the human imagination." It was the bridge between the self-conscious, introverted dreamer and the world he was obliged to live in. As such, it was celebrated by White, who had no desire to sever his connection with the world as it was, even if that commitment meant he must keep one tentative foot in a New York City changing for the worse. As living products of the imagination, Fords were the poetry of technological man possessed. They went from forward into reverse without any perceptible mechanical hiatus. As with all events that take place more in the imagination than in the physical world, White's affair with the Model T was part of his night life that still remained with him: "The days were golden, the nights were dim and strange. I still recall with trembling those loud, nocturnal crises when you drew up to a signpost and raced the engine so the lights would be bright enough to read destinations by. I have never been really planetary since." The Ford represented that night which White largely set aside in his maturity, seldom allowing it to disturb his lucid Apollonian day. Still, he never ceased to lament the "dim degeneracy of prog-

ress" and to regret the imaginative loss that modern men suffered with the passing of the temperamental Model T. For him, it was a decline from the natural and humane order that he was trying to construct for himself and his family in Maine.

In the story "The Morning of the Day They Did It" (1950) White describes a society so mechanized that shots are required to prevent death from chronically contaminated food; almost all pay is withheld to finance a welfare state. Men in a new military satellite cease to feel any commitment to the earth and destroy it. To abandon personal relationships with natural objects, White seems to be saying, is to take the first step toward dictatorship, which will manipulate men as soullessly as men have manipulated nature. White was saddened by the passage of the farmer's land into the hands of speculators, seeing in the ominous exchange a sign of America's decline into irreverent commercialism. White feared that man's arrogance toward nature, the cause of "declension," would lead to the destruction of both. "Petulance, coupled with insatiable curiosity, and the will to dominate" mark man's attitude toward his own environment. At the 1939 World's Fair, White had been particularly struck by an outsized mechanical man feeling the real girls in his lap. He wrote in "The World of Tomorrow": "the heroic man, bloodless and perfect and enormous, created in his own image, and in his hand (rubber, aseptic) the literal desire, the warm and living breast." The monstrous image represents the modern split between man's analytical powers and his intuition of what is good for him, a condition White made his central literary concern.

White was as disturbed over the erosion of artistic integrity as he was over the decline of man's relationship to nature. Both were linked in his mind to modern commercialism, especially to the prostitution of the mass media to manipulative advertisers. In a letter he had written in

1936 to Alexander Woollcott, White protested Woollcott's selling of his sophisticated image to support Seagram's whiskey. He objected on several grounds. One was the matter of snobbery: Woollcott's choice of this particular brand seemed to infer that the common man, if he wished to be a similarly superior being, should accept on Woollcott's authority the superiority of Seagram's. Another objection was more serious: as a journalist, Woollcott's views on public matters now had to be suspect, for he was being supported by a certain segment of the economy. Almost forty years later, White had had similar doubts about Xerox's sponsorship of an *Esquire* travel article by Harrison Salisbury, believing that such support would ultimately erode the freedom of the press (January 30, 1976), and with it, the basis of American democracy. (The company agreed and promised not to sponsor such articles in the future.)

Television posed a new threat to the free dissemination of opinion, White felt. In a magazine or newspaper, the advertisement and the news column compete for the reader's attention; he has a free choice of which of them he will look at. The television ad, however, "preempts" his attention against his will. A means must be found for supporting television programming from a general advertising fund, so that no program is identified with a particular sponsor, who inevitably would interfere with program content if he could. The economy must be simplified, White believed; advertising and consumerism are lesser priorities than the freedom of the press.

As Edward Sampson points out, White had been a simplifier long before he encountered Thoreau; and *Walden,* which he bought in 1927, confirmed all his own best intuitions and experiences, as well as his intention to find a Walden of his own. The work was both a celebration of Thoreau's transcendental "higher laws," which White had never much regarded, "and a practical enterprise." Rural life was not for White

the beachhead of eternity that it was for Thoreau but, rather, the place where one was obliged to confront the indifference of the higher laws to one's own welfare. In the late 1930's, while Chamberlain, Hitler, and Mussolini were swapping promises and countries like horsetraders at a fair, White had been shingling his barn roof against the elements, taking the "long view," and seeing grand designs—a Patton of the pumpkin patch. In a single sentence of the essay "Clear Days" (1938), White links world leadership to rural life: ". . . the barn is tight, and the peace is preserved." But he knows Chamberlain's ugly peace is as ephemeral as his own truce with the elements. He sits on the barn roof, like Ishmael on the masthead of the *Pequod,* comprehending the anarchic details of events with an artist's instant, ordering glance. Implied in the lone sentinel's preeminence over natural things is the conviction that the individual has a wisdom and honesty not to be found in groups, particularly in groups of leaders, and that the only way "higher laws" can be recognized or upheld is by a man alone upon a barn roof.

White puts a high premium on independence. While appearing to promote an alternative to the American materialist's dream, he in fact confirms the political-economic principles that make it work. In keeping with the sober American pattern of controlled or institutionalized revolution, White affirms the values of individual initiative, responsibility to a set of agreed upon and unquestioned principles, and a faith that if this initiative and responsibility are maintained, a better world will result.

On occasion, White said that yesterday's world was much like today's, in the face of evidence he himself knew better than to ignore. In "Removal" (1938), for instance, he was prophetically aware that television would tempt us to ". . . forget the primary and the near in favor of the secondary and remote." He felt that he stood at the fork of two worlds as they parted direction, "when the solid world becomes make-believe," rejecting the course Poirier believes the greatest American writers have followed: the creation of an imaginative environment out of whole cloth, rather than an imitation of the actual one. The manufactured, artificial world in which White felt Americans were beginning to live had to be corrected by the world of the artist's experience, where the appearance and feel of things were celebrated. Reality was being disintegrated by mechanical processes, broken up into small dots on a cathode-ray tube as it is in comic books or a Lichtenstein painting. The artist's responsibility was not to make his own private world, apart from the real one, but to preserve the link between art and reality. In the passage from "Clear Days" where he sees a likeness between himself and the leaders of the world, he makes a symbolic gesture that justifies their contiguity: he sets up a weather vane, so he will know which way the wind is blowing. As a journalist, he has an obligation to find out, and he thinks the roof of his barn is as good a place as any to start. As always, his action, however brave and positive, has an aspect of futility, underlined by its juxtaposition with the "horsetraders" who think they have achieved world peace.

Writing of young soldiers in the essay "First World War" (1939), White soberly examines the young man he was at the time and reflects that every man who does not keep what he can of his childhood is a fool. His determination to write about the land is part of his conviction that one must keep in touch with the sources of life in order to stay alive; this is of a piece with his belief that one must not despise the young, including one's own youthful self, with their posturing and idealism. And it seems to be for this reason that he wrote endless kind, interested letters to fifth-graders who wanted to know if Stuart Little ever found Margalo and to gloomy young writers in college who doubted their own powers.

For a similar reason, White felt an obligation to put back into the soil the strength he took from it. This obligation was rooted in his belief that he and the land were an inseparable unity and that it was possible to experience the world unmediated by language or calculation. Moments arose, even in the deliberately ordered life of his Maine farm, when events seemed to take place as much in White's imagination as in the physical world; the form in which he chose to write often acknowledges this double reality.

In his essay "Death of a Pig" (1948) he gives a running account of his own spiritual state along with the barnyard event that is his ostensible subject. As in "Farewell, My Lovely!" decline is the central concern of the essay. The same pattern of elevated expectation and trivial conclusion is followed, much as Swiftian satire puts high diction in the service of low subjects. Thus, White is telling two stories: his own sense of confusion and despair at an untidy universe is made into a humble comedy, while the sorry death of a "plugged-up pig" is given the dignity of tragedy.

In the first paragraph of the essay, White suggests his own consternation at the event, preparing the reader for a blurring of lines between sorrow and laughter. The time spent with his sick pig has passed as a dream, and he is no longer in charge of the world he had thought he controlled. He no longer knows on which night of his vigil the pig died and assigns his uncertainty to "personal deterioration." Not only has he failed to raise his pig properly, but he has failed to grasp the outside world in the assertive and omnipotent manner that he had been taught was desirable.

The second paragraph is a foil to the first; uncertainty and "personal deterioration" are followed by the clear, well-defined "scheme" that was to be expected in the management of pigs: they were bought, fed, and slaughtered according to the order established by the seasons. An "original script" exists for the death of pigs, and the tragedy is ". . . enacted on most farms with perfect fidelity to the original script." A ceremonial ending, the eating of smoked bacon and ham, assures a "fitness" in the order of things, both in the pig's proper cycle from birth to death and in the farmer's control over that cycle.

Early in the essay, the neat, abstract pattern established by the pride and omnipotence of the farmer goes awry. As always in White's work, the planned performance collapses when it must be enacted in real life: "Once in a while something slips—one of the actors goes up in his lines and the whole performance stumbles and halts. . . . The classic outline of the tragedy was lost." White, the innocent narrator and participant, was suddenly no longer the creator of his drama but a character suffering in it. He had lost his sense of omnipotent objectivity. No longer a mere producer of hams, he cares only that he is losing the animal that has become an extension of himself.

At this point White switches from his own perspective to that of the pig, as if acknowledging the bonds that this sickness has created between them. He no longer separates his own story from that of the animal. After hearing from a skilled neighboring farmer that he must purge the pig, White delays a bit, unwilling to do the deed that would ". . . officially recognize the collapse of the performance of raising a pig. . . ." The diction makes it unclear whether it is White whose performance has collapsed, or the animal, and for the purposes of the essay the distinction is unimportant. A few lines after he says that he wanted only to raise his pig "full meal after full meal," he remembers that it is time for him to go out to dinner and that he must dose his plugged pig with castor oil, pouring the stuff down its "pink, corrugated throat." The screaming and writhing of the indignant animal is not allowed to dominate the scene; White distances the violence with a typically laconic and almost heartless objectivity: "I had just time to read the label while the neck of the bottle was in his mouth. It said Puretest." No merely sentimental bond between himself and the animal exists here. White understands his role as "friend and physician," while the pig is only a pig: ". . . his wicked eyes, shaded by their coy little lashes, turned on me in disgust and hatred." The humanity and wisdom of animals, which is the source of the comedy in his children's books, never intrudes into the realism of White's essays. If anything, he means to intensify the sorrow and loneliness of both man and animal by presuming no tangible communion between them. The good will is all on the part of the man, who comes out to the barn late at night to feel the pig's ears, "as you might put your hand on the forehead of a child." Only when the pig is asleep can the illusion of solidarity between man and beast be maintained.

White broadens the landscape beyond himself and the animal, setting them both against a backdrop of their common misery:

We had been having an unseasonable spell of weather—hot, close days, with the fog shutting in every night, scaling for a few hours in midday, then creeping back again at dark, drifting in first over the trees on the point, then suddenly blowing across the fields, blotting out the world and taking possession of houses, men, and animals. Everyone kept hoping for a break, but the break failed to come.

The words carry a double burden. "Unseasonable" suggests White's earlier hope that the seasons would be observed with the regularity proper to the life cycle of a pig. More than the weather is "unseasonable" here. The desperate condition of the plugged pig and the anxious man, over whom "a depression had settled," are suggested by the words "close days" and by the fog that drifts back "at dark . . . taking possession of houses, men, and animals." In just this short description of the scene, then, White establishes the themes of irregularity, chance, entrapment, and ultimate loss. Only at the conclusion of the first section does he give a brief, overt statement that makes the conjunction of his life and the pig's explicit: "... the pig's imbalance becomes the man's, vicariously, and life seems insecure, displaced, transitory."

In keeping with White's custom, however, no single mood is allowed to prevail. He begins the second section: "As my own spirits declined, along with the pig's, the spirits of my vile old dachshund rose." The graphlines of life on the farm, here, follow compensating patterns, as they do in *Charlotte's Web*, where the spider dies so that her children may be born. For White, tragedy in the abstract is always mitigated by the comedy of the concrete, as loss of a sweetheart in youth was made bearable by the singing of frogs. The delight of Fred the dachshund at the enema of the wretched, dying pig obliges the reader to contend with two conflicting graphlines, one ascending, one descending. Only in a single sentence does White suggest where they converge: "... Fred will feverishly consume any substance that is associated with trouble —the bitter flavor is to his liking." Yet Fred goes on to preside over the pig's interment, looking down from his eminence above the grave, unsentimental as always, but "possessed of the vital spark" that makes it harder to drag him from the grave than to drag the pig to it.

The intimate incident of the enema has closed the conventional distance between farmer and beast: "The pig's lot and mine were inextricably bound now, as though the rubber tube were the silver cord. From then until the time of his death I held the pig steadily in the bowl of my mind. . . . His suffering soon became the embodiment of all earthly wretchedness." White carefully avoids mentioning his own wretchedness, skipping the personal term to move to mankind in general, relying instead on the specific link between tube and cord in the "bowl" of his mind

to indicate indirectly his own involvement with the fate of the pig.

At precisely the point when this involvement is absolute, he must surrender the care of his animal to a third party. Even his language here becomes deliberately detached: he "phoned the veterinary . . . and placed the case formally in his hands." The dialogue over the telephone is punctuated by the operator's anxious, disembodied interruptions: " 'Have they answered?' " They have, but she is right to be concerned about the connection. Little enough passes between the veterinary and White, and in fact the doctor can do the pig no good. He is late in coming because he has been picnicking with his fiancée, who had exclaimed coyly, " 'Poor piggledy-wiggledy!' " Nobody really cares about White's pig except White; and he knows it. His alienation from those around him and his union with the dying pig are confirmed by the carelessness of the doctor and the conviction that he himself has erysipelas, as he fears the pig does.

The animal's premature death, a violation of the scheme of the farmer in control, has severely shaken the farmer's certainty about his own fate:

I had assumed that there could be nothing much wrong with a pig during the months it was being groomed for murder; my confidence in the essential health and endurance of pigs had been strong and deep, particularly in the health of pigs . . . that were part of my proud scheme. The awakening had been violent and I minded it all the more because I knew that what could be true of my pig could be true also of the rest of my tidy world.

He had thought that his powers of command put him beyond loss and death, but his pig's illness had taught him the extent of his own vulnerability and the depth of his empathy for the animal. When the pig comes out of his pen to die, White mentions that he himself was just going to bed. The pig "had suffered a good deal." And "I went back up to the house and to bed, and cried internally—deep hemorrhagic intears.''

The language he had applied to the pig is now indiscriminately applied to himself. ''Never send to know for whom the grave is dug, I said to myself, it's dug for thee.'' As he watches the digging, he observes that an earthworm (''legendary bedfellow of the dead'') and an apple (''conventional garnish of a pig'') are in the grave. These two emblems, of decay and of nourishment, set the seal on his removal from the animal to the human world; he is himself again, ready to receive the calls of the community, resulting from ''a sorrow in which it feels fully involved,'' and to write his penitential account, explaining ''my deviation from the classic course of so many raised pigs.'' Even here the diction is ambiguous, leaving the reader in doubt as to who, ultimately, is the farmer, who the animal. The only way to tell is by the tale itself, for as White said at the beginning, ''. . . the pig died at last, and I lived, and things might easily have gone the other way round and none left to do the accounting.'' The distance between the pig and himself is, in the end, established by his own capacity for self-knowledge and grief. The pig will be remembered, on the ''flagless memorial days of our own choosing.'' But the pig could not even recall so much as the ''satisfaction of being scratched when in health.'' White parts with his animal as if he were being left alone in the world, having lost through pride and incompetence what it was his duty and his happiness to hold securely. His sorrow for himself is inseparable from his sorrow for the lost animal, and his language does not allow us to decide, at any moment, for which it is he grieves.

As White attempted to break free of personality, he also moved outside time, establishing a chronology drawn from nature, not history. The basic unifying device in his works is the season. Events are related not by cause and effect but by association. ''You remember one thing,'' he remarks in ''Once More to the Lake'' (1941), ''and that suddenly reminds you of another thing.'' The answer to the problem posed by a language that drains the life from experience is the creation of a living tissue of images and paragraphs. No part can be excised from the organic whole without leaving an open wound; no detail is so small that it can be sacrificed.

In translating the opus that is yourself, White explained to a student in 1951, you are to write not an advertisement but an objective, accurate description of what you see; the more faithful your description of what is not yourself, the more fully and honestly that self is ultimately revealed. The writer who uses devices and ornaments in order to impress, White seems to suggest, is probably mislabeling his product and himself, committing an advertising fraud to fool the public. The self-effacing writer, on the other hand, is so perfectly united with the subject that it inspires the language and style appropriate to itself. Language thus becomes a transparent window between the writer and the reader, not a wall plastered with posters.

From his early years, White tried to keep his emotions from interfering with the effect of a total situation upon him. In his preface to *A Subtreasury of American Humor* (1941), he describes the moment at which the emotional writer shaping his art with an eye to high seriousness and complex architecture, is stopped by an ''uninvited snicker (which may closely resemble a sob, at that)'' and becomes, irrevocably a humorist. What he approved in the author and playwright Don Marquis he tried to cultivate in himself, an ability ''to be profound without sounding self-important, or even self-conscious.'' White always kept modesty in mind, hoping to give the impression of spontaneity and effortlessness. He wrote to Cass Canfield, in 1964, that a writer has to get rid of tricks and formulas before he gets good. To James Thurber, who thought he ought to take drawing lessons to improve his cartoons, White said no: "if you ever got good, you'd be mediocre." The essays collected in *One Man's Meat* are apparently tossed off as by-products of everyday experience and seem as casual as if written without a line being blotted; to White, though, writing them had been "like trying to tend the furnace in a dinner jacket."

As his life in Maine was a counterweight to his life in New York, so nature was to be balanced against culture in his writing. Both art and science are dangerous preoccupations because they separate a man from his own experience, making him alienated and self-conscious. If he could not manage art and life at once, White clearly preferred to sacrifice art. Perhaps the reason he found work on the early *New Yorker* so congenial was that, as he later explained in a letter to Dale Kramer (August 25, 1950), for the first ten years at the magazine "fact and fiction lived together in sin." He was assigned to cover both, for the lines between editorial departments had not yet been drawn. In such a situation, he did not need to impose arbitrary meanings on imaginative constructs; the facts provided the meaning, and the "little pieces" that he built on those facts were their own meaning. No symbolic apparatus was presumed or desired. Unencumbered by artificial "meanings," things had a clear and satisfying meaning of their own. "I have had an entirely new feeling about life," White wrote to his wife in 1937, "ever since making an ax handle."

By taking things as they are and offering no interpretation of them, White broke cleanly with the twentieth-century symbolist writers. Unlike them, he was not on the track of pure art but of firsthand experience. He wanted that experience processed as little as possible by language or ideology. As a believer in the "eloquence of facts," he suspected the capacity of literature to imitate it, a paralyzing fear for a writer and one that brought him many unhappy hours at the typewriter. Words made it too easy to forget the thing they described, setting it at a comfortable distance requiring no immediate response. It was, for instance, hard to stay worked up about the war, White remarked in 1941. One heard the words "occupied France" so often that they expressed only a token outrage rather than the real thing. Throughout his writing, especially about farm life, White's method is to revive the original freshness of an experience, stripping it of its accumulated symbolic deadweight and restoring to it the original simplicity and power to move. Writing in "Coon Hunt" (1941) of an event that he was experiencing for the first time, White describes how the "stars leaned close, and some lost their hold and fell."

White's success as a writer of children's books owed much to his own capacity for astonishment at the obvious. He was aware that adults usually compensate with affected innocence for their loss of childlike directness and freshness of response. He describes himself in the essay "Speaking of Counterweights," as being afraid of a fragile little railcar that moved around the top of the Seattle *Times* building. Every experience moves, scares, amazes him, as if he had stumbled suddenly and for the first time into society, like Voltaire's Candide or Jakob Wassermann's Caspar Hauser.

White does not write without structure, any more than he would try to hatch eggs without heat or hen. To enjoy the freedom of creation, one must submit to the laws of the world as it is, otherwise any structure, be it a henhouse or a sentence, will collapse. His style expresses the classicist's concern for structure, discipline, and simplicity, qualities that are exemplified in "Maine Speech":

Country talk is alive and accurate, and contains more pictures and images than city talk. It usually has an unmistakable sincerity which gives it distinction. I think there is less talking merely for the sound which it makes. At any rate, I seldom tire listening to even the most commonplace stuff, directly and sincerely spoken; and I still recall with dread the feeling that occasionally used to come over me at parties in town when the air was crowded with loud intellectual formulations—the feeling that there wasn't a remark in the room that couldn't be brought down with a common pin.

The classic reserve, understatement, and vigor of Maine speech show respect both for the facts and for the audience, characteristics that mark White's own prose.

The purpose of writing, White believes, is "to break through the barriers that separate [the writer] from other minds." One reason that White objected to advertising jargon was for its use of language in order to manipulate and mislead; the genuine writer's purpose, according to *Elements of Style,* "is to engage, not paralyze, the reader's senses." A style of writing is no mere adornment to an idea, but rather, is inseparable from it and from the man: "Style has no . . . separate entity; it is nondetachable, unfilterable. The beginner should approach style warily, realizing that it is himself that he is approaching, no other." White's practice is to eliminate needless connective words and to use punctuation marks instead. In doing so, he allows relationships between things to emerge of themselves, without being forced out by his own linguistic manipulation. Words must not be played with; they have a life of their own, and a careless style can drain the reality out of them.

One reason, perhaps, for White's adherence to the spare, classical style that Strunk had taught him was that it allowed, even forced, him to forget himself and concentrate on what was before him. This concentration took several stylistic forms, all of which mark his most successful writing: the reduction of connective and qualifying words in order to increase the importance of nouns and verbs; sharpened outlines that are achieved by the device of the quick stop and the quick switch, as well as by the precise choice of nouns; the positive attack, which goes straight to the matter at hand rather than attracting attention to the doubts, opinions, and hedgings of the self-conscious writer; thematic parallels that cannot be made to converge as an abstract idea except in the mind of the determined reader.

In a letter (February 1954) to students who doubted the relevance of Latin to their education, White testified to its formative influence on him: "When you know Latin, you know enough to say 'guts' instead of 'intestinal fortitude.' " He associates classical style with condensation and simplicity, and prefers the use of one suggestive word, conveying "toughness and color," to the abstract and discursive explanatory phrase. He loves "the clear, the brief, and the bold."

The use of unnecessary words, and of overwriting in general, is a form of egotism, to which White objects in art, as he does in life. As Strunk had taught: the reader's attention should be drawn to the matter, not to the author. White wanted his audience to look not at him or at some idea that was a projection of himself, but directly at persons, events, and objects. In a letter to E. J. McDonald (January 14, 1948), he warned: "Thirty years of being a writer have convinced me that people are always trying to read something into a man's motives, and are finding hidden meanings that exist only in the eye of the beholder." Referring to *Charlotte's Web,* he wrote John Detmold in February 1953: "Any attempt to find allegorical meanings is bound to end disastrously, for no meanings are in there. I ought to know." Instead of finding a correspondence between what was in his own head and what was outside it, as the symbolist vogue of his day prescribed, White effaced himself and assumed the protective coloration of the natural landscape.

For White, the pruning of such qualifiers as very, pretty (as in "pretty much"), rather, and little, serves several related purposes. First, the writer gives up the nervous habit of questioning his own capacity to relay what he perceives, and lets the reader observe what is being described through a clear glass. And second, such a writer emphasizes verbs and nouns, which can move freely through the uncluttered sentence. A paragraph from the essay "Sootfall and Fallout" (1956) illustrates both the spareness and vividness of White's classical style:

If a candidate were to appear on the scene and come out for the dignity of mud turtles, I suppose people would hesitate to support him, for fear he had lost his reason. But he would have my vote, on the theory that in losing his reason he had kept his head. It is time men allowed their imagination to infect their intellect, time we all rushed headlong into the wilder regions of thought where the earth again revolves around the sun instead of around the Suez, regions where no individual and no group can blithely assume the right to sow the sky with seeds of mischief . . .

Like nudes on a Greek vase, the bare, startling nouns and verbs of this passage capture the reader's undistracted attention. It is a case of the plain being more elegant than the ornate and of omitting connectives for the sake of clarity, simplicity, immediacy, and grace. Adjectives and adverbs, and qualifiers in general, should be used sparingly, White believes, for it is nouns and verbs that are the strength and the beauty of good writing. He chooses his adjectives for their precision ("a frail soprano voice," and "small ungerminated thoughts") just as he selects his nouns.

White uses adverbs more for comic effect than for objective descriptiveness. A choir struggles "tentatively"; one does not sail a thirty-foot boat "expertly" but "courageously." The verb in the following sentence, from "Sabbath Morn" (1939) carries the entire burden of the humor, as well as reminding the reader of the title and theme of the essay: "one of the dogs has sinned under the piano. . . ." A scarcity of adjectives and a plethora of pictorial nouns mark this descriptive passage from the essay: the "seams in the floor have opened wide from the dry heat of the furnace, revealing the accumulation of a century of dust and crumbs and trouble, and giving quite a good view of the cellar." Conjunctions, not often used by White, are here marshaled in force. He uses them to move from the specific to the general, and then, with a crash, to the "view of the cellar."

When he undercuts a sentence, dropping from a rhetorical flight, he often ends on an apologetic, deprecatory troche, as he does with "cellar." More often, he ends his sentences, especially those that conclude paragraphs, with a firm monosyllable, perhaps following Strunk's advice to put the strongest words at the end, rather than burying them in the middle of the sentence. Some ringing, mock-solemn sentences from "Sabbath Morn" illustrate the technique: "I hear the bells, calling me to share God's grace." "This house, this house now held in Sunday's fearful grip, is a hundred and twenty years old. . . . My retriever comes in, from outdoors, full of greeting on a grand scale." The quick stop is intended to give people who are too active for their own good the "sense of something being wrong, when, in point of fact, it may be the beginning of something being right."

In addition to abrupt stops, made more abrupt by the omission of conjunctions to ease the jolt, White uses what Arthur Koestler calls "biosociation": "the perceiving of a situation or idea . . . in two self-consistent but habitually incompatible frames of reference." That is to say, White associates two orders of reality, usually the social and the natural (or personal), in order to reveal their unexpected and usually ludicrous similarities. "Sabbath Morn" offers some particularly happy examples of this juxtaposition.

White sets to work on his writing and turns on the radio to the local Sunday church service: "I sit down, opening the work folder. An organ prelude! The organ makes a curious whine, sentimental, grandiose—half cello, half bagpipes." He and the service are both engaged in beginnings, *are* their beginnings, and so, can be taken as one in intention. Later, hearing the radio voice read Psalm 66, he wonders, "where have I heard this voice before? was it the voice saying good night for Canada Dry, saying hello for Fels Naphtha? if mine eye follows down now to the twelfth verse, can I win a Buick by writing twenty-five words?" His child is on the floor, reading a book about subways, by Grof Conklin, having created a world for himself independent of his father's wireless Sunday: "On the child's face now a look of complete absorption, Grof Conklin triumphs over a terrible God, subways over the kingdom on high." Here White's use of commas instead of the expected conjunctions or periods creates a series of parallel phenomena. Strunk may have advised writers to use parallel constructions for expressions "similar in content," but White often stands the admonition on its head for comic effect.

At the heart of comedy lies the potential for pain. Conventional conjunctions of events are designed to fit logical expectations and to create a pleasing order in the anarchy of experience; the humorist must break up the pattern, risking the shock of unfamiliarity and the reminder of helplessness. If he has no new order of his own, he may leave us "stupefied and incapacitated," as Daniel E. Berlyne says. White takes this risk, for himself and for his reader. To Thurber, his closest collaborator in comedy, he wrote in October 1937:

I, too, know that the individual plight is the thing. . . . You spend your days chuckling . . . but always knowing that much of life is insupportable and that no individual play can have a happy ending. . . . your own inarticulateness only hastens the final heart attack. . . . Today with the radio yammering at you and the movies turning all human emotions into cup custard, the going is tough. Or I find it tough."

Humorists, like clowns, learn to mine the "deep vein of melancholy running through everyone's life. . . ." White writes in the essay "Some Remarks on Humor," and are

perhaps more sensible of it than some others, . . .

. . . there is often a rather fine line between laughing and crying, and if a humorous piece of writing brings a person to the point where his emotional responses are untrustworthy and seem likely to break over into the opposite realm, it is because humor, like poetry, has an extra content. It plays close to the big hot fire which is Truth, and sometimes the reader feels the heat.

At times it is difficult to say whether White wants us to laugh or cry, but perhaps he offers us the only way out of a bad situation: to cry at the general condition and to laugh at the individual one that is all we have to call our own. Louis Rubin may be right to observe that a Puritan grimness remains in American humor, blending despair with "idealist hope."

White advised, in a letter to a serious young writer, "I should not try to learn to write without learning first to be frivolous." What he seems to mean by frivolity is taking oneself lightly and seeing that experience, however terrible, does not make one pompous, self-pitying, or tragic. In the face of events, one must remain eager, naive, and perpetually capable of astonishment. To maintain this attitude, a writer must not think he is being funny. Although *Walden* was the most humorous of books, White writes in "A Slight Sound at Evening," ". . . its humor is almost continuously subsurface and there is nothing deliberately funny anywhere. . . ." Much the same can be said of many of White's pieces; the humor is offhand, or throwaway, as much a surprise to the author as to the reader. White admitted to Thurber, in his letter of June 14, 1951, "I haven't got any idea about humor except that I seldom think of anything funny to write. . . ."

White's refusal to maintain any "idea about humor" is of a piece with his rejection of theory in any form, political, literary, or personal. He relies instead on seeing a situation clearly and without preconceptions or conventions, as a child does, and on using language that conveys his astonishment and pleasure as precisely as possible. It is this shock of using the accurate word where one expects to see a commonplace one, as well as the impact of the concrete and real instead of the easy and familiar abstraction, that makes White funny. As his quick stops and juxtapositions put one "face-to-fact" with the unexpected, Rubin remarks, so do his "irrelevant asides and non-sequiturs," as for instance in the essay "Garter Motif" (1926): "Let a man's leg be never so shapely, sooner or later his garters wear out." When White begins a sentence with a formula, he is sure to end it with a shock, although often such a gentle one that the inattentive reader may miss it altogether. Let a man's leg be never so shapely, for sooner or later White will pull it.

As Rubin suggests, White's deadpan use of bogus authority and of "funny names, ludicrous juxtaposition, abrupt irrelevancy," repetition, and recounting of unnecessary details are particularly telling devices in his takeoffs on society, such as the mock gossip column "Fin de Saison—Palm Beach." The "correspondent" is in the resort town with a "CWA project for diverting the effluvia of the proletariat from Lake Worth," and he observes the social activities of such notables as Sir Horace Elsinore ("a charter member of the Automobile Club of Rangoon"), Serge Aspirin and Madame Aspirinskaya, Lady Herman Schulte ("descended from a band of Seminole Indians on her mother's side"), and

Baron Temple Irksome, who was bitten by a dog at the races. "The dog was sent away for examination but the veterinary reported that there was nothing much the matter with him. The Baron was given the Schick test." The whole piece is little more than a list of names, irrelevant details, stories that begin and end nowhere, the pointless activities of the decadent leisure class, interrupted from time to time by references to labor agitators, the fate of a "lady from the lower middle classes," and the proletariat whose effluvia makes the lake smell. Where Mencken mocked viciously, dissociating himself from a public scene that he found irredeemably vulgar, White, like Thurber, typically shared the condition of the victims. They created not just a scene but the narrative voice of a participant rather than of a judgmental onlooker. The writer's solidarity with the victim in his delusions, pretensions, and anxieties was characteristic of the tone of the *New Yorker* in Thurber's and White's time and was, as Rubin says, "an implicit recognition that only a fine line separates the satirist from his target, the humorist from his subject." Whether White was writing personal anecdotes or impersonal parables, his humor was neither the vulgar farce and slapstick of popular humor, nor the heavy sarcasm of elitists such as Mencken. Rubin calls it a humor turned "gentle, ruminative, even somber on occasion."

A change came over White's humor in the middle of his career, perhaps as part of his recognition that the world he had known was on its way out. Edward Sampson writes that "his humor becomes more and more a means to an end, not an end in itself," and that it supports "serious themes." "Once More to the Lake" (1941) marks this shift in style. The humor of the essay is muted, replaced by meaning, coherence, and unity of tone. "Once More" was for E. B. White what *Immortality Ode* and *Tintern Abbey* were for Wordsworth, a prose poem in celebration of memory, childhood, and a nation's past. The mood set in the very first sentence is partly that of a children's story, partly that of a fable, and rightly so, since in this essay White is defining one of the most compelling myths of America: "One summer, along about 1904, my father rented a camp on a lake in Maine and took us all there for the month of August." It is the "along about" that defines the atmosphere, the "once upon a time" world of father, family, and past. That world is now an interior one, because it no longer exists literally. But in "Once More" the world is not that of make-believe but of genuine myth.

As he returns to the lake with his own son, almost forty years later, White wonders how it will have changed and whether "the tarred road," symbol of progress, will have found it out. He remembers places that to a child had seemed "infinitely remote and primeval" and refers to the lake as "this holy spot." It is the world of childhood, the lake of beginnings. It is also the world of the inner man. White tells us he has been more a man of the ocean than a man of the lakes, but that inclement weather sent him to the placidity of a lake in the woods. The ocean, in myth and dream, is a symbol of the exterior world of action and event; the lake is a symbol of the contemplative mind. The literal story line is reinforced by the reverberation of these symbols; and as we follow the ripples from a rock thrown in water until they disappear against the shore, so we follow the shades of meaning to the understanding that life is not limited to a particular generation, and that there is an enormous satisfaction in seeing our children repeat the pattern that we ourselves repeated a generation before. Our satisfaction is not lessened, but made more acute, by the knowledge of our own inevitable death. This tragedy is made bearable by the knowledge that we and our children participate in a scheme of life that transcends the individual.

White fears the lake will have changed, but it has not, except in relatively unimportant details.

The bass are still there, as are the bathers and the American flags on the docks: "there having been no passage of time, only the illusion of it as in a dropped curtain. . . ." The absence of change is disconcerting. He seems to become his own father and his child becomes him, as the two leave the world of individuation and personality and enter that of myth. When he says "I was my father," he echoes Wordsworth's "The child is father of the man," although he intends a somewhat different meaning. For Wordsworth the child was wiser, in his "natural piety," than the man and passed on to the man the experience of that piety to strengthen him in dark days. For White the child becomes his own father by acting his father's role on the very stage where his father once acted it, thus partially losing his individual identity in the world of archetypes: "Everywhere I went I had trouble making out which was I." Since there is no place in the world of archetypes for individuality, upon entering this timeless world, "personality" is lost and the "self" is in confusion.

At night White and his son go to sleep with the smell of the swamp drifting in through the screened porch. The return is not only to childhood but also to "the infinitely remote and primeval," to prehistoric and subconscious origins of the self. There are, however, disconcerting changes in the landscape that do not allow White to leave the world of history altogether. He walks with his son up to the farm for dinner, but the road is not the same.

The middle track was missing, the one with the marks of the hooves and the splotches of dried, flaky manure. There had always been three tracks to choose from in choosing which track to walk in; now the choice was narrowed down to two. For a moment I missed terribly the middle alternative.

The vanished middle way was the old way of the self-sufficient dairy farm out of the rural past, suggested by the hooves and dried dung. That tradition and the living experience of that tradition defined the native populsim that lay at the mythic base of the Republic. In its absence one must choose either the left or the right. The political implications of such a dilemma are clear enough; the psychological implications are no less important but far less immediately clear. In being precipitated so abruptly out of its manorial and pastoral tradition by the Civil War and the Industrial Revolution, the American has lost contact with his mythic origins, with the Eden that White sought to regain in Maine, at the lake. The road, as well as "the petulant, irritable sound" of the outboard motors, is forgotten in the thunderstorm that concludes the essay, which links the present and the past as the rainbow does for Wordsworth.

In *Tintern Abbey*, Wordsworth forces the returned wanderer to admit that it is he who has changed and not the place. In "Once More," White's returned wanderer is forced by a dramatic epiphany to admit that although the place does not seem to have changed, and he himself seems to be the same, he must expect dissolution in time. That knowledge comes like cold to the groin. The pattern will continue: fathers will take their sons back to the lake, and in so doing will link the generations. But the finality of death is absolute for the individual.

The distinctly modern drama in the essay is that of an individual who participates in a pattern larger than himself, but who in the end cannot give himself up to that pattern. Like Keats, White is tolled back from the nightingale to his "sole self," which must face sickness, age, and death, alone. Although the lake is "holy," its holiness is conferred by man, by American man working, playing, and dreaming. It is a natural and not a supernatural consecration that renders the lake "holy"; the lake has been consecrated by activity, not by contemplation. Death ultimately does not bring White closer to coats, bathing children, and bass but, rather, removes them from him forever. He is driven by his own

self-consciousness and agnosticism out of Eden. As he watches his son pull on a wet bathing suit, he feels the chill of mortality. In a letter written in December 1951, about the essay, White explains to a young reader: "A child, by his very existence, makes a parent feel older, nearer death. . . . At your age this is perhaps hard to understand. It will become clearer to you later on. Meantime, be thankful that a wet bathing suit is just a wet bathing suit."

In the 1950's, White was not so quick to claim that his work had no meaning. Perhaps he no longer needed humor as a means of effacing himself, for self-consciousness was no longer the demon that it had been in his youth. Even in the *Letters,* the change is noticeable; the self-deprecatory humor and the ludicrous situations in which he plays the victim become scarcer, while a philosophical reflectiveness that is more cheerful than comic becomes increasingly evident.

A new seriousness had become noticeable as early as "The Door" (1939), White's most anthologized piece. A story about a man alienated by modern industrial technology, "The Door" is for the twentieth century what Charles Dickens' *Hard Times* was for the nineteenth. Instead of being infuriated by the steam-driven mills and the brutalized workers of the early industrial revolution, the author strikes out at the smooth, plasticized life of a modern city completely cut off from anything natural that would take man out of himself. The style of the story is cryptic. White, as is his custom, does not give the reader a code breaker, but the message and matter are clear.

As the story opens, a man wanders through an environment that is kept purposely vague. He is in a city and does not feel well. The names of things disturb him because they suggest a reality with which he is familiar, yet a reality that has passed away. "The names were tex and frequently koid . . . and the thing that you touched (the surface, washable, crease-resistent) was rubber, only it wasn't quite rubber and you didn't quite touch it. . . .'' The hero of ''The Door'' is seeking a way not only out of the artificial environment constructed by modern technology but a way into meaning for his life.

The rats in a maze provide the controlling metaphor; White drew the language of the rat maze from a *Life* article on the behavior of frustrated laboratory animals. They were trained to jump at cards to get food, but the professor changed the rules. Jumping at the correct card no longer produced the food, and the rats became first confused, then apathetic. The hero of ''The Door'' reacts the same way, having been ''trained'' by a different professor. First the man was taught to jump at the door which attracted him by prayers and psalms, and ''long sweet words with the holy sound.'' Then one day he jumps, and the door does not give way. Different doors are substituted. One door, displaying a picture of an amoeba reproducing itself, is obviously the door of science; another has a check for $32.50 on it, representing economic life. Both fail to provide a meaning that is worth jumping for. But the door with a picture of a girl was the hardest to give up on:

The time they changed that door on me, my nose bled for a hundred hours—how do you like that, Madam? Or would you prefer to show me further through this so strange house . . . although my heart has followed all my days something I cannot name, I am tired of the jumping and I do not know which way to go. . . .

He is a prime candidate for what *Life* magazine, in an article on lobotomy, called the operation that could correct ''the disease of civilization.'' It is the solution White feared modern man would adopt, whether by surgery or by some more subtle surrender to social pressure. The story ends with the man leaving the house and the exhibit. He has escaped, for the time being.

But the implication is that society is building an artificial house—and White will not live in it.

The style of the essay reinforces the content. The sentences are made jumpy and chaotic by the use of parentheses. ''Everything (he kept saying) is something it isn't.'' Dashes are used to similar effect. The resulting texture suggests a constant swinging between widely varied mental processes. Such instability, for White, is the mark of the modern mind at work in a Crystal Palace of confusion. The character in the story is no more mad than White himself, and his perceptions are only slightly more complex than is common for the narrative voice that is heard in all White's prose.

White's poetry is decidedly simple and has little of the deliberate mystery that gives such pieces as ''The Door'' their resonance. Morris Bishop, in his introduction to *One Man's Meat*, credits White for making poetry accessible to those who find themselves ''rebuffed by the hermeneutics of our time'' and for creating a ''new mid-form between Light Verse and Heavy Verse.'' The poems are slight, as one would expect of a writer who was essentially a journalist. As White was no ordinary journalist, however, his verse is also clever and lucid, sometimes taking literary forms seriously, sometimes mocking them and the culture that had already largely abandoned them. The titles in *The Fox of Peapack* speak well enough of White's acquaintance with English poetry. He had read *Lyric Forms From France* by the time he was twenty-three and had made those forms his own, as in ''Rondel for a September Day'' and ''Ballade of Meaty Inversions.'' Although he modestly claims not to have been a reader, he was obviously familiar with classics of his own literary tradition. ''Poet-or the Growth of a Lit'ry Figure'' is obviously a takeoff on Wordsworth's *Prelude: Or, Growth of a Poet's Mind,* which was first made available to modern readers in Ernest de Sélincourt's edition (1926). In the early

1930's there was considerable talk about the poem in academic circles, and White's familiarity with Wordsworth certainly suggested a more than ordinary acquaintance with serious literary affairs.

If certain titles suggest White's knowledge of European forms, many others are purely American in content: "H. L. Mencken Meets a Poet in the West Side Y.M.C.A.," "A Connecticut Lad," "Spain in Fifty-Ninth Street." White's literary consciousness was trained in the Anglo-American tradition. He feared that the tradition and the society upon which it was based were passing away in his own time. Essentially an alien in the twentieth century, White's poems comment humorously and caustically on manners that he regarded as foreign and on events he deplored. At all times, however, his poetry is formal and his consciousness controlled.

"The Fox of Peapack," the title poem of the volume, is subtitled "A Ballad of Somerset County." The title, meter, and rhyme scheme make it clear that White's manner of proceeding is suggested by the medieval ballads. The poem is in twenty stanzas of four tetrametric lines rhyming *abab*, with an extra syllable in the second line of each stanza. The medieval ballads often rhymed *abab*, and tetrameter was the preferred meter. In using it in "Fox," White matches the form of the poem to its mock-medieval content. The falling meter of the second and fourth lines is exploited for humor, a trick he may well have learned from Byron.

> He then went home, athwart with life,
>   To wash and do a little fixin',
> "I'm back from town," he told his wife.
>   "I see you are," replied the vixen.
>
> They ate a bit of sobel stew
>   And read a page or so from Genesis,
> They carried out a threat or two
>   And certain harmless little menaces.

To derive humor from outrageous rhymes is certainly Byronic, and much of the humor in White's poems comes from a similar manipulation. The actions and dialogues in the poem contain much to suggest the tradition of the English "dressed animal" tale and the Anglo-Saxon animal folk tale. The fox concludes that people neither smell nor act in an acceptable manner, and he and his wife set out for the hills, a conclusion that recalls White's own removal. White uses the traditional ballad form and folk content to reinforce his theme: the failure in modern life to retain the humanity and naturalness of an earlier age.

White could, however, be entirely original in form. He wrote a series of poems as book reviews. The conception alone is original; the execution is equally so. In his review of John Dewey's *Individualism, Old and New*, he wrote:

> Our grandsires bred, in pushing back frontiers,
> The individual. They were contented—
>   (One can relax, with an ax).
> Today, with Nature cowed, we engineers
> Should utilize the things we have invented.
>   We don't, says Mr. Dewey, do we?

He also reviewed the *Shaw-Terry Letters:*

> Wrote G.B.S. to Ellen Terry:
> "I am an intelligent person, very."
>
> Wrote Ellen T. to G.B.S.:
> "You certainly are, I must confess."

"H. L. Mencken Meets a Poet in the West Side Y.M.C.A." is arranged as a conversation between the poet, Mencken, and a bishop. It is clear that White, while preferring to rebound off traditionally accepted poetic forms, took pleasure in creating his own forms for particular, and especially for satiric, purposes.

The organization of *The Fox of Peapack* reveals much about the pattern of White's perceptions. The poems are collected in five sections:

"Ballads and Songs of an Eventful Nature," "Songs Having to Do With Greater New York," "Songs of Childbirth, Paternity, and Routine Domestic Disturbance," "Book Reviews," and "Love Songs. Also Two or Three Poems of a Cosmic Character." One senses that the light, whimsical touch throughout the book would with one more turn of the screw become serious and profound insight. In "Complicated Thoughts About a Small Son" he wrote:

> And that, to give you breath and blood
>   Was trick beyond my simple scope,
> Is everything I know of good
>   And everything I see of hope.
>
> And since, to write in blood and breath
>   Was fairer than my fairest dream,
> The manuscript I leave for death
>   Is you, whose life supplied its theme.

These lines are both a confession—that he did not believe himself capable of writing in "blood and breath"—and a testimony—to his commitment to elemental life (whether or not he was capable of writing about it passionately or profoundly). If White is ever serious, it is in writing about his wife and child, although he is certainly not always serious when he writes about them. He could joke, even about pregnancy, but the joking in "An Expectant Father Compares His Wife to a Rabbit" is prompted by love:

> The doe rabbit,
> Acting on impulse,
> Pulls the soft fur out of her belly
> And delivers her young into it,
> So they won't be cold suddenly.
>
> My wife,
> I am pleased to say,
> Acting more reasonably,
> Buys ten yards of McCutcheon's best nainsook
> To receive warmly the baby
> We so anxiously await.

Both the emotion and the humor are centered on "the baby/ We so anxiously await," and the domestic event is seen as an event in nature, also. In "Apostrophe to a Pram Rider" he addresses his young son Joel, in tetrametric couplets:

> Some day when I'm out of sight
> Travel far but travel light!
> Stalk the turtle on the log,
> Watch the heron spear the frog,
> Find the things you only find
> When you leave your bag behind;
> Raise the sail your old man furled,
> Hang your hat upon the world!

What White takes to be the world is clearly not the world of society but rather Thoreau's world of nature-out-the-back-door. White's nature is not quite Thoreau's, however, because it is always at one remove from home, wife, and children. If there is any society in the world of White's poetry, it is the society of the family. Yet nature *is* here more than anywhere else: as an Anglo-Saxon ideal and myth, which for many others was not a myth but a reality. Wife and children to love and care for and to love him back; the great world of nature just beyond the back door. It is that world that has a life of its own and not one that is simply mirrored in literature. In deeding the world of nature to his son, he gives what he himself values most.

White wrote in the age of the socialist ideologue, whose radicalism had been vindicated by the Great Depression and the apparent collapse of American capitalism. The rebels of the 1920's, Ernest Hemingway, e. e. cummings, Edmund Wilson, and Malcolm Cowley, had broken with their own class; those of the 1930's, as Alfred Kazin remarked, came from nowhere. They were immigrants without a stake in the American past, who had little reason to support American institutions. They no longer battled for a reform of art alone but were dedicated to a reform of society, drawing on other than American traditions to achieve their goals. James T. Farrell, Clifford Odets, and Kazin did what William Saroyan said he wanted to do: "escape from meaninglessness, unimportance . . . poverty . . . and all manner of other unattractive, natural, and inevitable things."

By and large, the writers of the 1930's took one of two directions. The socialists and communists submerged themselves in the historical process, while men such as White submerged themselves in the natural process, the old America of family and Emersonian idealism. In both cases, the movement was away from romantic assertions of independent power and identity. Both groups had a contempt for the merely literary and affirmed the need for firsthand experience. In April 1942, White wrote to Harry Lyford of small-town life: "I am a decentralist, at heart; I think the business of making the earth produce and bear fruit should be participated in by almost everybody. . . ." The artist of the 1930's in general lost himself in a subjective pursuit of his art or in a social cause; either he left society or he united himself with some kind of community. White, on the other hand, did both. By withdrawing to a private, rural life, he believed that he became a more representative American by being more thoroughly himself.

Even before the Great Depression, the *New Yorker* had caught the tone that was to characterize American humor after the Crash and to mark American fiction in the years after World War II. Its writers took the world lightly, making fun of the pretensions to permanence in social attitudes and structures, of the attempts of ideologues to impose their monolithic truths and institutions on others, and of the belief that men can discern a pattern and purpose behind the chaos of events. White and James Thurber, more than any of the other writers for the magazine, established its characteristic subject matter, rejecting large and heavy issues for the small and commonplace. They specialized in reporting the indignities suffered by the ordinary man, making private events carry an implicit social comment. With his "little pieces," in which the narrator survives the collapse of his illusions, White added what Marc Connelly called the "steel and the music to the magazine." Humor had traditionally allowed the writer a detachment from the constraints of the real world and, as Rubin points out, a flight into "dream, fantasy, and non-sense." White's humor, on the other hand, comes out of a total engagement with the real world instead of a flight from it.

White's tone is that of a man who takes on faith as little as possible and who has a temperamental preference for letting facts speak for themselves, not for his own mental state or some metaphysical truth. No given structure of ideas establishes priority and order among the parts of a poem or story; they are instead yoked in improbable juxtaposition, obliging the reader to stand like a conjunction between them. "Next thing that's going to happen is my birthday, then the total eclipse of the sun," White wrote to Beulah Hagen (June 1, 1963). Between the two terms, one prosaic and one apocalyptic, the reader learns to live along with White. His prose invites participation in the life it describes. Remove from White's reticent style his taste, good will, and decency, and it becomes that of the current cosmopolitan cynic—coarse, debunking, and manipulative, bearing the mark of what sociologist Pitirim Sorokin called "late sensate" culture, a phenomenon that White himself condemned.

White's stylistic revolution depended on the sense that a secure social and ideological structure existed in America. The disorder of his absurdities rebounds off the order of these given structures, against which the absurdities can be measured and appreciated. Both poles are necessary for full effect. Establishing relationships between opposites implies equal respect for both terms of the equation. When White's *New Yorker* style is revised by contemporary artists of the cool, it suffers in its humanity from the omission of accepted values. White's light touch assumes that some things are funny and some are not. The only sort of humorist he would consider worth laughing at is one who understands how to be melancholy on the appropriate occasion.

In the third decade of the twentieth century, the antiromantic neohumanists saw science as the great threat to civilization. They rejected the vestiges of romantic sentimentality, yet retained traditional moral values. If White belongs to any school, it is to this one. Religion, art, and ideas all were suspect, which is perhaps what kept this artist of the common and the small from creating any sustained work in which the subject is worthy of the style. Even so human and reflective a writer as White cannot omit absolute values from his work without making it seem to be all surface and no substance. The limitation is perhaps not White's but a weakness of the culture and century he so faithfully reflects.

Was it being a journalist, paid by the word, that made White prefer shingling his barn roof to writing? His *Letters* and children's books, written for love, not money, show signs of the life he might have given to the language had he found a tale worthy of the telling. White himself felt that a goal he could not name had always eluded him, that he remained an unfinished man. It may be that this was his choice, for as he once wrote, ''An unhatched egg is to me the greatest challenge of life.''

Selected Bibliography

WORKS OF E. B. WHITE

The Lady Is Cold. New York: Harper and Bros., 1929.
Is Sex Necessary? Or Why You Feel the Way You Do, with James Thurber. New York: Harper and Bros., 1929.
Every Day Is Saturday. New York: Harper and Bros., 1934.
Farewell to Model T. New York: Putnam, 1936. Published under the pseudonym Lee Strout White.
The Fox of Peapack and Other Poems. New York: Harper and Bros., 1938.
Quo Vadimus? Or the Case for the Bicycle. New York: Harper and Bros., 1939.
A Subtreasury of American Humor, with Katharine S. White. New York: Coward-McCann, 1941.
One Man's Meat. New York: Harper and Bros., 1942.
Stuart Little. New York: Harper and Row, 1945.
The Wild Flag. Boston: Houghton Mifflin, 1946.
Here Is New York. New York: Harper and Bros., 1949.
Charlotte's Web. New York: Harper and Bros., 1952.
The Second Tree From the Corner. New York: Harper and Bros., 1954.
Elements of Style, with William Strunk, Jr. New York: Macmillan, 1959.
The Points of My Compass. New York: Harper and Row, 1962.
E. B. White Reader, edited by William W. Watt and Robert W. Bradford. New York: Harper and Row, 1966.
Trumpet of the Swan. New York: Harper and Row, 1970.
Letters, ed. Dorothy L. Guth. New York: Harper and Row, 1976.
Essays of E. B. White. New York: Harper and Row, 1977.

UNCOLLECTED WORKS

''Where Do the New Eras Go?'' *Magazine of Business,* 54:505 (November 1928).
''What Should Children Tell Parents?'' *Harper's Magazine,* 160:120–22 (December 1929).
''Urgency of an Agency,'' *New Republic,* 66:180–81 (April 1, 1931).
''A Blessed Event—I,'' *New Yorker,* 11:32–34 (January 25, 1936).
''A Blessed Event—II,'' *New Yorker,* 11:31–35 (February 1, 1936).
''You Can't Resettle Me,'' *Saturday Evening Post,* 209:8 (October 10, 1936).
''How the Automobile Got into Bermuda,'' *New Yorker,* 14:22–23 (April 2, 1938).

"Huntsman, I'm in a Quarry!" *Country Life,* 77:45 (April 1940).

"Preaching Humorist" (with Katharine S. White), *Saturday Review of Literature,* 24:16 (October 18, 1941).

"I Accept with Pleasure," *New Yorker,* 19:16 (March 1943).

"Home Song," *New Yorker,* 19:30 (February 5, 1944).

"Breakfast on Quaker Hill," *New Yorker,* 20:27 (October 28, 1944).

"A Reporter at Large: The Eve of St. Francis," *New Yorker* 21:44 (May 5, 1945).

"A Reporter at Large: Beautiful Upon a Hill," *New Yorker,* 21:42 (May 12, 1945).

"Love Among the Foreign Offices," *New Yorker,* 22:24 (February 1, 1947).

"Noontime of an Advertising Man," *New Yorker,* 25:25–26 (June 25, 1949).

"Visitors to the Pond," *New Yorker,* 29:28–31 (May 23, 1953).

"A Stratagem for Retirement," *Holiday,* 19:84–87 (March 1956).

"Seven Steps to Heaven," *New Yorker,* 33:32–37 (September 7, 1957).

"Fred on Space," *New Yorker,* 33:46–47 (November 6, 1957).

"Khrushchev and I," *New Yorker,* 35:39–41 (September 26, 1959).

"Department of Amplification," *New Yorker,* 37:42 (August 5, 1961).

"Was Lifted by Ears as Boy, No Harm Done," *New Yorker,* 40:38 (May 9, 1964).

"Annals of Bird Watching: Mr. Forbush's Friends," *New Yorker,* 42:42–66 (February 26, 1966).

"Following Our Instincts," *Writer,* 79:22–23 (July 1966).

"The Deserted Nation," *New Yorker,* 42:53 (October 8, 1966).

"The Browning-off of Pelham Manor," *New Yorker,* 46:49 (November 14, 1970).

"Letter From the East," *New Yorker,* 47:35–37 (March 27, 1971).

"Letter From the East," *New Yorker,* 47:27–29 (July 24, 1971).

"Faith of a Writer: Remarks," *Publisher's Weekly,* 200:29 (December 2, 1971).

"Letter From the East," *New Yorker,* 51:36–40 (February 24, 1975).

SECONDARY SOURCES

Allen, Frederick L. *Only Yesterday.* New York: Blue Ribbon Books, 1931.

————. *Since Yesterday.* New York: Harper and Bros., 1939.

Beck, Warren. "E. B. White," *College English,* 7:367–73 (April 1946).

Bishop, Morris. Introduction to *One Man's Meat.* New York: Harper and Bros., 1950.

Fuller, J. W. "Prose Style in the Essays of E. B. White." University of Washington, 1959. Unpublished dissertation.

Gill, Brendan. *Here at the New Yorker.* New York: Random House. 1975.

Hall, Donald. "E. B. White on the Exercycle." *National Review,* 29:671–72 (June 10, 1977).

Hasley, Louis. "The Talk of the Town and the Country: E. B. White," *Connecticut Review,* 5:37–45 (October 1971).

Kramer, Dale. *Ross and the New Yorker.* Garden City: Doubleday and Co., 1951.

Krutch, Joseph Wood. "Profession of a New Yorker." *Saturday Review,* 37:15–16 (January 30, 1954).

Maloney, Russell. "Tilley the Toiler." *Saturday Review of Literature,* 30:7 (August 30, 1947).

Poirier, Richard. *A World Elsewhere: The Place of Style in American Literature.* New York: Oxford University Press, 1966.

Rubin, Louis D., ed. *Comic Imagination in American Literature.* New Brunswick, N.J.: Rutgers University Press, 1973.

Sampson, Edward C. *E. B. White.* Twayne Publishers: Boston, 1974.

Steinhoff, William R. " 'The Door,' 'The Professor,' 'My Friend the Poet (Deceased),' " *College English,* 23:229–32 (December 1961).

Thurber, James. "E.B.W." *Saturday Review,* 18:8–9 (October 15, 1938).

————. *The Years With Ross.* Boston: Little, Brown, and Co., 1959.

"Typewriter Man." *Newsweek,* 55:72 (February 22, 1960).

"Updike Lauds National Medalist E. B. White." *Wilson Library Bulletin,* 46:489 (February 1972).

–BARBARA J. ROGERS

John Greenleaf Whittier

1807–1892

NEAR the end of his life, John Greenleaf Whittier characterized his work by remarking: "I am not one of the master singers and don't pose as one. By the grace of God I am only what I am and don't wish to pass for more." Most readers and critics would agree with the first statement, for measured against such great nineteenth-century American poets as Edgar Allan Poe, Walt Whitman, or Emily Dickinson, Whittier is clearly a minor figure. Perhaps he and the other schoolroom poets have been justly criticized for their sentimentality, pietism, diffuse rhetoric—even their popular appeal now seems a devaluation of artistic worth. Whittier's own biographers often have answered the question of what he was by emphasizing his role as an abolitionist, a practical politician, or a religious humanist. They have taken Whittier at his word when he insisted that he was first of all a man, not a versemaker. But poet he was, and so he must be judged. In a casual critical aside, his official biographer Samuel T. Pickard noted that Whittier's verse was written first of all for the neighbors, a remark that illuminates the essence of Whittier's achievement. His poems preserve what was most particularly his and his neighbors': *his* Quaker heritage, *his* Haverhill boyhood, *his* Merrimack scenery, *his* love of local superstitions and legend, and *his* interest in colonial times. And in certain of these poems he can pass as a very fine poet indeed.

The farmhouse near Haverhill, Massachusetts, in which Whittier was born in 1807 was typical of the thousands of similar homesteads scattered throughout rural New England. Solidly constructed of hand-hewn logs, it was nearly 120 years old. The farm was set in a valley almost surrounded by hills, with the nearest neighbor a half-mile distant. This isolation made the Whittiers dependent on one another for companionship, entertainment, and even education. Strong links with the past also united the family, which had come to New England in 1638 and since then had been continuously associated with the Merrimack River valley of northeastern Massachusetts. Over the years the region's spirit of personal independence, belief in rigorous work, closeness to nature, and confidence in the natural rights of man had become Whittier characteristics.

Whittier's Quaker background was intimately connected with this New England heritage. His parents were devout Quakers who held daily worship at home and who attended First Day meetings in Amesbury, regardless of weather or the discomfort of the nine-mile trip. Whittier also read and literally made a part of his being the Quaker books in his father's small library.

The writings of William Penn and Richard Baxter schooled Whittier in the necessity of individual striving for personal perfection; the failure of outward rules and formalized creeds; the love, not the wrath, of Christ; and the humanitarian practice of social equality and individual rights. These basic ideas directly influenced his life by causing his enlistment in the abolitionist cause and by occasioning some of his finest religious lyrics.

Whittier's farm experiences also formed the man. The property was never free from debt, and only the strictest economy and husbandry kept it a going concern. Under such conditions Whittier's youth was hardly an idyllic one. The man-size tasks of planting, harvesting, and milking overtaxed his physical strength and permanently impaired his health. Unfit for heavy farm labor and temperamentally unsuited to the life of a farmer, he complained in his earliest verses (untitled and undated):

> And must I always swing the flail
> And help to fill the milking pail?
> I wish to go away to school;
> I do not wish to be a fool.

Whittier was attracted to the beauty hidden beneath the austerity of his family's life and the plain landscape around him. Although he responded to the old legends, the rural landscape, and the simple Quaker life, his realization of its inherent poetic value did not come until he was introduced, at the age of fourteen, to the poetry of Robert Burns. When a visiting schoolmaster read some of Burns's poetry to Whittier, the effect was instantaneous and lasting. In Burns he found one of his own: a farm boy like himself who had ruined his health on a farm, and who hated intolerance and hypocrisy. Burns's poetry appealed to ordinary people, and he wrote of their thoughts and feelings. The themes of his poems reflected Burns's dislike of harsh Calvinistic church rule, disdain for ostentation, love of nature, belief in the innate dignity of man, and hope for social equality. Primarily this introduction to Burns initiated Whittier's rhyme-making and dreams of literary fame. In his early works, praise for William Penn and early Quaker martyrs was mingled with admiration for Lord Byron and the Marquis de Lafayette; and romantic glimpses of distant lands were contrasted with nationalistic boasting about New England's Nahant beach.

By 1826 Whittier had written manuscripts of nearly thirty poems. His sister Mary launched the hesitant author by appropriating ''The Exile's Daparture'' and sending it in June to the Newburyport *Free Press*. The editor of the *Press* was William Lloyd Garrison, who was just starting his turbulent career as a humanitarian and reformer. He printed the piece and asked for more. In fact, Garrison was so impressed with the verses that he rode out to the Haverhill farm and pleaded with Whittier's parents to encourage the boy's ability by allowing him further education. As the year went on, Whittier's poems also were published in the Haverhill *Gazette;* and the persuasive urgings of its editor influenced Whittier's father to allow his son to attend the newly opened Haverhill Academy.

Undoubtedly the next two years in Haverhill broadened Whittier's intellectual range, allowing him to measure his poetic ambitions against the established masters of English literature. Having been publicly praised as a ''genius of a high order'' in a prospectus for his poems, Whittier must have envisioned poetic fame within his grasp. He earned his tuition by shoemaking and schoolteaching, frugally calculating his first-term expenses to within twenty-five cents. A collected edition of his poems did not materialize, however; and this failure, coupled with romantic disappointments and economic necessities, drove Whittier into posturing and gloom. From personal experience he viewed schoolteaching as a nightmare, and without further education the professions were closed to him. Consequently he turned to newspaper work, obtaining his first position as editor of the *American Manufacturer* in Boston from January to July 1829. The editorship was a complete education in itself, for Whittier served as his own proofreader, book reviewer, news analyst, poetry writer, and office boy. During his seven-month apprenticeship he brought this relatively obscure journal admiration for its lead articles and selection of news.

After a brief period as editor of the *Essex Gazette* in Haverhill, Whittier assumed editorship of the influential *New England Weekly Review* at Hartford in July 1830. He later recalled the eighteen months there as one of the happiest periods of his young life. Living at a congenial boardinghouse with attractive and admiring young female boarders, Whittier was entertained by their social gossip and flirtations, and his position as editor of the *Review* brought him into intimate contact with the leading men of the city. He entered fully into the literary circle that centered around Lydia Sigourney and included Willis Gaylord Clark and Frederick Barnard (later president of Columbia College).

During his editorship Whittier published more than fifty poems and much fiction; had his first book, *Legends of New England,* published (1831); wrote most of "Moll Pitcher" (1832); carried on a feud with a rival newspaper editor; vigorously backed the protective tariff system of Henry Clay; and, between bouts of illness, traveled to New York and New Haven. Still, his vacillating and impulsive emotional nature led him to make declarations like the following in a letter to Louisa Cavolne Tuthill (April 16, 1831):

Disappointment in a thousand ways has gone over my heart and left it dust. Yet I still look forward with high anticipation. I have placed the goal of my ambition high—but with the blessing of God, it shall be reached. The world has at last breathed into my bosom a portion of its own bitterness and I now feel as if I could wrestle manfully in the strife of men. If my life is spared, the world shall know me in a loftier capacity than *as a writer of rhymes*.

After resigning from the *Review* because of ill health, Whittier stayed at the Haverhill farm during the winter of 1831–32. There he daydreamed of publishing a novel to reconcile the North and South, projected a history of the Society of Friends, and planned a sketchbook dealing with local superstitions. However, the excitement and reality of an Essex County political race soon dispelled these airy literary dreams. Prose articles and political letters became Whittier's literary staples, and he plunged headlong into the maelstrom of a congressional race that pitted Caleb Cushing against two rivals. Whittier's letters to various Essex County politicians demonstrated his quick grasp of the political situation and his shrewd manipulation of events and people to mold public opinion. Unable to obtain majority support, Cushing withdrew, and for a time in the summer of 1832 Whittier was considered a possible candidate. Since he was underage (he would not be twenty-five until December), Whittier tried to foster a stalemate and prolong the contest until he could accept a nomination. For once, personal ambition dominated his Quaker conscience. The stratagem failed, however, and a substitute candidate was elected.

With the defeat of his political hopes, Whittier reached the bleak end of a journey that had begun so auspiciously when he left Haverhill Academy in 1828. Editorial positions had brought new friendships but no financial security; his poverty and Quaker background rendered him ineligible for the marriages he wanted; his poetry had achieved an ephemeral journalistic fame but not the national reputation he had envisioned. Now, burdened with ill health, he undertook the management of a large farm and the support of his family. The winter months of 1832–33 must have been depressing ones for Whittier, once again faced with the question of what to do with his life. The answer, which galvanized his entire being for the next twenty years, came in the spring of 1833: enlistment in the abolitionist cause.

By early 1833 Whittier had written more than 280 poems, a number equal to his entire output in the next thirty years. He disparaged his early verses as "wretched first appearances" and fought bitterly to have them excluded from his collected works. Still, they afford a valuable glimpse into the development of the young writer. Many of these poems teach moral lessons by paraphrasing familiar psalms or dramatizing crucial moments from Scripture. Others reflect his religious background, dealing with the customs, traditions, and martyrs of the Quaker faith. But in the main, the English Romantics and their American counterparts furnished the themes and literary models for Whittier.

The lure of the exotic and the mysterious captured his young imagination and, like thousands of Americans, Whittier responded to the excitement aroused by Sir Walter Scott's stirring tales. Scores of his poems imitated Scott's historical approach with its emphasis on battles, romantic interludes, thrilling rescues, and virtuous heroes. Although Whittier imitated Scott, Lord Byron, the symbol of the Romantic ego and the adventurous spirit, became his literary idol. He criticized Byron's immoral life and feared his "licentious" poetry, but was fascinated by Byron's investigation of the passions and psychological handling of sin and rebellion. For more than ten years Whittier's prose and poetry mirrored aspects of the Byronic hero's cynicism and disillusionment.

Since these pieces drew on sentiments quite foreign to Whittier's Quaker simplicity and common sense, their posturing and attempted sophistication rendered them artificial and unconvincing. Such poems show how impressionable and uncertain his taste was. The lack of revision, careless use of language, and uneven versification and rhyme of these early poems continued to plague his mature work; and the themes of lost love, melancholy, and poetic fame indicate how far Whittier had come from the homespun songs of Burns and the Quaker belief that art must be practical and moral. One of the main tensions in his literary career is here placed in focus: the lure of beauty in its own sphere and a moralistic view of literature that relegates beauty to a secondary position.

In the main, Whittier's writing up to 1833, when he entered the abolitionist movement, reveals three formative influences: his religious training, which led him to consider literature from an ethical viewpoint; his isolated rural background and Burns's poetry, which influenced him to seek poetic material within his own environment and experience; and the Romantic verse of Scott and Byron, which taught him the value of affections while the sentimental traits of their American imitators fashioned his literary style.

The catalyst needed to transform Whittier's melancholy and chastened ambitions came with Garrison's emotional appeal in March 1833: "This then, is a time for the philanthropist—any friend of his country, to put forth his energies, in order to let the oppressed go free and to sustain the republic. Whittier enlist!—Your talents, zeal, influence—all are needed." Garrison's plea quickened Whittier's latent reform interests, strengthened his still uncertain temperament, and touched the core of his Quaker humanitarian beliefs. For the next twenty years the events of his life were written on the pages of American reform history along with those of John Quincy Adams, John Parker Hale, and Charles Sumner.

During the few months following Garrison's letter, Whittier studied all the available publications on colonization and slavery, then printed in

June, at his own expense, *Justice and Expediency*. The pamphlet's relentlessly phrased logic and blunt style exposed the failure of the American Colonization Society and argued not only that immediate emancipation would be a safe, peaceable remedy, but also that the resulting free labor would be more productive than slave labor. Its publication had a profound and lasting effect on Whittier's life. It severely limited his hopes of political preferment, sharply curtailed the number of journals that would publish his verse, and earned him a notoriety second only to that of Garrison and a few other abolitionists. For distributing this pamphlet in Washington, Dr. Reuben Crandall, an abolitionist sympathizer, was arrested and imprisoned for eight months.

In December 1833, Whittier attended the first meeting of the American Anti-Slavery Society and helped to draft its declaration of sentiments that sounded the death knell for slavery. He soon recognized that political skill and editorial experience would be effective weapons in molding public opinion. He organized antislavery societies throughout Essex County, often served as secretary for local groups, attended conventions, reported on meetings, and even served in the Massachusetts legislature (1834–35). His correspondence broadened to include such nationally known figures as Henry Clay and John Quincy Adams, all the leading abolitionists, and numerous local politicians. Nothing was too insignificant for Whittier to handle as he traveled to the small towns of Massachusetts and New Hampshire, canvassing voters and contacting abolitionist leaders.

Whittier often was caught in mob action. In September 1835, while traveling with George Thompson, the eloquent and fiery British abolitionist, he was assaulted with rocks and debris by a Concord, New Hampshire, mob trying to tar and feather Thompson. Both escaped under the cover of darkness, with only minor injuries. Weeks later Whittier witnessed the near lynching of Garrison in Boston and, while attending an antislavery meeting in neighboring Newburyport, he was pelted with stones and rotten eggs. Even Whittier's editorships were affected. In 1838 he became editor of the *Pennsylvania Freeman* and helped shape it into one of the leading antislavery papers in the North. His actual editorship began with the sacking and burning of Pennsylvania Hall, Philadelphia, in May 1838. Erected by the abolitionists as a temple for free speech, the $40,000 building was destroyed by a proslavery mob a few days after its dedication. To save personal papers that were in the hall, Whittier adopted a disguise, mingled with the crowd, and entered the building. Outside, he could hear the shout "Hang Whittier!"

Whittier's maneuvering with Congressman Caleb Cushing is a classic example of political skill. Cushing's election in 1834 hinged on Whittier's antislavery support, and Whittier never let him abandon his pledge to support the abolition of slavery in the District of Columbia and to honor abolitionist petitions. When Cushing tried to repudiate his promise, Whittier so effectively controlled the votes in the district that Cushing was forced to write an open letter indicating his continued support of abolitionist aims. Whittier prodded Cushing and other congressmen to defend the constitutional rights of petition and to fight against the gag rules. The strategy of submitting abolitionist petitions reaped enormous dividends, for former president John Quincy Adams took up the fight in Congress against the gag rules. The struggle over the "gag" broadened the abolition appeal; instead of being viewed as a few fanatics trying to free the slaves, abolitionists now represented the majority of Americans in their attempts to secure freedom of press and of speech. Popular national support was further secured by the formation of the Liberty party in 1840 and its merger into the powerful Free-Soil party, which formed the nucleus for the Republican party by the mid-1850's.

Whittier's turn to open political action caused

an irreconcilable and bitter break with Garrison; but it also led to editorships of the *Middlesex Standard* (the Liberty party organ in Lowell) and of the *National Era* in Washington. Throughout the 1840's Whittier remained the poet laureate of the Liberty party, and he ringingly expressed his indignation at the annexation of Texas and the Mexican War. His outstanding political feat was, however, his drafting of Charles Sumner as candidate for the United States Senate in 1850. Sumner's election diminished Whittier's active participation in the abolitionist cause; but he was not immune to the violent passions swirling about him and repeatedly expressed his indignation over the North's compromises in stirring political verse that belied his Quaker hope for peace. From Daniel Webster's "Seventh of March" (1850) speech for conciliation came Whittier's denunciation of the betrayal, "Ichabod" (1850); the bloody fighting in Kansas occasioned "The Kansas Emigrants" (1854), "Le marais du cygne" (1858), and "Letter . . ." (1854); and the arrest of fugitive slaves and his hatred for church hypocrisy brought forth "Moloch in State Street" (1857) and "Official Piety" (1853). When war became inevitable, Whittier sadly perceived the bitter end of his reform efforts and wondered if perhaps disunion were not better than a civil war. Yet, when war came, he defended President Abraham Lincoln's position.

By the mid-1850's Whittier gradually turned to writing home legends and ballads. The twenty years of political activism had taken their toll, and he sought mental rest, saying, "I have crowded into a few years what should have been given to many." His experiences had far-reaching personal effects and important literary consequences. The vilification and mob abuse, the ostracism from literary life, and the bitter break with Garrison had toughened Whittier's mild Quaker soul and had given him hard-won knowledge of human nature. His dedicated absorption in a moral cause had refined the dross of earlier posturing, and the swirl of practical politics and unscrupulous ambition about him had intensified his regard for eternal standards and the consolation of the Inner Light. The abolitionist movement drew Whittier away from a love of poetry by itself to a universal awareness of man's spiritual significance, his need for love and respect, and his hunger for freedom. Expressing the writer's innermost belief in the power of the human will to overcome evil and his emotional response to slavery as a symbol of all oppression—physical, economic, or spiritual—Whittier's poems aroused an immediate popular response by substituting emotional feeling for the logic and dryness of political appeal.

Whittier recognized the shortcomings of his abolitionist poems, saying that they were all "written with no expectation that they would survive the occasions which called them forth: they were protests, alarm signals, trumpet calls to action, words wrung from the writer's heart, forged at white heat." A typical verse from "The Slave-Ships" illustrates his poetic difficulty in transforming his emotional and moral indignation at the barbarism of slavery into poetry. An early stanza reads:

> Hark! from the ship's dark bosom,
>   The very sounds of hell!
> The ringing clank of iron,
>   The maniac's short, sharp yell!
> The hoarse, low curse, throat-stifled;
>   The starving infant's moan,
> The horror of a breaking heart
>   Poured through a mother's groan.

This brief survey of the slaves imprisoned on the ship maintains them as abstractions without any real characterization, and consequently they are not perceived as human beings. Types, not individuals, are presented: a maniac, a starving child, a heartbroken mother. The threadbare, unimaginative phrasing fails to provide the concrete dramatization necessary to endow the idea with an emotional life. The imagery, rife with cliché and hampered by the rhetorical pattern, forces the emotion into bathos. Whittier editorializes, telling the reader that the scene is a "hell" and filled with "horror"; but there has been no tangible development of these emotions. Basically the appeal remains on a crude level of propaganda: the issue is starkly presented in terms of good and evil, and stereotyped images elicit desired emotional responses.

Whittier's most successful abolitionist poems depended on these propaganda elements and utilized all the available media for disseminating their message. They were printed in Northern newspapers, circulated in broadsides throughout the country, declaimed by orators and schoolchildren, set to music, and even presented as memorials to the state legislatures. Because of their topical interest, broad emotional appeal, and moral intensity, they affected thousands of readers who were rarely touched by sermons or newspaper editorials.

"Our Countrymen in Chains!" typifies Whittier's standard approach and in turn reveals another underlying conflict in his nature, the tension between the Quaker pacifist and the radical abolitionist. Originally printed in the *Liberator* in 1834, this poem was reissued as an antislavery broadside during the next six years. The top half of the broadside contained a cut of a kneeling black man who raised his manacled hands while crying, "Am I not a man and a Brother?" Below was Whittier's poem, consisting of a long series of rhetorical questions contrasting America and Europe that climaxed in the demand for the destruction of slavery. The poem opens with an incredulous tone, as Whittier contrasts the sordid reality of slave-dominated America with the bright dreams of the revolution. Stock phrases seek conventional emotional responses as the familiar "falling lash, the fetter's clank" lead into a depiction of the black mother whipped and driven from her child.

In the long central section of the poem, Whittier exhorts his audience, in the name of liberty, to "break the chain . . . And smite to earth Oppression's rod." Although his condemnation of war and plea to rise for freedom "not in strife" qualify this call to action, his hopes for peace sound hollow; and within the context of the poem they remain unconvincing. His emotional and moral outrage and the controlling images of bloodshed and war force the conclusion that slavery must be abolished immediately.

A similar theme guides "Massachusetts to Virginia" (1843), but here propaganda becomes art. The carefully controlled structure balances defiance with reconciliation. The opening five stanzas categorize the Northern man and briefly survey his individual occupations, while the next nine stanzas plead with Virginia to recollect its revolutionary heritage of freedom. The concluding ten stanzas return to the imagery and tone of the opening. Here Whittier's presentation of Northern power expands from individuals to a panoramic survey of the united strength of all Massachusetts communities—an overwhelming Northern "blast" to Virginia.

While the poem offers some hope for a peaceful solution, its heaviest stress falls on the North's determination to resist any renewed assaults on its basic freedoms. The opening lines exemplify this contrast as a warlike defiance breathes through the surface posture of peace and reconciliation.

The blast from Freedom's Northern hills,
    upon its Southern way,
Bears greeting to Virginia from Massachusetts
    Bay:
No word of haughty challenging, nor battle
    bugle's peal,
Nor steady tread of marching files, nor
    clang of horsemen's steel.
No trains of deep-mouthed cannon along
    our highways go;
Around our silent arsenals untrodden lies
    the snow;

Whittier's greeting, a "blast" of icy Northern resolution, is hardly a message of peace; and the following images all stress challenge, battle, soldiers, steel, and guns. The very term "blast" connotes destruction and annihilation, while its later associations with nature's storms and God's just anger imply both a physical and a moral sanction for the North's attitude. Although Whittier asserts the North's unwillingness to employ such force, the bleak picture of the "deep-mouthed cannon" and the silent arsenals in the snow emphasize the industrial might of the North and its military potential.

The next three stanzas develop these ideas by a definition of Northern manhood and a survey of its occupations. Significantly, the first images are of a worker's "brown, hard hand" and of a lumberman's swinging his axe against mountain oaks, an association of manhood with primitive natural forces. The "brown, hard hand" aptly conveys the strength of Northern free labor while suggesting the darker brown hand of the Southern slave, whose forced labor supported the South and whose potential freedom terrified. Coupled with this looms the image of the man with the axe, demolishing giant oaks. Countinuing his portrayal, Whittier emphasizes the Northern man's daily struggle with the natural forces around him—the wind, ice, fog, cold, storm; they toughen his character, develop an inner self-reliance, and foster an independent attitude that "laugh[s] to scorn the slaver's threat against their rocky home." The underlying pattern of images in these five introductory stanzas presents a defiant posture of natural strength that can well destroy any Southern opposition.

The ending stanzas repeat this martial pattern; and the final image in the poem, that of a fire-damp ready to be exploded by a Northern torch, underscores exactly what this poem urged and ultimately obtained: it ignited and coalesced a divided North into a vigorous force that would defy, and finally destroy, slavery. Perhaps some of these effects were unconscious, but the pattern of images and the emotional movement of the poem lead to this conclusion. The incongruous mixture of poet, abolitionist, and Quaker produced poetry as well as powerful propaganda.

In Whittier's most successful abolitionist poems an openly religious tone and sense of moral indignation help purge their topical and journalistic nature. At times extensive biblical allusions and a prophetic manner fuse with structure and imagery to develop wider spiritual dimensions. The assaults on the basic principles of free speech, free press, and free assembly occurring throughout the pre-Civil War period inspired Whittier's utterances as Israel's crises had moved its ancient prophets. Repeatedly Whittier describes his abolitionist poems as a "voice and vision" passing before his soul. In the classical manner of Amos or Isaiah, he interprets the North-South slavery conflict in terms of Israel's apostasy from God's law, uttering his vision of God's coming judgment and doom. As he surveys North (Israel) and South (Judah), Whittier curses them both and specifies the advent of God's wrathful anger on His chosen people. In the traditional prophetic manner he extends the hope that a response to the word of God might avert destruction. Such future salvation, reserved for a small "remnant," will come only after a "long night silence" and a purging holocaust. On the ruins of the old will arise a new Jerusalem, heralding an era of paradisiacal glory.

"Ichabod," Whittier's one antislavery poem that claims poetic immortality, fits into this biblical prophetic category. The work was occasioned by Whittier's grief, surprise, and prescience of evil when he read of Daniel Webster's speech in support of the Fugitive Slave Law. As a terse, tightly knit phillipic the poem perfectly blends biblical allusions, light-dark imagery, and a modulated elegiac tone to mourn the loss of freedom's defender. Its very title, which signifies "inglorious one," becomes the controlling image for the poem, the loss of the inner spiritual light that is contrasted with a fall into the dark world of sin and pride. The biblical allusions that open and close the poem link Webster's fall with defamation of the sacred ark by the high priest Eli and Noah's terrible, drunken betrayal of God's will. These two allusions suggest the vast, eternal moral dimensions of Webster's act, while Whittier and the nation perform the rites of burial for a living corpse, a formal ceremony that transcends personal rancor or vilification. Only a new high priest can restore the glory to Israel and America.

Whittier's poetic maturity came late—in his fifties and sixties—and only after his main reform efforts were completed. His ill-paid, physically exhausting dedication to moral principles yielded the proverbial hundredfold return. The death of the reformer marked the birth of the poet. Whittier once remarked, "My vehicles have been of the humbler sort—merely the farm wagon and buckboard of verse." This was his achievement: to have represented the common thoughts and feelings of a mainly agrarian society. Whittier wrote with the strong moral sense of his age and its complete confidence in progress and democratic concepts. Hardly a profound thinker, he remained, like his readers, strikingly unaware of the vast social and economic changes in the nineteenth century and only superficially understood that abolition alone was no panacea for the ills of his age. Nevertheless, he did have a tenacious grasp of a few fundamentals: farm life, nature, moral principles, freedom, and the Inner Light. If these realities were a narrow vein of poetic ore and mined nearly to exhaustion, their constant sifting and refining did produce a few finished poems.

In his mature poetry Whittier drew heavily on nature and his farm experience for imagery and pictorial description, but this background furnished him mainly with certain basic concepts—the value of hard work and rural simplicity, and

nature's role as a teacher of moral virtues—that were never absent from his work. Perhaps no other American poet has been so extremely devoted to the concept of freedom and the basic principles of democracy. In his better poems these basic moral beliefs are neither platitudinous nor sentimental, but refreshingly direct and certain in a relativistic age.

Another aspect of Whittier's mature poetry was his use of history and legend to vitalize his ideas on intolerance, moral courage, and reform. He once said that his tales often were written to give "far faint glimpses of the dual life of old/ Inward, grand with awe and reverence; outward, mean and coarse and cold." Whittier's nostalgic recalling of these past times in his ballads and genre pieces was an attempt to save a tradition and to record the passing of a social order. Tardily, he found in the ordinary things of life, his boyhood memories, local Haverhill scenery, and Essex County legends, the factual images that could be transmuted by personal associations and imaginative effort into authentic materials for poetry. The romance that he found in these familiar things was based on an awareness that humble experiences and simple feelings possessed as much wonder and beauty as any dream of loving knight and lady.

Of course theory is one thing, while practice is another. Whittier had more than the usual difficulty in properly organizing his material, and his mature method of composition reflects his early formative influences. Most noticeable is the didactic bent of certain recurring themes. The value of domestic emotions, the rewards of true love, the innocence of childhood, the necessity of social equality, and the nobility of ethical action repeat the stock ideas of the nineteenth century.

In presenting these moral lessons Whittier often took the nucleus of the story from another source—an old legend, an account from history, or even a contemporary event. This was recast in a realistic narrative with a concluding discussion of the moral application of the tale. This technique is found in such widely divergent ventures as the nature poem "The Vanishers" (1864), in which an Indian legend of the dead returning for their loved ones leads to the consolation that all the losses will be reclaimed in heaven; the ballad "The Garrison of Cape Ann" (1857), in which the colonial legend of specter warriors teaches the value of prayer; and the philosophic "Miriam" (1870), in which the Islamic concept of God affirms the universality of truth as Miriam uses Christian doctrine to quell the rage of Shah Akbar. The tagged-on moral is a serious aesthetic failing that plagued Whittier throughout his life. In his best poems, however, such as "Skipper Ireson's Ride" (1857) or "The Trailing Arbutus" (1879), the lesson achieves an organic harmony and artistically develops the implications of the narrative.

Whittier's mastery of local-color techniques and his painterly ability to describe accurately the native scene characterize his finest poems. In them the natural scene remains unchanged, for he transcribed rather than created, and represented rather than arranged. The artistic value of this approach depended on the skill and selectivity of his recording. The following lines from "The Countess" (1863) are a close literal picture of Rocks Village on the Merrimack River:

> Over the wooded northern ridge,
>   Between its houses brown,
> To the dark tunnel of the bridge
>   The street comes straggling down.
>
> .   .   .
>
> With salt sea-scents along its shores
>   The heavy hay-boats crawl,
> The long antennae of their oars
>   In lazy rise and fall.

Yet its salient characteristics are exaggerated and heightened to create an atmosphere of drowsiness and the "stranded" quality of a bypassed town. Closely connected with his pictorial cast of mind is Whittier's use of decorative imagery. Usually associated with his rural background, these images evoke a mild sensory response lacking the richness and complexity of the expansive imagery used by Walt Whitman and Emily Dickinson. The visual presentation of his ideas draws heavily on common farm images— planting, growth of crops, harvesting, husking, change of seasons—and on biblical analogues. Thus an old teacher's antiquarian interests are described as "threshing time's neglected sheaves," and a girl's mind is seen as "dew-moist and bright . . ./Unfolding like a morning flower."

Another characteristic of Whittier's style is the neoclassic bent of his versification, diction, and imagery. His poems use the simplest of meters, the ballad and octosyllabic, while eighteenth-century rhyming couplet and alternate rhyme are his usual stanzaic forms. Rhetorical balance and set parallelisms, such as appear in "The Barefoot Boy" (1855), dated his poems even in his own day. Similar devices that made his art somewhat old-fashioned are his pairing of adjectives and his characteristic inversions, which tend to create a slow, halting rhythm. These technical inadequacies, however, do not always detract from his artistic achievement. Whittier's realistic genre pieces and ballads show his art at its best, as a natural and intimate part of his own experience, for in them he firmly heeded the essential truth that he had first recognized in Burns's poems: that within the most commonplace objects lie rich poetic materials. These poems convey his inner love for the environment that molded him and the traditions that inspired him, and reveal his extensive knowledge of local scenery, custom, and history. Here his style is direct and sincere, purged of its glaring rhetorical and sentimental flaws; the descriptions are graphic and picturesque; and the materials of home, nature, and the affections are fashioned into enduring poetry.

Whittier's ballads probably represent his finest poetic achievement and the best re-creation of native folklore and legend written in the nineteenth century. They especially express his lifelong interest in New England history and wide knowledge of local customs and superstitions. Still, the formation of these ballads was a tortuous process that reveals how slowly Whittier's artistry matured and how tardily he recognized his own abilities. Only when dealing with material that was intimately associated with his Quaker beliefs, rural background, humanitarian interests, and Essex County region could he produce poetry of artistic merit.

In general, Whittier's ballads remain remarkably true to the characteristics of traditional folk balladry. Like Sir Walter Scott, he was genuinely responsive to the spirit of folk narrative, having the background knowledge necessary to embody popular feeling and legend in narrative song. His best ballads are realistic and direct, centering on dramatic action and developing one main theme. As in traditional ballads, the tragic overtones of the theme evolve from the basic emotions of love, hate, loyalty, and betrayal, with particular emphasis on individual rebellion against society. Whittier's diction usually is sparse and simple, his images commonplace and filled with folk expressions. Even so, lyric and pastoral effects often hinder dramatic action and mar the objectivity so necessary for good balladry. Nor do the ballads escape his habitual "moral squint."

Fortunately for Whittier, his earliest literary influences were the poems of Burns, which glorified rural life and local customs, and the romances of Scott, which centered on the heroism of Scottish warriors. His imitations of them, or at least his use of their themes as he saw them reflected in his own life, were the most promising verses of his early years. His first collection of poems and tales, *Legends of New England,* dealt entirely with local traditions and superstitions. The verses are marred by digressions and extravagant romantic phrasing, and employ the typical Gothic devices of doomed lovers, ghostly ships, and hidden horrors. However, one ballad, "The Black Fox," has a sure poetic beat and adapts its subject and content to the ballad tradition of simplicity. The introduction to the poem re-creates the atmosphere of a winter's evening in rural New England with a clearness of language and simplicity of diction that indicate Whittier's ballad capabilities. The grandmother, with her homespun descriptions and superstitious nature, is an excellent choice as narrator; and her account of the mysterious activities of the black fox effectively conveys a rural delight in the supernatural.

Another early ballad is "The Song of the Vermonters" (1833). Its theme, a rallying cry for all patriotic Vermonters to defend their state during the Revolutionary War, imitates Scott's border romances; its form, rhyming couplets with a basic anapestic beat, gives a martial ring to the whole:

Ho—all to the borders! Vermonters, come
    down,
With your breeches of deerskin and jackets of
    brown;
With your red woollen caps, and your
    moccasins, come,
To the gathering summons of trumpet and drum.

One of Whittier's first real ballads is "The Exiles," written in 1841. It shows how a decade of abolitionist work had matured him and, conversely, how far he had to go to achieve poetic maturity. The plot of "The Exiles" is suited to ballad demands for an exciting, realistic narrative, since it tells of Thomas Macy's flight down the Merrimack River to escape persecution for harboring a Quaker. Its theme, the dramatic struggle of one man against existing injustice, stresses the value of inner principle over outward law. Everything was within the range of Whittier's talents and interests, for he had grown up in the Merrimack Valley and had spent the greater part of his life fighting for freedom and resisting intolerance. Yet he failed to develop the poem artistically. It is overly long (sixty stanzas) and greatly weakened by numerous digressions and pious interjections; and its labored comparisons and sentimental tone ignore the realism of good balladry.

"Cassandra Southwick," written in 1843, shows a considerable advance in dramatic structure and presentation. Here, too, the incident is culled from the history of Quaker persecutions; but instead of relating the complete story behind Cassandra's imprisonment, Whittier concentrates on her fears and doubts as she waits to be sold into slavery. The early section of the poem probes Cassandra's fears and near despair. Her simple, trusting spirit is prey to all the distorted visions that the night and the unknown can bring. Fearfully she imagines the insults and pain to which her gentle nature will soon be subject. Once dawn breaks and Cassandra is led to the wharves, the movement is swift and dramatic. Though overly long and didactic, the poem is considerably better than the discursive and dramatically weak "The Exiles."

During the next ten years Whittier wrote mainly prose, but two ballads of this period merit attention. "Barclay of Ury" (1847) expands the general theme of "Cassandra Southwick" in dealing with the indignities heaped upon an old warrior for joining the Quakers. Again the story turns on the conflict of inner conviction versus outward ridicule, as Barclay's quiet reliance on the Inner Light is contrasted with the outbursts of the jeering mob. The slow, deliberate beat of the verse echoes the measured pace of Barclay's horse and conveys his unflinching religious confidence. At the climax of the poem, Barclay movingly tells an old warrior comrade that he will not fight the mob, and goes his own way, enduring alone. This portrait of Barclay is Whittier's first successful investigation of those reserved, dignified figures whose utter simplicity and tenacious faith capture one's imagination. The other ballad, "Kathleen" (1849), shows Whittier's complete mastery of ballad techniques. The story relates the selling of a beautiful Irish girl into slavery in the colonies by her cruel stepmother and a safe return to her sorrowing father. In traditional ballad fashion, dialogue conveys the feeling and action. No motivation is given for the stepmother's decision to sell Kathleen, nor is there an explanation for her triumph over the old lord's love for his daughter. Also noticeable is the absence of sophisticated imagery; only the most conventional descriptions are given as the ballad moves swiftly along. This ballad readily illustrates the progress Whittier had made from his early uneven, discursive efforts.

At the height of his poetic powers, Whittier wrote his best ballads during the 1850's and 1860's. While studying at Haverhill Academy, he had heard the song of Captain Ireson's being tarred and feathered by the women of Marblehead. It was a typical folk song familiar to all the inhabitants of the town—perfect material for a poet who knew the locale and understood the mentality of the people. At that time Whittier tried writing it down, but it was not finished until thirty years later. The gestation period proved valuable.

The ballad opens slowly, almost incongruously, as the strangeness of Ireson's ride is compared with other famous rides of story and rhyme. These outlandish references give a grotesque, grimly humorous tone to the opening. The refrain, repeated with slight variations in every stanza, contains the essence of the story, though it does not reveal why the skipper is being punished. In the next stanzas Ireson's disheveled condition is mocked as "Body of turkey, head of owl/ Wings a-droop like a rained on fowl,'' while the crowd, consisting of women, responds to his plight with raucous cries and violent jostling. Their wildness creates a half-mad, half-comic mood that catches the confusion and chaos of mob action.

The tone changes in the middle stanzas as the reasons for Ireson's shame are revealed: he sailed away from a sinking ship filled with his townspeople, betraying his own kin. We never know his motivation, nor is the event further elaborated; but the horror of his act is enlarged upon by the pathetic descriptions of the women of Marblehead wreaking revenge for their lost loved ones. All these things are but touched upon as the poem returns to the savage humor of the opening with this description:

Sea-worn grandsires, cripple-bound,
Hulks of old sailors run aground,
Shook head, and fist, and hat, and cane,
And cracked with curses the hoarse refrain:

.   .   .

Part of Whittier's achievement is seen in these lines. The shipwreck images echo Ireson's betrayal and ridicule the pitiful attempts of the old sailors to obtain revenge, and their feeble, cracking voices make the refrain childish and meaningless. The crippled quality of their acts and the female character of the mob indicate the utter failure of the townspeople to obtain any measure of satisfaction equal to their loss.

Suddenly the mood shifts; and in contrast with the harsh voices of the turbulent mob in the narrow, winding streets is the peace and serenity of the road leading to nearby Salem. As the physical setting changes for artistic contrast, so does the psychological tone. For the first time the skipper dominates the scene as he cries out:

What to me is this noisy ride?
What is the shame that clothes the skin
To the nameless horror that lives within?

The transition is sudden and complete, surprising the reader, who is engrossed in the outward narrative, and making him startlingly aware of the poem's chief theme—the torture and remorse of a man after his crime. Although the hate of the mob and his present physical disfigurement will pass with time, his own terrible awareness of the sin will not. Ireson's unexpected admission of guilt is perhaps unmotivated; but the change from hate to remorse is in keeping with the shifting pattern of the poem, its mixture of humor, pathos, and cruelty. The crowd's vengeance is now muted, and in ''half scorn, half pity'' they turn Ireson loose.

The final refrain changes ''old'' Floyd Ireson to ''poor'' Floyd Ireson, and so becomes a mournful dirge forever accusing and dooming the man, as well as emphasizing the emptiness remaining in the lives of the townspeople. The ballad makes Ireson live as an essentially tragic figure, who has betrayed the loyalties of his home and the traditions of the sea. He towers over the drama, coming from the sea, acting without apparent justification, and then vanishing to live alone with his shame.

At last Whittier had attained the artistry to express his feelings for the New England scene, its history, customs, and deeper psychological traditions. There followed the gems of his maturity: the lyric drama ''Telling the Bees'' (1858); the pastoral romance ballads ''Amy Wentworth'' (1862), ''The Countess'' (1863), and ''The Witch of Wenham'' (1877); the hardier ballads of history and superstition ''The Garrison of Cape Ann'' (1857), ''The Wreck of Rivermouth'' (1864), and ''The Palatine'' (1867); and his later dramatic ballads of Quaker persecution ''The King's Missive'' (1880) and ''How the Women Went from Dover'' (1883).

''Telling the Bees'' hinges on an Essex County superstition that a death in the family would drive away the bees and, to prevent this, the hives must be draped in mourning. The narrative records the delayed visit of a young man to the farmhouse of his beloved Mary. The tone of the poem is informal, almost conversational; and Whittier relates the tale as if he and the reader were rewalking the ground on which it took place. In the first lines, directly addressing this reader and insisting that he follow the scene closely, Whittier says:

Here is the place; right over the hill
    Runs the path I took;
You can see the gap in the old wall still,
    And the stepping-stones in the shallow brook.

There is the house, with the gate red-barred,
    And the poplars tall;
And the barn's brown length, and the cattle-
        yard,
    And the white horns tossing above the wall.

The details are plain and unelaborated, and a series of "ands" connects one detail to the next in almost childlike fashion. Then, as if pausing in his trip, the poet notes that, although a year has passed, the same rose blows, the same sun glows, and the same brook sings. This emphasis on the "sameness" of the previous visits and the scenery unifies the poem, giving assurance that the lover's previous meetings with Mary will be repeated.

But the mood shifts when the poet recalls, almost casually, that upon coming closer to the house he noticed "Nothing changed but the hives of bees." This one small detail breaks the continuity, and with increasing tension we hear with him again the drearily singing chore girl and see the ominous shreds of black on the hives. The warm June sun of the moment before now chills like snow as the eventual discovery is foreshadowed. Still, the boy refuses to abandon his former confidence and assumes that Mary's grandfather must be dead. But then he sees the old man sitting on the porch, "and the chore-girl still/ Sung to the bees. . . ." Finally he is close enough to understand the song of the chore girl:

"Stay at home, pretty bees, fly not hence!
Mistress Mary is dead and gone!"

With effective absence of comment, Whittier concludes the poem with this revelation of Mary's death, allowing the reader to supply the resulting horror and impact of the loss.

Only then is the reader aware of the skillful manipulation of theme, for the careful development of the attractiveness and assurance of external nature hides the inevitable destruction of human beauty and earthly love. The ironic contrast of the boy's trust and expectation with the true situation offers a psychological insight into the problem of death and man's inability to prepare for its shocking occurrence.

Whittier's mature ballads show many interesting variations. His most famous, "Barbara Frietchie" (1863), the story of an old woman waving a Union flag before the conquering Southern troops, was supposedly a true one. For Whittier she symbolized all who loved and fought for the Union, and the poem was his spontaneous expression of that feeling. The story is told in simple rhyming couplets of four beats to a line. The stage for the drama is set by a few suggestive details evoking the environs of Frederick town and the luxuriant land, ripe both for the actual corn harvest and for the harvest of blood and destruction. A continuing economy of detail sweeps the ballad along to its melodramatic climax: Barbara's defiant "Shoot, if you must, this old gray head" causes Stonewall Jackson to blush and to save her life. The poem's lack of subtlety and highly emotional presentation are in keeping with the manner of old ballads, while its final couplets bind the drama together as the stars shine over the graves of the protagonist, the town, and the Union itself, suggesting nature's full approval of the battle for "peace and order and beauty" represented in the flag. Few Civil War poems were so definitely the product of the hour and so quickly recognized by the people as an expression of their feelings.

"Amy Wentworth," like many other of Whittier's romantic ballads, lacks dramatic action as it portrays an aristocratic Amy disregarding her rank to marry a sea captain. Its sentimental theme, the power of true love, is developed by fine images as it contrasts the physical confinement of Amy's ancestral home with the freedom and love of the sea. The ballad opens with a graceful image of her fragile, delicate appearance, then presents an evocative sea image:

> Her heart is like an outbound ship
>   That at its anchor swings;
> The murmur of the stranded shell
>   Is in the song she sings.

Sections of "The Witch of Wenham" and "How the Women Went from Dover" contain some of Whittier's best rendering of colonial customs and illustrate his complete understanding of the psychology of witchcraft and local superstition. However, overlong digressions and sentimental touches mar the graphic descriptions and rustic phrases—indicating again how badly Whittier's art suffered from a lack of selection. "The Palatine" also catches the grim and foreboding atmosphere of past days in recording the legend of a specter ship. Throughout there is swiftness of narrative, and the ending remarks avoid Whittier's usual moralizing to hint at the complex relationship existing between the physical and spiritual worlds. In the ending conceit Whittier wonders if the return of the ship to haunt those who wrecked it is nature's grim comment on our past actions.

Two of Whittier's less well-known ballads also merit attention. "The Sisters" (1871) is based on a traditional ballad theme and in form and presentation bears a close resemblance to the original Scottish ballad "The Twa Sisters." The action of the story is concentrated on a single stormy night. The whole narrative is done in dialogue, with none of the "before" or "after" events included. Only one scene is given, the resulting effects of the tragedy; the reader must fill in the details. The presentation is bare, almost harsh, in its simplicity. Another of Whittier's later pieces, "The Henchman" (1877), also demonstrates his mastery of ballad techniques. Like "The Sisters" it has no moral, but it is entirely different in tone and presentation. The poem is a pure love song, chanted joyously by a young lover in praise of his lady. The imagery concentrates on the things of summer—birds, flowers, sun, and wind—and makes the lady superior to them all.

This type of ballad is the exception rather than the rule for most of Whittier's later pieces. Some of his mature ballads, such as "The Brown Dwarf of Rügen" (1888), "King Volmer and Elsie" (1872), and "Kallundborg Church" (1865), also convey the charm of a foreign land and create a fairy-tale atmosphere by the techniques used in "The Henchman." In general, however, Whittier's later ballads tend to take a concrete historical incident or some local tradition and dramatize it, using an actual locale for the setting. These tales fit in perfectly with his critical belief that there is romance underlying the simplest of incidents and that the writer should utilize the materials within his own experience.

"The Wreck of Rivermouth" is typical. The story is based on the historical character of Goody Cole of Hampton, New Hampshire, who was persecuted for being a witch in the latter half of the seventeenth century. Many of the deeds attributed to her probably were superstitions based on popular traditions, yet they were common in Whittier's youth. The setting is laid precisely, with an eye for picturesque detail:

And fair are the sunny isles in view
  East of the grisly Head of the Boar,
And Agamenticus lifts its blue
  Disk of a cloud the woodlands o'er;
And southerly, when the tide is down,
'Twixt white sea-waves and sand-hills brown,
The beach-birds dance and the gray gulls wheel
Over a floor of burnished steel.

The ballad proper begins with the boat full of "goodly company" sailing past the rocks to fish outside the bay. The idyllic atmosphere of the summer's day is conveyed by the picture of the mowers in the Hampton meadows, who listen to the songs coming from the passing boat and who longingly watch the joyous young girls. As the boat rounds the point where Goody Cole lives, the laughing group taunts her and sails on, but only after she answers their gibes with a bitter proverb: " 'The broth will be cold that waits at home;/ For it's one to go, but another to come!' " Ironically her prophecy proves true, as a sudden storm sweeps upon the ship, driving it to destruction on Rivermouth Rocks. In one brief moment all are lost, and the next stanzas mournfully reecho the previous happiness. A stunned and broken Goody Cole is left behind, pathetically cursing the sea for fulfilling her wish. Her tragedy, like Skipper Ireson's, is an inner thing—the torment she will have for the rest of her life, wondering if her angry words actually caused the death of the group. The final scene in church highlights the community's silent condemnation of those who dare to live outside its conventions. This scene is overlong and weakened by the heavy moral tone of the conclusion, "Lord, forgive us! we're sinners all!"

The poem illustrates Whittier's successes and failures in ballad presentation. The story itself is typical and probable, and Whittier's handling of it realistic. He places it exactly in Hampton, by employing details characteristic of that locale: fishing for haddock and cod, the scent of the pines of nearby Rye, the mowing of salt grass, and Goody Cole's use of familiar proverbs. There is a keynote of drama in the situation and a direct narrative appeal that fit ballad presentation, for Whittier allows us to view a most human Goody Cole, an old woman tragically destroyed by a village's narrow hate. Yet, like so many of Whittier's ballads, this one needs more concentration, especially an ending before the dramatic effect is lost. Also, there is a touch here of his overreaching for sentimental and melodramatic effects, a fault clearly seen in "The Changeling" (1865) and "How the Women Went from Dover."

Whittier's genre poems differ from his ballads in their lack of drama and objectivity; they are personal and subjective, fully revealing the poet and his ideas. They deal with the life and manners of common people, re-create a past agrarian society, or nostalgically remember boyhood experiences. Often they are longer, employing description and decorative imagery that minimize physical action and narrative pace; and the tone of wistful longing and romantic reminiscence replaces the impersonality and directness of the ballad. The best genre poems realistically portray the particular scenes, customs, traditions, and personages of nineteenth-century rural New England: the fields, drab and bare on a sleety winter day or green and growing under a summer sun; the plain colonial houses with their massive crossbeams, wide fireplaces, and rustic furniture; the barns filled with harvest or the excitement of a husking party; the isolation and narrowness of a small town with its delight in superstitions, eccentric wanderers, and local poets; the emotional effect of evangelical preaching on a farm populace; the traditional folk tales of stern "Yankee" forebears—the list is lengthy, a complete social history of the period. These genre poems most vividly exemplify Whittier's belief that the best materials for poetry lie in the commonplace objects of familiar experience.

"Maud Muller" (1854) shows Whittier's genre art at its most typical. The story is an unpretentious account of the popular American belief in romantic love, set in a quaint rural background; yet Whittier pauses to examine this trust and to question its validity. The poem's narrative sparseness and ironic undertones avoid his usual sentimentality and overelaboration. The occasion for the poem was Whittier's recollection of a trivial event—his meeting with a young farm girl and her shame at her torn attire and bare feet. To this matter-of-fact incident he added an unadorned story of the appearance of a wealthy judge and the effect of this meeting upon their lives. The surface theme illustrates the belief that romantic love is necessary for happiness, but Whittier undercuts the excessive sentiment by developing a series of ironic contrasts: reality versus dream, action versus thought.

The opening of the poem prepares for an objective treatment of the romance. A "mockbird" echoes Maud's daydreams; and the town at which she gazes, the symbol of her romantic aspirations, is "far-off" and causes "vague unrest." When the judge appears on his horse, Maud offers him some water. This simple placement of figures quietly indicates their basic irreconcilable differences. After their meeting Maud dreams of becoming his wife and of all its social benefits, while the judge longs for a simple farmer's life. Their dreams disappear in the harsh light of reality, however, and Whittier concludes by sadly musing about the "might have been." Within the context of the poem, the sorrow lies not in their failure to marry, but in their refusal to confront reality. The imaginative hopes of the judge and Maud reflect the sentiments of the "rags to riches" saga and trust in romantic love, yet the poem warns that, although one may believe in and cherish the dream, reality and life usually prove to be different. The ending remarks probe deeper as Whittier points out that only in heaven may our human dreams be realized (and even here the subjunctive "may" indicates his doubt that heaven would afford such romantic fulfillment), and that only a final spiritual goal provides consolation, not vain regrets. Rather than asking for a sentimental response to the story, he indicates his doubts and wonders who knows what is best after all. Therein lie the pathos and universality of the tale.

Just as he captured the naive aspirations of his age, Whittier also preserved the memories of the old order and the history of the local scene. His rustic anecdotes, "Yankee" character sketches, and humorous satires of legends and superstitions rank with his best poetic achievements. His fanciful handling of Cotton Mather's history of a fabled two-headed snake in "The Double-Headed Snake of Newbury" (1859) is a comic triumph. Whittier ridicules Mather's credulous account of the wonders worked by God's providence by thoroughly reshaping the tale with appropriate exaggeration and a mock-heroic tone that satirize the Puritan delight in superstition and moralizing. The section on the townspeople describes the ancient gossips "Shaking their heads in their dreary way" to parallel the coiling of the snake. The passage reaches its climax with Whittier's caricature of Mather's entrance:

Cotton Mather came galloping down
All the way to Newbury town,
With his eyes agog and his ears set wide,
And his marvellous inkhorn at his side;
Stirring the while in the shallow pool
Of his brains for the lore he learned at school,
To garnish the story, with here a streak
Of Latin and there another of Greek:

.   .   .

Even the ending preserves the burlesque mood as Whittier records the present-day life of the snake in a native proverb dealing with the quarreling of husband and wife: "One in body and two in will,/ The Amphisbaena is living still." This poem is the best among a group including "The

Preacher'' (1859), ''Birchbrook Mill'' (1884), and ''The Prophecy of Samuel Sewall'' (1859).

Whittier never had notable success with characterization, but in a few anecdotes of historical figures that strikingly foreshadow the work of Robert Frost and Edwin Arlington Robinson he did capture the essential characteristics of the New England mind. ''Abraham Davenport'' (1866) shows Whittier's genre art at its most realistic and enjoyable. The ''old preaching mood'' of the poem is at once dryly humorous and honestly respectful. Whittier pictures Davenport's granitelike determination and shrewd common sense as he calmly goes about his legislative duties amid the fear and religious hysteria occasioned by an eclipse of the sun, the famous Dark Day of May 19, 1780. The poem opens with a laconic observation on the slackness of the present age:

In the old days (a custom laid aside
With breeches and cocked hats) the people sent
Their wisest men to make the public laws.

The terror of the day, lampooned by the overdrawn setting and the farfetched comparisons, conveys the still strong Calvinist belief in a wrathful God and the presence of the supernatural in physical occurrences. The style, with its salient observations, keeps this formal description from being melodramatic.

Birds ceased to sing, and all the barn-yard fowls
Roosted; the cattle at the pasture bars
Lowed, and looked homeward; bats on leathern
    wings
Flitted abroad; the sounds of labor died;
Men prayed, and women wept; . . .

The humorous urgency of the verbs and the incongruity of such insignificant detail ridicule the solemnity of the event to make the ending human prayers and tears outrageously anticlimactic.

''Cobbler Keezar's Vision'' (1861), ''The Sycamores'' (1857), and ''Abram Morrison''

(1884) also exemplify Whittier's facility in rustic character sketches. Two of the poems contrast wine-loving and hard-drinking immigrant outsiders, a German cobbler and an Irish workman, with the grim, repressed existence of the early Puritans; the third follows the career of an Irish Quaker well-known in Whittier's youth. All three are filled with Whittier's native wit and dry turn of phrase. One other characterization, ''A Spiritual Manifestation'' (1870), reveals a most human Roger Williams who laconically satirizes the mob of dissenters and religious cranks who have descended upon his colony. Here shrewd social comment, realistic genre touches, and character insight balance the usual didactic passages and digressive material.

More and more Whittier turned to the memories of his own youth for poetic material, typifying and idealizing the barefoot days, the district school days, and lost childhood romances. Throughout all these poems run the strains of his sentimental longing for the simplicity of a past social order. ''The Barefoot Boy'' (1855), ''In School-Days'' (1870), ''My Playmate'' (1860), ''Memories'' (1841), and ''A Sea Dream'' (1874) captured the romantic aspirations of a wide reading public and were enshrined as part of traditional Americana along with Longfellow's verses and the songs of Stephen Foster.

Although ''The Barefoot Boy'' displays Whittier's most obvious artistic flaws, it also indicates why his verses were so popular. The introduction is sentimental and unreal, depending on hackneyed imagery and conventional poetic diction. The boy is styled ''little man,'' wears ''pantaloons,'' has lips ''kissed by strawberries on the hill,'' and is pompously addressed as ''Prince.'' These generalizations reveal nothing about a real boy or his background; rather, they show how responsive Whittier was to the Currier and Ives approach to local color. The central section of the poem does realistically examine the world and interests of a small boy. Forgetting the idealized little man, Whittier identifies himself with the scene:

> I was rich in flowers and trees,
> Humming-birds and honey-bees;
> For my sport the squirrel played,
> Plied the snouted mole his spade;
> For my taste the blackberry cone
> Purpled over hedge and stone;
>
> . . .
>
> All the world I saw or knew
> Seemed a complex Chinese toy,
> Fashioned for a barefoot boy!

The last stanzas return to the platitudes of the opening as Whittier concludes with the pious hope that the boy's bare feet will never sink in the "Quick and treacherous sands of sin." And yet this poem became a national tradition, symbolizing a romantic phase of America's past.

Its companion piece, "In School-Days," is correctly considered a poem for children, although its first four stanzas contain good local color. "My Playmate" is the best of three love lyrics that nostalgically recall the bittersweet pain of young love. Its blend of memory and reality, symbolized by the moaning pines and falling blossoms, artistically portrays an older man's sense of regret and longing.

One of Whittier's most neglected poems, "The Pennsylvania Pilgrim" (1872), shows how accurately and realistically he could re-create the past. His portrait of the seventeenth-century Quaker Francis Daniel Pastorius fully explores the varied nature of that settler, while the mood and image development convey Pastorius' quiet, secure personality. Employing a style similar to Jonathan Edwards' *Personal Narrative* with its insistent repetition of certain phrases, Whittier indicates the presence of the Inner Light in Pastorius. Throughout the poem terms such as "peace," "mild," "meek," "simple," "tender," "sober," and "mystical" are continually enlarged upon and reechoed. Decorative, pasto-

ral similes pervade the poem and create a quiet, almost dreamlike atmosphere. Rarely did Whittier achieve a more artistic fusion of his own interests and those of the actual story than in the following lines:

> Fair First-Day mornings, steeped in summer calm,
> Warm, tender, restful, sweet with woodland balm,
> Came to him, like some mother-hallowed psalm
>
> . . .
>
> There, through the gathered stillness multiplied
> And made intense by sympathy, . . .

Balancing these light images are references to planting, sowing, reaping, and blossoming that signify Pastorius' attempts to transplant Old World culture in the New World, his cultivation of religious tolerance, and his work to free the slaves. The portrait leaves the reader with a full impression of a complex, idealistic, and learned Quaker who was at the same time a simple, tolerant, humble man.

The most famous of Whittier's genre poems, and undoubtedly his masterpiece, is "Snow-Bound" (1866). Written a few months after the end of the Civil War, it was his memorial to the two women who were closest to him during his life—his mother, who had died eight years before, and his sister Elizabeth, who had died the previous year. The loss of Elizabeth, his favorite companion, left Whittier a lonely man; and the outcome of the Civil War completed the one great work of his life, the abolition of slavery. In this mood of sorrow and isolation, he turned to the happy past when the family was intact at the Haverhill birthplace, and constructed this winter idyll to express his feelings for the area and family that had produced and molded him. Its theme, the value of family affection, had always been deepest in his heart; and its locale, the homestead during a snowstorm, was one he knew intimately. Nowhere in Whittier's work, outside of some of his ballads, had the material so suited his capabilities and interest.

The movement of the poem turns on the poet's nostalgic recalling of the love and protection that his family once gave him, thereby emphasizing his painful sense of present loss and hope for spiritual consolation. These emotions are developed primarily by a series of contrasts—of fire and snow, past and present, people and elements—that combine to form the larger theme of love and immortality struggling against pain and death.

Perhaps the key to interpreting the poem is the symbolic development of the wood fire. Fire is associated not only with brightness, relaxation, and physical comfort, but also with the emotional and spiritual warmth of family love, with the "genial glow" of community brotherhood, and with divine protection against the evil spirits of nature and time. Artistically delayed by the description of the storm, the initial lighting of the fire introduces the Whittier household, and its blaze symbolizes the reality of family love. Its significance is highlighted as loving hands gather the wood and brush necessary to kindle the fire. The "curious art" displayed in these simple tasks suggests a ritual-like significance in their performance. The first red blaze metamorphoses the kitchen into "rosy bloom," but an even greater miracle occurs as the snowdrifts outside reflect the inner fire with their own "mimic flame." For the first time the fire controls, and the snow receives its burning imprint. Yet the outer elements are not so easily conquered, and the moon reveals an eerie world of "dead white" snows and "pitchy black" hemlocks suffused by an "unwarming" light. Once more the fire's "tropic heat" asserts its power; and the glowing light reveals a mug of simmering cider, a row of apples, and a basket of nuts—objects closely related to the inner world of personality and life.

Throughout the poem Whittier associates the vigor and happiness of family talk, games, and interests with the color and sparkle of the glowing logs, and unites the close bond of family love with the red heat of the fire. For example, the uncle's simple tales cause the listeners to forget "the outside cold,/The bitter wind." Whittier also weaves into the fire pattern the sunny richness, ripe crops, blooming hillsides, and full greenness associated with summer. Finally, the dying fire indicates the end of the evening's activities while also symbolizing the eventual crumbling of the security and protection of the family group.

By contrast, the storm evokes sensations of fear and awe, and illustrates the terrible anonymity of nature and death. It dominates the entire first section, transforming its principal antagonist, the sun, into a cheerless, dark, snow-blown wanderer, and enforcing on the family a "savage" isolation that obtains no comfort from "social smoke." The storm's assault on the house is likened to the later attack of death on its individual members as Whittier recalls "the chill weight of the winter snow" on Elizabeth's grave. Conversely, the storm's magical power changes a dull, commonplace farm into a wintry fairyland of beauty and wonder.

A second major contrast deals with the past versus the present. Whittier imaginatively recreates the past while echoing his present-day feelings of loneliness. Four main interpolations deal with this problem of time and change, contrasting past happiness with present pain and concluding with the hope for future social progress and spiritual consolation. For example, the first interpolation (lines 175–211) appropriately comes when the fire is lighted and the storm's force seems abated. As if lost in the scene he has recalled, Whittier cries: "What matter how the night behaved?/What matter how the north-wind raved?" But immediately the knowledge of "Time and Change" stops him; for what the elements failed to do that night, death has since accomplished. These stark reflections are contrasted with the strength of Whittier's faith as the section ends with his defiant affirmation that spiritual life is the "lord of Death," for a soul's love remains an eternal force. These major contrasts are further expanded by an increasing depth of images and by a movement from concrete physical description to an investigation of personality and emotions, with a final return to realistic depiction. All these aspects are blended into the total theme—the strength and bond of family love.

At the heart of the poem comes Whittier's portrait of his family and the winter visitors. The father, mother, and uncle are characterized by warm summer days, fishing and haying, ripening corn, steaming clambakes, and sunny hillsides. Their plain, childlike natures and interests are perfectly echoed by the quaint couplet rhythm, the rough unpolished lines, and the vernacular "Yankee" rhymes. To follow these innocent characters, Whittier introduces another group of three, the aunt and two sisters, whose more complex natures reflect some measure of life's pain, sacrifice, and loneliness. The tone becomes more introspective and the images more expansive and thoughtful. The aunt's still youthful charm and virgin freshness are expressed in a delicate summer figure of clouds and dew:

> Before her still a cloud-land lay,
> The mirage loomed across her way;
> The morning dew, that dries so soon
> With others, glistened at her noon.

The elder sister's death is described as an entrance "beneath the low green tent/Whose curtain never outward swings!" Significantly, her death is not snow-filled or chilling; rather, it is the lifting of a tent flap, with the later discovery that this light opening has been closed with the heavy weight of green sod. A following passage on Elizabeth introduces the second interpolation. Once again Whittier's faith struggles with the

brutal reality of death as the chilling snows of the grave cover the summer charm and violet beauty of Elizabeth's nature. Finally the poet asks:

> Am I not richer than of old?
> Safe in thy immortality,
>   What change can reach the wealth I hold?

At first glance the figure appears paradoxical, for how can Elizabeth's death make the poet "richer" and "safe"? On one level his rich memories of her vibrant personality and spiritual perfection are now "safe," secured forever from realistic tarnish and inexorable change; but also her "immortality" secures him, since it illuminates his final spiritual goal and provides him with a standard for judging all his future acts.

The following two characterizations portray the visiting schoolmaster and the "not unfeared, half-welcome guest" (Harriet Livermore) while also introducing the third interpolation. The realistic sketch of the schoolmaster's entertaining knowledge of the classics and of rural games, his boyish humor, and his self-reliant, yet humble, nature is a fine genre portrait that matches the earlier ones of the father and uncle. Indeed, the schoolmaster's intimacy with the family is underscored by the lines that introduce him as one who "Held at the fire his favored place,/Its warm glow lit a laughing face." His further delineation as one of "Freedom's young apostles" completes Whittier's portrait of the fearless young leader whose moral strength will destroy social injustice such as slavery and will open a new era of peace and progress.

The final figure, Harriet Livermore, presents an interesting variation of the fire imagery as she combines characteristics of the spirits of light and of blackness. Her warm and lustrous eyes flash light, but also hold "dark languish" and wrath; her brows are "black with night" and shoot out a "dangerous light." This tortured nature warps and twists the "Celestial Fire," for she enters the family group without sharing its close affection or receiving the warm benefits of love from the wood fire. Her complex characterization is appropriately concluded by the uneasy observation that in some natures "will and fate" form a tangled skein. Structurally these two outsiders represent the contrasting "warm-cold" aspects of a forgotten external world. The schoolmaster offers the warmth of companionship, the balance of learning, and eventual hope for social responsibility; while Harriet Livermore reveals the chill of fanaticism and the failure of personal, emotional efforts to correct injustice. Their intrusion also foreshadows the unavoidable demands that society is soon to make upon the secure family group.

The final section of the poem returns briefly to the physical world of the opening stanzas. The teamsters and plows control the effects of the storm; and the children find sport, instead of terror, in the whiteness. Signalizing the larger social union that radiates from the smaller family bond, the visiting doctor utilizes the mother's nursing skill to aid a sick neighbor. With the arrival of the local newspaper, "the chill embargo" of the storm is completely broken; and a joyous Whittier cries out that the world was his once more.

While this seems to be the logical conclusion for the poem, it disregards the reality of time's ultimate victory. So in a final interpolation Whittier asks the "Angel of the backward look" to close the volume in which the angel has been writing. With difficulty he shakes off this mood of regret and nostalgia to respond to present-day demands (much as he had pictured the young schoolmaster doing), and employs the image of the century-blooming aloe dramatically to portray the successful flowering of his abolitionist's aim of eradicating slavery. The ending lines further console Whittier with the hope that his "Flemish" artistry has truly re-created "pictures of old days" and that others may gather a similar spiritual and emotional comfort from them by stretching the "hands of memory forth/To warm them at the wood-fire's blaze!"

A final summer image completes the poem; the thought of future readers enjoying his efforts refreshes the poet as odors blown from unseen meadows or the sight of lilies in some half-hidden pond. These lines reflect the inner serenity and imperturbable peace that offer final solace. The dread of time and change is assuaged by the confidence that social reform will improve the future, by the knowledge that art often outlasts time's ravages, and by the certainty that spiritual immortality does conquer it completely. So the poem moves in artistic transitions from the physical level of storm and fire to the psychological world of death and love, utilizing the wood fire as the dominant symbol. It is for this skillful fusing of form and theme that Whittier deserves to have future readers send him "benediction of the air."

The publication of "Snow-Bound" in 1866 brought Whittier national fame and financial security, and changed his reputation from that of a reform poet to the "wood thrush" of Essex County. When "The Tent on the Beach" appeared the next year and sold at the rate of a thousand copies a day, a delighted but slightly shocked Whittier remarked that it seemed to be a greater swindle on the public than P. T. Barnum ever perpetrated. A responsive reading public asked for more; and so "Among the Hills" was published in 1868, then "Miriam" in 1870, followed by five new volumes of poetry in the next fifteen years. This late flowering continued unabated and vigorous past Whittier's seventieth year, with the themes of love, peace, and acceptance of God's will pervading these poems. The tumultuous problems of the Reconstruction, of swift westward expansion, and of developing industrial power did not find the emotional response in the poet that contemporary events of pre-Civil War America had aroused. Far removed from actual reform struggle, Whittier had only mild interest in strikes, woman suffrage, and corruption in government.

In these later years Whittier searched poetically for the meaning of life, and the intense spiritual consciousness that had permeated all aspects of his life found its natural outlet in religious lyrics and hymns. Certainly his own age read him primarily as a religious poet; and his verses openly reflect his admiration of spiritual strength, his deep faith in the goodness of God, and his love of fellow man as a sharer in the divine essence. The widespread hymnal use of these lyrics testifies to their worth as expressions of universal religious beliefs. Although few of Whittier's poems were written expressly for that purpose, the adaptations of "The Eternal Goodness" (1865), "Our Master" (1866), "At Last" (1882), and "The Brewing of Soma" (1872) have enshrined his religious verses among the finest expressions of American Protestant thought. Without metaphysical complexities or any dogmatic stance, Whittier simply and directly expressed the age's trust in God's love and captured its innermost hopes in lines like these from "The Eternal Goodness":

> And so beside the Silent Sea
>   I wait the muffled oar;
> No harm from Him can come to me
>   On ocean or on shore.
>
> I know not where His islands lift
>   Their fronded palms in air;
> I only know I cannot drift
>   Beyond His love and care.

Whittier's popularity in the late nineteenth century surpassed even that of Longfellow, and his later years brought a series of uninterrupted literary and personal triumphs. The popular image of the fiery reformer hammering out incendiary verses softened to the revered portrait of a white-bearded old man gently spinning out rustic tales of long ago. Oliver Wendell Holmes

was only reflecting the taste of his age when he wrote that Whittier's poems brought him "the morning air of a soul that breathes freely, and always the fragrance of a loving spirit." Under such conditions of religious security, glorification of virtue, and public pride in the abolition of slavery, Whittier became an object of veneration and near awe; and his birthday was a national holiday.

As he grew older, Whittier found relaxation and comfort with a restricted group of relatives and friends who sheltered him from an increasingly curious public. After the death of his sister, literary friends like the Claflins and the Fieldses opened their Boston homes to him; and a host of minor women writers, pleased with Whittier's interest in their writings and responsive to his bachelorhood, became frequent visitors. Newspapers continually manufactured romances and engagements for Whittier; but he remained single and, despite the attentions of close friends, his final years were lonely. His humor and tolerance saved him from the worst of isolated old age; but the crowd of interviewers, autograph seekers, and aspiring writers who descended on Amesbury as pilgrims going to Mecca exasperated even the patient Whittier. He invented all sorts of stratagems to escape them; but, as he ruefully remarked, he could lose a "him" but never a "her."

In 1876 Whittier left his Amesbury home to spend the spring and autumn with relatives at a secluded, beautifully landscaped estate in Danvers that he named Oak Knoll. Severe winters were passed with his Cartland relatives in Newburyport, while the New Hampshire coast and inland mountains drew him in the summer. Whittier remained alert and active throughout the 1880's: he published numerous volumes of new verse, received what he called a "nickname" from Harvard—an LL.D.—edited the definitive collection of his prose and poetry, and had his last volume, *At Sundown*, privately printed in

1890. On December 17, 1891, Whittier was eighty-four years old. Shortly afterward he had an almost fatal attack of grippe; but his health improved in the spring, and by summer he was strong enough to visit with friends in Hampton Falls, New Hampshire, near the coast he loved so well. He took excursions around the countryside and even wrote two poems in honor of Oliver Wendell Holmes. However, on September 3 he suffered a severe paralytic stroke and died on September 7, 1892.

At his death Whittier seemingly was enshrined as one of America's great poets. Less than fifty years later that opinion was completely reversed. Although he was definitely a minor poet, Whittier's ballads and genre pieces place him midway in the direct line of American poetic expression that stretches from Anne Bradstreet to Robert Frost. Certainly his poems fall short of the richness and imaginative depth of poets like Whitman or Dickinson, but his verses exhibit more spiritual illumination and downright "grit" than the poems of the other schoolroom writers. His place in American literature seems secure. He will continue to be read and enjoyed as long as people respond to their traditions and heritage, and want to find honest expression of their fundamental democratic and religious feelings. Winfield Townley Scott's penetrating poem "Mr. Whittier" aptly characterizes the man and illuminates the lasting quality of Whittier's achievement:

It is easier to leave *Snow-Bound* and a dozen
    other items in or out of
The school curriculum than it is to have written
    them. Try it and see.
            .   .   .
It is so much easier to forget than to have been
    Mr. Whittier.
He put the names of our places into his poems
    and he honored us with himself;
And is for us but not altogether, because larger
    than us.

Selected Bibliography

WORKS OF JOHN GREENLEAF WHITTIER

The Writings of John Greenleaf Whittier, edited by Horace E. Scudder. 7 vols. Boston—New York: Houghton Mifflin, 1888–89.

Whittier Correspondence from the Oak Knoll Collections, 1830–1892, edited by John Albree. Salem, Mass.: Essex Book and Print Club, 1911.

Cady, Edwin Harrison, and Harry Hayden Clark. *Whittier on Writers and Writing: The Uncollected Critical Writings of John Greenleaf Whittier*. Syracuse, N.Y.: Syracuse University Press, 1950.

The Letters of John Greenleaf Whittier, edited by John B. Pickard. 3 vols. Cambridge, Mass.: Harvard University Press, 1975.

BIBLIOGRAPHIES

Currier, Thomas Franklin. *A Bibliography of John Greenleaf Whittier*. Cambridge, Mass.: Harvard University Press, 1937.

von Frank, Albert J. *Whittier: A Comprehensive Annotated Bibliography*. New York: Garland, 1976.

CRITICAL AND BIOGRAPHICAL STUDIES

BIOGRAPHIES

Bennett, Whitman. *Whittier: Bard of Freedom*. Chapel Hill: University of North Carolina Press, 1941.

Currier, Thomas Franklin, ed. *Elizabeth Lloyd and the Whittiers*. Cambridge: Harvard University Press, 1939.

Keller, Karl. "John Greenleaf Whittier," *Fifteen American Authors Before 1900: Bibliographic Essays on Research and Criticism*, edited by Robert A. Rees and Earl N. Harbert. Madison: University of Wisconsin Press, 1971.

Kennedy, William Sloane. *John G. Whittier: The*

Poet of Freedom. New York: Funk and Wagnalls, 1892.

Mordell, Albert. *Quaker Militant: John Greenleaf Whittier*. Boston: Houghton Mifflin, 1933.

Perry, Bliss. *John Greenleaf Whittier: A Sketch of His Life*. Boston: Houghton Mifflin, 1907.

Pickard, Samuel T. *Life and Letters of John Greenleaf Whittier*. Boston–New York: Houghton Mifflin, 1907.

Pollard, John A. *John Greenleaf Whittier: Friend of Man*. Boston: Houghton Mifflin, 1949.

Wagenknecht, Edward. *John Greenleaf Whittier: A Portrait in Paradox*. New York: Oxford University Press, 1967.

Woodwell, Roland B. "The Life of John Greenleaf Whittier." (Unpublished manuscript on deposit at the Haverhill Public Library. Completed in 1974, this is the definitive life of Whittier.)

CRITICAL STUDIES

Carpenter, George Rice. *John Greenleaf Whittier*. Boston–New York: Houghton Mifflin, 1903.

Leary, Lewis. *John Greenleaf Whittier*. New York: Twayne, 1961.

Pickard, John B. *John Greenleaf Whittier: An Introduction and Interpretation*. New York: Barnes and Noble, 1961.

Warren, Robert Penn. *John Greenleaf Whittier's Poetry: An Appraisal and a Selection*. Minneapolis: University of Minnesota Press, 1971.

SPECIAL TOPICS

Arms, George W. *The Fields Were Green: A New View of Bryant, Whittier, Holmes, Lowell, and Longfellow, with a Selection of Their Poems*. Stanford, Calif.: Stanford University Press, 1953.

Pearce, Roy Harvey. *The Continuity of American Poetry*. Princeton, N.J.: Princeton University Press, 1961.

Pickard, John B., ed. *Memorabilia of John Greenleaf Whittier*, Hartford, Conn.: Emerson Society, 1968.

———, and others, eds. *Whittier and Whittierland: Portrait of a Poet and His World*. North Andover, Mass.: Eagle-Tribune Press, 1976.

Pickard, Samuel T. *Whittier-Land: A Handbook of North Essex*. Boston: Houghton Mifflin, 1904.

Waggoner, Hyatt H. *American Poets: From the Puritans to the Present*. Boston: Houghton Mifflin, 1968.

Wright, Donald P. *John G. Whittier: A Profile in Pictures*. Groveland, Mass.: Boyd James Press, 1967.

CRITICAL ARTICLES

Hall, Donald. "Whittier," *Texas Quarterly*, 3:165–74 (Autumn 1960).

Jones, Howard Mumford. "Whittier Reconsidered," *Essex Institute. Historical Collections*, 93:231–46 (October 1957).

Jones, Rufus. "Whittier's Fundamental Religious Faith," *Byways of Quaker History*, edited by Howard H. Brinton. Wallingford, Conn.: Pendel Hill, 1944.

Powell, Desmond. "Whittier," *American Literature*, 9:335–42 (November 1937).

Ringe, Donald. "The Artistry of Whittier's *Margaret Smith's Journal*," *Essex Institute. Historical Collections*, 108:235–43 (July 1972).

Scott, Winfield Townley. "Poetry in American: A New Consideration of Whittier's Verse," *New England Quarterly*, 7:258–75 (June 1934).

Trawick, Leonard M. "Whittier's *Snow-Bound*: A Poem About the Imagination," *Essays in Literature*, 1:46–53 (Spring 1974).

Whittier Newsletter (1966–   ), edited by John B. Pickard and others, is an annual review of Whittier scholarship and research.

—*JOHN B. PICKARD*

Elinor Wylie

1885–1928

WHEN Elinor Wylie first appeared on the literary scene in 1921, she was already a public figure. For the next seven years her public life was less glamorous as she applied herself to the task of writing three books of poetry and four novels. But in spite of this serious investment of her time and energy in artistic and intellectual work, her remarkable beauty, her elegance of dress and person, and her exquisite taste made her an almost too perfect embodiment of the "poetess." The 1920's in America was a period when the woman poet flourished: Sara Teasdale, Amy Lowell, Marianne Moore, Hilda Doolittle, Edna St. Vincent Millay, Louise Bogan, Léonie Adams were all writing at the same time as Elinor Wylie.

Wylie's earliest years, however, could not have been more respectable and less imbued with poetry than with public service. Elinor Morton Hoyt was born in 1885 at Somerville, New Jersey. The first of five children, she was the great-granddaughter of Morton McMichael, a mayor of Philadelphia, and the granddaughter of Henry Martyn Hoyt, a governor of Pennsylvania. Her father, Henry Hoyt, was assistant attorney general of the United States under William McKinley and solicitor general under Theodore Roosevelt. For the first two years of her life, Elinor lived in Somerville. Then the family moved to Philadelphia, where she attended Miss Baldwin's School in Bryn Mawr, and spent summers at North East Harbor, Maine. Love of Maine lasted throughout her life, influencing her choice of the Yankee David Butternut as a companion for Shiloh in *The Orphan Angel* and being reflected in such poems as "Wild Peaches," "Silver Filigree," "Spring Pastoral," "An American in England," and "The Golden Heifer."

The Hoyt family moved to Washington, D.C., when Elinor was twelve years old. She attended Mrs. Flint's (later Holton Arms) School and took classes at the Corcoran Gallery of Art; and she was so passionately interested in her schoolwork that she was considered a "bluestocking" by the time she was sixteen. Rosalba Berni, the heroine of *The Venetian Glass Nephew* who is called the "Infant Sappho," and Rosalie Lillie of *The Orphan Angel*, who writes poetry and plays the Spanish guitar, must owe something to this period of Wylie's life.

Like most girls of her time and class, Elinor left school at eighteen and "came out" as a debutante in Washington society. She and her sister Constance were taken to Europe by her grandfather, to whom, she later told Carl Van Doren, she owed a great deal of her education. Caught up in parties and other social engagements, Elinor Hoyt became engaged to Philip Hichborn, the son of an admiral. Her early married life, during which she spent much time on motor launches and at dinner parties, must have involved a great deal of hidden misery. She said of it more than a decade later, "My marriage was a prison. I felt stifled. There was no room for my mind at all. I had to get away. While my father was alive I had him to turn to. But after he died I was desperate."

And so in December 1910 Elinor Hichborn, then twenty-four and the mother of a young son, eloped with Horace Wylie. The scandal was the talk of Washington. Horace, the father of five children, was unable to obtain his wife's consent to a divorce. Under the circumstances, life in the United States seemed impossible for them. Elinor therefore left her two-year-old son with his father and went abroad with Horace Wylie. Calling themselves Mr. and Mrs. Waring, they lived in Burley, a village in the heart of the New Forest, some two hours from London. Horace, who was fifteen years older than Elinor, devoted part of each day to instructing her in literature. He saw himself as Jonathan Swift and Elinor as both Stella and Vanessa. Speaking many years later to Mary Colum, Elinor said that Horace "really opened the world of poetry and literature" to her.

Most of the time she was very happy, but there were embarrassing incidents. Once, while visiting an English country house for a weekend, she met a woman who had known Horace in Washington and who told their hostess that Elinor and Horace were not married and were using a false name. Such humiliations made Elinor very wary of people. The haughty and beautiful face of the famous Nicholas Muray photograph that frequently forms the frontispiece for volumes of her poetry reflects great defensiveness. That same defensiveness against a hostile world is central to *Black Armour,* and perhaps Elinor Wylie is speaking of her personal experience when she writes about Mr. Hazard in her novel *Mr. Hodge and Mr. Hazard:*

Years of the severest lessons of adversity had rendered Mr. Hazard's outward composure so nearly flawless that the sharp lancet of his self-contempt was blunted upon its surface. This superhuman armour was divided by no clumsy cracks and joinings; rather it resembled a coat of flexible mail, a cool marvel of contrived providence, a knitting up of nerves into invulnerable proof. Mr. Hazard's skill had woven it; he might have been proud of its difficult fabric. Yet he disliked the thing. It was a tough and stringent shield against the world, but after all it was only a makeshift. Even if his own skin had been but a beggarly tissue, he missed it sadly. He wished he might have patched and mended its tatters to last him into eternity.

Philip Hichborn shot and killed himself in 1912, and Elinor felt hounded by gossip as she and Horace moved from Burley to Merrow Down to Witley. Meanwhile, her mother had paid for the private printing of sixty copies of *Incidental Numbers* (1912), a volume of her poems modeled upon and inspired by William Blake's *Songs of Innocence.* In later years Wylie discounted the importance of these poems, and she never wished them to be considered part of her literary production.

Elinor and Horace Wylie returned to America in 1915, when, as a war measure, the English government required all persons living under assumed names to report to the police. Horace Wylie's wife agreed to a divorce, and he and Elinor were married in August 1916. They then went first to Bar Harbor, and later to Somesville, Maine, where her eleven-year-old son joined them for a visit. The boy, who had not seen her since he was two, lived with his paternal grandparents.

After a short time in Augusta, Georgia, Horace and Elinor Wylie settled in Washington, D.C., in 1919. Horace took a job with the Interstate Commerce Commission and was away a good deal in connection with railroads on the West Coast. Elinor was writing now and meeting some of her brother Henry's friends, particularly

Sinclair Lewis and William Rose Benét, with whom she discussed literature. After she published *Nets to Catch the Wind* (1921) and was invited to read at the New York Poetry Society, Wylie decided to live in New York, where her circle included Edmund Wilson and John Peale Bishop. She was now submitting poetry to *Century Magazine, Outlook, New Republic,* and *Poetry.* Her literary career had begun in earnest by the time she became poetry editor of *Vanity Fair* at a salary of fifty dollars a week. In 1923 she and Horace agreed to a friendly divorce, and she married William Rose Benét.

Wylie spent the summer of 1923 writing at the MacDowell Colony in New Hampshire. That same year her second volume of poetry, *Black Armour,* and her first novel, *Jennifer Lorn,* appeared. Her next three works were novels: *The Venetian Glass Nephew* (1925), *The Orphan Angel* (1926), and *Mr. Hound and Mr. Hazard* (1928). It was unfortunate that Wylie spent so much time writing fiction although it was a more remunerative way of using her talent. *The Orphan Angel* was a Book of the Month Club selection and earned her $8,000 in an immediate lump sum, $1,800 of which she spent to buy part of an original manuscript by Percy Bysshe Shelley and a signed check from Shelley to William Godwin. Although the public response to *Jennifer Lorn* was spectacular and the critical acclaim almost irresistible for any author, Wylie's fame as a novelist was clearly the result of a fad for the precious and the exotic.

Trivial Breath appeared in 1928. Clearly an advance on all her poetry that had preceded it, this volume announced the advent of a more mature poet. But Wylie had only a short time to live. She spent that time in England, at London and Henley-on-Thames. In the spring of 1928 Wylie fell and hurt her back. The high blood pressure that had threatened her life since 1923 became complicated by incipient Bright's disease. When Carl Van Doren visited her in June of that year at her house in Chelsea, she read him some of the sonnets from "One Person." She told him that at last she absolutely loved someone; always before she had been loved. There had been three "trysts": "We had met under an oak, an ash, and a thorn." In October she suffered a mild stroke that resulted in partial paralysis of one side of her face.

Wylie sailed for America on December 1, 1928. On December 12 she recited her new sonnets to a small group of friends in New York. Mary Colum, to whom she spoke about her love for the man in the sonnets, remarked, "It seemed a simple and rather pathetic relationship where two people with obligations to others were attracted to each other in a romantic and intellectual way." Wylie intended to live near this man, but not to make her life with him. On December 16, after preparing the final manuscript for what would become her posthumous volume of poetry, *Angels and Earthly Creatures,* she died in her New York apartment.

Wylie's life was certainly passionate and romantic. Her poetry, however, is more remarkable for its clarity and discipline than for its emotional content. Writing in 1923 about the craft of poetry, she argues:

. . . in the remote possibility that some of us are not geniuses, but only adroit and talented young people with a passion for writing verse, it may be an excellent thing after all that we have cultivated a small clean technique. A number of minor poets are far better employed in being brittle and bright and metallic than in being soft and opulently luscious. It keeps the workshop tidier, and leaves a little elbow-room in which the very great may move their hammers and chisels in serenity.

Although Elinor Wylie is frequently thought of as a peculiarly artificial and precious poet, the epitome of the female poet of the American 1920's, she is an amazingly strong and, in some senses, hard poet. Perhaps Mary Colum, a friend as well as a critic, goes too far when she says that she "brought in a new despair—a despair which seemed to be another name for courage and combat." But her insight is much truer than the more recent assessment by Thomas Gray, who describes her as "primarily an artificer rather than an interpreter of life."

Wylie was thirty-six when her first volume of poetry, *Nets to Catch the Wind*, appeared. Nevertheless, the book was a very precocious piece of work. There was simply no preparation for it. She had not gone through the usual apprenticeship to develop the musical and rhetorical skills that clearly were there. Her poetry would grow and deepen in the short space of years left to her, but in her first volume she showed herself to be an accomplished poet.

Many things that must be said of Wylie's poetry in general can be said of *Nets to Catch the Wind*. Already some of her most important characteristics are in evidence: extreme contrasts of heat and coolness, of darkness and light, of smoothness and angularity, of height and depth; technical experiments with variations of vowel sounds; a love of close rhyme schemes and set meters; thematic development within a sonnet sequence; subtle handling of couplets; delicate observations of animals, insects, and plants; an intellectual power that strengthens the apparent musical quality of each line.

The first three poems in this volume speak on behalf of what is wild, adventuresome, alive—a persistent theme in Wylie's poetry. In "Beauty" she places what is beautiful outside the realm of good and bad, cautioning against any attempt to turn the wild gull of beauty into the tame dove of goodness. In the last two lines of the three-stanza poem she conveys the sense of the absolute integrity, the unrestrainable freedom of beauty. Attaching moral value to beauty means either cursing or enshrining it, in either case vitiating it. By connecting the innocence of beauty with the hard heart of a child, she suggests both the strength and the fragility of beauty's aloofness.

One of Wylie's most frequently anthologized poems, "The Eagle and the Mole," is an arrogant statement recommending two ways of retaining an uncorrupted self: the eagle's and the mole's. The poem enjoins us either to live above the clouds or to burrow underground, but in either case to shun the crowd. The advice is given in language full of contempt for the "reeking herd," "the polluted flock," "the huddled warmth of crowds," "the lathered pack," "the steaming sheep." These strong sensory words communicate extreme physical distaste. In the first part of the poem, where she develops the eagle's way, what is sought by avoiding the herd is a heady freedom, a sense of unhampered movement. Security and comfort are disdained by the "stoic bird" that does not fear storm or sun. In the second part, which develops the mole's way, what is sought by avoiding the "lathered pack" is a kind of protection. Even the word "pack" suggests pursuit and flight. And whereas the eagle remains alone, the mole holds intercourse

> With roots of trees and stones,
> With rivers at their source,
> And disembodied bones.

The two ways, therefore, represent widely different choices.

The intense appeal of the poem resides, no doubt, partly in the vivid invective. Denigrating the foe is an exhilarating experience even for spectators. This is particularly true when the anger and contempt become, as they do here, a mode of self-protection. But there is also a peaceful resolution to the poem that is immensely satisfying. The restlessness that continues through the first five stanzas disappears in the final stanza, most of which is quoted above, where a quiet and almost communal haven is found. That harmony is increased if a reader associates the concluding lines with William

Wordsworth's description of a dead woman in her grave:

> Rolled round in earth's diurnal course,
> With rocks, and stones, and trees.

The third poem, "Madman's Song," illustrates Wylie's strengths and weaknesses. The song is mad indeed; the maddening repetition of the sound "o" that imitates the music of the hunting horn resounds obsessively through the three stanzas in all its variations. Except for the central idea that it is better to grow worn and old by living an intense, physical life than to live comfortably unaware of the wild world outside, the sense of individual lines is unimportant. Wylie is intoxicated with the sounds she can create. There is a vacuousness about the poem's content that no amount of technically achieved beauty of sound can dispel.

In her justly famous "Velvet Shoes," also in this volume, sound and sense work together in a tight and rigorous discipline. The poem begins with the invitation "Let us walk in the white snow" and ends with the acceptance "We shall walk in the snow." Between these lines the shoes become velvet shoes as details and sounds create a sense of the snow in the air and on the ground and of feet walking upon it.

> Let us walk in the white snow
>   In a soundless space;
> With footsteps quiet and slow,
>   At a tranquil pace,
>   Under veils of white lace.
>
> I shall go shod in silk,
>   And you in wool,
> White as a white cow's milk,
>   More beautiful
>   Than the breast of a gull.
>
> We shall walk through the still town
>   In a windless peace;

> We shall step upon white down,
>   Upon silver fleece,
>   Upon softer than these.
>
> We shall walk in velvet shoes:
>   Wherever we go
> Silence will fall like dews
>   On white silence below.
>   We shall walk in the snow.

Here the softly sibilant "s" predominates, creating the monotony and repetition that simulate the snow falling. The main visual, kinetic, tactile sensations cluster around shoes, silence, snow. Numerous other "s" words support these three, contributing to the effect first of snow falling and then of snow falling upon snow, first of shoes lifting and falling until snow accumulates on the bottom of those shoes, when snow presses upon snow, and the snowy shoes feel like velvet.

Like so many of the poems in this volume, "Velvet Shoes" describes a retreat from the vulgar world. Written in the period following Wylie's years of seclusion abroad, when she felt hounded by gossip and newspaper scandalmongering, it is not surprising that this first book of poetry reflects hostility toward the crowd. The longing to be "quit of the cruel cold," to be "under the roots of the balsam tree," as she says in "Winter Sleep," suggests a desire for protection that we have already seen in the description of the mole's way in "The Eagle and the Mole." The poem "Sanctuary," however, indicates that Wylie recognized the danger in her desire to flee to a cell built to contain herself and her cool and quiet dreams. As the last brick is put in place, leaving not even a chink, she asks, "How can I breathe?" and is answered, "You can't, you fool!" Reacting to a cruel and painful world by building a sanctuary in which to hide from its attacks, one is left in a prison.

In "Proud Lady" Wylie describes her determination not to be marred and molded by the world's hatred, not to define herself merely by opposition to it, but to turn the "pain to a grace," "the scorn to a charm." For in addition to her hostility toward the crowd, these first poems express her hunger for experience. The four sonnets of "Wild Peaches" emphasize the one as much as the other. After describing the Baltimore landscape with its short winter and long summer where "spring begins before winter's over," its abundance of squirrels and chestnuts in autumn, its early-summer lush superfluity of strawberries and blue plums, she writes:

Down to the Puritan marrow of my bones
There's something in this richness that I hate.
I love the look, austere, immaculate,
Of landscapes drawn in pearly monotones.
There's something in my very blood that owns
Bare hills, cold silver on a sky of slate,
A thread of water, churned to milky spate
Streaming through slanted pastures fenced with
    stones.

I love those skies, thin blue or snowy gray,
Those fields sparse-planted, rendering meagre
    sheaves;
That spring, briefer than apple-blossom's breath,
Summer, so much too beautiful to stay,
Swift autumn, like a bonfire of leaves,
And sleepy winter, like the sleep of death.

The kind of austerity described here does not, of course, exclude sensual delight. But the pleasure is subtle, deep, tinged with mortality. The promise of constantly renewed largess is not here; instead, there is the threat of scarcity. Such meagerness does not decrease hunger; it makes it go beyond a surface appetite, to become a hunger of the marrow of the bone, of the very blood.

Nets to Catch the Wind introduced a new poet to the world, but one who came already equipped with her particular voice, already in control of the techniques to express that voice and the themes worthy of being expressed.

Black Armour: A Book of Poems, Wylie's second volume of poetry, is an emblem book in which the poet meditates on five pieces of a knight's traditional armament: breastplate, gauntlet, helmet, beaver, plumes. There is an inordinate concentration on the head and face, as the last three divisions indicate. The beaver is the only piece of armor that is more than named; in calling one section of the book "Beaver Up," Wylie suggests a momentary willingness to expose her vulnerable flesh.

Poem after poem in "Breastplate" describes the poet's weariness with being brave, her desire to let the wave close over her head. She records in technically brilliant poems her longing to rid herself of her soul, that nuisance that will not stop seductiveness and the horror of drowning, inviting us to look down into the "subaqueous shade" and imagine "a rainbow world," bright sea birds, and "dancing clouds about the sun" flashing before the eyes as we sink. In another she sees herself as dead in a house with back door bolted and front door locked.

"Peregrine," the poem that opens "Gauntlet," is doubly welcome, therefore, after the heavily narcissistic and escapist poems of the first section. In throwing down the gauntlet, Wylie begins with moral imperiousness by describing Peregrine as a liar and a bragger without a friend. The poem gallops along with its bright dimeters and their outrageous rhymes. It is a swaggering, bantering, posturing piece that is completely successful. Unlike so many other Elinor Wylie poems of bravado, this one is in the third person. She avoids, consequently, any taint of narcissism, achieving instead an invigorating portrait that turns our attention outward rather than inward. Peregrine's gargantuan drinking of whole vineyards, the extravagance of his traveling to Brittany for its cider, are matched by a regal insouciance concerning food, clothing, his ultimate fate:

As a king goes
He went, not minding

That he lived seeking
And never finding.

The poem ends with an epigrammatic suc-
cinctness that echoes the moral imperiousness of
its beginning.

> "The noose draws tighter;
> This is the end;
> I'm a good fighter,
> But a bad friend:
> I've played the traitor
> Over and over;
> I'm a good hater,
> But a bad lover."

This robust fighting spirit is rarely displayed in
Wylie's poetry. Her love of wildness in eagle
and antelope, in hounds and foxes and gulls,
recurs; but human wildness in the form of a
warm participation in the rough-and-tumble
physical world does not often appear. Her usual
stance is one of cold haughtiness; she proclaims
an untamable spirit through her power to endure
and reject. "Peregrine" embraces man's lot,
rejoicing in the physical pleasures and discom-
forts of human experience, and discounting the
need for conventional and respectable safeguards
against their intense proximity.

In contrast, the overrefined "Preference," in
the same volume, proclaims the value of the
"mournful mouth" and "small bones in wrists
and ankles." The beautiful people the poet professes to prefer "carry a dagger in the heart" and
are the antithesis of Peregrine, who carries his in
his hand to scare cravens. For one poem like
"Peregrine" Wylie wrote a dozen as fastidious
as "Preference." Not until she came to her last
poems, in *Angels and Earthly Creatures,* did she
write any substantial body of poetry affirming
boisterous humanity.

But in *Black Armour,* as "Simon Gerty," her
poem about a man "Who Turned Renegade and
Lived with the Indians," shows, Wylie fears that
wildness is too closely akin to cruelty for comfort. Although she can understand what motivated Simon Gerty, for she too can see how
clean-muscled Indians could be preferred to tallow, greasy-fat faces, she still thinks he was mistaken in his choice.

Perhaps no poem so clearly expresses Wylie's
awareness of how beleaguered is the human
being as "Let No Charitable Hope." One of her
most elegant and simple utterances, it has the
power of absolute sincerity and truth. The im-
peccable diction, the restraint and clarity, make
it a classical statement on the human condition.
She tempers the advice given in "The Eagle and
the Mole," recognizing essential differences between herself and all other animals:

> Now let no charitable hope
> Confuse my mind with images
> Of eagle and of antelope:
> I am in nature none of these.
>
> I was, being human, born alone;
> I am, being woman, hard beset;
> I live by squeezing from a stone
> The little nourishment I get.
>
> In masks outrageous and austere
> The years go by in single file;
> But none has merited my fear,
> And none has quite escaped my smile.

The first two stanzas have that perfect inevitability of word and rhythm that is the hallmark of
great poetry. The last two lines, however, have a
slightly pretentious, self-congratulatory air that
is perhaps unavoidable when a poet asks us to
join her in looking admiringly at herself. "This
Hand," the last poem in "Gauntlet," is not so
finely wrought; and yet, because Wylie limits
herself to a physical description, leaving the
emotional response entirely to us, the poem is
free of this particular weakness. The last lines of
"Let No Charitable Hope" mar an otherwise
exquisite poem. It almost persuades us that any
stance other than her proud endurance is childish and undignified.

Nothing in the rest of the volume rivals "Peregrine" or "Let No Charitable Hope." At times, as in "Castilian" or "Parting Gift," Wylie does little more than versify a rather uninteresting sentiment or coy feeling. Indulging her pleasures in the macabre, she writes in "Fable" of a raven dipping its bloody beak in the crack of a dead knight's breastbone and sipping his brains from the broken cup of his skull while his eye sockets suck light. Here both her lifelong enjoyment of ballads and the emblem of the helmet have led her astray.

This second volume of poetry, although it has been praised by some critics as more warmly passionate, less purely intellectual than *Nets to Catch the Wind,* is really much less impressive than her first book. Wylie seems to shrink from life, taking refuge behind her black armor as though, as James Branch Cabell said, "the writer has found life to be unendurably ugly."

Although Wylie's poetry has not, since her death, received the popular acclaim accorded Edna St. Vincent Millay's or Amy Lowell's, it has continued to be anthologized. At least three of her poems—"Velvet Shoes," "The Eagle and the Mole," and "Let No Charitable Hope"—are still widely known. But her novels have been almost totally neglected. It is difficult to believe that New Yorkers turned out in a twilight procession to celebrate the publication of her first novel or that her next novel was so enthusiastically praised by English critics that she was entertained by the Sitwells and Virginia Woolf when she visited England, and was the only New York writer Aldous Huxley asked to meet when he visited America. One of her novels was even a Book of the Month Club choice in 1926. Cabell said that if her novels did not last, and they probably would not, then posterity was to be pitied. Whether or not his judgment is valid, his prediction has been realized.

Wylie wrote four novels: *Jennifer Lorn: A Sedate Extravaganza* (1923), *The Venetian Glass Nephew* (1925), *The Orphan Angel* (1926), and *Mr. Hodge and Mr. Hazard* (1928). *Jennifer Lorn* was a remarkable first novel, a completely original performance for an American writer that has had no imitators. *Zuleika Dobson* (1911) is the only English novel of the period remotely comparable, but Max Beerbohm's vein is comic where Wylie's is satiric. The eighteenth-century setting is not fortuitous; the age of Swift and Alexander Pope seems particularly well suited to her intention. Wylie's notebooks, which are now the property of Yale University, reveal how scrupulously she researched the background for this novel. Every page of *Jennifer Lorn* reflects her knowledge of eighteenth-century literary history. Gerald, we learn, is enamored of Voltaire. When he arrives in France with Jennifer, he remembers having had breakfast with Laurence Sterne once in Calais when the author was writing *A Sentimental Journey.* Jennifer reads *Clarissa,* Pope, William Collins, Oliver Goldsmith; Horace Walpole is a friend of the Cleverly-Nevilles, Jennifer's mother's family. Wylie describes in great detail fashionable clothes of the period, jewelry, hairstyles. Her knowledge of incunabula and of bookbinding is extensive. She scatters historical anecdotes connected with painters such as Titian and Jean Baptiste Greuze across the pages. At some points the novel is almost a travel guide to India, particularly the area around Delhi. Wylie describes Humayan's tomb and the private audience hall in Shah Jehan's Red Fort, even quoting the inscription on the wall around one of the chambers: "If Paradise be on this earth, it is this, it is this, it is this." The beautiful site of the Taj Mahal at Agra is also mentioned. Her knowledge of Indian food includes not only curries but also favorite Indian sweets such as elephant's ears.

As the eighteenth-century author of *Robinson Crusoe* knew, nothing so completely persuades us that a fictional world is real as quantities of particular details that sound like true facts. *Jennifer Lorn* was praised for its fantasy, but Wylie built her extravaganza on a solid body of facts.

The peculiar blend of fact and fancy that so delighted readers of *Jennifer Lorn* is characteristic of all her novels. Each required tremendous erudition, but the author carried her learning lightly. Her scholarship is there, but so transmogrified that it carries us further into fantasy rather than bringing us back to the real world of brick and mortar.

Although Carl Van Vechten was content to see Gerald Poynyard, the hero of this extravaganza, as an irresistibly decorative figure, he functions much more seriously as the main subject of Wylie's satire. The novel opens with his return to England from India in the state that, as Jane Austen noted, makes a male essentially interesting: in need of a wife. At twenty-seven he has amassed a fortune of £50,000. He acquires as a bride Jennifer Lorn, the daughter of the earl of Tam Linn, "the most beautiful girl in Devonshire," much as he sought and took possession of various pieces of Meissen, enameled snuffboxes, and amethyst signet rings. After a honeymoon in Bath and a short visit to Paris, they travel to India, where, on a trip from Delhi, they are set upon by Turcoman bandits. After romantically engaging his attackers in single combat, Gerald is supposedly killed and buried with a stake through his heart, while Jennifer is seized as booty.

At one time the novel was to be entitled *The Lady Stuffed with Pistachios,* for in the next episode Jennifer's slight figure does not suit the voluptuous taste of the wife of the old Indian khan whose bed she is supposed to grace. While futile attempts are made to fatten her, she is courted by Prince Abbas, a devotee of the art of cooking. Thinking her husband is dead, Jennifer disguises herself as a boy and runs away with him. The young couple wander platonically over the countryside, vaguely in the direction of Europe, until they reach Persepolis, where Jennifer sees Gerald but is not observed by him. She rejects Prince Abbas' pleas that she leave Gerald, and instead follows him to the khan's palace. Captured once more, she dies of fright when an infernal contraption, the bowstring, encircles her throat. There follows a very melodramatic burial at which an Irish Jesuit, Father O'Donnell, officiates. Prince Abbas flings himself down at the graveside and is expiring in grief when Gerald passes by and takes from the prince's hand a tiny Byzantine ivory bas-relief. Noting the resemblance of the carved face to Jennifer's, Gerald thinks how fortunate he is to have this lovely antique object, "both rare and valuable."

At every point in the novel, Wylie stresses Gerald's exquisite taste and his human insensitivity. He is a lover of precious things. Jennifer cowers before his aesthetic standards. She is thoroughly intimidated when he finds fault with hotel furniture that she thinks is magnificent. For a while the little bride is a highly prized ornament. Gerald fancies how lovely she would look transformed into marble, with flying draperies. But then he realizes she "would undoubtedly be the property of the king" and so dispels the vision. But he spares himself the pain of that necessity. Jennifer lives with him as though in a museum.

Wylie describes Jennifer as languid, wilting, enervated. At one point Gerald, who has ignored her existence for two days, feels an urge to converse with her; he swoops her from her bed in the middle of the night and carries her about like a lifeless doll. Both before her marriage and during her short domestic life with Gerald, Jennifer lacks any natural vitality or curiosity. She has a dream before their departure for Paris in which a young man offers to save her, but she is so unaware of any possibility of a more vital existence that she asks, "From what?"

Sometime before that dream Jennifer lies awake one night for hours. Thoughts drift through her mind:

"Dear Gerald assures me that Paris will restore my spirits," she thought, as she lay watching the bluish flame of her night-light diffused in a dim radiance beside her bed, spreading thinly, like milk in a muddy pool, through a darkness rendered more brown than black by filtrations of fog from without; beyond the window-panes an evil yellow gloom mirrored and magnified the ring of brightness. ''He is extraordinarily kind to me; I ought not to allow myself to fall into these moods of melancholy. I think the climate of London must be ill-suited to my constitution; I remember that the east wind in Paris is said to be decidedly bracing; I must ask Gerald about a new fur pelisse to-morrow, without fail. 'So shines a good deed in a naughty world.'—Shakespeare. The French consider him barbarous. It is a pity that Mr. Gray should have died after all, in spite of the Duke's kindness. I had so wished to meet him; I prefer his 'Country Churchyard' to Mr. Goldsmith's 'Deserted Village'; I believe Mr. Goldsmith to be a little lacking in elegance. 'Out, out, brief candle.' Shakespeare again. Papa admires Shakespeare. How dreadful it would be if the light were actually to be extinguished; this room is very draughty. ' 'Tis but a night, a long and moonless night. . . .' Blair's Grave . . . my Aunt Susanna's favourite poem. 'To paint the gloomy horror of the tomb. . . .' I wish I did not remember it so well; my aunt continually read it aloud to me when I was a child. Paris . . . Paris . . . how delightful to see it once more! I trust the good sisters have none of them died; impossible to conceive of Paris without them. La Rêve . . . Racine . . . Corneille. 'Ne verse point de pleurs sur cette sepulture passant: ce lit funèbre est un lit précieux.' Death; poets are forever writing about death. These purple curtains always turn black at night; they are too sombre a shade. 'My love is dead, gone to his death-bed. . . .' Ah, that unfortunate youth Chatterton . . . dead by his own hand! Dead . . . dead . . . I am becoming excessively morbid; let me resolutely think of something else . . . the beauties of nature . . .

Devon. . . . Ah, no, not that! Pictures; I have seen many beautiful pictures in London. . . . I wish Sir Joshua had given the Academy's gold medal to young Mr. Flaxman . . . Gerald says he is a most deserving person. I am to have my miniature taken in Paris . . . à Paris . . . Paradis . . .''

This passage not only illustrates the elegant, slightly stilted diction, the careful observation, the use of historical allusions so characteristic of the whole novel, but also supplies an unusual example of Wylie's handling of stream of consciousness. The mind she exposes is a very literary one, full of tags of poetry. Jennifer, who has been homesick ever since her marriage, thinks frequently of her family: father, Aunt Susanna; but she cannot bear to think of her beloved Devonshire. She remembers her childhood, her short time with the good sisters in the convent; she anticipates a fur pelisse, having her miniature taken. France and England mingle as she anticipates arrival and departure. That final ''à Paris . . . Paradis'' that signals the moment of sleep mimics the drifting mind associating sounds in a last effort to establish order and relatedness among its contents. The revery is unified, of course, by the theme of death, which makes her normal languor even more apparent; and yet, in these moments before sleep, Jennifer and her plight are more sharply focused than almost anywhere else in the novel. Here we see most clearly the exhausting attempt to reconcile herself to life with Gerald.

Still later, in India, Saint Amond, a Frenchman who reminds Jennifer of her father, offers to provide her with a safe retreat because he thinks a trip with Gerald to Delhi would be unwise and unhealthy. Although she repeatedly asks him to remain with her, she responds apathetically to his suggestion that she go with him.

This unnatural lethargy, this congenital laziness, suddenly disappears when Jennifer starts to respond to Prince Abbas. For the first time in her life, she wants to be strong and bold. This change seems to arise from her discovery of a robust emotion and her awareness of extreme danger. She has lived a pampered and conventional life in which the lady has lived at the expense of the woman. After a week of walking through the countryside, she and Prince Abbas are transformed. Abbas is "no longer spoiled and peevish, nor Jennifer vain and melancholy." The two "sickly pigeons" have turned into "meadow larks." With the resurrection of Gerald, Jennifer and Prince Abbas resume their old forms. The sight of him revives both her fear and her awe. After the prince has said his last farewell: " 'Good-bye,' Jennifer replied softly; the little word, shorn of every title of endearment or courtesy, fell through the air like a bird without wings." The conventional return to the loveless marriage, here satirized, is foiled, of course, by Jennifer's death.

Jennifer Lorn is indeed a novel that turns everyday life into an enchantment. But Wylie's purpose is not to suggest that the world of ideals is more beautiful than the world of reality, that love and marriage are even more beautiful than we realize. On the contrary, as she wrote in 1928: "If you call a spade a diamond some people will think you are frivolous and affected, but other people will understand how much blacker things may be said about spades by the simple trick of pretending that they are diamonds." *Jennifer Lorn* is a fiercely satirical book.

Her next novel is another satire on the institution of marriage. *The Venetian Glass Nephew* was Wylie's only novel to be serialized. Carl Van Doren, the editor of *Century Magazine,* wrote, "The first part was in type before there was any second or third." By the time it was published as a book, Wylie was already writing *The Orphan Angel* and thought the more lively characters of that novel, Shiloh and David, made Virginio seem relatively "gutless."

The story is an unlikely one. The naive Cardinal Peter Innocent Bon, whose heart at eighty-one is still a "blue balloon," wishes he had a nephew. Accompanying Pope Pius VI on a visit to Venice, he befriends the glassblower Luna, who takes him to his workshop. There he meets the worldly-wise Chastelneuf and is entertained by a display of animated glass objects. When he tells the pair of his desire for a nephew, Virginio is hand-blown for him by the ingenious Luna and the lecherous Chastelneuf. The beautiful glass figurine falls in love instantly and forever when he meets the notorious bluestocking Rosalba, daughter of Abbé de Bernis and the nun Caterina. Called the Infant Sappho, the beautiful girl, who at twelve had been an intimate friend of Voltaire, is learned and gifted, especially in poetry. Once she falls in love, however, she grows quite wild and flighty, and flaunts an interest in yellow gowns rather than old books. Brought up to be a deist and to feel guilty about her secret preference for fairy tales over the encyclopedists, she is free through Virginio's miraculous birth from sand, holy water, extreme heat, and human breath. "Magic was justified by experiment; it was become a verity, true, rational and possible, like mathematics or the rights of man."

Although Virginio is a suitable husband, he cannot, Rosalba learns after marriage, be a playmate because he splinters too easily to engage in her hoydenish games. She is a child of sunshine; he, a creature of moonlight. Unable to bear Virginio's physical fear of living with her, Rosalba flings herself into a bonfire. Chastelneuf, who is modeled on Casanova, saves her; thinking she is worth a million pale Virginios, he offers her human love. Instead of accepting the aged suitor, Rosalba rushes off to Virginio, who, injured earlier in a fall while chasing her during a game, has an arm in a sling. Peter Innocent sees no solution for their dilemma except a convent for Rosalba, a monastery for Virginio. Chastelneuf suggests black magic instead. The little fable concludes with Rosalba having successfully submitted to the fiery furnace in order to be turned into a piece of fine Sèvres porcelain to match Virginio's Venetian glass.

Carl Van Doren said of this novel, "Sympathy is on the side of Nature but skill is on the side of Art." Rosalba is a warm and vibrant girl. When she first meets Virginio, her talk is full of impertinence and self-importance. She has a sharp tongue and an imperious manner. Virginio, on the other hand, begins with some gusto but grows steadily more abject. One weakness in this almost flawless tale is the inexplicable change in his character after marriage. The young man enters life judging a glass of wine as a little too heavy for his taste. He then asks for a *viola da gamba* and starts humming a tune by Cimarosa. When courting Rosalba he strikes her as rather unbending in his notion of duty. He presses his suit by discouraging her deistic propensities and encouraging her to love him by giving her a ring with the inscription "Fear God and love me." In the last chapters of the book Virginio has no personality at all. Like Jennifer Lorn he is a "person" whose remarkable beauty seems to have replaced all other aspects of selfhood. But in *Jennifer Lorn* Wylie supplies a psychological explanation for the changes from lassitude to vivacity in Jennifer. Virginio's change is more unbelievable than Rosalba's fiery transformation—all the more reason, therefore, for a reader's sympathies to be with the natural girl rather than with the artificial boy.

And yet the fable is delightfully artificial. Wylie has employed a mass of alchemical facts, topographical data about Venice, details from Casanova's memoirs and ecclesiastical history, and information on glassblowing and porcelain firing. The more factual she becomes, the more fantastic the story grows. This perhaps is her unique contribution to the American novel of the period. The British novelist Virginia Woolf makes facts gallop and cavort in *Orlando* (1928), but it would be difficult to find an American novelist who achieves the same kind of effect through the use of historical facts. James Branch Cabell, for example, constructs his fantasies out of dreams and imaginary creatures. In *Jurgen* (1919) we are in the world of legend rather than of history. But Wylie uses historical research to turn eighteenth-century Italy and France into a fabulous land.

The worlds of art and nature, of fantasy and reality, are brought together in satire. In *The Venetian Glass Nephew,* as well as in *Jennifer Lorn,* Wylie is a true disciple of Shelley, among whose many indictments of modern marriage "Epipsychidion" is only the most famous. Here, where Rosalba has exchanged her human warmth and vitality for an aesthetic beauty and purity, the cost of becoming a fit bride is painfully clear. Jennifer never becomes a marble figure, but Gerald would have liked her to be one. She does, however, learn to become a fit bride for him, traveling to Paris and India when her heart longs for Devonshire. A glass man may not be able to share the physical joy of running and playing, but he can fulfill all the physical requirements of the marriage bed. From the very beginning Chastelneuf is concerned that the glass nephew be sexually complete. When Peter Innocent decides to name his nephew Virginio, Chastelneuf responds, "A pretty name, but I trust it may not long be strictly appropriate; I have spared no pains to make our young friend a complete work of art, after the best natural patterns. . . ."

The elderly men surrounding the young lovers—Peter Innocent Bon, the happy celibate; Chastelneuf, the confirmed rake; Count Gazzi, the voyeuristic writer of fairy tales—provide a chorus, giving their opinions on love and marriage. It is they who have arranged the marriage; in spite of their expressions of guilt, it is they who will suggest and then execute the plan for turning Rosalba into a Sèvres figure. Rosalba goes into the furnace claiming that the choice is freely hers. In this world of men, it is the woman who must be transformed before she can be a proper bride for Virginio.

Wylie's prose gifts seem to be those of the satirist rather than of the more ordinary novelist. Unfortunately, her next novel is not a satire. The title that she had chosen for her novel about Shelley was *Mortal Image;* but Willa Cather published *My Mortal Enemy* in the same year (1926), and so the American title of Wylie's book was changed to *The Orphan Angel*. It is the story of what might have happened to Shelley if he had not drowned off Lerici in July 1822, but had been rescued by an American ship.

The story begins on board the *Witch of the West*, where David Butternut, a young seaman from Maine, has recently quarreled with and accidentally killed Jasper Cross, another sailor. In the midst of an ensuing storm, David rescues a beautiful youth who resembles the dead sailor and whom he christens Shiloh (a name Byron had used for Shelley). The two men decide to go in search of Jasper's twin sister, Silver, when the ship docks in Boston. They set off on a series of adventures that has led Alfred Kazin to describe the novel as a "boy's book." They hike all day and sleep out at night, hunting their food and cooking it over campfires in the woods; they bathe in streams, go down the Ohio on a raft, eat quantities of bacon and johnnycake, get captured by Indians and almost burned at the stake, cross the desert (where they run out of water), and manage finally to reach a California mission.

Unlike a boy's book, however, the novel is full of romantic incidents. David and Shiloh are constantly rescuing or fleeing from ladies who are overly susceptible to Shiloh's charms: Melissa, the fourteen-year-old girl with a drunken father, who will not accept David as a replacement for Shiloh (as a husband); Rosalie, the professor's intended bride, who almost ruins her wedding by falling in love with Shiloh; Annie, the daughter of dead Protestant missionaries, who is softened by her love for Shiloh but reveals herself as even more cruel than her Indian captors; and Silver, whose picture Shiloh has often kissed but whom he gives up rather than compromise.

David's weakness for whiskey and Shiloh's penchant for poetry also are not the usual ingredients for a boy's book. Unfortunately, neither are they enough to constitute adult characterization. Wylie has settled for the roughest approximations in both instances. Shiloh is the epitome of elegance, grace, beauty, courtesy. David is the embodiment of simplicity, naturalness, generosity. Shiloh is described both by the author and by other characters as an angel. David at one point dons the skin of a bear, which is the animal he most resembles—a nice, friendly one. Neither character achieves human stature.

Part of the reason is the language. Shiloh's dialogue is so outrageous that Wylie wrote an essay to defend her judgment against the critics. In "Mr. Shelley Speaking" (1927), she argues that Keats's language was his own London dialect mixed with literary borrowings from Edmund Spenser and the Elizabethans, that Byron's was the language of a Regency wit, but that Shelley's was a slightly inflated version of the eighteenth-century language of his teachers and elders. She notes further that Shelley always affected a stilted and distant vocabulary, that he told Godwin, "I have experienced a decisive pulmonary attack" when he meant his lungs were slightly touched, that he would never say "sailor" when he could say "mariner."

In the following passages, therefore, Wylie is attempting to imitate Shelley's ordinary cadence and vocabulary:

"If there were any lake or sequestered pool in the neighbourhood, I should be most grateful for directions which might enable me to find it . . .'' (A woman asked him if he would like to wash up.)

"I shall go to her to-night, alone, and in the very hush and suspension of mortality I shall give her a single parting kiss, thus mingling for a moment our extremest souls in hallowed chaste communion.''

"A happy augury of the perfectibility of the human mind!'' cried Shiloh.

Three hundred pages of such language, no matter on what grounds, remain fairly indefensible. And unfortunately Wylie's own narrative is not very different from Shiloh's dialogue. She describes him as answering questions "with an ambiguous shake of his romantic locks, and a glance of darkling fire.'' Here she is describing Shiloh as he gives the good-night kiss spoken of in the second passage above: "He leaned above her in the moonlight, and the flood of silver poured from his shoulders in feathery flakes like the bright cataract of archangelic wings.''

David's dialogue is, of course, different; but his "rustic'' speech is as painful as Shiloh's exquisite refinement. At one point he says, "I remember when I first seen you, Shiloh, I thought as how you was sort of an unearthly critter, but now there ain't none of us can touch you for nimbleness and spunk.'' And at another point, he protests, "Aw, Shiloh, you ain't never done it, and you don't rightly understand how goldarned slow it can be. . . .'' Because of such dialogue it is extremely difficult for a reader to accept any kind of conversation between David and Shiloh.

The language of the main characters is not the only problem in the novel. Completely free to invent whatever adventures she likes, Wylie roots herself in the factual world of steamboats, American geography, the food and drink, the wildfowl and fish, the flowers and street names of America on the one hand, the people and places, poetry and habits of Shelley's life and work and times on the other. The backdrop of this novel is meticulously and vividly realistic. But the characters and actions she introduces into this historical world are absurd and ridiculous. Her seamen, innkeepers, pioneers, and Indians behave like opéra buffe characters. A European, an Asian, or an African might be excused for understanding and reflecting so little of American life beyond its physical surface; but *The Orphan Angel* is an extraordinary book for an American to have written.

The cause of this discrepancy between the treatment of characters and setting can perhaps be traced to the subject. Hardly anyone who knew her fails to mention the strength of her attachment to the poet and his works or the breadth of her knowledge of both his poetry and his life. Amy Lowell, whose two-volume critical study of John Keats appeared in the year of her death, had a similar feeling for Keats. Alice Meynell, her daughter Viola says, was so attached to Shakespeare that if a biography of her mother recorded only the history of her feelings and thoughts about him, there would be very few biographical facts left out. Women poets of the period seem to have had a tendency to develop deeply personal relations with a deceased poet. After her death Wylie was to be adopted in a somewhat similar fashion by the British novelist Winifred Holtby, whose poems written to the dead Wylie reveal how often Holtby viewed her own fatal illness within the context of Wylie's chronic high blood pressure.

But there is something unique about Wylie's feelings for Shelley. In her essay "Excess of Charity'' (1927), she describes her discovery of the poet at the age of eleven, some years after being introduced to "The Cloud'' and "To a Skylark'' in her Third Reader.

It was September in Washington and the air was warm and sweet as if all the grapes and peaches of Maryland and Virginia had flavored it to my taste. I stood before the smallest bookcase in the library, and from its shelves I drew Trelawny's "Recollections." The window was wide open; there was plenty of light and soft autumnal wind in the room. I did not move except to turn the pages. Even the black leather chair was too far away from the scene within the covers of the book. I stood quite still and turned the pages, and the curtains blew in at the window and a few golden leaves blew in between them.

So I read for the first time of Shelley's death and burial. I can remember what I felt in that moment of past time, but never what I thought. It is therefore impossible to tell of it except to draw the picture of the room full of light and softer air and the child standing in the center of the room and turning pages of the book, afraid to move, afraid to cry for fear the scene within the pages of the book might be hidden from her eyes, wondering and wondering why the bright creature who had lived within that scene should have died and fallen into dust no stronger than the golden leaves blowing in at the window.

Stories, essays, poems, novels all attest to the amazing persistence of this childhood feeling. Emotionally unable to accept the early death of Shelley, Wylie went on resurrecting him in her imagination. In 1927, the year after *The Orphan Angel*, Shelley was the central figure in two of her essays and a short story. "A Birthday Cake for Lionel" is a light piece in which she permits herself to mock a Shelley, now grown gray, who has come to the end of an educational experiment with two little girls, Artemis and Jezebel. The children mother him as though he were a little boy and they a pair of matrons. Although their adoration of him is too syrupy, Wylie tries to temper it with humor, noting, for example, that the children's noisy expressions of their love for him gives him neuralgia.

There is little mockery in *The Orphan Angel,* in which she adopts an attitude of idolatry. Although David Butternut makes a few disparaging remarks about Shiloh, Wylie is so painfully uncritical of Shelley in *The Orphan Angel* that he emerges as the romantic image of an adolescent daydream. In spite of all her erudition, Wylie does not really create or re-create the poet at age thirty, for, to her, Shelley inhabited not a period in history but a place in her emotional life. Her failure to make him or any other of the characters live in the historically accurate world she has provided for them suggests that there is some truth in Morton Zabel's claim that Wylie did not have a grasp of history in the sense that Robert Bridges, Ezra Pound, or T. S. Eliot did.

Where her purpose was satire—as in *Jennifer Lorn* and *The Venetian Glass Nephew*—this lack in Wylie's ability to grasp the historical dimensions of character and action was not felt. Since the characters were supposed to be fantastic and unreal, there was no need for her to convince us that they belonged to a real eighteenth-century world in England, India, or Italy. Furthermore, she invested the houses, food, furniture, and clothing of those eighteenth-century countries with a dazzling unreality. Her intention had nothing to do with verisimilitude. But in *The Orphan Angel* both character and setting are presented as stimulants to our historical imagination. The characters, however, elicit incredulity rather than conviction.

Few readers would be as harsh as James Branch Cabell, who found *The Orphan Angel* "one of the most gloomy errors in all literary history" and "a waste of woodpulp." But almost all critics have found *Mr. Hodge and Mr. Hazard* (1928), Wylie's next novel and her last, considerably more successful.

The novel is in three books: "Mr. Hazard," "The Young Huntings," and "Mr. Hodge." When Mr. Hazard returns to England, he is met by an old friend, Mr. Hartleigh, who takes him to visit his family in Marylebone. Here Mr. Hazard falls ill with influenza and spends a great deal of his time avoiding the doctor and revisiting his old London haunts. In book II, Mr. Hazard,

722 / AMERICAN WRITERS

longing for the country, leaves London and goes in the springtime to Gravelow, where he meets Lady Clara Hunting through her young daughters Allegra and Penserosa. For some time he lives an idyllic life, reading Milton and Job, writing his own poetry, and visiting the Huntings once or twice a week at Lyonnesse, their home. Infatuated with Allegra, Hazard is also much moved by Lady Clara's kindness and sensitivity. In book III, Hodge, the tutor of Lady Clara's two sons, arrives with the boys at Lyonnesse for their holidays. He very much disapproves of Hazard and encourages Lady Clara to break with him. At first she refuses but yields when the emotionally clumsy Hodge refers to the inappropriateness of Hazard's feelings for Allegra. Lady Clara and her daughters therefore fail to appear at a tea party that Hazard has specially arranged for them. Hazard recognizes that he has lost the battle to Hodge and seizes upon an excuse to leave Gravelow.

The language of *Mr. Hodge and Mr. Hazard* is considerably different from *The Orphan Angel*. The novel opens thus:

When Mr. Hazard was forty years old, he decided to revisit England. Having been out of it for precisely fifteen years, he had half forgotten its climate; his memory was incurably romantic, and through veils of far-away mist he saw the blackthorn more clearly than the mud. Also, it was true that he, who so dearly loved the sun, had been rather too much in the sun of late.

This language is spare, pointed, fast-paced, eminently more readable. We are in for a very different novel.

Some of the poems in *Trivial Breath*, the volume of poetry published in the same year as this final novel, reveal important changes in Wylie. She has begun to turn from her admiration of "flesh refined to glass" toward a more earthy approval of the fact that

The flesh survives at last
Because it is not pure.

In *Mr. Hodge and Mr. Hazard* the figure who embodies the values of Shiloh/Shelley has grown ten years older in two years. The author also seems to have gone through a period of rapid growth, for she now sees the forty-year-old Hazard through the eyes of experience as well as of dream. His conflict and defeat are as much a result of defects in his own character as of inadequacies in the social and natural world.

"Malediction upon Myself," one of the poems in *Trivial Breath*, records a personal experience that went into the writing of the novel. In mounting crescendos of "if" clauses, the poet pronounces a curse to follow her possible denigration of beauty in its baser and everyday forms. If her heart is so dull that it says London is no longer fair because all the beautiful people have gone to the country and left it to common men and women, if she can't see beauty in rooftops and a polluted Thames, then the strings of her heart should be loosened, her veins emptied, and her pulses stopped; her eyes should be blinded and her nostrils and mouth stuffed; her ankles should be broken and her legs and throat twisted. This orgy of self-punishment concludes with dismemberment and trampling.

In *Mr. Hodge and Mr. Hazard,* Wylie has written a novel that satirizes both the bathos and dull industriousness of the middle class and the languor and withdrawal of the romantic poet. She does not merely deplore the drab world; she also deplores the airy spirits who are too pure to engage a world of flesh and blood. Mr. Hazard, who has a talent for making himself uncomfortable, rejects every opportunity to enter "the England of the time." Such effeteness is not seen as exotic and precious in this novel, but as a malediction upon the self. Mr. Hazard has damned himself to decay. He has come to England seeking his coffin. When offered the possibility of something alive but imperfect—Lady Clara, who is both malicious and amiable—he is content to retreat without making any effort to win her.

Mr. Hodge, the representative materialist and opportunist, does not defeat Mr. Hazard through any direct confrontation. There is an enemy within Mr. Hazard who works on Hodge's behalf. As in much of Wylie's poetry, there is a split between mind and spirit in Hazard. The mind "was a scorner, a tyrant, a torturer." The spirit can believe in the enchanting world of Lyonnesse and its place in it only as long as the mind is kept silent. Hodge's arrival has "unlocked the prison and let loose the demoniacal mind" that now speeds "through the high chambers of the soul, splintering the crystal roofs, breaking the looking-glass walls with the vibrations of its laughter. His mind was no friend to Mr. Hazard; his mind was the sworn friend of Mr. Hodge."

In "True Vine," another poem in *Trivial Breath,* Wylie describes the dangers of such dependence of happiness upon the abeyance of the activity of the mind. The kind of heaven that is contrived of "immaculate blossoms" that cannot stand "malicious verity" is quick to languish; it has "ruin for its centre."

Not so the obdurate and savage lovely
Whose roots are set profoundly upon trouble;
This flower grows so fiercely and so bravely
It does not even know that it is noble.

This is the vine of love, whose balsams flourish
Upon a living soil corrupt and faulty,
Whose leaves have drunk the skies, and stooped
    to nourish
The earth again with honey sweet and salty.

Trivial Breath reveals a kind of pagan joy in mortal beauty. Many of the poems describe an acceptance of man's short span of life along with great joy in the physicality of his passage. "The Puritan's Ballad," for example, is a simple,

open statement of love at twenty: the young woman's wedding ring clinks on the pan as she skims the cream, the man's clanks on the knife as he slits the fish's head. The homeliness of their daily tasks is lit up by the physical union. Similarly, "As I Went Down by Havre de Grace" affirms the beauty of this transitory life, taking comfort in what an imperfect world affords despite its hardness: laurel, dogwood, wild strawberries, balsam trees, the mayflower. In "A Strange Story" the poet describes dying in various sections of London: Berners Street, Houndsditch, Holborn, Marylebone, Lincoln's Inn. Finally

When I died in Bloomsbury
In the bend of your arm,
At the end I died merry
And comforted and warm.

Throughout Wylie's poetry there are references to death. But in this volume death has become a friendly visitor of flesh and blood. She sees the physical signs of approaching death in herself, and

The vanishing dust of my heart is proud
To watch me wither and grow old.

In one of her most compassionate poems, "The Coast Guard's Cottage," she offers to share her bed with a dead man, giving him human warmth and pity with no question about his former beauty and no fear of what the waters have made of him. Sleeping in this house so recently occupied by the coast guard, she experiences a close and physical bond between the living and the dead:

No creature flies or swims
Which can dismay my heart; you have come
    home.

Mr. Hodge and Mr. Hazard also explores that relationship. Hazard feels as though he is a ghost in England. The author remarks, "The ghost of a living man must be a poor creature at best; a stuffless thing, projected into sunshine by a sick brain. But the ghosts of the dead are different; they are sustained and animated by spirits whole and entire, they possess their proper souls.'' By accepting his own view of himself as a ghost, Hazard cuts himself off more completely from life than he could have by actually dying. He thinks of the lovely girls, Allegra and Rosa, and their mother, Clara, as enchanting creatures, and would no more consider stealing them ''for mortal employ than to fling a noose around the moon and pull it earthward to be cherished in his breast.'' In *The Orphan Angel*, Shiloh has the same attitude toward the women he meets, preferring to gaze at the picture of Silver rather than involve himself with an actual woman. But whereas Wylie asks us to view Shiloh's angelic distance from common humanity as a sign of his superior worth, in *Mr. Hodge and Mr. Hazard* she suggests that such a romantic view of experience is timid and lazy.

Mr. Hodge, of course, has every intention of mortally employing the lovely Lady Clara if he can. Although Wylie sees the inadequacies of Hazard, she by no means endorses the Hodges of the world. ''Tragic Dialogue,'' the last poem in *Trivial Breath*, gives some idea of what her new attitude involves. She answers a question raised about the hundred years that separate her from Shelley by saying that they would never have been kindred even if they had lived at the same time and in the same place:

> Ah no, both happily and alas!
> A clover field, a river,
> A hawthorn hedge, a pane of glass
> Had parted us forever.

In *The Orphan Angel*, Wylie attempts to resurrect Shelley by pretending he has not died, that he has walked the streets of Boston and traveled the Camino Real. But this Shelley is the ghost of a living man rather than the ghost of a dead man.

As she says in her four sonnets ''A Red Carpet for Shelley,'' also in *Trivial Breath*, the only way the dead Shelley can walk this world now is through her own mortal veins. And in *Mr. Hodge and Mr. Hazard*, Wylie has given us that Shelley rather than Shelley viewed from the outside. By blending herself and Shelley (and a host of other romantics) in the character of Mr. Hazard, she has replaced her idolatry of Shelley with a more critical—because a more internal—awareness of the dangers of excessive sensibility. The author, therefore, is clearly on the side of Mr. Hazard in this contest with Mr. Hodge. For Mr. Hodge is cruel, petty, unimaginative; in his heart of hearts, he loathes Milton as well as Hazard, although he dares only to sneer at that ''horrid apparition'' who appears, drenched with rain, at Lady Clara's home.

Although Hazard is defeated in the contest for Lady Clara, Wylie allows him a humorous triumph. In our last sight of him, Hazard is seated ''in the most comfortable arm-chair that the room afforded,'' watching Mr. Hodge sweat as he packs up Hazard's books for his departure. Clearly, Wylie has moved a great distance from the saccharine conclusion of *The Orphan Angel*.

The novels of Elinor Wylie are not among the more important literary achievements of the 1920's. *Jennifer Lorn* and *The Venetian Glass Nephew* are highly successful, but very minor, fantasies. *Mr. Hodge and Mr. Hazard* is nothing more than the ''brief symbolic romance of the mind'' that Wylie said it was. Some of her best poems in *Trivial Breath* communicate that romance much more effectively. If she had written only her novels, Wylie's reputation would have perished with her death. Fortunately she had one more year to live, and she spent it writing poetry.

The nineteen sonnets in the ''One Person'' section of her last volume of poetry, *Angels and Earthly Creatures*, are for many critics the apex and triumph of Elinor Wylie's poetry. The first sonnet is not numbered as part of the sequence, for it is an introduction to the whole series. In the purity and restraint of its diction we can hear her long acquaintance with the poetry of John Donne, a volume of whose poems she always carried with her during her last summer in England.

Although these words are false, none shall
    prevail
To prove them in translation less than true
Or overthrow their dignity, or undo
The faith implicit in a fabulous tale;
The ashes of this error shall exhale
Essential verity, and two by two
Lovers devout and loyal shall renew
The legend, and refuse to let it fail.

Even the betrayer and the fond deceived,
Having put off the body of this death,
Shall testify with one remaining breath,
From sepulchres demand to be believed:
These words are true, although at intervals
The unfaithful clay contrive to make them false.

Wylie, who had spent her life creating fabulous and fantastic worlds from her "jeweled brain," reached in this volume, and particularly in these sonnets, a fabulous world whose truth is beyond contesting. Biographical information only confirms what the unaided reader finds: a voyage of sensual and emotional discovery that is both painful and exhilarating.

In sonnet I the poet begins with simple happiness:

Now shall the long homesickness have an end
Upon your heart. . . .

But even here the conclusion of the poem brings us to death and burial. Just as the introductory sonnet calls upon other lovers to testify to the truth of words that the flesh has often made false, this first sonnet unites the "you" and "I" involved in this present love to all those dead lovers, with whom they are coeval, who now lie bound to "one another's bosom in the ground." The homecoming is to love and death. Sonnet XVII, the next to last in the series, returns to that homecoming and reiterates its connection with death. In both sonnets the "I" finds heaven or paradise, but always this side of the grave. For the lover has but lately discovered this earth and sky; the new land has only now become beloved. In sonnet IX, Wylie renounces the heavenly aid of the protective spirit who, she says, accompanied her throughout life and made her a "woman by an archangel befriended." In ending her archangel's "knightly servitude," she becomes vulnerable to the arrows against which he once defended her. She and her lover "are but perishable things." The sense of imminent death that pervades these poems makes the ecstatic discovery of physical joy quite poignant.

The unexpected joy is conveyed with great delicacy. Whereas before, her "flesh was but a fresh-embroidered shroud" and she was blind to "those sharp ecstasies the pulses give," now—although she grieves that time "sets sickle to our Aprils"—she declares:

We grow beyond vagaries of the weather
And make a summer of our mingled breath. . . .

She writes:

I have survived to see the heavens fall
Into my hands, which on your hands depend.

Throughout the sequence Wylie suggests the deepest physical intimacy through simple references to hands. In sonnet III she pleads, "Put forth your hand, put forth your hand to bless." When she wishes that she could make her flesh subliminal and arrive to comfort him in her absence, his letter "cries, 'My hands are cold as ice.' " Just as the lovers in sonnet I lie "side by side and hand in hand," the lovers in the last sonnet wake "and touch each other's hands." In sonnet X, thinking how often her lover has been fretted and wounded by life, she asks:

How is it possible that this hand of clay,
Though white as porcelain, can contrive a touch
So delicate it shall not hurt too much?

All the exquisite and delicate qualities that Wylie had sought in her poetry and fiction now seem to have found a commensurate subject in this record of the awakening of passionate love in the shadow of imminent death. To glimpse beauty as the result of wars between "the upper and the nether stars," to feel happiness as the "cool and chaste, the iridescent sphere" is not to distort or exaggerate the intense physical reality of that fabulous world known only to lovers, or that equally precious and heightened reality seen only by those close to death.

The luminous experiences that Wylie writes about in the "One Person" sonnets cannot be separated from their lucid expression. All of the sonnets follow the same Italian rhyme scheme for the octave: *abbaabba*. The self-imposed limit of two rhymes for the first eight lines requires verbal facility and richness. By the time she wrote these last sonnets, Wylie had made herself master of the form through constant practice. The sestet varies, although most of the sonnets follow the pattern *cddcee*. The concluding couplet is a favorite sonnet device with Wylie. The last "sonnet" actually has sixteen lines and two concluding couplets. The introductory sonnet has a structural joke because it follows the standard *abbaabbacddc* and then concludes—since the final word is "false"—with *ef* instead of *ee*.

Louise Bogan complained about the compulsion that women poets felt to write sonnets, but there is no denying that in the hands of Edna St. Vincent Millay and Elinor Wylie the form was made to advance new and delightful intentions. For example, sonnet XVI does more than employ architectural imagery in ways that suggest Donne's "Batter my heart, three person'd God":

I hereby swear that to uphold your house
I would lay my bones in quick destroying lime
Or turn my flesh to timber for all time;

Cut down my womanhood; lop off the boughs
Of that perpetual ecstasy that grows
From the heart's core; condemn it as a crime
If it be broader than a beam, or climb
Above the stature that your roof allows.

I am not the hearthstone nor the cornerstone
Within this noble fabric you have builded;
Not by my beauty was its cornice gilded;
Not by my courage were its arches thrown:
My lord, adjudge my strength, and set me where
I bear a little more than I can bear.

The parts of the house assemble themselves: timber, beam, roof, hearthstone, cornerstone, cornice, arches. Wylie achieves an aesthetically pleasing effect by taking up emotional and ornamental parts of a house in the sestet after describing the more structurally necessary parts in the octave. But what unifies the sonnet as an organic whole is the rhyme established between the last phrase of the final line and the first phrase of the initial line of the poem: "I hereby swear" and "more than I can bear." Since the last line begins "I bear" and ends "I can bear," the thing sworn to becomes not the supposedly extreme offers but the "little more" of the last line. That "little more" assumes a tremendous weight from the context. A caryatid emerges in the last line to uphold the house.

But, as in a number of other sonnets in "One Person," the poem embodies more self-abasement than we are altogether comfortable with. Here the poet says she would lay her bones in lime. Elsewhere she would turn her flesh to warm air to wind around his body, or vanish, as even her "body's core and pith dissolves in air." Over and over she claims that she is not good enough for him. He is her lord; she is a child or a faithful hound. He requires a pretense of equality, but she knows that she is the "savage" and he the "fine," that there is "intrinsic difference in our dust." She is so imperfect that she will need an eternity to be made fit to be his bride.

In sonnet XV the poet begs forgiveness from a depth of pain that is full of self-abasement:

My honoured lord, forgive the unruly tongue
That utters blasphemies; forgive the brain
Borne on a whirlwind of unhallowed pain:
Remember only the intrepid song;
The flag defended and the gauntlet flung;
The love that speech can never render plain;
The mind's resolve to turn and strive again;
The fortitude that has endured so long.

My cherished lord, in charity forgive
A starveling hope that may at times desire
To warm its frozen fingers at your fire;
'Tis by such trifles that your lovers live,
And so rise up, and in the starlight cold
Frighten the foxes from your loneliest fold.

The poem is punctuated by the explosive *f*: *f*orgive the tongue its blas*ph*emies, *f*orgive the brain; remember the *f*lag de*f*ended, the gauntlet *f*lung, the *f*ortitude; *f*orgive the hope, the *f*rozen *f*ingers at your *f*ire. The final line not only begins and ends with a word having an initial *f*, but includes two additional *f* words within the line. Although the line scans as a normal line of iambic pentameter, it is so full of initial *f* sounds that it suggests an Anglo-Saxon alliterative line. Such an echo is appropriate to the physically elemental situation that is described. The relationship between the speaker and the honored lord is that of a servant and master. The actions of defending a flag and flinging down a gauntlet have a military significance that carries us to the Middle Ages. Warming frozen fingers at another's fire, when juxtaposed with frightening foxes from a fold, introduces the more peaceful idea of a shepherd at a feudal fire. If the poem were not part of this particular sonnet sequence, the religious connotations of such words as "blasphemies," "unhallowed," and "charity" would suggest an address to God rather than to a human lover.

In this request for forgiveness, the speaker has widened the difference between the lovers to the distance between a human suppliant and a divine auditor. Although this may reflect the anguish felt by a lover who wishes to regain a lost esteem and love, the almost frantic and desperate repetition of the word "forgive," which is reinforced by all the other words beginning with an initial *f*, is related to the extreme self-abasement found in other poems in the sequence.

Despite any discomfort we may feel because of this self-abasement, the sonnet sequence remains a moving record of a late and consuming love. Carl Van Doren said of "One Person": "The heart of sixteen spoke with the tongue of forty." The range of feeling, the extent to which emotion is permeated by intellect, the passionate simplicity of diction, the musical beauty of many lines and whole sonnets reveal an emotional and poetic growth in Elinor Wylie that suggests she may have been on the verge of crossing over from that special category of minor poet to take her place among the major poets of her period. At last she was ready to use her disciplined craft to re-create in poetry a vision of those fabulous lands opened to men and women through the deepest joys and sorrows. Her argument with the naturalists and realists continued to the end of her life. But in this last volume of poetry, we glimpse the deeper reality that she had always felt resided at the heart of experience. Her exotic world is no longer Persia or Venice: human flesh is now more fragile than glass; the grave yields more voluptuous ease than "silver fleece" or "bloom on grape" ever provided, and more jeweled veins than ever a "deep vault" or "phosphorescent gloom" revealed.

The remaining twenty poems in *Angels and Earthly Creatures* are necessarily less cumulatively effective. Nevertheless, here is more gold per ounce than ever before. At least seven of these poems—"Absent Thee from Felicity Awhile," "Felo de Se," "Hymn to Earth," "This Corruptible," "Bread Alone," "To a Cough in the Street at Midnight," "Farewell

Sweet Dust''—are among the finest she ever wrote. One, ''Hymn to Earth,'' may be her masterpiece.

''Hymn to Earth'' is imbued with the spirit of Shelley. Julia Cluck has quite rightly noted its resemblance to the opening lines of ''Alastor.'' It leaps to poetry, as Shelley's poems so often do, through scientific awareness. We find here the exactitude in the description of natural phenomena that is so compelling an aspect, for instance, of his ''Ode to the West Wind.'' But in place of Shelley's desire to be a leaf or a cloud, which is laid to rest only by his poetic ambition to be scattered even more widely through the world, Wylie accepts her physical fate by freely choosing to be ''a particle of earth'' containing the seed that, being consumed in the ''embrace of clay,'' lives again in a cypress grove.

By reversing Catullus' ''Hail and farewell'' uttered over his brother's grave to her own ''Farewell and hail,'' Wylie charts her resignation to death. Man has no part in fire, air, water; but both in life and in death he has sown himself in the earth, in the form of sweat and effort behind the plow and in the form of decomposing matter in the grave. Man says farewell to something immaterial from which he arose, and hails the earth as his urn, in which he will now be consumed as he once consumed the fruits of the earth. Catullus also mingled the four elements in his poem: he speaks of coming over the water (*per aequora*) to the grave (*ad inferias*) to speak to his brother's ashes (*adloquerer cinerem*). The Latin poem concludes with a sense of peace: ''and so forever, brother, hail and farewell'' (*atque in perpetuum, frater, ave atque vale*). Wylie's hymn ends with earth receiving man, who sleeps as her lover for a little while.

But rich as the literary echoes of Shelley and Catullus are, the poem has its unique ideas and music. In the second stanza, for example, Wylie speaks of fire in both scientific and mythological terms. Referring to it as ''secret at the core'' suggests the story of Prometheus, who stole the secret of fire from the gods and gave it to man. Then she says man draws the emanation of fire from the skies—as, of course, he does through sun and lightning. The theft now becomes man's use of an element that, she says, he ''has no part in.'' Similarly, in stanza three, which is devoted to air, the poet describes man's coming and going—into and out of the world—in terms of his inhaling and exhaling breath. Air is only borrowed by the lungs. It is an element that man constantly returns to the atmosphere. Fire has been stolen, then, and air borrowed. Water, as the fourth and fifth stanzas declare, is the element that has rejected man. Since man came from the water, he once did have a part in this element; but he was cast forth from it and now retains only the salt of his tears as his gift from the sea. However, when earth receives man in its ''kind embrace,'' he is returned to the elements: in the slow-burning fire of the soil as it is warmed by the sun, the body is devoured and then mingled, at full tide, with the sea. The sleep at the end of Wylie's poem is not Catullus' *in perpetuum,* but only for a little while.

As in so much of Wylie's poetry, the music of ''Hymn to Earth'' is largely the result of carefully controlled assonance and alliteration. Although sometimes the music in her earlier poems has little or no effect on the meaning of a line, here each phrase is a sudden illumination. She refers to the ''twin minutes'' of birth and death, to the ''last ashes'' or the ''perfect urn,'' to ''harvests . . . sparsely given,'' to waves that ''grow shallow.'' She describes the sea as casting off man with ''his dead weight of burdens nothing worth,'' and asks the earth to ''cherish'' at its ''charitable breast'' this ''man, this mongrel beast.''

Like D. H. Lawrence's ''Ship of Death,'' the ''Hymn to Earth'' is a modern meditation on dying. The hymn reflects a culmination of the poet's thoughts about man's relation to the elements that support life. At various points in her career she had raised the question of man's relation to other forms of life, particularly to animals. "Cold-blooded Creatures" in *Black Armour* is a poem that speaks of the "intolerable load" that lies "on all living creatures," and accuses man of being an "egregious egoist" because he lacks the imagination to think of the sentient life of snakes and fish. Man's biological alliance with both animals and the elements recurs in a number of Wylie's poems: "The Eagle and the Mole," "Madman's Song," "Winter Sleep," "Song," "Self-portrait," "Pity Me," "Desolation Is a Delicate Thing," "Address to My Soul." However, "Let No Charitable Hope" is an admonitory poem that sets up clear distinctions between man and eagle and antelope (two of her favorite living things). "Hymn to Earth" does the same for the elements. Although man asks to be received by the earth, he is not really of it any more than he is of fire, air, or water. He is of an "incomparable element" to which, in "Hymn to Earth," there is no return.

In another poem, "This Corruptible," Wylie eschews the traditional notion concerning the relation of body to soul. The body, not the soul, is freed by death in this poem in which mortality gives matter an advantage over mind, heart, and soul, which can never slough off their chains. Although the poem does not seriously advance the notion of transmigration of souls any more than Wordsworth's "Intimations of Immortality" makes a case for the preexistence of souls, it is difficult to see what other explanation there might be for such captivity. But in "Absent Thee from Felicity Awhile" Wylie accepts the traditional idea that in death the spirit puts off the "bonds of body and sense." The last stanza even suggests a homecoming for the soul when it will meet other souls after death. Here there is a promise of a return to the "incomparable element."

Such thoughts must have preoccupied Wylie in the last months of her life. It is not surprising that she gives more than one view of what death means for the individual. In "Felo de Se," however, one aspect of dying is incontrovertible: death means taking leave of an earthly lover. Even preparing to do this requires, in the context of this poem, a kind of suicide. In the three stanzas the poet progressively attempts to put him from her heart. She begins by addressing him as "my heart's delight"; then she calls him "my dearest heart"; in the last stanza he is "heart of my heart." In the first two stanzas she repeats the word "must" three times, as she tries to exert her will to do what she must: first, put him out of her mind, forget him; then, eject his image from her soul, cease to "see" him. But in the last stanza there is no "must"; what the will cannot do, the "heart alone has courage" to do. She can relinquish him only when his heart and her heart become identified as one heart, so that it is he himself who helps her let go, stilling himself where he most deeply lives—in her pulse. Only when he is killed in her heart's core can he die in her mind and soul as well. Such a killing of him is suicide, not murder.

In such a poem as "Felo de Se" there is a kind of humility that recognizes the limits of one's personal power and accepts another's help. "To a Cough in the Street at Midnight" gives one of the emotional effects of this kind of humility: an immediate compassion for all human beings who share one's own vulnerability. The poem is only six lines long.

God rest you if you're dead;
And bless, and send you safely home to bed
If you are only old:
God cure your cold,
Whether it be but a cold in the head
Or the more bitter cold which binds the dead.

The common human fate is death; old age, which is only a temporary alternative, takes its smaller role in the two rhymes that describe the two conditions: old, dead. The cold will be cured one way or another. Nevertheless, the poem takes the form of a prayer, asking for rest, a blessing, a cure. The cough is like Donne's tolling bell. It not only reminds man that he must die; it also arouses in him a sense of shared humanity. Asking for what is going to come in any event is a way of becoming part of the experience of that cough in the street.

The poet's personal experience with love and death have been a route to this deeper feeling for others. Caught up in the passion of love and the expectation of death, Wylie continued to write intellectually brilliant poetry. But these last poems blend mind, heart, and soul in the single identity that she had sought, and failed to find, throughout her life. Her reputation as a poet depends on the estimation of a dozen poems from her three earlier volumes and the heights attained in *Angels and Earthly Creatures*.

Selected Bibliography

WORKS OF ELINOR WYLIE

Nets to Catch the Wind. New York: Harcourt, Brace, 1921.

Black Armour: A Book of Poems. New York: Doran, 1923.

Jennifer Lorn: A Sedate Extravaganza. New York: Doran, 1923.

The Venetian Glass Nephew. New York: Doran, 1925.

The Orphan Angel. New York: Knopf, 1926.

Mr. Hodge and Mr. Hazard. New York: Knopf, 1928.

Trivial Breath. New York: Knopf, 1928.

Angels and Earthly Creatures. New York: Knopf, 1929.

Collected Poems of Elinor Wylie. New York: Knopf, 1932.

Collected Prose of Elinor Wylie. New York: Knopf, 1933.

Last Poems of Elinor Wylie. New York: Knopf, 1943. (Transcribed by Jane D. Wise.)

CRITICAL AND BIOGRAPHICAL STUDIES

Benét, William Rose. *The Prose and Poetry of Elinor Wylie*. Norton, Mass.: Wheaton College Press, 1934.

Cabell, James Branch. *Some of Us*. New York: McBride, 1930. Pp. 13–26.

Cluck, Julia. "Elinor Wylie's Shelley Obsession," *PMLA*, 56:841–60 (September 1941).

Colum, Mary. *Life and the Dream*. New York: Doubleday, 1947.

Gorman, Herbert S. "Daughter of Donne," *North American Review*, 219:679–86 (May 1924).

Gray, Thomas A. *Elinor Wylie*. New York: Twayne, 1969.

Hoyt, Nancy. *Elinor Wylie: The Portrait of an Unknown Lady*. New York: Bobbs-Merrill, 1935.

Kazin, Alfred. "The Exquisites," in *On Native Grounds*. New York: Reynal and Hitchcock, 1942.

Kohler, Dayton. "Elinor Wylie: Heroic Mask," *South Atlantic Quarterly*, 36:218–28 (April 1937).

Moore, Virginia. *Distinguished Women Writers*. New York: Dutton, 1934. Pp. 221–33.

Saul, G. B. *Quintet: Essays on Five American Women Poets*. The Hague: Mouton, 1967.

Sergeant, Elizabeth S. *Fire Under the Andes*. New York: Knopf, 1927. Pp. 107–21.

Tate, Allen. "Elinor Wylie's Poetry," *New Republic*, 72:107 (September 7, 1932).

Untermeyer, Louis. *American Poetry Since 1900*. New York: Holt, 1923. Pp. 221–26.

Van Doren, Carl. *Three Worlds*. New York: Harper, 1936.

Wilson, Edmund. *The Shores of Light*. New York: Farrar, Straus and Young, 1952.

————, and Mary Colum. "In Memory of Elinor Wylie," *New Republic*, 57:316–19 (February 6, 1929).

Wright, Celeste T. "Elinor Wylie: The Glass Chimaera and the Minotaur," *Twentieth Century Literature*, 12:15–26 (April 1966).

Zabel, Morton D. "The Pattern of the Atmosphere," *Poetry*, 40:273–82 (August 1932).

—*JOSEPHINE O'BRIEN SCHAEFER*

Index

*Arabic numbers printed in bold-face type refer
to extended treatment of a subject*